CALIFORNIA

Made in the United States
Text printed on 90%
recycled paper

Houghton Mifflin Harcourt

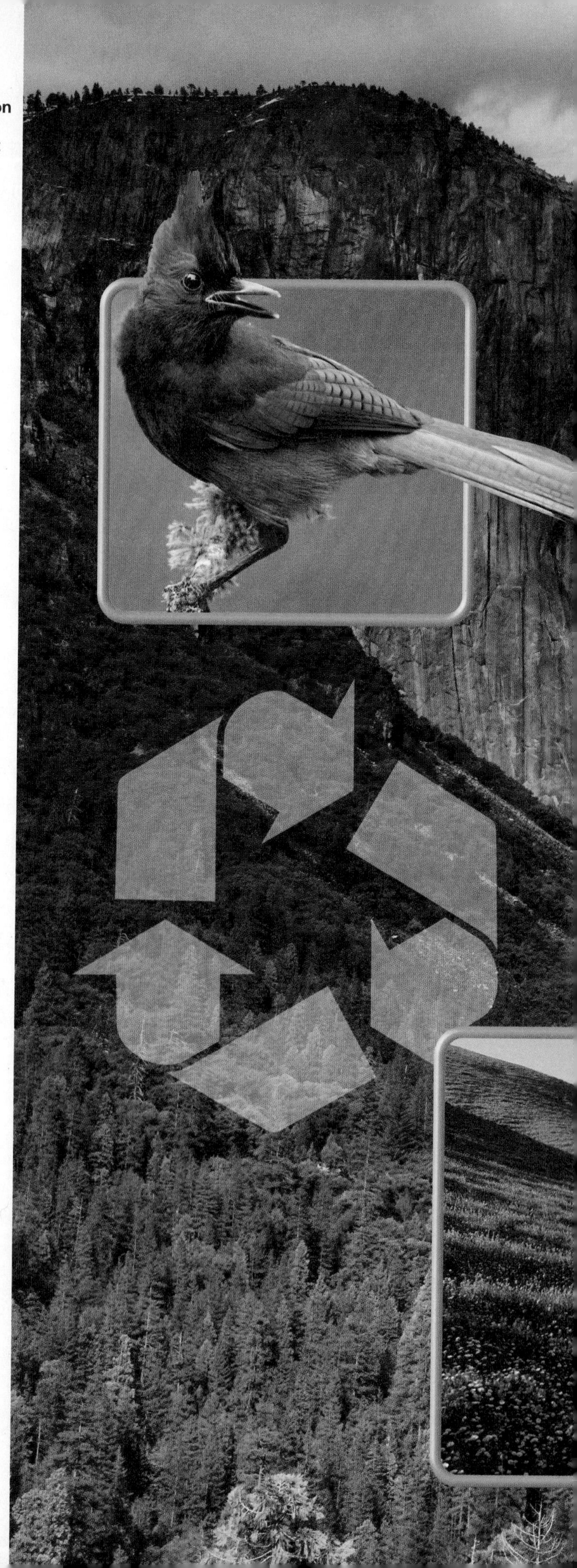

Printed in the U.S.A.

ISBN 978-0-544-20405-8

12 13 14 15 16 17 18 19 0029 27 26 25 24 23 22 21 20

4500790731 E F G

Dear Students and Families,

Welcome to **California Go Math!**, Grade X! In this exciting mathematics program, there are hands-on activities to do and real-world problems to solve. Best of all, you will write your ideas and answers right in your book. In **California Go Math!**, writing and drawing on the pages helps you think deeply about what you are learning, and you will really understand math!

By the way, all of the pages in your **California Go Math!** book are made using recycled paper. We wanted you to know that you can Go Green with **California Go Math!**

Sincerely,

The Authors

Made in the United States
Text printed on 90% recycled paper

CALIFORNIA

GO MATH!

Authors

Juli K. Dixon, Ph.D.
Professor, Mathematics Education
University of Central Florida
Orlando, Florida

Edward B. Burger, Ph.D.
President, Southwestern University
Georgetown, Texas

Steven J. Leinwand
Principal Research Analyst
American Institutes for Research (AIR)
Washington, D.C.

Matthew R. Larson, Ph.D.
K-12 Curriculum Specialist for Mathematics
Lincoln Public Schools
Lincoln, Nebraska

Martha E. Sandoval-Martinez
Math Instructor
El Camino College
Torrance, California

Contributor

Rena Petrello
Professor, Mathematics
Moorpark College
Moorpark, CA

English Language Learners Consultant

Elizabeth Jiménez
CEO, GEMAS Consulting
Professional Expert on English Learner Education
Bilingual Education and Dual Language
Pomona, California

Place Value and Operations with Whole Numbers

Critical Area

Critical Area Developing understanding and fluency with multi-digit multiplication, and developing understanding of dividing to find quotients involving multi-digit dividends

1 Place Value, Addition, and Subtraction to One Million 3

Domain Number and Operations in Base Ten

CALIFORNIA COMMON CORE STANDARDS 4.NBT.1, 4.NBT.2, 4.NBT.3, 4.NBT.4

GO DIGITAL

Go online! Your math lessons are interactive. Use *i*Tools, Animated Math Models, the Multimedia *e*Glossary, and more.

Chapter 1 Overview

In this chapter, you will explore and discover answers to the following **Essential Questions**:

- How can you use place value to compare, add, subtract, and estimate with whole numbers?
- How do you compare and order whole numbers?
- What are some strategies you can use to round whole numbers?
- How is adding 5- and 6-digit numbers similar to adding 3-digit numbers?

Chapter 2 Overview

In this chapter, you will explore and discover answers to the following **Essential Questions**:

- What strategies can you use to multiply by 1-digit numbers?
- How can you use models to multiply a multi-digit number by a 1-digit number?
- How can you use estimation to check your answer?
- How does the partial products strategy use place value?

2 Multiply by 1-Digit Numbers 45

Domains Operations and Algebraic Thinking
Number and Operations in Base Ten

CALIFORNIA COMMON CORE STANDARDS 4.OA.1, 4.OA.2, 4.OA.3, 4.NBT.5

Chapter 3 Overview

In this chapter, you will explore and discover answers to the following **Essential Questions**:

- What strategies can you use to multiply 2-digit numbers?
- How can you use place value to multiply 2-digit numbers?
- How can you choose the best method to multiply 2-digit numbers?

3 Multiply 2-Digit Numbers 103

Domains Operations and Algebraic Thinking
Number and Operations in Base Ten

CALIFORNIA COMMON CORE STANDARDS 4.OA.3, 4.NBT.5

4 Divide by 1-Digit Numbers 141

Domains Operations and Algebraic Thinking
Number and Operations in Base Ten

CALIFORNIA COMMON CORE STANDARDS 4.OA.3, 4.NBT.6

Chapter 4 Overview

In this chapter, you will explore and discover answers to the following **Essential Questions**:

- How can you divide by 1-digit numbers?
- How can you use remainders in division problems?
- How can you estimate quotients?
- How can you model division with a 1-digit divisor?

Chapter 5 Overview

In this chapter, you will explore and discover answers to the following **Essential Questions**:

- How can you find factors and multiples, and how can you generate and describe number patterns?
- How can you use models or lists to find factors?
- How can you create a number pattern?

5 Factors, Multiples, and Patterns 199

Domain Operations and Algebraic Thinking

CALIFORNIA COMMON CORE STANDARDS 4.OA.4, 4.OA.5

GAS ST

Fractions and Decimals

Critical Area Developing an understanding of fraction equivalence, addition and subtraction of fractions with like denominators, and multiplication of fractions by whole numbers

Critical Area

GO DIGITAL

Go online! Your math lessons are interactive. Use *i*Tools, Animated Math Models, the Multimedia *e*Glossary, and more.

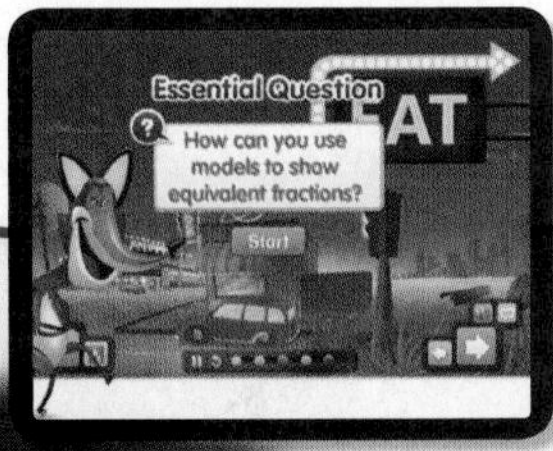

Chapter 6 Overview

Essential Questions:

- What strategies can you use to compare fractions and write equivalent fractions?
- What models can help you compare and order fractions?
- How can you find equivalent fractions?
- How can you solve problems that involve fractions?

Chapter 7 Overview

Essential Questions:

- How do you add or subtract fractions that have the same denominator?
- Why do you add or subtract the numerators and not the denominators?
- Why do you rename mixed numbers when adding or subtracting fractions?
- How do you know that your sum or difference is reasonable?

Chapter 8 Overview

In this chapter, you will explore and discover answers to the following **Essential Questions**:

- How do you multiply fractions by whole numbers?
- How can you write a product of a whole number and a fraction as a product of a whole number and a unit fraction?

8 Multiply Fractions by Whole Numbers 327

Domain Number and Operations–Fractions

CALIFORNIA COMMON CORE STANDARDS 4.NF.4a, 4.NF.4b, 4.NF.4c

Chapter 9 Overview

In this chapter, you will explore and discover answers to the following **Essential Questions**:

- How can you record decimal notation for fractions and compare decimal fractions?
- Why can you record tenths and hundredths as decimals and fractions?
- What are some different models you can use to find equivalent fractions?
- How can you compare decimal fractions?

9 Relate Fractions and Decimals 357

Domains Number and Operations–Fractions
Measurement and Data

CALIFORNIA COMMON CORE STANDARDS 4.NF.5, 4.NF.6, 4.NF.7, 4.MD.2

Geometry, Measurement, and Data

Critical Area Understanding that geometric figures can be analyzed and classified based on their properties, such as having parallel sides, perpendicular sides, particular angle measures, and symmetry

10 Two-Dimensional Figures 397

Domains Operations and Algebraic Thinking
Geometry

CALIFORNIA COMMON CORE STANDARDS 4.OA.5, 4.G.1, 4.G.2, 4.G.3

11 Angles 439

Domain Measurement and Data

CALIFORNIA COMMON CORE STANDARDS 4.MD.5a, 4.MD.5b, 4.MD.6, 4.MD.7

Critical Area

GO DIGITAL

Go online! Your math lessons are interactive. Use *i*Tools, Animated Math Models, the Multimedia eGlossary, and more.

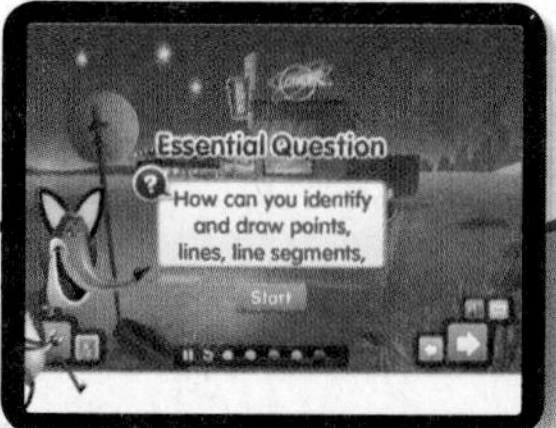

Chapter 10 Overview

Essential Questions:

- How can you draw and identify lines and angles, and how can you classify shapes?
- What are the building blocks of geometry?
- How can you classify triangles and quadrilaterals?
- How do you recognize symmetry in a polygon?

Chapter 11 Overview

Essential Questions:

- How can you measure angles and solve problems involving angle measures?
- How can you use fractions and degrees to understand angle measures?
- How can you use a protractor to measure and classify angles?
- How can equations help you find the measurement of an angle?

Chapter 12 Overview

In this chapter, you will explore and discover answers to the following **Essential Questions**:

- How can you use relative sizes of measurements to solve problems and to generate measurement tables that show a relationship?
- How can you compare metric units of length, mass, or liquid volume?
- How can you compare customary units of length, weight, or liquid volume?

12 Relative Sizes of Measurement Units 469

Domain Measurement and Data

CALIFORNIA COMMON CORE STANDARDS 4.MD.1, 4.MD.2, 4.MD.4

Chapter 13 Overview

In this chapter, you will explore and discover answers to the following **Essential Questions**:

- How can you use formulas for perimeter and area to solve problems?
- How are area and perimeter different?
- What are some methods you can use to find area and perimeter of a figure?
- How could two different rectangles have the same perimeter or the same area?

13 Algebra: Perimeter and Area 523

Domain Measurement and Data

CALIFORNIA COMMON CORE STANDARDS 4.MD.3

Critical Area

Place Value and Operations with Whole Numbers

CRITICAL AREA Developing understanding and fluency with multi-digit multiplication, and developing understanding of dividing to find quotients involving multi-digit dividends

Space Shuttle launching from Kennedy Space Center ▶

Project

Food in Space

The United States is planning a manned mission to Mars. The crew must take all of its food along on the journey, because there is no food available on Mars.

Get Started

Work with a partner. You are in charge of planning the amount of food needed for the Mars mission. Decide how much food will be needed for the entire trip. Use the Important Facts to help you plan. **Explain** your thinking.

Important Facts

- Length of trip to Mars: 6 months
- Length of stay on Mars: 6 months
- Length of return trip to Earth: 6 months
- Number of astronauts: 6
- 2 cups of water weigh 1 pound.
- 1 month = 30 days (on average).
- Each astronaut needs 10 cups of water and 4 pounds of food each day.

Completed by ____________

Chapter 1

Place Value, Addition, and Subtraction to One Million

Show What You Know 

Check your understanding of important skills.

Name ______________________________

▶ Tens and Ones Write the missing numbers.

1. 27 = _____ tens _____ ones

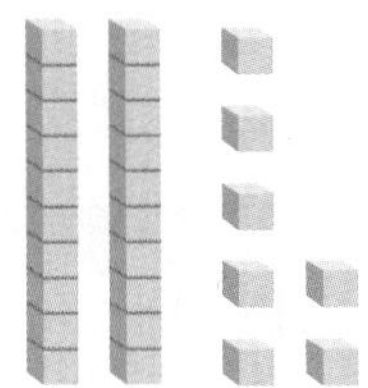

2. 93 = _____ tens _____ ones

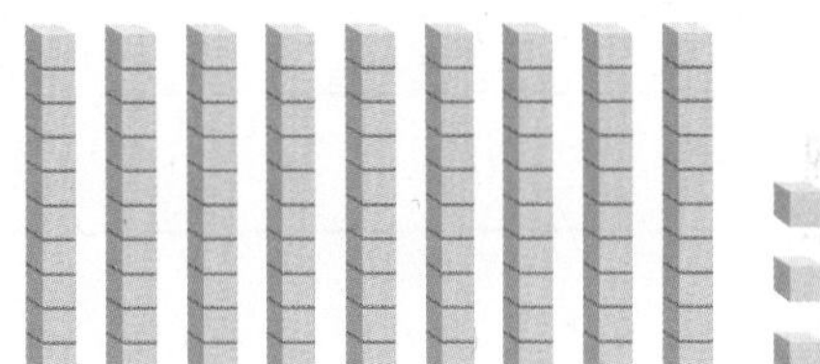

▶ Regroup Hundreds as Tens Regroup. Write the missing numbers.

3. 5 hundreds 4 tens = _____ tens

4. 8 hundreds 9 tens = _____ tens

▶ Two-Digit Addition and Subtraction Add or subtract.

5. $\begin{array}{r} 27 \\ +\ 34 \\ \hline \end{array}$

6. $\begin{array}{r} 95 \\ +\ 46 \\ \hline \end{array}$

7. $\begin{array}{r} 84 \\ -\ 27 \\ \hline \end{array}$

Math Detective

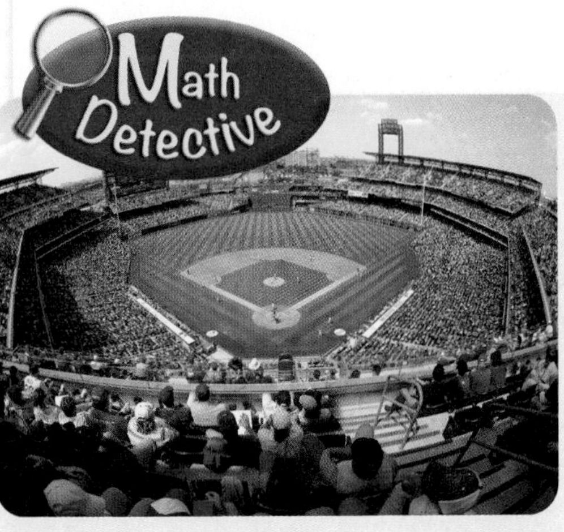

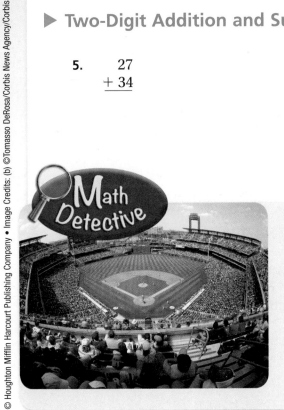

The home stadium of the Philadelphia Phillies is a large baseball park in Philadelphia, PA. Be a Math Detective. Use the following clues to find the stadium's maximum capacity.

- The 5-digit number has a 4 in the greatest place-value position and a 1 in the least place-value position.
- The digit in the thousands place has a value of 3,000.
- The digit in the hundreds place is twice the digit in the thousands place.
- There is a 5 in the tens place.

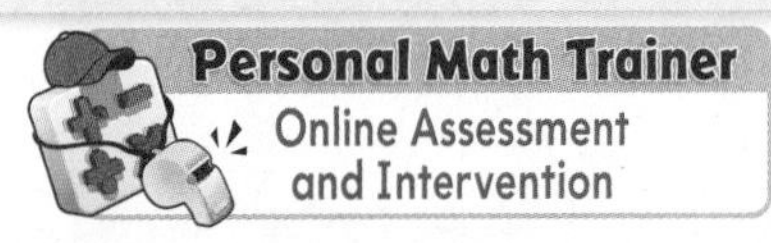

Vocabulary Builder

▶ Visualize It

Write the review words with a ✓ on the Word Line, from greatest to least place value.

Place Value

greatest | ____________________

| ____________________

| ____________________

| ____________________

least | ____________________

Review Words

✓ hundreds

inverse operations

✓ ones

✓ tens

✓ ten thousands

✓ thousands

Preview Words

estimate

expanded form

period

round

standard form

word form

▶ Understand Vocabulary

Read the definition. Which word does it describe?

1. To replace a number with another number that tells about how many or how much ____________

2. A way to write numbers by showing the value of each digit ____________

3. A number close to an exact amount ____________

4. Each group of three digits separated by commas in a multi-digit number ____________

5. A way to write numbers by using the digits 0–9, with each digit having a place value ____________

GO DIGITAL • Interactive Student Edition • Multimedia *e*Glossary

Name ______________________________

Model Place Value Relationships

Essential Question How can you describe the value of a digit?

Number and Operations in Base Ten—4.NBT.1

MATHEMATICAL PRACTICES
MP.4, MP.6, MP.7

Unlock the Problem

Hands On

Activity Build numbers through 10,000.

Materials ■ base-ten blocks

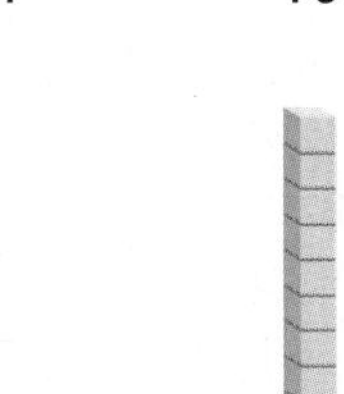
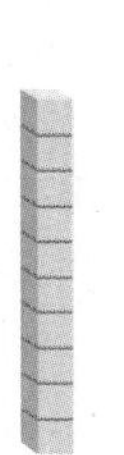

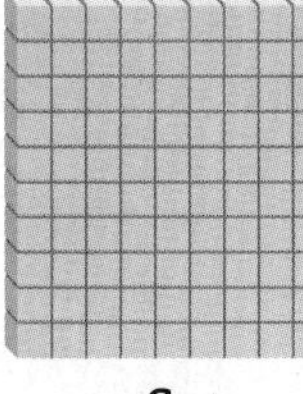
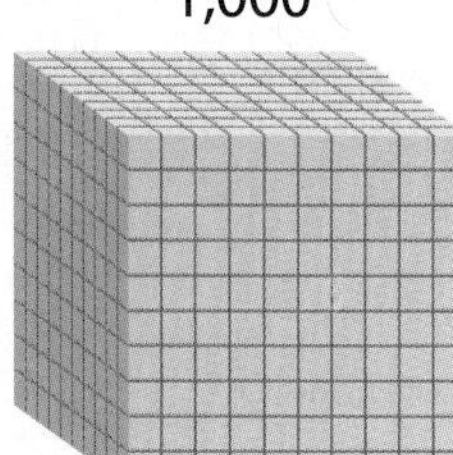
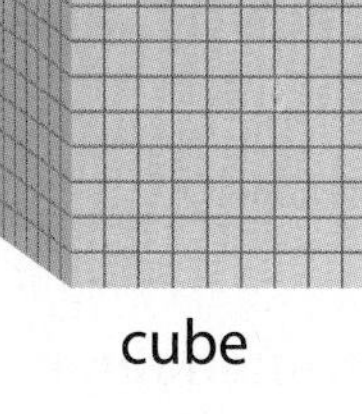

1	10	100	1,000	10,000
				?
cube	long	flat	cube	_____
1	10 ones	_____ tens	_____ hundreds	_____ thousands

A small cube represents 1.

_____ small cubes make a long. The long represents _____.

_____ longs make a flat. The flat represents _________.

_____ flats make a large cube. The large cube represents _________.

1. Describe the pattern in the shapes of the models. What will be the shape of the model for 10,000?

____

____

____

Math Talk — Mathematical Practices

Explain how you can use ten thousands longs to model 100,000.

2. Describe the pattern you see in the sizes of the models. How will the size of the model for 100,000 compare to the size of the model for 10,000?

____

____

____

Value of a Digit The value of a digit depends on its place-value position in the number. A place-value chart can help you understand the value of each digit in a number. The value of each place is 10 times the value of the place to the right.

 **Write 894,613 in the chart. Find the value of the digit 9.**

MILLIONS			THOUSANDS			ONES		
Hundreds	Tens	Ones	Hundreds	Tens	Ones	Hundreds	Tens	Ones

			8 hundred thousands	9 ten thousands	4 thousands	6 hundreds	1 ten	3 ones
			800,000	90,000	4,000	600	10	3

The value of the digit 9 is 9 ten thousands, or ________________.

Compare the values of the underlined digits.

2,304 16,135

Math Talk **Mathematical Practices**

Explain how you can compare the values of the digits without drawing a model.

STEP 1 Find the value of 3 in 2,304.

Show 2,304 in a place-value chart.

THOUSANDS			ONES		
Hundreds	Tens	Ones	Hundreds	Tens	Ones

Think: The value of the digit 3 is ____________.

Model the value of the digit 3.

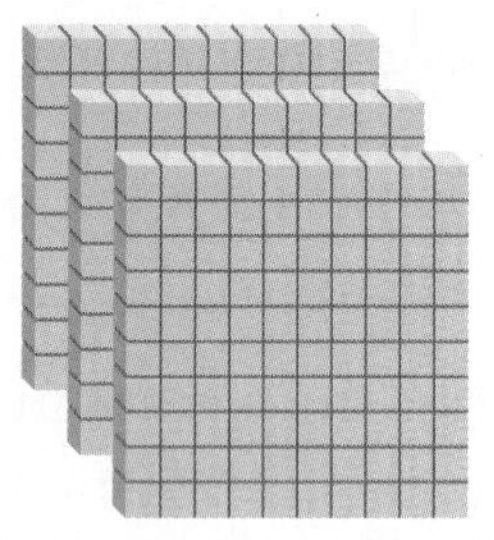

STEP 2 Find the value of 3 in 16,135.

Show 16,135 in a place-value chart.

THOUSANDS			ONES		
Hundreds	Tens	Ones	Hundreds	Tens	Ones

Think: The value of the digit 3 is ______.

Model the value of the digit 3.

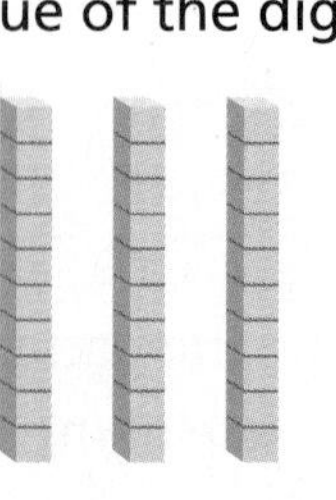

Each hundred is 10 times as many as 10, so 3 hundreds is ten times as many as 3 tens.

So, the value of 3 in 2,304 is ______ times the value of 3 in 16,135.

Name ______________________________

Share and Show

1. Complete the table below.

Number	1,000,000	100,000	10,000	1,000	100	10	1
Model	?	?	?				
Shape				cube	flat	long	cube
Group				10 hundreds	10 tens	10 ones	1 one

Find the value of the underlined digit.

2. 703,890 ________

3. 63,540 ________

4. 182,034 ________

5. 345,890 ________

Compare the values of the underlined digits.

6. 2,000 and 200

The value of 2 in __________ is ______ times the value of 2 in __________.

7. 40 and 400

The value of 4 in __________ is ______ times the value of 4 in ______.

On Your Own

Find the value of the underlined digit.

8. 230,001 ________

9. 803,040 ________

10. 46,842 ________

11. 980,650 ________

Compare the values of the underlined digits.

12. 67,908 and 76,908

The value of 7 in ______________ is ______ times the value of 7 in ______________.

13. 546,300 and 3,456

The value of 3 in ______________ is ______ times the value of 3 in ______________.

Problem Solving • Applications

Use the table for 14.

14. GO DEEPER What is the value of the digit 7 in the population of Memphis? How many times as much is the value of the place that the 7 is in than the value of the place to the right?

____

15. THINK SMARTER How many models of 100 do you need to model 3,200? Explain.

____

____

____

City Populations

City	Population*
Cleveland	431,369
Denver	610,345
Memphis	676,640

*2009 U. S. Census Bureau Estimation

16. MATHEMATICAL PRACTICE 6 Sid wrote 541,309 on his paper. Using numbers and words, **explain** how the number would change if he exchanged the digits in the hundred thousands and tens places.

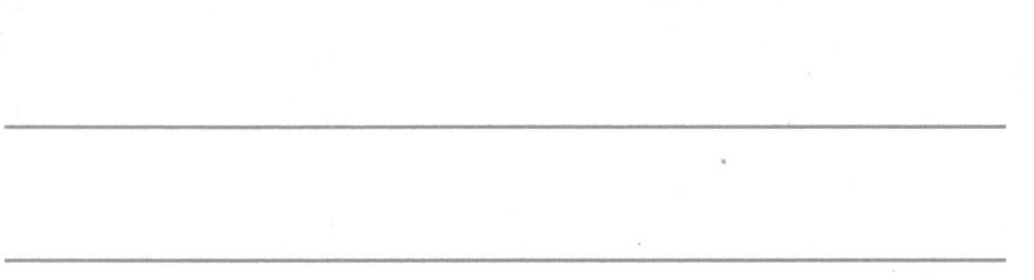

____

____

____

____

WRITE Math • Show Your Work

17. THINK SMARTER For numbers 17a–17e, select True or False for each statement.

17a. The value of 7 in 375,081 is 7,000. ○ True ○ False

17b. The value of 6 in 269,480 is 600,000. ○ True ○ False

17c. The value of 5 in 427,593 is 500. ○ True ○ False

17d. The value of 1 in 375,081 is 10. ○ True ○ False

17e. The value of 4 in 943,268 is 40,000. ○ True ○ False

FOR MORE PRACTICE: Standards Practice Book

Name ______________________________

Read and Write Numbers

Essential Question How can you read and write numbers through hundred thousands?

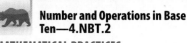

Number and Operations in Base Ten—4.NBT.2

MATHEMATICAL PRACTICES
MP.2, MP.7

Unlock the Problem

The International Space Station uses 262,400 solar cells to change sunlight to electricity.

Write 262,400 in standard form, word form, and expanded form.

Use a place-value chart.

Each group of three digits separated by a comma is called a **period**. Each period has hundreds, tens, and ones. The greatest place-value position in the thousands period is hundred thousands.

Write 262,400 in the place-value chart below.

THOUSANDS			ONES		
Hundreds	Tens	Ones	Hundreds	Tens	Ones

The number 262,400 has two periods, thousands and ones.

Standard Form: 262,400

Word Form: two hundred sixty-two thousand, four hundred

Expanded Form: 200,000 + 60,000 + 2,000 + 400

Math Talk — **Mathematical Practices**

Which digit has the greatest value in 262,400? Explain.

Try This! **Use place value to read and write numbers.**

Standard Form: ______________

Word Form: ninety-two thousand, one hundred seventy

Expanded Form:

90,000 + 2,000 + __________ + 70

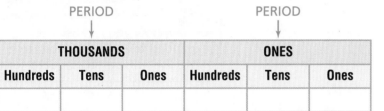

Standard Form: 200,007

Word Form:
two hundred __________, __________

Expanded Form:

__________ + 7

Share and Show

1. How can you use place value and period names to read and write 324,904 in word form?

Read and write the number in two other forms.

2. four hundred eight thousand, seventeen

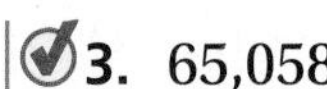

3. 65,058

Math Talk — Mathematical Practices

Explain how you can use the expanded form of a number to write the number in standard form.

On Your Own

Read and write the number in two other forms.

4. five hundred eight thousand

5. forty thousand, six hundred nineteen

6. 570,020

7. $400{,}000 + 60{,}000 + 5{,}000 + 100$

Use the number 145,973.

8. Write the name of the period that has the digits 145.

9. Write the name of the period that has the digits 973.

10. Write the digit in the ten thousands place.

11. Write the value of the digit 1.

Name ________________________

THINK SMARTER **Find the sum. Then write the answer in standard form.**

12. 5 thousands 2 tens 4 ones
+ 4 thousands 3 hundreds 2 ones

13. 6 thousands 5 hundreds
+ 1 thousand 3 hundreds 4 tens

14. 4 ten thousands + 3 ten thousands
4 hundreds 8 tens

15. 4 ten thousands 3 ones + 1 ten thousand
9 hundreds 5 ones

Problem Solving • Applications

Use the table for 16–17.

Major Cities in North Carolina

City	Population*
Durham	229,171
Greensboro	255,124
Raleigh	405,612

*U.S. Census Bureau 2008 Estimated Population

16. MATHEMATICAL PRACTICE 4 **Use Graphs** Which city has a population of two hundred fifty-five thousand, one hundred twenty-four?

17. Write the population of Raleigh in expanded form and word form.

18. **THINK SMARTER** **What's the Error?** Sophia said that the expanded form for 605,970 is 600,000 + 50,000 + 900 + 70. Describe Sophia's error and give the correct answer.

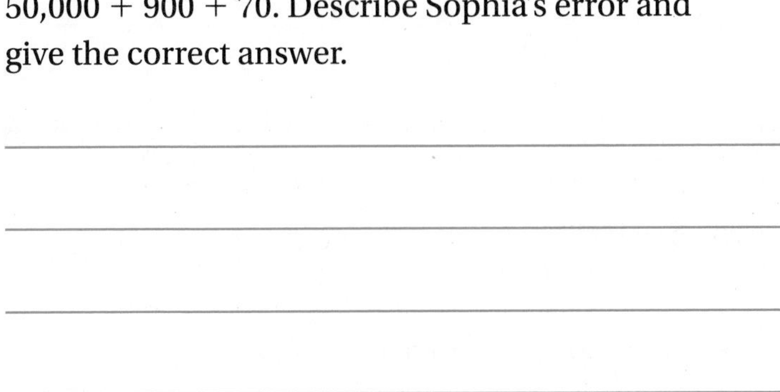

Unlock the Problem

19. GO DEEPER Mark tossed six balls while playing a number game. Three balls landed in one section, and three balls landed in another section. His score is greater than one hundred thousand. What could his score be?

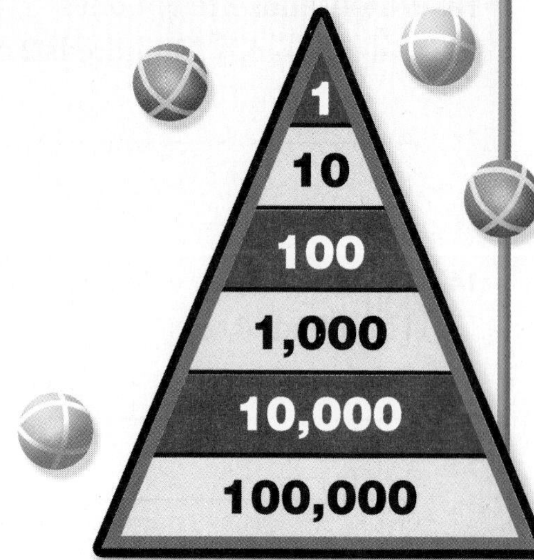

a. What do you know? ______________________________

____

____

b. How can you use what you know about place value

to find what Mark's score could be? ______________________________

____

____

____

____

____

____

c. Draw a diagram to show one way to solve the problem.

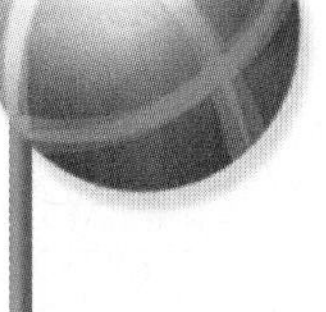

d. Complete the sentences.

Three balls could have landed in the

______________________ section.

Three balls could have landed in the

______________________ section.

Mark's score could be ______________

______________.

20. THINK SMARTER What is another way to write 615,004? Mark all that apply.

- (A) six hundred fifteen thousand, four
- (B) six hundred five thousand, fourteen
- (C) 60,000 + 10,000 + 5,000 + 4
- (D) 600,000 + 10,000 + 5,000 + 4

FOR MORE PRACTICE: Standards Practice Book

Name ___________________________

Compare and Order Numbers

Essential Question How can you compare and order numbers?

Number and Operations in Base Ten—4.NBT.2

MATHEMATICAL PRACTICES
MP.2, MP.4, MP.5

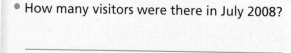

Unlock the Problem Real World

Grand Canyon National Park in Arizona had 651,028 visitors in July 2008 and 665,188 visitors in July 2009. In which year did the park have more visitors during the month of July?

- How many visitors were there in July 2008?

____

- How many visitors were there in July 2009?

____

Example 1 Use a place-value chart.

You can use a place-value chart to line up the digits by place value. Line up the ones with the ones, the tens with the tens, and so on. Compare 651,028 and 665,188.

Write 651,028 and 665,188 in the place-value chart below.

THOUSANDS			ONES		
Hundreds	Tens	Ones	Hundreds	Tens	Ones

Start at the left. Compare the digits in each place-value position until the digits differ.

STEP 1 Compare the hundred thousands.

651,028

665,188

6 hundred thousands ◯ 6 hundred thousands

↑ Write <, >, or =.

The digits in the hundred thousands place are the same.

STEP 2 Compare the ten thousands.

651,028

665,188

5 ten thousands ◯ 6 ten thousands

↑ Write <, >, or =.

5 ten thousands is less than 6 ten thousands so, 651,028 < 665,188.

Since 651,028 < 665,188, there were more visitors in July 2009 than in July 2008.

Example 2 **Use a number line to order 10,408; 10,433; and 10,416 from least to greatest.**

Locate and label each point on the number line. The first one is done for you.

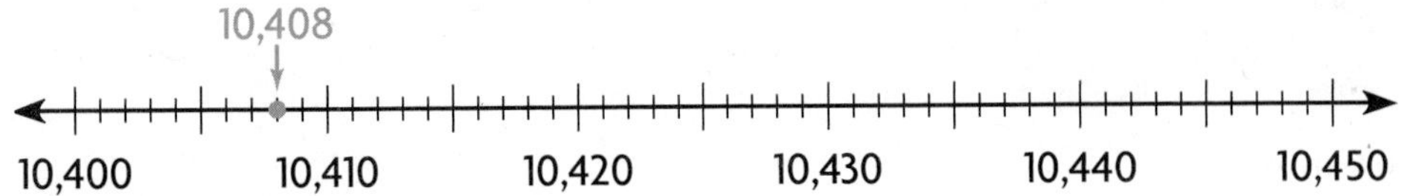

Think: Numbers to the left are closer to 0.

So, the numbers from least to greatest are 10,408; 10,416; and 10,433.
10,408 < 10,416 < 10,433

Share and Show

1. Compare 15,327 and 15,341.
   Write <, >, or =. Use the number line to help.

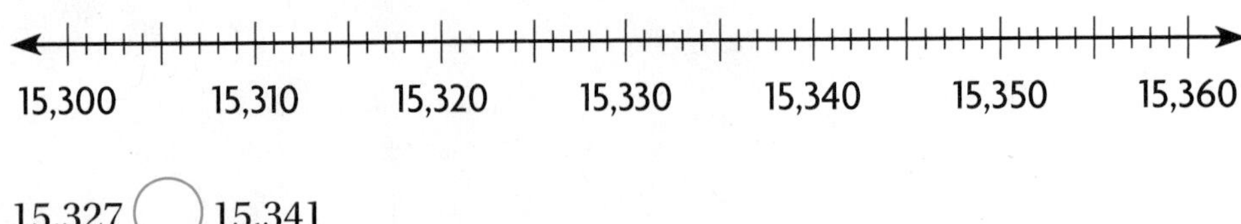

15,327 ◯ 15,341

Compare. Write <, >, or =.

2. \$631,328 ◯ \$640,009

3. 56,991 ◯ 52,880

4. 708,561 ◯ 629,672

5. 143,062 ◯ 98,643

Order from greatest to least.

6. 20,650; 21,150; 20,890

____

Math Talk — **Mathematical Practices**

Explain how you ordered the numbers from greatest to least in Exercise 6.

Name ______________________

On Your Own

Compare. Write <, >, or =.

7. \$2,212 ◯ \$2,600

8. 88,304 ◯ 88,304

9. \$524,116 ◯ \$61,090

10. 751,272 ◯ 851,001

Order from least to greatest.

11. 41,090; 41,190; 40,009

12. 910,763; 912,005; 95,408

MATHEMATICAL PRACTICE 7 Identify Relationships **Algebra** **Write all of the digits that can replace each** $\blacksquare$**.**

13. $567 < 5\blacksquare 5 < 582$

14. $464{,}545 > 4\blacksquare 3{,}535 > 443{,}550$

15. Which digits can replace the $\blacksquare$ to make a true statement?
$6{,}456 < 6{,}\blacksquare 12 < 6{,}788$

16. GO DEEPER At Monica's Used Cars, the sales staff set a goal of \$25,500 in sales each week. The sales for three weeks were \$28,288; \$25,369; and \$25,876. Which total did not meet the goal?

17. THINK SMARTER Max said that 36,594 is less than 5,980 because 3 is less than 5. Describe Max's error and give the correct answer.

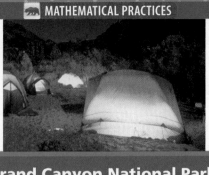

Problem Solving • Applications Real World

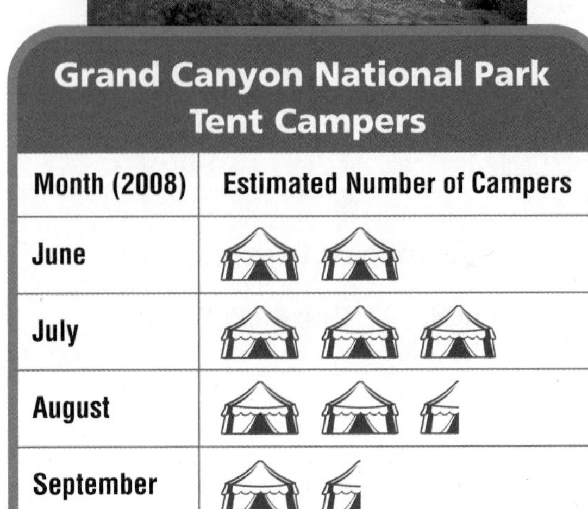

Grand Canyon National Park Tent Campers

Month (2008)	Estimated Number of Campers
June	2 tents
July	3 tents
August	2 and a half tents
September	1 and a half tents

Key: Each tent = 5,000.

Use the picture graph for 18–20.

18. MATHEMATICAL PRACTICE 4 **Use Graphs** In which month shown did Grand Canyon National Park have about 7,500 tent campers?

____

19. Which months had more than 10,000 tent campers?

____

20. What if during the month of October, the park had 22,500 tent campers? How many symbols would be placed on the pictograph for October?

____

21. THINK SMARTER **What's the Question?** Compare: 643,251; 633,512; and 633,893. The answer is 633,512.

____

____

Personal Math Trainer

22. THINK SMARTER + Zachary's school set a goal of collecting 12,155 cans of food each day. In the first 3 days they collected 12,250 cans; 10,505 cans; and 12,434 cans. Write each number in the box that tells whether or not they met their goal.

12,434 | 10,505 | 12,250

Met the daily goal	Did not meet the daily goal

FOR MORE PRACTICE: Standards Practice Book

Name ____________________

Round Numbers

Essential Question How can you round numbers?

Number and Operations in Base Ten—4.NBT.3

MATHEMATICAL PRACTICES
MP.1, MP.2, MP.5, MP.7

Unlock the Problem Real World

During May 2008, the Mount Rushmore National Monument in South Dakota welcomed 138,202 visitors. A website reported that about 1 hundred thousand people visited the park during that month. Was the estimate reasonable?

- Underline what you are asked to find.
- Circle the information you will use.

An **estimate** tells you about how many or about how much. It is close to an exact amount. You can **round** a number to find an estimate.

One Way Use a number line.

To round a number to the nearest hundred thousand, find the hundred thousands it is between.

________ < 138,202 < ________

Use a number line to see which hundred thousand 138,202 is closest to.

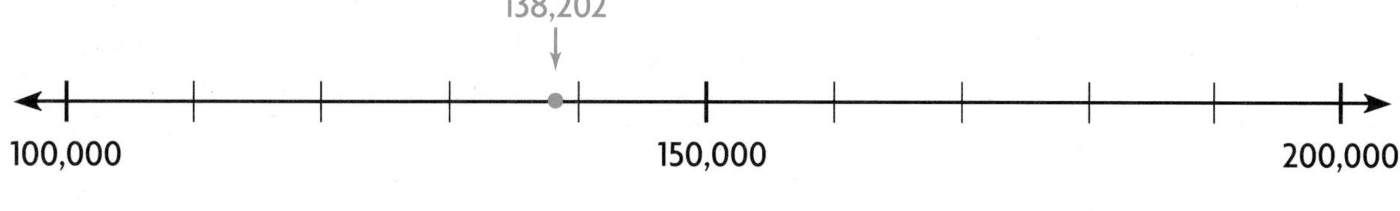

138,202 is closer to ________ than ________.

So, 1 hundred thousand is a reasonable estimate for 138,202.

Math Talk **Mathematical Practices**
Is 155,000 closer to 100,000 or 200,000? **Explain.**

1. What number is halfway between 100,000 and 200,000?

____

2. How does knowing where the halfway point is help you find which hundred thousand 138,202 is closest to? Explain.

____

____

____

Another Way Use place value.

Mount Rushmore is located 5,725 feet above sea level. About how high is Mount Rushmore above sea level, to the nearest thousand feet?

To round a number to the nearest thousand, find the thousands it is between.

__________ < 5,725 < __________

Look at the digit in the place-value position to the right.

5,725

Think: The digit in the hundreds place is 7.
So, 5,725 is closer to 6,000 than 5,000.

So, Mount Rushmore is about __________ feet above sea level.

Math Talk **Mathematical Practices**

Explain how you know that 5,700 is closer to 6,000 than to 5,000.

3. What number is halfway between 70,000 and 80,000?

____

4. What is 75,000 rounded to the nearest ten thousand? Explain.

____

____

____

Math Idea

When a number is exactly half way between two rounding numbers, round to the greater number.

Try This! **Round to the place value of the underlined digit.**

A $\underline{6}4{,}999$

____

B $\underline{8}50{,}000$

____

C $30\underline{1}{,}587$

____

D $1\underline{0}{,}832$

____

Name ____________________

Share and Show

1. Suppose 255,113 people live in a city. Is it reasonable to say that about 300,000 people live in the city? Use the number line to help you solve the problem. Explain.

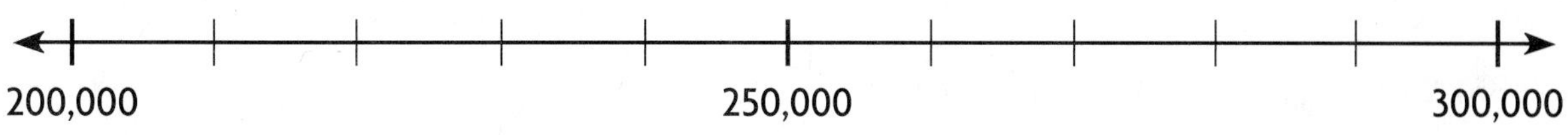

____

____

Round to the place value of the underlined digit.

2. 934,567 ____________
3. 641,267 ____________
4. 234,890 ____________
5. 347,456 ____________

On Your Own

Round to the place value of the underlined digit.

6. 562,408 ____________
7. 284,792 ____________
8. 199,814 ____________
9. 923,718 ____________

Problem Solving • Applications

10. THINK SMARTER The number 2,■00 is missing a digit. The number rounded to the nearest thousand is 3,000. List all of the possibilities for the missing digit. Explain your answer.

____

____

____

____

____

11. GO DEEPER What is 277,300 rounded to the nearest thousand? to the nearest ten thousand?

____

12. THINK SMARTER About 300,000 people attended a festival. For numbers 12a–12e, choose Yes or No to show whether each number could be the exact number of people that attended the festival.

12a.	351,213	○ Yes	○ No
12b.	249,899	○ Yes	○ No
12c.	252,348	○ Yes	○ No
12d.	389,001	○ Yes	○ No
12e.	305,992	○ Yes	○ No

Connect to Science

Data Gathering

Some scientists count and measure groups of things. Benchmarks can be used to estimate the size of a group or a population. A *benchmark* is a known number of things that helps you understand the size or amount of a different number of things.

Use the benchmark to find a reasonable estimate for the number of coquina shells it would take to fill a jar.

It would take about 5 times the benchmark to fill the jar.
$100 + 100 + 100 + 100 + 100 = 500$

Benchmark
100 shells

200; 500; or 5,000

The most reasonable estimate for the number of coquina shells it would take to fill the jar is 500 shells.

MATHEMATICAL PRACTICE 1 Evaluate Reasonableness **Use the benchmark to find a reasonable estimate. Circle the reasonable estimate.**

13.

500 beads

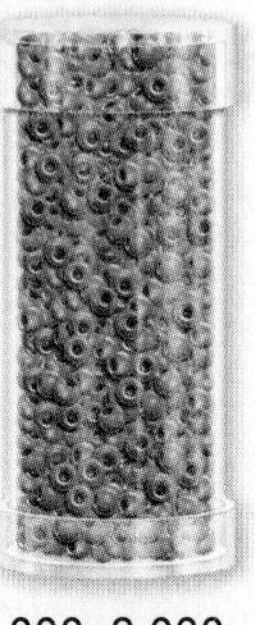
1,000; 2,000; or 3,000

14.

10,000 blades of grass

1,000; 10,000; or 100,000

FOR MORE PRACTICE: Standards Practice Book

Name ____________________

Mid-Chapter Checkpoint

Vocabulary

Choose the best term from the box.

Vocabulary
expanded form
period
round
standard form

1. The ____________ of 23,850 is 20,000 + 3,000 + 800 + 50. (p. 9)

2. You can ____________ to find *about* how much or how many. (p. 17)

3. In 192,860 the digits 1, 9, and 2 are in the same

____________. (p. 9)

Concepts and Skills

Find the value of the underlined digit. (4.NBT.1)

4. 3$\underline{8}$0,671 ____________

5. 10,6$\underline{9}$8 ____________

6. $\underline{6}$50,234 ____________

Write the number in two other forms. (4.NBT.2)

7. 293,805

____

____

____

8. 300,000 + 5,000 + 20 + 6

____

____

____

Compare. Write <, >, or =. (4.NBT.2)

9. 457,380 ◯ 458,590

10. 390,040 ◯ 39,040

11. 11,809 ◯ 11,980

Round to the place of the underlined digit. (4.NBT.3)

12. $\underline{1}$40,250 ____________

13. 10,$\underline{4}$50 ____________

14. 12$\underline{6}$,234 ____________

15. Last year, three hundred twenty-three thousand people visited the museum. What is this number written in standard form? (4.NBT.2)

16. Rounded to the nearest thousand, what number will 4,645 be rounded to? (4.NBT.3)

17. What is the highest volcano in the Cascade Range? (4.NBT.2)

Cascade Range Volcanoes

Name	State	Height (ft)
Lassen Peak	CA	10,457
Mt. Rainier	WA	14,410
Mt. Shasta	CA	14,161
Mt. St. Helens	WA	8,364

18. Richard got 263,148 hits when he did an Internet search. What is the value of the digit 6 in this number? (4.NBT.1)

Name ____________________

Rename Numbers

Essential Question How can you rename a whole number?

Number and Operations in Base Ten—4.NBT.1 *Also 4.NBT.2*

MATHEMATICAL PRACTICES
MP.2, MP.4, MP.7

Investigate

Materials ■ base-ten blocks

You can regroup numbers to rename them.

A. Use large cubes and flats to model 1,200. Draw a quick picture to record your model.

The model shows ______ large cube and ______ flats.

Another name for 1,200 is ______ thousand ______ hundreds.

B. Use only flats to model 1,200.
Draw a quick picture to record your model.

The model shows ______ flats.

Another name for 1,200 is ______ hundreds.

Draw Conclusions

1. How is the number of large cubes and flats in the first model related to the number of flats in the second model?

____

____

2. Can you model 1,200 using only longs? Explain.

____

____

3. You renamed 1,200 as hundreds. How can you rename 1,200 as tens? Explain.

____

____

4. **THINK SMARTER** What would the models in Step A and Step B look like for 5,200? How can you rename 5,200 as hundreds?

____

____

____

Make Connections

You can also use a place-value chart to help rename numbers.

THOUSANDS			ONES		
Hundreds	Tens	Ones	Hundreds	Tens	Ones
5	0	0,	0	0	0

5 hundred thousands
50 ten thousands
500 thousands
5,000 hundreds
50,000 tens
500,000 ones

Write 32 hundreds on the place-value chart below. What is 32 hundreds written in standard form?

THOUSANDS			ONES		
Hundreds	Tens	Ones	Hundreds	Tens	Ones

32 hundreds

32 hundreds written in standard form is __________.

Mathematical Practices

Explain how you can rename 4 ten thousands 3 thousands as thousands.

Name ________________________________

Share and Show

Rename the number. Draw a quick picture to help.

1. 150

_____ tens

2. 1,400

_____ hundreds

3. 2 thousands 3 hundreds

_____ hundreds

4. 13 hundreds

_____ thousand _____ hundreds

Rename the number. Use the place-value chart to help.

5. 18 thousands = ________________

THOUSANDS			ONES		
Hundreds	Tens	Ones	Hundreds	Tens	Ones

6. 570,000 = 57 ________________

THOUSANDS			ONES		
Hundreds	Tens	Ones	Hundreds	Tens	Ones

Rename the number.

7. 580 = _____ tens

8. 740,000 = _____ ten thousands

9. 8 hundreds 4 tens = 84 _____

10. 29 thousands = __________

Unlock the Problem — Real World

11. THINK SMARTER A toy store is ordering 3,000 remote control cars. The store can order the cars in sets of 10. How many sets of 10 does the store need to order?

a. What information do you need to use?

b. What do you need to find?

c. How can renaming numbers help you solve this problem?

d. Describe a strategy you can use to solve the problem.

e. How many sets of 10 remote control cars does the store need to buy?

12. GO DEEPER Ivan sold 53 boxes of oranges on Friday and 27 boxes on Saturday during a citrus sale. There were 10 oranges in each box. How many oranges did he sell in all?

13. MATHEMATICAL PRACTICE 2 **Use Reasoning** A store sold a total of 15,000 boxes of buttons last month. If the store sold 150,000 buttons, how many buttons were in each box?

14. THINK SMARTER For numbers 14a–14d, select True or False for each statement.

14a. 9 hundreds 3 tens can be renamed as 39 tens. ○ True ○ False

14b. 370,000 can be renamed as 37 ten thousands. ○ True ○ False

14c. 780 can be renamed as 78 tens. ○ True ○ False

14d. 42,000 can be renamed as 42 thousands. ○ True ○ False

FOR MORE PRACTICE: Standards Practice Book

Name ________________________________

Add Whole Numbers

Essential Question How can you add whole numbers?

Number and Operations in Base Ten—4.NBT.4 *Also 4.OA.3, 4.NBT.3*

MATHEMATICAL PRACTICES
MP.1, MP.5, MP.8

Unlock the Problem (Real World)

Alaska is the largest state in the United States by area. Its land area is 570,374 square miles and its water surface area is 86,051 square miles. Find the total area of Alaska.

- Underline what you are asked to find.
- Circle the information you will use.

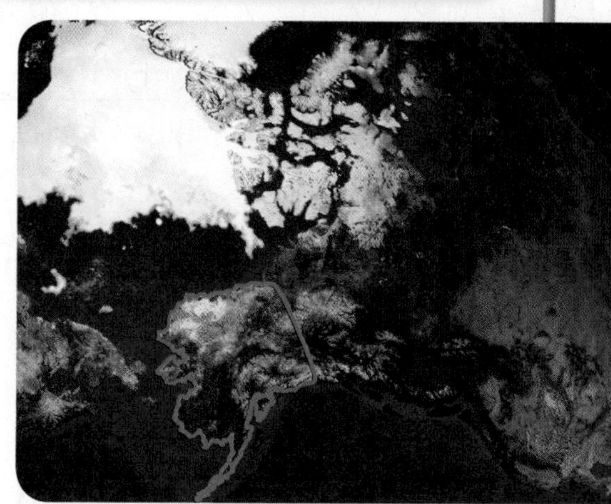

▲ The area of Alaska is outlined in the photo above.

Find the sum.

Add. 570,374 + 86,051

Think: It is important to line up the addends by place value when adding two numbers.

STEP 1 Add the ones.

Add the tens. Regroup.

12 tens = 1 hundred ______ tens

$$\begin{array}{r} \overset{1}{} \\ 570{,}374 \\ +\ 86{,}051 \\ \hline \end{array}$$

STEP 2 Add the hundreds.

Add the thousands.

$$\begin{array}{r} 570{,}374 \\ +\ 86{,}051 \\ \hline 25 \end{array}$$

STEP 3 Add the ten thousands.

Regroup.

15 ten thousands =

1 hundred thousand ______ ten thousands

$$\begin{array}{r} 570{,}374 \\ +\ 86{,}051 \\ \hline 6{,}425 \end{array}$$

STEP 4 Add the hundred thousands.

$$\begin{array}{r} 570{,}374 \\ +\ 86{,}051 \\ \hline 56{,}425 \end{array}$$

So, the total area of Alaska is __________ square miles.

Math Talk — Mathematical Practices

Explain how you know when to regroup when adding.

Estimate You can estimate to tell whether an answer is reasonable. To estimate a sum, round each addend before you add.

Example Estimate. Then find the sum.

Juneau has an area of 2,717 square miles. Valdez has an area of 222 square miles. What is their combined area?

A Estimate. Use the grid to help you align the addends by place value.

2, 7 1 7 → 3, 0 0 0
2 2 2 → +

Round to the nearest thousand.

Round to the nearest hundred.

So, the combined area of Juneau and Valdez is about ________ square miles.

ERROR Alert

Remember to align the addends by place value.

B Find the sum.

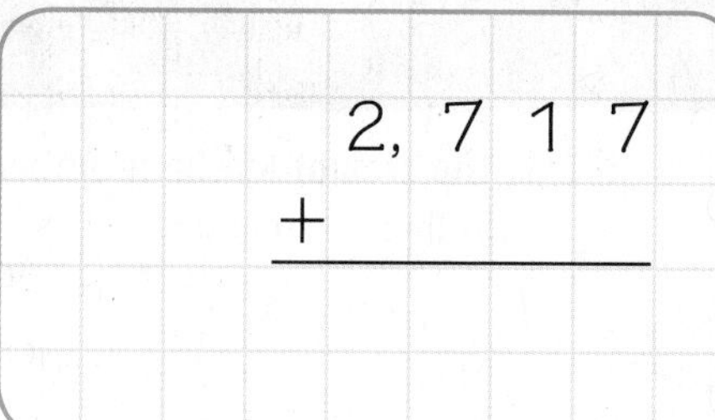

Think: Begin by adding the ones.

So, the combined area of Juneau and Valdez is ________ square miles.

- Is the sum reasonable? Explain.

____

Share and Show

1. Use the grid to find 738,901 + 162,389.

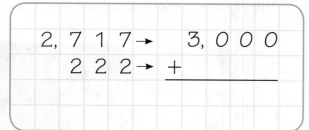

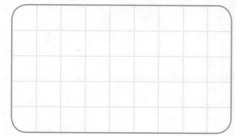

Use the grid to align the addends by place value.

Name ________________

Estimate. Then find the sum.

2. Estimate: ________

$$\begin{array}{r} 72{,}931 \\ +18{,}563 \\ \hline \end{array}$$

3. Estimate: ________

$$\begin{array}{r} 432{,}068 \\ +239{,}576 \\ \hline \end{array}$$

4. Estimate: ________

$$\begin{array}{r} 64{,}505 \\ +38{,}972 \\ \hline \end{array}$$

Math Talk — Mathematical Practices

Explain how you know your answer for Exercise 2 is reasonable.

On Your Own

Estimate. Then find the sum.

5. Estimate: ________

$$\begin{array}{r} 839{,}136 \\ +120{,}193 \\ \hline \end{array}$$

6. Estimate: ________

$$\begin{array}{r} 186{,}231 \\ +\ 88{,}941 \\ \hline \end{array}$$

7. Estimate: ________

$$\begin{array}{r} 744{,}201 \\ +168{,}900 \\ \hline \end{array}$$

8. Estimate: ________

$$\begin{array}{r} 374{,}096 \\ +187{,}543 \\ \hline \end{array}$$

9. Estimate: ________

$$\begin{array}{r} 100{,}738 \\ +19{,}553 \\ \hline \end{array}$$

10. Estimate: ________

$$\begin{array}{r} 512{,}335 \\ +297{,}866 \\ \hline \end{array}$$

MATHEMATICAL PRACTICE 2 Reason Abstractly **Algebra** **Find the missing number and name the property you used to find it. Write *Commutative* or *Associative*.**

Remember

Commutative Property

4 + 5 = 5 + 4

Associative Property

4 + (7 + 3) = (4 + 7) + 3

11. (4,580 + 5,008) + 2,351 = 4,580 + (+ 2,351)

____

12. 7,801 +   = 4,890 + 7,801 ________________

13. 2,592 + 3,385 = 3,385 +   ________________

Problem Solving • Applications

Use the table for 14–15.

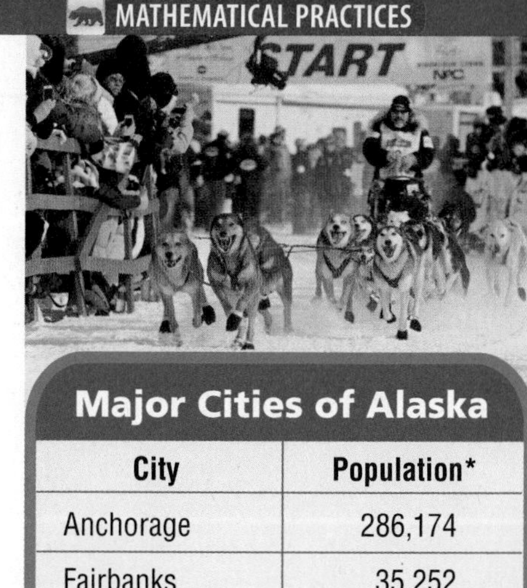

Major Cities of Alaska

City	Population*
Anchorage	286,174
Fairbanks	35,252
Juneau	30,796

*2009 U.S. Census Bureau estimates

14. THINK SMARTER What is the combined population of the three major Alaskan cities? Estimate to verify your answer.

15. MATHEMATICAL PRACTICE 6 The digit 5 occurs two times in the population of Fairbanks. What is the value of each 5? **Explain** your answer.

16. GO DEEPER Kaylie has 164 stamps in her collection. Her friend Nellie has 229 more stamps than Kaylie. How many stamps do Kaylie and Nellie have?

WRITE ▸ *Math* • **Show Your Work**

17. THINK SMARTER Alaska's Glacier Bay National Park had 431,986 visitors one year. The next year, the park had 22,351 more visitors than the year before. How many people visited during the two years? Show your work and explain how you found your answer.

Name ______________________________

Subtract Whole Numbers

Essential Question How can you subtract whole numbers?

Number and Operations in Base Ten—4.NBT.4 *Also 4.NBT.3, 4.OA.3*

MATHEMATICAL PRACTICES
MP.1, MP.5, MP.8

Unlock the Problem (Real World)

Mt. Bear and Mt. Bona are two mountains in Alaska. Mt. Bear is 14,831 feet tall and Mt. Bona is 16,421 feet tall. How much taller is Mt. Bona than Mt. Bear?

▲ Mt. Bear and Mt. Bona are in the St. Elias Mountain Range located in the Wrangell-St. Elias National Park and Preserve in Alaska.

Estimate. 16,000 − 15,000 = ______

Subtract. 16,421 − 14,831

STEP 1 Subtract the ones.

Regroup to subtract the tens.

4 hundreds 2 tens =

3 hundreds ______ tens

```
   312
 16,421
-14,831
```

STEP 2 Regroup to subtract the hundreds.

6 thousands 3 hundreds =

5 thousands ______ hundreds

```
    13
  5 312
 16,421
-14,831
     90
```

STEP 3 Subtract the thousands.

Subtract the ten thousands.

```
    13
  5 312
 16,421
-14,831
   ,590
```

So, Mt. Bona is ______ feet taller than Mt. Bear. Since ______ is close to the estimate of ______, the answer is reasonable.

Try This! **Use addition to check your answer.**

1$\not{3}$ 5 $\not{3}$12 1$\not{6}$,4$\not{2}$1 −14,831 1,590	1 1 1,590 +14,831

So, the answer checks.

Math Idea

Inverse operations undo each other. Addition and subtraction are inverse operations, so you can use addition to check a subtraction problem.

Share and Show

1. Subtract. Use the grid to record the problem.

   637,350 − 43,832

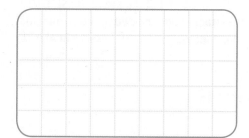

Math Talk **Mathematical Practices**

Explain how you know which places to regroup to subtract.

Estimate. Then find the difference.

2. Estimate: ________

$$\begin{array}{r} 14,659 \\ -11,584 \\ \hline \end{array}$$

3. Estimate: ________

$$\begin{array}{r} 456,912 \\ -\ 37,800 \\ \hline \end{array}$$

4. Estimate: ________

$$\begin{array}{r} 407,001 \\ -184,652 \\ \hline \end{array}$$

On Your Own

Estimate. Then find the difference.

5. Estimate: ________

$$\begin{array}{r} 942,385 \\ -461,803 \\ \hline \end{array}$$

6. Estimate: ________

$$\begin{array}{r} 798,300 \\ -348,659 \\ \hline \end{array}$$

7. Estimate: ________

$$\begin{array}{r} 300,980 \\ -159,000 \\ \hline \end{array}$$

Name ______________________________

Practice: Copy and Solve **Subtract. Add to check.**

8. 653,809 − 256,034

9. 258,197 − 64,500

10. 496,004 − 398,450

11. 500,000 − 145,609

MATHEMATICAL PRACTICE 2 **Reason Abstractly** **Algebra** Find the missing digit.

12.
$$\begin{array}{r} 6{,}532 \\ -\,4{,}1\square5 \\ \hline 2{,}407 \end{array}$$

13.
$$\begin{array}{r} \square08{,}665 \\ -\,659{,}420 \\ \hline 149{,}245 \end{array}$$

14.
$$\begin{array}{r} 697{,}320 \\ -\,432{,}\square08 \\ \hline 264{,}712 \end{array}$$

Problem Solving • Applications

Use the table for 15–18.

15. MATHEMATICAL PRACTICE 1 **Estimate Reasonableness** How many more acres were grown in 1996 than in 1986? Estimate to check the reasonableness of your answer.

____

____

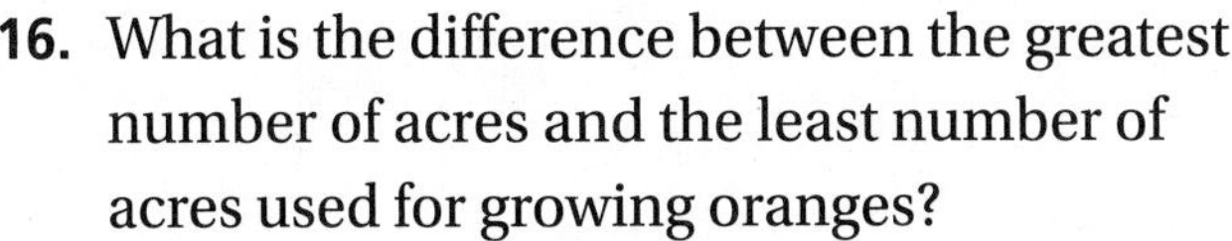

16. What is the difference between the greatest number of acres and the least number of acres used for growing oranges?

____

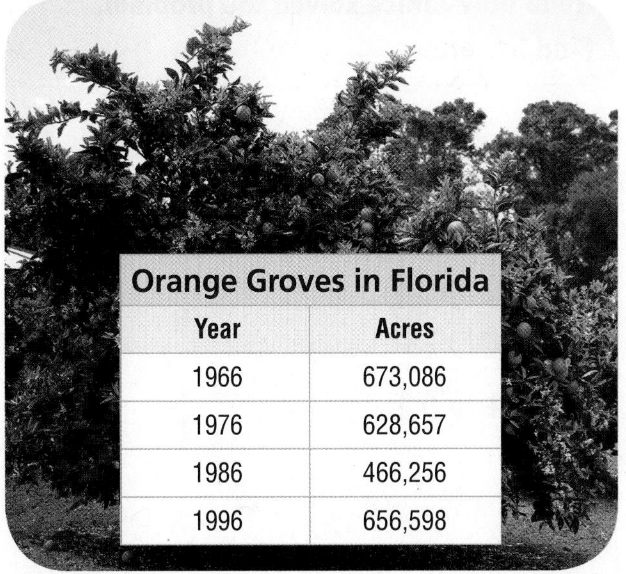

Orange Groves in Florida

Year	Acres
1966	673,086
1976	628,657
1986	466,256
1996	656,598

17. Grapefruit was grown on 144,416 acres in 1996. What is the total number of acres for oranges and grapefruit in 1996?

____

18. GO DEEPER Round the number of acres in 1966 and 1996 to the nearest ten thousand. What is the estimated difference between these two years?

____

19. THINK SMARTER There are 135,663 kilometers of U.S. coastline that border the Pacific Ocean. There are 111,866 kilometers of U.S. coastline that border the Atlantic Ocean. How many more kilometers of U.S. coastline border the Pacific Ocean than the Atlantic Ocean? Solve the problem and show how to check your answer.

____

____

20. THINK SMARTER **What's the Error?** Maryland has an area of 12,407 square miles. Texas has an area of 268,601 square miles. How much larger is Texas than Maryland?

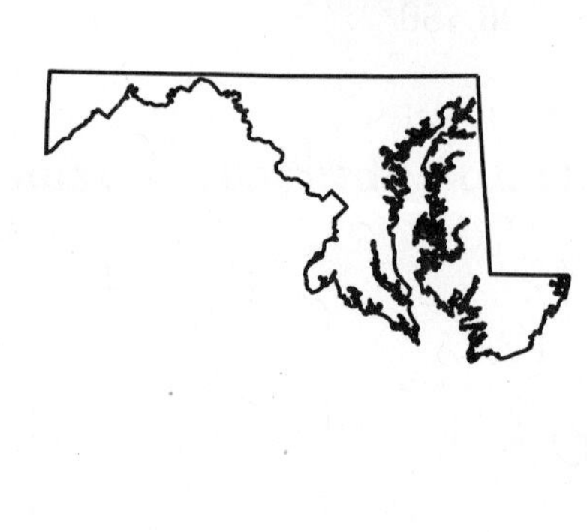

Read how Janice solved the problem. Find her error.

Texas: 268,601 square miles
Maryland: 12,407 square miles
I can subtract to find the difference.

$$\begin{array}{r} 268{,}601 \\ -\ 12{,}407 \\ \hline 144{,}531 \end{array}$$

Solve the problem and correct her error.

So, Texas is ________________ square miles larger than Maryland.

- MATHEMATICAL PRACTICE 3 **Verify Reasoning of Others** Describe Janice's error.

____

____

FOR MORE PRACTICE: Standards Practice Book

Name ______________________

Problem Solving • Comparison Problems with Addition and Subtraction

PROBLEM SOLVING
Lesson 1.8

Essential Question How can you use the strategy *draw a diagram* to solve comparison problems with addition and subtraction?

Number and Operations in Base Ten— 4.NBT.4

MATHEMATICAL PRACTICES
MP.3, MP.4, MP.5, MP.8

Unlock the Problem

Hot air balloon festivals draw large crowds of people. The attendance on the first day of one festival was 17,350. On the second day the attendance was 18,925. How many more people attended the hot air balloon festival on the second day?

Use the graphic organizer to help you solve the problem.

Read the Problem

What do I need to find?	What information do I need to use?	How will I use the information?
Write what you need to find. ______________ ______________ ______________ ______________	______________ people attended on the first day, ______________ people attended on the second day.	What strategy can you use? ______________ ______________ ______________ ______________

Solve the Problem

I can draw a bar model and write an equation to represent the problem.

18,925
17,350

18,925 − 17,350 = ______

So, ______ more people attended the festival on the second day.

Try Another Problem

During an event, a hot air balloon traveled a distance of 5,110 feet during the first trip and 850 feet more during the second trip. How far did it travel during the second trip?

Read the Problem

What do I need to find?	What information do I need to use?	How will I use the information?

Solve the Problem

- Is your answer reasonable? Explain how you know.

Mathematical Practices

Explain how inverse operations can be used to check your answer.

Name ____________________

Share and Show

1. Hot air balloons are able to fly at very high altitudes. A world record height of 64,997 feet was set in 1988. In 2005, a new record of 68,986 feet was set. How many feet higher was the 2005 record than the 1988 record?

   First, draw a diagram to show the parts of the problem.

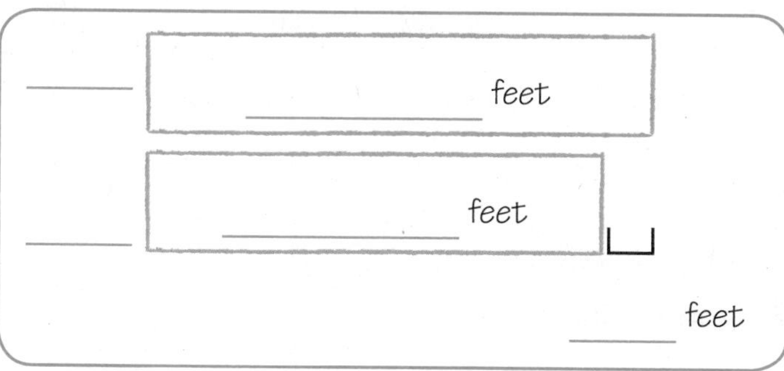

   Next, write the problem you need to solve.

   ____

   Last, solve the problem to find how many feet higher the 2005 record was than the 1988 record.

   So, the 2005 record was ________ feet higher.

2. What if a new world altitude record of 70,000 feet was set? How many feet higher would the new record be than the 2005 record?

   ____

3. Last year, the ticket sales for a commercial hot air balloon ride were $109,076. This year, the ticket sales were $125,805. How much more were the ticket sales this year?

   ____

4. A musician's first album sells 234,499 copies the first week it was released. During the second week, another 432,112 albums were sold. How many more albums were sold during the second week than the first week?

   ____

Unlock the Problem

- √ Use the Problem Solving MathBoard
- √ Underline important facts.
- √ Choose a strategy you know.

▲ Dr. Vijaypat Singhania flew the world's largest hot-air balloon when he made his record-breaking flight. The balloon he flew was over 20 stories tall.

On Your Own

Use the information in the table for 5–6.

5. MATHEMATICAL PRACTICE 4 **Use Models** Steve Fossett attempted to fly around the world in a balloon several times before he succeeded in 2002. How many more miles did he fly during the 2002 flight than during the August 1998 flight?

Steve Fossett's Balloon Flights

Year	Distance in Miles
1996	2,200
1997	10,360
1998 (January)	5,803
1998 (August)	14,235
2001	3,187
2002	20,482

____

6. GO DEEPER Is the combined distance for the 1998 flights more or less than the distance for the 2002 flight? Explain.

____

____

____

7. THINK SMARTER There were 665 hot air balloon pilots at a hot air balloon race. There were 1,550 more ground crew members than there were pilots. How many pilots and ground crew members were there all together?

____

Personal Math Trainer

8. THINK SMARTER + The first year Becky owned her car she drove it 14,378 miles. The second year she drove it 422 fewer miles than the first year. She bought the car with 16 miles on it. How many miles were on the car at the end of the second year? Show your work.

____

____

____

____

FOR MORE PRACTICE:
Standards Practice Book

Name ___________________________________

Chapter 1 Review/Test

1. Select a number for ▢ that will make a true comparison. Mark all that apply.

703,209 > ▢

Ⓐ 702,309 Ⓒ 703,209 Ⓔ 730,029

Ⓑ 703,029 Ⓓ 703,290 Ⓕ 730,209

2. Nancy wrote the greatest number that can be made using each of these digits exactly once.

5	3	4	9	8	1

Part A

What was Nancy's number? How do you know this is the greatest possible number for these digits?

Part B

What is the least number that can be made using each digit exactly once? Explain why the value of the 4 is greater than the value of the 5.

GO DIGITAL Assessment Options Chapter Test

For 3–4, use the table.

U.S. Mountain Peaks					
Name	**State**	**Height (ft)**	**Name**	**State**	**Height (ft)**
Blanca Peak	CO	14,345	Mount Whitney	CA	14,494
Crestone Peak	CO	14,294	University Peak	AK	14,470
Humboldt Peak	CO	14,064	White Mountain	CA	14,246

3. Write the name of each mountain peak in the box that describes its height, in feet.

Between 14,000 feet and 14,300 feet	Between 14,301 feet and 14,500 feet

4. Circle the name of the tallest peak. Explain how you know which of the mountain peaks is the tallest.

5. Mr. Rodriguez bought 420 pencils for the school. If there are 10 pencils in a box, how many boxes did he buy?

Ⓐ 42

Ⓑ 420

Ⓒ 430

Ⓓ 4,200

6. Bobby and Cheryl each rounded 745,829 to the nearest ten thousand. Bobby wrote 750,000 and Cheryl wrote 740,000. Who is correct? Explain the error that was made.

Name ________________________________

7. The total season attendance for a college team's home games, rounded to the nearest ten thousand, was 270,000. For numbers 7a–7d, select Yes or No to tell whether the number could be the exact attendance.

7a. 265,888 ○ Yes ○ No

7b. 260,987 ○ Yes ○ No

7c. 274,499 ○ Yes ○ No

7d. 206,636 ○ Yes ○ No

For 8–10, use the table.

The table shows recent population data for Sacramento, California.

Population of Sacramento, CA			
Age in years	**Population**	**Age in years**	**Population**
Under 5	35,010	20 to 34	115,279
5 to 9	31,406	35 to 49	92,630
10 to 14	30,253	50 to 64	79,271
15 to 19	34,219	65 and over	49,420

8. How many children are under 10 years old? Show your work.

9. How many people are between the ages of 20 and 49? Show your work.

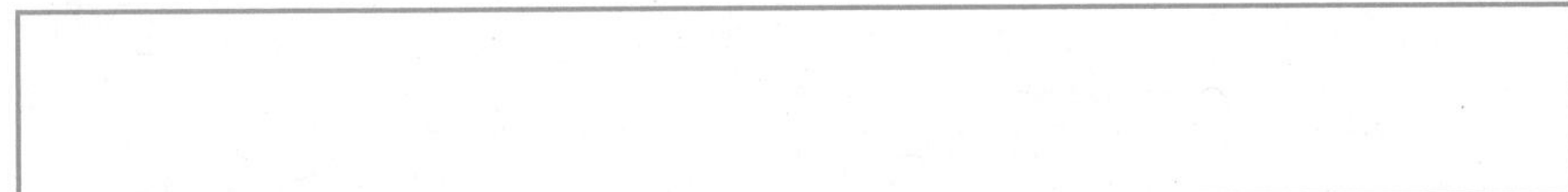

10. How many more children are under the age of 5 than between the ages of 10 and 14? Show your work.

11. For numbers 11a–11d, select True or False for each sentence.

11a. The value of 7 in 375,092 is 7,000. ○ True ○ False

11b. The value of 5 in 427,593 is 500. ○ True ○ False

11c. The value of 2 in 749,021 is 200. ○ True ○ False

11d. The value of 4 in 842,063 is 40,000. ○ True ○ False

12. Select another way to show 403,871. Mark all that apply.

(A) four hundred three thousand, eight hundred one

(B) four hundred three thousand, seventy-one

(C) four hundred three thousand, eight hundred seventy-one

(D) 400,000 + 38,000 + 800 + 70 + 1

(E) 400,000 + 3,000 + 800 + 70 + 1

(F) 4 hundred thousands + 3 thousands + 8 hundreds + 7 tens + 1 one

13. Lexi, Susie, and Rial are playing an online word game. Rial scores 100,034 points. Lexi scores 9,348 fewer points than Rial and Susie scores 9,749 more points than Lexi. What is Susie's score? Show your work.

14. There were 13,501 visitors to a museum in June. What is this number rounded to the nearest ten thousand? Explain how you rounded.

Name ______________________________

15. New Mexico has an area of 121,298 square miles. California has an area of 155,779 square miles. How much greater is the area, in square miles, of California than the area of New Mexico? Show your work and explain how you know the answer is reasonable.

16. Circle the choice that completes the statement.

10,000 less than 24,576 is [equal to / greater than / less than] 1,000 less than 14,576

17. Match the number to the value of its 5.

45,678 •	• 500
757,234 •	• 50
13,564 •	• 50,000
3,450 •	• 5,000

18. During September and October, a total of 825,150 visitors went to Grand Canyon National Park. If 448,925 visitors went to the park in September, how many visitors went to the park in October? Show your work.

19. A college baseball team had 3 games in April. Game one had an attendance of 14,753 people. Game two had an attendance of 20,320 people. Game three had an attendance of 14,505 people. Write the games in order from the least attendance to the greatest attendance. Use pictures, words, or numbers to show how you know.

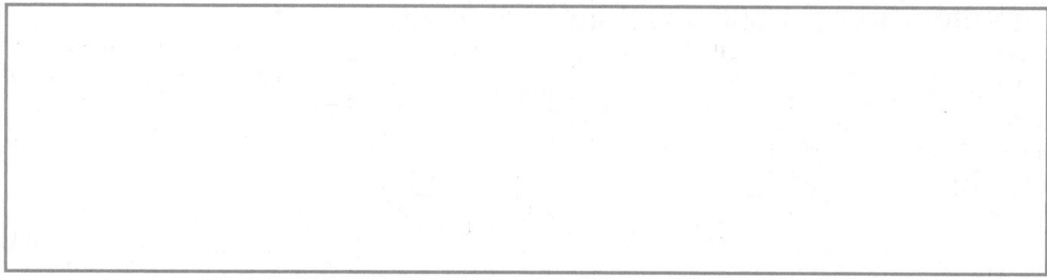

20. Caden made a four-digit number with a 5 in the thousands place, a 5 in the ones place, a 6 in the tens place, and a 4 in the hundreds place. What was the number?

Chapter 2

Multiply by 1-Digit Numbers

Show What You Know

Check your understanding of important skills.

Name ______________________

▶ Arrays Write a multiplication sentence for the array.

1.  

______ ______

2. 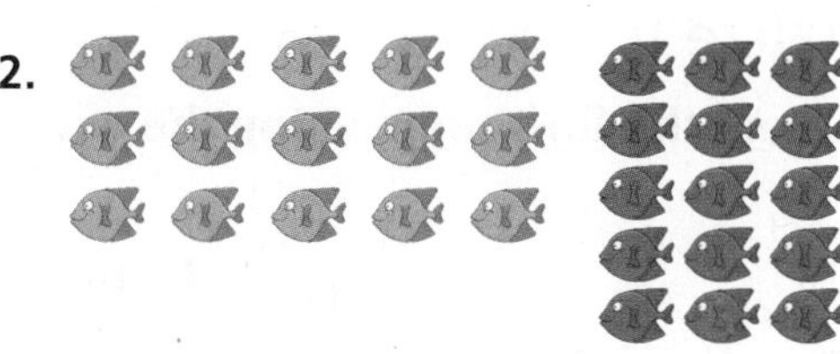

______ ______

▶ Multiplication Facts Find the product.

3. ______ $= 9 \times 6$

4. ______ $= 7 \times 8$

5. $8 \times 4 =$ ______

▶ Regroup Through Thousands

Regroup. Write the missing numbers.

6. 9 tens 10 ones = ______ hundred

7. 60 hundreds = ______ thousands

8. 25 tens = ______ hundreds 5 tens

9. 14 ones = ______ ten ______ ones

10. 3 tens 12 ones = ______ tens 2 ones

The Arctic Lion's Mane Jellyfish is one of the largest known animals. Its tentacles can be as long as 120 feet. Be a Math Detective to find how this length compares to your height. Round your height to the nearest foot.
120 feet is ______ times as long as ______ feet.

Personal Math Trainer
Online Assessment and Intervention

Vocabulary Builder

Review Words			Preview Words
✓ estimate	✓ place value	✓ rounding	Distributive Property
expanded form	product		partial product
factor	✓ regroup		

▶ Visualize It

Complete the flow map, using the words with a ✓.

Multiplying

What can you do?		What can you use?		What are some examples?
______________ products.	→	Use ______________ and mental math.	→	3 × 48 = ■ ↓ ↓ 3 × 50 = 150
______________ ones as tens.	→	Use ______________.	→	12 ones = 1 ten 2 ones

▶ Understand Vocabulary

Complete the sentences.

1. The ______________ states that multiplying a sum by a number is the same as multiplying each addend by the number and then adding the products.

2. A number that is multiplied by another number to find a product is called a ______________.

3. A method of multiplying in which the ones, tens, hundreds, and so on are multiplied separately and then the products are added together is called the ______________ method.

GO DIGITAL
• Interactive Student Edition
• Multimedia eGlossary

Name ____________________

ALGEBRA
Lesson 2.1

Multiplication Comparisons

Essential Question How can you model multiplication comparisons?

Operations and Algebraic Thinking—4.OA.1
MATHEMATICAL PRACTICES
MP.1, MP.4, MP.7

You can use multiplication to compare amounts. For example, you can think of $15 = 3 \times 5$ as a comparison in two ways:

15 is 3 times as many as 5.

15

5	5	5

5

15 is 5 times as many as 3.

15

3	3	3	3	3

3

Remember

The Commutative Property states that you can multiply two factors in any order and get the same product.

Unlock the Problem

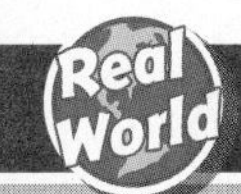

Carly has 9 pennies. Jack has 4 times as many pennies as Carly. How many pennies does Jack have?

- What do you need to compare?

____

____

Draw a model and write an equation to solve.

MODEL

Carly [___]

Jack [___ | ___ | ___ | ___]

RECORD

Use the model to write an equation and solve.

$n =$ ______ $\times$ ______

$n =$ ______

The value of n is 36.

Think: n is how many pennies Jack has.

So, Jack has ______ pennies.

Mathematical Practices

Describe what is being compared and explain how the comparison model relates to the equation.

- THINK SMARTER Explain how the equation for *4 is 2 more than 2* is different from the equation for *4 is 2 times as many as 2.*

____

____

____

Example Draw a model and write an equation to solve.

Miguel has 3 times as many rabbits as Sara. Miguel has 6 rabbits. How many rabbits does Sara have?

- How many rabbits does Miguel have? _____
- How many rabbits does Sara have?

_____

_____

MODEL

Think: You don't know how many rabbits Sara has. Use n for Sara's rabbits.

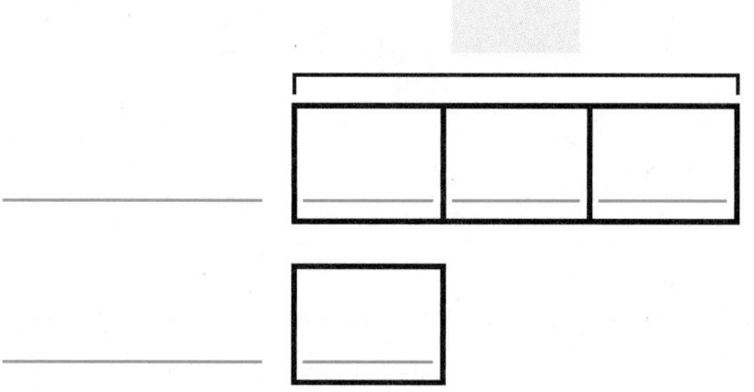

So, Sara has 2 rabbits.

RECORD

Use the model to write an equation and solve.

$6 =$ _____ $\times$ _____

$6 = 3 \times$ _____ Think: 3 times what number equals 6?

The value of n is 2.

Think: n is how many rabbits Sara has.

Try This! Write an equation or a comparison sentence.

A Write an equation.

21 is 7 times as many as 3.

_____ $=$ _____ $\times$ _____

B Write a comparison sentence.

$8 \times 5 = 40$

_____ times as many as _____ is _____.

Share and Show

1. There are 8 students in the art club. There are 3 times as many students in chorus. How many students are in chorus?

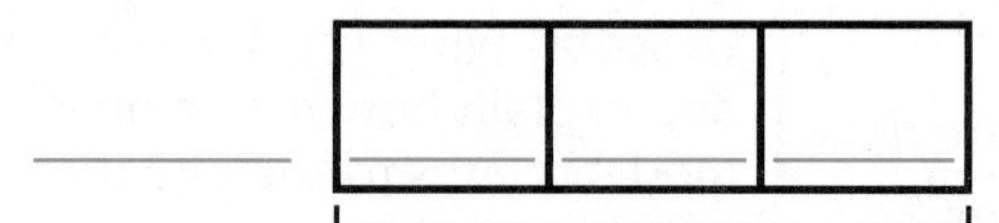

Write an equation and solve.

$n =$ _____ $\times$ _____

$n =$ _____

The value of n is _____.

So, there are _____ students in chorus.

Mathematical Practices

Could you write the equation a different way? **Explain.**

Name ____________________

Draw a model and write an equation.

2. 6 times as many as 2 is 12.

____

3. 20 is 4 times as many as 5.

____

Write a comparison sentence.

4. $18 = 9 \times 2$

_____ is _____ times as many as _____.

5. $8 \times 4 = 32$

_____ times as many as _____ is _____.

On Your Own

Write a comparison sentence.

6. $5 \times 7 = 35$

_____ times as many as _____ is _____.

7. $54 = 6 \times 9$

_____ is _____ times as many as _____.

Write an equation.

8. 3 times as many as 7 is 21.

____

9. 40 is 5 times as many as 8.

____

10. GO DEEPER Nando has 4 goldfish. Jill has 3 goldfish. Cooper has 2 times as many goldfish as Nando and Jill combined. Write an equation that compares the number of goldfish Cooper has with the number of goldfish that Nando and Jill have.

____

11. MATHEMATICAL PRACTICE 2 **Represent a Problem** Write a comparison sentence about pet food that could be represented using the equation $12 = 4 \times 3$.

____

____

____

Unlock the Problem

12. THINK SMARTER Luca has 72 baseball cards. This is 8 times as many cards as Han has. How many baseball cards does Han have?

a. What do you need to find? ______________________

____

b. How can you use a model to find the number of cards Han has?

____

c. Draw the model.

d. Write an equation and solve.

_____ = _____ × _____

_____ = _____

So, Han has _____ baseball cards.

13. THINK SMARTER Complete the statements to describe each model.

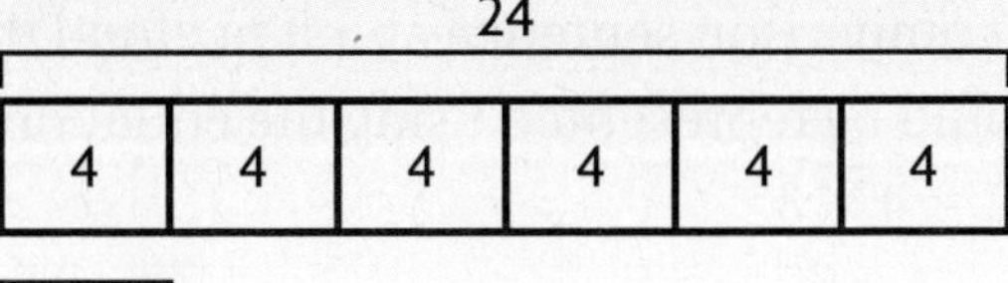

24

6	6	6	6

6

24 is ☐ times as many as ☐.

24 is ☐ times as many as ☐.

FOR MORE PRACTICE:
Standards Practice Book

Name ______________________

Comparison Problems

Essential Question How does a model help you solve a comparison problem?

Operations and Algebraic Thinking—4.OA.2

MATHEMATICAL PRACTICES
MP.1, MP.3, MP.4, MP.7

Unlock the Problem

Evan's dog weighs 7 times as much as Oxana's dog. Together, the dogs weigh 72 pounds. How much does Evan's dog weigh?

Example 1 Use a multiplication model.

STEP 1 Draw a model. Let n represent the unknown.

Think: Let n represent how much Oxana's dog weighs. Together, the dogs weigh 72 pounds.

Evan's	____	____	____	____	____	____	____
Oxana's	____						

STEP 2 Use the model to write an equation. Find the value of n.

$\_\_\_\_ \times n = \_\_\_\_$ Think: There are 8 parts. The parts together equal 72.

$8 \times \_\_\_\_ = 72$ Think: What times 8 equals 72?

The value of n is 9.

n is how much __________ weighs.

STEP 3 Find how much Evan's dog weighs.

Think: Evan's dog weighs 7 times as much as Oxana's dog.

Evan's dog = ____ × ____ Multiply.

= ____

So, Evan's dog weighs 63 pounds.

Math Talk **Mathematical Practices**

Explain how you know you have found the weight of Evan's dog.

To find how many times as much, use a multiplication model. To find how many more or fewer, model the addition or subtraction.

Evan's dog weighs 63 pounds. Oxana's dog weighs 9 pounds. How much more does Evan's dog weigh than Oxana's dog?

Example 2 Use an addition or subtraction model.

STEP 1 Draw a model. Let *n* represent the unknown.

Think: Let *n* represent the difference.

STEP 2 Use the model to write an equation. Find the value of *n*.

_____ − _____ = *n* **Think:** The model shows a difference.

63 − 9 = _____ Subtract.

The value of *n* is _____.

n is ______________________________.

So, Evan's dog weighs 54 pounds more than Oxana's dog.

Share and Show

MATH BOARD

1. Maria's dog weighs 6 times as much as her rabbit. Together the pets weigh 56 pounds. What does Maria's dog weigh?

Draw a model. Let n represent the unknown.

Write an equation to find the value of n. $7 \times n =$ _____. n is _____ pounds.

Multiply to find how much Maria's dog weighs. $8 \times 6 =$ _____

So, Maria's dog weighs _____ pounds.

Math Talk **Mathematical Practices**

Explain how you can choose a model to help solve a comparison problem.

Name ____________________

Draw a model. Write an equation and solve.

✓ **2.** Last month Kim trained 3 times as many dogs as cats. If the total number of cats and dogs she trained last month is 28, how many cats did Kim train?

Draw a model.

Write an equation and solve.

✓ **3.** How many more dogs than cats did Kim train?

Draw a model.

Write an equation and solve.

On Your Own

Practice: Copy and Solve **Draw a model.**

Write an equation and solve.

4. At the dog show, there are 4 times as many boxers as spaniels. If there are a total of 30 dogs, how many dogs are spaniels?

5. There are 5 times as many yellow labs as terriers in the dog park. If there are a total of 18 dogs, how many dogs are terriers?

6. Ben has 3 times as many guppies as goldfish. If he has a total of 20 fish, how many guppies does he have?

7. Carlita saw 5 times as many robins as cardinals while bird watching. She saw a total of 24 birds. How many more robins did she see than cardinals?

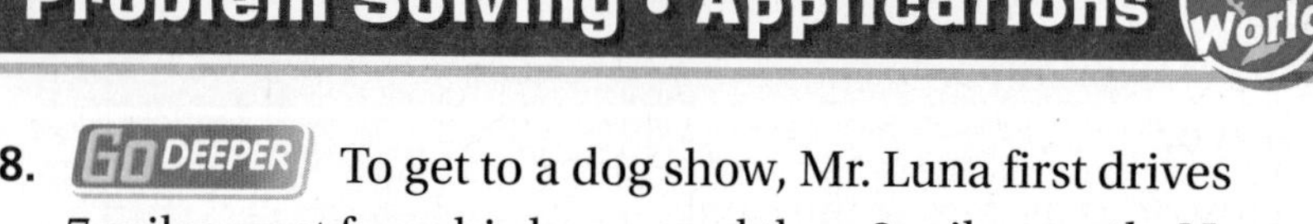

8. GO DEEPER To get to a dog show, Mr. Luna first drives 7 miles west from his home and then 3 miles north. Next, he turns east and drives 11 miles. Finally, he turns north and drives 4 miles to the dog show. How far north of Mr. Luna's home is the dog show?

25 miles

7 miles 3 miles 11 miles 4 miles

Dara's Diagram

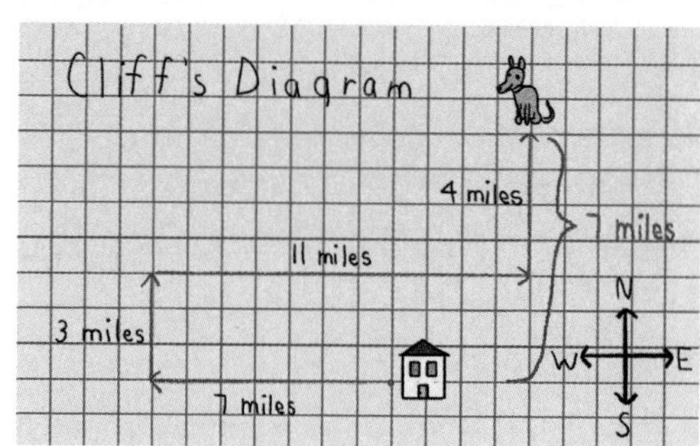

To solve the problem, Dara and Cliff drew diagrams. Which diagram is correct? Explain.

____

____

____

____

WRITE ▸ Math
Show Your Work

9. MATHEMATICAL PRACTICE 2 **Use Reasoning** Valerie and Bret have a total of 24 dog show ribbons. Bret has twice as many ribbons as Valerie. How many ribbons does each have?

____

____

10. THINK SMARTER Noah built a fenced dog run that is 8 yards long and 6 yards wide. He placed posts at every corner and every yard along the length and width of the run. How many posts did he use?

____

11. THINK SMARTER Last weekend, Mandy collected 4 times as many shells as Cameron. Together, they collected 40 shells. How many shells did Mandy collect? Complete the bar model. Then write an equation and solve.

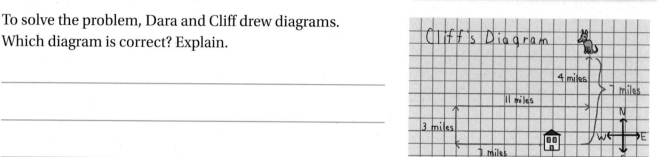

FOR MORE PRACTICE:
Standards Practice Book

Name ____________________

Multiply Tens, Hundreds, and Thousands

Essential Question How does understanding place value help you multiply tens, hundreds, and thousands?

Number and Operations in Base Ten—4.NBT.5 *Also 4.NBT.1*

MATHEMATICAL PRACTICES
MP.4, MP.5, MP.7, MP.8

Unlock the Problem

Each car on a train has 200 seats. How many seats are on a train with 8 cars?

Find 8 × 200.

One Way Draw a quick picture.

Think: 10 hundreds = 1,000

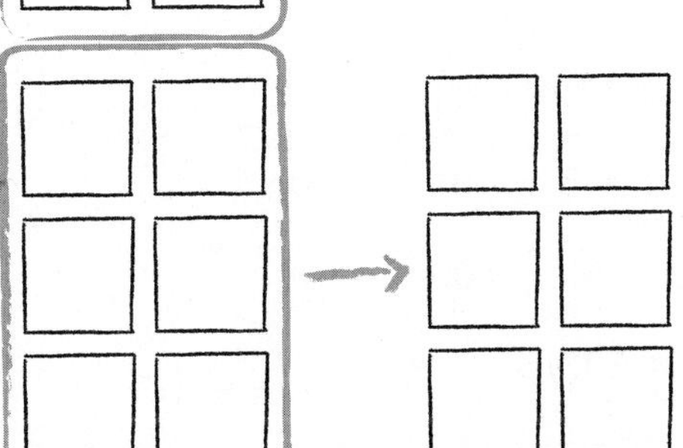

Think: 6 hundreds = 600

1,000 + 600 = ________

Another Way Use place value.

8 × 200 = 8 × ________ hundreds

= ________ hundreds

= ________ Think: 16 hundreds is 1 thousand, 6 hundreds.

So, there are ________ seats on a train with 8 cars.

Mathematical Practices

Explain how finding 8 × 2 can help you find 8 × 200.

Other Ways

A **Use a number line.**

Bob's Sled Shop rents 4,000 sleds each month. How many sleds does the store rent in 6 months?

Find 6 × 4,000.

Multiplication can be thought of as repeated addition. Draw jumps to show the product.

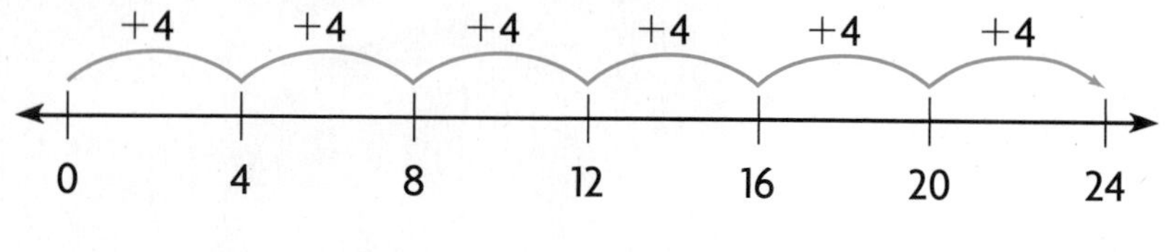

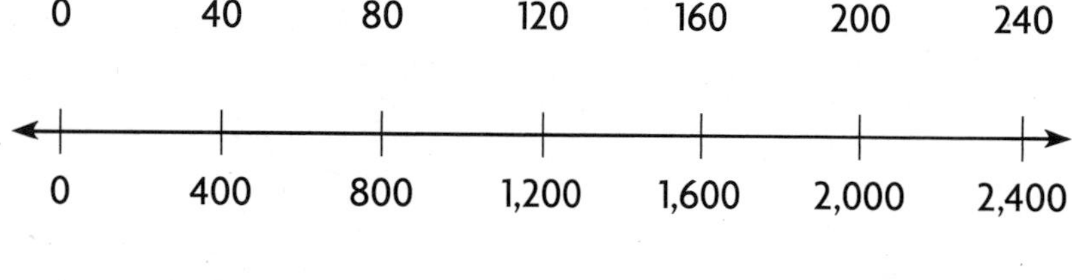

6 × 40 = 240

6 × 400 = 2,400

0 4,000 8,000 12,000 16,000 20,000 24,000

6 × 4,000 = 24,000

So, Bob's Sled Shop rents ________ sleds in 6 months.

B **Use patterns.**

Basic fact:

3 × 7 = 21 ← basic fact

3 × 70 = 210

3 × 700 = ____________

3 × 7,000 = ____________

Basic fact with a zero:

8 × 5 = 40 ← basic fact

8 × 50 = 400

8 × 500 = ____________

8 × 5,000 = ____________

- How does the number of zeros in the product of 8 and 5,000 compare to the number of zeros in the factors? Explain.

____

____

Math Talk **Mathematical Practices**

Describe how the number of zeros in the factors and products changes in Example B.

Name ______________________

Share and Show

1. Use the drawing to find 2×500.

$2 \times 500 =$ ______

Math Talk — Mathematical Practices

Explain how to use place value to find 2×500.

Complete the pattern.

2. $3 \times 8 = 24$

   $3 \times 80 =$ ______

   $3 \times 800 =$ ______

   $3 \times 8{,}000 =$ ______

3. $6 \times 2 = 12$

   $6 \times 20 =$ ______

   $6 \times 200 =$ ______

   $6 \times 2{,}000 =$ ______

4. $4 \times 5 =$ ______

   $4 \times 50 =$ ______

   $4 \times 500 =$ ______

   $4 \times 5{,}000 =$ ______

Find the product.

5. $6 \times 500 = 6 \times$ ______ hundreds

   $=$ ______ hundreds

   $=$ ______

6. $9 \times 5{,}000 = 9 \times$ ______ thousands

   $=$ ______ thousands

   $=$ ______

On Your Own

Find the product.

7. $7 \times 6{,}000 =$ ______

8. $4 \times 80 =$ ______

9. $3 \times 500 =$ ______

MATHEMATICAL PRACTICE 2 Use Reasoning **Algebra** **Find the missing factor.**

10. ______ $\times 9{,}000 = 63{,}000$

11. $7 \times$ ______ $= 56{,}000$

12. $8 \times$ ______ $= 3{,}200$

13. MATHEMATICAL PRACTICE 5 **Communicate** How does the number of zeros in the product of 8 and 5,000 compare to the number of zeros in the factors? Explain.

____

____

Unlock the Problem

14. THINK SMARTER Joe's Fun and Sun rents beach chairs. The store rented 300 beach chairs each month in April and in May. The store rented 600 beach chairs each month from June through September. How many beach chairs did the store rent during the 6 months?

a. What do you need to know? ______________________

____

b. How will you find the number of beach chairs? ______________________

____

c. Show the steps you use to solve the problem.

d. Complete the sentences.

For April and May, a total of ________ beach chairs were rented.

For June through September, a total of ________ beach chairs were rented.

Joe's Fun and Sun rented ________ beach chairs during the 6 months.

15. GO DEEPER Mariah makes bead necklaces. Beads are packaged in bags of 50 and bags of 200. Mariah bought 4 bags of 50 beads and 3 bags of 200 beads. How many beads did Mariah buy? ______________________

16. THINK SMARTER Carmen has three books of 20 stamps and five books of 10 stamps. How many stamps does Carmen have? Complete the equation using the numbers on the tiles.

______ × 20 + ______ × 10 = ______

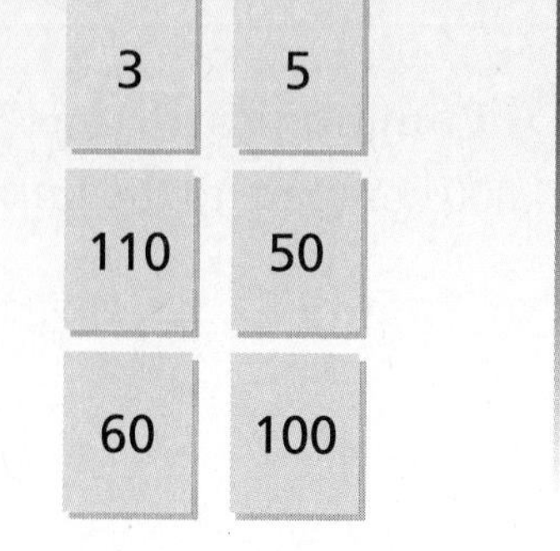

FOR MORE PRACTICE:
Standards Practice Book

Name ______________________________

Estimate Products

Essential Question How can you estimate products by rounding and determine if exact answers are reasonable?

Number and Operations in Base Ten—4.NBT.5 *Also 4.NBT.3*

MATHEMATICAL PRACTICES
MP.1, MP.6, MP.7, MP.8

Unlock the Problem — Real World

An elephant can reach as high as 23 feet with its trunk. It uses its trunk to pick up objects that weigh up to 3 times as much as a 165-pound person. About how much weight can an African elephant pick up with its trunk?

- Cross out the information you will not use.
- Circle the numbers you will use.
- How will you use the numbers to solve the problem?

____

One Way Estimate by rounding.

STEP 1 Round the greater factor to the nearest hundred.

3×165

↓

3×200

STEP 2 Use mental math.

Think: $3 \times 200 = 3 \times 2$ hundreds

$= 6$ hundreds

$=$ ______

So, an African elephant can pick up about 600 pounds with its trunk.

Another Way Estimate by finding two numbers the exact answer is between.

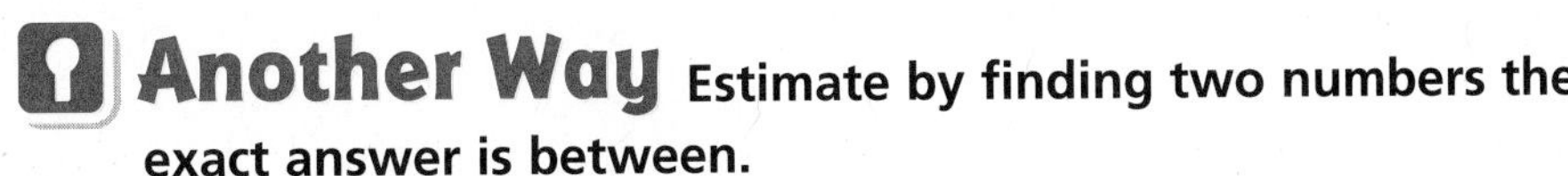

3×165

↓

$3 \times 100 =$ ______

3×165

↓

$3 \times 200 =$ ______

Think: 165 is between 100 and 200. Use those numbers to estimate.

So, the African elephant can pick up between 300 and 600 pounds.

An African elephant is the largest living land mammal.

1. Is 200 less than or greater than 165? ______________________

2. So, would the product of 3 and 165 be less than or greater than 600? ______________________

Math Talk — **Mathematical Practices**

Is the exact answer closer to 300 or 600? Why?

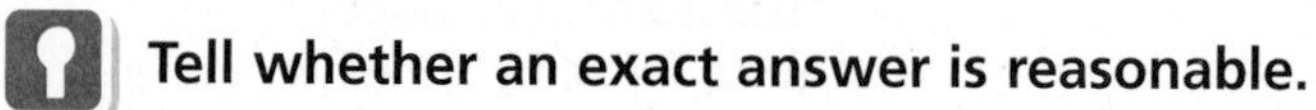

Describe Reasonableness You can estimate a product to find whether an exact answer is reasonable.

Tell whether an exact answer is reasonable.

Eva's horse eats 86 pounds each week. Eva solved the equation below to find how much feed she needs for 4 weeks.

$4 \times 86 = \blacksquare$

Eva says she needs 344 pounds of feed.
Is her answer reasonable?

One Way Estimate.

4 × 86

↓ **Think:** Round to the nearest ten.

_____ × _____ = _____

344 is close to 360.

Another Way Find two numbers the exact answer is between.

4 × 86

↓

_____ × _____ = _____

4 × 86

↓

_____ × _____ = _____

_____ is between _____ and _____.

So, 344 pounds of feed is reasonable.

Share and Show

Math Talk — **Mathematical Practices**

Is an exact answer of 11,065 reasonable? **Explain.**

1. Estimate the product by rounding.

   5 × 2,213

   ↓

   _____ × _____ = _____

2. Estimate the product by finding two numbers the exact answer is between.

   5 × 2,213

   _____ × _____ = _____

   5 × 2,213

   _____ × _____ = _____

Name ______________________

Tell whether the exact answer is reasonable.

3. Kira needs to make color copies of a horse show flyer. The printer can make 24 copies in 1 minute. Kira says the printer makes 114 copies in 6 minutes.

____

____

____

4. Jones Elementary is having a car wash to raise money for a community horse trail. Each car wash ticket costs $8. Tiara says the school will receive $1,000 if 125 tickets are sold.

____

____

____

On Your Own

Tell whether the exact answer is reasonable.

5. MATHEMATICAL PRACTICE 1 **Evaluate Reasonableness** Mrs. Hense sells a roll of coastal Bermuda horse hay for $58. She says she will make $174 if she sells 3 rolls.

____

____

____

6. Mr. Brown sells horse supplies. A pair of riding gloves sells for $16. He says he will make $144 if he sells 9 pairs.

____

____

____

7. A walking path for horses is 94 feet long. Carlos says that if a horse walks the length of the path 3 times, it will have walked 500 feet.

____

____

____

8. THINK SMARTER Students in the third grade sell 265 tickets to the school play. Students in the fourth grade sell 3 times as many tickets as the third grade students. Estimate the number of tickets the fourth grade students sold by finding the two numbers the exact answer is between.

The students sold between

0		300	
300	and	600	tickets.
600		900	
800		1,200	

Connect to Reading

Make Predictions

As you read a story, you make predictions about what might happen next or about how the story will end.

When you solve a math problem, you make predictions about what your answer might be.

An *estimate* is a prediction because it helps you to determine whether your answer is correct. For some problems, it is helpful to make two estimates—one that is less than the exact answer and one that is greater.

Predict whether the exact answer will be *less than* or *greater than* the estimate. Explain your answer.

9. THINK SMARTER The food stand at the zoo sold 2,514 pounds of hamburger last month. The average cost of a pound of hamburger is $2. Jeremy estimates that about $6,000 worth of hamburger was sold last month.

10. GO DEEPER A zoo bought 2,240 pounds of fresh food for the bears this month. The average cost of a pound of food is $4. Jeremy estimates that about $8,000 was spent on fresh food for the bears this month.

FOR MORE PRACTICE: Standards Practice Book

Name ______________________________

Multiply Using the Distributive Property

Essential Question How can you use the Distributive Property to multiply a 2-digit number by a 1-digit number?

Number and Operations in Base Ten—4.NBT.5

MATHEMATICAL PRACTICES
MP.1, MP.7

Investigate

Materials ■ color pencils, grid paper

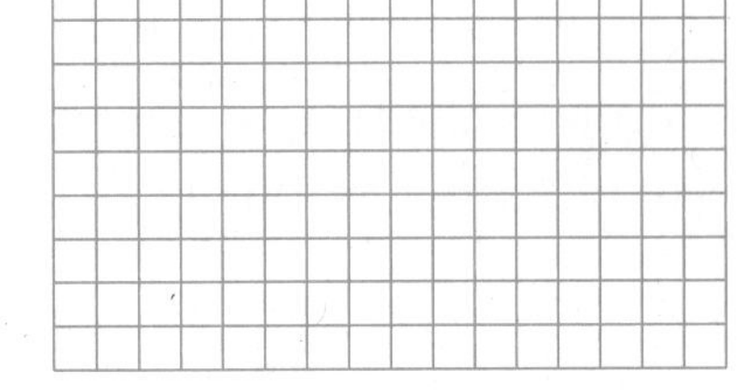

You can use the Distributive Property to break apart numbers to make them easier to multiply.

The **Distributive Property** states that multiplying a sum by a number is the same as multiplying each addend by the number and then adding the products.

A. Outline a rectangle on the grid to model 6×13.

B. Think of 13 as $5 + 8$. Break apart the model to show $6 \times (5 + 8)$. Label and shade the smaller rectangles. Use two different colors.

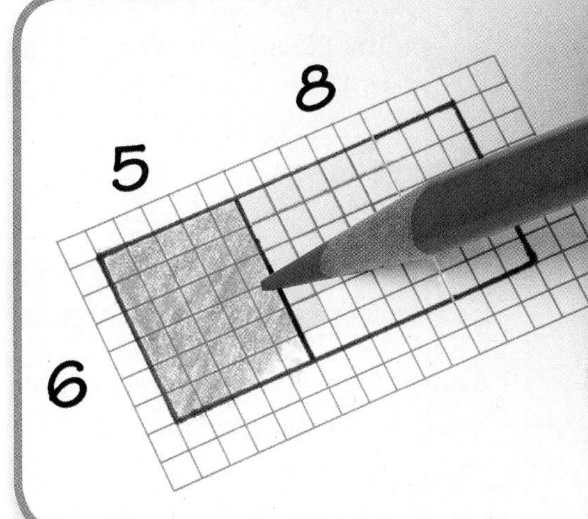

Use the Distributive Property. Find the product each smaller rectangle represents. Then find the sum of the products. Record your answers.

_____ × _____ = _____

_____ × _____ = _____

_____ + _____ = _____

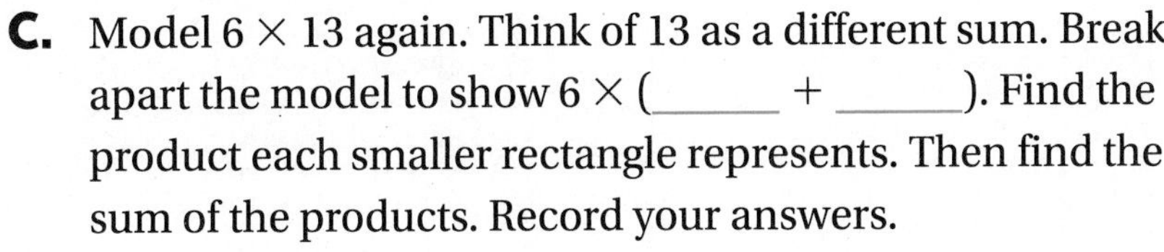

C. Model 6×13 again. Think of 13 as a different sum. Break apart the model to show $6 \times$ (_____ + _____). Find the product each smaller rectangle represents. Then find the sum of the products. Record your answers.

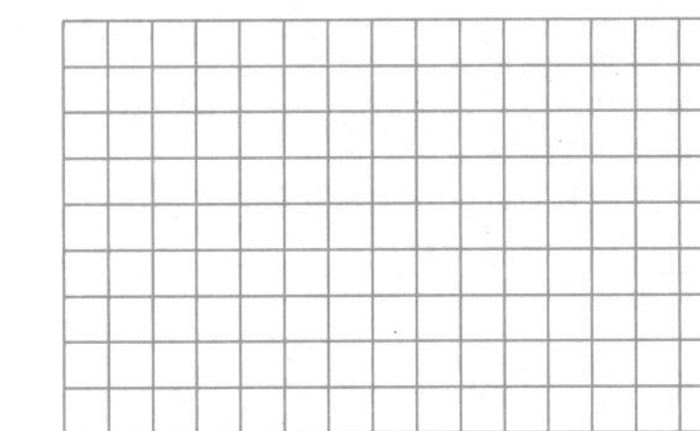

_____ × _____ = _____

_____ × _____ = _____

_____ + _____ = _____

Draw Conclusions

1. Explain how you found the total number of squares in each model in Steps B and C.

2. Compare the sums of the products in Steps B and C with those of your classmates. What can you conclude?

3. THINK SMARTER To find 7×23, is it easier to break apart the factor, 23, as $20 + 3$ or $15 + 8$? Explain.

Make Connections

Another way to model the problem is to use base-ten blocks to show tens and ones.

STEP 1

Use base-ten blocks to model 6×13.

6 rows of 1 ten 3 ones

STEP 2

Break the model into tens and ones.

($6 \times$ 1 ten) ($6 \times$ 3 ones)

(6×10) (6×3)

STEP 3

Add the tens and the ones to find the product.

$(6 \times 10) + (6 \times 3)$

60 + 18

So, $6 \times 13 = 78$.

In Step 2, the model is broken into two parts. Each part shows a **partial product**. The partial products are 60 and 18.

Math Talk **Mathematical Practices**

How does breaking apart the model into tens and ones make finding the product easier?

Name ______________________

Share and Show

Model the product on the grid. Record the product.

1. $3 \times 13 =$ ______

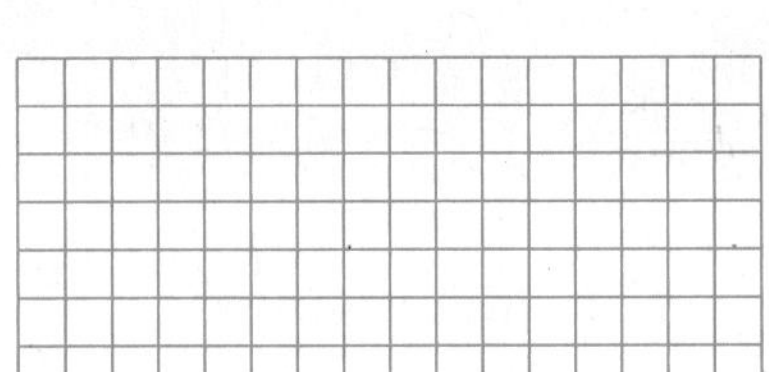

2. $5 \times 14 =$ ______

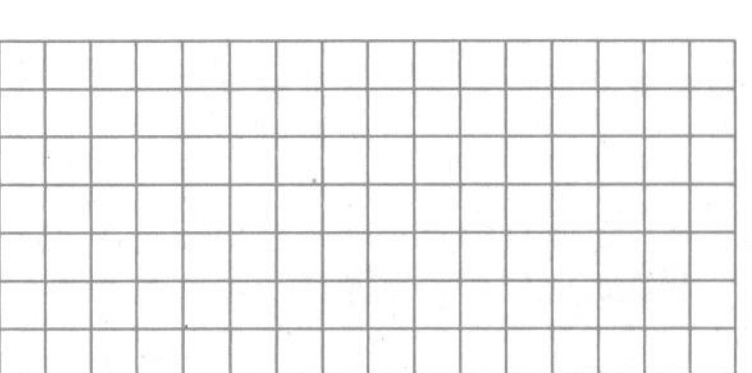

Find the product.

3. $6 \times 14 =$ ______

4. $5 \times 18 =$ ______

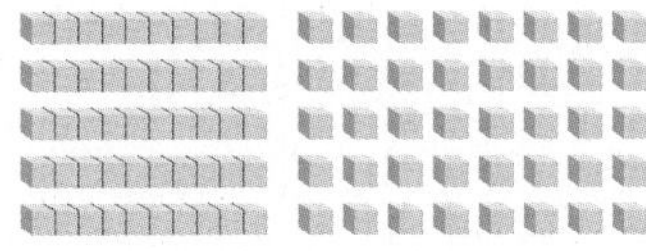

5. $4 \times 16 =$ ______

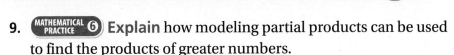

Use grid paper or base-ten blocks to model the product. Then record the product.

6. $7 \times 12 =$ ______

7. $5 \times 16 =$ ______

8. $9 \times 13 =$ ______

Problem Solving • Applications

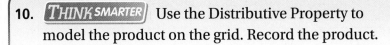

9. MATHEMATICAL PRACTICE 6 **Explain** how modeling partial products can be used to find the products of greater numbers.

____

____

____

10. THINK SMARTER Use the Distributive Property to model the product on the grid. Record the product.

$4 \times 14 =$ ______

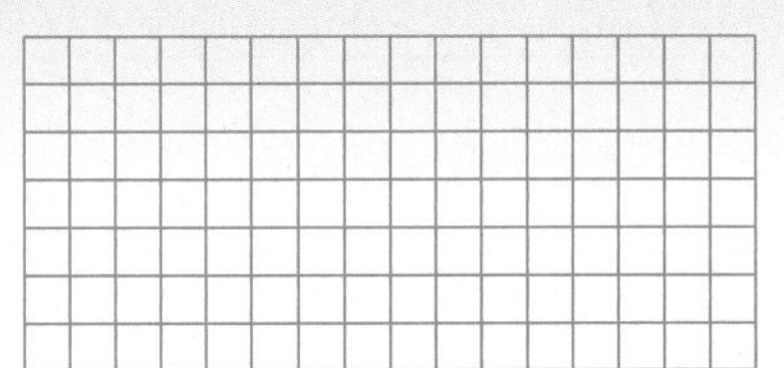

11. THINK SMARTER Kyle went to a fruit market. The market sells a wide variety of fruits and vegetables. The picture at the right shows a display of oranges.

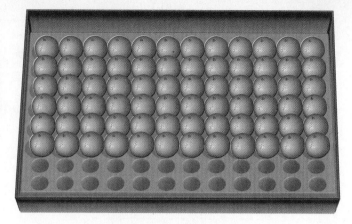

Write a problem that can be solved using the picture.

Pose a problem.

Solve your problem.

- GO DEEPER Describe how you could change the problem by changing the number of rows of oranges and the number of empty spaces in the picture. Then solve the problem.

FOR MORE PRACTICE:
Standards Practice Book

Name ______________________________

Multiply Using Expanded Form

Essential Question How can you use expanded form to multiply a multidigit number by a 1-digit number?

Number and Operations in Base Ten—4.NBT.5

MATHEMATICAL PRACTICES
MP.1, MP.2, MP.4

Unlock the Problem — Real World

Example 1 Use expanded form.

Multiply. 5×143

$5 \times 143 = 5 \times (\_\_\_\_ + \_\_\_\_ + \_\_\_\_)$ Write 143 in expanded form.

$= (5 \times 100) + (\_\_\_\_ \times \_\_\_\_) + (\_\_\_\_ \times \_\_\_\_)$ Use the Distributive Property.

SHADE THE MODEL | **THINK AND RECORD**

STEP 1

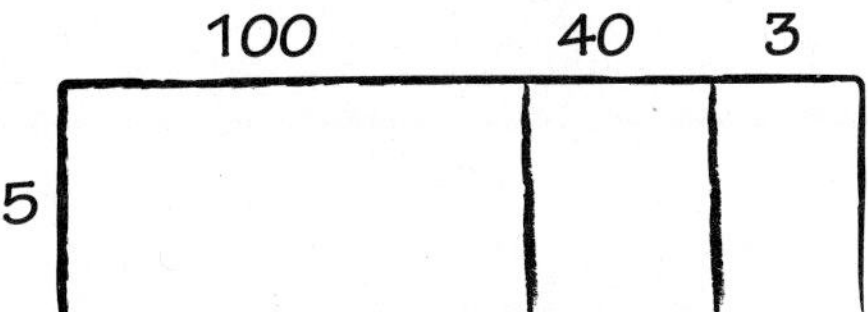

Multiply the hundreds.

$(5 \times 100) + (5 \times 40) + (5 \times 3)$

$\_\_\_\_ + (5 \times 40) + (5 \times 3)$

STEP 2

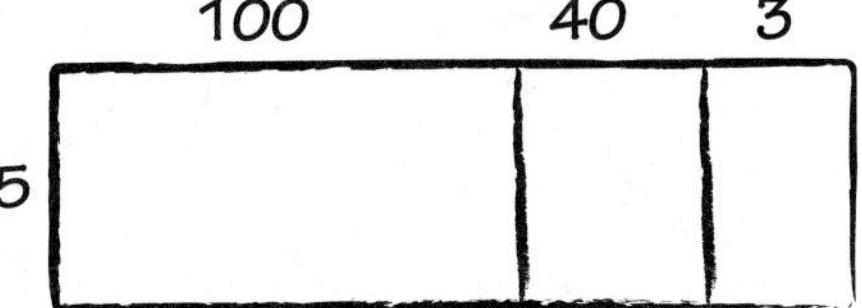

Multiply the tens.

$(5 \times 100) + (5 \times 40) + (5 \times 3)$

$500 + \_\_\_\_ + (5 \times 3)$

STEP 3

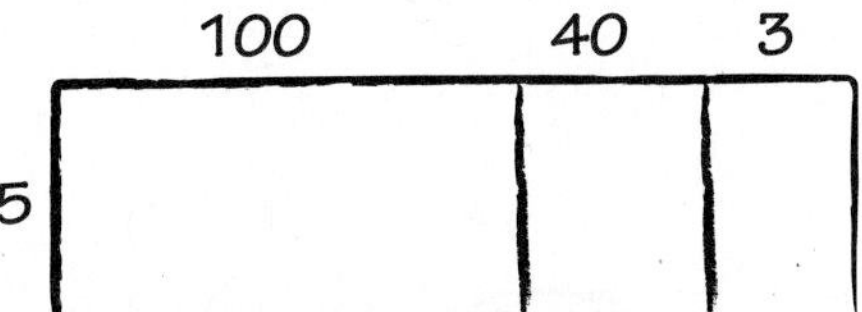

Multiply the ones.

$(5 \times 100) + (5 \times 40) + (5 \times 3)$

$500 + 200 + \_\_\_\_$

STEP 4

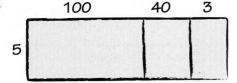

Add the partial products.

$$\begin{array}{r} 500 \\ 200 \\ +\ 15 \\ \hline \end{array}$$

So, $5 \times 143 = \_\_\_\_$.

Mathematical Practices

Is your answer reasonable? **Explain.**

Example 2 Use expanded form.

The gift shop at the animal park orders 3 boxes of toy animals. Each box has 1,250 toy animals. How many toy animals does the shop order?

Multiply. $3 \times 1,250$

STEP 1

Write 1,250 in expanded form. Use the Distributive Property.

$3 \times 1,250 = 3 \times (\_\_\_\_ + \_\_\_\_ + \_\_\_\_)$

$= (3 \times 1,000) + (\_\_\_\_ \times \_\_\_\_) + (\_\_\_\_ \times \_\_\_\_)$

STEP 2

Add the partial products.

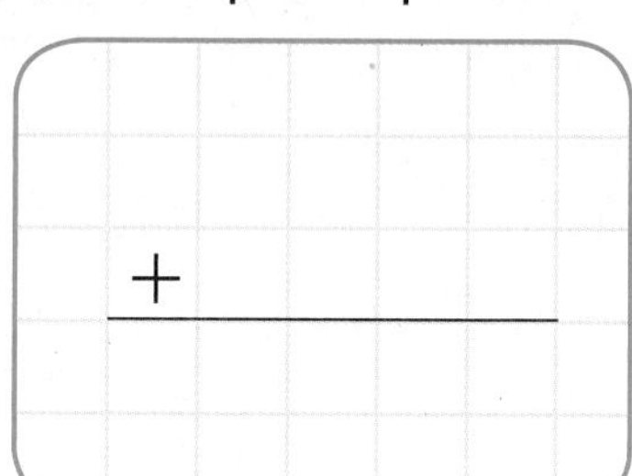

So, the shop ordered ________ animals.

Share and Show

1. Find 4×213. Use expanded form.

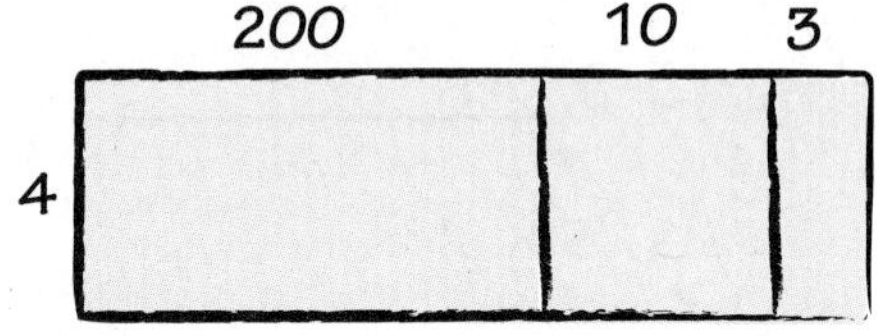

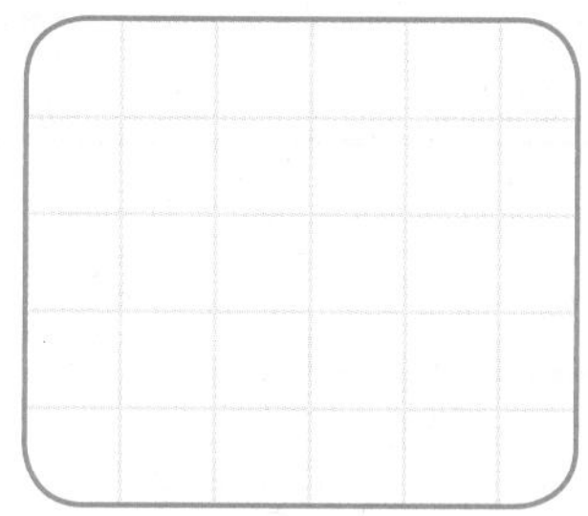

$4 \times 213 = \_\_\_\_ \times (\_\_\_\_ + \_\_\_\_ + \_\_\_\_)$

$= (\_\_\_\_ \times \_\_\_\_) + (\_\_\_\_ \times \_\_\_\_) + (\_\_\_\_ \times \_\_\_\_)$ Use the Distributive Property.

$= \_\_\_\_ + \_\_\_\_ + \_\_\_\_$

$= \_\_\_\_$

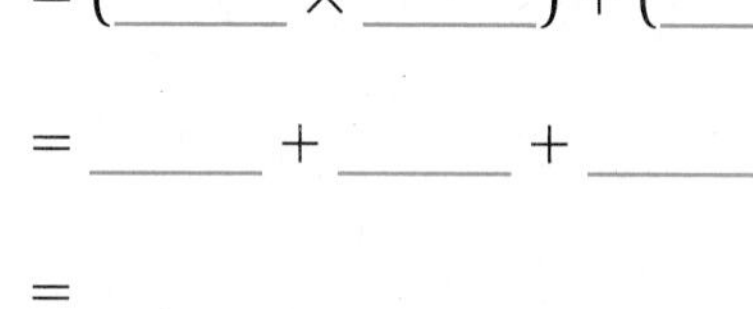

Math Talk **Mathematical Practices**

Explain how using the Distributive Property makes finding the product easier.

Record the product. Use expanded form to help.

2. $4 \times 59 = \_\_\_\_$

3. $3 \times 288 = \_\_\_\_$

Name ____________________

On Your Own

Record the product. Use expanded form to help.

4. $4 \times 21 =$ ________

5. $6 \times 35 =$ ________

6. $5 \times 479 =$ ________

7. $6 \times 4{,}121 =$ ________

WRITE ▸ Math
Show Your Work

8. A jeweler has 36 inches of silver chain. She needs 5 times that much to make some necklaces. How much silver chain does the jeweler need to make her necklaces?

____

9. Gretchen walks her dog 3 times a day. Each time she walks the dog, she walks 1,760 yards. How many yards does she walk her dog in 1 day?

____

10. MATHEMATICAL PRACTICE 4 **Write an Expression** Which expression could you write to show how to multiply 9×856 using place value and expanded form?

____

11. GO DEEPER Jennifer bought 4 packages of tacks. There are 48 tacks in a package. She used 160 of the tacks to put up posters. How many tacks does she have left? Explain.

____

____

____

____

Problem Solving • Applications Real World

Use the table for 12–13.

Sacco Nursery Plant Sale		
Tree	Regular Price	Discounted Price (4 or more)
Flowering Cherry	$59	$51
Italian Cypress	$79	$67
Muskogee Crape Myrtle	$39	$34
Royal Empress	$29	$25

12. What is the total cost of 3 Italian cypress trees?

____

13. THINK SMARTER What's the Error? Tanya says that the difference in the cost of 4 flowering cherry trees and 4 Muskogee crape myrtles is $80. Is she correct? Explain.

____

____

____

14. WRITE ▸ Math What is the greatest possible product of a 2-digit number and a 1-digit number? Explain how you know.

____

____

____

WRITE ▸ Math • Show Your Work

15. THINK SMARTER Multiply 5×381 using place value and expanded form. Select a number from each box to complete the expression.

$(5 \times$ [30 / 300] $) + (5 \times$ [8 / 80] $) + (5 \times$ [1 / 10] $)$

FOR MORE PRACTICE:
Standards Practice Book

Name ________________

Multiply Using Partial Products

Essential Question How can you use place value and partial products to multiply by a 1-digit number?

Number and Operations in Base Ten—4.NBT.5

MATHEMATICAL PRACTICES
MP.1, MP.7

Unlock the Problem (Real World)

CONNECT How can you use what you know about the Distributive Property to break apart numbers to find products of 3-digit and 1-digit numbers?

- How can you write 182 as a sum of hundreds, tens, and ones? ________

Use place value and partial products.

Multiply. 6 × 182 **Estimate.** 6 × 200 = ________

SHADE THE MODEL | THINK AND RECORD

STEP 1

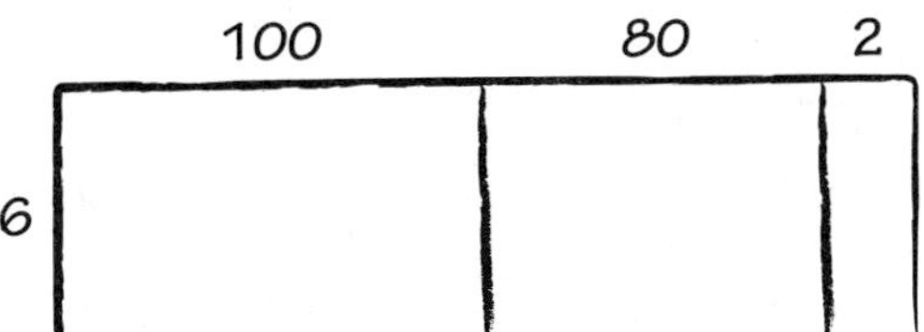

$$\begin{array}{r} 182 \\ \times \quad 6 \\ \hline \end{array}$$

← Multiply the hundreds.
6 × 1 hundred = 6 hundreds

STEP 2

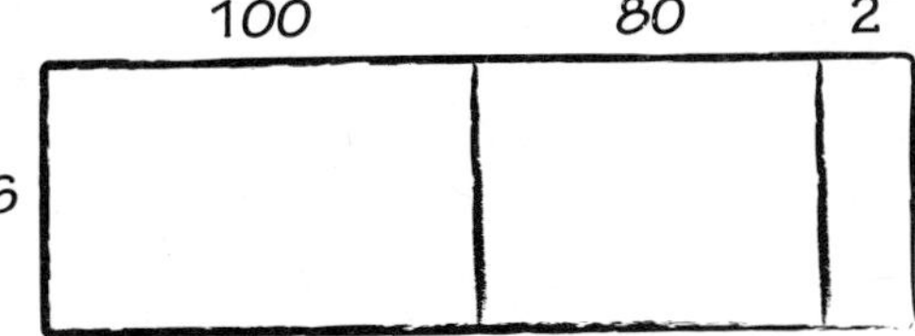

$$\begin{array}{r} 182 \\ \times \quad 6 \\ \hline 600 \end{array}$$

← Multiply the tens.
6 × 8 tens = 48 tens

STEP 3

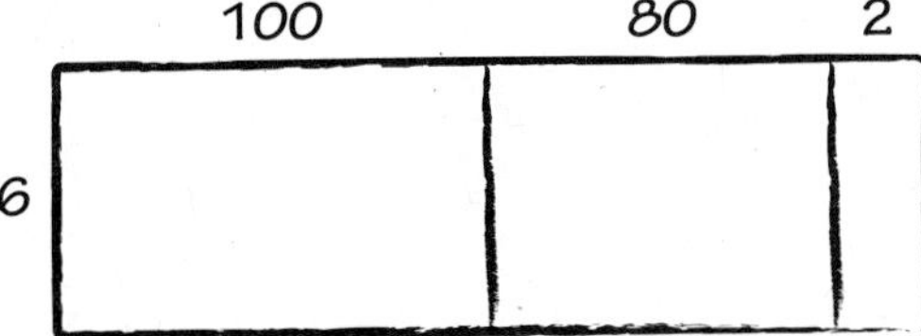

$$\begin{array}{r} 182 \\ \times \quad 6 \\ \hline 600 \\ 480 \end{array}$$

← Multiply the ones.
6 × 2 ones = 12 ones

STEP 4

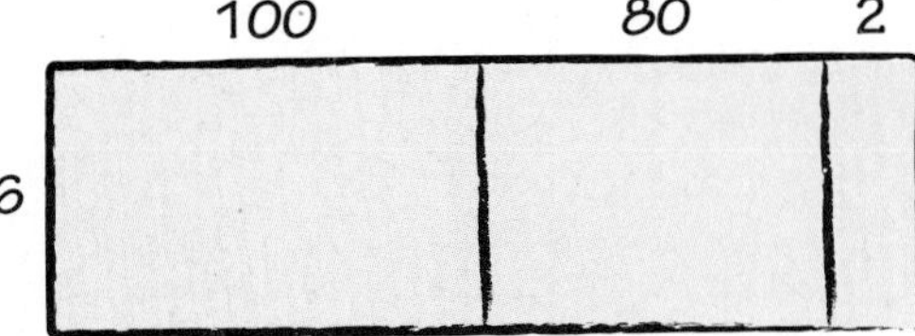

$$\begin{array}{r} 182 \\ \times \quad 6 \\ \hline 600 \\ 480 \\ +\ \ 12 \\ \hline \end{array}$$

← Add the partial products.

So, 6 × 182 = 1,092. Since 1,092 is close to the estimate of 1,200, it is reasonable.

Math Talk — Mathematical Practices
How can you use the Distributive Property to find 4 × 257?

Example

Use place value and partial products.

Multiply. 2 × 4,572. **Estimate.** 2 × 5,000 = ______

```
   4,572
 ×     2
```

← 2 × 4 thousands = 8 thousands

← 2 × 5 hundreds = 1 thousand

← 2 × 7 tens = 1 hundred, 4 tens

← 2 × 2 ones = 4 ones

\+ ______

← Add the partial products.

Share and Show

1. Use the model to find 2 × 137.

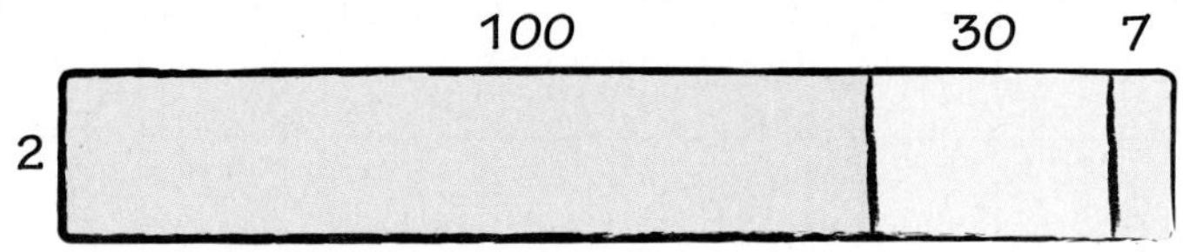

Model: a rectangle with height 2, divided into sections labeled 100, 30, 7.

```
  137
×   2

+
______
```

Estimate. Then record the product.

2. Estimate: ______

```
  190
×   3

+
______
```

3. Estimate: ______

```
  471
×   4

+
______
```

4. Estimate: ______

```
$3,439
×    7
```

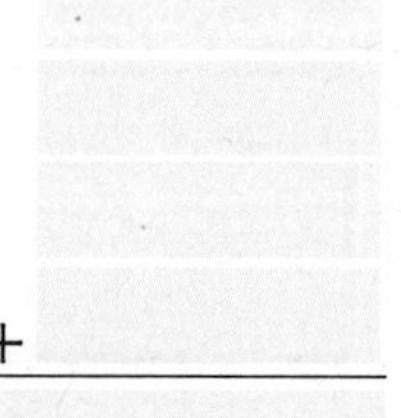

\+ ______

Mathematical Practices

Explain how using place value and expanded form makes it easier to find products.

Name ______________________________

On Your Own

Estimate. Then record the product.

5. Estimate: __________

$$\begin{array}{r} \$53 \\ \times \quad 4 \\ \hline \\ + \\ \hline \end{array}$$

6. Estimate: __________

$$\begin{array}{r} \$473 \\ \times \quad 9 \\ \hline \\ \\ + \\ \hline \end{array}$$

7. Estimate: __________

$$\begin{array}{r} 608 \\ \times \quad 6 \\ \hline \\ \\ + \\ \hline \end{array}$$

Practice: Copy and Solve **Estimate. Then record the product.**

8. 2 × 78

9. 2 × $210

10. 9 × $682

11. 8 × 8,145

MATHEMATICAL PRACTICE 2 Use Reasoning **Algebra** **Find the missing digit.**

12.

$$\begin{array}{r} \square 5 \\ \times \quad 7 \\ \hline 455 \end{array}$$

13.

$$\begin{array}{r} 248 \\ \times \quad 3 \\ \hline \square 44 \end{array}$$

14.

$$\begin{array}{r} \$395 \\ \times \quad \square \\ \hline \$2,370 \end{array}$$

15.

$$\begin{array}{r} 3,748 \\ \times \quad 4 \\ \hline 1\square,992 \end{array}$$

16. A store bought 9 cases of light bulbs. There are 48 light bulbs in a case. How many light bulbs does the store buy?

____

17. Hugo drives 208 miles to and from work each week. How many miles does he drive in 4 weeks?

____

18. Coach Ramirez bought 8 cases of bottled water for a road race. There are 24 bottles in each case. After the race, 34 bottles of water were left. How many bottles were used at the race? Explain.

____

____

____

Problem Solving • Applications

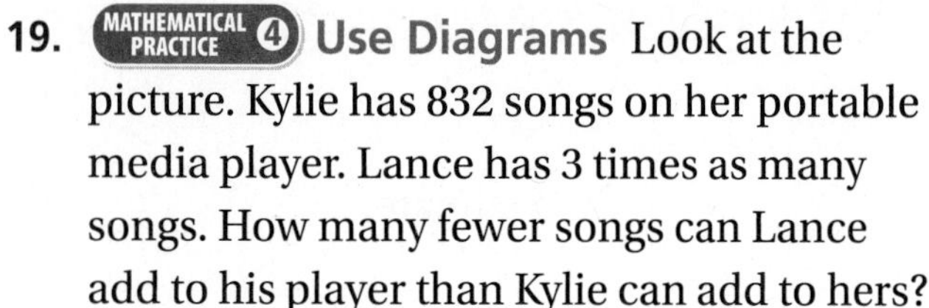

19. MATHEMATICAL PRACTICE 4 **Use Diagrams** Look at the picture. Kylie has 832 songs on her portable media player. Lance has 3 times as many songs. How many fewer songs can Lance add to his player than Kylie can add to hers?

____

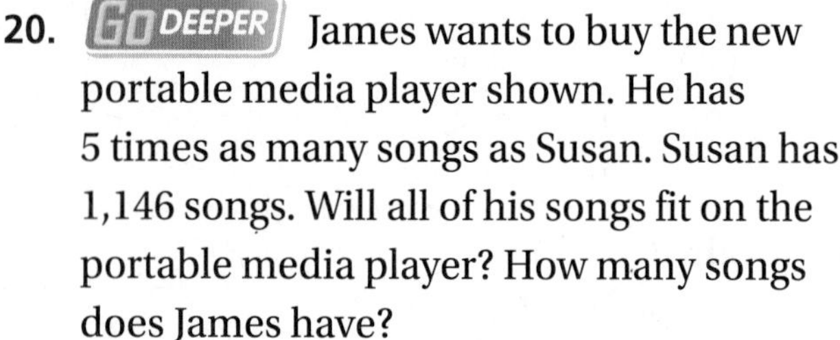

20. GO DEEPER James wants to buy the new portable media player shown. He has 5 times as many songs as Susan. Susan has 1,146 songs. Will all of his songs fit on the portable media player? How many songs does James have?

____

WRITE ▸Math • Show Your Work

21. THINK SMARTER The sum of a 3-digit number and a 1-digit number is 217. The product of the numbers is 642. If one number is between 200 and 225, what are the numbers?

____

22. THINK SMARTER Mrs. Jackson bought 6 gallons of juice for a party. Each gallon has 16 cups. After the party, 3 cups of juice were left over. At the party, how many cups did people drink? Show your work and explain how you found your answer.

____

____

____

FOR MORE PRACTICE:
Standards Practice Book

Name ___

Mid-Chapter Checkpoint

Vocabulary

Choose the best term from the box to complete the sentence.

Vocabulary
Distributive Property
factor
partial products

1. To find the product of a two-digit number and a 1-digit number, you can multiply the tens, multiply the ones, and find the sum of each ___. (p. 64)

2. The ___ states that multiplying a sum by a number is the same as multiplying each addend by the number and then adding the products. (p. 63)

Concepts and Skills

Write a comparison sentence. (4.OA.1)

3. $5 \times 9 = 45$

___ times as many as ___ is ___.

4. $24 = 6 \times 4$

___ is ___ times as many as ___.

5. $54 = 6 \times 9$

___ is ___ times as many as ___.

6. $8 \times 6 = 48$

___ times as many as ___ is ___.

Estimate. Then record the product. (4.NBT.5)

7. Estimate: ___

$$\begin{array}{r} 75 \\ \times \ 5 \\ \hline \end{array}$$

8. Estimate: ___

$$\begin{array}{r} 12 \\ \times \ 6 \\ \hline \end{array}$$

9. Estimate: ___

$$\begin{array}{r} 28 \\ \times \ 3 \\ \hline \end{array}$$

10. Estimate: ___

$$\begin{array}{r} \$43 \\ \times \ 6 \\ \hline \end{array}$$

Record the product. Use expanded form to help. (4.NBT.5)

11. $5 \times 64 =$ ___

12. $3 \times 272 =$ ___

13. There are 6 times as many dogs as cats. If the total number of dogs and cats is 21, how many dogs are there? (4.OA.2)

---

14. The table below shows the number of calories in 1 cup of different kinds of berries. How many calories are in 4 cups of blackberries? (4.NBT.5)

Berry Nutrition

Berry	Number of Calories in 1 Cup
Blackberries	62
Blueberries	83
Raspberries	64
Strawberries	46

---

15. The skating rink rents 200 pairs of skates in a month. How many pairs of skates does the rink rent in 4 months? (4.NBT.5)

Name ______________________

Multiply Using Mental Math

Essential Question How can you use mental math and properties to help you multiply numbers?

Number and Operations in Base Ten—4.NBT.5
MATHEMATICAL PRACTICES
MP.1, MP.7, MP.8

Unlock the Problem Real World

Properties of Multiplication can make multiplication easier.

There are 4 sections of seats in the Playhouse Theater. Each section has 7 groups of seats. Each group has 25 seats. How many seats are there in the theater?

Find 4 × 7 × 25.

$4 \times 7 \times 25 = 4 \times 25 \times 7$ Commutative Property

$= \_\_\_\_\_\_ \times 7$ **Think:** $4 \times 25 = 100$

$= \_\_\_\_\_\_$ **Think:** $100 \times 7 = 700$

So, there are 700 seats in the theater.

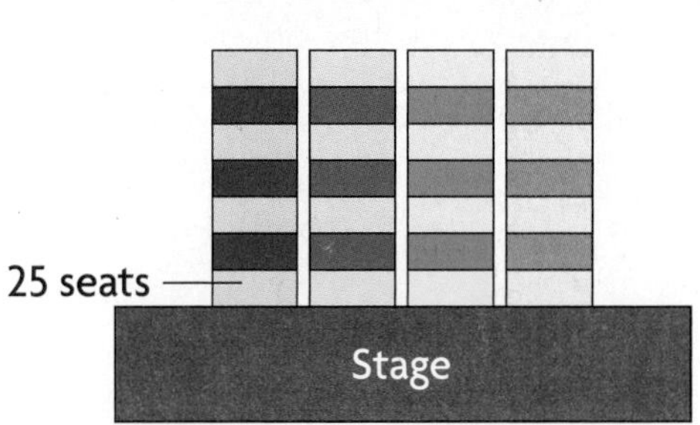

Math Talk Mathematical Practices

How could knowing 4 × 25 help you find 6 × 25?

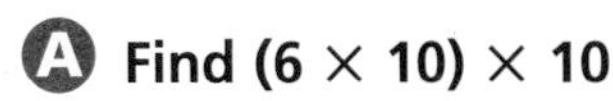

Try This! Use mental math and properties.

A Find (6 × 10) × 10.

$(6 \times 10) \times 10 = 6 \times (10 \times 10)$ Associative Property

$= 6 \times \_\_\_\_\_\_$

$= \_\_\_\_\_\_$

B Find (4 × 9) × 250.

$(4 \times 9) \times 250 = 250 \times (4 \times 9)$ Commutative Property

$= (250 \times 4) \times 9$ Associative Property

$= \_\_\_\_\_\_ \times 9$

$= \_\_\_\_\_\_$

Remember

The Associative Property states that you can group factors in different ways and get the same product. Use parentheses to group the factors you multiply first.

More Strategies Choose the strategy that works best with the numbers in the problems.

Examples

A Use friendly numbers.

Multiply. 24×250

Think: $24 = 6 \times 4$ and $4 \times 250 = 1,000$

$24 \times 250 = 6 \times 4 \times 250$

$= 6 \times$ ______

$=$ ______

B Use halving and doubling.

Multiply. 16×50

Think: 16 can be divided evenly by 2.

$16 \div 2 = 8$ Find half of 16.

$8 \times 50 =$ ______ Multiply.

$2 \times 400 =$ ______ Double 400.

C Use addition.

Multiply. 4×625

Think: 625 is 600 plus 25.

$4 \times 625 = 4 \times (600 + 25)$

$= (4 \times 600) + (4 \times 25)$

$=$ ______ $+$ ______

$=$ ______

D Use subtraction.

Multiply. 5×398

Think: 398 is 2 less than 400.

$5 \times 398 = 5 \times (400 - 2)$

$= (5 \times$ ______ $) - (5 \times 2)$

$= 2,000 -$ ______

$=$ ______

- What property is being used in Examples C and D? ______

Share and Show

1. Break apart the factor 112 to find 7×112 by using mental math and addition.

$7 \times 112 = 7 \times ($ ______ $+ 12)$

$=$ ______

$=$ ______

$=$ ______

Name ____________________

Find the product. Tell which strategy you used.

2. $4 \times 6 \times 50$

3. 5×420

4. 6×298

On Your Own

Math Talk — Mathematical Practices

Explain how using an addition strategy is related to using a subtraction strategy.

Find the product. Tell which strategy you used.

5. 14×50

6. 32×25

7. $14 \times 25 \times 4$

8. $4 \times 15 \times 25$

9. 5×198

10. 5×250

Practice: Copy and Solve **Use a strategy to find the product.**

11. 16×400

12. $3 \times 31 \times 10$

13. 3×199

14. $3 \times 1{,}021$

MATHEMATICAL PRACTICE 7 Identify Relationships **Algebra** **Use mental math to find the unknown number.**

15. $21 \times 40 = 840$, so $21 \times 42 =$ ______.

16. $9 \times 60 = 540$, so $18 \times 30 =$ ______.

Problem Solving • Applications Real World

Use the table for 17–19.

Arena Ticket Prices Per Game

Section	Full Season	15-Game Plan	Gate Price
K	$44	$46	$48
L	$30	$32	$35
M	$25	$27	$30
N	$20	$22	$25

17. GO DEEPER Three thousand, forty-three people buy tickets at the gate for Section N and one hundred people buy tickets at the gate for Section L. How much money is collected for Section N and Section L at the gate?

18. MATHEMATICAL PRACTICE 1 **Use Diagrams** Tina and 3 of her friends buy the full season plan for Section M. If there are 45 games in the full season, how much money do they spend?

19. THINK SMARTER When the full season tickets first went on sale, 2,000 Full Season tickets sold for Section N. Two weeks after the tickets first went on sale, another 1,500 full season tickets were sold for Section N. How much money was spent on full season tickets for Section N in total? How much more money was spent when the tickets first went on sale than after the first two weeks?

Personal Math Trainer

20. THINK SMARTER + Find 6×407. Show your work and explain why the strategy you chose works best with the factors.

WRITE ▸Math • Show Your Work

FOR MORE PRACTICE: Standards Practice Book

Name ______________________

Problem Solving • Multistep Multiplication Problems

Essential Question When can you use the *draw a diagram* strategy to solve a multistep multiplication problem?

Operations and Algebraic Thinking—4.OA.3 *Also 4.NBT.5*

MATHEMATICAL PRACTICES
MP.1, MP.4, MP.8

Unlock the Problem

At the sea park, one section in the stadium has 9 rows with 18 seats in each row. In the center of each of the first 6 rows, 8 seats are in the splash zone. How many seats are not in the splash zone?

Use the graphic organizer to help you solve the problem.

Read the Problem

What do I need to find?

I need to find the number of seats that __________ in the splash zone.

What information do I need to use?

There are 9 rows with __________ seats in each row of the section.

There are 6 rows with __________ seats in each row of the splash zone.

How will I use the information?

I can __________ to find both the number of seats in the section and the number of seats in the splash zone.

Solve the Problem

I drew a diagram of the section to show 9 rows of 18 seats. In the center, I outlined a section to show the 6 rows of 8 seats in the splash zone.

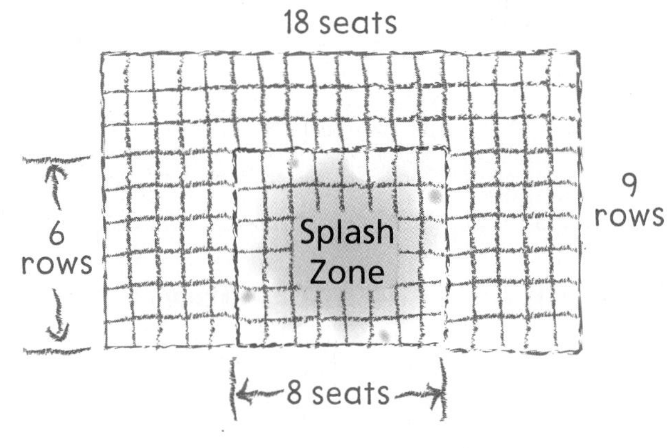

$$\begin{array}{r} 18 \\ \times\ 9 \\ \hline \end{array}$$ ← total number of seats in the section

$$\begin{array}{r} 8 \\ \times 6 \\ \hline \end{array}$$ ← seats in the splash zone

1. What else do you need to do to solve the problem?

____

____

Try Another Problem

At the sea park, one section of the shark theater has 8 rows with 14 seats in each row. In the middle of the section, 4 rows of 6 seats are reserved. How many seats are not reserved?

Read the Problem	Solve the Problem
What do I need to find?	
What information do I need to use?	
How will I use the information?	

2. How did your diagram help you solve the problem?

____

____

Math Talk **Mathematical Practices**

Explain how you can check your answer.

Name ______________________________

Share and Show

Unlock the Problem

- ✓ Use the Problem Solving MathBoard
- ✓ Underline important facts.
- ✓ Choose a strategy you know.

1. The seats in Sections A and B of the stadium are all taken for the last show. Section A has 8 rows of 14 seats each. Section B has 6 rows of 16 seats each. How many people are seated in Sections A and B for the last show?

   First, draw and label a diagram. **Next**, find the number of seats in each section.

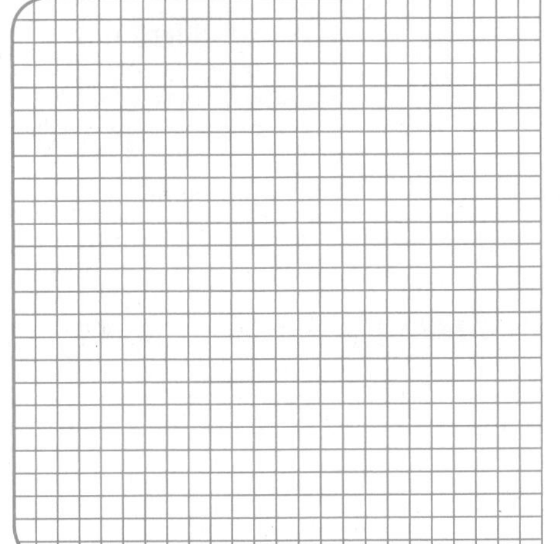

Section A **Section B**

Last, find the total number of seats. ________ + ________ = ________

There are ________ people seated in Sections A and B for the last show.

WRITE ▸ Math
Show Your Work

2. What if Sections A and B each had 7 rows? How many people would have been seated in Sections A and B?

   ____

3. Brenda's vegetable garden has 13 rows with 8 plants in each row. Brenda plans to plant peppers in the first 2 rows and the last 2 rows of the garden. The rest of the rows will be tomatoes. How many tomato plants will Brenda plant?

   ____

4. There are 8 rows of 22 chairs set up for an awards ceremony at the school. In each row, the 2 chairs on each end are reserved for students receiving awards. The rest of the chairs are for guests. How many chairs are there for guests?

   ____

On Your Own

Use the graph for 5–6.

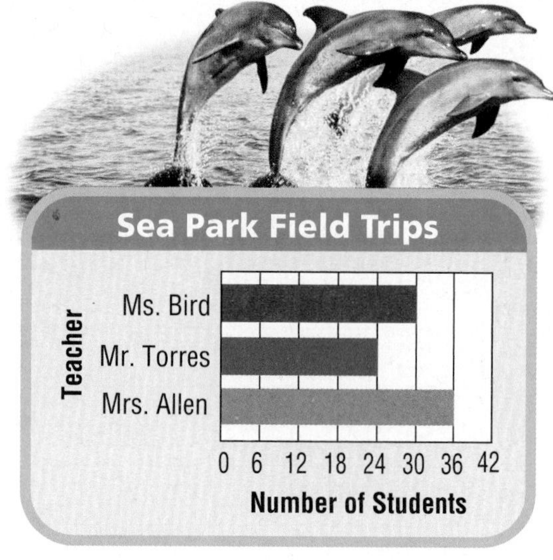

5. GO DEEPER Mr. Torres took his students to the dolphin show. Each row in the stadium had 11 seats. One adult sat at each end of a row, and each group of 4 students was seated between 2 adults. Mr. Torres sat by himself. How many adults were there?

6. WRITE Math Another stadium section has 24 rows of 10 seats each. Describe at least two ways Mrs. Allen's class can sit if an equal number of students sits in each row.

WRITE Math • Show Your Work

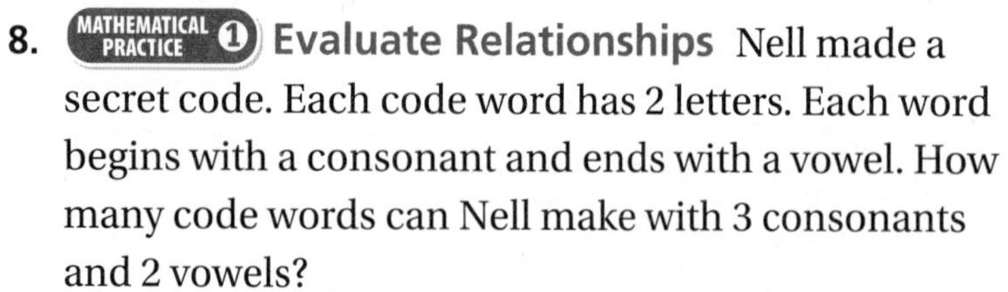

7. THINK SMARTER Carol, Ann, and Liz each bought a toy fish. Carol's fish is 10 inches longer than Ann's fish. Liz's fish is 2 inches longer than twice the length of Ann's fish. Ann's fish is 12 inches long. Find the length of each toy fish.

8. MATHEMATICAL PRACTICE 1 **Evaluate Relationships** Nell made a secret code. Each code word has 2 letters. Each word begins with a consonant and ends with a vowel. How many code words can Nell make with 3 consonants and 2 vowels?

9. THINK SMARTER Allie is building a patio. The patio will have 8 tiles in each of 13 rows. Allie built the center section with 4 tiles in each of 7 rows. How many tiles are needed to complete the patio? Show your work.

FOR MORE PRACTICE: Standards Practice Book

Name ____________________

Multiply 2-Digit Numbers with Regrouping

Essential Question How can you use regrouping to multiply a 2-digit number by a 1-digit number?

Number and Operations in Base Ten—4.NBT.5 *Also 4.OA.3*

MATHEMATICAL PRACTICES
MP.1, MP.4. MP.7

Unlock the Problem (Real World)

A Thoroughbred racehorse can run at speeds of up to 60 feet per second. During practice, Celia's horse runs at a speed of 36 feet per second. How far does her horse run in 3 seconds?

- Underline important information.
- Is there information you will not use? If so, cross out the information.

Example 1

Multiply. 3 × 36 **Estimate.** 3 × 40 = ______

	MODEL	THINK	RECORD
STEP 1	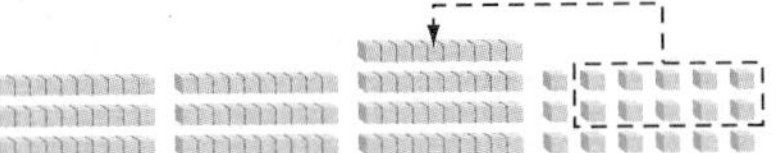	Multiply the ones. 3 × 6 ones = 18 ones Regroup the 18 ones.	$\begin{array}{r} {}^{1} \\ 36 \\ \times\ 3 \\ \hline 8 \end{array}$ Regroup 18 ones as 1 ten 8 ones.
STEP 2	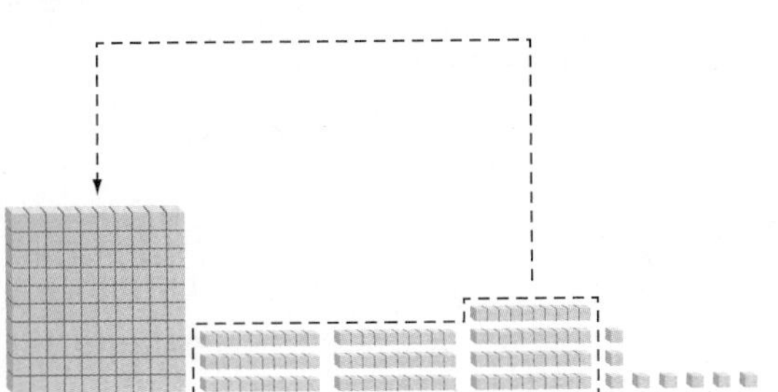	Multiply the tens. 3 × 3 tens = 9 tens Add the regrouped ten. 9 tens + 1 ten = 10 tens	$\begin{array}{r} {}^{1} \\ 36 \\ \times\ 3 \\ \hline 108 \end{array}$ 10 tens is the same as 1 hundred 0 tens.

So, Celia's racehorse runs ______ feet in 3 seconds.

Since ______ is close to the estimate of ______, the answer is reasonable.

Math Talk **Mathematical Practices**

Look at Step 1. **Explain** how the blocks show the regrouping of the 18 ones.

Example 2

Multiply. 8 × 22 **Estimate.** 8 × 20 = ________

MODEL | **THINK** | **RECORD**

STEP 1

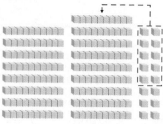

Multiply the ones.
8 × 2 ones = 16 ones

Regroup the 16 ones.

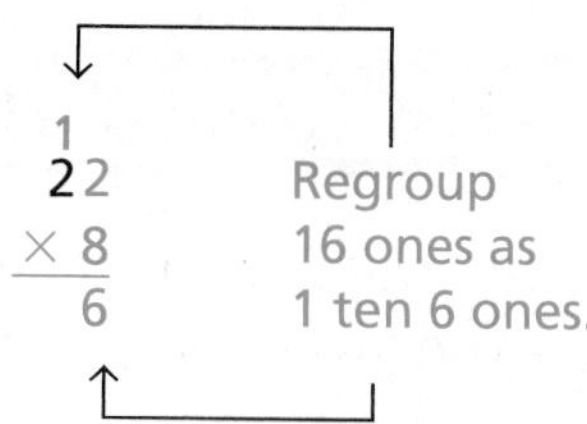

STEP 2

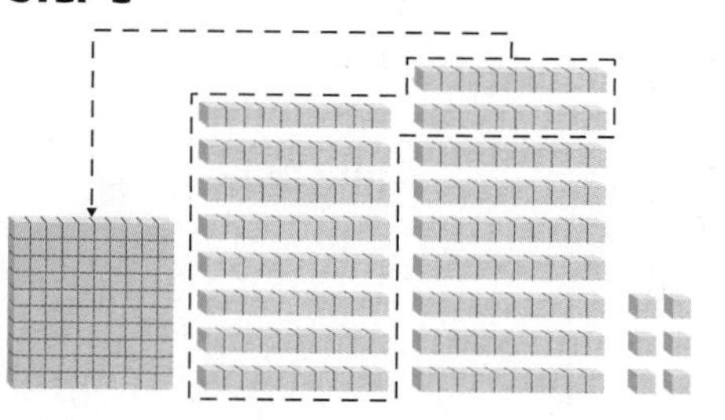

Multiply the tens.
8 × 2 tens = 16 tens

Add the regrouped ten.
16 tens + 1 ten = 17 tens

1
22
× 8
176

17 tens is the same as 1 hundred 7 tens.

So, 8 × 22 = ________. Since ________ is close to the estimate

of ________, it is reasonable.

Try This! Multiply. 7 × $68

Estimate. 7 × $68

Use partial products.

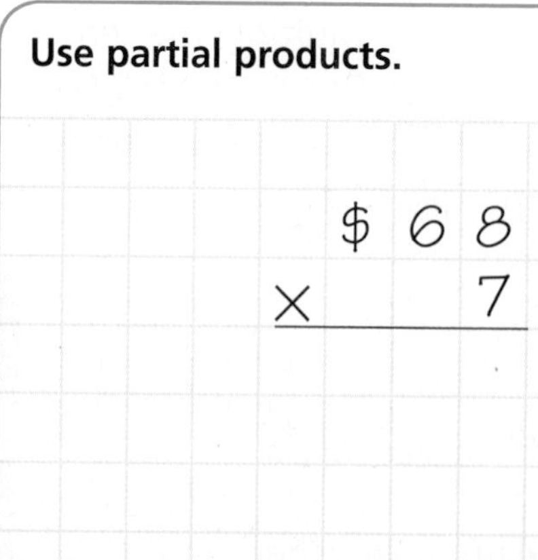

Use regrouping.

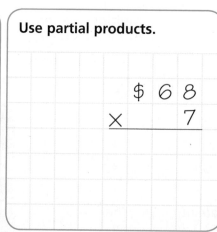

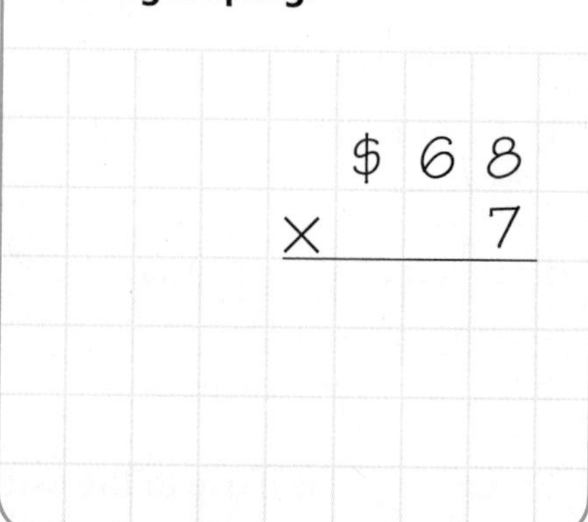

- MATHEMATICAL PRACTICE 7 **Identify Relationships** Look at the partial products and regrouping methods above. How are the partial products 420 and 56 related to 476?

____

Name ______

Share and Show

1. Use the model to find the product.

$2 \times 36 =$ ____

Estimate. Then record the product.

2. Estimate: ____ 42×4

3. Estimate: ____ 32×2

4. Estimate: ____ 81×5

5. Estimate: ____ $\$63 \times 7$

Math Talk — Mathematical Practices

Describe the steps for using place value and regrouping to find 3×78.

On Your Own

Estimate. Then record the product.

6. Estimate: ____ 33×2

7. Estimate: ____ $\$25 \times 3$

8. Estimate: ____ 36×8

9. Estimate: ____ $\$94 \times 5$

Practice: Copy and Solve **Estimate. Then record the product.**

10. 3×82
11. 9×41
12. 6×75
13. $7 \times \$23$
14. $8 \times \$54$
15. 5×49
16. 8×97
17. 4×68
18. $9 \times \$68$
19. $6 \times \$73$

MATHEMATICAL PRACTICE 7 **Identify Relationships** **Algebra** **Write a rule. Find the unknown numbers.**

20.

Carton	____	1	2	3	4	5
Eggs	____	12	24		48	

______

21.

Row	____	2	3	4	5	6
Seats	____	32	48	64		

______

Problem Solving • Applications Real World

Use the table for 22–23.

22. At the speeds shown, how much farther could a black-tailed jackrabbit run than a desert cottontail in 7 seconds?

23. A black-tailed jackrabbit hops about 7 feet in a single hop. How far can it hop in 5 seconds?

Running Speeds	
Animal	**Speed (feet per second)**
Black-tailed Jackrabbit	51
Desert Cottontail	22

▲ Desert Cottontail

24. GO DEEPER Mr. Wright bought a 3-pound bag of cat food and a 5-pound bag of dog food. There are 16 ounces in each pound. How many ounces of pet food did Mr. Wright buy?

25. THINK SMARTER The sum of two numbers is 31. The product of the two numbers is 150. What are the numbers?

26. MATHEMATICAL PRACTICE 2 **Use Reasoning** 6×87 is greater than 5×87. How much greater? Explain how you know without multiplying.

27. THINK SMARTER Multiply 6×73. For 27a–27d, select True or False for each statement.

27a. A reasonable estimate of the product is $420. ○ True ○ False

27b. Using partial products, the products are 42 and 180. ○ True ○ False

27c. Using regrouping, 18 ones are regrouped as 8 tens and 1 one. ○ True ○ False

27d. The product is 438. ○ True ○ False

FOR MORE PRACTICE: Standards Practice Book

Name ______________________________

Multiply 3-Digit and 4-Digit Numbers with Regrouping

Essential Question How can you use regrouping to multiply?

Number and Operations in Base Ten—4.NBT.5

MATHEMATICAL PRACTICES
MP.4, MP.8

Unlock the Problem

Alley Spring, in Missouri, produces an average of 567 million gallons of water per week. How many million gallons of water do the springs produce in 3 weeks?

Multiply. 3×567

Estimate. $3 \times$ __________ $=$ __________

THINK	RECORD
STEP 1 Multiply the ones. 3×7 ones $=$ ______ ones Regroup the 21 ones.	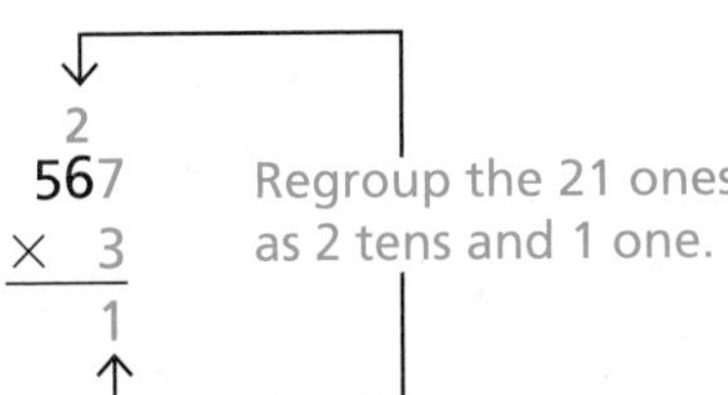
STEP 2 Multiply the tens. 3×6 tens $=$ ______ tens Add the regrouped tens. 18 tens + 2 tens = 20 tens Regroup the 20 tens.	22 567 × 3 01 Regroup 20 tens as 2 hundreds 0 tens.
STEP 3 Multiply the hundreds. 3×5 hundreds $=$ ______ hundreds Add the regrouped hundreds. 15 hundreds + 2 hundreds = 17 hundreds	22 567 × 3 1,701 17 hundreds is the same as 1 thousand 7 hundreds.

So, Alley Spring produces ______ million gallons of water in 3 weeks.

Example

Use an estimate or an exact answer.

The table shows the prices of three vacation packages. Jake, his parents, and his sister want to choose a package.

Lakefront Vacations

	Adult	Child
Package A	$1,299	$619
Package B	$849	$699
Package C	$699	$484

A About how much would Package C cost Jake's family?

STEP 1

Estimate the cost for 2 adults.

2 × $699

↓

2 × $700 = ______

STEP 2

Estimate the cost for 2 children.

2 × $484

↓

2 × $500 = ______

STEP 3

Add to estimate the total cost.

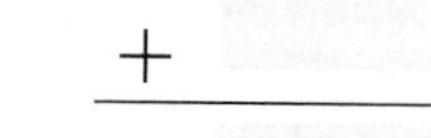

\+ ______

So, Package C would cost Jake's family about $2,400.

Math Talk — **Mathematical Practices**

Explain how you know you can use an estimate.

B Jake's family wants to compare the total costs of Packages A and C. Which plan costs more? How much more does it cost?

Package A

Adults	Children	Total Cost
$1,299 × 2	$619 × 2	+

Package C

Adults	Children	Total Cost
$699 × 2	$484 × 2	+

Subtract to compare the total costs of the packages.

$3,836
− $2,366

So, Package ______ would cost ________ more than Package ______.

Math Talk — **Mathematical Practices**

Explain why you need an exact answer.

Name ____________________

Share and Show

1. Tell what is happening in Step 1 of the problem.

STEP 1	STEP 2	STEP 3	STEP 4
2	42	1 42	1 42
1,274	1,274	1,274	1,274
× 6	× 6	× 6	× 6
4	44	644	7,644

____

____

Estimate. Then find the product.

2. Estimate: ________ 603 × 4

✓ 3. Estimate: ________ 1,935 × 7

✓ 4. Estimate: ________ $8,326 × 5

Math Talk **Mathematical Practices**

Explain how you can use estimation to find how many digits the product 4 × 1,861 will have.

On Your Own

Estimate. Then find the product.

5. Estimate: ________ $3,316 × 8

6. Estimate: ________ $2,900 × 7

7. Estimate: ________ $4,123 × 6

8. Estimate: ________ $1,893 × 4

9. Estimate: ________ $9,042 × 8

10. Estimate: ________ 3,286 × 5

Practice: Copy and Solve **Compare. Write <, >, or =.**

11. 5 × 352 ◯ 4 × 440

12. 6 × 8,167 ◯ 9,834 × 5

13. 3,956 × 4 ◯ 5 × 7,692

14. 740 × 7 ◯ 8 × 658

15. 4 × 3,645 ◯ 5 × 2,834

16. 6,573 × 2 ◯ 4,365 × 3

Problem Solving • Applications

17. GO DEEPER Airplane tickets to Fairbanks, Alaska, will cost $958 each. Airplane tickets to Vancouver, Canada, will cost $734. How much can the four members of the Harrison family save on airfare by vacationing in Vancouver?

____

WRITE ▸Math • Show Your Work

18. THINK SMARTER Philadelphia, Pennsylvania, is 2,147 miles from Salt Lake City, Utah, and 2,868 miles from Portland, Oregon. What is the difference in the round-trip distances between Philadelphia and each of the other two cities? Explain whether you need an estimate or an exact answer.

____

____

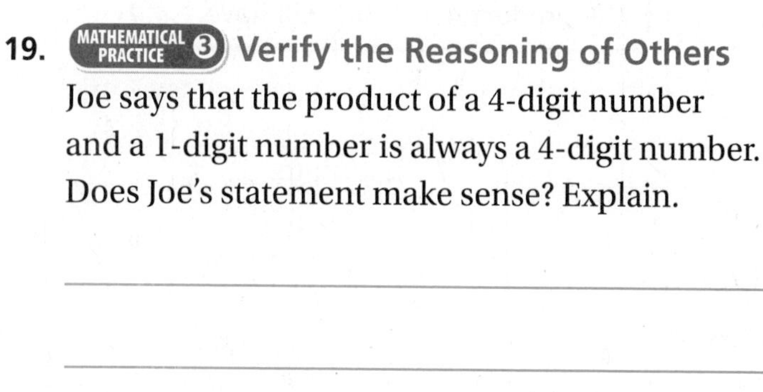

19. MATHEMATICAL PRACTICE 3 **Verify the Reasoning of Others** Joe says that the product of a 4-digit number and a 1-digit number is always a 4-digit number. Does Joe's statement make sense? Explain.

____

____

____

____

20. THINK SMARTER What number is 150 more than the product of 5 and 4,892? Explain how you found the answer.

____

____

____

FOR MORE PRACTICE:
Standards Practice Book

Name ______________________

Solve Multistep Problems Using Equations

Essential Question How can you represent and solve multistep problems using equations?

Operations and Algebraic Thinking—4.OA.3

MATHEMATICAL PRACTICES
MP.2, MP.4, MP.7

Unlock the Problem

Crismari's computer has 3 hard drives with 64 gigabytes of space each and 2 hard drives with 16 gigabytes of space each. The files on her computer use 78 gigabytes of space. How much hard drive space does her computer have left?

- Underline the important information.

One Way Use multiple single-step equations.

STEP 1 Find how much hard drive space is on 3 hard drives with 64 gigabytes of space each.

64	64	64

← 3 hard drives with 64 gigabytes.

n ← Total space on 3 hard drives with 64 gigabytes.

$3 \times 64 = n$

$\_\_\_\_ = n$

STEP 2 Find how much hard drive space is on 2 hard drives with 16 gigabytes of space.

16	16

← 2 hard drives with 16 gigabytes.

p ← Total space on 2 hard drives with 16 gigabytes.

$2 \times 16 = p$

$\_\_\_\_ = p$

STEP 3 Find the total hard drive space on the computer.

Total space on 64-gigabyte hard drives. ↓ Total space on 16-gigabyte hard drives. ↓

192	32

A ← Total space on computer.

$192 + 32 = A$

$\_\_\_\_ = A$

STEP 4 The files use 78 gigabytes of space. Find how much hard drive space the computer has left.

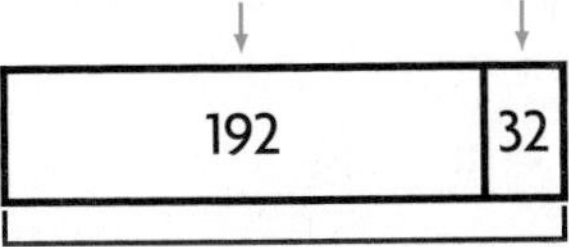

space left ↓ space used ↓

y	78

224 ← Total hard drive space on the computer.

$224 - 78 = y$

$\_\_\_\_ = y$

So, Crismari has ______ gigabytes of hard drive space left on her computer.

Order of Operations The Order of Operations is a special set of rules that gives the order in which calculations are done in an expression. First, multiply and divide from left to right. Then, add and subtract from left to right.

Another Way Use one multistep equation.

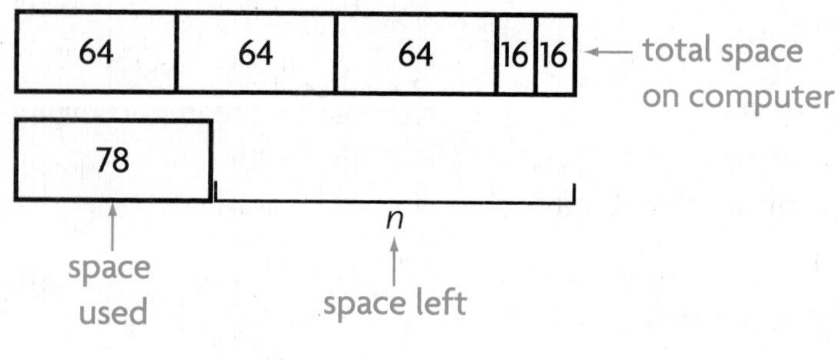

$3 \times 64 + 2 \times 16 - 78 = n$

_____ + _____ × _____ − _____ = *n*

_____ + _____ − _____ = *n*

_____ − _____ = *n*

_____ = *n*

Share and Show

1. Use the order of operations to find the value of *n*.

$5 \times 17 + 5 \times 20 - 32 = n$

_____ + _____ × _____ − _____ = *n* ← First, multiply 5 × 17.

_____ + _____ − _____ = *n* ← Next, multiply 5 × 20.

_____ − _____ = *n* ← Then, add the two products.

_____ = *n* ← Finally, subtract to find *n*.

Find the value of *n*.

2. $3 \times 22 + 7 \times 41 - 24 = n$

_____ = *n*

3. $4 \times 34 + 6 \times 40 - 66 = n$

_____ = *n*

4. $2 \times 62 + 8 \times 22 - 53 = n$

_____ = *n*

5. $6 \times 13 + 9 \times 34 - 22 = n$

_____ = *n*

Math Talk **Mathematical Practices**

If you add before multiplying, will you get the same answer? **Explain.**

Name ______________________________

On Your Own

Find the value of *n*.

6. $8 \times 42 + 3 \times 59 - 62 = n$

_____ $= n$

7. $6 \times 27 + 2 \times 47 - 83 = n$

_____ $= n$

Problem Solving • Applications Real World

WRITE ▸ Math
Show Your Work

8. GO DEEPER Maggie has 3 binders with 25 stamps in each binder. She has 5 binders with 24 baseball cards in each binder. If she gives 35 stamps to a friend, how many stamps and cards does she have left?

____

9. MATHEMATICAL PRACTICE 1 **Evaluate** Maddox has 4 boxes with 32 marbles in each box. He has 7 boxes with 18 shells in each box. If he gets 20 marbles from a friend, how many marbles and shells does he have?

____

Personal Math Trainer

10. THINK SMARTER + The soccer team sells 54 bagels with cream cheese for \$2 each and 36 muffins for \$1 each during a bake sale. The coach uses the money to buy socks for the 14 players. The socks cost \$6 per pair. How much money does the coach have left? Explain how you found your answer.

____

____

____

____

____

11. THINK SMARTER **What's the Error?** Dominic has 5 books with 12 postcards in each book. He has 4 boxes with 20 coins in each box. If he gives 15 post cards to a friend, how many postcards and coins does he have?

Dominic drew this model.

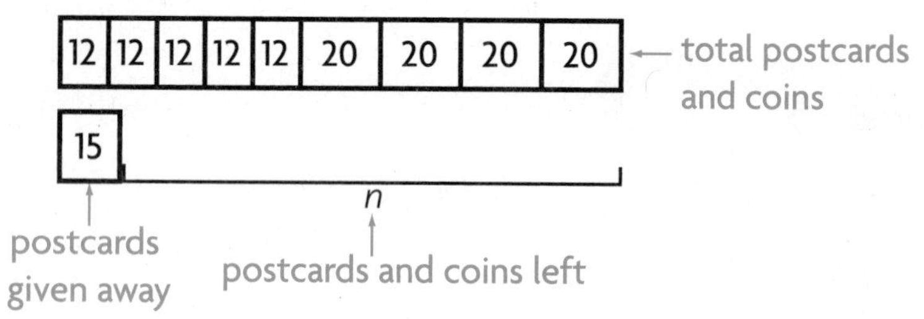

Dominic used these steps to solve.

$5 \times 12 + 4 \times 20 - 15 = n$

$60 + 4 \times 20 - 15 = n$

$64 \times 20 - 15 = n$

$1{,}280 - 15 = n$

$1{,}265 = n$

Look at the steps Dominic used to solve this problem. Find and describe his error.

Use the correct steps to solve the problem.

So, there are ______ postcards and coins left.

FOR MORE PRACTICE:
Standards Practice Book

Name ______________________________

Chapter 2 Review/Test

For 1–3, use the table.

Prices for Trees					
Tree	**Regular Price**	**Price for 3 or more**	**Tree**	**Regular Price**	**Price for 3 or more**
Ivory Silk Lilac	$25	$22	Hazelnut	$9	$8
White Pine	$40	$37	Red Maple	$9	$8
Bur Oak	$35	$32	Birch	$9	$8

1. What is the cost of 3 Bur Oak trees? Show your work.

2. Mr. Tan buys 4 White Pine trees and 5 Birch trees. What is the cost of the trees? Show your work and explain how you found the answer.

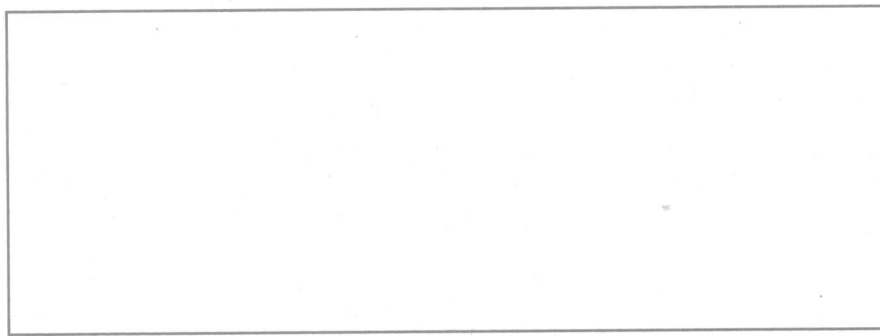

3. Rudy will buy 3 Ivory Silk Lilac trees or 2 Bur Oak trees. He wants to buy the trees that cost less. What trees will he buy? How much will he save? Show your work.

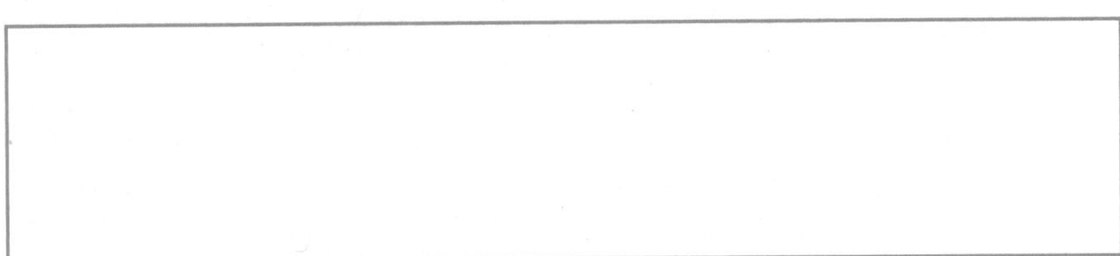

GO DIGITAL Assessment Options Chapter Test

4. For numbers 4a–4d, select True or False for each equation.

4a. $7 \times 194 = 1{,}338$ ○ True ○ False

4b. $5 \times 5{,}126 = 25{,}630$ ○ True ○ False

4c. $8 \times 367 = 2{,}926$ ○ True ○ False

4d. $4 \times 3{,}952 = 15{,}808$ ○ True ○ False

5. **Part A**

Draw a line to match each section in the model to the partial product it represents.

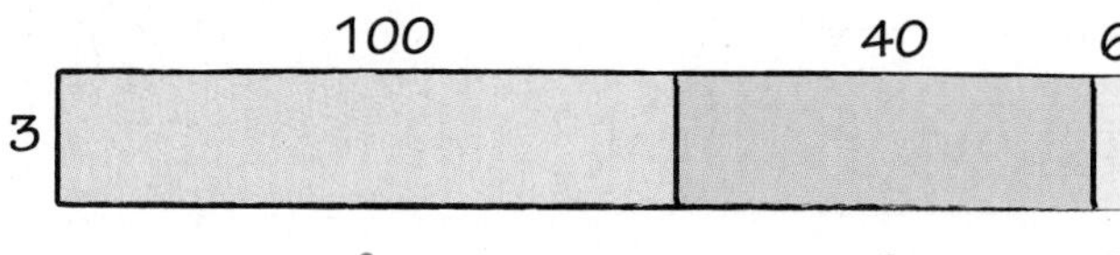

3×6 3×100 3×40

Part B

Then find 3×146. Show your work and explain.

Name ______________________________

6. For numbers 6a–6c, write an equation or a comparison sentence using the numbers on the tiles.

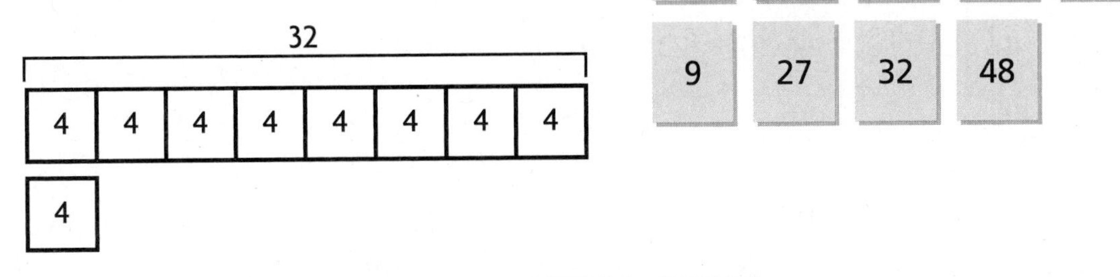

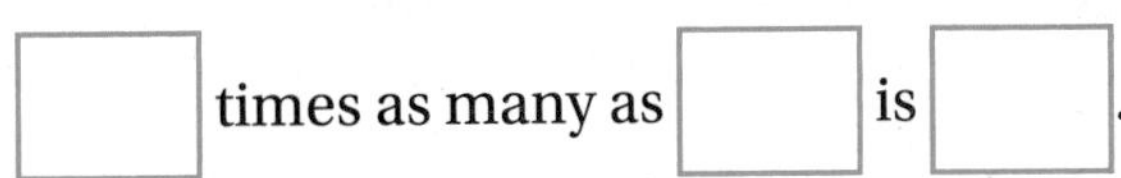

☐ times as many as ☐ is ☐.

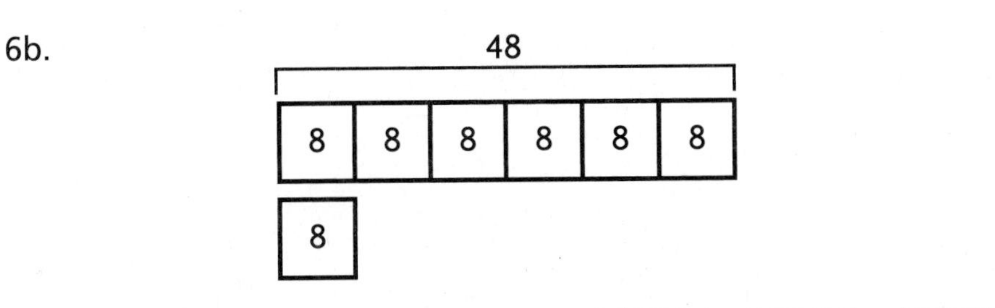

☐ × ☐ = ☐

6c. $9 \times 3 = 27$

☐ times as many as ☐ is ☐.

7. Multiply 7×43. For 7a–7d, select True or False for each statement.

7a. A reasonable estimate of the product is 280. ○ True ○ False

7b. Using partial products, the products are 21 and 28. ○ True ○ False

7c. Using regrouping, 21 ones are regrouped as 1 ten and 2 ones. ○ True ○ False

7d. The product is 301. ○ True ○ False

8. It costs 9,328 points to build each apartment building in the computer game *Big City Building*. What is the cost to build 5 apartment buildings? Show your work.

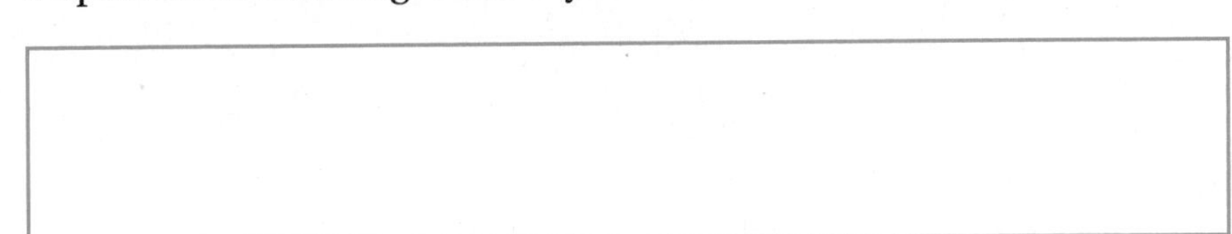

9. Multiply 7 × 462 using place value and expanded form.
Choose the number from the box to complete the expression.

(7 × [4 / 40 / 400]) + (7 × [600 / 60 / 6]) + (7 × [2 / 20 / 200])

	4		600		2	
(7 ×	40	) + (7 ×	60	) + (7 ×	20	)
	400		6		200	

10. For numbers 10a–10b, use place value to find the product.

10a. 3 × 600 = 3 × ☐ hundreds

= ☐ hundreds

= ☐

10b. 5 × 400 = 5 × ☐ hundreds

= ☐ hundreds

= ☐

11. Liam has 3 boxes of baseball cards with 50 cards in each box. He also has 5 boxes with 40 basketball cards in each box. If Liam goes to the store and buys 50 more baseball cards, how many baseball and basketball cards does Liam have? Show your work.

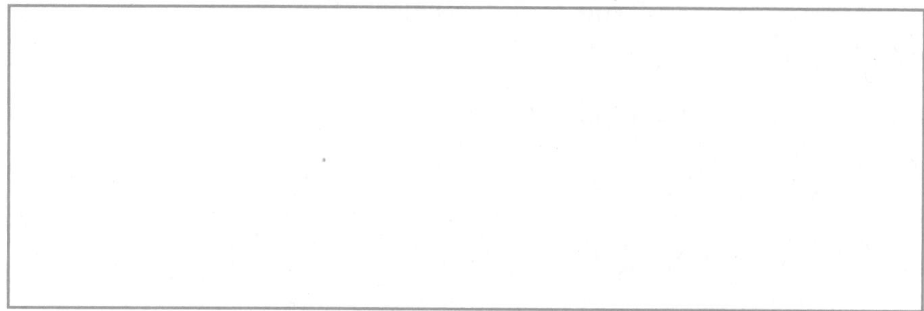

Name ______________________________

12. There is a book sale at the library. The price for each book is $4. Which expression can be used to show how much money the library will make if it sells 289 books? Use the numbers on the tiles to complete your answer.

2	4	8	9
80	90	200	

$(4 \times$ ______ $) + (4 \times$ ______ $) + (4 \times$ ______ $)$

13. Find 8×397. Show your work and explain why the strategy you chose works best with the factors.

14. A clown bought 6 bags of round balloons with 24 balloons in each bag. The clown also bought 3 bags of long balloons with 36 balloons in each bag.

Part A

How many more long balloons than round balloons did the clown buy? Show your work.

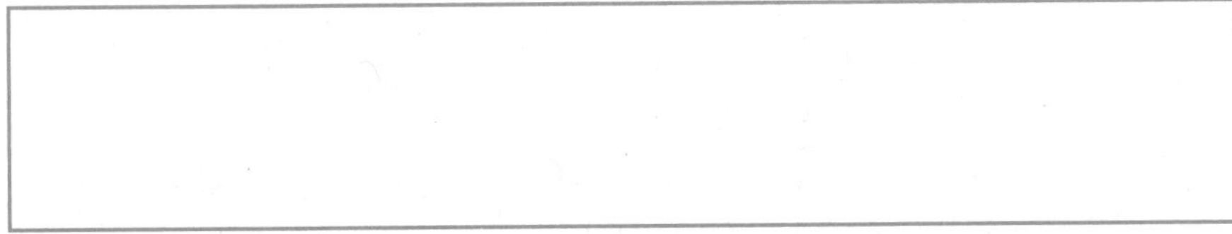

Part B

The clown also bought 5 bags of heart-shaped balloons with 14 balloons in each bag. When the clown blew up all of the round, long, and heart-shaped balloons, 23 balloons burst. How many blown-up balloons were left? Explain your answer.

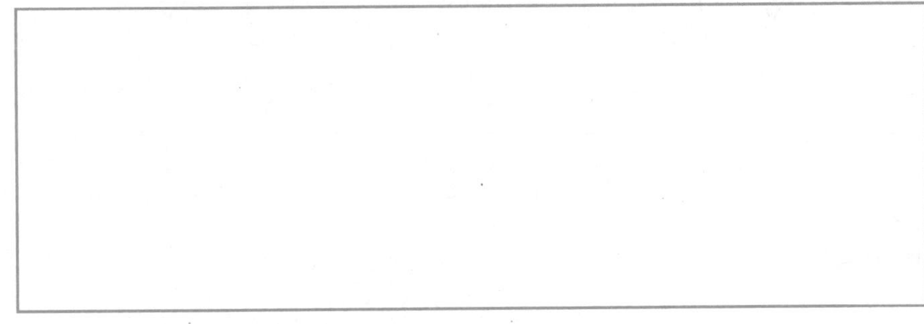

15. Hector planted 185 flowers in 2 days. There were 5 volunteers, including Hector, who each planted about the same number of flowers. About how many flowers did they plant?

185
400
500
1,000

16. Jay and Blair went fishing. Together, they caught 27 fish. Jay caught 2 times as many fish as Blair. How many fish did Jay and Blair each catch? Write an equation and solve. Explain your work.

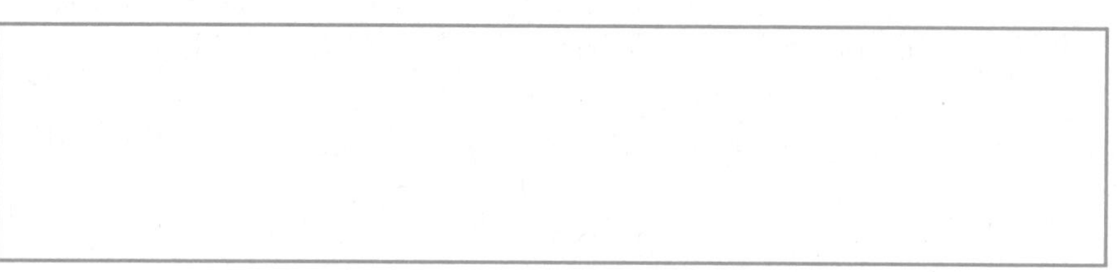

17. At the pet fair, Darlene's dog weighed 5 times as much as Leah's dog. Together, the dogs weighed 84 pounds. How much did each dog weigh? Complete the bar model. Write an equation and solve.

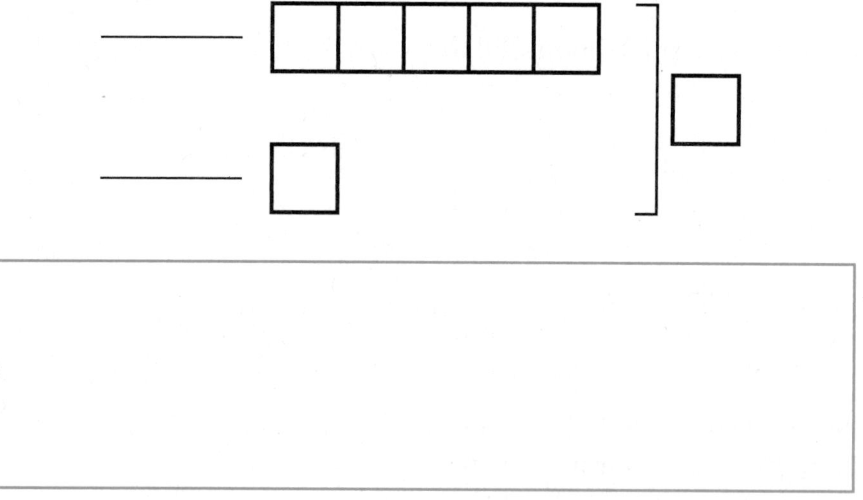

18. Use the Distributive Property to model the product on the grid. Record the product.

$4 \times 12 =$ ________

Chapter 3

Multiply 2-Digit Numbers

Show What You Know 

Check your understanding of important skills.

Name ____________________

▶ Practice Multiplication Facts Find the product.

1. $8 \times 7 =$ ______

   $7 \times 8 =$ ______

2. $3 \times (2 \times 4) =$ ______

   $(3 \times 2) \times 4 =$ ______

▶ 2-Digit by 1-Digit Multiplication Find the product.

3. 28×3

4. 56×6

5. 71×5

6. 69×8

7. 36×4

▶ Multiply by 1-Digit Numbers Find the product.

8. 72×4

9. 456×5

10. 804×7

11. $1{,}341 \times 9$

12. 65×6

13. 392×8

14. $1{,}478 \times 3$

15. $\$1{,}627 \times 2$

16. 584×7

17. $2{,}837 \times 4$

Math Detective

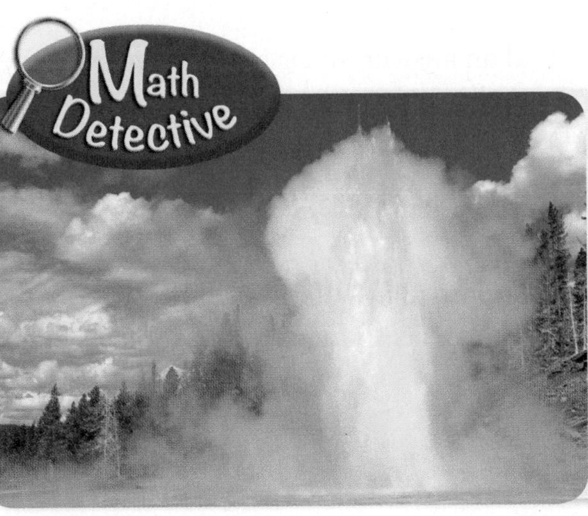

Yellowstone National Park, which is located in Wyoming, Montana, and Idaho, was America's first National Park. The park has over 500 geysers. Grand Geyser erupts about every 8 hours.

Be a Math Detective. Based on this estimate, how many times would you see this geyser erupt if you could watch it for 1 year? There are 24 hours in a day and 365 days in a year.

Personal Math Trainer
Online Assessment and Intervention

Vocabulary Builder

▶ Visualize It

Complete the H-diagram using the words with a ✓.

Multiplication Words		Estimation Words

Review Words

Associative Property of Multiplication
Commutative Property of Multiplication
✓ estimate
✓ factor
✓ partial product
✓ place value
✓ product
regroup
✓ round

Preview Words

✓ compatible numbers

▶ Understand Vocabulary

Draw a line to match each word or phrase with its definition.

Word

1. Commutative Property of Multiplication
2. estimate
3. compatible numbers
4. factor
5. regroup

Definition

- A number that is multiplied by another number to find a product
- To exchange amounts of equal value to rename a number
- To find an answer that is close to the exact amount
- Numbers that are easy to compute mentally
- The property that states when the order of two factors is changed, the product is the same.

GO DIGITAL
- Interactive Student Edition
- Multimedia eGlossary

Name ________________________

Multiply by Tens

Essential Question What strategies can you use to multiply by tens?

Number and Operations in Base Ten—4.NBT.5 *Also 4.NBT.1*

MATHEMATICAL PRACTICES
MP.1, MP.4, MP.7

Unlock the Problem

Animation for a computer-drawn cartoon requires about 20 frames per second. How many frames would need to be drawn for a 30-second cartoon?

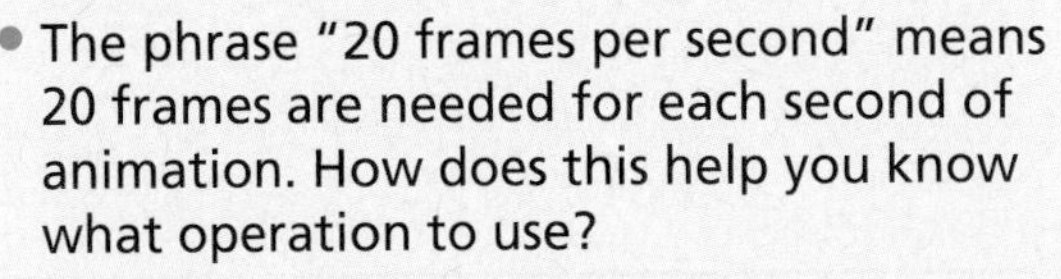

- The phrase "20 frames per second" means 20 frames are needed for each second of animation. How does this help you know what operation to use?

____

____

One Way Use place value.

Multiply. 20×30

You can think of 30 as 3 tens.

$20 \times 30 = 20 \times$ ______ tens

$=$ ______ tens

$= 600$

Remember

The Associative Property states that you can group factors in different ways and get the same product. Use parentheses to group the factors you multiply first.

Another Way Use the Associative Property.

You can think of 30 as 3×10.

$20 \times 30 = 20 \times (3 \times 10)$

$= (20 \times 3) \times 10$

$=$ ______ $\times$ ______

$=$ ______

Mathematical Practices

How can you use place value to tell why $60 \times 10 = 600$? **Explain.**

So, ______ frames would need to be drawn.

- Compare the number of zeros in each factor to the number of zeros in the product. What do you notice?

____

____

Other Ways

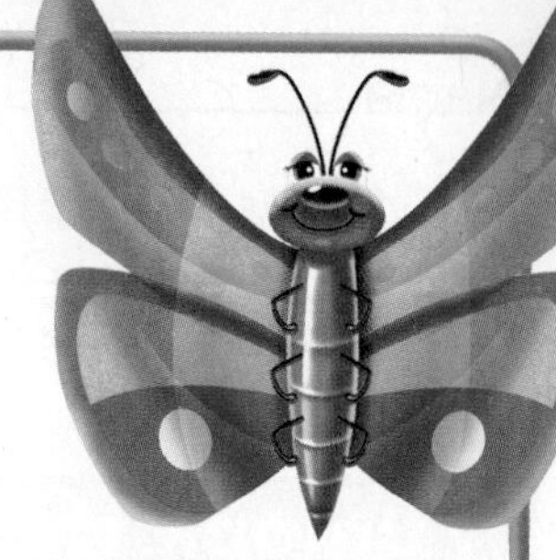

A Use a number line and a pattern to multiply 15×20.

Draw jumps to show the product.

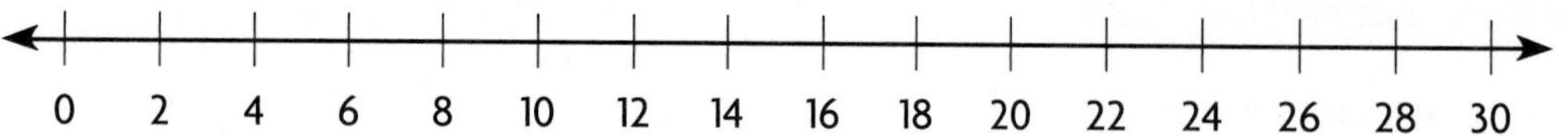

$15 \times 2 =$ ______

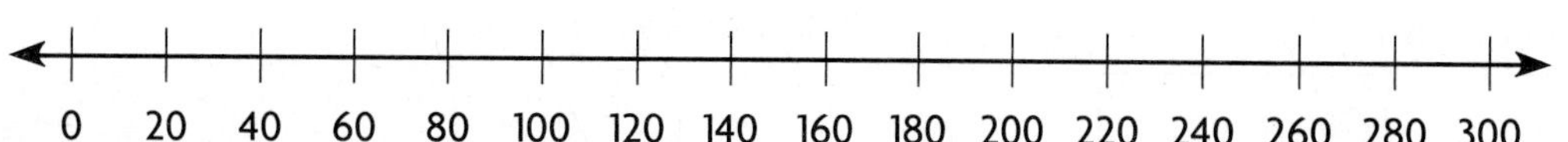

$15 \times 20 =$ ______

B Use mental math to find 14×30.

Use the halving-and-doubling strategy.

STEP 1 Find half of 14 to make the problem simpler.

Think: To find half of a number, divide by 2.

$14 \div 2 =$ ______

STEP 2 Multiply.

$7 \times 30 =$ ______

STEP 3 Double 210.

Think: To double a number, multiply by 2.

$2 \times 210 =$ ______

So, $14 \times 30 = 420$.

Try This! Multiply.

Use mental math to find 12×40.

Use place value to find 12×40.

Share and Show

1. Find 20×27. Tell which method you chose. Explain what happens in each step.

______

______

Name ___________________________

Choose a method. Then find the product.

2. 10×12

3. 20×20

4. 40×24

5. 11×60

Mathematical Practices

Explain how you can use $30 \times 10 = 300$ to find 30×12.

On Your Own

Choose a method. Then find the product.

6. 70×55

7. 17×30

8. 30×60

9. 12×90

MATHEMATICAL PRACTICE 2 Reason Quantitatively **Algebra** **Find the unknown digit in the number.**

10. $64 \times 40 = 2{,}56\blacksquare$

    ■ = ______

11. $29 \times 50 = 1{,}\text{⬟}50$

    ⬟ = ______

12. $3\blacklozenge \times 47 = 1{,}410$

    ◆ = ______

13. A factory makes 80 bicycles a day. How many bicycles do they make in 22 days?

    ____

14. Malala has 20 vases. She puts 12 flowers into each vase. How many flowers does she use?

    ____

Problem Solving • Applications Real World

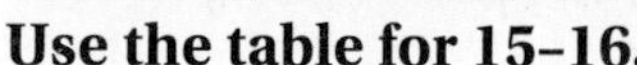

Use the table for 15–16.

15. MATHEMATICAL PRACTICE 4 **Use Graphs** How many frames did it take to produce 50 seconds of *Pinocchio*?

Animated Productions

Title	Date Released	Frames per Second
The Enchanted Drawing©	1900	20
Little Nemo©	1911	16
Snow White and the Seven Dwarfs©	1937	24
Pinocchio©	1940	19
The Flintstones™	1960–1966	24

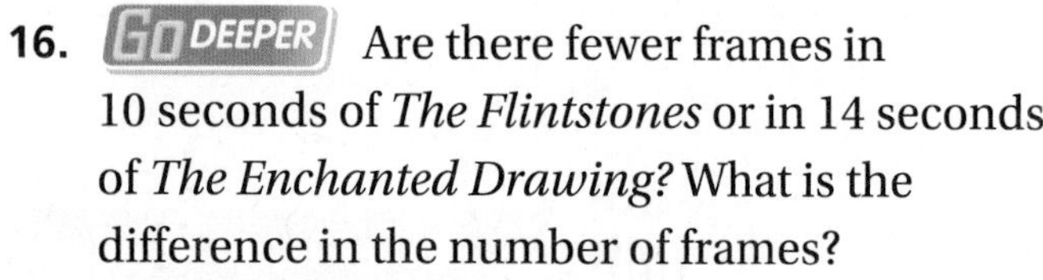

16. GO DEEPER Are there fewer frames in 10 seconds of *The Flintstones* or in 14 seconds of *The Enchanted Drawing?* What is the difference in the number of frames?

17. THINK SMARTER The product of my number and twice my number is 128. What is half my number? Explain how you solved the problem.

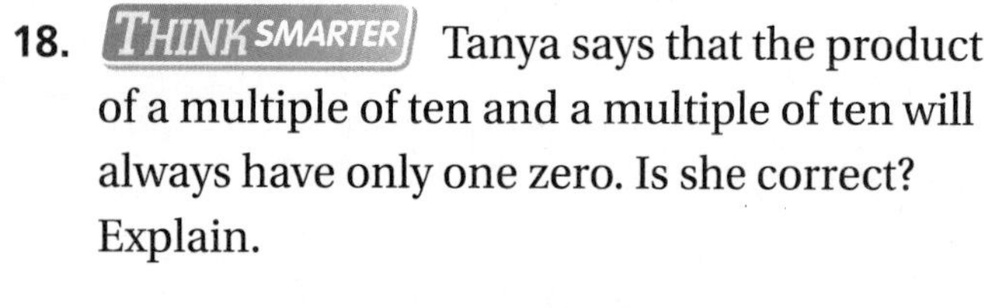

18. THINK SMARTER Tanya says that the product of a multiple of ten and a multiple of ten will always have only one zero. Is she correct? Explain.

WRITE ▸ Math
Show Your Work

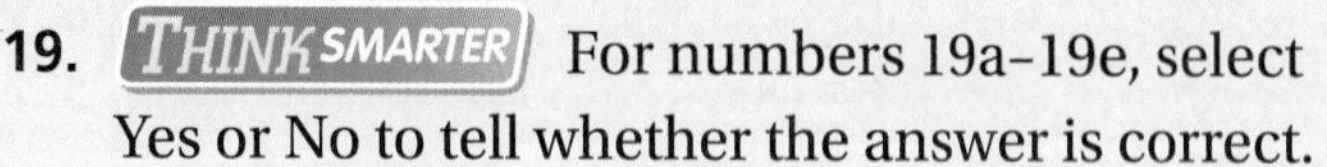

19. THINK SMARTER For numbers 19a–19e, select Yes or No to tell whether the answer is correct.

19a. $28 \times 10 = 280$ ○ Yes ○ No

19b. $15 \times 20 = 300$ ○ Yes ○ No

19c. $17 \times 10 = 17$ ○ Yes ○ No

19d. $80 \times 10 = 800$ ○ Yes ○ No

19e. $16 \times 30 = 1{,}800$ ○ Yes ○ No

FOR MORE PRACTICE:
Standards Practice Book

Name ______________________________

Estimate Products

Essential Question What strategies can you use to estimate products?

Number and Operations in Base Ten—4.NBT.5 *Also 4.NBT.3*

MATHEMATICAL PRACTICES
MP.1, MP.2, MP.5, MP.7

Unlock the Problem (Real World)

The Smith family opens the door of their refrigerator 32 times in one day. There are 31 days in May. About how many times is it opened in May?

- Underline any information you will need.

One Way Use rounding and mental math.

Estimate. 32×31

STEP 1 Round each factor.

32×31

↓ ↓

30×30

STEP 2 Use mental math.

$3 \times 3 = 9$ ← basic fact

$30 \times 30 =$ ____________

So, the Smith family opens the refrigerator door about 900 times during the month of May.

Math Talk — Mathematical Practices

Will the actual number of times the refrigerator is opened in a year be greater than or less than 900? **Explain.**

1. On average, a refrigerator door is opened 38 times each day. About how many fewer times in May is the Smith family's refrigerator door opened than the average refrigerator door?

Show your work.

All 24 light bulbs in the Park family's home are CFL light bulbs. Each CFL light bulb uses 28 watts to produce light. About how many watts will the light bulbs use when turned on all at the same time?

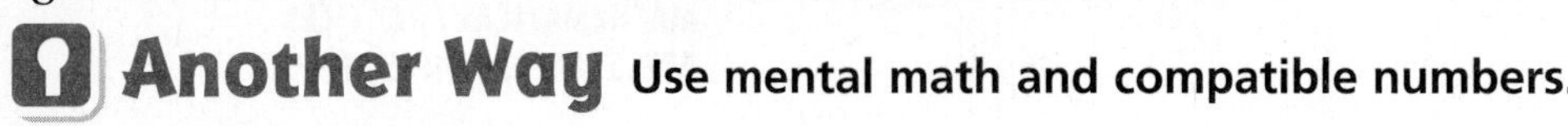

Use mental math and compatible numbers.

Compatible numbers are numbers that are easy to compute mentally.

Estimate. 24×28

STEP 1 Use compatible numbers.

24×28

↓ ↓

25×30 Think: $25 \times 3 = 75$

STEP 2 Use mental math.

$25 \times 3 = 75$

$25 \times 30 =$ ____________

So, about 750 watts are used.

Try This! **Estimate 26 × $79.**

A **Round to the nearest ten**

26 × $79

↓ ↓

________ × ________ = ________

26 × $79 is about ____________.

B **Compatible numbers**

26 × $79

↓ ↓

25 × $80 = ____________

Think: How can you use $25 \times 4 = 100$ to help find 25×8?

26 × $79 is about ____________.

2. Explain why $2,400 and $2,000 are both reasonable estimates.

____

____

3. In what situation might you choose to find an estimate rather than an exact answer?

____

____

Share and Show

1. To estimate the product of 62 and 28 by rounding, how would you round the factors? What would the estimated product be?

____

Name ______________________

Estimate the product. Choose a method.

2. 96×34

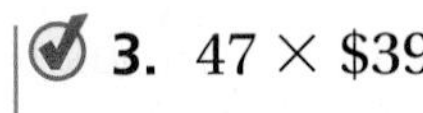

3. $47 \times \$39$

4. 78×72

Math Talk — **Mathematical Practices**

Describe how you know if an estimated product will be greater than or less than the exact answer.

On Your Own

Estimate the product. Choose a method.

5. 41×78

6. 51×73

7. 34×80

8. 84×23

9. $27 \times \$56$

10. 45×22

Practice: Copy and Solve **Estimate the product. Choose a method.**

11. 61×31

12. 52×68

13. 26×44

14. $57 \times \$69$

15. 55×39

16. 51×81

17. $47 \times \$32$

18. 49×64

THINK SMARTER **Find two possible factors for the estimated product.**

19. 2,800

____

____

20. 8,100

____

____

21. 5,600

____

____

22. 2,400

____

____

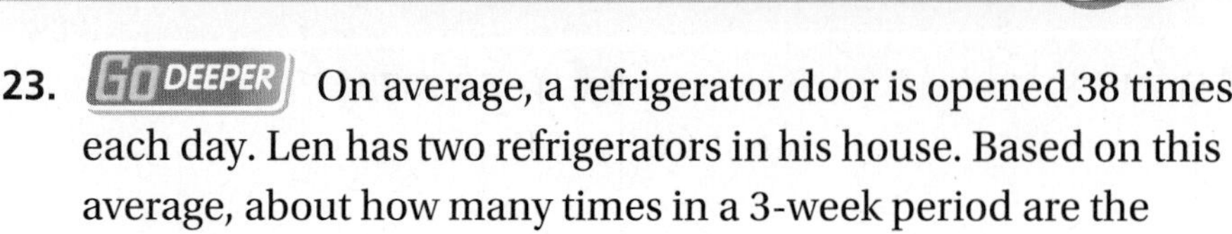

23. GO DEEPER On average, a refrigerator door is opened 38 times each day. Len has two refrigerators in his house. Based on this average, about how many times in a 3-week period are the refrigerator doors opened?

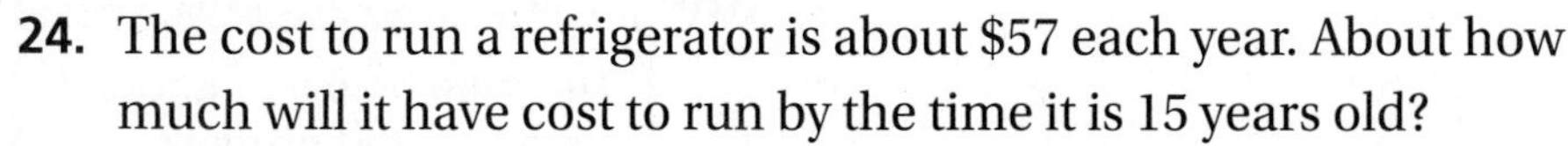

24. The cost to run a refrigerator is about $57 each year. About how much will it have cost to run by the time it is 15 years old?

25. THINK SMARTER If Mel opens his refrigerator door 36 times every day, about how many times will it be opened in April? Will the exact answer be more than or less than the estimate? Explain.

26. MATHEMATICAL PRACTICE 2 **Represent a Problem** What question could you write for this answer? The estimated product of two numbers, that are not multiples of ten, is 2,800.

27. THINK SMARTER Which is a reasonable estimate for the product? Write the estimate. An estimate may be used more than once.

30×20	25×50	20×20

26×48		28×21	
21×22		51×26	

 FOR MORE PRACTICE: Standards Practice Book

Name ______________________________

Area Models and Partial Products

Essential Question How can you use area models and partial products to multiply 2-digit numbers?

Number and Operations in Base Ten—4.NBT.5

MATHEMATICAL PRACTICES
MP.2, MP.4, MP.5, MP.8

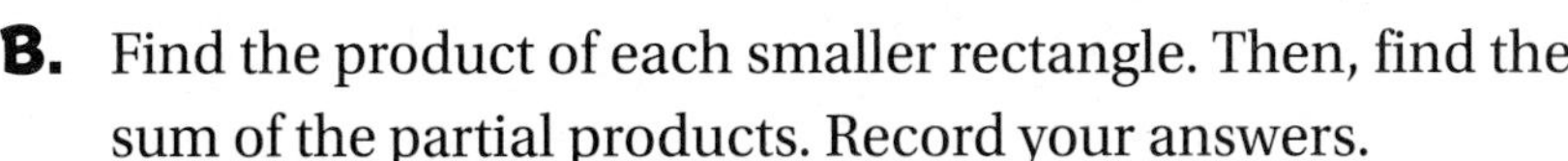

Materials ■ color pencils

How can you use a model to break apart factors and make them easier to multiply?

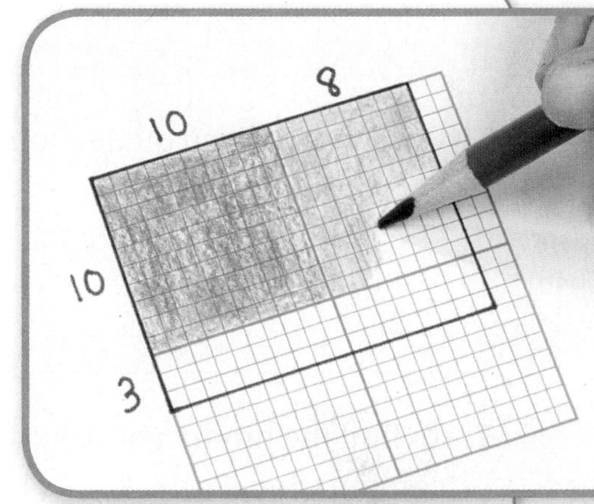

A. Outline a rectangle on the grid to model 13 × 18. Break apart the model into smaller rectangles to show factors broken into tens and ones. Label and shade the smaller rectangles. Use the colors below.

B. Find the product of each smaller rectangle. Then, find the sum of the partial products. Record your answers.

☐ = 10 × 10

☐ = 10 × 8

☐ = 3 × 10

☐ = 3 × 8

100 + ____ + ____ + ____ = ____

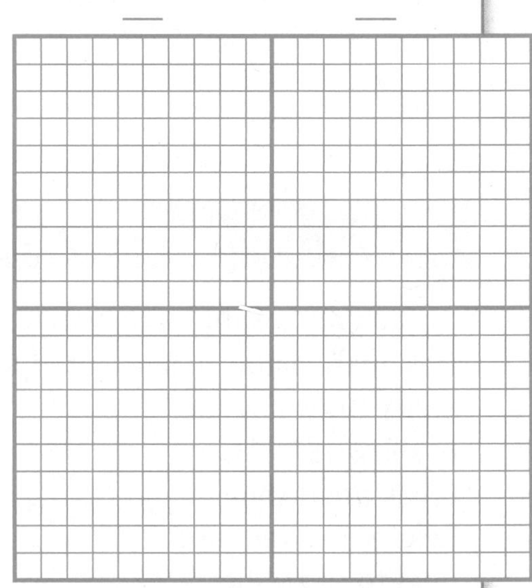

C. Draw the model again. Break apart the whole model to show factors different from those shown the first time. Label and shade the four smaller rectangles and find their products. Record the sum of the partial products to represent the product of the whole model.

____ + ____ + ____ + ____ = ____

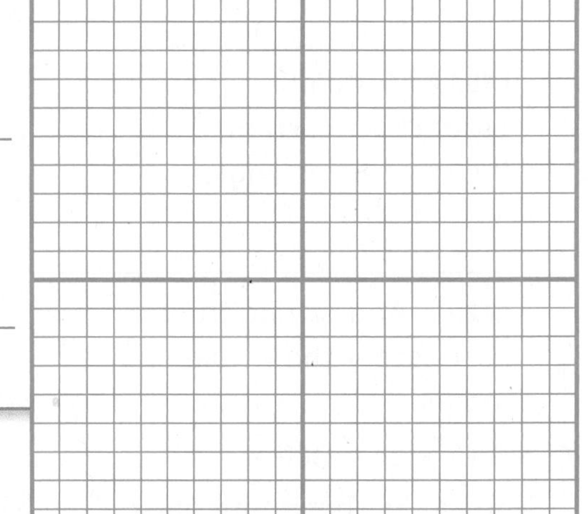

Draw Conclusions

1. Explain how you found the total number of squares in the whole model.

2. Compare the two models and their products. What can you conclude? Explain.

3. To find the product of 10 and 33, which is the easier computation, $(10 \times 11) + (10 \times 11) + (10 \times 11)$ or $(10 \times 30) + (10 \times 3)$? Explain.

Make Connections

You can draw a simple diagram to model and break apart factors to find a product. Find 15×24.

Remember

24 is 2 tens 4 ones.

STEP 1 Draw a model to show 15×24. Break apart the factors into tens and ones to show the partial products.

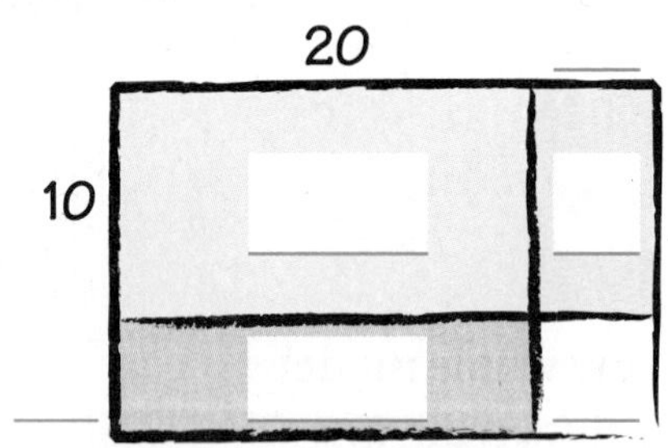

STEP 2 Write the product for each of the smaller rectangles.

(10 × 2 tens)	(10 × 4 ones)	(5 × 2 tens)	(5 × 4 ones)
(10 × 20)	(10 × 4)	(5 × 20)	(5 × 4)
____	____	____	____

STEP 3 Add to find the product for the whole model.

____ + ____ + ____ + ____ = ____

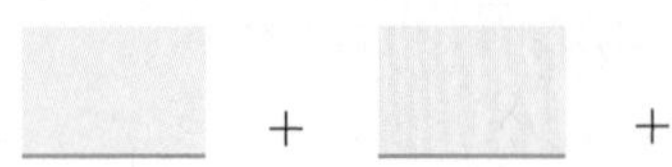

So, $15 \times 24 = 360$.

The model shows four parts. Each part represents a partial product. The partial products are 200, 40, 100, and 20.

Mathematical Practices

Explain how breaking apart the factors into tens and ones makes finding the product easier.

Name ______________________________

Share and Show

Find the product.

1. $16 \times 19 =$ ________

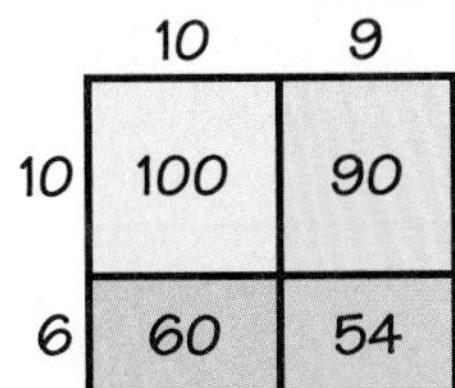

2. $18 \times 26 =$ ________

	20	6
10		
8		

3. $27 \times 39 =$ ________

	30	9
20		
7		

Draw a model to represent the product. Then record the product.

4. $14 \times 16 =$ ________

5. $23 \times 25 =$ ________

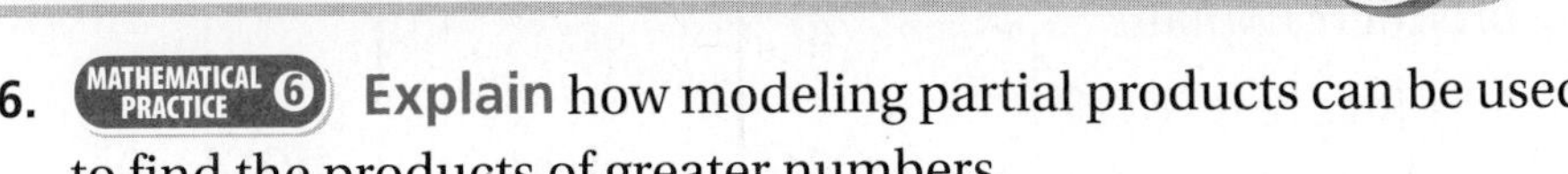

Problem Solving • Applications

6. MATHEMATICAL PRACTICE 6 **Explain** how modeling partial products can be used to find the products of greater numbers.

____

____

7. GO DEEPER Emma bought 16 packages of rolls for a party. There were 12 rolls in a package. After the party there were 8 rolls left over. How many rolls were eaten? Explain.

____

____

Sense or Nonsense?

8. THINK SMARTER Jamal and Kim used different ways to solve 12×15 by using partial products. Whose answer makes sense? Whose answer is nonsense? Explain your reasoning.

Jamal's Work

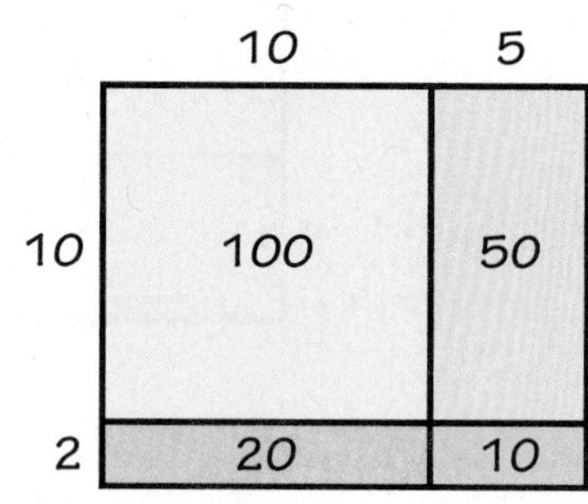

$100 + 20 + 10 = 130$

____

____

____

Kim's Work

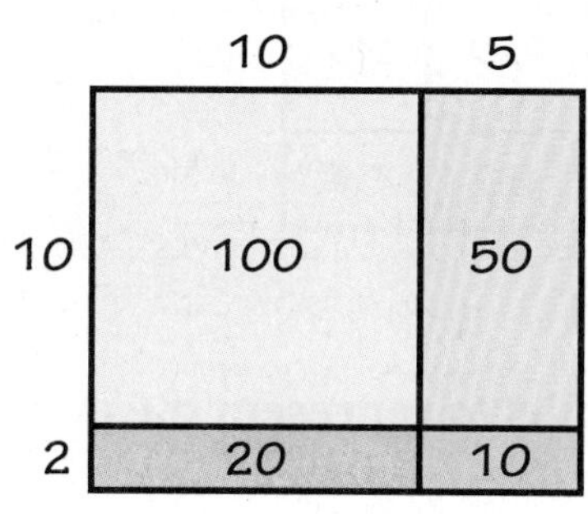

$120 + 60 = 180$

____

____

____

a. For the answer that is nonsense, write an answer that makes sense.

____

b. Look at Kim's method. Can you think of another way Kim could use the model to find the product? Explain.

	10	5
10	100	50
2	20	10

____

____

____

9. THINK SMARTER Look at the model in 8b. How would the partial products change if the product was 22×15? Explain why you think the products changed.

____

____

FOR MORE PRACTICE:
Standards Practice Book

Name ______________________

Multiply Using Partial Products

Essential Question How can you use place value and partial products to multiply 2-digit numbers?

Number and Operations in Base Ten—4.NBT.5

MATHEMATICAL PRACTICES
MP.4, MP.7, MP.8

Unlock the Problem (Real World)

CONNECT You know how to break apart a model to find partial products. How can you use what you know to find and record a product?

Multiply. 34 × 57 **Estimate.** 30 × 60 = ________

SHADE THE MODEL | **THINK AND RECORD**

STEP 1

57
× 34
_____

← Multiply the tens by the tens.
30 × 5 tens = 150 tens

STEP 2

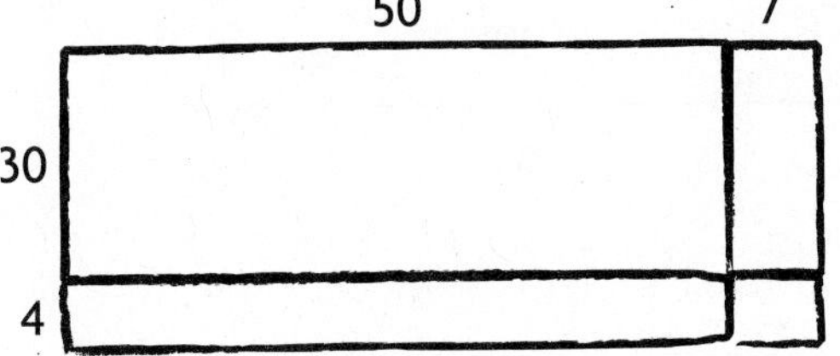

57
×34
1,500

← Multiply the ones by the tens.
30 × 7 ones = 210 ones

STEP 3

57
×34
1,500
210

← Multiply the tens by the ones.
4 × 5 tens = 20 tens

STEP 4

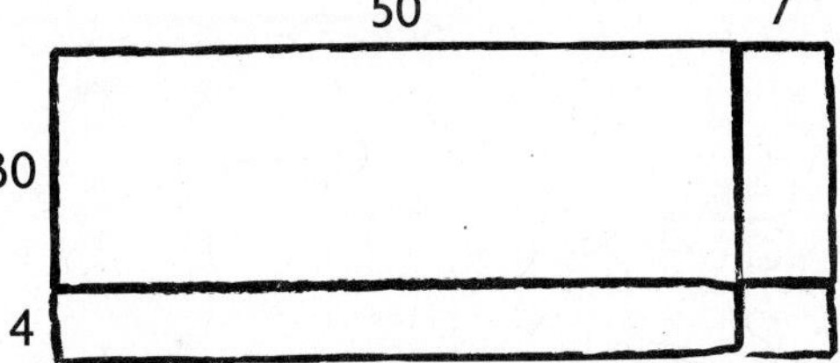

57
×34
1,500
210
200
+ ____

← Multiply the ones by the ones.
4 × 7 ones = 28 ones
← Add the partial products.

So, 34 × 57 = 1,938. Since 1,938 is close to the estimate of 1,800, it is reasonable.

Math Talk — **Mathematical Practices**

You can write 10 × 4 ones = 40 ones as 10 × 4 = 40. What is another way to write 10 × 3 tens = 30 tens?

Example

The apples from each tree in an orchard can fill 23 bushel baskets. If 1 row of the orchard has 48 trees, how many baskets of apples can be filled?

Multiply. 48×23 **Estimate.** $50 \times 20 =$ ______

THINK	RECORD	
STEP 1 Multiply the tens by the tens.	23 × 48 ____	← 40 × ______ tens = ______ tens
STEP 2 Multiply the ones by the tens.	23 × 48 800 ____	← 40 × ______ ones = ______ ones
STEP 3 Multiply the tens by the ones.	23 × 48 800 120 ____	← 8 × ______ tens = ______ tens
STEP 4 Multiply the ones by the ones. Then add the partial products.	23 × 48 800 120 160 + ____ ____	← 8 × ______ ones = ______ ones

So, 1,104 baskets can be filled.

Mathematical Practices

How do you know your answer is reasonable?

Share and Show

1. Find 24×34.

	30	4
20	600	80
4	120	16

$$\begin{array}{r} 34 \\ \times\ 24 \\ \hline \end{array}$$

Name ____________________

Record the product.

2. $\begin{array}{r} 12 \\ \times\ 12 \\ \hline \end{array}$

3. $\begin{array}{r} 31 \\ \times\ 24 \\ \hline \end{array}$

4. $\begin{array}{r} 25 \\ \times\ 43 \\ \hline \end{array}$

5. $\begin{array}{r} 37 \\ \times\ 26 \\ \hline \end{array}$

Math Talk **Mathematical Practices**

Explain how to model and record 74 × 25.

On Your Own

Record the product.

6. $\begin{array}{r} 54 \\ \times\ 15 \\ \hline \end{array}$

7. $\begin{array}{r} 87 \\ \times\ 16 \\ \hline \end{array}$

8. $\begin{array}{r} 62 \\ \times\ 56 \\ \hline \end{array}$

9. $\begin{array}{r} 49 \\ \times\ 63 \\ \hline \end{array}$

Practice: Copy and Solve Record the product.

10. 38 × 47
11. 46 × 27
12. 72 × 53
13. 98 × 69
14. 53 × 68
15. 76 × 84
16. 92 × 48
17. 37 × 79

MATHEMATICAL PRACTICE 2 Reason Abstractly **Algebra** Find the unknown digits. Complete the problem.

18. $\begin{array}{r} \square 6 \\ \times\ \square 4 \\ \hline 1{,}400 \\ 120 \\ 280 \\ +\ 24 \\ \hline \square \end{array}$

19. $\begin{array}{r} \square 2 \\ \times\ \square 7 \\ \hline 7{,}200 \\ 180 \\ 560 \\ +\ 14 \\ \hline \square \end{array}$

20. $\begin{array}{r} \square 6 \\ \times\ 5\square \\ \hline 1{,}500 \\ 300 \\ 90 \\ +\ 18 \\ \hline \square \end{array}$

21. $\begin{array}{r} 3\square \\ \times\ \square 8 \\ \hline 600 \\ 80 \\ 240 \\ +\ 32 \\ \hline \square \end{array}$

Problem Solving • Applications

Use the picture graph for 22–24.

Pounds of Citrus Fruit per Box

Citrus Fruit	Weight per Box (in pounds)
Grapefruit	
Orange	
Tangelo	
Tangerine	

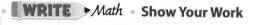

Key: Each = 10 pounds.

22. MATHEMATICAL PRACTICE 4 **Use Graphs** A fruit-packing warehouse is shipping 15 boxes of grapefruit to a store in Santa Rosa, California. What is the total weight of the shipment?

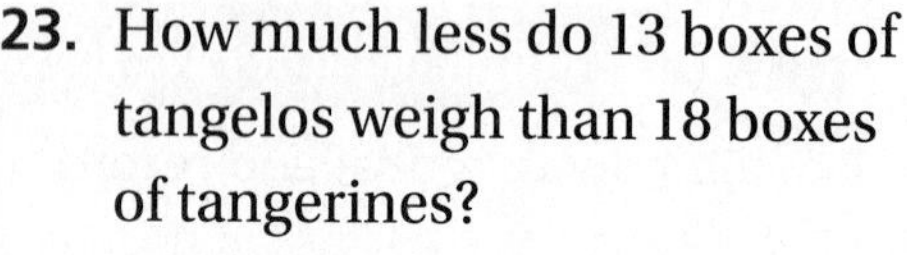

23. How much less do 13 boxes of tangelos weigh than 18 boxes of tangerines?

24. What is the weight of 12 boxes of oranges?

WRITE ▸Math • Show Your Work

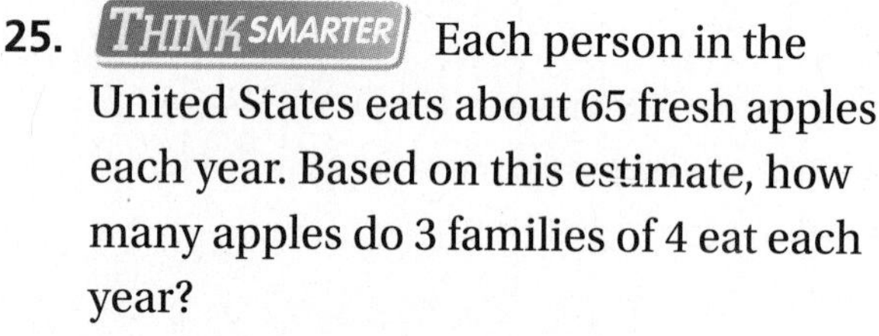

25. THINK SMARTER Each person in the United States eats about 65 fresh apples each year. Based on this estimate, how many apples do 3 families of 4 eat each year?

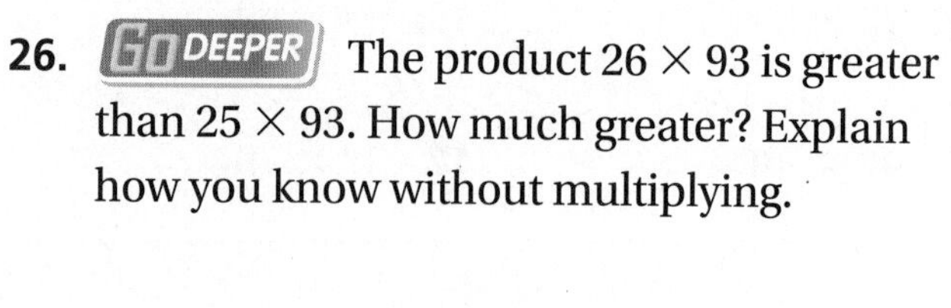

26. GO DEEPER The product 26×93 is greater than 25×93. How much greater? Explain how you know without multiplying.

27. THINK SMARTER Margot wants to use partial products to find 22×17. Write the numbers in the boxes to show 22×17.

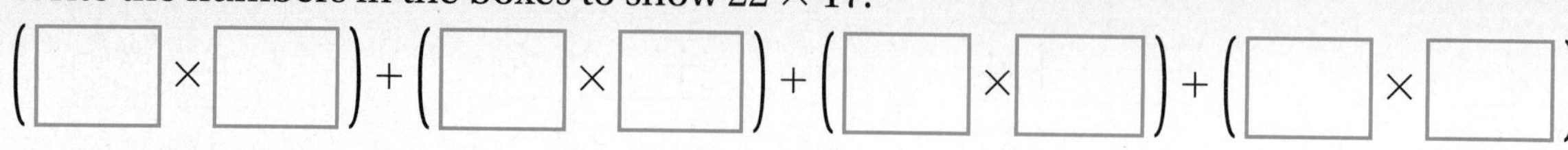

$(\square \times \square) + (\square \times \square) + (\square \times \square) + (\square \times \square)$

FOR MORE PRACTICE: Standards Practice Book

Name ____________________

Mid-Chapter Checkpoint

Concepts and Skills

1. Explain how to find 40×50 using mental math. (4.NBT.5)

____

____

2. What is the first step in estimating 56×27? (4.NBT.5)

____

Choose a method. Then find the product. (4.NBT.5)

3. 35×10 ______
4. 19×20 ______
5. 12×80 ______
6. 70×50 ______
7. 58×40 ______
8. 30×40 ______
9. 14×60 ______
10. 20×30 ______
11. 16×90 ______

Estimate the product. Choose a method. (4.NBT.5)

12. 81×38 ______
13. $16 \times \$59$ ______
14. 43×25 ______
15. 76×45 ______
16. $65 \times \$79$ ______
17. 92×38 ______
18. 37×31 ______
19. $26 \times \$59$ ______
20. 54×26 ______
21. 52×87 ______
22. 39×27 ______
23. 63×58 ______

24. Ms. Traynor's class is taking a field trip to the zoo. The trip will cost \$26 for each student. There are 22 students in her class. What is a good estimate for the cost of the students' field trip? (4.NBT.5)

---

25. Tito wrote the following on the board. What is the unknown number? (4.NBT.5)

$$
\begin{aligned}
50 \times 80 &= 50 \times (8 \times 10) \\
&= (50 \times 8) \times 10 \\
&= ? \times 10 \\
&= 4{,}000
\end{aligned}
$$

---

26. What are the partial products that result from multiplying 15×32? (4.NBT.5)

---

27. The cost of a ski-lift ticket is \$31. How much will 17 tickets cost? (4.NBT.5)

Lesson 3.5

Name ______________________

Multiply with Regrouping

Essential Question How can you use regrouping to multiply 2-digit numbers?

Number and Operations in Base Ten—4.NBT.5 *Also 4.OA.3*

MATHEMATICAL PRACTICES
MP.2, MP.7, MP.8

Unlock the Problem

By 1914, Henry Ford had streamlined his assembly line to make a Model T Ford car in 93 minutes. How many minutes did it take to make 25 Model Ts?

▲ The first production Model T Ford was assembled on October 1, 1908.

Use place value and regrouping.

Multiply. 93 × 25 **Estimate.** 90 × 30 = ______

THINK	RECORD
STEP 1 • Think of 93 as 9 tens and 3 ones. • Multiply 25 by 3 ones.	$\begin{array}{r} \scriptstyle 1 \\ 25 \\ \times\ 93 \\ \hline \square \end{array}$ ← 3 × 25
STEP 2 • Multiply 25 by 9 tens.	$\begin{array}{r} \scriptstyle 4 \\ \scriptstyle \not{1} \\ 25 \\ \times\ 93 \\ \hline 75 \\ \square \end{array}$ ← 90 × 25
STEP 3 • Add the partial products.	$\begin{array}{r} \scriptstyle 4 \\ \scriptstyle \not{1} \\ 25 \\ \times\ 93 \\ \hline 75 \\ 2,250 \\ \hline \square \end{array}$

So, 93 × 25 is 2,325. Since ____________ is close to the estimate of ____________, the answer is reasonable.

Math Talk — Mathematical Practices

Explain why you will get the same answer whether you multiply 93 × 25 or 25 × 93.

Different Ways to Multiply You can use different ways to multiply and still get the correct answer. Shawn and Patty both solved 67×40 correctly, but they used different ways.

Look at Shawn's paper.

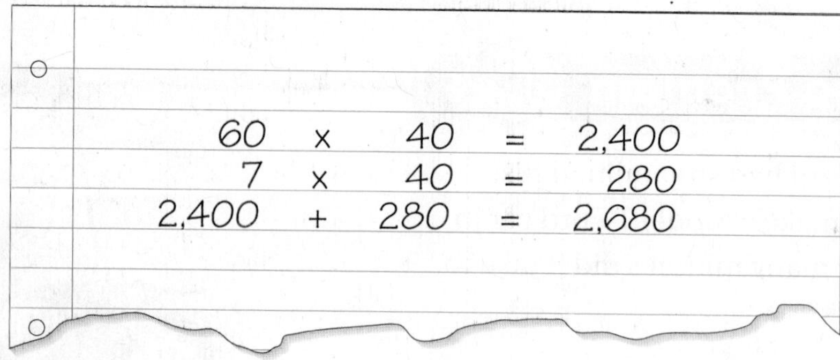

So, Shawn's answer is $67 \times 40 = 2{,}680$.

Look at Patty's paper.

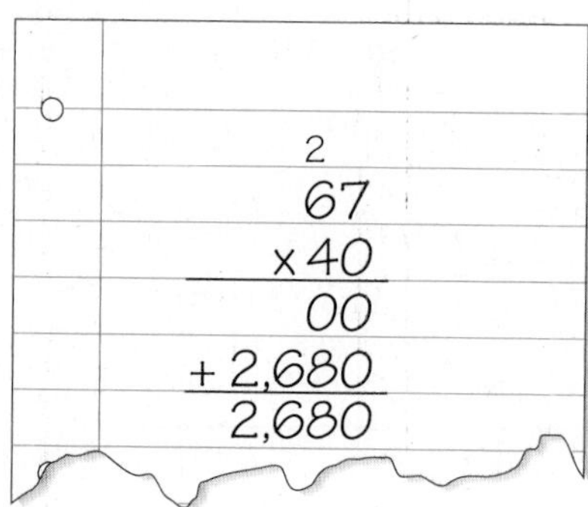

So, Patty also found $67 \times 40 = 2{,}680$.

1. What method did Shawn use to solve the problem?

____

2. What method did Patty use to solve the problem?

____

Share and Show

1. Look at the problem. Complete the sentences.

Multiply ______ and ______ to get 0.

Multiply ______ and ______ to get 1,620.

Add the partial products.

$0 + 1{,}620 =$ __________

$$\begin{array}{r} {}^{4} \\ 27 \\ \times 60 \\ \hline 0 \\ +1{,}620 \\ \hline \end{array}$$

Name ______________________________

Estimate. Then find the product.

2. Estimate: __________

$$\begin{array}{r} 68 \\ \times\ 53 \\ \hline \end{array}$$

3. Estimate: __________

$$\begin{array}{r} 61 \\ \times\ 54 \\ \hline \end{array}$$

4. Estimate: __________

$$\begin{array}{r} 90 \\ \times\ 27 \\ \hline \end{array}$$

Mathematical Practices

Explain why you can omit zeros of the first partial product when you multiply 20 × 34.

On Your Own

Estimate. Then find the product.

5. Estimate: __________

$$\begin{array}{r} 30 \\ \times\ 47 \\ \hline \end{array}$$

6. Estimate: __________

$$\begin{array}{r} 78 \\ \times\ 56 \\ \hline \end{array}$$

7. Estimate: __________

$$\begin{array}{r} 27 \\ \times\ 25 \\ \hline \end{array}$$

Practice: Copy and Solve **Estimate. Then find the product.**

8. 34 × 65 **9.** 42 × $13 **10.** 60 × 17 **11.** 62 × 45 **12.** 57 × $98

13. 92 × $54 **14.** 75 × 20 **15.** 66 × 55 **16.** 73 × $68 **17.** 72 × 40

MATHEMATICAL PRACTICE 7 **Look for a Pattern** **Algebra** **Write a rule for the pattern. Use your rule to find the unknown numbers.**

18.

Hours	*h*	5	10	15	20	25
Minutes	*m*	300	600	900		

Rule: ______________________

19.

Minutes	*m*	12	14	16	18	20
Seconds	*s*	720	840		1,080	

Rule: ______________________

Unlock the Problem Real World

20. THINK SMARTER Machine A can label 11 bottles in 1 minute. Machine B can label 12 bottles in 1 minute. How many bottles can both machines label in 15 minutes?

a. What do you need to know? ______________________

____

b. What numbers will you use? ______________________

c. Tell why you might use more than one operation to solve the problem.

____

____

____

d. Solve the problem.

So, both machines can label ______ bottles in ______ minutes.

21. MATHEMATICAL PRACTICE 1 **Make Sense of Problems** A toy company makes wooden blocks. A carton holds 85 blocks. How many blocks can 19 cartons hold?

____

22. GO DEEPER A company is packing cartons of candles. Each carton can hold 75 candles. So far, 50 cartons have been packed, but only 30 cartons have been loaded on a truck. How many more candles are left to load on the truck?

____

Personal Math Trainer

23. THINK SMARTER + Mr. Garcia's class raised money for a field trip to the zoo. There are 23 students in his class. The cost of the trip will be $17 for each student. What is the cost for all the students? Explain how you found your answer.

____

____

FOR MORE PRACTICE: Standards Practice Book

Name ______________________

Choose a Multiplication Method

Essential Question How can you find and record products of two 2-digit numbers?

Number and Operations in Base Ten—4.NBT.5

MATHEMATICAL PRACTICES
MP.2, MP.3, MP.8

Unlock the Problem

Did you know using math can help prevent you from getting a sunburn?

The time it takes to burn without sunscreen multiplied by the SPF, or sun protection factor, is the time you can stay in the sun safely with sunscreen.

If today's UV index is 8, Erin will burn in 15 minutes without sunscreen. If Erin puts on lotion with an SPF of 25, how long will she be protected?

- Underline the sentence that tells you how to find the answer.
- Circle the numbers you need to use. What operation will you use?

____

▲ Sunscreen helps to prevent sunburn.

One Way Use partial products to find 15 × 25.

$$\begin{array}{r} 25 \\ \times\ 15 \\ \hline \end{array}$$

☐ ← 10 × 2 tens = 20 tens

☐ ← 10 × 5 ones = 50 ones

☐ ← 5 × 2 tens = 10 tens

\+ ☐ ← 5 × 5 ones = 25 ones

☐ ← Add.

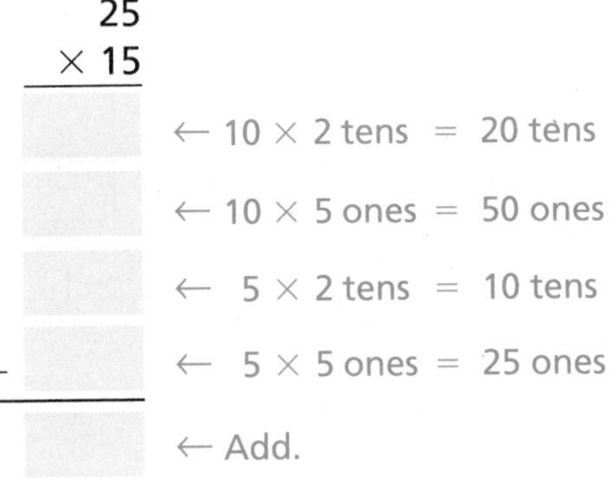

Draw a picture to check your work.

Math Talk **Mathematical Practices**

The product is 375. **Explain** what 375 means for Erin.

Another Way Use regrouping to find 15 × 25.

Estimate. 20 × 20 = ______

STEP 1

Think of 15 as 1 ten 5 ones. Multiply 25 by 5 ones, or 5.

```
   2
   25
 × 15
 ----
      ← 5 × 25
```

STEP 2

Multiply 25 by 1 ten, or 10.

```
   2
   25
 × 15
 ----
  125
      ← 10 × 25
```

STEP 3

Add the partial products.

```
    2
    25
  × 15
  ----
   125
 + 250
 -----
```

Try This! **Multiply. 57 × $43**

Estimate. 57 × $43

Use partial products.

```
  $43
×  57
-----
```

Use regrouping.

```
  $43
×  57
-----
```

1. How do you know your answer is reasonable?

____

____

2. Look at the partial products and regrouping methods above. How are the partial products 2,000 and 150 related to 2,150?

____

How are the partial products 280 and 21 related to 301?

____

Name ___________________________

Share and Show

1. Find the product.

			5	4	
	×		2	9	

Math Talk — **Mathematical Practices**

Explain why you begin with the ones place when you use the regrouping method to multiply.

Estimate. Then choose a method to find the product.

2. Estimate: ______

$$\begin{array}{r} 36 \\ \times\ 14 \\ \hline \end{array}$$

3. Estimate: ______

$$\begin{array}{r} 63 \\ \times\ 42 \\ \hline \end{array}$$

✓4. Estimate: ______

$$\begin{array}{r} 84 \\ \times\ 53 \\ \hline \end{array}$$

✓5. Estimate: ______

$$\begin{array}{r} 71 \\ \times\ 13 \\ \hline \end{array}$$

On Your Own

Practice: Copy and Solve **Estimate. Find the product.**

6. 29 × $82
7. 57 × 79
8. 80 × 27
9. 32 × $75
10. 55 × 48
11. 19 × $82
12. 25 × $25
13. 41 × 98

MATHEMATICAL PRACTICE 7 **Identify Relationships** **Algebra** **Use mental math to find the number.**

14. 30 × 14 = 420, so 30 × 15 = ______.

15. 25 × 12 = 300, so 25 × ______ = 350.

16. MATHEMATICAL PRACTICE 6 The town conservation manager bought 16 maple trees for $26 each. She paid with five $100 bills. How much change will the manager receive? **Explain.**

____

____

17. GO DEEPER Each of 25 students in Group A read for 45 minutes. Each of 21 students in Group B read for 48 minutes. Which group read for more minutes? Explain.

____

Unlock the Problem (Real World)

18. THINK SMARTER Martin collects stamps. He counted 48 pages in his collector's album. The first 20 pages each have 35 stamps in 5 rows. The rest of the pages each have 54 stamps. How many stamps does Martin have in his album?

a. What do you need to know? ______________________

____

b. How will you use multiplication to find the number of stamps? ______________________

____

c. Tell why you might use addition and subtraction to help solve the problem.

____

____

d. Show the steps to solve the problem.

e. Complete the sentences.

Martin has a total of ________ stamps on the first 20 pages.

There are ________ more pages after the first 20 pages in Martin's album.

There are ________ stamps on the rest of the pages.

There are ________ stamps in the album.

19. THINK SMARTER Select the expressions that have the same product as 35×17. Mark all that apply.

- ○ $(30 \times 10) + (30 \times 7) + (5 \times 10) + (5 \times 7)$
- ○ $(35 \times 30) + (35 \times 5) + (35 \times 10) + (35 \times 7)$
- ○ $(35 \times 10) + (30 \times 10) + (5 \times 10) + (5 \times 7)$
- ○ $(30 \times 17) + (5 \times 17)$
- ○ $(35 \times 10) + (35 \times 7)$
- ○ $(35 \times 30) + (35 \times 5)$

FOR MORE PRACTICE: Standards Practice Book

Name ______________________________

Problem Solving • Multiply 2-Digit Numbers

PROBLEM SOLVING
Lesson 3.7

Essential Question How can you use the strategy *draw a diagram* to solve multistep multiplication problems?

Operations and Algebraic Thinking—4.OA.3 *Also 4.NBT.5*

MATHEMATICAL PRACTICES
MP.1, MP.2, MP.5

Unlock the Problem

During the 2010 Great Backyard Bird Count, an average of 42 bald eagles were counted in each of 20 locations throughout Alaska. In 2009, an average of 32 bald eagles were counted in each of 26 locations throughout Alaska. Based on this data, how many more bald eagles were counted in 2010 than in 2009?

Use the graphic organizer to help you solve the problem.

Read the Problem

What do I need to find?

I need to find ____________ bald eagles were counted in 2010 than in 2009.

What information do I need to use?

In 2010, _____ locations counted an average of _____ bald eagles each.

In 2009 _____ locations counted an average of _____ bald eagles each.

How will I use the information?

I can solve simpler problems.

Find the number of bald eagles counted in _____.

Find the number of bald eagles counted in _____.

Then draw a bar model to compare the _____ count to the _____ count.

Solve the Problem

- First, find the total number of bald eagles counted in 2010.

  _____ × _____

  = _____ bald eagles counted in 2010

- Next, find the total number of bald eagles counted in 2009.

  = _____ × _____

  = _____ bald eagles counted in 2009

- Last, draw a bar model. I need to subtract.

840 bald eagles in 2010
832 bald eagles in 2009	?

840 − 832 = _____

So, there were _____ more bald eagles counted in 2010 than in 2009.

Try Another Problem

Prescott Valley, Arizona, reported a total of 29 mourning doves in the Great Backyard Bird Count. Mesa, Arizona, reported 20 times as many mourning doves as Prescott Valley. If Chandler reported a total of 760 mourning doves, how many more mourning doves were reported in Chandler than in Mesa?

Mourning dove ▲

Read the Problem	Solve the Problem
What do I need to find?	
What information do I need to use?	760 mourning doves in Chandler 580 mourning doves in Mesa ?
How will I use the information?	

- Is your answer reasonable? Explain. ______________________

____

____

Math Talk **Mathematical Practices**

Describe another way you could solve this problem.

Name ____________________

Share and Show

1. An average of 74 reports with bird counts were turned in each day in June. An average of 89 were turned in each day in July. How many reports were turned in for both months? (Hint: There are 30 days in June and 31 days in July.)

First, write the problem for June.

____

Next, write the problem for July.

____

Last, find and add the two products.

__________ reports were turned in for both months.

2. What if an average of 98 reports were turned in each day for the month of June? How many reports were turned in for June? Describe how your answer for June would be different.

____

____

____

3. There are 48 crayons in a box. There are 12 boxes in a carton. Mr. Johnson ordered 6 cartons of crayons for the school. How many crayons did he get?

____

4. MATHEMATICAL PRACTICE 1 **Make Sense of Problems** Each of 5 bird-watchers reported seeing 15 roseate spoonbills in a day. If they each reported seeing the same number of roseate spoonbills over 14 days, how many would be reported?

____

Unlock the Problem

- ✓ Underline important facts.
- ✓ Choose a strategy.
- ✓ Use the Problem Solving MathBoard.

WRITE ▸ *Math* • **Show Your Work**

On Your Own

5. THINK SMARTER On each of Maggie's bird-watching trips, she has seen at least 24 birds. If she has taken 4 of these trips each year over the past 16 years, at least how many birds has Maggie seen?

6. MATHEMATICAL PRACTICE 1 **Make Sense of Problems** There are 12 inches in a foot. In September, Mrs. Harris orders 32 feet of ribbon for the Crafts Club. In January, she orders 9 fewer feet. How many inches of ribbon does Mrs. Harris order? Explain how you found your answer.

7. GO DEEPER Lydia is having a party on Saturday. She decides to write a riddle on her invitations to describe her house number on Cypress Street. Use the clues to find Lydia's address.

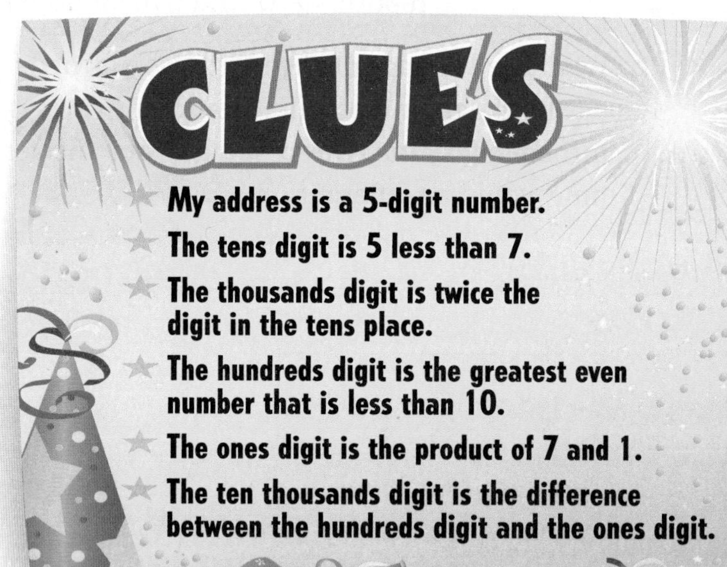

CLUES
My address is a 5-digit number.
The tens digit is 5 less than 7.
The thousands digit is twice the digit in the tens place.
The hundreds digit is the greatest even number that is less than 10.
The ones digit is the product of 7 and 1.
The ten thousands digit is the difference between the hundreds digit and the ones digit.

Personal Math Trainer

8. THINK SMARTER + A school is adding 4 rows of seats to the auditorium. There are 7 seats in each row. Each new seat costs $99. What is the total cost for the new seats? Show your work.

Name ___________________________________

Chapter 3 Review/Test

1. Explain how to find 40×50 using mental math.

2. Mrs. Traynor's class is taking a field trip to the zoo. The trip will cost $26 for each student. There are 22 students in her class.

Part A

Round each factor to estimate the total cost of the students' field trip.

Part B

Use compatible numbers to estimate the total cost of the field trip.

Part C

Which do you think is the better estimate? Explain.

GO DIGITAL Assessment Options Chapter Test

3. For numbers 3a–3e, select Yes or No to show if the answer is correct.

3a. 35 × 10 = 350 ○ Yes ○ No

3b. 19 × 20 = 380 ○ Yes ○ No

3c. 12 × 100 = 120 ○ Yes ○ No

3d. 70 × 100 = 7,000 ○ Yes ○ No

3e. 28 × 30 = 2,100 ○ Yes ○ No

4. There are 23 boxes of pencils in Mr. Shaw's supply cabinet. Each box contains 100 pencils. How many pencils are in the supply cabinet?

_______________ pencils

5. Which would provide a reasonable estimate for each product? Write the estimate beside the product. An estimate may be used more than once.

50 × 20	25 × 40	30 × 30

23 × 38 [ ] 46 × 18 [ ]

31 × 32 [ ] 39 × 21 [ ]

6. There are 26 baseball teams in the league. Each team has 18 players. Write a number sentence that will provide a reasonable estimate for the number of players in the league. Explain how you found your estimate.

7. The model shows 48 × 37. Write the partial products.

	40	8
30		
7		

Name ______________________________

8. Jess made this model to find the product 32 × 17. Her model is incorrect.

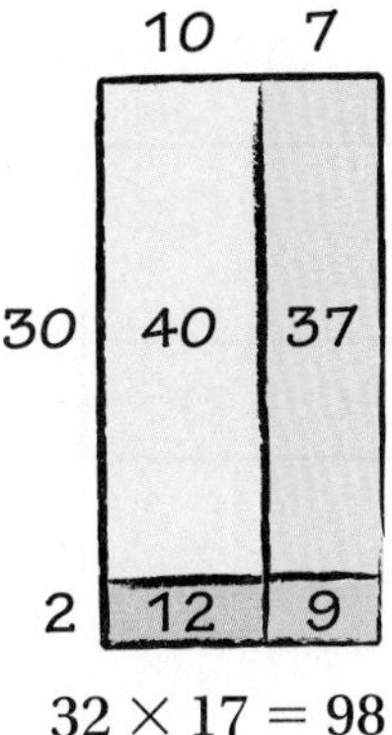

32 × 17 = 98

Part A

What did Jess do wrong?

Part B

Redraw the model so that it is correct.

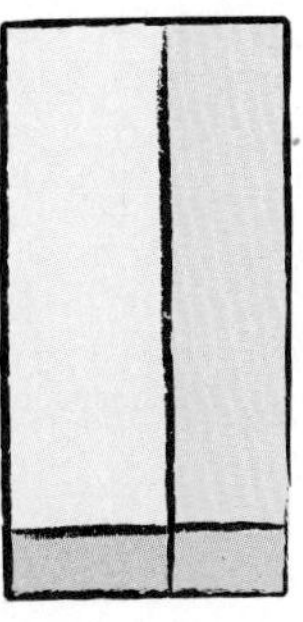

Part C

What is the actual product 32 × 17?

____

9. Tatum wants to use partial products to find 15 × 32. Write the numbers in the boxes to show 15 × 32.

(☐ × ☐) + (☐ × ☐) + (☐ × ☐) + (☐ × ☐)

10. Which product is shown by the model? Write the letter of the product on the line below the model.

Ⓐ 17×36 Ⓑ 24×14 Ⓒ 13×13

	10	3
10	100	30
3	30	9

______

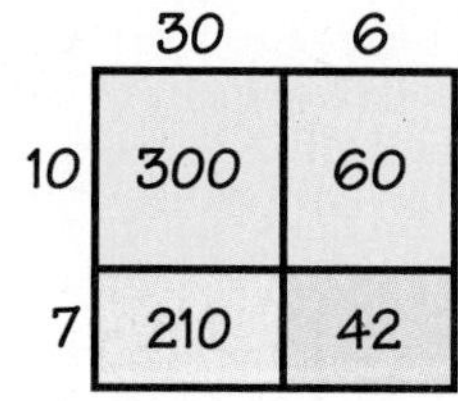

______

	10	4
20	200	80
4	40	16

______

11. Mrs. Jones places 3 orders for school T-shirts. Each order has 16 boxes of shirts and each box holds 17 shirts. How many T-shirts does Mrs. Jones order? Use partial products to help you.

12. Write the unknown digits. Use each digit exactly once.

```
     46
   × 93
  ------
 3, □00
    5□0
    □20
 +  1□
  ------
 4, □78
```

1 2 4 6 8

13. Mike has 16 baseball cards. Niko has 17 times as many baseball cards as Mike does. How many baseball cards does Niko have?

______ baseball cards

14. Multiply.

$36 \times 28 =$ ______

Name ____

15. A farmer planted 42 rows of tomatoes with 13 plants in each row. How many tomato plants did the farmer grow?

$42 \times 13 =$ ______________ tomato plants

16. Select another way to show 25×18. Mark all that apply.

○ $(20 \times 10) + (20 \times 8) + (5 \times 10) + (5 \times 8)$

○ $(25 \times 20) + (25 \times 5) + (25 \times 10) + (25 \times 8)$

○ $(20 \times 18) + (5 \times 10) + (5 \times 8)$

○ $(25 \times 10) + (25 \times 8)$

○ $(25 \times 20) + (25 \times 5)$

17. Terrell runs 15 sprints. Each sprint is 65 meters. How many meters does Terrell run? Show your work.

18. There are 3 new seats in each row in a school auditorium. There are 15 rows in the auditorium. Each new seat cost $74. What is the cost for the new seats? Explain how you found your answer.

19. Ray and Ella helped move their school library to a new building. Ray packed 27 boxes with 25 books in each box. Ella packed 23 boxes with 30 books in each box. How many more books did Ella pack? Show your work.

20. Julius and Walt are finding the product of 25 and 16.

Julius	Walt
25	25
× 16	× 16
150	200
+ 250	50
500	120
	+ 300
	670

Part A

Julius' answer is incorrect. What did Julius do wrong?

Part B

What did Walt do wrong?

Part C

What is the correct product?

21. A clothing store sells 26 shirts and 22 pairs of jeans. Each item of clothing costs $32.

Part A

What is a reasonable estimate for the total cost of the clothing? Show or explain how you found your answer.

Part B

What is the exact answer for the total cost of the clothing? Show or explain how you found your answer.

Chapter

4 Divide by 1-Digit Numbers

Show What You Know

Check your understanding of important skills.

Name ______________________

▶ **Use Arrays to Divide** **Draw to complete each array. Then complete the number sentence.**

1. 

$8 \div 4 =$ _____

2. 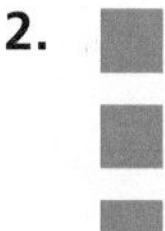

$21 \div 3 =$ _____

▶ **Multiples** **Write the first six multiples of the number.**

3. 4: ______________________

4. 10: ______________________

▶ **Subtract Through 4-Digit Numbers** **Find the difference.**

5. $\begin{array}{r} 626 \\ -\ \ 8 \\ \hline \end{array}$

6. $\begin{array}{r} 744 \\ -\ 36 \\ \hline \end{array}$

7. $\begin{array}{r} 5{,}413 \\ -2{,}037 \\ \hline \end{array}$

8. $\begin{array}{r} 8{,}681 \\ -\ 422 \\ \hline \end{array}$

Each digit in the division example has been replaced with the same letter throughout. (r stands for remainder.) The digits used were 1, 2, 3, 4, 5, 7, and 9. Be a Math Detective and find the numbers. Clue: U is 5.

```
    SU rE
U)CAN
 -CU
   IN
  -IU
    E
```

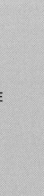

Personal Math Trainer
Online Assessment and Intervention

Vocabulary Builder

▶ Visualize It

Sort the words into the Venn diagram.

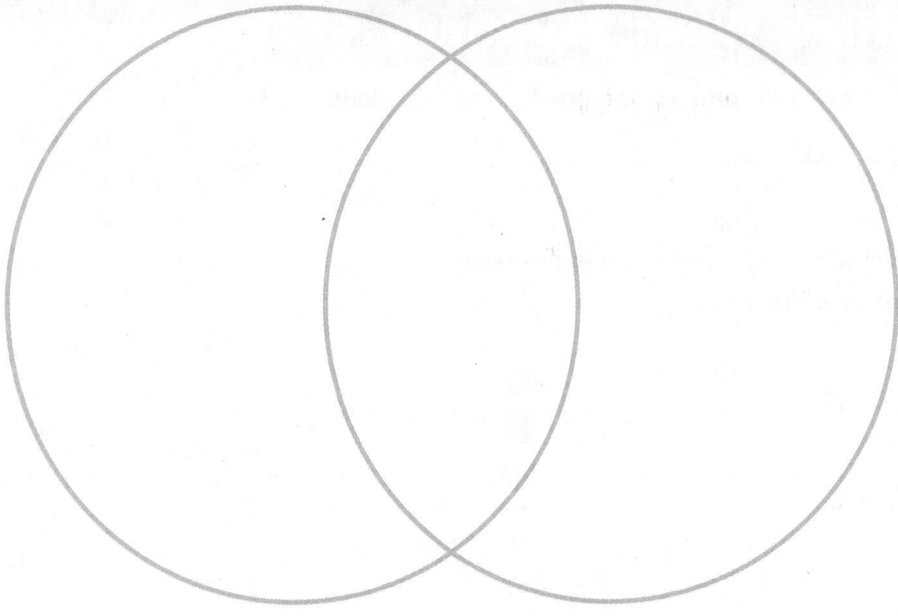

Review Words

Distributive Property
divide
dividend
division
divisor
factor
multiplication
product
quotient

Preview Words

compatible numbers
multiple
partial quotient
remainder

▶ Understand Vocabulary

Write the word that answers the riddle.

1. I am the method of dividing in which multiples of the divisor are subtracted from the dividend and then the quotients are added together.

____

2. I am the number that is to be divided in a division problem.

____

3. I am the amount left over when a number cannot be divided equally. _______________

4. I am the number that divided the dividend.

____

• Interactive Student Edition
• Multimedia eGlossary

Name ______________________

Estimate Quotients Using Multiples

Essential Question How can you use multiples to estimate quotients?

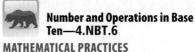

Number and Operations in Base Ten—4.NBT.6

MATHEMATICAL PRACTICES
MP.2, MP.5, MP.7

Unlock the Problem (Real World)

The bakery made 110 pumpkin muffins. They will be packed in boxes with 8 muffins in each box. About how many boxes will there be?

You can use multiples to estimate.

A **multiple** of a number is the product of a number and a counting number. 1, 2, 3, 4, and so on, are counting numbers.

Estimate. 110 ÷ 8

Think: What number multiplied by 8 is about 110?

STEP 1 List the multiples of 8 until you reach 110 or greater.

Counting number	1	2	3	4	5	6	7	8	9	10	11	12	13	14
Multiple of 8	8	16	24	32			56	64				96		112

STEP 2 Find the multiples of 8 that 110 is between.

13 × 8 = __________

14 × 8 = __________

110 is between ______ and ______, so 110 ÷ 8 is between 13 and 14.

110 is closest to __________, so 110 ÷ 8 is about __________.

So, there will be about ______ boxes.

Math Talk — Mathematical Practices

When estimating a quotient, how do you know which two numbers it is between? **Explain.**

Try This!

List the next 8 multiples of 10.

10, 20, ______________________

List the next 7 multiples of 100.

100, 200, ______________________

Example Estimate 196 ÷ 4

Think: What number times 4 is about 196?

STEP 1 List the next 6 multiples of 4.

4, 8, 12, 16, ______________________________

Are any multiples close to 196? ______

____

Think: If I multiply by multiples of 10, the products will be greater. Using multiples of 10 will get me to 196 faster.

STEP 2 Multiply 4 by multiples of 10.

$10 \times 4 = 40$

$20 \times 4 = 80$

$30 \times 4 =$ ____________

$40 \times 4 =$ ____________

$50 \times 4 =$ ____________

The quotient is between 40 and 50.

______ $\times$ 4 is closest to ______, so 196 ÷ 4 is about ______.

Share and Show

1. A restaurant has 68 chairs. There are six chairs at each table. About how many tables are in the restaurant?

Estimate. 68 ÷ 6

Think: What number times 6 is about 68?

$10 \times 6 =$ ______

$11 \times 6 =$ ______

$12 \times 6 =$ ______

68 is closest to ______, so the best estimate is

about ______ tables are in the restaurant.

Mathematical Practices

When do you multiply the divisor by multiples of 10 to estimate a quotient? **Explain.**

Name ______________________

Find two numbers the quotient is between. Then estimate the quotient.

2. 41 ÷ 3

3. 192 ÷ 5

On Your Own

Find two numbers the quotient is between. Then estimate the quotient.

4. 90 ÷ 7

5. 67 ÷ 4

6. 281 ÷ 9

7. 102 ÷ 7

8. 85 ÷ 6

9. 220 ÷ 8

10. 443 ÷ 5

11. 95 ÷ 8

12. 49 ÷ 3

Decide whether the actual quotient is greater than or less than the estimate given. Write < or >.

13. 83 ÷ 8 ◯ 10

14. 155 ÷ 4 ◯ 40

15. 70 ÷ 6 ◯ 11

16. **What's the Question?** A dolphin's heart beats 688 times in 6 minutes. Answer: about 100 times.

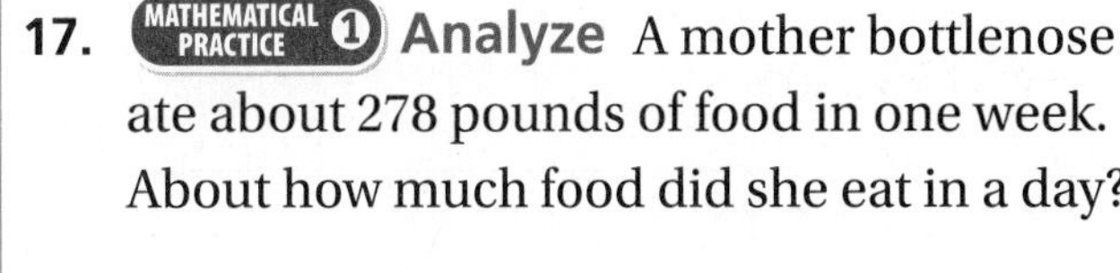

17. MATHEMATICAL PRACTICE 1 **Analyze** A mother bottlenose ate about 278 pounds of food in one week. About how much food did she eat in a day?

Problem Solving • Applications Real World

18. THINK SMARTER If a bottlenose dolphin can eat 175 pounds of fish, squid, and shrimp in a week, about how many pounds of food does it eat in a day? Milo says the answer is about 20 pounds. Leah says the answer is about 30 pounds. Who is correct? Explain.

____

____

____

____

19. GO DEEPER Four families went out for lunch. The total food bill came to $167. The families also left a $30 tip for the waitress. If each family spent the same amount, about how much did each family spend on dinner? Explain how you found your answer.

____

____

____

Show Your Work

20. THINK SMARTER There are 6 showings of a film about Van Gogh at the Art Museum. A total of 459 people saw the film. The same number of people were at each showing. About how many people were at each showing? Circle the numbers the quotient is between. Then explain how you found your answer.

40 50 60 70 80

____

____

FOR MORE PRACTICE:
Standards Practice Book

Name ____________________________

Remainders

Essential Question How can you use models to divide whole numbers that do not divide evenly?

Number and Operations in Base Ten—4.NBT.6

MATHEMATICAL PRACTICES
MP.4, MP.5

Investigate

Hands On

Materials ■ counters

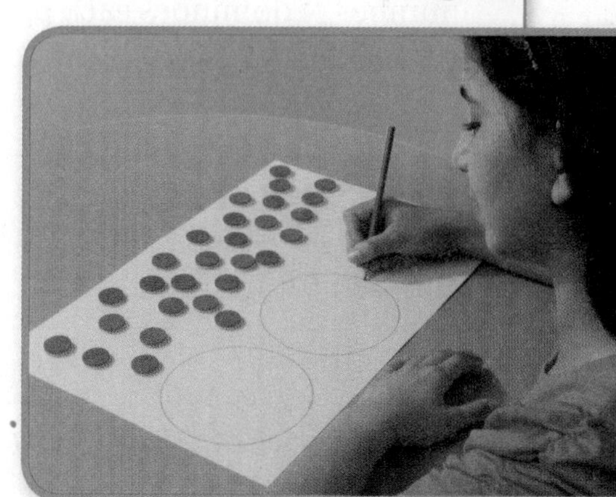

Andrea and 2 friends are playing a game of dominoes. There are 28 dominoes in the set. Andrea wants each player to receive the same number of dominoes. Can she divide them equally among the 3 players? Why or why not?

You can use division to find the number of dominoes each player will receive.

A. Use 28 counters to represent the 28 dominoes. Then draw 3 circles to represent the 3 players.

B. Share the counters equally among the 3 groups by placing them in the circles.

Draw a quick picture to show your work.

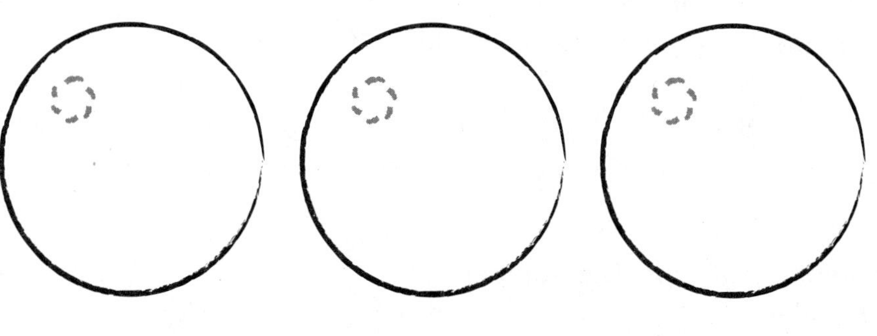

C. Find the number of counters in each group and the number of counters left over. Record your answer.

_____ counters in each group

_____ counter left over

Draw Conclusions

1. How many dominoes does each player receive? ______

   How many dominoes are left over? ______

2. THINKSMARTER Explain how the model helped you find the number of dominoes each player receives. Why is 1 counter left outside the equal groups?

   ______

   ______

   ______

3. Use counters to represent a set of 28 dominoes. How many players can play dominoes if each player receives 9 dominoes? Will any dominoes be left over? Explain.

   ______

   ______

Make Connections

When a number cannot be divided evenly, the amount left over is called the **remainder**.

Use counters to find 39 ÷ 5.

- Use 39 counters.
- Share the counters equally among 5 groups. The number of counters left over is the remainder.

Draw a quick picture to show your work.

For 39 ÷ 5, the quotient is ______ and the remainder is ______, or 7 r4.

Math Talk **Mathematical Practices**

How do you know when there will be a remainder in a division problem?

Name ______________________

Share and Show 

Use counters to find the quotient and remainder.

1. $10 \div 3$ ______
2. $28 \div 5$ ______
3. $15 \div 6$ ______
4. $11 \div 3$ ______
5. $29 \div 4$ ______
6. $34 \div 5$ ______
7. $25 \div 3$ ______
8. $7\overline{)20}$ ______

Divide. Draw a quick picture to help.

9. $4\overline{)35}$ ______

10. $23 \div 8$ ______

Problem Solving • Applications Real World

11. MATHEMATICAL PRACTICE 6 **Explain** how you use a quick picture to find the quotient and remainder.

____

____

____

____

12. GO DEEPER Alyson has 46 beads to make bracelets. Each bracelet has 5 beads. How many more beads does Alyson need so that all the beads she has are used? Explain.

____

____

____

13. THINK SMARTER For 13a–13d, choose Yes or No to tell whether the division expression has a remainder.

13a.	$36 \div 9$	○ Yes	○ No
13b.	$23 \div 3$	○ Yes	○ No
13c.	$82 \div 9$	○ Yes	○ No
13d.	$28 \div 7$	○ Yes	○ No

What's the Error?

14. THINK SMARTER Macy, Kayley, Maddie, and Rachel collected 13 marbles. They want to share the marbles equally. How many marbles will each of the 4 girls get? How many marbles will be left over?

Oscar used a model to solve this problem. He says his model represents $4\overline{)13}$. What is his error?

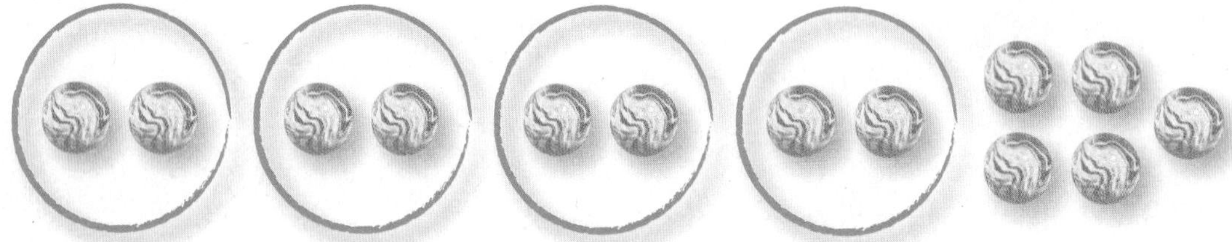

Look at the way Oscar solved this problem. Find and describe his error.

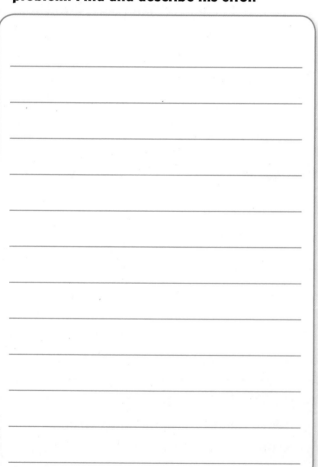

Draw a correct model and solve the problem.

So, each of the 4 girls will get ______ marbles and ______ marble will be left over.

FOR MORE PRACTICE:
Standards Practice Book

Lesson 4.3

Name ____________________

Interpret the Remainder

Essential Question How can you use remainders in division problems?

Operations and Algebraic Thinking—4.OA.3 *Also 4.NBT.6*

MATHEMATICAL PRACTICES
MP.2, MP.7, MP.8

Unlock the Problem

Magda has some leftover wallpaper 73 inches long. She wants to cut it into 8 pieces to use around the photos in her scrapbook. Each piece will have equal length. How long will each piece be?

When you solve a division problem with a remainder, the way you interpret the remainder depends on the situation and the question.

One Way Write the remainder as a fraction.

The divisor is ______ pieces.

The ____________ is 73 inches.

Divide to find the quotient and remainder. $8\overline{)73}$ 9 r1

Remember

You can use multiples, counters, or draw a quick picture to divide.

The remainder represents 1 inch left over, which can also be divided into 8 equal parts and written as a fraction.

$\frac{\text{remainder}}{\text{divisor}} =$ ______

Write the quotient with the remainder written as a fraction. ______

So, each piece will be ______ inches long.

Try This!

Daniel made 32 ounces of soup for 5 people. How many ounces will each person get? Complete the division.

$5\overline{)32}$

Each person gets ______ ounces.

Math Talk **Mathematical Practices**

Explain what the 2 in the answer represents.

Other Ways

A Use only the quotient.

Ben is a tour guide at a glass-blowing studio. He can take no more than 7 people at a time on a tour. If 80 people want to see the glass-blowing demonstration, how many groups of 7 people will Ben show around?

First, divide to find the quotient and remainder.
Then, decide how to use the quotient and remainder.

The quotient is ______.

$$7\overline{)80} \quad 11 \text{ r } \square$$

The remainder is ______.

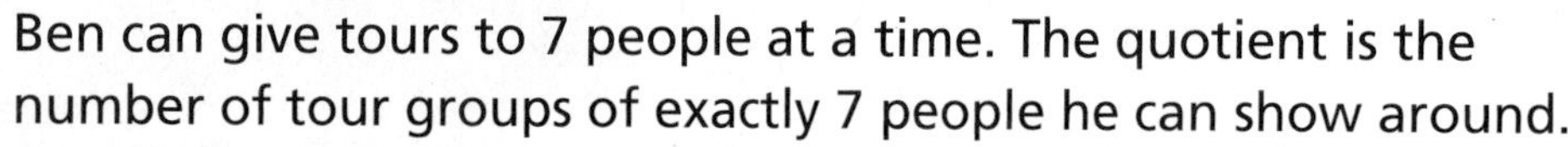

Ben can give tours to 7 people at a time. The quotient is the number of tour groups of exactly 7 people he can show around.

So, Ben gives tours to ______ groups of 7 people.

B Add 1 to the quotient.

If Ben gives tours to all 80 people, how many tours will he give? A tour can have no more than 7 people. To show all 80 people around, Ben will have to give 1 more tour.

So, Ben will give ______ tours in all for 80 people.

C Use only the remainder.

Ben gives tours to all 80 people. After he completes the tours for groups of 7 people, how many people are in his last tour?

The remainder is 3.

So, Ben's last tour will have ______ people.

Math Talk **Mathematical Practices**

Explain why you would not write the remainder as a fraction when you find the number of vans needed.

Try This!

Students are driven to soccer games in vans. Each van holds 9 students. How many vans are needed for 31 students?

Divide. 31 ÷ 9 ______

Since there are ______ students left over, ______ vans are needed to carry 31 students.

Name ____________________

Share and Show

1. Olivia baked 53 mini-loaves of banana bread to be sliced for snacks at a craft fair. She will place an equal number of loaves in 6 different locations. How many loaves will be at each location?

   a. Divide to find the quotient and remainder.

   $6\overline{)53}$ ___ r ___

   b. Decide how to use the quotient and remainder to answer the question.

   ____

Interpret the remainder to solve.

✓ 2. What if Olivia wants to put only whole loaves at each location? How many loaves will be at each location?

____

✓ 3. Ed carves 22 small wooden animals to sell at the craft fair. He displays them in rows with 4 animals in a row. How many animals will not be in equal rows?

____

On Your Own

Interpret the remainder to solve.

4. Myra has a 17-foot roll of crepe paper to make 8 streamers to decorate for a party. How long will each streamer be if she cuts the roll into equal pieces?

____

5. THINK SMARTER Juan has a piano recital next month. Last week he practiced for 8 hours in the morning and 7 hours in the afternoon. Each practice session is 2 hours long. How many full practice sessions did Juan complete?

____

6. A total of 25 students sign up to be hosts on Parent's Night. Teams of 3 students greet parents. How many students cannot be on a team? Explain.

____

____

____

Problem Solving • Applications Real World

Use the picture for 7–9.

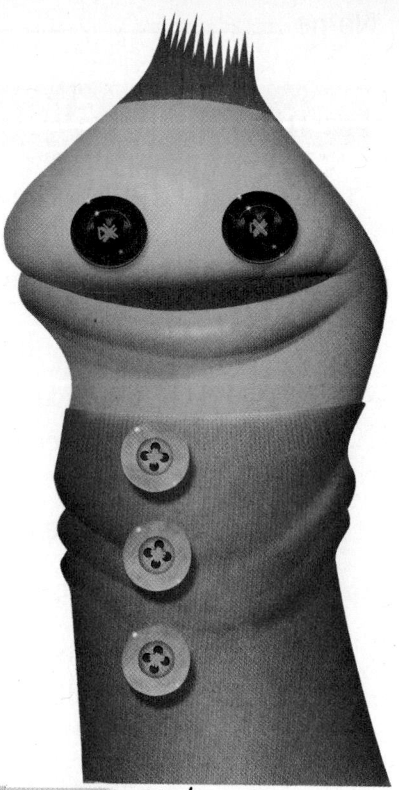

7. Teresa is making sock puppets just like the one in the picture. If she has 53 buttons, how many puppets can she make?

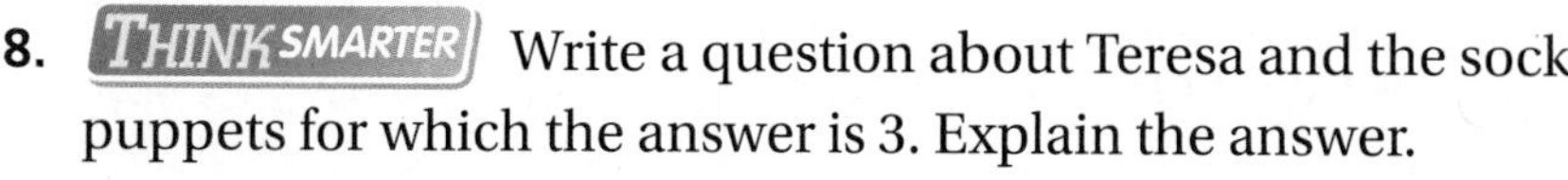

8. THINK SMARTER Write a question about Teresa and the sock puppets for which the answer is 3. Explain the answer.

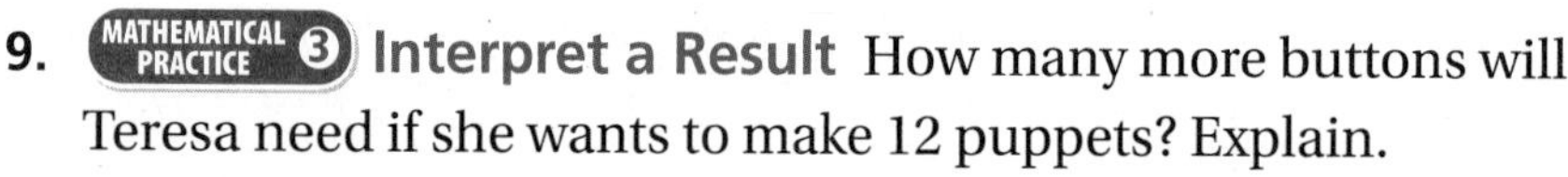

9. MATHEMATICAL PRACTICE 3 **Interpret a Result** How many more buttons will Teresa need if she wants to make 12 puppets? Explain.

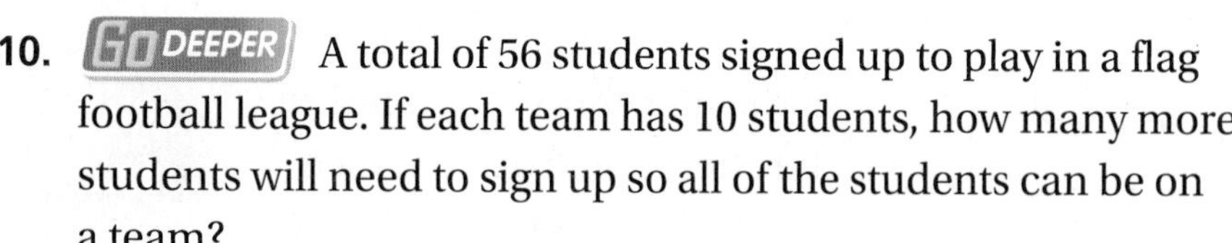

WRITE ▸ Math
Show Your Work

10. GO DEEPER A total of 56 students signed up to play in a flag football league. If each team has 10 students, how many more students will need to sign up so all of the students can be on a team?

Personal Math Trainer

11. THINK SMARTER + A teacher plans for groups of her students to eat lunch at tables. She has 34 students in her class. Each group will have 7 students. How many tables will she need? Explain how to use the quotient and remainder to answer the question.

FOR MORE PRACTICE:
Standards Practice Book

Name ___________________________

Divide Tens, Hundreds, and Thousands

Essential Question How can you divide numbers through thousands by whole numbers through 10?

Number and Operations in Base Ten—4.NBT.6 *Also 4.NBT.1*

MATHEMATICAL PRACTICES
MP.2, MP.7, MP.8

Unlock the Problem

Dustin is packing apples in gift boxes. Each gift box holds 4 apples. How many boxes can Dustin pack with 120 apples?

You can divide using basic facts and place value.

Example 1 Divide. 120 ÷ 4

STEP 1 Identify the basic fact. 12 ÷ 4

STEP 2 Use place value. 120 = ______ tens

STEP 3 Divide. 12 tens ÷ 4 = ______ tens ← **Think:** 4 × 3 tens = 12 tens

= ______

120 ÷ 4 = 30

So, Dustin can pack ______ boxes.

Example 2 Divide. 1,200 ÷ 4

STEP 1 Identify the basic fact. 12 ÷ 4

STEP 2 Use place value. 1,200 = ______ hundreds

STEP 3 Divide. 12 hundreds ÷ 4 = ______ hundreds ← **Think:** 4 × 3 hundreds = 12 hundreds

= ______

1,200 ÷ 4 = 300

Math Talk — **Mathematical Practices**

Describe the pattern in the place value of the dividends and quotients.

- MATHEMATICAL PRACTICE 6 **Explain** how to use a basic fact and place value to divide 4,000 ÷ 5.

____

____

Share and Show

1. Divide. 2,800 ÷ 7

What basic fact can you use? ______

2,800 = 28 ______

28 hundreds ÷ 7 = ______

2,800 ÷ 7 = ______

Math Talk **Mathematical Practices**

Explain how Exercises 1 and 2 are alike and different.

2. Divide. 280 ÷ 7

What basic fact can you use? ______

280 = 28 ______

28 tens ÷ ______ = 4 ______

280 ÷ 7 = ______

Use basic facts and place value to find the quotient.

3. 360 ÷ 6 = ______

4. 2,000 ÷ 5 = ______

5. 4,500 ÷ 9 = ______

On Your Own

Use basic facts and place value to find the quotient.

6. 560 ÷ 8 = ______

7. 200 ÷ 5 = ______

8. 240 ÷ 4 = ______

9. 810 ÷ 9 = ______

10. 6,400 ÷ 8 = ______

11. 3,500 ÷ 7 = ______

12. 5,000 ÷ 5 = ______

13. 9,000 ÷ 3 = ______

14. 3,000 ÷ 5 = ______

MATHEMATICAL PRACTICE 5 Use Patterns **Algebra** **Find the unknown number.**

15. 420 ÷ ■ = 60 ______

16. ■ ÷ 4 = 30 ______

17. 810 ÷ ■ = 90 ______

18. THINK SMARTER Divide 400 ÷ 40. Explain how patterns and place value can help.

______

______

______

Name ________________________

Problem Solving • Applications

19. Jamal put 600 pennies into 6 equal rolls. How many pennies were in each roll?

____

20. Sela has 6 times as many coins now as she had 4 months ago. If Sela has 240 coins now, how many coins did she have 4 months ago?

____

21. THINK SMARTER Chip collected 2,090 dimes. Sue collected 1,910 dimes. They divided all their dimes into 8 equal stacks. How many dimes are in each stack?

____

22. MATHEMATICAL PRACTICE 5 **Communicate** Mr. Roberts sees a rare 1937 penny. The cost of the penny is $210. If he saves $3 each week, will Mr. Roberts have enough money to buy the penny in one year? Explain.

____

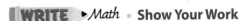

23. GO DEEPER Mrs. Fletcher bought 5 coins for $32 each. Later, she sold all the coins for $300. How much more did Mrs. Fletcher receive for each coin than she paid? Explain.

____

24. THINK SMARTER Which quotients are equal to 20? Mark all that apply.

Ⓐ 600 ÷ 2
Ⓑ 1,200 ÷ 6
Ⓒ 180 ÷ 9
Ⓓ 140 ÷ 7
Ⓔ 500 ÷ 5

Connect to Science

Insect Flight

True flight is shared only by insects, bats, and birds. Flight in insects varies from the clumsy flight of some beetles to the acrobatic moves of dragonflies.

The wings of insects are not moved by muscles attached to the wings. Muscles in the middle part of the body, or thorax, move the wings. The thorax changes shape as the wings move.

Insect Wing Beats in 3 Minutes

Insect	Approximate Number of Wing Beats
Aeschnid Dragonfly	6,900
Damselfly	2,700
Large White Butterfly	2,100
Scorpion Fly	5,000

25. About how many times does a damselfly's wings beat in 1 minute?

______

26. About how many times do a scorpion fly's wings beat in 6 minutes?

______

27. THINK SMARTER In one minute, about how many more times do a damselfly's wings beat than a large white butterfly's wings?

______

28. **What's the Question?** The answer is about 2,300 times.

______

______

FOR MORE PRACTICE: Standards Practice Book

Name ______________________

Estimate Quotients Using Compatible Numbers

Essential Question How can you use compatible numbers to estimate quotients?

Number and Operations in Base Ten—4.NBT.6

MATHEMATICAL PRACTICES
MP.1, MP.5, MP.7

Unlock the Problem (Real World)

A horse's heart beats 132 times in 3 minutes. About how many times does it beat in 1 minute?

- Will a horse's heart beat more or fewer than 132 times in 1 minute?

____

- What operation will you use to solve the problem?

____

You can use compatible numbers to estimate quotients.

Compatible numbers are numbers that are easy to compute mentally.

Example 1 Estimate. 132 ÷ 3

STEP 1 Find a number close to 132 that divides easily by 3. Use basic facts.

12 ÷ 3 is a basic fact. 120 divides easily by 3.

15 ÷ 3 is a basic fact. 150 divides easily by 3.

Think: Choose 120 because it is closer to 132.

STEP 2 Use place value.

120 = ______ tens

12 ÷ 3 = ______

12 tens ÷ 3 = ______ tens

120 ÷ 3 = ______

So, a horse's heart beats about ______ times a minute.

Example 2 Use compatible numbers to find two estimates that the quotient is between. 1,382 ÷ 5

STEP 1 Find two numbers close to 1,382 that divide easily by 5.

______ ÷ 5 is a basic fact.
1,000 divides easily by 5.

______ ÷ 5 is a basic fact.
1,500 divides easily by 5.

1,382 is between ______ and ______.

STEP 2 Divide each number by 5. Use place value.

1,000 ÷ 5

______ hundreds ÷ 5 = ______ hundreds, or ______

1,500 ÷ 5

______ hundreds ÷ 5 = ______ hundreds, or ______

So, 1,382 ÷ 5 is between ______ and ______.

Math Talk — Mathematical Practices

Explain which estimate you think is more reasonable.

Share and Show

1. Estimate. 1,718 ÷ 4 | Think: What number close to 1,718 is easy to divide by 4?

_____ is close to 1,718. | What basic fact can you use? _____ ÷ 4

_____ is close to 1,718. | What basic fact can you use? _____ ÷ 4

Choose 1,600 because _______________________________.

16 ÷ 4 = _____

1,600 ÷ _____ = _____

1,718 ÷ 4 is about _____

Mathematical Practices

Explain how your estimate might change if the problem were 1,918 ÷ 4.

Use compatible numbers to estimate the quotient.

2. 455 ÷ 9 _____

3. 1,509 ÷ 3 _____

4. 176 ÷ 8 _____

5. 2,795 ÷ 7 _____

On Your Own

Use compatible numbers to estimate the quotient.

6. 163 ÷ 2 _____

7. 500 ÷ 7 _____

8. 1,421 ÷ 5 _____

9. 2,642 ÷ 8 _____

Use compatible numbers to find two estimates that the quotient is between.

10. 5,321 ÷ 6 _____

11. 1,765 ÷ 6 _____

12. 1,189 ÷ 3 _____

13. 2,110 ÷ 4 _____

MATHEMATICAL PRACTICE 2 **Reason Abstractly** **Algebra** **Estimate to compare. Write <, >, or =.**

14. 613 ÷ 3 ◯ 581 ÷ 2

_____ estimate _____ estimate

15. 364 ÷ 4 ◯ 117 ÷ 6

_____ estimate _____ estimate

16. 2,718 ÷ 8 ◯ 963 ÷ 2

_____ estimate _____ estimate

Name ______________________________

Problem Solving • Applications

Use the table for 17–19.

Animal Heartbeats in 5 Minutes

Animal	Number of Heartbeats
Whale	31
Cow	325
Pig	430
Dog	520
Chicken	1,375

17. About how many times does a chicken's heart beat in 1 minute?

____

18. GO DEEPER About how many times does a cow's heart beat in 2 minutes?

____

19. MATHEMATICAL PRACTICE 2 **Use Reasoning** About how many times faster does a cow's heart beat than a whale's?

____

20. THINK SMARTER Martha had 154 stamps and her sister had 248 stamps. They combined their collections and put the stamps in an album. If they want to put 8 stamps on each page, about how many pages would they need?

____

21. Jamie and his two brothers divided a package of 125 toy cars equally. About how many cars did each of them receive?

____

WRITE ▸ Math • Show Your Work

22. THINK SMARTER Harold and his brother collected 2,018 cans over a 1-year period. Each boy collected the same number of cans. About how many cans did each boy collect? Explain how you found your answer.

____

____

____

Connect to Reading

Cause and Effect

The reading skill *cause and effect* can help you understand how one detail in a problem is related to another detail.

Chet wants to buy a new bike that costs $276. Chet mows his neighbor's lawn for $15 each week. Since Chet does not have money saved, he needs to decide which layaway plan he can afford to buy the new bike.

Bike Shop Layaway Plans

Plan A	3 months (3 equal payments)
Plan B	6 months (6 equal payments)

Cause:		**Effect:**
Chet does not have money saved to purchase the bike.	→	Chet will have to decide which layaway plan he can afford to purchase the bike.

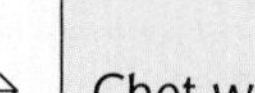

Which plan should Chet choose?

3-month layaway:

$276 ÷ 3

Estimate.

$270 ÷ 3 ____________

6-month layaway:

$276 ÷ 6

Estimate.

$300 ÷ 6 ____________

Chet earns $15 each week. Since there are usually 4 weeks in a month, multiply to see which payment he can afford.

$15 × 4 = ____________

So, Chet can afford the ____________ layaway plan.

Use estimation to solve.

23. Sofia wants to buy a new bike that costs $214. Sofia helps her grandmother with chores each week for $18. Estimate to find which layaway plan Sofia should choose and why.

____

____

____

____

24. WRITE ▸ *Math* Describe a situation when you have used cause and effect to help you solve a math problem.

____

____

____

____

____

FOR MORE PRACTICE: Standards Practice Book

Name ______________________________

Division and the Distributive Property

Essential Question How can you use the Distributive Property to find quotients?

Number and Operations in Base Ten—4.NBT.6

MATHEMATICAL PRACTICES
MP.1, MP.4, MP.5

Investigate

Materials ■ color pencils ■ grid paper

You can use the Distributive Property to break apart numbers to make them easier to divide.

The Distributive Property of division says that dividing a sum by a number is the same as dividing each addend by the number and then adding the quotients.

A. Outline a rectangle on a grid to model $69 \div 3$.

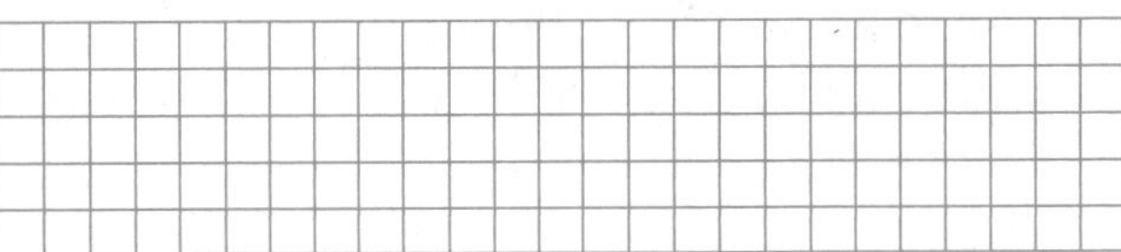

Shade columns of 3 until you have 69 squares.

How many groups of 3 can you make? ______

B. Think of 69 as $60 + 9$. Break apart the model into two rectangles to show $(60 + 9) \div 3$. Label and shade the smaller rectangles. Use two different colors.

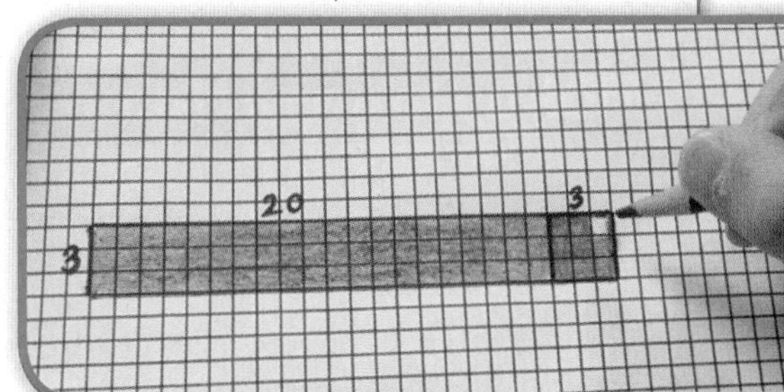

C. Each rectangle models a division.

$69 \div 3 = (\_\_\_\_\_\_ \div 3) + (\_\_\_\_\_\_ \div 3)$

$= \_\_\_\_\_\_ + \_\_\_\_\_\_$

$= \_\_\_\_\_\_$

D. Outline another model to show $68 \div 4$.

How many groups of 4 can you make? ______

E. Think of 68 as $40 + 28$. Break apart the model, label, and shade to show two divisions.

$68 \div 4 = (\_\_\_\_\_\_ \div 4) + (\_\_\_\_\_\_ \div 4)$

$= \_\_\_\_\_\_ + \_\_\_\_\_\_$

$= \_\_\_\_\_\_$

Draw Conclusions

1. Explain how each small rectangle models a quotient and a product in Step C.

____

____

____

2. Compare your answer in Step A to the final quotient in Step C. What can you conclude?

____

____

3. THINK SMARTER To find the quotient $91 \div 7$, would you break up the dividend into $90 + 1$ or $70 + 21$? Explain.

____

____

Make Connections

Math Talk — Mathematical Practices

Describe another way you could use the Distributive Property to solve $68 \div 4$.

You can also model $68 \div 4$ using base-ten blocks.

STEP 1 Model 68.

$68 =$ ______ $+$ ______

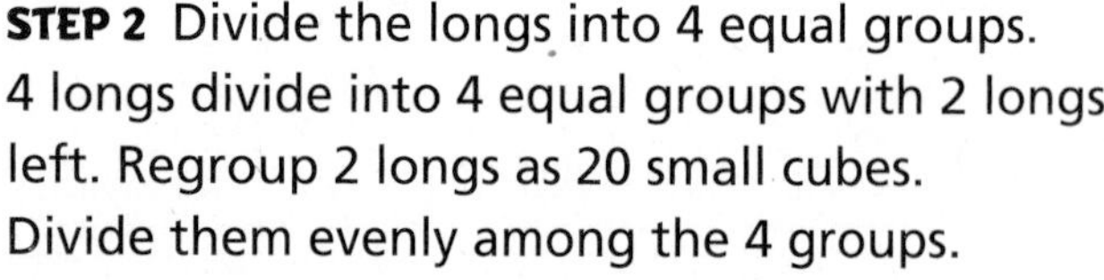

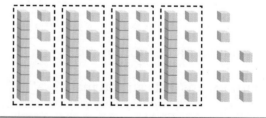

STEP 2 Divide the longs into 4 equal groups. 4 longs divide into 4 equal groups with 2 longs left. Regroup 2 longs as 20 small cubes. Divide them evenly among the 4 groups.

$60 \div 4 =$ ______

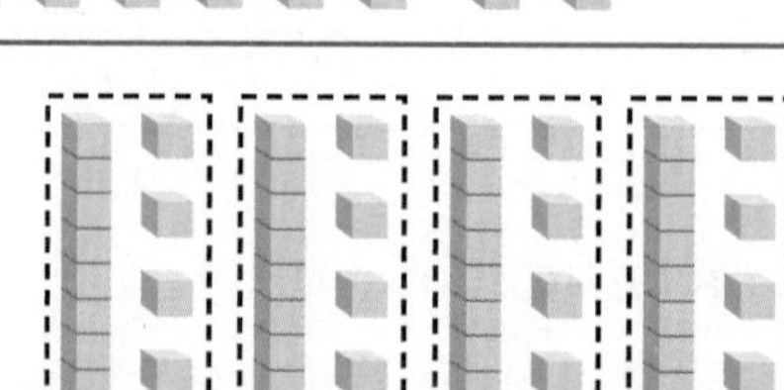

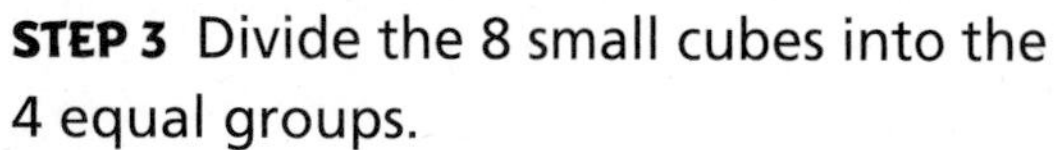

STEP 3 Divide the 8 small cubes into the 4 equal groups.

$8 \div 4 =$ ______

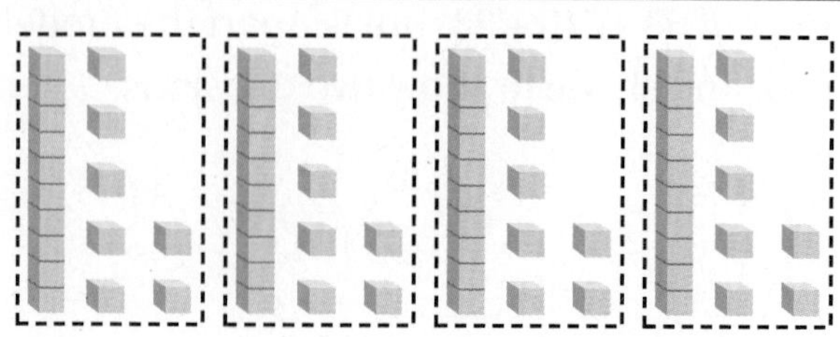

So, $68 \div 4 = (60 \div 4) + (8 \div 4) =$ ______ $+$ ______ $=$ ______

Name ______________________________

Share and Show

Model the division on the grid.

1. $26 \div 2 = (\_\_\_\_ \div 2) + (\_\_\_\_ \div 2)$

$= \_\_\_\_ + \_\_\_\_$

$= \_\_\_\_$

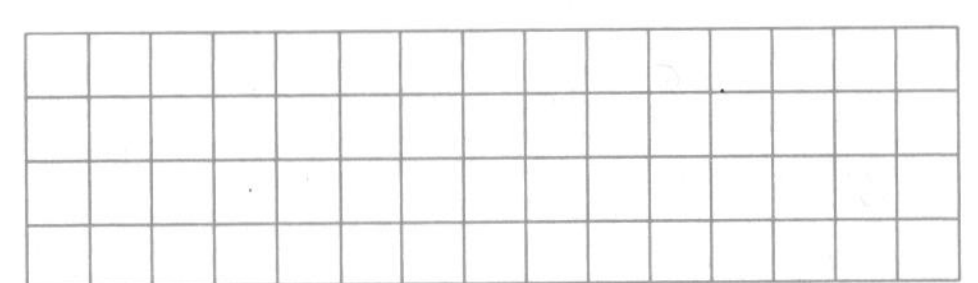

2. $45 \div 3 = (\_\_\_\_ \div 3) + (\_\_\_\_ \div 3)$

$= \_\_\_\_ + \_\_\_\_$

$= \_\_\_\_$

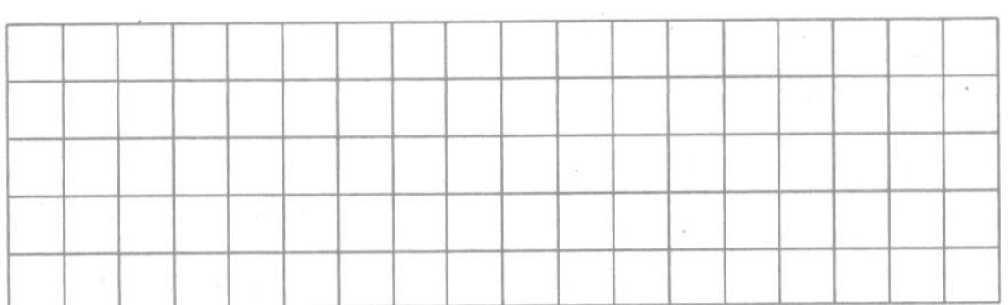

Find the quotient.

3. $86 \div 2$

$= (\_\_\_\_ \div 2) + (\_\_\_\_ \div 2)$

$= \_\_\_\_ + \_\_\_\_$

$= \_\_\_\_$

4. $208 \div 4$

$= (\_\_\_\_ \div 4) + (\_\_\_\_ \div 4)$

$= \_\_\_\_ + \_\_\_\_$

$= \_\_\_\_$

Use base-ten blocks to model the quotient.
Then record the quotient.

5. $88 \div 4 = \_\_\_\_$

6. $36 \div 3 = \_\_\_\_$

7. $186 \div 6 = \_\_\_\_$

Problem Solving • Applications Real World

8. WRITE ▸*Math* Explain how you can model finding quotients using the Distributive Property.

9. GO DEEPER Justin earned \$50 mowing yards and \$34 washing cars. He wants to divide his money into 3 equal accounts. How much will he put in each account? Explain.

Pose a Problem

10. THINK SMARTER Christelle went to a gift shop. The shop sells candles in a variety of sizes and colors. The picture shows a display of candles.

Write a problem that can be solved using the picture.

Pose a problem.

Solve your problem.

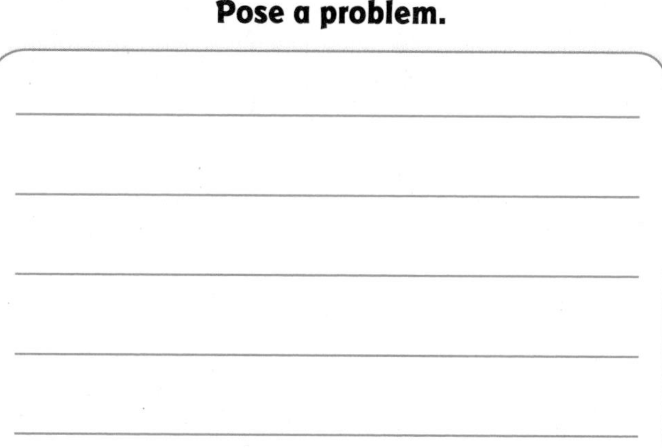

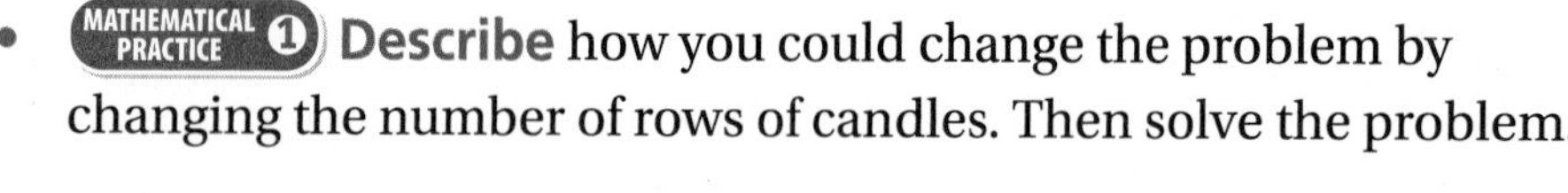

- MATHEMATICAL PRACTICE 1 **Describe** how you could change the problem by changing the number of rows of candles. Then solve the problem.

11. THINK SMARTER For 11a–11d, choose Yes or No to indicate if the expression shows a way to break apart the dividend to find the quotient $147 \div 7$.

11a. $(135 \div 7) + (10 \div 7)$ ○ Yes ○ No

11b. $(147 \div 3) + (147 \div 4)$ ○ Yes ○ No

11c. $(140 \div 7) + (7 \div 7)$ ○ Yes ○ No

11d. $(70 \div 7) + (77 \div 7)$ ○ Yes ○ No

FOR MORE PRACTICE: Standards Practice Book

Name ______________________________

Mid-Chapter Checkpoint

Vocabulary

Vocabulary
counting numbers
compatible numbers
multiple
remainder

Choose the best term from the box to complete the sentence.

1. A number that is the product of a number and a counting number is called a ________________. (p. 143)

2. Numbers that are easy to compute mentally are called ________________. (p. 159)

3. When a number cannot be divided evenly, the amount left over is called the ________________. (p. 148)

Concepts and Skills

Divide. Draw a quick picture to help. (4.NBT.6)

4. $26 \div 3$ ______

5. $19 \div 4$ ______

Use basic facts and place value to find the quotient. (4.NBT.6)

6. $810 \div 9 =$ ______

7. $210 \div 7 =$ ______

8. $3{,}000 \div 6 =$ ______

Use compatible numbers to estimate the quotient. (4.NBT.6)

9. $635 \div 9$ ______

10. $412 \div 5$ ______

11. $490 \div 8$ ______

Use grid paper or base-ten blocks to model the quotient. Then record the quotient. (4.NBT.6)

12. $63 \div 3 =$ ______

13. $85 \div 5 =$ ______

14. $168 \div 8 =$ ______

15. Ana has 296 coins in her coin collection. She put the same number of coins in each of 7 jars. About how many coins are in each jar? (4.NBT.6)

____

16. Which two estimates is the quotient 345 ÷ 8 between? (4.NBT.6)

____

17. A peanut vendor had 640 bags of peanuts. She sold the same number of bags of peanuts at each of 8 baseball games. How many bags of peanuts did she sell at each game? (4.NBT.6)

____

18. There are 4 students on a team for a relay race. How many teams can be made from 27 students? (4.OA.3)

____

19. Eight teams of high school students helped clean up trash in the community. Afterwards, they shared 23 pizzas equally. How many pizzas did each team get? (4.OA.3)

____

Name ______________________

Divide Using Repeated Subtraction

Essential Question How can you use repeated subtraction and multiples to find quotients?

Number and Operations in Base Ten—4.NBT.6

MATHEMATICAL PRACTICES
MP.3, MP.6, MP.8

Investigate

Materials ■ counters ■ grid paper

John is building a backyard pizza oven with an arch opening. He has 72 bricks. He will place 6 bricks at a time as he builds the oven. If he arranges the bricks in piles of 6, how many piles will he have?

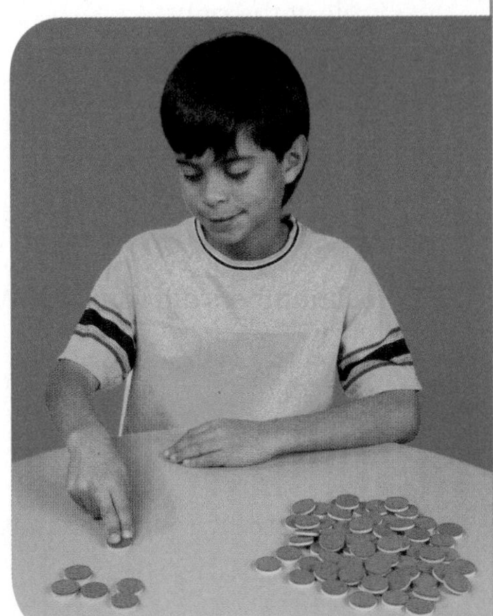

You can use repeated subtraction to divide 72 ÷ 6.

A. Begin with 72 counters. Subtract 6 counters.

How many are left? _____

B. Record the subtraction on grid paper as shown. Record the number of counters left and the number of times you subtracted.

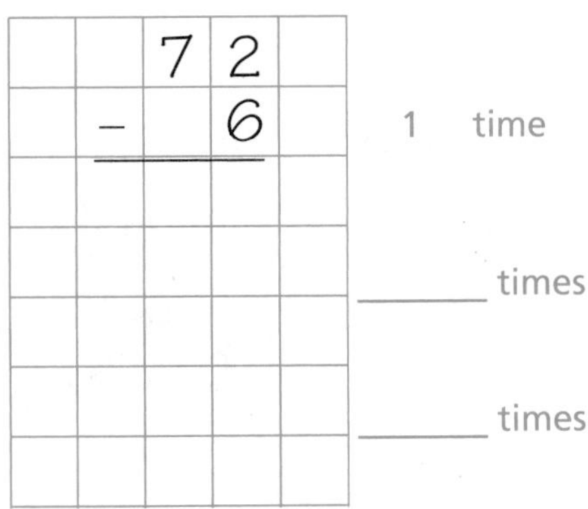

C. Can you reach zero evenly? Explain.

____

____

D. Count the number of times you subtracted 6 counters. _____________

So, there are _____ piles of 6 bricks.

Draw Conclusions

1. Explain the relationship between the divisor, the dividend, the quotient, and the number of times you subtracted the divisor from the dividend.

____

____

2. What happens if you subtract multiples of 6? Complete the example at the right.

$6\overline{)72}$
$-60 \leftarrow$ ___ $\times 6$ 10
___
$-12 \leftarrow$ ___ $\times 6 +$ ___
___ ___

- What multiples of 6 did you use? How did you use them?

____

____

- What numbers did you add? Why?

____

____

- How did using multiples of the divisor help you?

____

____

3. THINK SMARTER Why should you subtract 10×6 and not 9×6 or 20×6?

____

____

____

Math Talk **Mathematical Practices**

Explain subtracting counters and counting back on a number line help you divide.

Make Connections

Another way to divide by repeated subtraction is to use a number line. Count back by 4s from 52 to find 52 ÷ 4.

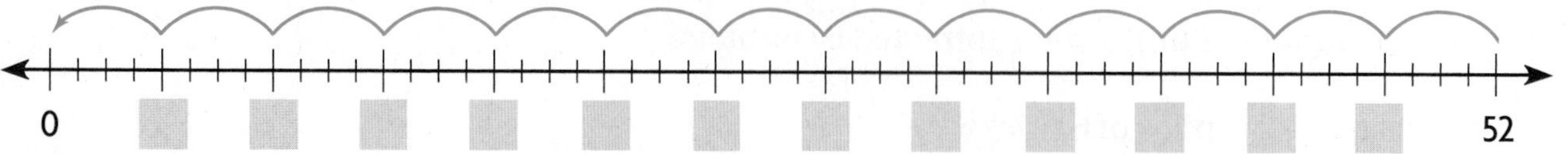

How many equal groups of 4 did you subtract? ______

So, 52 ÷ 4 = ______.

Name ________________________________

Share and Show 

Use repeated subtraction to divide.

1. 84 ÷ 7 __________

 2. 60 ÷ 4 __________

3. 91 ÷ 8 __________

Draw a number line to divide.

4. 65 ÷ 5 = ______

Problem Solving • Applications 

5. MATHEMATICAL PRACTICE 5 **Use Appropriate Tools** Can you divide 32 by 3 evenly? Use the number line to explain your answer.

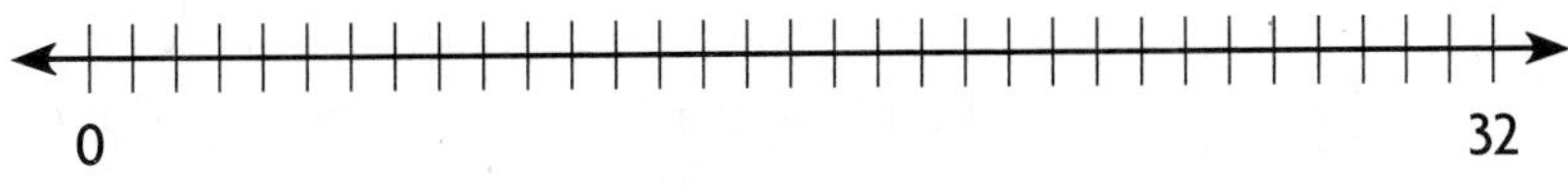

____

____

____

6. GO DEEPER John has $40 to spend at the yard sale. He buys 6 books for $2 each. He would like to spend the rest of his money on model cars for his collection. If the cars cost $7 each, how many can he buy? Explain.

____

____

____

Unlock the Problem (Real World)

7. THINK SMARTER A new playground will be 108 feet long. Builders need to allow 9 feet of space for each piece of climbing equipment. They want to put as many climbers along the length of the playground as possible. How many climbers can they place?

a. What are you asked to find?

____

b. How can you use repeated subtraction to solve the problem?

____

____

c. Tell why you might use multiples of the divisor to solve the problem.

____

____

d. Show steps to solve the problem.

e. Complete the sentences.

There are _____ equal parts of the playground, each _____ feet long.

So, _____ climbers can fit along the length of the playground.

8. THINK SMARTER Which model matches each expression? Write the letter on the line next to the model.

Ⓐ 240 ÷ 80

Ⓑ 240 ÷ 60

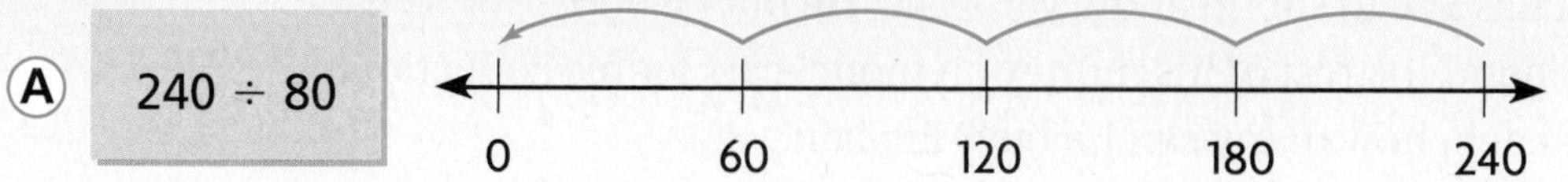

_____

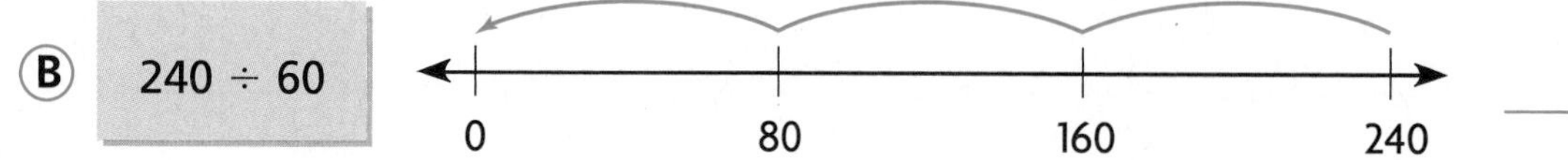

_____

Name ______________________________

Divide Using Partial Quotients

Essential Question How can you use partial quotients to divide by 1-digit divisors?

Number and Operations in Base Ten—4.NBT.6

MATHEMATICAL PRACTICES
MP.2, MP.7, MP.8

Unlock the Problem (Real World)

At camp, there are 5 players on each lacrosse team. If there are 125 people on lacrosse teams, how many teams are there?

- Underline what you are asked to find.
- Circle what you need to use.
- What operation can you use to find the number of teams?

____

One Way Use partial quotients.

In the **partial quotient** method of dividing, multiples of the divisor are subtracted from the dividend and then the partial quotients are added together.

Divide. 125 ÷ 5 **Write.** $5\overline{)125}$

STEP 1

Start by subtracting a greater multiple, such as 10 times the divisor. For example, you know that you can make at least 10 teams of 5 players.

Continue subtracting until the remaining number is less than the multiple, 50.

STEP 2

Subtract smaller multiples, such as 5, 2, or 1 times the divisor until the remaining number is less than the divisor. In other words, keep going until you no longer have enough players to make a team.

Then add the partial quotients to find the quotient.

		Partial Quotients
$5\overline{)125}$		↓
− ____	10 × ____	10
− ____	10 × ____	10
− ____	5 × ____	+ 5

So, there are ______ lacrosse teams.

Math Talk — Mathematical Practices

Explain how you found the total number of teams after finding the partial quotients.

Another Way Use rectangular models to record the partial quotients.

Jarod and Ana also found the number of teams using partial quotients. They recorded the partial quotients using rectangular models. They each still had 25 as the quotient.

Jarod

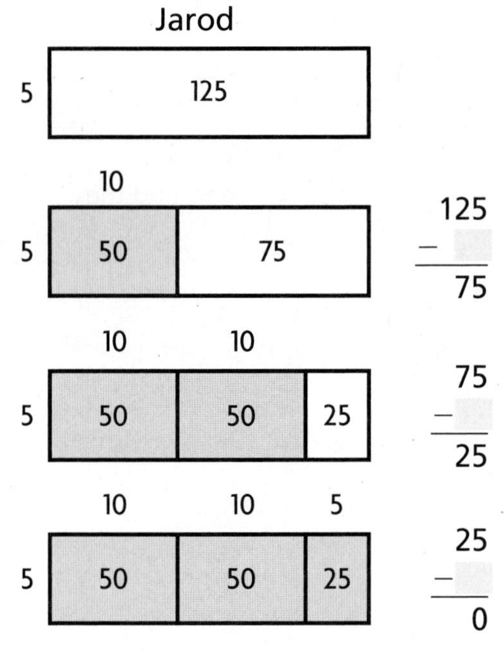

10 + 10 + 5 = ______

Ana

5 | 125

20

5 | 100 | 25

125
− ___
25

20 5

5 | 100 | 25

25
− ___
0

20 + 5 = ______

Math Talk — Mathematical Practices

Explain why you might prefer to use one method rather than the other.

Share and Show

1. Lacrosse is played on a field 330 ft long. How many yards long is a lacrosse field? (3 feet = 1 yard)

Divide. Use partial quotients.

3)330
− ___ 100 × ___ 100
___
___ 10 × ___ + 10
___ ___

So, the lacrosse field is ______ yards long.

Name ____________________

Divide. Use partial quotients.

2. $3\overline{)225}$

Divide. Use rectangular models to record the partial quotients.

3. $428 \div 4 =$ ______

Math Talk — Mathematical Practices

Explain how you could solve Problems 2 and 3 a different way.

On Your Own

Divide. Use partial quotients.

4. $9\overline{)198}$

5. $7\overline{)259}$

6. $8\overline{)864}$

7. $6\overline{)738}$

Divide. Use rectangular models to record the partial quotients.

8. $328 \div 2 =$ ______

9. $475 \div 5 =$ ______

10. $219 \div 3 =$ ______

11. $488 \div 4 =$ ______

12. MATHEMATICAL PRACTICE 2 **Use Reasoning** What is the least number you can divide by 5 to get a three-digit quotient? Explain how you found your answer.

____

____

____

Problem Solving • Applications Real World

Use the table for 13–15.

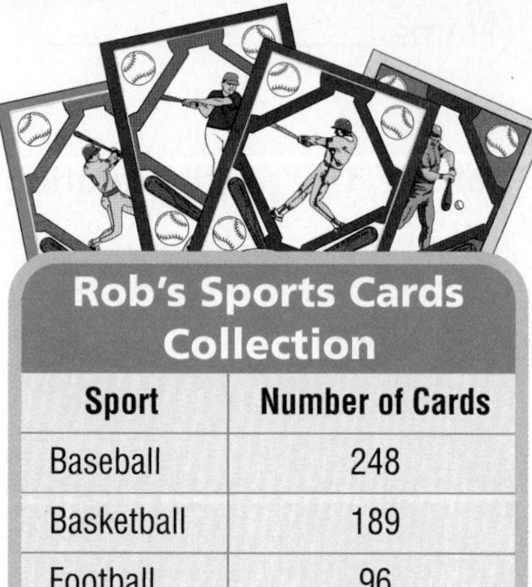

Rob's Sports Cards Collection	
Sport	**Number of Cards**
Baseball	248
Basketball	189
Football	96
Hockey	64

13. Rob wants to put 8 baseball cards on each page in an album. How many pages will he fill?

______

14. Rob filled 9 plastic boxes with basketball cards with the same number of cards in each box. How many cards did he put in each box?

______

15. THINK SMARTER Rob filled 3 fewer plastic boxes with football cards than basketball cards. He filled 9 boxes with basketball cards. How many boxes did he fill with football cards? How many football cards were in each box?

______

16. GO DEEPER Marshall can buy 5 tee shirts for \$60. If each shirt costs the same amount, what is the cost of 4 tee shirts?

______

17. THINK SMARTER Use partial quotients. Fill in the blanks.

$$5\overline{)485}$$

− ______ 80×5

− ______ 10×5

− ______ 7×5 + ______

FOR MORE PRACTICE: Standards Practice Book

Name ________________________

Model Division with Regrouping

Essential Question How can you use base-ten blocks to model division with regrouping?

Number and Operations in Base Ten—4.NBT.6

MATHEMATICAL PRACTICES
MP.2, MP.4, MP.6

Investigate

Materials ■ base-ten blocks

The librarian wants to share 54 books equally among 3 classes. How many books will she give to each class?

A. Draw 3 circles to represent the classes. Then use base-ten blocks to model 54. Show 54 as 5 tens and 4 ones.

B. Share the tens equally among the 3 groups.

C. If there are any tens left, regroup them as ones. Share the ones equally among the 3 groups.

D. There are ______ ten(s) and ______ one(s) in each group.

So, the librarian will give ______ books to each class.

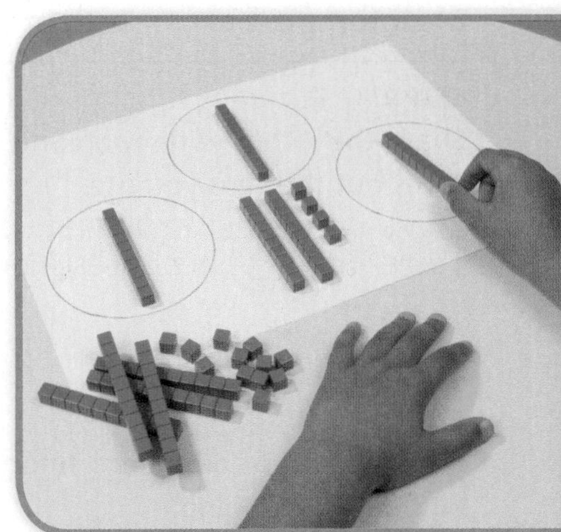

Draw Conclusions

1. THINK SMARTER Explain why you needed to regroup in Step C.

____

____

2. How you can use base-ten blocks to find the quotient of 92 ÷ 4?

____

____

____

____

Make Connections

Use the quick picture at the bottom of the page to help you divide. Record each step.

Find 76 ÷ 3.

STEP 1
Model 76 as 7 tens 6 ones.
Draw three circles to represent equal groups.

$3\overline{)76}$

STEP 2
Share the 7 tens equally among the 3 groups.
Cross out the tens you use.

There are ______ tens in each group.

______ tens were used. There is ______ ten left over.

STEP 3
One ten cannot be shared among 3 groups without regrouping.
Regroup 1 ten by drawing 10 ones.

There are now ______ ones to share.

STEP 4
Share the ones equally among the 3 groups.
Cross out the ones you use.

There are ______ ones in each group.

______ ones were used. There is ______ one left over.

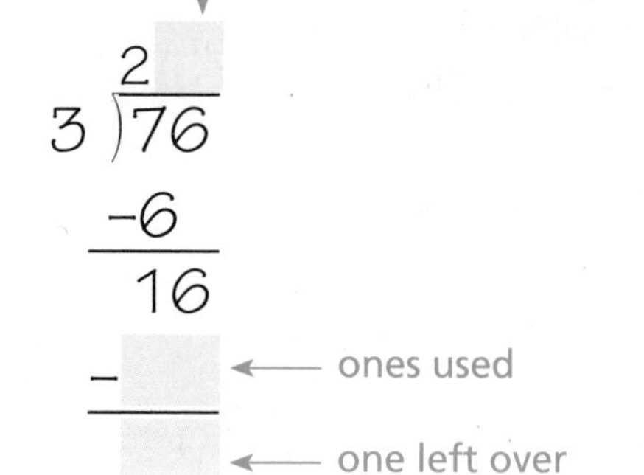

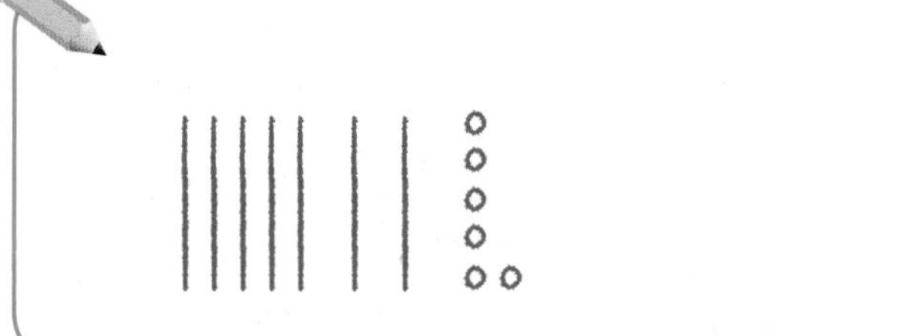

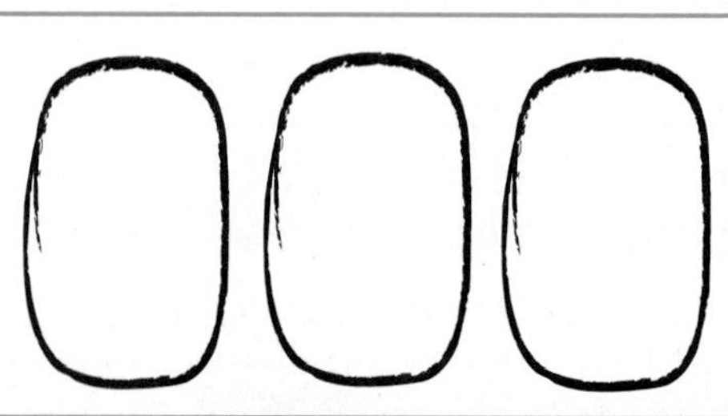

There are 3 groups of ______ and ______ left over.

So, for 76 ÷ 3, the quotient is ______ and the remainder is ______.

This can be written as __________.

Mathematical Practices

Why do you share tens equally among groups before sharing ones?

Name ________________________________

Share and Show

Divide. Use base-ten blocks.

1. 48 ÷ 3 ______

2. 84 ÷ 4 ______

3. 72 ÷ 5 ______

4. Divide. Draw a quick picture. Record the steps.

84 ÷ 3 ____________

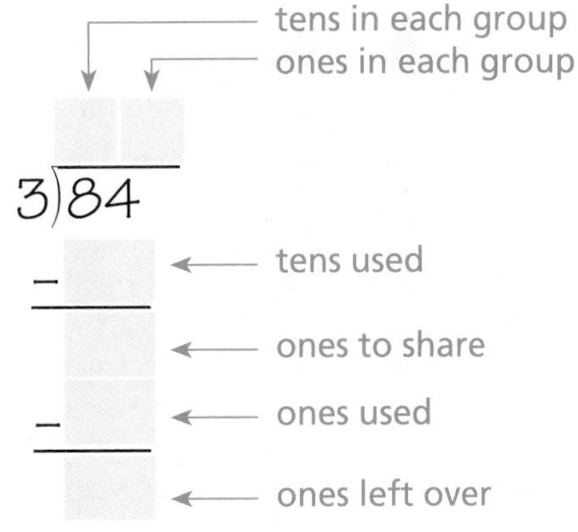

Problem Solving • Applications

5. WRITE ▸ *Math* Explain why you did not need to regroup in Exercise 2.

____

6. GO DEEPER Mindy is preparing fruit boxes for gifts. She divides 36 apples evenly into 6 boxes. Then she divided 54 bananas evenly into the same 6 boxes. How many pieces of fruit are in each of Mindy's boxes?

____

7. THINK SMARTER Ami needs to divide these base-ten blocks into 4 equal groups.

Describe a model that would show how many are in each group.

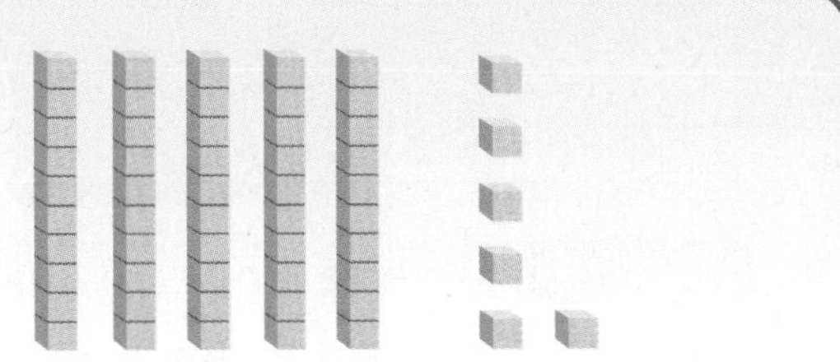

____

Sense or Nonsense?

8. THINK SMARTER Angela and Zach drew quick pictures to find $68 \div 4$. Whose quick picture makes sense? Whose quick picture is nonsense? Explain your reasoning.

I drew 1 ten and 2 ones in each group.

I drew 1 ten and 7 ones in each group.

Angela's Quick Picture

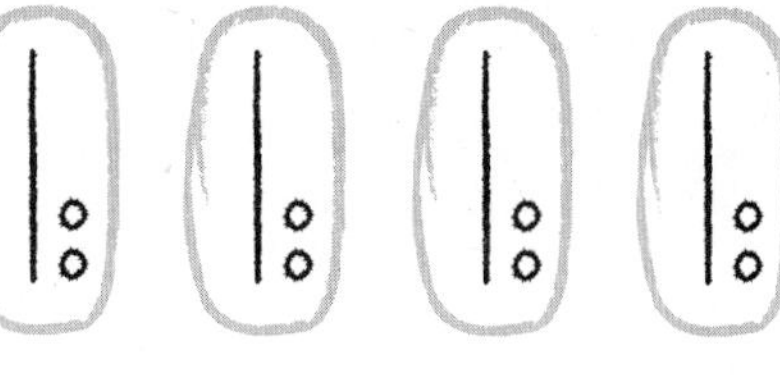

Zach's Quick Picture

9. MATHEMATICAL PRACTICE 1 **Analyze** What did Angela forget to do after she shared the tens equally among the 4 groups?

FOR MORE PRACTICE:
Standards Practice Book

Name ______________________________

Place the First Digit

Essential Question How can you use place value to know where to place the first digit in the quotient?

Number and Operations in Base Ten—4.NBT.6

MATHEMATICAL PRACTICES
MP.2, MP.7, MP.8

Unlock the Problem (Real World)

Victor took 144 photos on a digital camera. The photos are to be placed equally in 6 photo albums. How many photos will be in each album?

- Underline what you are asked to find.
- Circle what you need to use.

Example 1 Divide. 144 ÷ 6

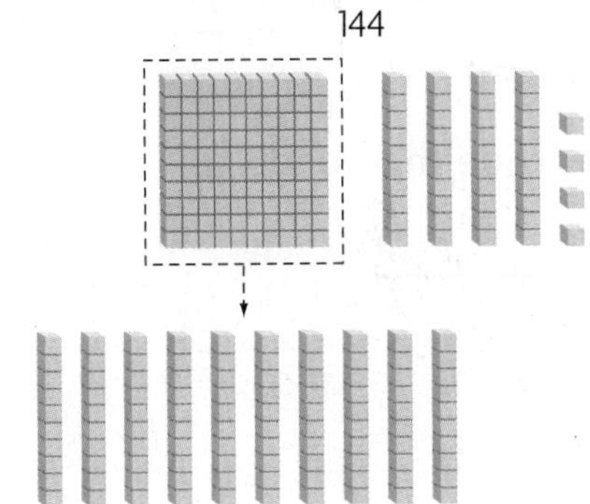

STEP 1 Use place value to place the first digit.
Look at the hundreds in 144.
1 hundred cannot be shared among 6 groups without regrouping.
Regroup 1 hundred as 10 tens.

Now there are ______ tens to share among 6 groups.

The first digit of the quotient will be in the ______ place.

STEP 2 Divide the tens.

$$6\overline{)144}$$ quotient 2, − ____ , ____

Divide. 14 tens ÷ 6

Multiply. 6 × 2 tens

Subtract. 14 tens − 12 tens
Check. 2 tens cannot be shared among 6 groups without regrouping.

STEP 3 Divide the ones.
Regroup 2 tens as 20 ones.

Now there are ______ ones to share among 6 groups.

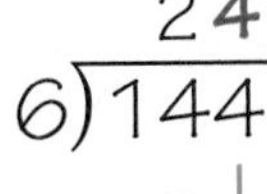

24
6)144
−12↓
24
− ____
____

Divide. ______ ones ÷ ______

Multiply. ______ × ______ ones

Subtract. ______ ones − ______ ones
Check. 0 ones cannot be shared among 6 groups.

So, there will be ______ photos in each album.

Math Idea

After you divide each place, the remainder should be less than the divisor.

Math Talk — Mathematical Practices

Explain how the answer would change if Jaime had 146 photos.

Example 2 Divide. 287 ÷ 2

Omar has 287 photographs of animals. If he wants to put the photos into 2 groups of the same size, how many photos will be in each group?

STEP 1

Use place value to place the first digit.
Look at the hundreds in 287.
2 hundreds can be shared between 2 groups.

So, the first digit of the quotient will be in the ________ place.

STEP 2

Divide the hundreds.

$$\begin{array}{r} 1 \\ 2\overline{)287} \\ -\square \\ \hline \square \end{array}$$

Divide. 2 hundreds ÷ 2

Multiply. 2 × 1 hundred

Subtract. 2 hundreds − 2 hundreds.

0 hundreds are left.

STEP 3

Divide the tens.

$$\begin{array}{r} 14 \\ 2\overline{)287} \\ -2\downarrow \\ \hline 0\square \\ -\square \\ \hline \square \end{array}$$

Divide. ______ tens ÷ ______

Multiply. ______ × ______ tens

Subtract. ______ tens − ______ tens 0 tens are left.

STEP 4

Divide the ones.

$$\begin{array}{r} 143\text{ r1} \\ 2\overline{)287} \\ -2 \\ \hline 08 \\ -8\downarrow \\ \hline 07 \\ -\square \\ \hline \square \end{array}$$

Divide. ______ ones ÷ ______

Multiply. ______ × ______ ones

Subtract. ______ ones − ______ ones
1 one cannot be equally shared between 2 groups.

So, there will be ________ photos in each group with 1 photo left.

Name ______________________

Share and Show

1. There are 452 pictures of dogs in 4 equal groups. How many pictures are in each group? Explain how you can use place value to place the first digit in the quotient.

$4\overline{)452}$

____

____

Divide.

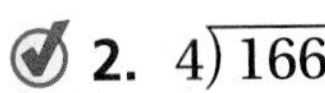

2. $4\overline{)166}$

3. $5\overline{)775}$

Mathematical Practices

Explain how you placed the first digit of the quotient in Exercise 2.

On Your Own

Divide.

4. $4\overline{)284}$

5. $5\overline{)394}$

6. $3\overline{)465}$

7. $8\overline{)272}$

8. $2\overline{)988}$

9. $3\overline{)504}$

10. $6\overline{)734}$

11. $4\overline{)399}$

Practice: Copy and Solve **Divide.**

12. $516 \div 2$

13. $516 \div 3$

14. $516 \div 4$

15. $516 \div 5$

16. MATHEMATICAL PRACTICE 6 Look back at your answers to Exercises 12–15. What happens to the quotient when the divisor increases? **Explain.**

____

____

Unlock the Problem Real World

17. THINK SMARTER Nan wants to put 234 pictures in an album with a blue cover. How many full pages will she have in her album?

Photo Albums

Color of cover	Pictures per page
Blue	4
Green	6
Red	8

a. What do you need to find?

____

b. How will you use division to find the number of full pages?

____

____

____

c. Show the steps you will use to solve the problem.

d. Complete the following sentences.

Nan has ______ pictures.

She wants to put the pictures in an album with pages that each hold ______ pictures.

She will have an album with ______ full pages and ______ pictures on another page.

18. GO DEEPER Mr. Parsons bought 293 apples to make pies for his shop. Six apples are needed for each pie. If Mr. Parsons makes the greatest number of apple pies possible, how many apples will be left?

____

19. THINK SMARTER Carol needs to divide 320 stickers equally among 4 classes. In which place is the first digit of the quotient? Choose the word that completes the sentence.

The first digit of the quotient is in

the [ones / tens / hundreds / thousands] place.

FOR MORE PRACTICE: Standards Practice Book

Name ______________________

Divide by 1-Digit Numbers

Essential Question How can you divide multidigit numbers and check your answers?

Number and Operations in Base Ten—4.NBT.6

MATHEMATICAL PRACTICES
MP.2, MP.7, MP.8

Unlock the Problem

Students in the third, fourth, and fifth grades made 525 origami animals to display in the library. Each grade made the same number of animals. How many animals did each grade make?

Example 1 Divide. 525 ÷ 3

STEP 1 Use place value to place the first digit. Look at the hundreds in 525. 5 hundreds can be shared among 3 groups without regrouping. The first digit of the quotient will be in the __________ place.

Math Talk Mathematical Practices

At the checking step, what would you do if the number is greater than the divisor?

STEP 2 Divide the hundreds.

```
    1
3)525
 -
 ___
```

Divide. Share ______ hundreds equally among ______ groups.

Multiply. ______ × __________

Subtract. __________ − __________.

Check. ______ hundreds cannot be shared among 3 groups without regrouping.

STEP 3 Divide the tens.

```
   17
3)525
 -3↓
  22
 -
 ___
```

Divide. Share __________ equally among ______ groups.

Multiply. ____________________

Subtract. __________ − __________

Check. ____________________

____

____________________.

STEP 4 Divide the ones.

```
  175
3)525
 -3
  22
 -21↓
   15
  -
  ___
```

Divide. Share __________ equally among ______ groups.

Multiply. ____________________

Subtract. __________ − __________

Check. __________ are left.

So, each class made __________ origami animals.

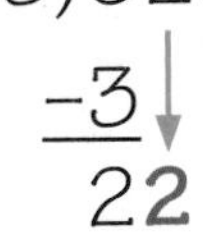

There are 8,523 sheets of origami paper to be divided equally among 8 schools. How many sheets of origami paper will each school get?

Example 2 Divide. 8,523 ÷ 8

STEP 1 Use place value to place the first digit.

Look at the thousands in 8,523.
8 thousands can be shared among 8 groups without regrouping.

The first digit of the quotient will be

in the ________ place.

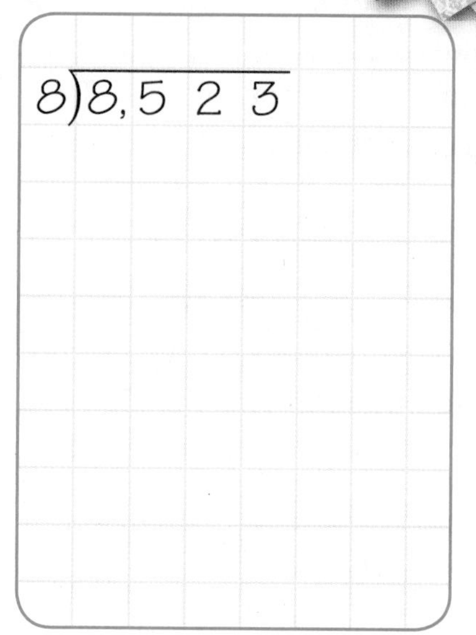

STEP 2 Divide the thousands.

STEP 3 Divide the hundreds.

STEP 4 Divide the tens.

STEP 5 Divide the ones.

So, each school will get ______ sheets of origami paper.

There will be ______ sheets left.

ERROR Alert

Place a zero in the quotient when a place in the dividend cannot be divided by the divisor.

CONNECT Division and multiplication are inverse operations. You can use multiplication to check your answer to a division problem.

Multiply the quotient by the divisor. If there is a remainder, add it to the product. The result should equal the dividend.

Divide.

quotient → 1,065 r3 ← remainder
divisor → 8)8,523 ← dividend

Check.

	1,065	← quotient
×	8	← divisor
	8,520	
+	3	← remainder
	8,523	← dividend

The check shows that the division is correct.

Name ____________________

Share and Show

1. Ollie used 852 beads to make 4 bracelets. He put the same number of beads on each bracelet. How many beads does each bracelet have? Check your answer.

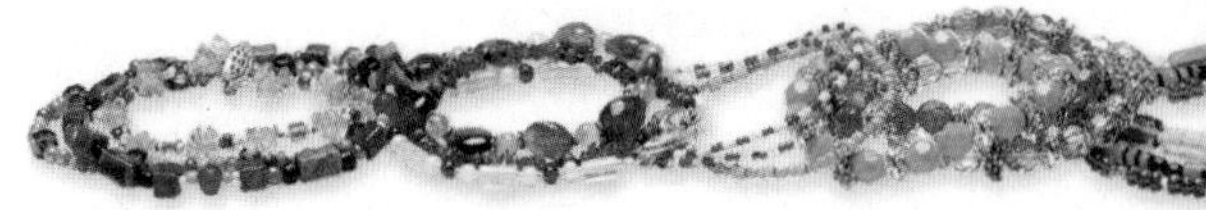

Divide.

Check.

Math Talk — **Mathematical Practices**

Explain how you could check if your quotient is correct.

So, each bracelet has ______ beads.

Divide and check.

2. $2\overline{)394}$

3. $2\overline{)803}$

4. $4\overline{)3,448}$

On Your Own

Divide and check.

5. $2\overline{)816}$

6. $4\overline{)709}$

7. $3\overline{)267}$

8. $6\overline{)1,302}$

9. $8\overline{)9,232}$

10. $9\overline{)1,020}$

Problem Solving • Applications Real World

Use the table for 11–13.

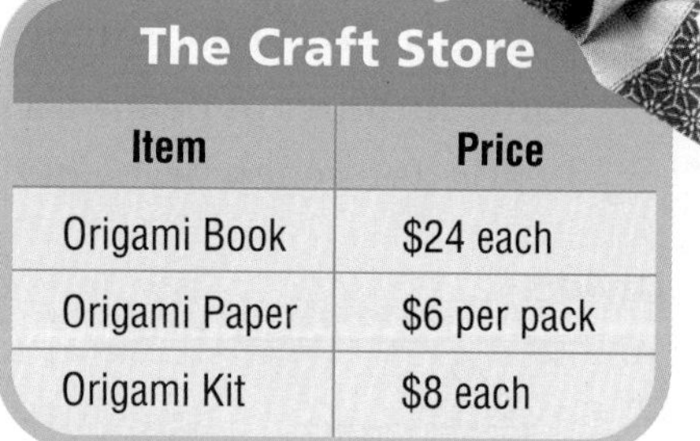

The Craft Store	
Item	**Price**
Origami Book	$24 each
Origami Paper	$6 per pack
Origami Kit	$8 each

11. THINK SMARTER Four teachers bought 10 origami books and 100 packs of origami paper for their classrooms. They will share the cost of the items equally. How much should each teacher pay?

12. MATHEMATICAL PRACTICE 5 **Communicate** Six students shared equally the cost of 18 of one of the items in the chart. Each student paid $24. What item did they buy? Explain how you found your answer.

13. Ms. Alvarez has $1,482 to spend on origami paper. How many packs can she buy?

14. GO DEEPER Evan made origami cranes with red, blue, and yellow paper. The number of cranes in each color is the same. If there are 342 cranes, how many of them are blue or yellow?

15. THINK SMARTER On Monday 336 fourth graders went on a field trip to a local park. The teachers divided the students into 8 groups.

Use a basic fact. Estimate the number of students in each group. Show your work.

WRITE ▸ *Math* • **Show Your Work**

FOR MORE PRACTICE:
Standards Practice Book

Name ____________________

Problem Solving • Multistep Division Problems

Essential Question How can you use the strategy *draw a diagram* to solve multistep division problems?

Operations and Algebraic Thinking—4.OA.2 *Also 4.OA.3, 4.NBT.6*

MATHEMATICAL PRACTICES
MP.1, MP.2, MP.4

Unlock the Problem

Lucia picked 3 times as much corn as Eli. Together, they picked 96 ears of corn. Eli wants to divide the number of ears he picked equally among 8 bags. How many ears of corn will Eli put in each of the 8 bags?

Read the Problem

What do I need to find?

I need to find the number of ____________ that will go in each bag.

What information do I need to use?

Lucia picked ______ times as much corn as Eli.

Together they picked ______ ears of corn. The number of ears Eli picked are divided equally among ______ bags.

How will I use the information?

I will make a bar model for each step to visualize the information. Then I will ______ to find the number of ears Eli picked and ______ to find the number for each bag.

Solve the Problem

I can draw bar models to visualize the information given.

First, I will model and compare to find the number of ears of corn that Eli picked.

Lucia's [___ | ___ | ___]
Eli's [___]
96

96 ÷ 4 = ______

number of parts

Then I will model and divide to find how many ears of corn Eli will put in each bag.

[___ | ___ | ___ | ___ | ___ | ___ | ___ | ___]
24

1. How many ears of corn will Eli put in each bag? ____________________

2. How can you check your answers? ____________________

____

Try Another Problem

There are 8 dinner rolls in a package. How many packages will be needed to feed 64 people if each person has 2 dinner rolls?

Read the Problem	Solve the Problem
What do I need to find?	
What information do I need to use?	
How will I use the information?	

3. How many packages of rolls will be needed? ____________

4. How did drawing a bar model help you solve the problem?

____

____

____

Math Talk — **Mathematical Practices**

Describe another method you could have used to solve the problem.

Name ______________________________

Share and Show

1. A firehouse pantry has 52 cans of vegetables and 74 cans of soup. Each shelf holds 9 cans. What is the least number of shelves needed for all the cans?

   First, draw a bar model for the total number of cans.

   Next, add to find the total number of cans.

   Then, draw a bar model to show the number of shelves needed.

   Finally, divide to find the number of shelves needed.

So, ______ shelves are needed to hold all of the cans.

2. THINK SMARTER What if 18 cans fit on a shelf? What is the least number of shelves needed? Describe how your answer would be different.

____

____

3. Julio's dad bought 10 dozen potatoes. The potatoes were equally divided into 6 bags. How many potatoes are in each bag?

____

4. At the garden shop, each small tree costs $125 and each large tree costs $225. How much will 3 small trees and 1 large tree cost?

____

Unlock the Problem

- ✓ Use the Problem Solving MathBoard.
- ✓ Underline important facts.
- ✓ Choose a strategy you know.

Math Talk — **Mathematical Practices**

Explain how you could check that your answer is correct.

WRITE ▸ *Math*
Show Your Work

On Your Own

5. THINK SMARTER Ms. Johnson bought 6 bags of balloons. Each bag has 25 balloons. She fills all the balloons and puts 5 balloons in each bunch. How many bunches can she make?

6. THINK SMARTER An adult's dinner costs $8. A family of 2 adults and 2 children pays $26 for their dinners. How much does a child's dinner cost? Explain.

7. MATHEMATICAL PRACTICE 5 **Communicate** Use the table at the right. Maria bought 80 ounces of apples. She needs 10 apples to make a pie. How many apples will be left over? Explain.

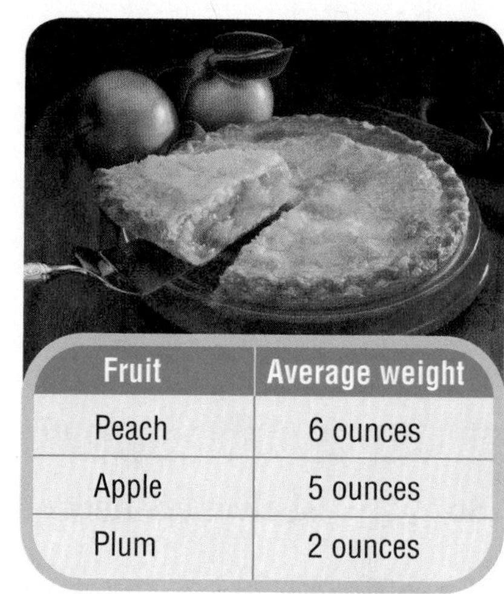

Fruit	Average weight
Peach	6 ounces
Apple	5 ounces
Plum	2 ounces

8. GO DEEPER Taylor has 16 tacks. She buys 2 packages of 36 tacks each. How many garage sale posters can she put up if she uses 4 tacks for each poster?

Personal Math Trainer

9. THINK SMARTER + Ryan bought 8 dozen bandages for the track team first aid kit. The bandages were divided equally into 4 boxes.

How many bandages are in each box?

FOR MORE PRACTICE:
Standards Practice Book

Name ________________________________

Chapter 4 Review/Test

1. There are 9 showings of a film about endangered species at the science museum. A total of 459 people saw the film. The same number of people were at each showing. About how many people were at each showing? Select the numbers the quotient is between.

   Ⓐ  40 Ⓑ 50 Ⓒ 60 Ⓓ 70 Ⓔ 80

2. Between which two numbers is the quotient of 87 ÷ 5? Write the numbers in the boxes.

   5  10 15 20 25

   The quotient is between 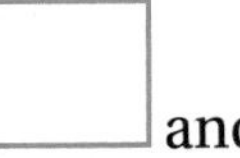 and ☐.

3. Look at the model. What division does it show?

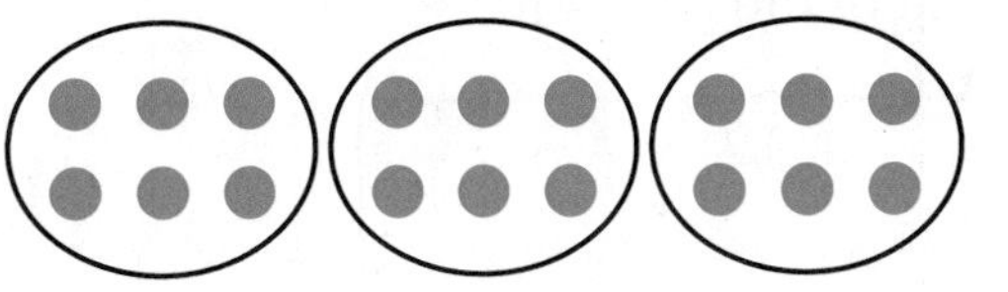

   ______ ÷ ______ → ______ r ______

4. For 4a–4d, choose Yes or No to tell whether the division sentence has a remainder.

   4a. 28 ÷ 4 ○ Yes ○ No

   4b. 35 ÷ 2 ○ Yes ○ No

   4c. 40 ÷ 9 ○ Yes ○ No

   4d. 45 ÷ 5 ○ Yes ○ No

GO DIGITAL Assessment Options Chapter Test

5. A park guide plans the swan boat rides for 40 people. Each boat can carry 6 people at a time. What is the best way to interpret the remainder in this situation so that everyone gets a ride?

____

6. Nolan divides his 88 toy cars into boxes. Each box holds 9 cars. How many boxes does Nolan need to store all of his cars?

______ boxes

7. A group of 140 tourists are going on a tour. The tour guide rents 15 vans. Each van holds 9 tourists.

Part A

Write a division problem that can be used to find the number of vans needed to carry the tourists. Then solve.

Part B

What does the remainder mean in the context of the problem?

Part C

How can you use your answer to determine if the tour guide rented enough vans? Explain.

8. Solve.

$3{,}200 \div 8 =$ ______

Name ____________________

9. Which quotients are equal to 300? Mark all that apply.

Ⓐ 1,200 ÷ 4 Ⓒ 2,400 ÷ 8 Ⓔ 90 ÷ 3

Ⓑ 180 ÷ 9 Ⓓ 2,100 ÷ 7 Ⓕ 3,000 ÷ 3

10. Margo estimated 188 ÷ 5 to be between 30 and 40. Which basic facts did she use to help her estimate? Mark all that apply.

Ⓐ 10 ÷ 5 Ⓑ 15 ÷ 5 Ⓒ 20 ÷ 5 Ⓓ 25 ÷ 5

11. Mathias and his brother divided 2,029 marbles equally. About how many marbles did each of them receive?

12. For 12a–12d, choose Yes or No to show how to use the Distributive Property to break apart the dividend to find the quotient 132 ÷ 6.

12a. (115 ÷ 6) + (17 ÷ 6) ○ Yes ○ No

12b. (100 ÷ 6) + (32 ÷ 6) ○ Yes ○ No

12c. (90 ÷ 6) + (42 ÷ 6) ○ Yes ○ No

12d. (72 ÷ 6) + (60 ÷ 6) ○ Yes ○ No

13. There are 60 people waiting for a river raft ride. Each raft holds 15 people. Silvia used the work below to find the number of rafts needed. Explain how Silvia's work can be used to find the number of rafts needed.

```
15)60
  −15
   45
  −15
   30
  −15
   15
  −15
    0
```

14. A traveling circus brings along everything it needs for a show in big trucks.

Part A

The circus sets up chairs in rows with 9 seats in each row. How many rows will need to be set up if 513 people are expected to attend the show?

______ rows

Part B

Can the rows be divided into a number of equal sections? Explain how you found your answer.

Part C

Circus horses eat about 250 pounds of horse food per week. About how many pounds of food does a circus horse eat each day? Explain.

15. Hilda wants to save 825 digital photographs in an online album. Each folder of the album can save 6 photographs. She uses division to find out how may full folders she will have. In what place is the first digit of the quotient?

____

Name ______________________________

16. Which model matches each expression? Write the letter in the box next to the model.

 160 ÷ 80 Ⓑ 150 ÷ 30 Ⓒ 160 ÷ 40 Ⓓ 150 ÷ 50

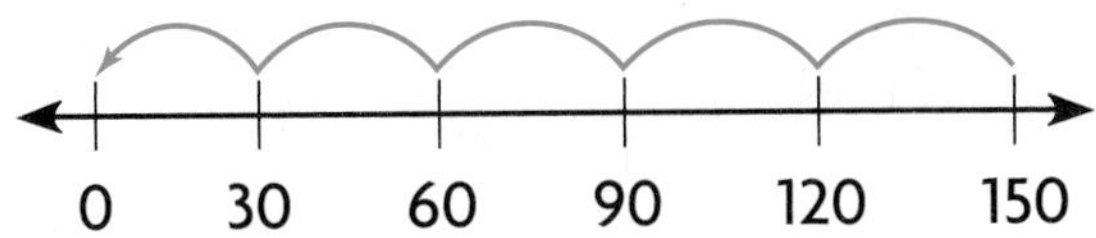

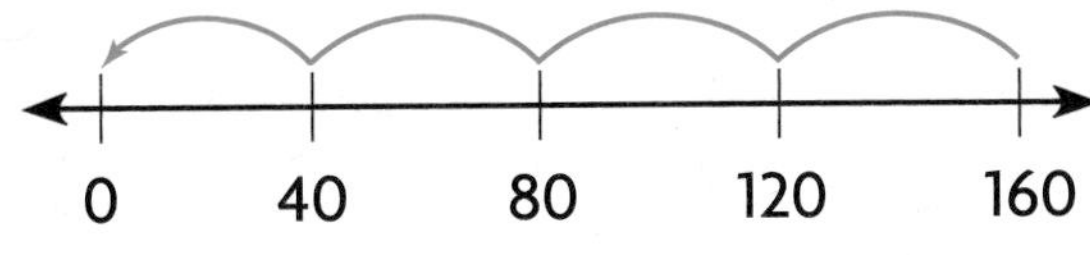

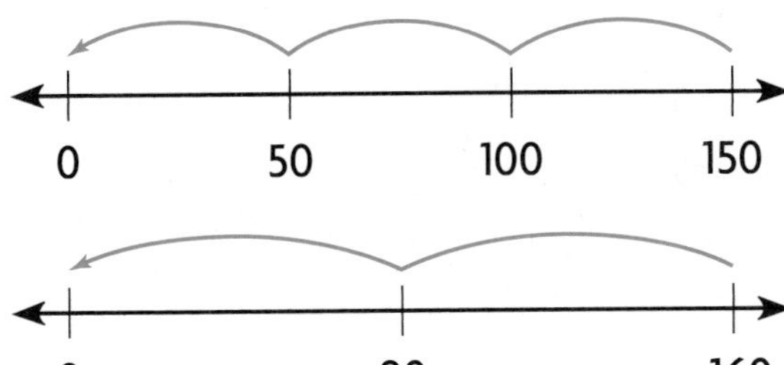

17. Popcorn was donated for the school fair by 3 different popcorn vendors. They donated a total of 636 bags of popcorn. Each vendor donated the same number of bags. How many bags of popcorn did each vendor donate?

______ bags

18. Use partial quotients. Fill in the blanks.

$8\overline{)832}$

$-$ ______ 100×8 ______

______

$-$ ______ 4×8 ______

______ ______

19. Zack needs to divide these base-ten blocks into 3 equal groups.

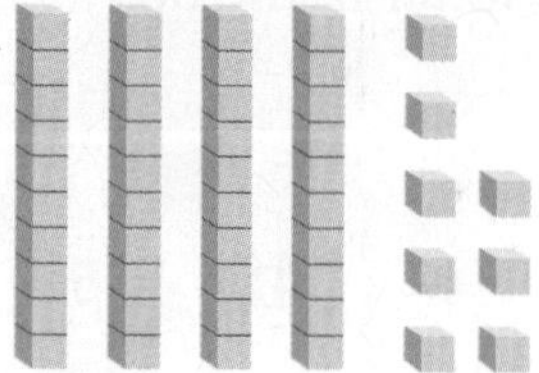

Draw or describe a model to show how many are in each group.

20. Jim needs to divide 750 coupon books equally among 9 stores. In which place is the first digit of the quotient? Choose the word that makes the sentence true.

The first digit of the quotient is in the [ones / tens / hundreds / thousands] place.

21. Ursula bought 9 dozen rolls of first aid tape for the health office. The rolls were divided equally into 4 boxes. How many rolls are in each box?

______ rolls

22. There are 112 seats in the school auditorium. There are 7 seats in each row. There are 70 people seated, filling up full rows of seats. How many rows are empty?

______ rows

Chapter 5 Factors, Multiples, and Patterns

Show What You Know 

Check your understanding of important skills.

Name ______________________

Skip-Count **Skip-count to find the unknown numbers.**

1. Skip count by 3s.

3 , ______, ______, ______

2. Skip count by 5s.

5 , ______, ______, ______

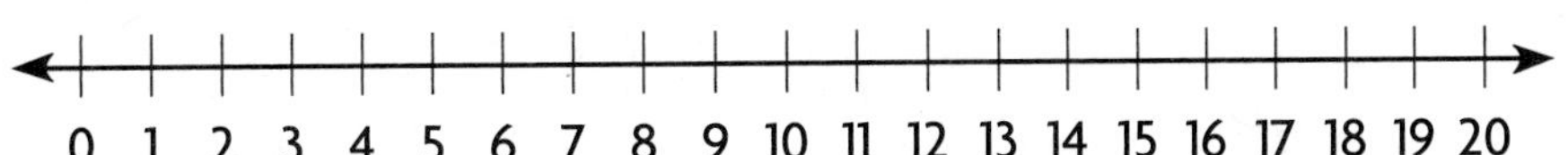

Arrays **Use the array to find the product.**

3. 

______ rows of ______ = ______

4. ■ ■ ■ ■ ■
■ ■ ■ ■ ■
■ ■ ■ ■ ■

______ rows of ______ = ______

Multiplication Facts **Find the product.**

5. $4 \times 5 =$ ______

6. $9 \times 4 =$ ______

7. $6 \times 7 =$ ______

Recycled plastic helps keep people warm. Some factories use recycled plastic, combined with other fabrics, to make winter jackets. A warehouse has 46 truckloads of recycled plastic. They use 8 truckloads each day. When there are fewer than 16 truckloads, more needs to be ordered. Be a Math Detective. Figure out how many truckloads will be left after 2 days. After 3 days. When will more need to be ordered?

Personal Math Trainer
Online Assessment and Intervention

Vocabulary Builder

▶ Visualize It

Complete the flow map by using the words with a ✓.

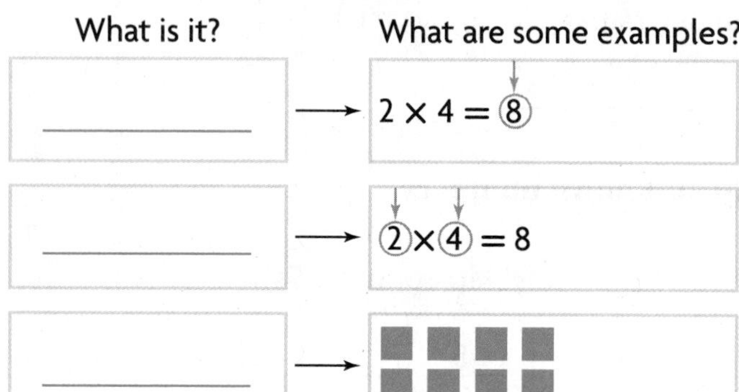

Review Words
✓ array
multiple
✓ product

Preview Words
common factor
common multiple
composite number
divisible
✓ factor
pattern
prime number
term

▶ Understand Vocabulary

Complete the sentences by using preview words.

1. A number that is a factor of two or more numbers is a ________________.

2. A number that is a multiple of two or more numbers is a ________________.

3. A number that has exactly two factors, 1 and itself, is a ________________.

4. A number that has more than two factors is a ________________.

5. A number is ________________ by another number if the quotient is a counting number and the remainder is 0.

6. An ordered set of numbers or objects is a ________________.

7. Each number in a pattern is called a ________________.

GO DIGITAL
• Interactive Student Edition
• Multimedia eGlossary

Name ______________________________

Model Factors

Essential Question How can you use models to find factors?

Operations and Algebraic Thinking—4.OA.4

MATHEMATICAL PRACTICES
MP.1, MP.4

Unlock the Problem 

A **factor** is a number multiplied by another number to find a product. Every whole number greater than 1 has at least two factors, that number and 1.

$18 = 1 \times 18$ (factor, factor) $\quad 7 = 7 \times 1 \quad 342 = 1 \times 342$

Many numbers can be broken into factors in different ways.

$16 = 1 \times 16 \quad 16 = 4 \times 4 \quad 16 = 2 \times 8$

Math Idea

When you are asked to find factors of a whole number, only list factors that are also whole numbers.

 **Activity** Model and record the factors of 24.

Materials ■ square tiles

Use all 24 tiles to make as many different arrays as you can. Record the arrays in the grid, and write the factors modeled.

$2 \times 12 = 24$

Factors: ______, ______

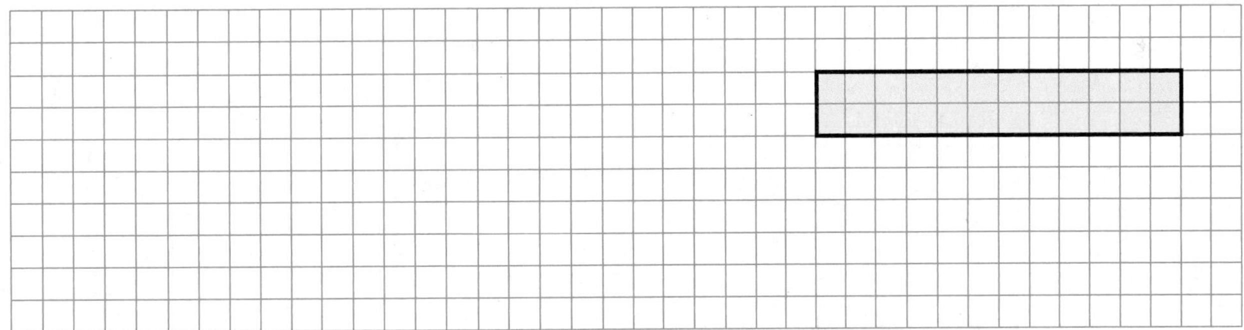

______ × ______ = 24 ______ × ______ = 24 ______ × ______ = 24

Factors: ______, ______ Factors: ______, ______ Factors: ______, ______

The factors of 24, from least to greatest, are

______, ______, ______, ______, ______, ______, ______, and ______.

Two factors that make a product are sometimes called a factor pair. How many factor pairs does 24 have? Explain.

____

Mathematical Practices

Can you arrange the tiles in each array another way and show the same factors? **Explain.**

Share and Show 

1. Use the arrays to name the factors of 12.

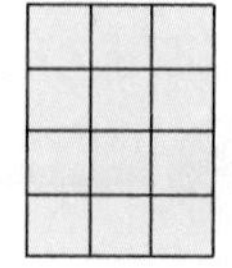

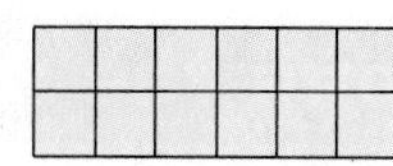

_____ × _____ = 12   _____ × _____ = 12   _____ × _____ = 12

The factors of 12 are 1, _____, 3, _____, 6, and _____.

Math Talk — **Mathematical Practices**

Explain how the numbers 3 and 12 are related. Use the word *factor* in your explanation.

Use tiles to find all the factors of the product. Record the arrays and write the factors shown.

2. 5: ____________________

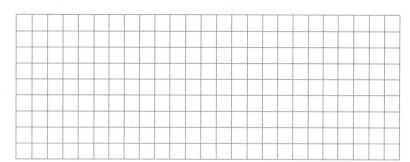

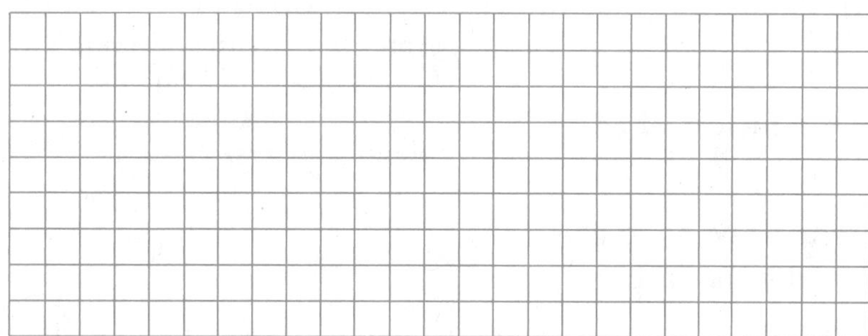

3. 20: ____________________

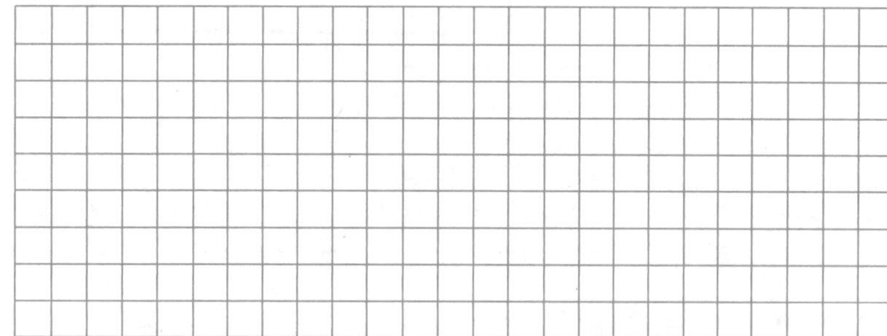

4. 25: ____________________

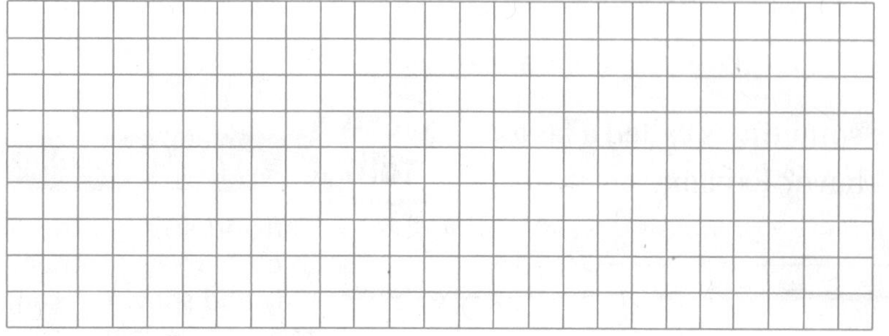

Name ____________________

On Your Own

Practice: Copy and Solve **Use tiles to find all the factors of the product. Record the arrays on grid paper and write the factors shown.**

5. 9 **6.** 21 **7.** 17 **8.** 18

Problem Solving • Applications

Use the diagram for 9–10.

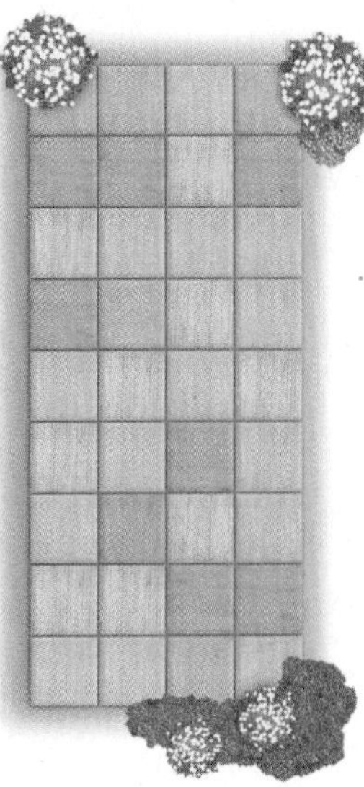

9. MATHEMATICAL PRACTICE 6 Pablo is using 36 tiles to make a patio. Can he arrange the tiles in another way and show the same factors? Draw a quick picture and **explain**.

10. THINKSMARTER How many different rectangular arrays can Pablo make with all 36 tiles, so none of the arrays show the same factors?

11. If 6 is a factor of a number, what other numbers must be factors of the number?

12. Jean spent $16 on new T-shirts. If each shirt cost the same whole-dollar amount, how many could she have bought?

Unlock the Problem

13. GO DEEPER Carmen has 18 connecting cubes. She wants to model a house shaped like a rectangle. If the model has a height of one connecting cube, how many different ways can Carmen model the house using all 18 connecting cubes?

a. What do you need to know? ______

______

b. How is finding the number of ways to model a rectangular house related to finding factor pairs? ______

______

______

c. Why is finding the factor pairs only the first step in solving the problem? ______

______

______

d. Show the steps you used to solve the problem.

______

______

______

______

e. Complete the sentences. Factor pairs for 18 are ______

______

There are ______ different ways Carmen can arrange the cubes to model the house.

14. THINK SMARTER Sarah was organizing vocabulary words using index cards. She arranged 40 index cards in the shape of a rectangle on a poster. For 14a–14e, choose Yes or No to tell whether a possible arrangement of cards is shown.

14a. 4 rows of 10 cards ○ Yes ○ No

14b. 6 rows of 8 cards ○ Yes ○ No

14c. 20 rows of 2 cards ○ Yes ○ No

14d. 40 rows of 1 card ○ Yes ○ No

14e. 35 rows of 5 cards ○ Yes ○ No

FOR MORE PRACTICE:
Standards Practice Book

Name ______________________________

Factors and Divisibility

Essential Question How can you tell whether one number is a factor of another number?

Operations and Algebraic Thinking—4.OA.4
MATHEMATICAL PRACTICES
MP.2, MP.4, MP.6

Unlock the Problem

Students in Carlo's art class painted 32 square tiles for a mosaic. They will arrange the tiles to make a rectangle. Can the rectangle have 32 tiles arranged into 3 equal rows, without gaps or overlaps?

▲ Mosaics are decorative patterns made with pieces of glass or other materials.

One Way Draw a model.

Think: Try to arrange the tiles into 3 equal rows to make a rectangle.

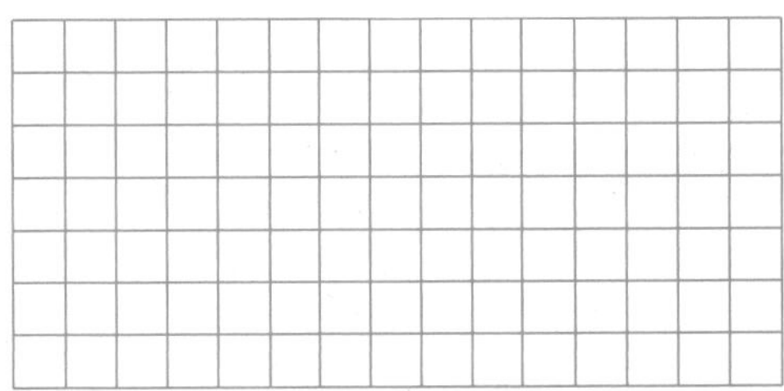

A rectangle ____________ have 32 tiles arranged into 3 equal rows.

Another Way Use division.

If 3 is a factor of 32, then the unknown factor in $3 \times \blacksquare = 32$ is a whole number.

Math Idea
A factor of a number divides the number evenly. This means the quotient is a whole number and the remainder is 0.

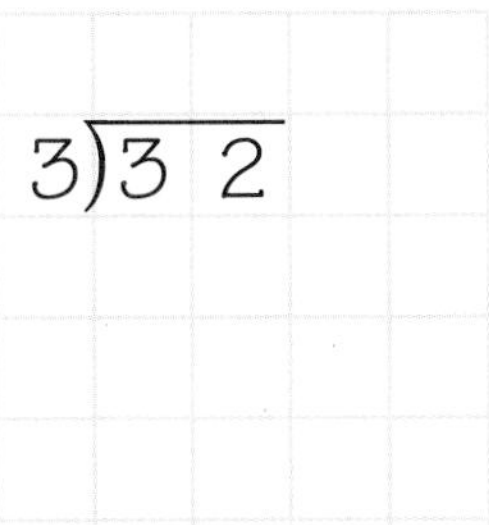

Think: Divide to see whether the unknown factor is a whole number.

The unknown factor in $3 \times \blacksquare = 32$ ____________ a whole number.

So, a rectangle ____________ have 32 tiles arranged in 3 rows.

- Explain how you can tell if 4 is a factor of 30.

____

____

Math Talk **Mathematical Practices**

Explain how the model relates to the quotient and remainder for $32 \div 3$.

Divisibility Rules A number is **divisible** by another number if the quotient is a counting number and the remainder is 0.

Some numbers have a divisibility rule. You can use a divisibility rule to tell whether one number is a factor of another.

Is 6 a factor of 72?

Think: If 72 is divisible by 6, then 6 is a factor of 72.

Test for divisibility by 6:

Is 72 even? ______

What is the sum of the digits of 72?

______ + ______ = ______

Is the sum of the digits divisible by 3?

____

72 is divisible by ______.

So, 6 is a factor of 72.

Divisibility Rules	
Number	**Divisibility Rule**
2	The number is even.
3	The sum of the digits is divisible by 3.
5	The last digit is 0 or 5.
6	The number is even and divisible by 3.
9	The sum of the digits is divisible by 9.

Try This! **List all the factor pairs for 72 in the table.**

Complete the table.

Factors of 72	
1 × 72 = 72	1, 72
____ × ____ = ____	____, ____
____ × ____ = ____	____, ____
____ × ____ = ____	____, ____
____ × ____ = ____	____, ____
____ × ____ = ____	____, ____

Show your work.

Math Talk **Mathematical Practices**

How are divisibility and factors related? **Explain.**

- How did you check if 7 is a factor of 72? Explain.

____

____

Name ________________________

Share and Show

1. Is 4 a factor of 28? Draw a model to help.

Think: Can you make a rectangle with 28 squares in 4 equal rows?

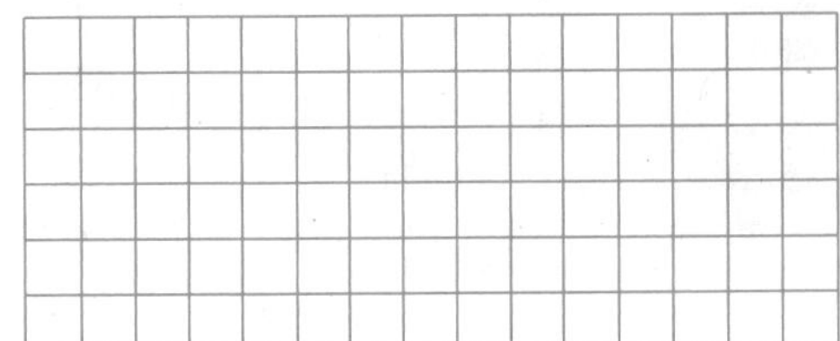

4 ______ a factor of 28.

Math Talk — **Mathematical Practices**

If 3 is a factor of a number, is 6 always a factor of the number? **Explain.**

Is 5 a factor of the number? Write *yes* or *no*.

2. 27 ______

3. 30 ______

4. 36 ______

5. 53 ______

On Your Own

Is 9 a factor of the number? Write *yes* or *no*.

6. 54 ______

7. 63 ______

8. 67 ______

9. 93 ______

List all the factor pairs in the table.

10.

Factors of 24	
___ × ___ = ___	___, ___
___ × ___ = ___	___, ___
___ × ___ = ___	___, ___
___ × ___ = ___	___, ___

11.

Factors of 39	
___ × ___ = ___	___, ___
___ × ___ = ___	___, ___

Practice: Copy and Solve **List all the factor pairs for the number. Make a table to help.**

12. 56

____

____

13. 64

____

____

Problem Solving • Applications Real World

Use the table to solve 14–15.

Stamps Sets	
Country	**Number of stamps**
Germany	90
Sweden	78
Japan	63
Canada	25

14. THINK SMARTER Dirk bought a set of stamps. The number of stamps in the set he bought is divisible by 2, 3, 5, 6, and 9. Which set is it?

15. GO DEEPER Geri wants to put 6 stamps on some pages in her stamp book and 9 stamps on other pages. Explain how she could do this with the stamp set for Sweden.

WRITE Math
Show Your Work

16. MATHEMATICAL PRACTICE 3 **Use Counterexamples** George said if 2 and 4 are factors of a number, then 8 is a factor of the number. Is he correct? Explain.

17. THINK SMARTER Classify the numbers. Some numbers may belong in more than one box.

27 45 54 72 81 84

Divisible by 5 and 9	Divisible by 3 and 9	Divisible by 2 and 6

FOR MORE PRACTICE:
Standards Practice Book

Name ____________________

Problem Solving • Common Factors

Essential Question How can you use the *make a list* strategy to solve problems with common factors?

Operations and Algebraic Thinking—4.OA.4

MATHEMATICAL PRACTICES
MP.1, MP.5

Unlock the Problem

Chuck has a coin collection with 30 pennies, 24 quarters, and 36 nickels. He wants to arrange the coins into rows. Each row will have the same number of coins, and all the coins in a row will be the same. How many coins can he put in each row?

The information in the graphic organizer below will help you solve the problem.

Read the Problem

What do I need to find?

I need to find ____________ that can go in each row so that each row has ____________ ____________.

What information do I need to use?

Chuck has ____________ ____________. Each row has ____________ ____________ ____________.

How will I use the information?

I can make a list to find all the factors of ____________. Then I can use the list to find the common factors. A **common factor** is a factor of two or more numbers.

Solve the Problem

I can list all the factors of each number. Then I can circle the factors that are common to all three numbers.

Factors of: 30 24 36

The common factors are ____________.

So, Chuck can put ______, ______, ______, or ______ coins in each row.

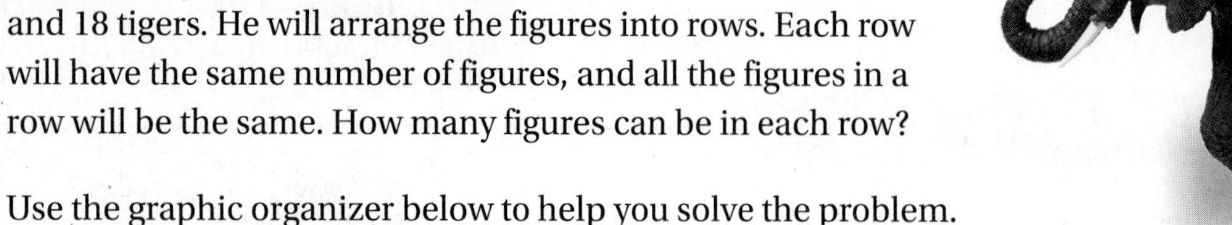

Try Another Problem

Ryan collects animal figures. He has 45 elephants, 36 zebras, and 18 tigers. He will arrange the figures into rows. Each row will have the same number of figures, and all the figures in a row will be the same. How many figures can be in each row?

Use the graphic organizer below to help you solve the problem.

Read the Problem	Solve the Problem
What do I need to find?	
What information do I need to use?	
How will I use the information?	

So, Ryan can put ______, ______, or ______ figures in each row.

Math Talk — **Mathematical Practices**

How did making a list help you solve the problem?

Name ______________________________

Share and Show

Unlock the Problem

√ Use the Problem-Solving MathBoard.

√ Underline the important facts.

1. Lucy has 40 bean plants, 32 tomato plants, and 16 pepper plants. She wants to put the plants in rows with only one type of plant in each row. All rows will have the same number of plants. How many plants can Lucy put in each row?

First, read the problem and think about what you need to find. What information will you use? How will you use the information?

____

____

Next, make a list. Find the factors for each number in the problem.

____

____

____

Finally, use the list. Circle the common factors.

So, Lucy can put ______, ______, ______, or ______ plants in each row.

2. What if Lucy has 64 bean plants instead of 40 bean plants? How many plants can Lucy put in each row?

____

3. THINK SMARTER One common factor of two numbers is 40. Another common factor is 10. If both numbers are less than 100, what are the two numbers?

____

4. The sum of two numbers is 136. One number is 51. What is the other number? What are the common factors of these two numbers?

____

WRITE Math
Show Your Work

On Your Own

5. MATHEMATICAL PRACTICE 1 **Analyze** A number is called a *perfect number* if it equals the sum of all of its factors except itself. For instance, 6 is a perfect number because its factors are 1, 2, 3, and 6, and $1 + 2 + 3 = 6$. What is the next greater perfect number?

6. THINK SMARTER Sona knits 10 squares a day for 7 days. Can she sew together the squares to make 5 equal-sized blankets? Explain.

7. Julianne earned $296 working at a grocery store last week. She earns $8 per hour. How many hours did Julianne work?

WRITE Math
Show Your Work

8. GO DEEPER There are 266 students watching a play in the auditorium. There are 10 rows with 20 students in each row and 5 rows with 8 students in each row. How many students are sitting in each of the 2 remaining rows if each of those rows has an equal number of students?

Personal Math Trainer

9. THINK SMARTER + Ben is planting a garden with 36 zinnias, 18 marigolds, and 24 petunias. Each row will have only one type of plant. Ben says he can put 9 plants in each row. He listed the common factors of 36, 18 and 24 below to support his reasoning.

36: 1, 2, 3, 4, 6, 9, 12, 18, 36
18: 1, 2, 3, 6, 8, 9, 18
24: 1, 2, 3, 4, 6, 8, 9, 12, 24

Is he correct? Explain your answer. If his reasoning is incorrect, explain how he should have found the answer.

FOR MORE PRACTICE:
Standards Practice Book

Name ______________________________

Mid-Chapter Checkpoint

Vocabulary

Vocabulary
common factor
divisible
factor

Choose the best term from the box.

1. A number that is multiplied by another number to find a product is called a ______________. (p. 201)

2. A number is ______________ by another number if the quotient is a counting number and the remainder is zero. (p. 206)

Concepts and Skills

List all the factors from least to greatest. (4.OA.4)

3. 8 ______________

4. 14 ______________

Is 6 a factor of the number? Write *yes* or *no*. (4.OA.4)

5. 81 ______

6. 45 ______

7. 42 ______

8. 56 ______

List all the factor pairs in the table. (4.OA.4)

9.

Factors of 64	
___ × ___ = ___	___ , ___
___ × ___ = ___	___ , ___
___ × ___ = ___	___ , ___
___ × ___ = ___	___ , ___

10.

Factors of 44	
___ × ___ = ___	___ , ___
___ × ___ = ___	___ , ___
___ × ___ = ___	___ , ___

List the common factors of the numbers. (4.OA.4)

11. 9 and 18 ______________

12. 20 and 50 ______________

13. Sean places 28 tomato plants in rows. All rows contain the same number of plants. There are between 5 and 12 plants in each row. How many plants are in each row? (4.OA.4)

____

14. Ella bought some key chains and spent a total of $24. Each key chain cost the same whole-dollar amount. She bought between 7 and 11 key chains. How many key chains did Ella buy? (4.OA.4)

____

15. Sandy has 16 roses, 8 daisies, and 32 tulips. She wants to arrange all the flowers in bouquets. Each bouquet has the same number of flowers and the same type of flower. What is the greatest number of flowers that could be in a bouquet? (4.OA.4)

____

16. Amir arranged 9 photos on a bulletin board. He put the photos in rows. Each row contains the same number of photos. How many photos could be in each row? (4.OA.4)

____

Name ______________________________

Factors and Multiples

Essential Question How are factors and multiples related?

Operations and Algebraic Thinking—4.OA.4
MATHEMATICAL PRACTICES
MP.6, MP.7

Unlock the Problem

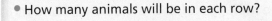

Toy animals are sold in sets of 3, 5, 10, and 12. Mason wants to make a display with 3 animals in each row. Which sets could he buy, if he wants to display all of the animals?

- How many animals will be in each row?
  ____
- How many animals are sold in each set?
  ____

The product of two numbers is a multiple of each number. Factors and multiples are related.

$$3 \times 4 = 12$$

↑ factor ↑ factor ↑ multiple of 3, multiple of 4

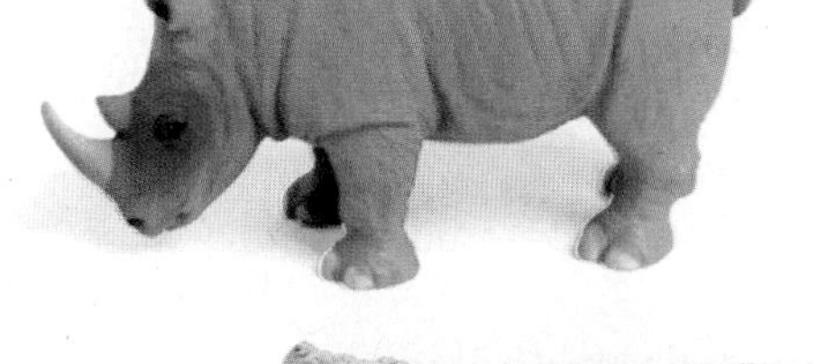

One Way Find factors.

Tell whether 3 is a factor of each number.

Think: If a number is divisible by 3, then 3 is a factor of the number.

Is 3 a factor of 3? ______________________________

Is 3 a factor of 5? ______________________________

Is 3 a factor of 10? ______________________________

Is 3 a factor of 12? ______________________________

3 is a factor of ______ and ______.

Another Way Find multiples.

Multiply and make a list. 3, ______, ______, ______, ______, . . .

3	______	______	______	______
1×3	2×3	3×3	4×3	5×3

______ and ______ are multiples of 3.

So, Mason could buy sets of ______ and ______ toy animals.

Math Talk Mathematical Practices

Explain how you can use what you know about factors to determine whether one number is a multiple of another number.

Common Multiples A **common multiple** is a multiple of two or more numbers.

Example Find common multiples.

Tony works every 3 days and Amanda works every 5 days. If Tony works June 3 and Amanda works June 5, on what days in June will they work together?

Circle multiples of 3. Draw a box around multiples of 5.

June						
Sun	Mon	Tue	Wed	Thu	Fri	Sat
	1	2	3	4	5	6
7	8	9	10	11	12	13
14	15	16	17	18	19	20
21	22	23	24	25	26	27
28	29	30				

Think: The common multiples have both a circle and a box.

The common multiples are _____ and _____.

So, Tony and Amanda will work together on June _____ and June _____.

Share and Show

Math Talk **Mathematical Practices**

How are the numbers 5 and 15 related? **Explain.**

1. Multiply to list the next five multiples of 4.

4, _____, _____, _____, _____, _____

1 × 4

Is the number a factor of 6? Write *yes* or *no*.

2. 3 _____

3. 6 _____

4. 16 _____

5. 18 _____

Is the number a multiple of 6? Write *yes* or *no*.

6. 3 _____

7. 6 _____

8. 16 _____

9. 18 _____

Name ___________________________

On Your Own

Is the number a multiple of 3? Write *yes* or *no.*

10. 4 ______

11. 8 ______

12. 24 ______

13. 38 ______

14. List the next nine multiples of each number. Find the common multiples.

Multiples of 2: 2, ______________________

Multiples of 8: 8, ______________________

Common multiples: ______________________

Generalize **Algebra** **Find the unknown number.**

15. 12, 24, 36, ______

16. 25, 50, 75, 100, ______

Tell whether 20 is a factor or multiple of the number.
Write *factor, multiple,* or *neither.*

17. 10 ______

18. 20 ______

19. 30 ______

THINK SMARTER **Write *true* or *false.* Explain.**

20. Every whole number is a multiple of 1.

____

____

21. Every whole number is a factor of 1.

____

____

22. THINK SMARTER Julio wears a blue shirt every 3 days. Larry wears a blue shirt every 4 days. On April 12, both Julio and Larry wore a blue shirt. What is the next date that they will both wear a blue shirt?

____

April

Sun	Mon	Tue	Wed	Thu	Fri	Sat
1	2	3	4	5	6	7
8	9	10	11	12	13	14
15	16	17	18	19	20	21
22	23	24	25	26	27	28
29	30					

Problem Solving • Applications

Complete the Venn diagram. Then use it to solve 23–25.

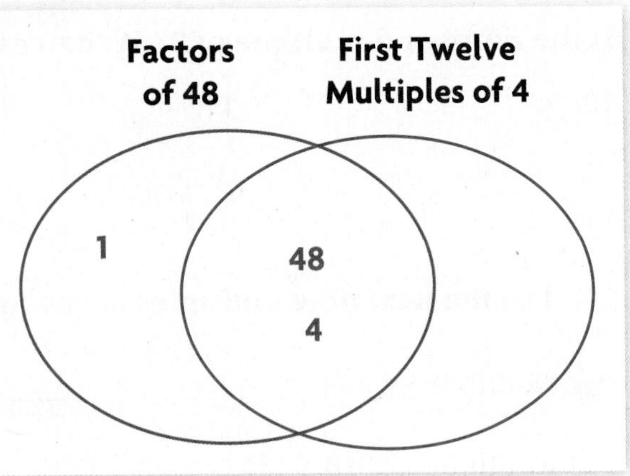

23. What multiples of 4 are not factors of 48?

____

24. What factors of 48 are multiples of 4?

____

25. GO DEEPER **Pose a Problem** Look back at Problem 24. Write a similar problem by changing the numbers. Then solve.

____

____

WRITE ▸Math
Show Your Work

26. Kia paid $10 for two charms. The price of each charm was a multiple of $2. What are the possible prices of the charms?

____

27. MATHEMATICAL PRACTICE 7 **Look for Structure** The answer is 9, 18, 27, 36, 45. What is the question?

____

28. WRITE ▸Math How do you know whether a number is a multiple of another number?

____

____

29. THINK SMARTER For numbers 29a–29e, select True or False for each statement.

29a. The number 45 is a multiple of 9. ○ True ○ False

29b. The number 4 is a multiple of 16. ○ True ○ False

29c. The number 28 is a multiple of 4. ○ True ○ False

29d. The number 4 is a factor of 28. ○ True ○ False

29e. The number 32 is a factor of 8. ○ True ○ False

FOR MORE PRACTICE:
Standards Practice Book

Name ____________________________

Prime and Composite Numbers

Essential Question How can you tell whether a number is prime or composite?

Operations and Algebraic Thinking—4.OA.4
MATHEMATICAL PRACTICES
MP.4, MP.6, MP.7

Unlock the Problem Real World

Students are arranging square tables to make one larger, rectangular table. The students want to have several ways to arrange the tables. Should they use 12 or 13 tables?

- What are the factors of 12?

____

Use a grid to show all the possible arrangements of 12 and 13 tables.

Draw all of the possible arrangements of 12 tables and 13 tables. Label each drawing with the factors modeled.

1×12

ERROR Alert

The same factors in a different order should be counted only once. For example, 3×4 and 4×3 are the same factor pair.

So, there are more ways to arrange ______ tables.

Math Talk Mathematical Practices

Explain how knowing whether 12 and 13 are prime or composite could have helped you solve the problem above.

- A **prime number** is a whole number greater than 1 that has exactly two factors, 1 and itself.
- A **composite number** is a whole number greater than 1 that has more than two factors.

Factors of 12: ______, ______, ______, ______, ______, ______

Factors of 13: ______, ______

12 is a __________ number, and 13 is a __________ number.

Divisibility You can use divisibility rules to help tell whether a number is prime or composite. If a number is divisible by any number other than 1 and itself, then the number is composite.

Tell whether 51 is *prime* or *composite*.

Is 51 divisible by 2?

____

Is 51 divisible by 3?

____

Think: 51 is divisible by a number other than 1 and 51.
51 has more than two factors.

So, 51 is ______________.

Math Idea

The number 1 is neither prime nor composite, since it has only one factor: 1.

Share and Show

MATH BOARD

1. Use the grid to model the factors of 18. Tell whether 18 is *prime* or *composite*.

Factors of 18: _____, _____, _____, _____, _____, _____

Think: 18 has more than two factors.

So, 18 is ______________.

Math Talk **Mathematical Practices**

Is the product of two prime numbers prime or composite? **Explain.**

Tell whether the number is *prime* or *composite*.

2. 11
Think: Does 11 have other factors besides 1 and itself?
____

3. 73
____

4. 69
____

5. 42
____

Name ______________________

On Your Own

Tell whether the number is *prime* or *composite*.

6. 18 ______

7. 49 ______

8. 29 ______

9. 64 ______

10. 33 ______

11. 89 ______

12. 52 ______

13. 76 ______

Write *true* or *false* for each statement. Explain or give an example to support your answer.

14. Only odd numbers are prime numbers.

______

______

15. THINK SMARTER A composite number cannot have three factors.

______

______

Problem Solving • Applications Real World

16. GO DEEPER I am a number between 60 and 100. My ones digit is two less than my tens digit. I am a prime number. What number am I?

______

17. Name a 2-digit odd number that is prime. Name a 2-digit odd number that is composite.

______

______

18. THINK SMARTER Choose the words that correctly complete the sentence.

The number 9 is [prime / composite] because it has [exactly / more than] two factors.

Connect to Social Studies

The Sieve of Eratosthenes

Eratosthenes was a Greek mathematician who lived more than 2,200 years ago. He invented a method of finding prime numbers, which is now called the Sieve of Eratosthenes.

19. Follow the steps below to circle all prime numbers less than 100. Then list the prime numbers.

STEP 1

Cross out 1, since 1 is not prime

STEP 2

Circle 2, since it is prime. Cross out all other multiples of 2.

STEP 3

Circle the next number that is not crossed out. This number is prime. Cross out all the multiples of this number.

STEP 4

Repeat Step 3 until every number is either circled or crossed out.

1	2	3	4	5	6	7	8	9	10
11	12	13	14	15	16	17	18	19	20
21	22	23	24	25	26	27	28	29	30
31	32	33	34	35	36	37	38	39	40
41	42	43	44	45	46	47	48	49	50
51	52	53	54	55	56	57	58	59	60
61	62	63	64	65	66	67	68	69	70
71	72	73	74	75	76	77	78	79	80
81	82	83	84	85	86	87	88	89	90
91	92	93	94	95	96	97	98	99	100

So, the prime numbers less than 100 are

____
____
____
____
____
____
____

20. MATHEMATICAL PRACTICE 6 **Explain** why the multiples of any number other than 1 are not prime numbers.

____

FOR MORE PRACTICE: Standards Practice Book

Name ______________________________

Number Patterns

Essential Question How can you make and describe patterns?

Operations and Algebraic Thinking—4.OA.5
MATHEMATICAL PRACTICES
MP.1, MP.4, MP.5, MP.7

Unlock the Problem (Real World)

Daryl is making a pattern for a quilt. The pattern shows 40 squares. Every fourth square is blue. How many blue squares are in the pattern?

- Underline what you are asked to find.
- Circle what you need to use.

A **pattern** is an ordered set of numbers or objects. Each number or object in the pattern is called a **term**.

Activity Find a pattern.

Materials ■ color pencils

Shade the squares that are blue.

1	2	3	4	5	6	7	8	9	10
11	12	13	14	15	16	17	18	19	20
21	22	23	24	25	26	27	28	29	30
31	32	33	34	35	36	37	38	39	40

Math Talk — Mathematical Practices
Describe another number pattern in Daryl's quilt.

Which squares are blue? ______________________

So, there are ______ blue squares in the pattern.

1. What patterns do you see in the arrangement of the blue squares?

____

____

2. What patterns do you see in the numbers of the blue squares?

____

____

Example Find and describe a pattern.

The rule for the pattern is *add* 5. The first term in the pattern is 5.

A **Use the rule to write the numbers in the pattern.**

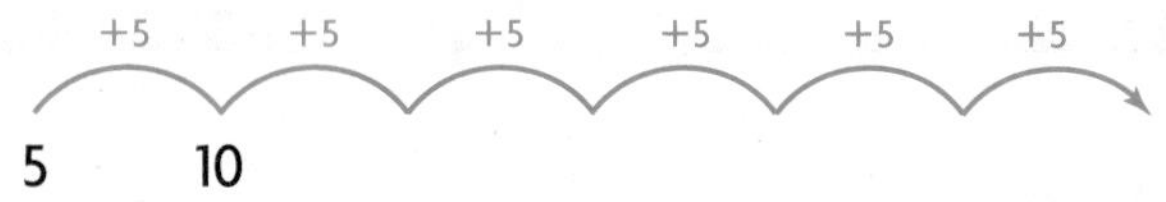

5 10 ____ ____ ____ ____ ____

5, 10, ______, ______, ______, ______, ______, ______, ______, ...

B **Describe other patterns in the numbers.**

What do you notice about the digits in the ones place?

____

____

Describe the pattern using the words *odd* and *even*.

____

____

Describe the pattern using the word *multiples*.

____

____

Try This! **Find and describe a pattern.**

The rule for the pattern is *add* 3, *subtract* 1. The first term in the pattern is 6.

Add 3. Subtract 1. Add 3.

6 ____ ____ ____ ____ ____ ____ ____ ____ ____

Describe another pattern in the numbers.

____

____

____

Name ______________________________

Share and Show

Use the rule to write the numbers in the pattern.

1. Rule: Subtract 10. First term: 100

Think Subtract 10

100 ____ ____ ____ ____

100, ______, ______, ______, ______, ...

Use the rule to write the numbers in the pattern. Describe another pattern in the numbers.

2. Rule: Multiply by 2. First term: 4

4, ______, ______, ______, ______, ...

____

3. Rule: Skip-count by 6. First term: 12

12, ______, ______, ______, ______, ...

____

Math Talk — **Mathematical Practices**

Explain how the first term in a pattern helps you find the next term.

On Your Own

Use the rule to write the first twelve numbers in the pattern. Describe another pattern in the numbers.

4. Rule: Add 7. First term: 3

____

____

5. Rule: Add 2, add 1. First term: 12

____

____

6. MATHEMATICAL PRACTICE 5 **Use Patterns** Marcie likes to collect stickers, but she also likes to give them away. Currently, Marcie has 87 stickers in her collection. If Marcie collects 5 new stickers each week and gives away 3 stickers each week, how many stickers will Marcie have in her collection after 5 weeks?

____

Problem Solving • Applications

7. THINK SMARTER John is saving for his trip to see the Alamo. He started With $24 in his savings account. Every week he earns $15 for baby sitting. Out of that, he spends $8 and saves the rest. John uses the rule *add 7* to find out how much money he has at the end of each week. What are the first 8 numbers in the pattern?

____

Personal Math Trainer

8. THINK SMARTER + Draw a check under the column that describes the number.

	Prime	Composite
81		
29		
31		
62		

Pose a Problem

9. GO DEEPER An activity at the Math Fair shows two charts.

Numbers
2
3
5
6
10

Operations
addition
subtraction
multiplication

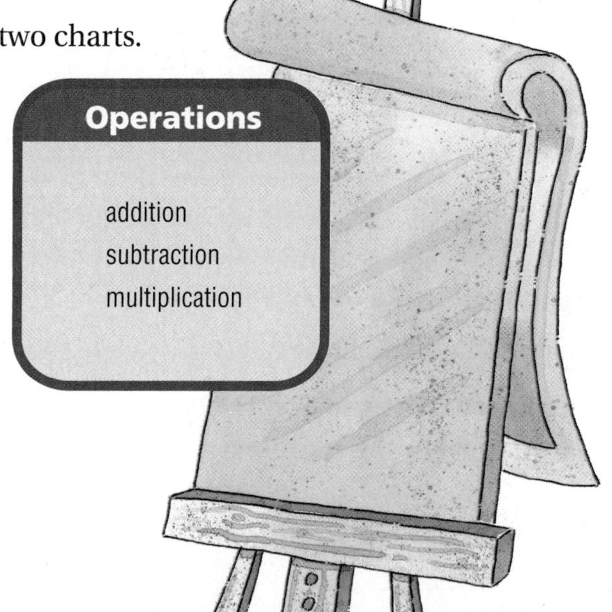

Use at least two of the numbers and an operation from the charts to write a pattern problem. Include the first five terms of your pattern in the solution to your problem.

Pose a problem.	Solve your problem.

- Describe other patterns in the terms you wrote.

____

FOR MORE PRACTICE:
Standards Practice Book

Name ____________________

Chapter 5 Review/Test

1. List all the factors of the number.

   14: ________

2. Select the numbers that have a factor of 5. Mark all that apply.

   (A) 15
   (B) 3
   (C) 45
   (D) 5
   (E) 50
   (F) 31

3. Jackson was making a poster for his room. He arranged 50 trading cards in the shape of a rectangle on the poster. For 3a–3e, choose Yes or No to tell whether a possible arrangement of cards is shown.

3a.	5 rows of 10 cards	○ Yes	○ No
3b.	7 rows of 8 cards	○ Yes	○ No
3c.	25 rows of 2 cards	○ Yes	○ No
3d.	50 rows of 1 card	○ Yes	○ No
3e.	45 rows of 5 cards	○ Yes	○ No

4. List all the factor pairs in the table.

Factors of 48	
____ × ____ = ____	____, ____
____ × ____ = ____	____, ____
____ × ____ = ____	____, ____
____ × ____ = ____	____, ____
____ × ____ = ____	____, ____

GO DIGITAL Assessment Options Chapter Test

5. Classify the numbers. Some numbers may belong in more than one box.

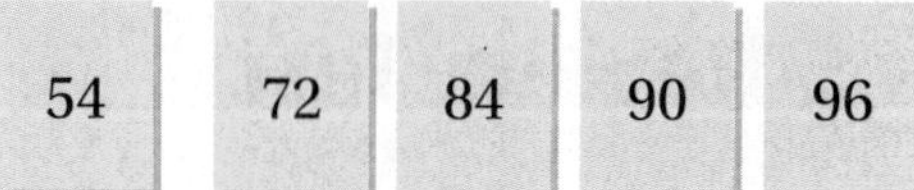

Divisible by 5 and 9	Divisible by 6 and 9	Divisible by 2 and 6

6. James works in a flower shop. He will put 36 tulips in vases for a wedding. He must use the same number of tulips in each vase. The number of tulips in each vase must be greater than 1 and less than 10. How many tulips could be in each vase?

_______________ tulips

7. Brady has a card collection with 64 basketball cards, 32 football cards, and 24 baseball cards. He wants to arrange the cards in equal piles, with only one type of card in each pile. How many cards can he put in each pile? Mark all that apply.

Ⓐ 1 Ⓑ 2 Ⓒ 3 Ⓓ 4 Ⓔ 8 Ⓕ 32

8. The Garden Club is designing a garden with 24 cosmos, 32 pansies, and 36 marigolds. Each row will have only one type of plant in each row. Ben says he can put 6 plants in each row. He listed the common factors of 24, 32, and 36 below to support his reasoning.

24: 1, 2, 3, 4, 6, 8, 12, 24

32: 1, 2, 4, 6, 9, 16, 32

36: 1, 2, 3, 4, 6, 8, 12, 18, 36

Is he correct? Explain your answer. If his reasoning is incorrect, explain how he should have found the answer.

Name ______________________________

9. The number of pieces of art at a museum is shown in the table.

Art	
Type of Art	**Number of Pieces**
Oil paintings	30
Photographs	24
Sketches	21

Part A

The museum is hosting a show for July that features the oil paintings by different artists. All artists show the same number of paintings and each will show more than 1 painting. How many artists could be featured in the show?

______________ artists

Part B

The museum wants to display all the art pieces in rows. Each row has the same number of pieces and the same type of pieces. How many pieces could be in each row? Explain how you found your answer.

10. Charles was skip counting at the Math Club meeting. He started to count by 8s. He said 8, 16, 24, 32, 40, and 48. What number will he say next?

____

11. Jill wrote the number 40. If her rule is *add 7*, what is the fourth number in Jill's pattern? How can you check your answer?

12. For numbers 12a–12e, select True or False for each statement.

12a.	The number 36 is a multiple of 9.	○ True	○ False
12b.	The number 3 is a multiple of 9.	○ True	○ False
12c.	The number 54 is a multiple of 9.	○ True	○ False
12d.	The number 3 is a factor of 9.	○ True	○ False
12e.	The number 27 is a factor of 9.	○ True	○ False

13. What multiple of 7 is also a factor of 7?

____

14. Manny makes dinner using 1 box of pasta and 1 jar of sauce. If pasta is sold in packages of 6 boxes and sauce is sold in packages of 3 jars, what is the least number of dinners that Manny can make without any supplies leftover?

__________ dinners

15. Serena has several packages of raisins. Each package contains 3 boxes of raisins. Which could be the number of boxes of raisins Serena has? Mark all that apply.

Ⓐ 9 Ⓑ 18 Ⓒ 23 Ⓓ 27 Ⓔ 32

16. Choose the words that make the sentence true.

The number 7 is [prime / composite] because it has [exactly / more than] two factors.

Name ____________________

17. Winnie wrote the following riddle: I am a number between 60 and 100. My ones digit is two less than my tens digit. I am a prime number.

Part A

What number does Winnie's riddle describe? Explain.

Part B

Winnie's friend Marco guessed that her riddle was about the number 79. Why can't 79 be the answer to Winnie's riddle? Explain.

18. Classify the numbers as prime or composite.

Prime	Composite

37 65 71 82

19. Erica knits 18 squares on Monday. She knits 7 more squares each day from Tuesday through Thursday. How many squares does Erica knit on Friday?

________ squares

20. Use the rule to write the first five terms of the pattern.

Rule: Add 10, subtract 5 First term: 11

____

21. Elina had 10 tiles to arrange in a rectangular design. She drew a model of the rectangles she could make with the ten tiles.

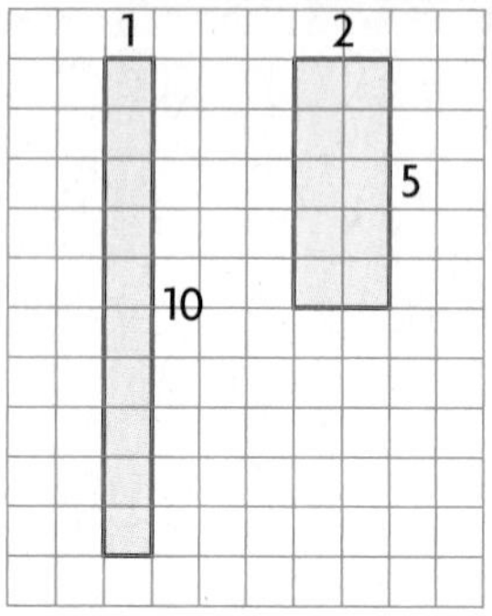

Part A

How does Elina's drawing show that the number 10 is a composite number?

Part B

Suppose Elina used 15 tiles to make the rectangular design. How many different rectangles could she make with the 15 tiles? Write a list or draw a picture to show the number and dimensions of the rectangles she could make.

Part C

Elina's friend Luke said that he could make more rectangles with 24 tiles than with Elina's 10 tiles. Do you agree with Luke? Explain.

Critical Area

Fractions and Decimals

CRITICAL AREA Developing an understanding of fraction equivalence, addition and subtraction of fractions with like denominators, and multiplication of fractions by whole numbers

A *luthier,* or guitar maker, at his workshop

Project

Building Custom Guitars

Do you play the guitar, or would you like to learn how to play one? The guitar size you need depends on your height to the nearest inch and on *scale length*. Scale length is the distance from the *bridge* of the guitar to the *nut*.

Get Started

Order the guitar sizes from the least size to the greatest size, and complete the table.

Important Facts

Guitar Sizes for Students

Age of Player	Height of Player (to nearest inch)	Scale Length (shortest to longest, in inches)	Size of Guitar
4–6	3 feet 3 inches to 3 feet 9 inches	19	
6–8	3 feet 10 inches to 4 feet 5 inches	20.5	
8–11	4 feet 6 inches to 4 feet 11 inches	22.75	
11–Adult	5 feet or taller	25.5	

Size of Guitar: $\frac{1}{2}$ size, $\frac{4}{4}$ size, $\frac{1}{4}$ size, $\frac{3}{4}$ size

Adults play $\frac{4}{4}$-size guitars. You can see that guitars also come in $\frac{3}{4}$, $\frac{1}{2}$, and $\frac{1}{4}$ sizes. Figure out which size guitar you would need according to your height and the scale length for each size guitar. Use the Important Facts to decide. **Explain** your thinking.

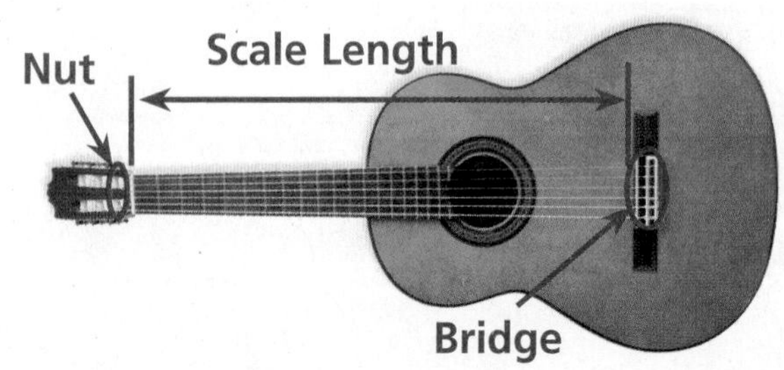

____

____

Completed by ______________________________

Chapter 6

Fraction Equivalence and Comparison

Show What You Know

Check your understanding of important skills.

Name ____________________

▶ **Part of a Whole** **Write a fraction for the shaded part.**

1. ______

2. ______

3. ______

▶ **Name the Shaded Part** **Write a fraction for the shaded part.**

4. 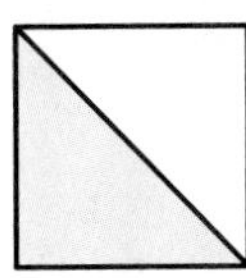 ______

5. 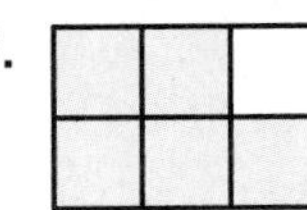 ______

6. 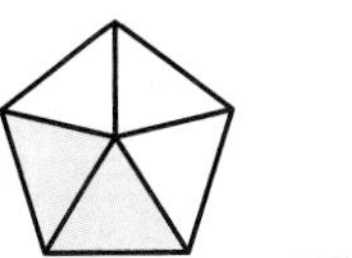 ______

▶ **Compare Parts of a Whole** **Color the fraction strips to show the fractions. Circle the greater fraction.**

7. $\frac{1}{2}$

$\frac{1}{3}$

8. $\frac{1}{5}$

$\frac{1}{3}$

Math Detective

Earth's surface is covered by more than 57 million square miles of land. The table shows about how much of Earth's land surface each continent covers. Be a Math Detective. Which continent covers the greatest part of Earth's land surface?

Continent	Part of Land Surface
Asia	$\frac{3}{10}$
Africa	$\frac{1}{5}$
Antarctica	$\frac{9}{100}$
Australia	$\frac{6}{100}$
Europe	$\frac{7}{100}$
North America	$\frac{1}{6}$
South America	$\frac{1}{8}$

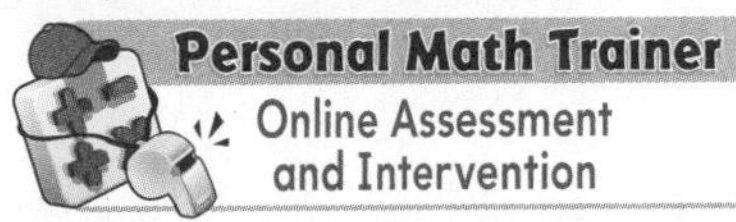

Vocabulary Builder

▶ Visualize It

Complete the flow map by using the words with a ✓.

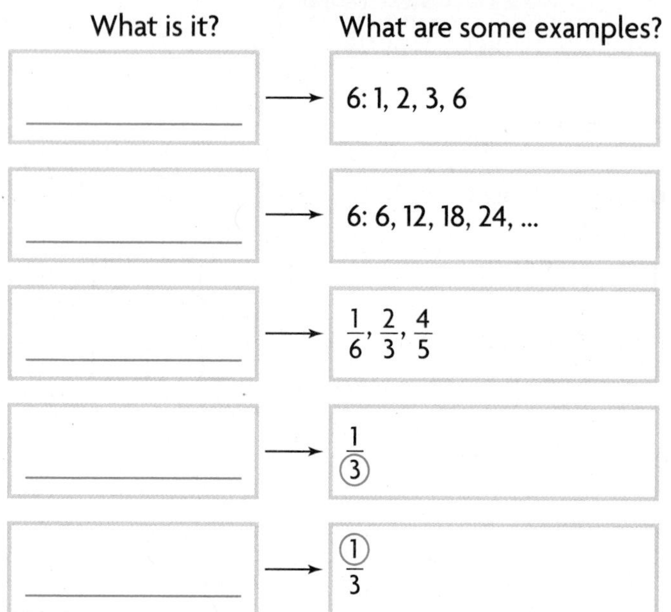

Review Words

- common multiple
- ✓ denominator
- ✓ factor
- ✓ fraction
- ✓ multiple
- ✓ numerator

Preview Words

- benchmark
- common denominator
- equivalent fractions
- simplest form

▶ Understand Vocabulary

Complete the sentences by using preview words.

1. A fraction is in ______________________ if the numerator and denominator have only 1 as a common factor.

2. ______________________ name the same amount.

3. A ______________________ is a common multiple of two or more denominators.

4. A ______________________ is a known size or amount that helps you understand a different size or amount.

GO DIGITAL • Interactive Student Edition • Multimedia eGlossary

Name ______________________

Equivalent Fractions

Essential Question How can you use models to show equivalent fractions?

MATHEMATICAL PRACTICES
MP.2, MP.4, MP.7

Investigate

Hands On

Materials ■ color pencils

Joe cut a pan of lasagna into third-size pieces. He kept $\frac{1}{3}$ and gave the rest away. Joe will not eat his part all at once. How can he cut his part into smaller, equal-size pieces?

A. Draw on the model to show how Joe could cut his part of the lasagna into 2 equal pieces.

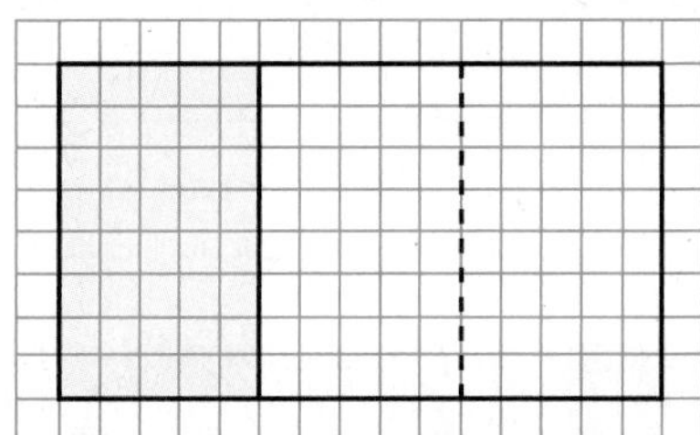

You can rename these 2 equal pieces as a fraction of the original pan of lasagna.

Suppose Joe had cut the original pan of lasagna into equal pieces of this size.

How many pieces would there be? ______

What fraction of the pan is 1 piece? ______

What fraction of the pan is 2 pieces? ______

You can rename $\frac{1}{3}$ as ______.

B. Now draw on the model to show how Joe could cut his part of the lasagna into 4 equal pieces.

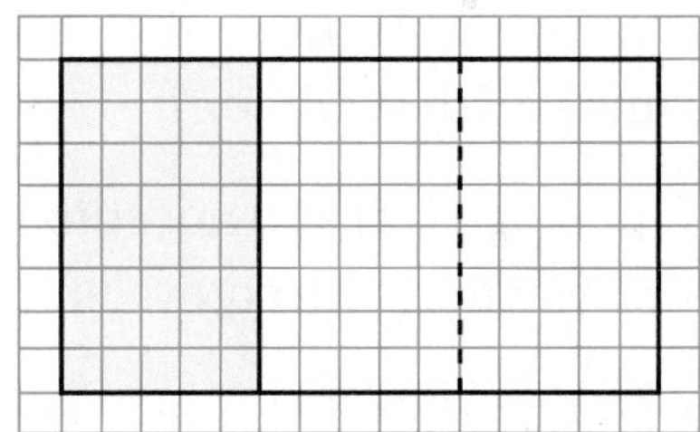

You can rename these 4 equal pieces as a fraction of the original pan of lasagna.

Suppose Joe had cut the original pan of lasagna into equal pieces of this size.

How many pieces would there be? ______

What fraction of the pan is 1 piece? ______

What fraction of the pan is 4 pieces? ______

You can rename $\frac{1}{3}$ as ______.

C. Fractions that name the same amount are **equivalent fractions**. Write the equivalent fractions.

$\frac{1}{3} = \frac{\square}{\square} = \frac{\square}{\square}$

Draw Conclusions

1. Compare the models for $\frac{1}{3}$ and $\frac{2}{6}$. How does the number of parts relate to the sizes of the parts?

2. Describe how the numerators are related and how the denominators are related in $\frac{1}{3} = \frac{2}{6}$.

3. THINK SMARTER Does $\frac{1}{3} = \frac{3}{9}$? Explain.

Make Connections

Savannah has $\frac{2}{4}$ yard of ribbon, and Isabel has $\frac{3}{8}$ yard of ribbon. How can you determine whether Savannah and Isabel have the same length of ribbon?

The equal sign (=) and not equal to sign (≠) show whether fractions are equivalent.

Tell whether $\frac{2}{4}$ and $\frac{3}{8}$ are equivalent. Write = or ≠.

STEP 1 Shade the amount of ribbon Savannah has.

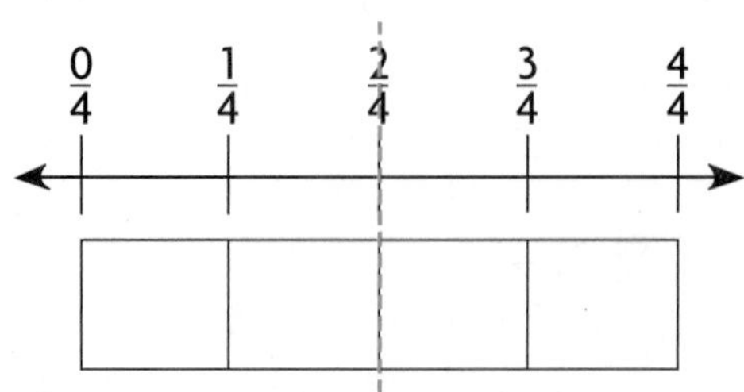

STEP 2 Shade the amount of ribbon Isabel has.

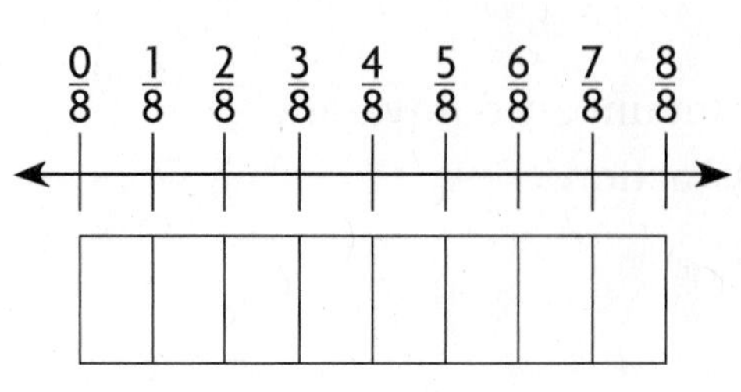

Think: $\frac{2}{4}$ yard is not the same amount as $\frac{3}{8}$ yard.

So, $\frac{2}{4}$ ◯ $\frac{3}{8}$.

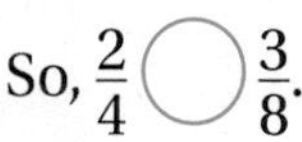

Math Talk — Mathematical Practices

How could you use a model to show that $\frac{4}{8} = \frac{1}{2}$?

Name ________________________________

Share and Show

Use the model to write an equivalent fraction.

1. 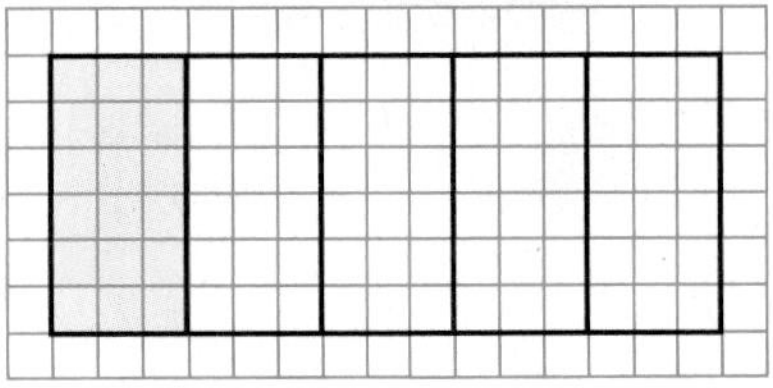 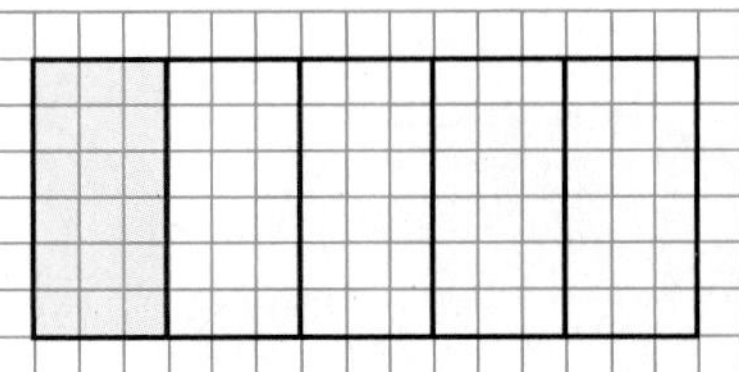

$\frac{1}{5}$ = ______

✓ 2. 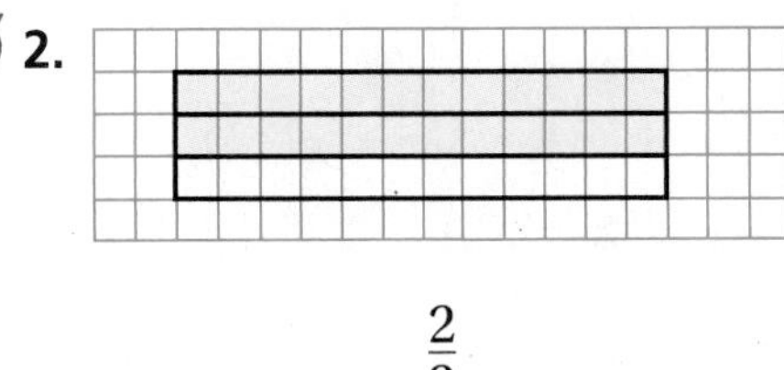 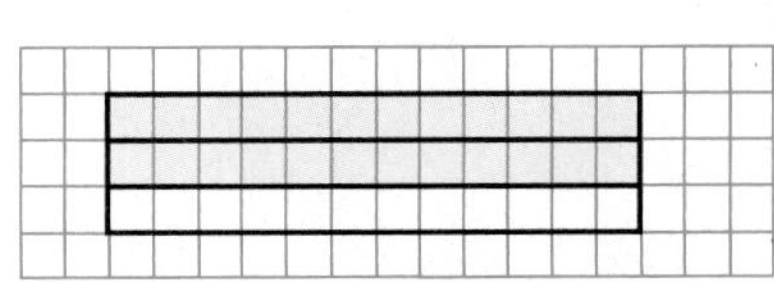

$\frac{2}{3}$ = ______

Tell whether the fractions are equivalent. Write = or ≠.

3. $\frac{1}{6}$ ◯ $\frac{2}{12}$

4. $\frac{2}{5}$ ◯ $\frac{6}{10}$

5. $\frac{4}{12}$ ◯ $\frac{1}{3}$

✓ 6. $\frac{5}{8}$ ◯ $\frac{2}{4}$

7. $\frac{5}{6}$ ◯ $\frac{10}{12}$

8. $\frac{1}{2}$ ◯ $\frac{5}{10}$

Problem Solving • Applications

9. GO DEEPER Manny used 8 tenth-size parts to model $\frac{8}{10}$. Ana used fewer parts to model an equivalent fraction. How does the size of a part in Ana's model compare to the size of a tenth-size part? What size part did Ana use?

____

____

____

____

10. MATHEMATICAL PRACTICE 5 **Use a Concrete Model** How many eighth-size parts do you need to model $\frac{3}{4}$? Explain.

____

____

____

____

____

What's the Error?

11. THINK SMARTER Ben brought two pizzas to a party. He says that since $\frac{1}{4}$ of each pizza is left, the same amount of each pizza is left. What is his error?

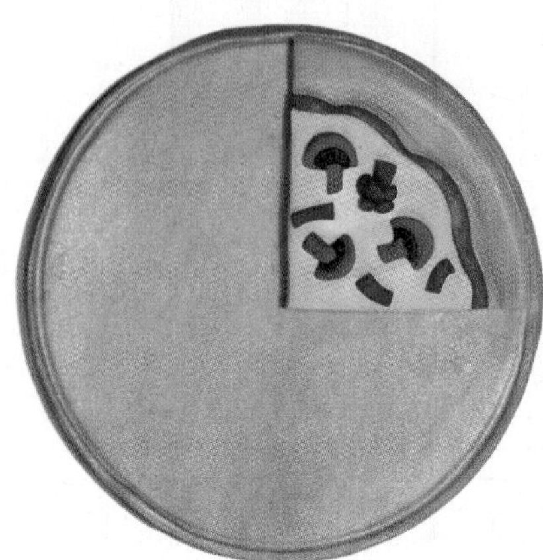

Describe Ben's error.

Draw models of 2 pizzas with a different number of equal pieces. Use shading to show $\frac{1}{4}$ of each pizza.

12. THINK SMARTER For numbers 12a–12d, tell whether the fractions are equivalent by selecting the correct symbol.

12a. $\frac{3}{15}$ [= / ≠] $\frac{1}{6}$

12b. $\frac{3}{4}$ [= / ≠] $\frac{16}{20}$

12c. $\frac{2}{3}$ [= / ≠] $\frac{8}{12}$

12d. $\frac{8}{10}$ [= / ≠] $\frac{4}{5}$

FOR MORE PRACTICE:
Standards Practice Book

Name ______________________________

Generate Equivalent Fractions

Essential Question How can you use multiplication to find equivalent fractions?

Number and Operations—Fractions—4.NF.1

MATHEMATICAL PRACTICES
MP.4, MP.7, MP.8

Unlock the Problem — Real World

Sara needs $\frac{3}{4}$ cup of dish soap to make homemade bubble solution. Her measuring cup is divided into eighths. What fraction of the measuring cup should Sara fill with dish soap?

- Is an eighth-size part of a measuring cup bigger or smaller than a fourth-size part?

____

Find how many eighths are in $\frac{3}{4}$.

STEP 1 Compare fourths and eighths.

Shade to model $\frac{1}{4}$.
Use fourth-size parts.

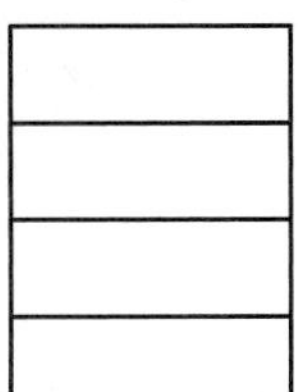

1 part

Shade to model $\frac{1}{4}$.
Use eighth-size parts.

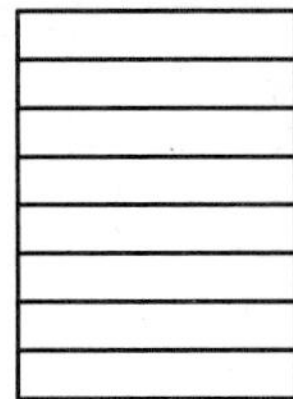

2 parts

You need ______ eighth-size parts to make 1 fourth-size part.

STEP 2 Find how many eighths you need to make 3 fourths.

Shade to model $\frac{3}{4}$.
Use fourth-size parts.

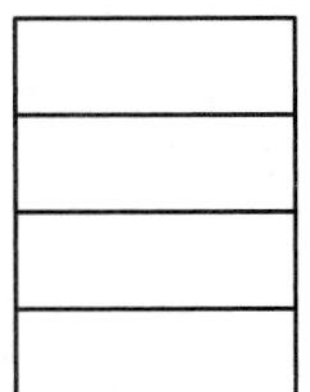

3 parts

Shade to model $\frac{3}{4}$.
Use eighth-size parts.

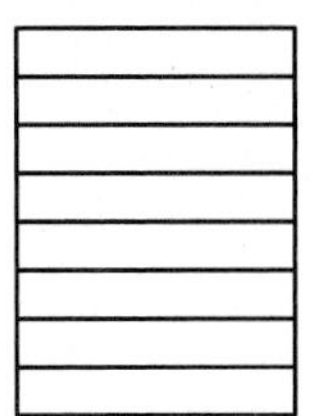

6 parts

You needed 2 eighth-size parts to make 1 fourth-size part.

So, you need ______ eighth-size parts to make 3 fourth-size parts.

So, Sara should fill $\frac{\square}{8}$ of the measuring cup with dish soap.

Mathematical Practices

How did you know how many eighth-size parts you needed to make 1 fourth-size part? **Explain.**

1. Explain why 6 eighth-size parts is the same amount as 3 fourth-size parts.

____

Example Write four fractions that are equivalent to $\frac{1}{2}$.

MODEL	WRITE EQUIVALENT FRACTIONS	RELATE EQUIVALENT FRACTIONS
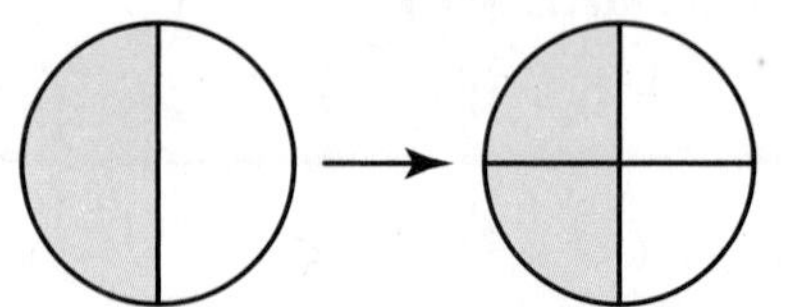	$\frac{1}{2} = \frac{2}{4}$	$\frac{1 \times 2}{2 \times 2} = \frac{2}{4}$
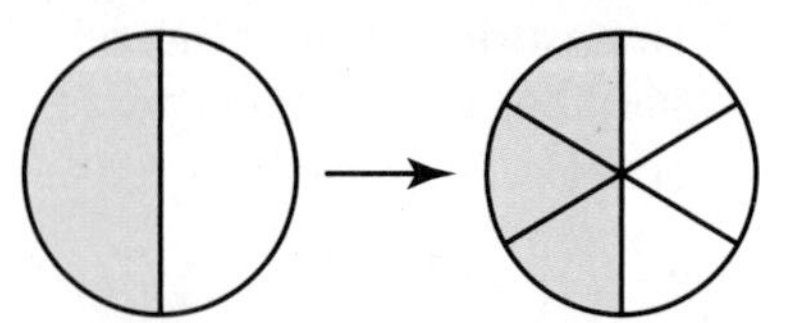	$\frac{1}{2} = \frac{\square}{6}$	$\frac{1 \times \square}{2 \times 3} = \frac{\square}{6}$
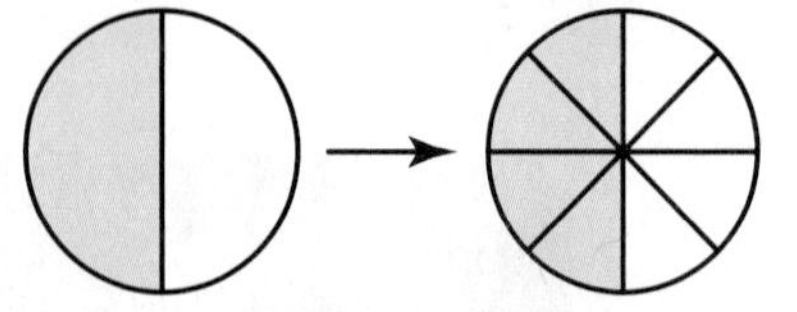	$\frac{1}{2} = \frac{\square}{\square}$	$\frac{1 \times \square}{2 \times \square} = \frac{\square}{\square}$
	$\frac{1}{2} = \frac{\square}{\square}$	$\frac{1 \times \square}{2 \times \square} = \frac{\square}{\square}$

So, $\frac{1}{2} = \frac{2}{4} = \frac{\square}{6} = \frac{\square}{\square} = \frac{\square}{\square}$.

2. Look at the model that shows $\frac{1}{2} = \frac{3}{6}$. How does the number of parts in the whole affect the number of parts that are shaded? Explain.

3. Explain how you can use multiplication to write a fraction that is equivalent to $\frac{3}{5}$.

4. Are $\frac{2}{3}$ and $\frac{6}{8}$ equivalent? Explain.

Name ____________________

Share and Show

1. Complete the table below.

MODEL	WRITE EQUIVALENT FRACTIONS	RELATE EQUIVALENT FRACTIONS
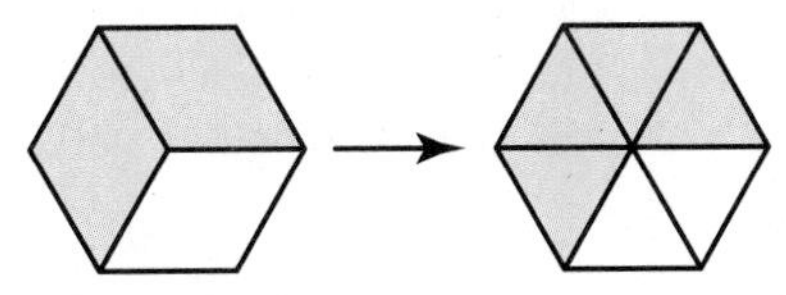	$\frac{2}{3} = \frac{4}{6}$	$\frac{2 \times \square}{3 \times \square} = \frac{\square}{\square}$
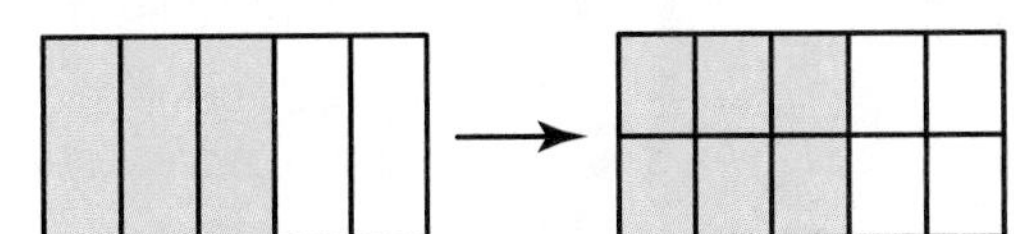	$\frac{3}{5} = \frac{6}{10}$	$\frac{3 \times \square}{5 \times \square} = \frac{\square}{\square}$
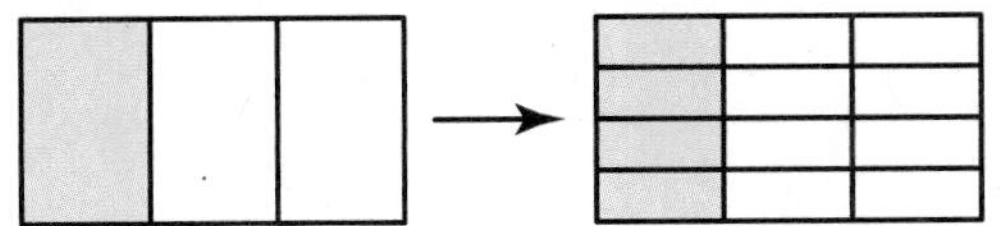	$\frac{1}{3} = \frac{4}{12}$	$\frac{1 \times \square}{3 \times \square} = \frac{\square}{\square}$

Math Talk — **Mathematical Practices**

Can you multiply the numerator and denominator of a fraction by 0? **Explain.**

Write two equivalent fractions.

2. $\frac{4}{5}$

$\frac{4}{5} = \frac{4 \times \square}{5 \times \square} = \frac{\square}{\square}$

$\frac{4}{5} = \frac{4 \times \square}{5 \times \square} = \frac{\square}{\square}$

$\frac{4}{5} = \frac{\square}{\square} = \frac{\square}{\square}$

3. $\frac{2}{4}$

$\frac{2}{4} = \frac{2 \times \square}{4 \times \square} = \frac{\square}{\square}$

$\frac{2}{4} = \frac{2 \times \square}{4 \times \square} = \frac{\square}{\square}$

$\frac{2}{4} = \frac{\square}{\square} = \frac{\square}{\square}$

On Your Own

Write two equivalent fractions.

4. $\frac{3}{6}$

$\frac{3}{6} = \frac{\square}{\square} = \frac{\square}{\square}$

5. $\frac{3}{10}$

$\frac{3}{10} = \frac{\square}{\square} = \frac{\square}{\square}$

6. $\frac{2}{5}$

$\frac{2}{5} = \frac{\square}{\square} = \frac{\square}{\square}$

Tell whether the fractions are equivalent. Write $=$ or $\neq$.

7. $\frac{5}{6} \bigcirc \frac{10}{18}$

8. $\frac{4}{5} \bigcirc \frac{8}{10}$

9. $\frac{1}{5} \bigcirc \frac{4}{10}$

10. $\frac{1}{4} \bigcirc \frac{2}{8}$

Problem Solving • Applications Real World

Use the recipe for 11–12.

Face Paint Recipe

$\frac{2}{8}$ cup cornstarch
1 tablespoon flour
$\frac{9}{12}$ cup light corn syrup
$\frac{1}{4}$ cup water
$\frac{1}{2}$ teaspoon food coloring

11. THINK SMARTER Kim says the amount of flour in the recipe can be expressed as a fraction. Is she correct? Explain.

____

____

____

12. GO DEEPER How could you use a $\frac{1}{8}$-cup measuring cup to measure the light corn syrup?

____

____

13. MATHEMATICAL PRACTICE 5 **Communicate** Explain using words how you know a fraction is equivalent to another fraction.

____

____

____

____

WRITE ▸ Math
Show Your Work

14. THINK SMARTER Kyle drank $\frac{2}{3}$ cup of apple juice. Fill in each box with a number from the list to generate equivalent fractions for $\frac{2}{3}$. Not all numbers will be used.

$\frac{2}{3} = \frac{\square}{6} = \frac{12}{\square} = \frac{\square}{\square}$

2	4	6	8
12	15	16	18

FOR MORE PRACTICE: Standards Practice Book

Name ______________________________

Simplest Form

Essential Question How can you write a fraction as an equivalent fraction in simplest form?

Number and Operations—Fractions—4.NF.1

MATHEMATICAL PRACTICES
MP.2, MP.4, MP.6

Unlock the Problem (Real World)

Vicki made a fruit tart and cut it into 6 equal pieces. Vicki, Silvia, and Elena each took 2 pieces of the tart home. Vicki says she and each of her friends took $\frac{1}{3}$ of the tart home. Is Vicki correct?

- Into how many pieces was the tart cut?

____

- How many pieces did each girl take?

____

Activity

Materials ■ color pencils

STEP 1 Use a blue pencil to shade the pieces Vicki took home.

STEP 2 Use a red pencil to shade the pieces Silvia took home.

STEP 3 Use a yellow pencil to shade the pieces Elena took home.

The tart is divided into ______ equal-size pieces. The 3 colors on the model show how to combine sixth-size pieces to make

______ equal third-size pieces.

So, Vicki is correct. Vicki, Silvia, and Elena each took $\frac{\square}{\square}$ of the tart home.

Math Talk **Mathematical Practices**

Compare the models for $\frac{2}{6}$ and $\frac{1}{3}$. **Explain** how the sizes of the parts are related.

- What if Vicki took 3 pieces of the tart home and Elena took 3 pieces of the tart home. How could you combine the pieces to write a fraction that represents the part each friend took home? Explain.

____

____

____

Simplest Form A fraction is in **simplest form** when you can represent it using as few equal parts of a whole as possible. You need to describe the part you have in equal-size parts. If you can't describe the part you have using fewer parts, then you cannot simplify the fraction.

One Way Use models to write an equivalent fraction in simplest form.

MODEL	WRITE EQUIVALENT FRACTIONS	RELATE EQUIVALENT FRACTIONS
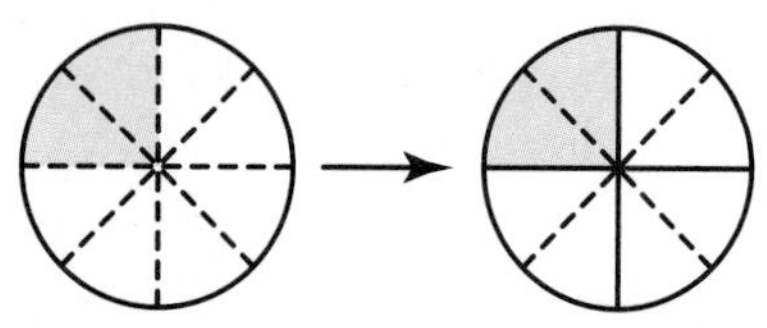	$\frac{2}{8} = \frac{1}{4}$	$\frac{2 \div 2}{8 \div 2} = \frac{1}{4}$
	$\frac{6}{10} = \frac{\square}{5}$	$\frac{6 \div \square}{10 \div \square} = \frac{\square}{5}$
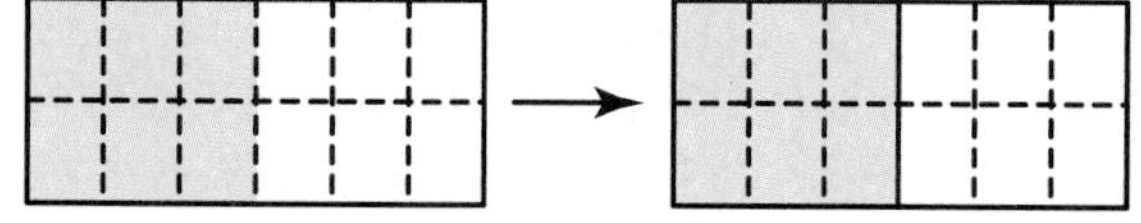	$\frac{6}{12} = \frac{\square}{\square}$	$\frac{6 \div \square}{12 \div \square} = \frac{\square}{\square}$

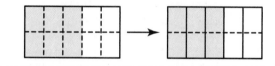

To simplify $\frac{6}{10}$, you can combine tenth-size parts into equal groups with 2 parts each.

So, $\frac{6}{10} = \frac{6 \div \square}{10 \div \square} = \frac{\square}{\square}$.

Another Way Use common factors to write $\frac{6}{10}$ in simplest form.

A fraction is in simplest form when 1 is the only factor that the numerator and denominator have in common. The parts of the whole cannot be combined into fewer equal-size parts to show the same fraction.

STEP 1 List the factors of the numerator and denominator. Circle common factors.	Factors of 6: ____, ____, ____, ____ Factors of 10: ____, ____, ____, ____
STEP 2 Divide the numerator and denominator by a common factor greater than 1.	$\frac{6}{10} = \frac{6 \div \square}{10 \div \square} = \frac{\square}{\square}$

Since 1 is the only factor that 3 and 5 have in common, ______ is written in simplest form.

Name ____________________

Share and Show

1. Write $\frac{8}{10}$ in simplest form.

$$\frac{8}{10} = \frac{8 \div \square}{10 \div \square} = \frac{\square}{\square}$$

Write the fraction in simplest form.

2. $\frac{6}{12}$ ______

3. $\frac{2}{10}$ ______

4. $\frac{6}{8}$ ______

5. $\frac{4}{6}$ ______

Math Talk — **Mathematical Practices**

Explain how you know a fraction is in simplest form.

On Your Own

Write the fraction in simplest form.

6. $\frac{9}{12}$ ______

7. $\frac{4}{8}$ ______

8. $\frac{10}{12}$ ______

9. $\frac{20}{100}$ ______

Tell whether the fraction is in simplest form. Write *yes* or *no*.

10. $\frac{2}{8}$ ______

11. $\frac{9}{12}$ ______

12. $\frac{5}{6}$ ______

13. $\frac{4}{10}$ ______

Tell whether the fractions are equivalent. Write = or ≠. Use simplest form to help.

14. $\frac{3}{6} \bigcirc \frac{5}{10}$

15. $\frac{9}{12} \bigcirc \frac{1}{3}$

16. $\frac{3}{12} \bigcirc \frac{2}{4}$

17. $\frac{6}{8} \bigcirc \frac{9}{12}$

Problem Solving • Applications 

Use the map for 18–19.

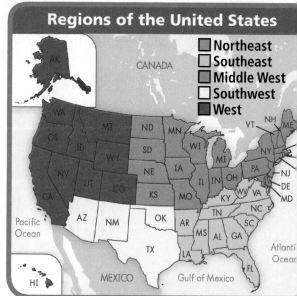

Regions of the United States

Northeast
Southeast
Middle West
Southwest
West

18. MATHEMATICAL PRACTICE 7 **Identify Relationships** What fraction of the states in the southwest region share a border with Mexico? Is this fraction in simplest form?

____

19. THINK SMARTER **What's the Question?** $\frac{1}{3}$ of the states in this region are on the Gulf of Mexico.

____

____

____

WRITE ▸Math
Show Your Work

20. GO DEEPER Pete says that to write $\frac{4}{6}$ as $\frac{2}{3}$, you combine pieces, but to write $\frac{4}{6}$ as $\frac{8}{12}$, you break apart pieces. Does this make sense? Explain.

____

____

____

Personal Math Trainer

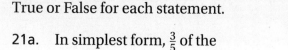

21. THINK SMARTER + In Michelle's homeroom, $\frac{9}{15}$ of the students ride the bus to school, $\frac{4}{12}$ get a car ride, and $\frac{2}{30}$ walk to school. For numbers 21a–21c, select True or False for each statement.

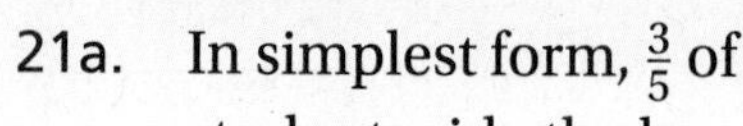

21a. In simplest form, $\frac{3}{5}$ of the students ride the bus to school. ○ True ○ False

21b. In simplest form, $\frac{1}{4}$ of the students get a car ride to school. ○ True ○ False

21c. In simplest form, $\frac{1}{15}$ of the students walk to school. ○ True ○ False

FOR MORE PRACTICE: Standards Practice Book

Name ____________________

Common Denominators

Essential Question How can you write a pair of fractions as fractions with a common denominator?

Number and Operations—Fractions—4.NF.1

MATHEMATICAL PRACTICES
MP.2, MP.4, MP.6

Unlock the Problem

Hands On

Martin has two rectangles that are the same size. One rectangle is cut into $\frac{1}{2}$-size parts. The other rectangle is cut into $\frac{1}{3}$-size parts. He wants to cut the rectangles so they have the same size parts. How can he cut each rectangle?

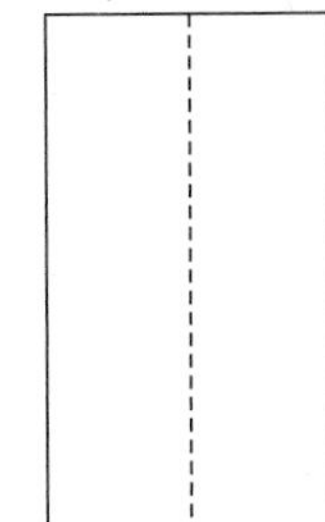

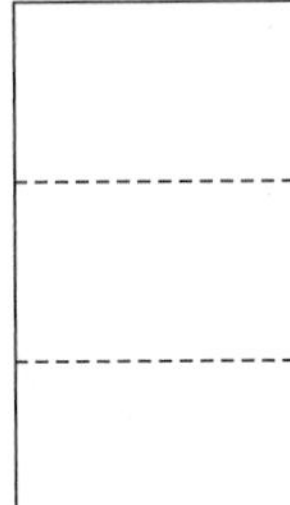

A **common denominator** is a common multiple of the denominators of two or more fractions. Fractions with common denominators represent wholes cut into the same number of parts.

Activity Use paper folding and shading.

Materials ■ 2 sheets of paper

Find a common denominator for $\frac{1}{2}$ and $\frac{1}{3}$.

STEP 1

Model the rectangle cut into $\frac{1}{2}$-size parts. Fold one sheet of paper in half. Draw a line on the fold.

STEP 2

Model the rectangle cut into $\frac{1}{3}$-size parts. Fold the other sheet of paper into thirds. Draw lines on the folds.

STEP 3

Fold each sheet of paper so that both sheets have the same number of parts. Draw lines on the folds. How many equal parts does each sheet of paper have? __________

STEP 4

Draw a picture of your sheets of paper to show how many parts each rectangle could have.

So, each rectangle could be cut into ______ parts.

Math Talk — **Mathematical Practices**

Does Martin need to cut each rectangle the same number of times? **Explain.**

Example Write $\frac{4}{5}$ and $\frac{1}{2}$ as a pair of fractions with common denominators.

You can use common multiples to find a common denominator. List multiples of each denominator. A common multiple can be used as a common denominator.

STEP 1 List multiples of 5 and 2. Circle common multiples.

5: 5, 10, ____, ____, ____, ____

2: ____, ____, ____, ____, ____, ____

STEP 2 Write equivalent fractions.

$$\frac{4}{5} = \frac{4 \times \square}{5 \times \square} = \frac{\square}{10}$$

$$\frac{1}{2} = \frac{1 \times \square}{2 \times \square} = \frac{\square}{10}$$

Choose a denominator that is a common multiple of 5 and 2.

You can write $\frac{4}{5}$ and $\frac{1}{2}$ as ____ and ____.

ERROR Alert

Remember that when you multiply the denominator by a factor, you must multiply the numerator by the same factor to write an equivalent fraction.

1. Are $\frac{4}{5}$ and $\frac{1}{2}$ equivalent? Explain.

2. Describe another way you could tell whether $\frac{4}{5}$ and $\frac{1}{2}$ are equivalent.

Share and Show

1. Find a common denominator for $\frac{1}{3}$ and $\frac{1}{12}$ by dividing each whole into the same number of equal parts. Use the models to help.

common denominator: ____

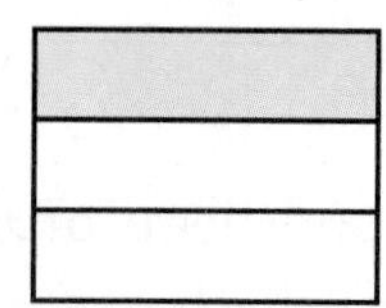

$\frac{1}{3}$

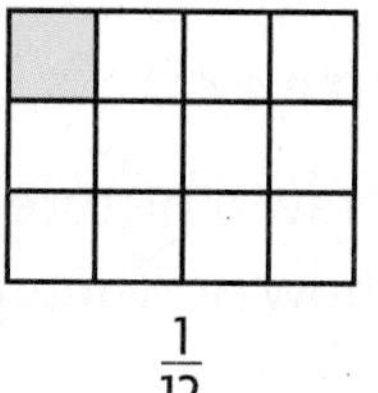

$\frac{1}{12}$

Name ________________________________

Write the pair of fractions as a pair of fractions with a common denominator.

2. $\frac{1}{2}$ and $\frac{1}{4}$

____

3. $\frac{3}{4}$ and $\frac{5}{8}$

____

4. $\frac{1}{3}$ and $\frac{1}{4}$

____

5. $\frac{4}{12}$ and $\frac{5}{8}$

____

Math Talk — Mathematical Practices

Explain how using a model or listing multiples helps you find a common denominator.

On Your Own

Write the pair of fractions as a pair of fractions with a common denominator.

6. $\frac{1}{4}$ and $\frac{5}{6}$

____

7. $\frac{3}{5}$ and $\frac{4}{10}$

____

Tell whether the fractions are equivalent. Write = or ≠.

8. $\frac{3}{4}$ ◯ $\frac{1}{2}$

9. $\frac{3}{4}$ ◯ $\frac{6}{8}$

10. $\frac{1}{2}$ ◯ $\frac{4}{8}$

11. $\frac{6}{8}$ ◯ $\frac{4}{8}$

12. $\frac{1}{3}$ ◯ $\frac{2}{6}$

13. $\frac{1}{3}$ ◯ $\frac{4}{12}$

14. $\frac{2}{6}$ ◯ $\frac{4}{12}$

15. $\frac{4}{12}$ ◯ $\frac{4}{12}$

Problem Solving • Applications Real World

16. GO DEEPER Carrie has a red streamer that is $\frac{3}{4}$ yard long and a blue streamer that is $\frac{5}{6}$ yard long. She says the streamers are the same length. Does this make sense? Explain.

17. THINK SMARTER Leah has two same-size rectangles divided into the same number of equal parts. One rectangle has $\frac{1}{3}$ of the parts shaded, and the other has $\frac{2}{5}$ of the parts shaded. What is the least number of parts into which both rectangles could be divided?

Math on the Spot

18. MATHEMATICAL PRACTICE 6 Julian says a common denominator for $\frac{3}{4}$ and $\frac{2}{5}$ is 9. What is Julian's error? **Explain.**

WRITE ▸Math
Show Your Work

Personal Math Trainer

19. THINK SMARTER + Miguel has two same-size rectangles divided into the same number of equal parts. One rectangle has $\frac{2}{3}$ of the parts shaded, and the other has $\frac{3}{5}$ of the parts shaded.

Into how many parts could each rectangle be divided? Show your work by sketching the rectangles.

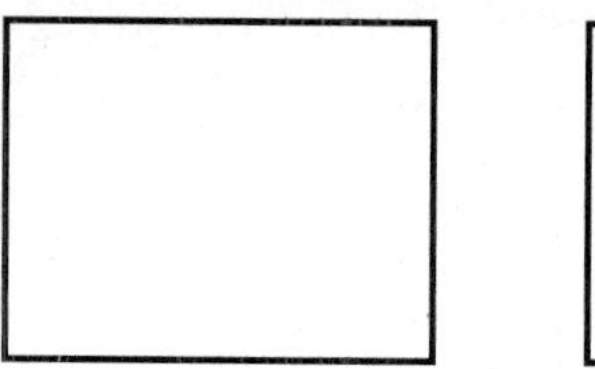

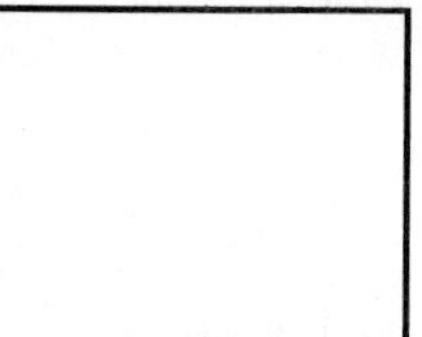

FOR MORE PRACTICE:
Standards Practice Book

Name ______________________________

Problem Solving • Find Equivalent Fractions

Essential Question How can you use the strategy *make a table* to solve problems using equivalent fractions?

Number and Operations—Fractions—4.NF.1

MATHEMATICAL PRACTICES
MP.1, MP.3, MP.4

Anaya is planting a flower garden. The garden will have no more than 12 equal sections. $\frac{3}{4}$ of the garden will have daisies. What other fractions could represent the part of the garden that will have daisies?

Read the Problem

What do I need to find?

__________ that could represent the part of the garden that will have daisies

What information do I need to use?

______ of the garden will have daisies. The garden will not have more than ______ equal sections.

How will I use the information?

I can make a __________ to find __________ fractions to solve the problem.

Solve the Problem

I can make a table and draw models to find equivalent fractions.

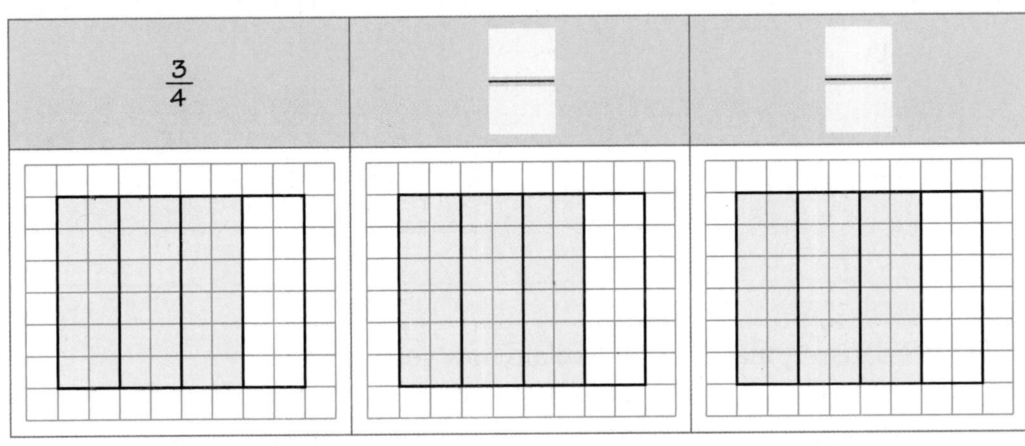

1. What other fractions could represent the part of the garden that will have daisies? Explain. ______________________

____

____

Math Talk **Mathematical Practices**

Compare the models of the equivalent fractions. How does the number of parts relate to the size of the parts? **Explain.**

Try Another Problem

Two friends are knitting scarves. Each scarf has 3 rectangles, and $\frac{2}{3}$ of the rectangles have stripes. If the friends are making 10 scarves, how many rectangles do they need? How many rectangles will have stripes?

Read the Problem

What do I need to find?	What information do I need to use?	How will I use the information?

Solve the Problem

2. Does your answer make sense? Explain how you know.

Math Talk **Mathematical Practices** What strategy did you use and why?

Name ______________________________

Share and Show

Unlock the Problem

- ✓ Use the Problem Solving Mathboard.
- ✓ Underline important facts.
- ✓ Choose a strategy you know.

1. Keisha is helping plan a race route for a 10-kilometer charity run. The committee wants to set up the following things along the course.

Viewing areas: At the end of each half of the course

Water stations: At the end of each fifth of the course

Distance markers: At the end of each tenth of the course

Which locations have more than one thing located there?

First, make a table to organize the information.

	Number of Locations	First Location	All the Locations
Viewing Areas	2	$\frac{1}{2}$	$\frac{1}{2}$
Water Stations	5	$\frac{1}{5}$	$\frac{1}{5}$
Distance Markers	10	$\frac{1}{10}$	$\frac{1}{10}$

Next, identify a relationship. Use a common denominator, and find equivalent fractions.

Finally, identify the locations at which more than one thing will be set up. Circle the locations.

____

____

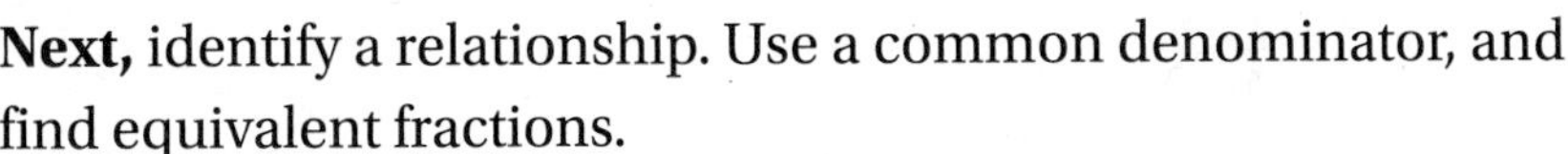

2. THINK SMARTER What if distance markers will also be placed at the end of every fourth of the course? Will any of those markers be set up at the same location as another distance marker, a water station, or a viewing area? Explain. ______________________________

____

____

3. Fifty-six students signed up to volunteer for the race. There were 4 equal groups of students, and each group had a different task.

How many students were in each group? ______________

On Your Own

4. THINK SMARTER A baker cut a pie in half. He cut each half into 3 equal pieces and each piece into 2 equal slices. He sold 6 slices. What fraction of the pie did the baker sell?

____

5. GO DEEPER Andy cut a tuna sandwich and a chicken sandwich into a total of 15 same-size pieces. He cut the tuna sandwich into 9 more pieces than the chicken sandwich. Andy ate 8 pieces of the tuna sandwich. What fraction of the tuna sandwich did he eat?

____

WRITE Math
Show Your Work

6. MATHEMATICAL PRACTICE 6 Luke threw balls into these buckets at a carnival. The number on the bucket gives the number of points for each throw. What is the least number of throws needed to score exactly 100 points? **Explain.**

____

____

____

7. THINK SMARTER Victoria arranges flowers in vases at her restaurant. In each arrangement, $\frac{2}{3}$ of the flowers are yellow. What other fractions can represent the part of the flowers that are yellow? Shade the models to show your work.

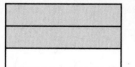

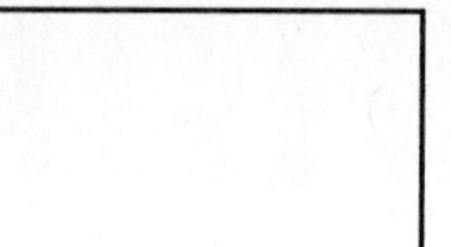

$\frac{2}{3}$ $\qquad \frac{}{12}$ $\qquad \frac{}{}$

FOR MORE PRACTICE:
Standards Practice Book

Name ____________________

Mid-Chapter Checkpoint

Vocabulary

Choose the best term from the box.

Vocabulary
common denominator
equivalent fractions
factor

1. ____________ name the same amount. (p. 237)

2. A ____________ is a common multiple of two or more denominators. (p. 249)

Concepts and Skills

Write two equivalent fractions. (4.NF.1)

3. $\frac{2}{5} = \_\_\_\_ = \_\_\_\_$

4. $\frac{1}{3} = \_\_\_\_ = \_\_\_\_$

5. $\frac{3}{4} = \_\_\_\_ = \_\_\_\_$

Tell whether the fractions are equivalent. Write = or ≠. (4.NF.1)

6. $\frac{2}{3} \bigcirc \frac{4}{12}$

7. $\frac{5}{6} \bigcirc \frac{10}{12}$

8. $\frac{1}{4} \bigcirc \frac{4}{8}$

Write the fraction in simplest form. (4.NF.1)

9. $\frac{6}{8}$ ____________

10. $\frac{25}{100}$ ____________

11. $\frac{8}{10}$ ____________

Write the pair of fractions as a pair of fractions with a common denominator. (4.NF.1)

12. $\frac{3}{10}$ and $\frac{2}{5}$ ____________

13. $\frac{1}{3}$ and $\frac{3}{4}$ ____________

14. Sam needs $\frac{5}{6}$ cup mashed bananas and $\frac{3}{4}$ cup mashed strawberries for a recipe. He wants to find whether he needs more bananas or more strawberries. How can he write $\frac{5}{6}$ and $\frac{3}{4}$ as a pair of fractions with a common denominator? (4.NF.1)

15. Karen will divide her garden into equal parts. She will plant corn in $\frac{8}{12}$ of the garden. What is the fewest number of parts she can divide her garden into? (4.NF.1)

16. Olivia is making scarves. Each scarf will have 5 rectangles, and $\frac{2}{5}$ of the rectangles will be purple. How many purple rectangles does she need for 3 scarves? (4.NF.1)

17. Paul needs to buy $\frac{5}{8}$ pound of peanuts. The scale at the store measures parts of a pound in sixteenths. What measure is equivalent to $\frac{5}{8}$ pound? (4.NF.1)

Name ____________________

Compare Fractions Using Benchmarks

Essential Question How can you use benchmarks to compare fractions?

Number and Operations—Fractions—4.NF.2

MATHEMATICAL PRACTICES
MP.1, MP.3, MP.4

Unlock the Problem

David made a popcorn snack. He mixed $\frac{5}{8}$ gallon of popcorn with $\frac{1}{2}$ gallon of dried apple rings. Did he use more dried apple rings or more popcorn?

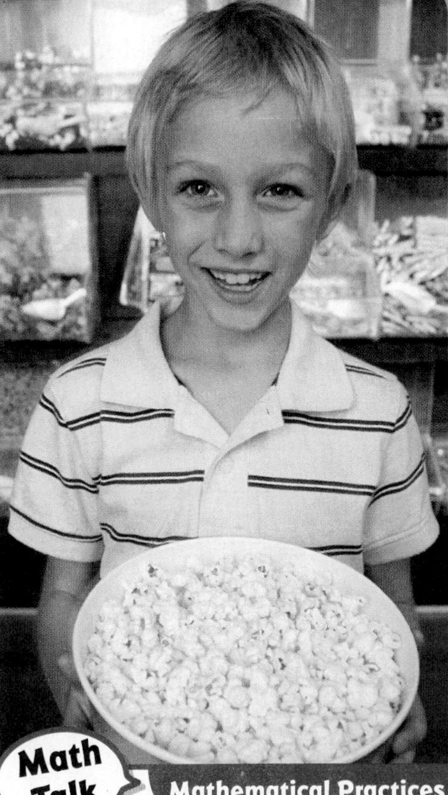

Activity Compare $\frac{5}{8}$ and $\frac{1}{2}$.

Materials ■ fraction strips

Use fraction strips to compare $\frac{5}{8}$ and $\frac{1}{2}$. Record on the model below.

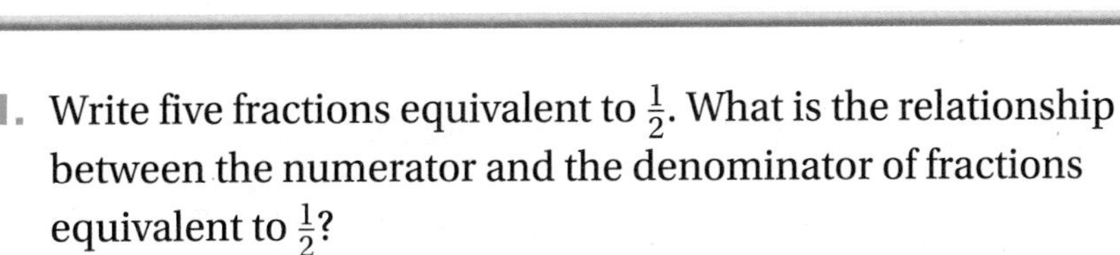

$\frac{1}{2}$	$\frac{1}{2}$				$\frac{1}{2}$			
$\frac{5}{8}$	$\frac{1}{8}$	$\frac{1}{8}$	$\frac{1}{8}$	$\frac{1}{8}$	$\frac{1}{8}$	$\frac{1}{8}$	$\frac{1}{8}$	$\frac{1}{8}$

$\frac{5}{8}$ ◯ $\frac{1}{2}$

So, David used more ____________.

Math Talk Mathematical Practices

Explain how the number of eighth-size parts in $\frac{5}{8}$ is related to the number of eighth-size parts you need to make $\frac{1}{2}$.

1. Write five fractions equivalent to $\frac{1}{2}$. What is the relationship between the numerator and the denominator of fractions equivalent to $\frac{1}{2}$?

____

____

2. How many eighths are equivalent to $\frac{1}{2}$?

____

3. How can you compare $\frac{5}{8}$ and $\frac{1}{2}$ without using a model?

____

____

Benchmarks A **benchmark** is a known size or amount that helps you understand a different size or amount. You can use $\frac{1}{2}$ as a benchmark to help you compare fractions.

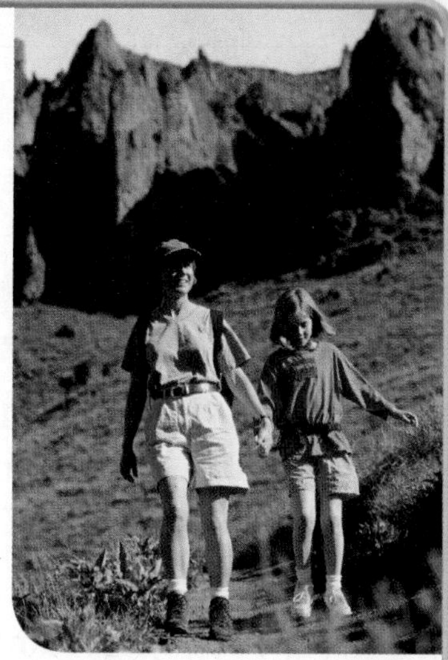

Example Use benchmarks to compare fractions.

A family hiked the same mountain trail. Evie and her father hiked $\frac{5}{12}$ of the trail before they stopped for lunch. Jill and her mother hiked $\frac{9}{10}$ of the trail before they stopped for lunch. Who hiked farther before lunch?

Compare $\frac{5}{12}$ and $\frac{9}{10}$ to the benchmark $\frac{1}{2}$.

STEP 1 Compare $\frac{5}{12}$ to $\frac{1}{2}$.

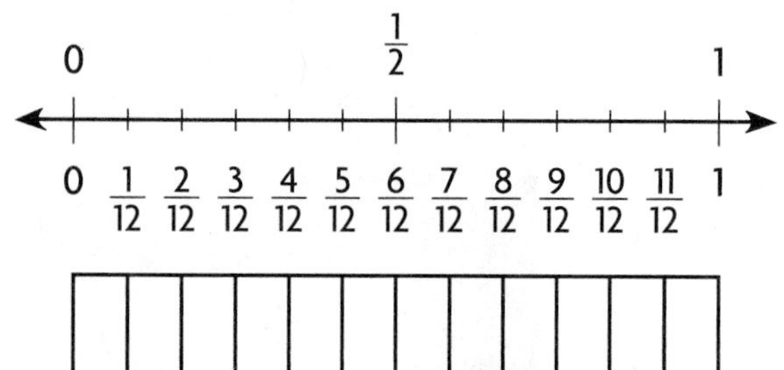

Think: Shade $\frac{5}{12}$.

$\frac{5}{12}$ ◯ $\frac{1}{2}$

STEP 2 Compare $\frac{9}{10}$ to $\frac{1}{2}$.

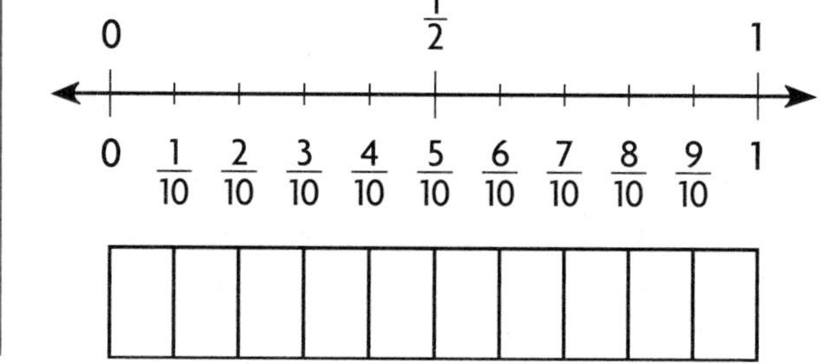

Think: Shade $\frac{9}{10}$.

$\frac{9}{10}$ ◯ $\frac{1}{2}$

Since $\frac{5}{12}$ is ____________ than $\frac{1}{2}$ and $\frac{9}{10}$ is ____________ than $\frac{1}{2}$, you know that $\frac{5}{12}$ ◯ $\frac{9}{10}$.

So, ____________________ hiked farther before lunch.

4. Explain how you can tell $\frac{5}{12}$ is less than $\frac{1}{2}$ without using a model.

____

____

5. Explain how you can tell $\frac{7}{10}$ is greater than $\frac{1}{2}$ without using a model.

____

____

Name ____________________

Share and Show

1. Compare $\frac{2}{5}$ and $\frac{1}{8}$. Write $<$ or $>$.

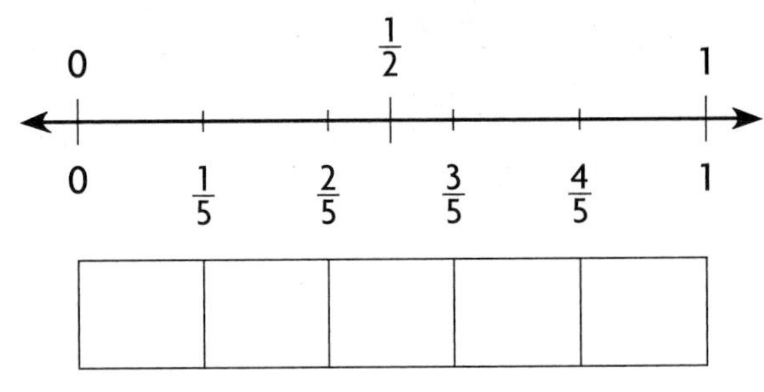

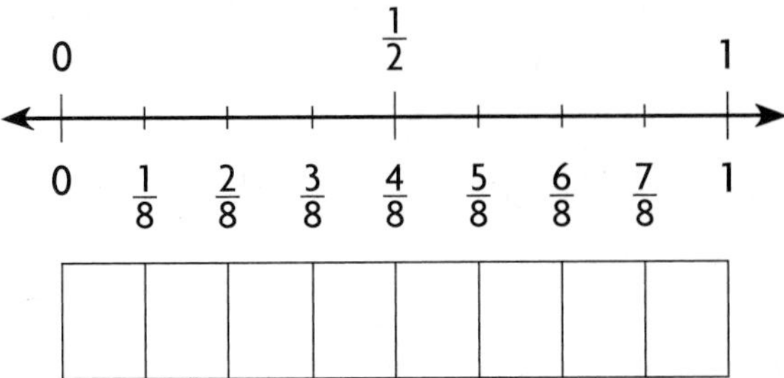

$\frac{2}{5} \bigcirc \frac{1}{8}$

Compare. Write $<$ or $>$.

✓ 2. $\frac{1}{2} \bigcirc \frac{4}{6}$	3. $\frac{3}{10} \bigcirc \frac{1}{2}$	✓ 4. $\frac{11}{12} \bigcirc \frac{4}{8}$	5. $\frac{5}{8} \bigcirc \frac{2}{5}$

Math Talk — Mathematical Practices

Explain how you know $\frac{1}{3} < \frac{1}{2}$.

On Your Own

Compare. Write $<$ or $>$.

6. $\frac{8}{10} \bigcirc \frac{3}{8}$	7. $\frac{1}{3} \bigcirc \frac{7}{12}$	8. $\frac{2}{6} \bigcirc \frac{7}{8}$	9. $\frac{4}{8} \bigcirc \frac{2}{10}$
10. $\frac{3}{4} \bigcirc \frac{1}{2}$	11. $\frac{6}{6} \bigcirc \frac{1}{3}$	12. $\frac{4}{5} \bigcirc \frac{1}{6}$	13. $\frac{5}{8} \bigcirc \frac{9}{10}$

MATHEMATICAL PRACTICE 2 Reason Quantitatively **Algebra** **Find a numerator that makes the statement true.**

14. $\frac{2}{4} < \frac{\square}{6}$	15. $\frac{8}{10} > \frac{\square}{8}$	16. $\frac{10}{12} > \frac{\square}{4}$	17. $\frac{2}{5} < \frac{\square}{10}$

18. When two fractions are between 0 and $\frac{1}{2}$, how do you know which fraction is greater? Explain.

____

____

____

Problem Solving • Applications

19. THINK SMARTER Saundra ran $\frac{7}{12}$ of a mile. Lamar ran $\frac{3}{4}$ of a mile. Who ran farther? Explain.

____

____

____

____

WRITE Math • Show Your Work

20. **What's the Question?** Selena ran farther than Manny.

____

____

21. GO DEEPER Chloe made a small pan of ziti and a small pan of lasagna. She cut the ziti into 8 equal parts and the lasagna into 9 equal parts. Her family ate $\frac{2}{3}$ of the lasagna. If her family ate more lasagna than ziti, what fraction of the ziti could have been eaten?

____

22. THINK SMARTER James, Ella, and Ryan biked around Eagle Lake. James biked $\frac{2}{10}$ of the distance in an hour. Ella biked $\frac{4}{8}$ of the distance in an hour. Ryan biked $\frac{2}{5}$ of the distance in an hour. Compare the distances biked by each person by matching the statements to the correct symbol. Each symbol may be used more than once or not at all.

$\frac{2}{10}$ ● $\frac{4}{8}$ • • $=$

$\frac{4}{8}$ ● $\frac{2}{5}$ • • $<$

$\frac{2}{10}$ ● $\frac{2}{5}$ • • $>$

FOR MORE PRACTICE: Standards Practice Book

Name ________________________

Compare Fractions

Essential Question How can you compare fractions?

Number and Operations—Fractions—4.NF.2

MATHEMATICAL PRACTICES
MP.2, MP.4, MP.6

Unlock the Problem

Every year, Avery's school has a fair. This year, $\frac{3}{8}$ of the booths had face painting and $\frac{1}{4}$ of the booths had sand art. Were there more booths with face painting or sand art?

Compare $\frac{3}{8}$ and $\frac{1}{4}$.

One Way Use a common denominator.

When two fractions have the same denominator, they have equal-size parts. You can compare the number of parts.

THINK

Think: 8 is a multiple of both 4 and 8. Use 8 as a common denominator.

$$\frac{1}{4} = \frac{1 \times \square}{4 \times \square} = \frac{\square}{8}$$

$\frac{3}{8}$ already has 8 as a denominator.

MODEL AND RECORD

Shade the model. Then compare.

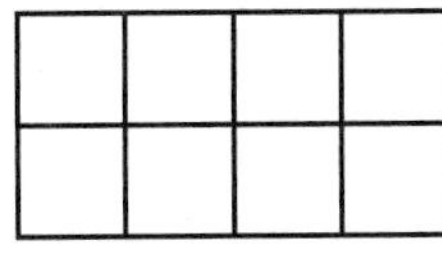

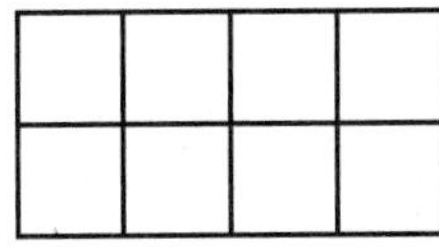

$\frac{3}{8}$ ◯ $\frac{2}{8}$

Another Way Use a common numerator.

When two fractions have the same numerator, they represent the same number of parts. You can compare the size of the parts.

THINK

Think: 3 is a multiple of both 3 and 1. Use 3 as a common numerator.

$\frac{3}{8}$ already has 3 as a numerator.

$$\frac{1}{4} = \frac{1 \times \square}{4 \times \square} = \frac{3}{\square}$$

MODEL AND RECORD

Shade the model. Then compare.

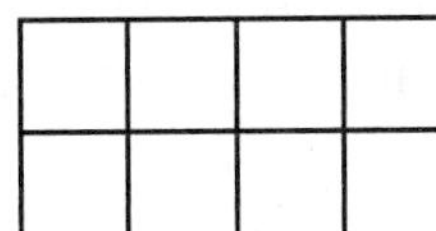

$\frac{3}{8}$ ◯ $\frac{3}{12}$

Since $\frac{3}{8}$ ◯ $\frac{1}{4}$, there were more booths with ________________.

Math Talk Mathematical Practices

Explain why you cannot use $\frac{1}{2}$ as a benchmark to compare $\frac{3}{8}$ and $\frac{1}{4}$.

Try This! **Compare the fractions. Explain your reasoning.**

A $\frac{3}{4} \bigcirc \frac{1}{3}$

B $\frac{3}{5} \bigcirc \frac{3}{8}$

C $\frac{3}{4} \bigcirc \frac{7}{8}$

D $\frac{4}{5} \bigcirc \frac{2}{3}$

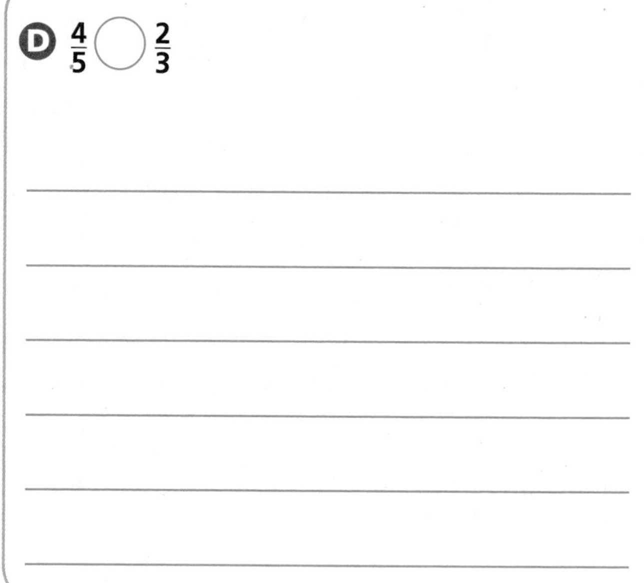

1. Which would you use to compare $\frac{11}{12}$ and $\frac{5}{6}$, a common numerator or a common denominator? Explain.

2. Can you use simplest form to compare $\frac{8}{10}$ and $\frac{3}{5}$? Explain.

Name ______________________________

Share and Show

1. Compare $\frac{2}{5}$ and $\frac{1}{10}$.

Think: Use ______ as a common denominator.

$\frac{2}{5} = \frac{\square \times \square}{\square \times \square} = \frac{\square}{\square}$

$\frac{1}{10}$

Think: 4 tenth-size parts ◯ 1 tenth-size part.

$\frac{2}{5}$ ◯ $\frac{1}{10}$

2. Compare $\frac{6}{10}$ and $\frac{3}{4}$.

Think: Use ______ as a common numerator.

$\frac{6}{10}$

$\frac{3}{4} = \frac{\square \times \square}{\square \times \square} = \frac{\square}{\square}$

Think: A tenth-size part ◯ an eighth-size part.

$\frac{6}{10}$ ◯ $\frac{3}{4}$

Compare. Write <, >, or =.

3. $\frac{7}{8}$ ◯ $\frac{2}{8}$

4. $\frac{5}{12}$ ◯ $\frac{3}{6}$

5. $\frac{4}{10}$ ◯ $\frac{4}{6}$

6. $\frac{6}{12}$ ◯ $\frac{2}{4}$

Math Talk Mathematical Practices

Explain why using a common numerator or a common denominator can help you compare fractions.

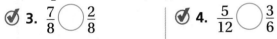

On Your Own

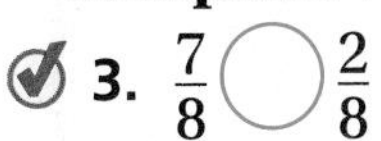

Compare. Write <, >, or =.

7. $\frac{1}{3}$ ◯ $\frac{1}{4}$

8. $\frac{4}{5}$ ◯ $\frac{8}{10}$

9. $\frac{3}{4}$ ◯ $\frac{2}{6}$

10. $\frac{1}{2}$ ◯ $\frac{5}{8}$

11. $\frac{3}{10}$ ◯ $\frac{2}{4}$

12. $\frac{75}{100}$ ◯ $\frac{8}{10}$

13. $\frac{4}{6}$ ◯ $\frac{2}{3}$

14. $\frac{3}{10}$ ◯ $\frac{4}{100}$

MATHEMATICAL PRACTICE 2 Reason Quantitatively **Algebra** **Find a number that makes the statement true.**

15. $\frac{1}{2} > \frac{\square}{3}$

16. $\frac{3}{10} < \frac{\square}{5}$

17. $\frac{5}{12} < \frac{\square}{3}$

18. $\frac{2}{3} > \frac{4}{\square}$

Unlock the Problem — Real World

19. THINKSMARTER Jerry is making a strawberry smoothie. Which measure is greatest, the amount of milk, cottage cheese, or strawberries?

Strawberry Smoothie

3 ice cubes
$\frac{3}{4}$ cup milk
$\frac{2}{6}$ cup cottage cheese
$\frac{8}{12}$ cup strawberries
$\frac{1}{4}$ teaspoon vanilla
$\frac{1}{8}$ teaspoon sugar

a. What do you need to find?

____

b. How will you find the answer?

____

____

c. Show your work.

d. Jerry needs more __________ than the other two ingredients.

20. GO DEEPER Angie, Blake, Carlos, and Daisy went running. Angie ran $\frac{1}{3}$ mile, Blake ran $\frac{3}{5}$ mile, Carlos ran $\frac{7}{10}$ mile, and Daisy ran $\frac{1}{2}$ mile. Which runner ran the shortest distance? Who ran the greatest distance?

____

21. THINKSMARTER Elaine bought $\frac{5}{8}$ pound of potato salad and $\frac{4}{6}$ pound of macaroni salad for a picnic. Use the numbers to compare the amounts of potato salad and macaroni salad Elaine bought.

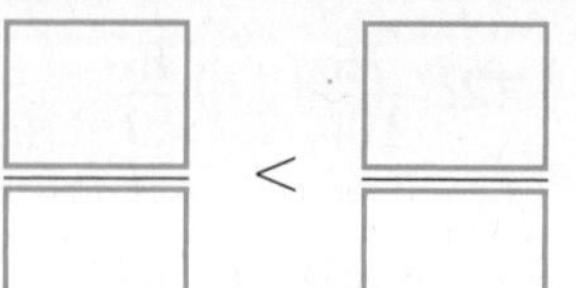

$\frac{\square}{\square} < \frac{\square}{\square}$

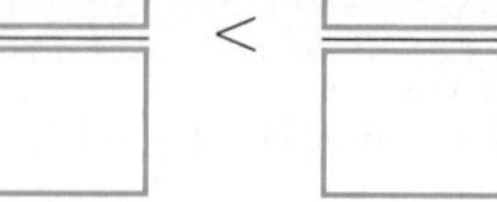

4

5

6

8

FOR MORE PRACTICE: Standards Practice Book

Name ______________________________

Compare and Order Fractions

Essential Question How can you order fractions?

Number and Operations—Fractions—4.NF.2

MATHEMATICAL PRACTICES
MP.2, MP.4, MP.6

Unlock the Problem (Real World)

Jody has equal-size bins for the recycling center. She filled $\frac{3}{5}$ of a bin with plastics, $\frac{1}{12}$ of a bin with paper, and $\frac{9}{10}$ of a bin with glass. Which bin is the most full?

- Underline what you need to find.
- Circle the fractions you will compare.

Example 1 Locate and label $\frac{3}{5}$, $\frac{1}{12}$, and $\frac{9}{10}$ on the number line.

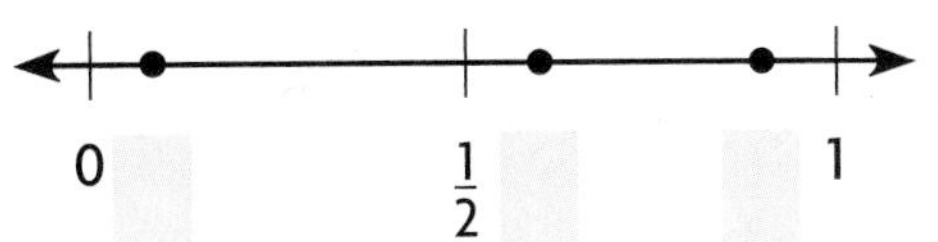

Math Idea

Sometimes it is not reasonable to find the exact location of a point on a number line. Benchmarks can help you find approximate locations.

STEP 1 Compare each fraction to $\frac{1}{2}$.

$\frac{3}{5} \bigcirc \frac{1}{2}$ $\quad \frac{1}{12} \bigcirc \frac{1}{2}$ $\quad \frac{9}{10} \bigcirc \frac{1}{2}$

______ and ______ are both greater than $\frac{1}{2}$.

______ is less than $\frac{1}{2}$.

Label $\frac{1}{12}$ on the number line above.

STEP 2 Compare $\frac{3}{5}$ and $\frac{9}{10}$.

Think: Use 10 as a common denominator.

$$\frac{3}{5} = \frac{\square \times \square}{\square \times \square} = \frac{\square}{\square}$$

Since $\frac{6}{10} \bigcirc \frac{9}{10}$, you know that $\frac{3}{5} \bigcirc \frac{9}{10}$.

Label $\frac{3}{5}$ and $\frac{9}{10}$ on the number line above.

The fraction the greatest distance from 0 has the greatest value.

The fraction with the greatest value is ______.

So, the bin with ____________ is the most full.

Math Talk — Mathematical Practices

Explain how you know you located $\frac{3}{5}$ on the number line correctly.

- Compare the distance between $\frac{3}{5}$ and 0 and the distance between $\frac{9}{10}$ and 0. What can you conclude about the relationship between $\frac{3}{5}$ and $\frac{9}{10}$? Explain.

____

____

Example 2 Write $\frac{7}{10}$, $\frac{1}{3}$, $\frac{7}{12}$, and $\frac{8}{10}$ in order from least to greatest.

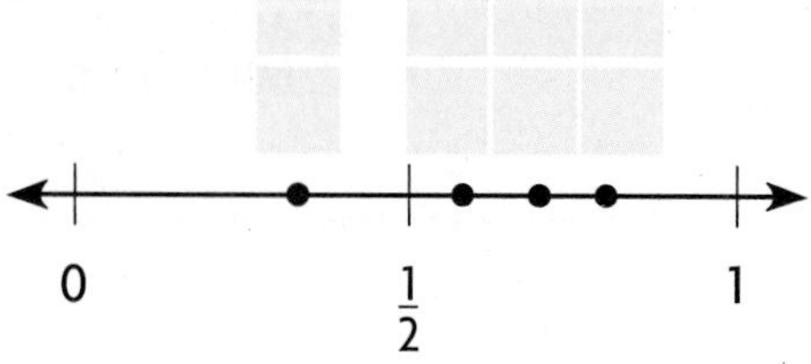

STEP 1 Compare each fraction to $\frac{1}{2}$.

List fractions that are less than $\frac{1}{2}$: ________________

List fractions that are greater than $\frac{1}{2}$: ________________

The fraction with the least value is ______.

Locate and label $\frac{1}{3}$ on the number line above.

STEP 2 Compare $\frac{7}{10}$ to $\frac{7}{12}$ and $\frac{8}{10}$.

Think: $\frac{7}{10}$ and $\frac{7}{12}$ have a common numerator.

$\frac{7}{10} \bigcirc \frac{7}{12}$

Think: $\frac{7}{10}$ and $\frac{8}{10}$ have a common denominator.

$\frac{7}{10} \bigcirc \frac{8}{10}$

Locate and label $\frac{7}{10}$, $\frac{7}{12}$, and $\frac{8}{10}$ on the number line above.

The fractions in order from least to greatest are ________________.

So, _____ < _____ < _____ < _____.

Try This! Write $\frac{3}{4}$, $\frac{3}{6}$, $\frac{1}{3}$, and $\frac{2}{12}$ in order from least to greatest.

_____ < _____ < _____ < _____

Name ________________________________

Share and Show

1. Locate and label points on the number line to help you write $\frac{3}{10}$, $\frac{11}{12}$, and $\frac{5}{8}$ in order from least to greatest.

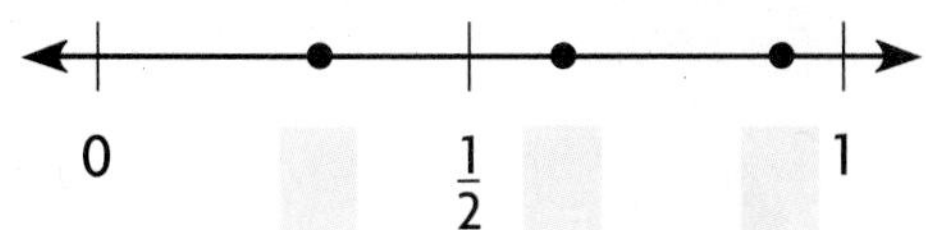

____

Write the fraction with the greatest value.

2. $\frac{7}{10}, \frac{1}{5}, \frac{9}{10}$ ____________

3. $\frac{5}{6}, \frac{7}{12}, \frac{7}{10}$ ____________

4. $\frac{2}{8}, \frac{1}{8}, \frac{2}{4}, \frac{2}{6}$ ____________

Write the fractions in order from least to greatest.

5. $\frac{1}{4}, \frac{5}{8}, \frac{1}{2}$ ____________

6. $\frac{3}{5}, \frac{2}{3}, \frac{3}{10}, \frac{4}{5}$ ____________

7. $\frac{3}{4}, \frac{7}{12}, \frac{5}{12}$ ____________

Math Talk **Mathematical Practices**

Explain how benchmarks can help you order fractions.

On Your Own

Write the fractions in order from least to greatest.

8. $\frac{2}{5}, \frac{1}{3}, \frac{5}{6}$ ____________

9. $\frac{4}{8}, \frac{5}{12}, \frac{1}{6}$ ____________

10. $\frac{7}{100}, \frac{9}{10}, \frac{4}{5}$ ____________

MATHEMATICAL PRACTICE 2 Reason Quantitatively **Algebra** **Write a numerator that makes the statement true.**

11. $\frac{1}{2} < \frac{\square}{10} < \frac{4}{5}$

12. $\frac{1}{4} < \frac{5}{12} < \frac{\square}{6}$

13. $\frac{\square}{8} < \frac{3}{4} < \frac{7}{8}$

Unlock the Problem

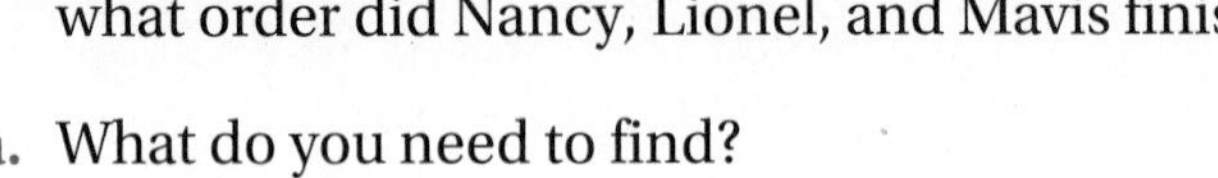

14. THINK SMARTER Nancy, Lionel, and Mavis ran in a 5-kilometer race. The table shows their finish times. In what order did Nancy, Lionel, and Mavis finish the race?

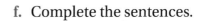

Finish line

5-Kilometer Race Results

Name	Time
Nancy	$\frac{2}{3}$ hour
Lionel	$\frac{7}{12}$ hour
Mavis	$\frac{3}{4}$ hour

a. What do you need to find?

____

____

b. What information do you need to solve the problem?

____

____

c. What information is not necessary?

____

d. How will you solve the problem?

____

____

e. Show the steps to solve the problem.

f. Complete the sentences.

The runner who finished first is ______.

The runner who finished second is ______.

The runner who finished third is ______.

15. GO DEEPER Alma used 3 beads to make a necklace. The lengths of the beads are $\frac{5}{6}$ inch, $\frac{5}{12}$ inch, and $\frac{1}{3}$ inch. What are the lengths in order from shortest to longest?

____

16. THINK SMARTER Victor has his grandmother's recipe for making mixed nuts.

$\frac{3}{4}$ cup pecans	$\frac{2}{12}$ cup peanuts
$\frac{1}{2}$ cup almonds	$\frac{7}{8}$ cup walnuts

Order the ingredients used in the recipe from least to greatest.

____

FOR MORE PRACTICE: Standards Practice Book

Name ______________________________

Chapter 6 Review/Test

1. For numbers 1a–1d, tell whether the fractions are equivalent by selecting the correct symbol.

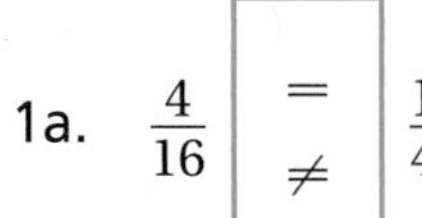

1a. $\frac{4}{16}$ [= / ≠] $\frac{1}{4}$

1c. $\frac{5}{6}$ [= / ≠] $\frac{25}{30}$

1b. $\frac{3}{5}$ [= / ≠] $\frac{12}{15}$

1d. $\frac{6}{10}$ [= / ≠] $\frac{5}{8}$

2. Juan's mother gave him a recipe for trail mix.

$\frac{3}{4}$ cup cereal	$\frac{2}{3}$ cup almonds
$\frac{1}{4}$ cup peanuts	$\frac{1}{2}$ cup raisins

Order the ingredients used in the recipe from least to greatest.

3. Taylor cuts $\frac{1}{5}$ sheet of construction paper for an arts and crafts project. Write $\frac{1}{5}$ as an equivalent fraction with the denominators shown.

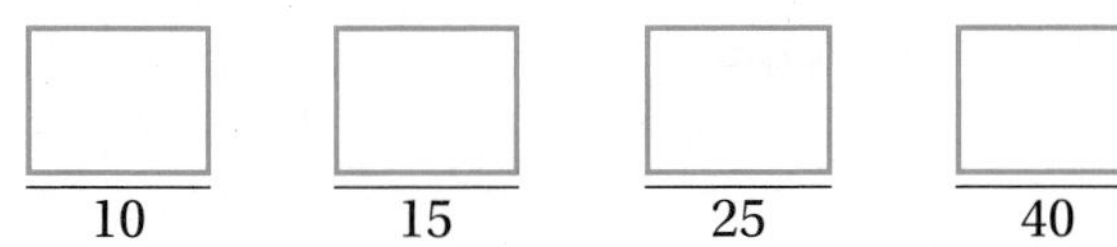

$\frac{\square}{10}$ $\frac{\square}{15}$ $\frac{\square}{25}$ $\frac{\square}{40}$

4. A mechanic has sockets with the sizes shown below. Write each fraction in the correct box.

$\frac{7}{8}$ in. $\frac{3}{16}$ in. $\frac{1}{4}$ in. $\frac{3}{8}$ in. $\frac{4}{8}$ in. $\frac{11}{16}$ in.

less than $\frac{1}{2}$ in.	equal to $\frac{1}{2}$ in.	greater than $\frac{1}{2}$ in.

GO DIGITAL Assessment Options Chapter Test

5. Darcy bought $\frac{1}{2}$ pound of cheese and $\frac{3}{4}$ pound of hamburger for a barbecue. Use the numbers to compare the amounts of cheese and hamburger Darcy bought.

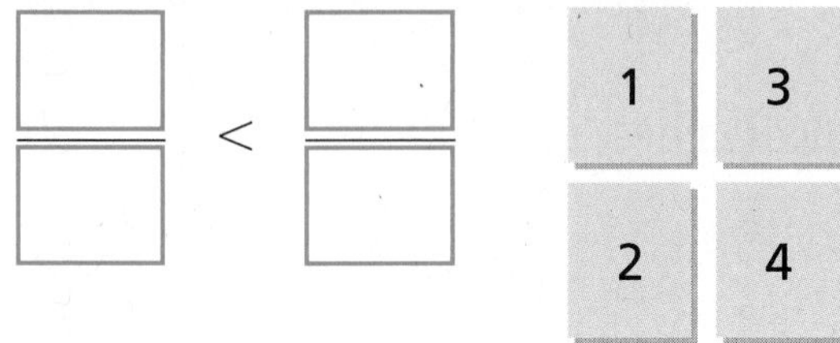

6. Brad is practicing the piano. He spends $\frac{1}{4}$ hour practicing scales and $\frac{1}{3}$ hour practicing the song for his recital. For numbers 6a–6c, select Yes or No to tell whether each of the following is a true statement.

6a. 12 is a common denominator of $\frac{1}{4}$ and $\frac{1}{3}$. ○ Yes ○ No

6b. The amount of time spent practicing scales can be rewritten as $\frac{3}{12}$. ○ Yes ○ No

6c. The amount of time spent practicing the song for the recital can be rewritten as $\frac{6}{12}$. ○ Yes ○ No

7. In the school chorus, $\frac{4}{24}$ of the students are fourth graders. In simplest form, what fraction of the students in the school chorus are fourth graders?

_______ of the students

8. Which pairs of fractions are equivalent? Mark all that apply.

○ $\frac{8}{12}$ and $\frac{2}{3}$

○ $\frac{4}{5}$ and $\frac{12}{16}$

○ $\frac{3}{4}$ and $\frac{20}{28}$

○ $\frac{7}{10}$ and $\frac{21}{30}$

9. Sam worked on his science fair project for $\frac{1}{4}$ hour on Friday and $\frac{1}{2}$ hour on Saturday. What are four common denominators for the fractions? Explain your reasoning.

Name ________________________________

10. Morita works in a florist shop and makes flower arrangements. She puts 10 flowers in each vase, and $\frac{2}{10}$ of the flowers are daisies.

Part A

If Morita makes 4 arrangements, how many daisies does she need? Show how you can check your answer.

__________ daisies

Part B

Last weekend, Morita used 10 daisies to make flower arrangements. How many flowers other than daisies did she use to make the arrangements? Explain your reasoning.

__________ other flowers

11. In Mary's homeroom, $\frac{10}{28}$ of the students have a cat, $\frac{6}{12}$ have a dog, and $\frac{2}{14}$ have a pet bird. For numbers 11a–11c, select True or False for each statement.

11a. In simplest form, $\frac{5}{14}$ of the students have a cat. ○ True ○ False

11b. In simplest form, $\frac{2}{4}$ of the students have a dog. ○ True ○ False

11c. In simplest form, $\frac{1}{7}$ of the students have a pet bird. ○ True ○ False

12. Regina, Courtney, and Ellen hiked around Bear Pond. Regina hiked $\frac{7}{10}$ of the distance in an hour. Courtney hiked $\frac{3}{6}$ of the distance in an hour. Ellen hiked $\frac{3}{8}$ of the distance in an hour. Compare the distances hiked by each person by matching the statements to the correct symbol. Each symbol may be used more than once or not at all.

$\frac{7}{10}$ ◯ $\frac{3}{6}$ •	• $<$
$\frac{3}{8}$ ◯ $\frac{3}{6}$ •	• $>$
$\frac{7}{10}$ ◯ $\frac{3}{8}$ •	• $=$

13. Ramon is having some friends over after a baseball game. Ramon's job is to make a vegetable dip. The ingredients for the recipe are given.

Ingredients in Vegetable Dip	
$\frac{3}{4}$ cup parsley	$\frac{5}{8}$ cup buttermilk
$\frac{1}{3}$ cup dill	$\frac{1}{2}$ cup cream cheese
$\frac{6}{8}$ cup scallions	$\frac{1}{16}$ cup lemon juice

Part A

Which ingredient does Ramon use the greater amount of, buttermilk or cream cheese? Explain how you found your answer.

Part B

Ramon says that he needs the same amount of two different ingredients. Is he correct? Support your answer with information from the problem.

Name ______________________________

14. Sandy is ordering bread rolls for her party. She wants $\frac{3}{5}$ of the rolls to be whole wheat. What other fractions can represent the part of the rolls that will be whole wheat? Shade the models to show your work.

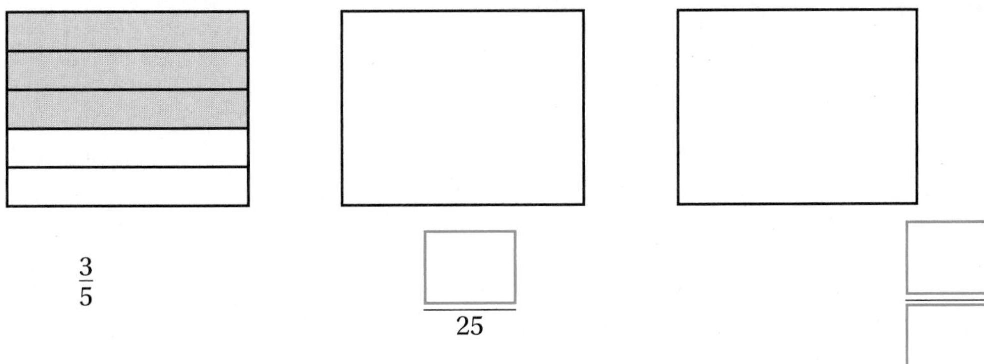

$\frac{3}{5}$ $\frac{\square}{25}$ $\frac{\square}{\square}$

15. Angel has $\frac{4}{8}$ yard of ribbon and Lynn has $\frac{3}{4}$ yard of ribbon. Do Angel and Lynn have the same amount of ribbon? Shade the model to show how you found your answer. Explain your reasoning.

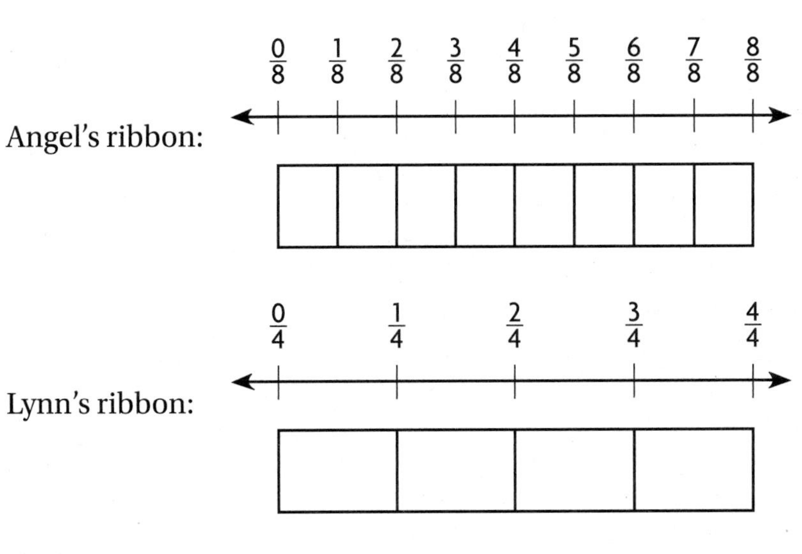

16. Ella used $\frac{1}{4}$ yard of red ribbon. Fill in each box with a number from the list to show equivalent fractions for $\frac{1}{4}$. Not all numbers will be used.

$\frac{1}{4} = \frac{\square}{8} = \frac{4}{\square} = \frac{\square}{\square}$

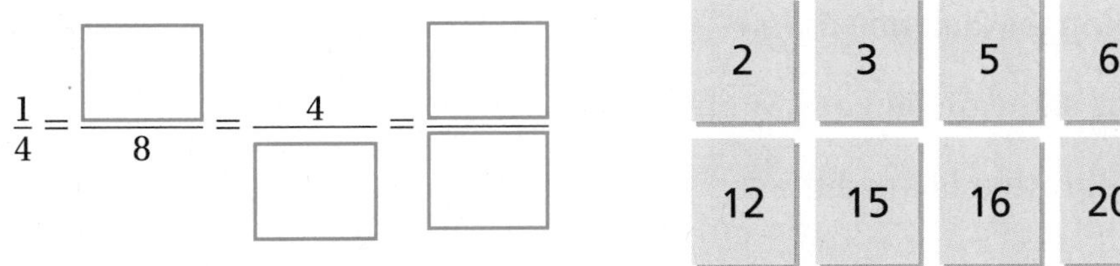

2	3	5	6
12	15	16	20

17. Frank has two same-size rectangles divided into the same number of equal parts. One rectangle has $\frac{3}{4}$ of the parts shaded, and the other has $\frac{1}{3}$ of the parts shaded.

Part A

Into how many parts could each rectangle be divided? Show your work by drawing the parts of each rectangle.

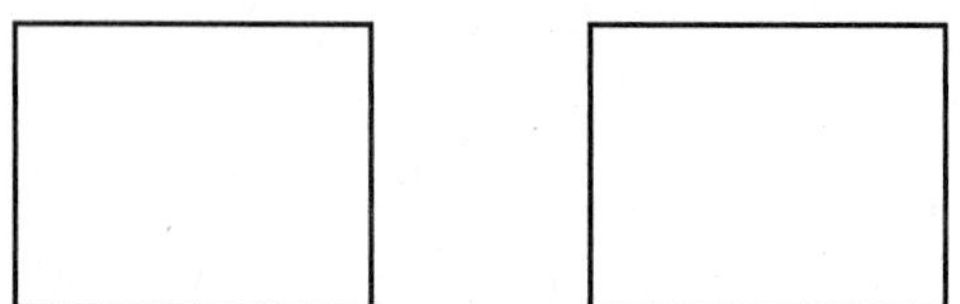

Part B

Is there more than one possible answer to Part A? If so, did you find the least number of parts into which both rectangles could be divided? Explain your reasoning.

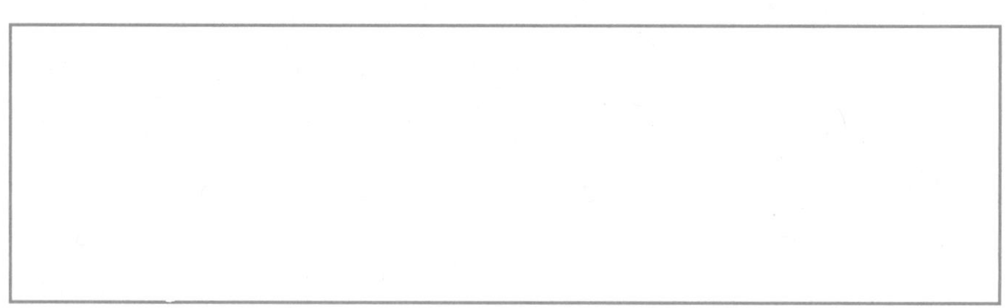

18. Suki rode her bike $\frac{4}{5}$ mile. Claire rode her bike $\frac{1}{3}$ mile. They want to compare how far they each rode their bikes using the benchmark $\frac{1}{2}$. For numbers 18a–18c, select the correct answers to describe how to solve the problem.

18a. Compare Suki's distance to the benchmark: $\frac{4}{5}$ [$<$ | $>$ | $=$] $\frac{1}{2}$.

18b. Compare Claire's distance to the benchmark: $\frac{1}{3}$ [$<$ | $>$ | $=$] $\frac{1}{2}$.

18c. Suki rode her bike [a longer distance than | the same distance as | a shorter distance than] Claire.

Chapter 7

Add and Subtract Fractions

Show What You Know 

Check your understanding of important skills.

Name ______________________

▶ **Fractions Equal to 1** **Write the fraction that names the whole.**

1. 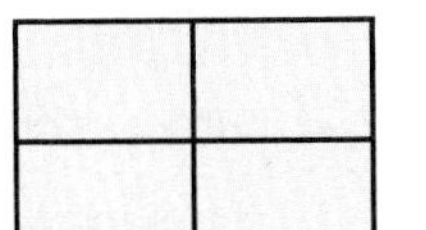 ______

2.  ______

▶ **Parts of a Whole** **Write a fraction that names the shaded part.**

3. 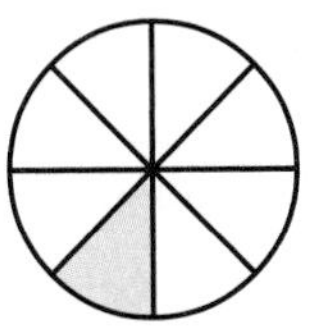 ______

4. 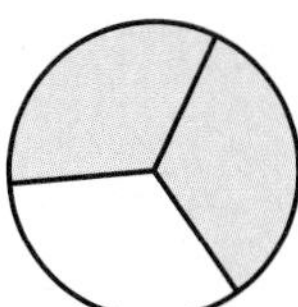 ______

5. 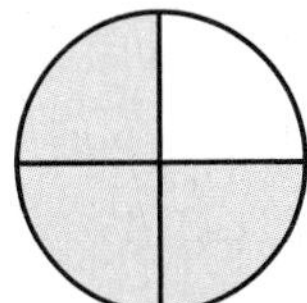 ______

▶ **Read and Write Fractions** **Write a fraction for the shaded part. Write a fraction for the unshaded part.**

6. 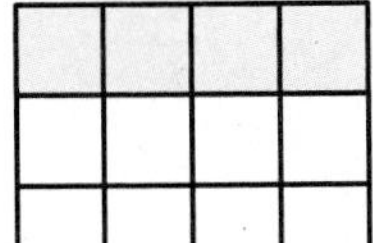 shaded: ______ unshaded: ______

7. 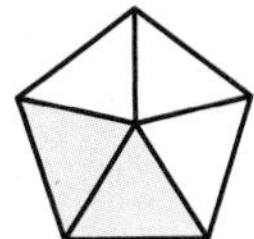 shaded: ______ unshaded: ______

The electricity that powers our appliances is converted from many sources of energy. About $\frac{5}{10}$ is made from coal, about $\frac{2}{10}$ from natural gas, and about $\frac{2}{10}$ from nuclear power. Be a Math Detective. About how much of our electricity comes from sources other than coal, natural gas, or nuclear power?

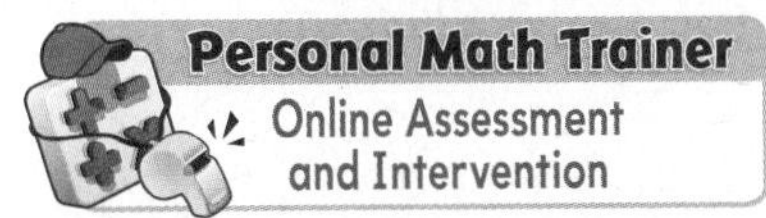

Vocabulary Builder

▶ Visualize It

Complete the bubble map using the words with a ✓.

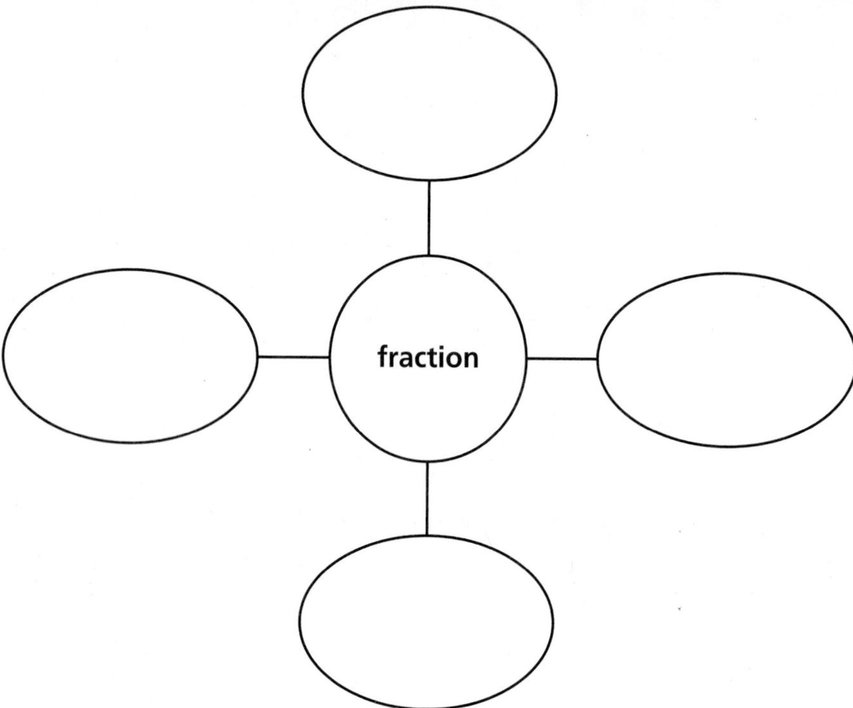

Review Words
Associative Property of Addition
Commutative Property of Addition
✓ denominator
fraction
✓ numerator
simplest form
Preview Words
✓ mixed number
✓ unit fraction

▶ Understand Vocabulary

Write the word or phrase that matches the description.

1. When the numerator and denominator have only 1 as a common factor

   ____

2. A number that names a part of a whole or part of a group

   ____

3. An amount given as a whole number and a fraction

   ____

4. The number in a fraction that tells how many equal parts are in the whole or in the group ____________________

5. A fraction that has a numerator of one ____________________

• Interactive Student Edition
• Multimedia eGlossary

Name ____________________

Add and Subtract Parts of a Whole

Essential Question When can you add or subtract parts of a whole?

Numbers and Operations—Fractions—4.NF.3a

MATHEMATICAL PRACTICES
MP.4, MP.5

Investigate

Hands On

Materials ■ fraction circles ■ color pencils

Ms. Clark has the following pie pieces left over from a bake sale.

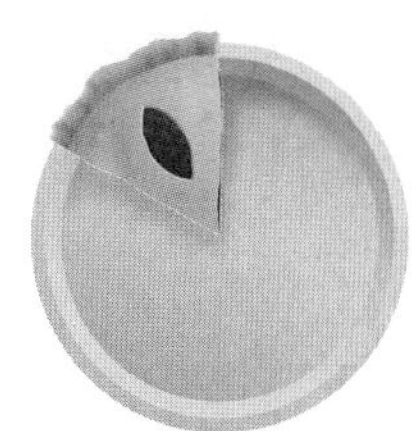

She will combine the pieces so they are on the same dish. How much pie will be on the dish?

A. Model the problem using fraction circles. Draw a picture of your model. Then write the sum.

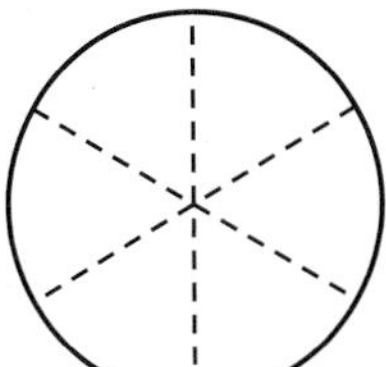 + 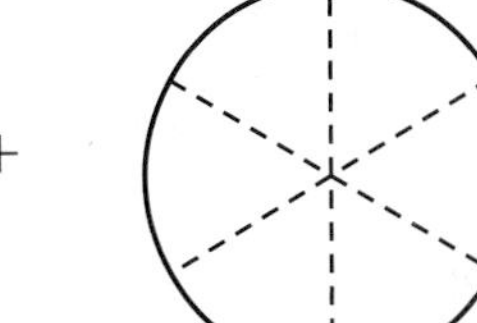 = 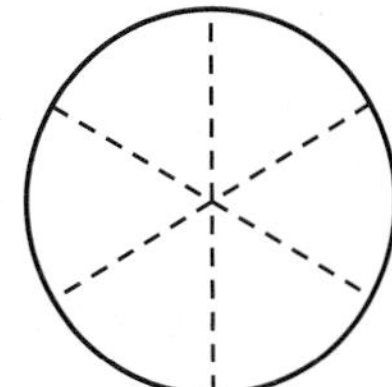

_______ + _______ = _______

So, _______ of a pie is on the dish.

B. Suppose Ms. Clark eats 2 pieces of the pie. How much pie will be left on the dish? Model the problem using fraction circles. Draw a picture of your model. Then write the difference.

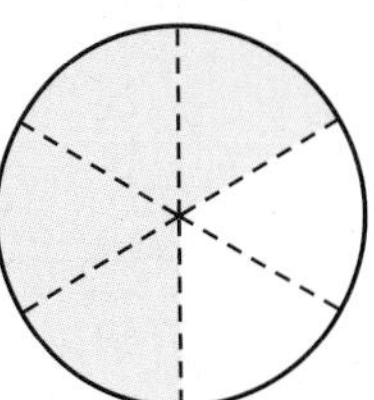

_______ − _______ = _______

So, _______ of the pie is left on the dish.

Draw Conclusions

1. Kevin says that when you combine 3 pieces of pie and 1 piece of pie, you have 4 pieces of pie. Explain how Kevin's statement is related to the equation $\frac{3}{6} + \frac{1}{6} = \frac{4}{6}$.

2. Isabel wrote the equation $\frac{1}{2} + \frac{1}{6} = \frac{4}{6}$ and Jonah wrote $\frac{3}{6} + \frac{1}{6} = \frac{4}{6}$ to represent combining the pie pieces. Explain why both equations are correct.

3. THINK SMARTER If there is $\frac{4}{6}$ of a pie on a plate, what part of the pie is missing from the plate? Write an equation to justify your answer.

Make Connections

You can only join or separate parts that refer to the same whole.

Suppose Randy has $\frac{1}{4}$ of a round cake and $\frac{1}{4}$ of a square cake.

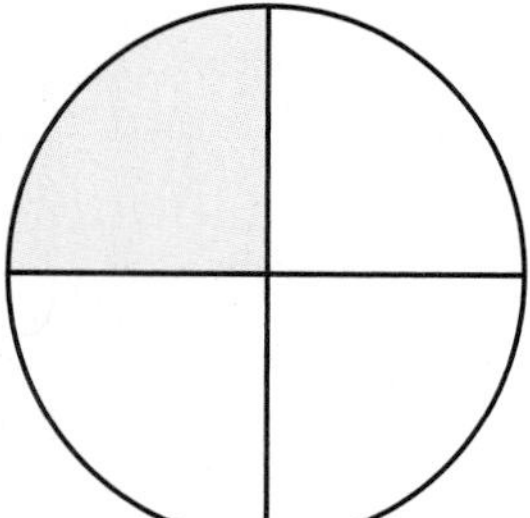

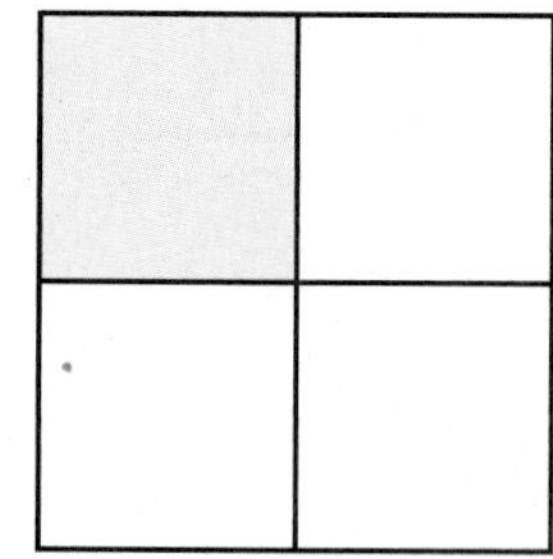

Mathematical Practices

Give an example of a situation where the equation $\frac{1}{4} + \frac{1}{4} = \frac{2}{4}$ makes sense. **Explain** your reasoning.

a. Are the wholes the same? Explain.

b. Does the sum $\frac{1}{4} + \frac{1}{4} = \frac{2}{4}$ make sense in this situation? Explain.

Name ________________________________

Share and Show

Use the model to write an equation.

1\.

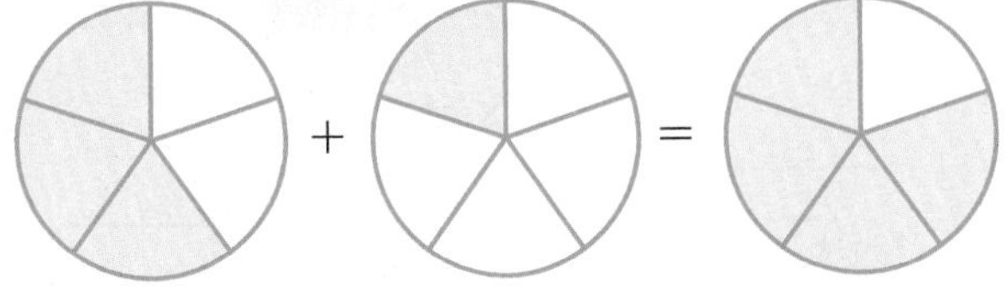

____

2\.

____

3\.

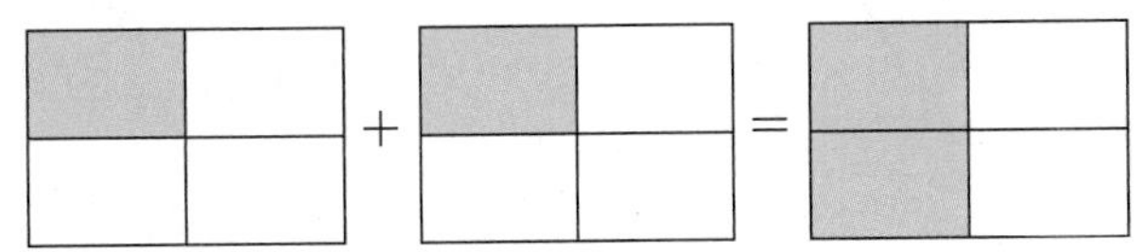

____

4\.

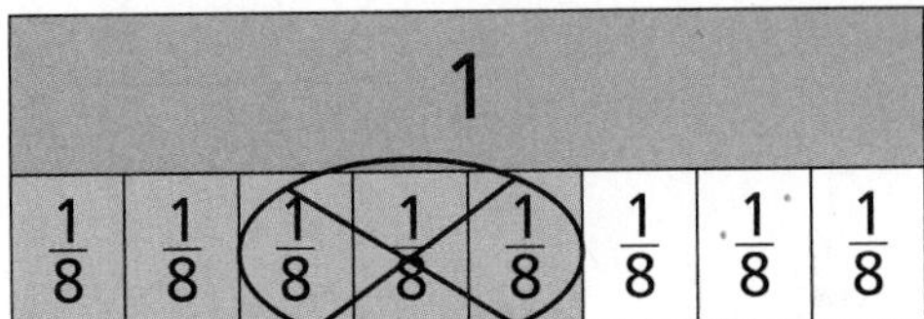

____

Use the model to solve the equation.

5\. $\frac{3}{4} - \frac{1}{4} =$ ____________

1			
$\frac{1}{4}$	$\frac{1}{4}$	$\frac{1}{4}$	$\frac{1}{4}$

6\. $\frac{5}{6} + \frac{1}{6} =$ ____________

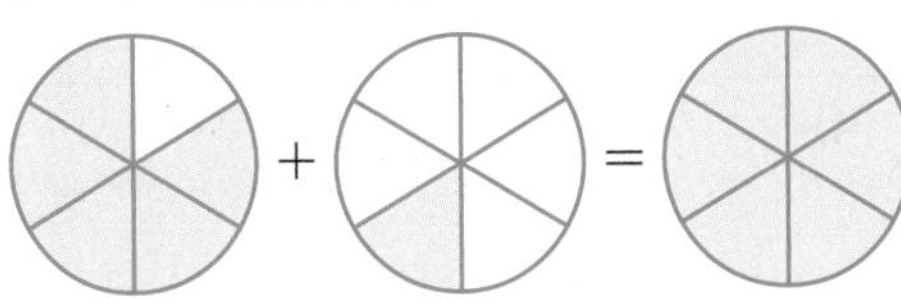

Problem Solving • Applications

7\. MATHEMATICAL PRACTICE 2 **Reason Abstractly** Sean has $\frac{1}{5}$ of a cupcake and $\frac{1}{5}$ of a large cake.

a. Are the wholes the same? Explain.

____

b. Does the sum $\frac{1}{5} + \frac{1}{5} = \frac{2}{5}$ make sense in this situation? Explain.

____

8\. GO DEEPER Carrie's dance class learned $\frac{1}{5}$ of a new dance on Monday, and $\frac{2}{5}$ of the dance on Tuesday. What fraction of the dance is left for the class to learn on Wednesday?

____

Sense or Nonsense?

9. THINK SMARTER Samantha and Kim used different models to help find $\frac{1}{3} + \frac{1}{6}$. Whose model makes sense? Whose model is nonsense? Explain your reasoning below each model.

Samantha's Model

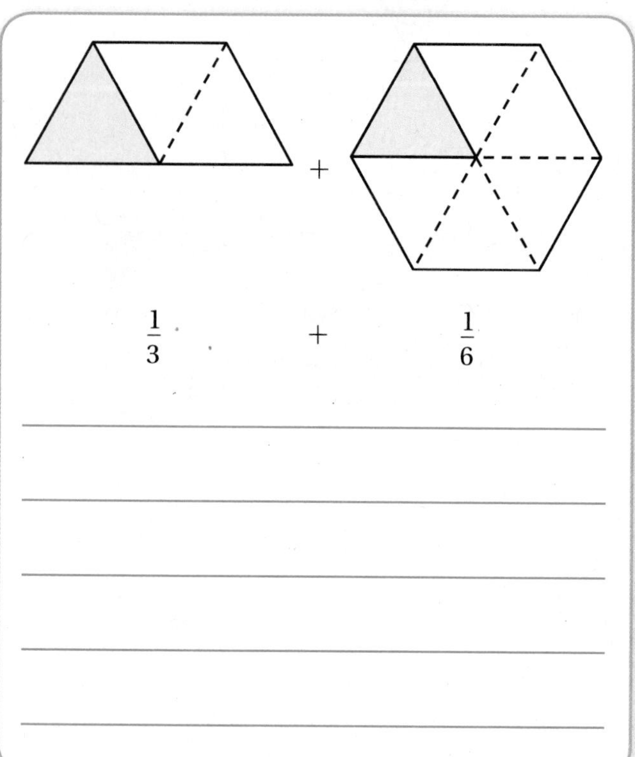

$\frac{1}{3} + \frac{1}{6}$

Kim's Model

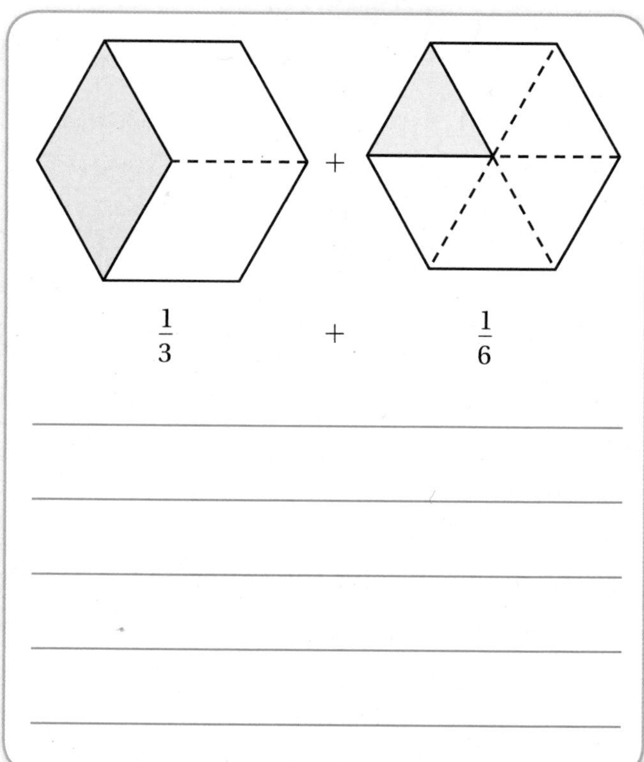

$\frac{1}{3} + \frac{1}{6}$

10. GO DEEPER Draw a model you could use to add $\frac{1}{4} + \frac{1}{2}$.

Personal Math Trainer

11. THINK SMARTER + Cindy has two jars of paint. One jar is $\frac{3}{8}$ full. The other jar is $\frac{2}{8}$ full.

Use the fractions to write an equation that shows the amount of paint Cindy has.

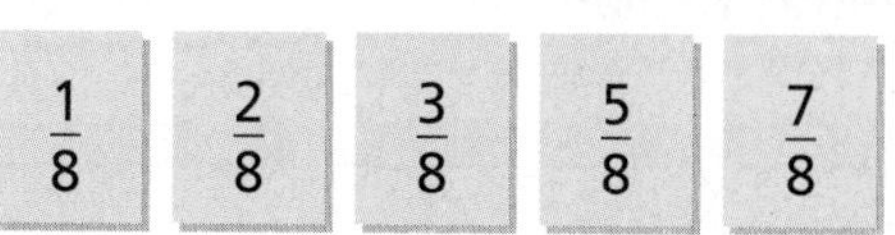

$\frac{3}{8}$ $\frac{2}{8}$

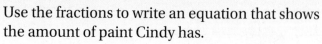

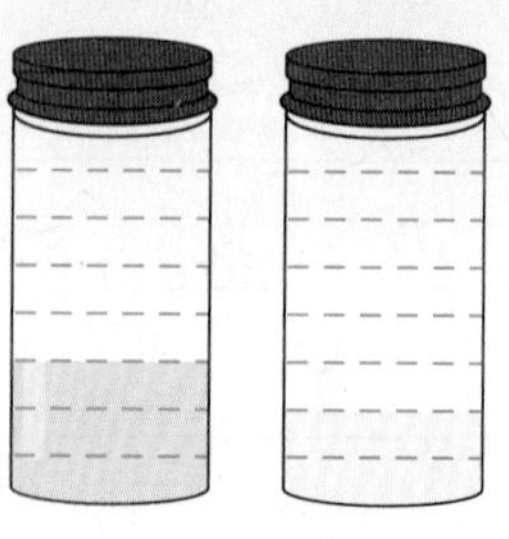

_____ + _____ = _____

FOR MORE PRACTICE: Standards Practice Book

Name ______________________

Write Fractions as Sums

Essential Question How can you write a fraction as a sum of fractions with the same denominators?

Numbers and Operations—Fractions—4.NF.3b

MATHEMATICAL PRACTICES
MP.2, MP.4, MP.8

Unlock the Problem (Real World)

Emilio cut a sandwich into 8 equal pieces and ate 1 piece. He has $\frac{7}{8}$ of the sandwich left. Emilio put each remaining piece on a snack plate. How many snack plates did he use? What part of the sandwich did he put on each plate?

Each piece of the sandwich is $\frac{1}{8}$ of the whole. $\frac{1}{8}$ is called a **unit fraction** because it tells the part of the whole that 1 piece represents. A unit fraction always has a numerator of 1.

Example 1 Write $\frac{7}{8}$ as a sum of unit fractions.

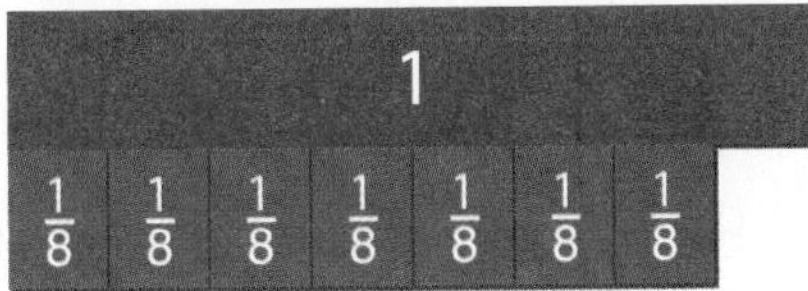

$\frac{7}{8}$ = ______ + ______ + ______ + ______ + ______ + ______ + ______

The number of addends represents the number of plates used.

The unit fractions represent the part of the sandwich on each plate.

So, Emilio used ______ plates. He put ______ of a sandwich on each plate.

1. What if Emilio ate 3 pieces of the sandwich instead of 1 piece? How many snack plates would he need? What part of the sandwich would be on each plate? Explain.

____

____

____

____

Example 2 Write a fraction as a sum.

Kevin and Isabel are going to share a whole pizza. The pizza is cut into 6 equal slices. They will put the slices on two separate dishes. What part of the whole pizza could be on each dish?

Shade the models to show three different ways Kevin and Isabel could share the pizza. Write an equation for each model.

Think: $\frac{6}{6}$ = 1 whole pizza.

$\frac{1}{6}$ $\frac{1}{6}$ $\frac{1}{6}$ $\frac{1}{6}$ $\frac{1}{6}$ $\frac{1}{6}$ = +

= ____ + ____

$\frac{1}{6}$ $\frac{1}{6}$ $\frac{1}{6}$ $\frac{1}{6}$ $\frac{1}{6}$ $\frac{1}{6}$ = +

= ____ + ____

$\frac{1}{6}$ $\frac{1}{6}$ $\frac{1}{6}$ $\frac{1}{6}$ $\frac{1}{6}$ $\frac{1}{6}$ = +

= ____ + ____

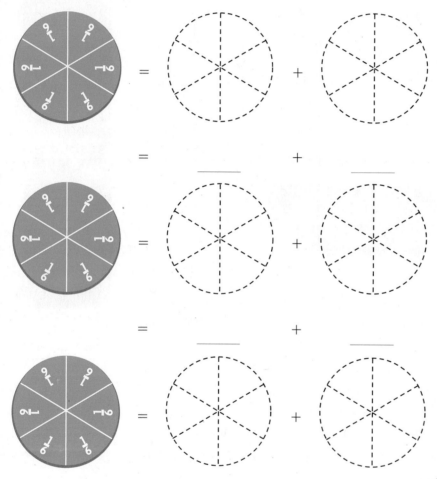

Math Talk **Mathematical Practices**

If there were 8 dishes, could $\frac{1}{6}$ of the whole pizza be on each dish? **Explain.**

2. What if 3 friends share the pizza and they put the pizza slices on three separate dishes? What part of the pizza could be on each dish? Write equations to support your answer.

____

____

Name ______________________________

Share and Show

1. Write $\frac{3}{4}$ as a sum of unit fractions.

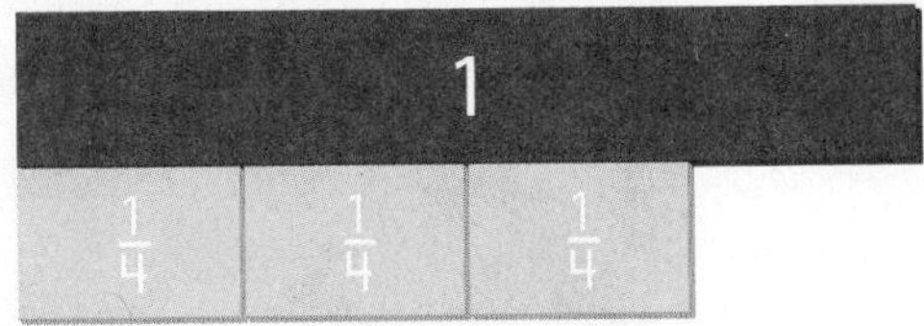

$\frac{3}{4} =$ ______ + ______ + ______

Write the fraction as a sum of unit fractions.

2.

1					
$\frac{1}{6}$	$\frac{1}{6}$	$\frac{1}{6}$	$\frac{1}{6}$	$\frac{1}{6}$	$\frac{1}{6}$

$\frac{5}{6} =$ ____________________

3.

1		
$\frac{1}{3}$	$\frac{1}{3}$	$\frac{1}{3}$

$\frac{2}{3} =$ ____________________

Math Talk — Mathematical Practices

Explain how the numerator in $\frac{5}{6}$ is related to the number of addends in the sum of its unit fractions.

On Your Own

Write the fraction as a sum of unit fractions.

4. $\frac{4}{12} =$ ____________________

5. $\frac{6}{8} =$ ____________________

Write the fraction as a sum of fractions three different ways.

6. $\frac{8}{10}$

____

____

____

7. $\frac{6}{6}$

____

____

____

8. MATHEMATICAL PRACTICE 3 **Compare Representations** How many different ways can you write a fraction that has a numerator of 2 as a sum of fractions? Explain.

____

____

Unlock the Problem 

9. THINKSMARTER Holly's garden is divided into 5 equal sections. She will fence the garden into 3 areas by grouping some equal sections together. What part of the garden could each fenced area be?

a. What information do you need to use?

____

____

b. How can writing an equation help you solve the problem? _______________

____

____

c. How can drawing a model help you write an equation?

____

____

d. Show how you can solve the problem.

e. Complete the sentence.

The garden can be fenced into ______, ______, and ______ parts or ______, ______, and ______ parts.

10. GO DEEPER Leena walked $\frac{2}{3}$ of a mile. What is $\frac{2}{3}$ written as a sum of unit fractions with a denominator of 9?

____

11. THINKSMARTER Ellie's mom sells toys. She sold $\frac{7}{10}$ of the toys. Select a way $\frac{7}{10}$ can be written as a sum of fractions. Mark all that apply.

Ⓐ $\frac{4}{10} + \frac{1}{10} + \frac{1}{10} + \frac{1}{10}$

Ⓑ $\frac{4}{10} + \frac{3}{10} + \frac{1}{10} + \frac{1}{10} + \frac{1}{10}$

Ⓒ $\frac{1}{10} + \frac{2}{10} + \frac{3}{10} + \frac{1}{10}$

FOR MORE PRACTICE:
Standards Practice Book

Name ______________________

Add Fractions Using Models

Essential Question How can you add fractions with like denominators using models?

Numbers and Operations—Fractions—4.NF.3d *Also 4.MD.2*

MATHEMATICAL PRACTICES
MP.2, MP.3, MP.5

Unlock the Problem (Real World)

Ms. Clark made a loaf of bread. She used $\frac{1}{8}$ of the bread for a snack and $\frac{5}{8}$ of the bread for lunch. How much did she use for a snack and lunch?

One Way Use a picture.

$\frac{1}{8}$ is ______ eighth-size piece of bread.

$\frac{5}{8}$ is ______ eighth-size pieces of bread.

Shade 1 eighth-size piece. Then shade 5 eighth-size pieces.

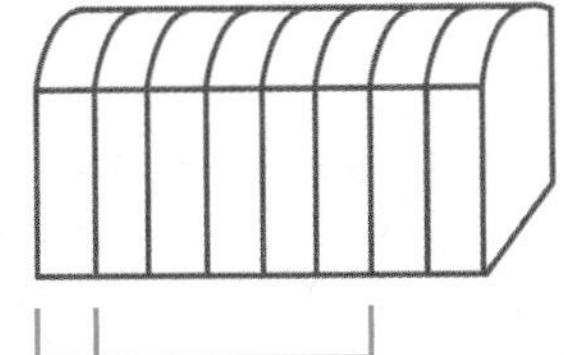

snack lunch

Think: The pieces you shaded represent the pieces Ms. Clark used.

So, Ms. Clark used ______ eighth-size pieces, or $\frac{}{8}$ of the bread.

Another Way Use fraction strips.

The 1 strip represents the whole loaf.

Each $\frac{1}{8}$ part represents 1 eighth-size piece of bread.

Shade $\frac{1}{8}$. Then shade $\frac{5}{8}$.

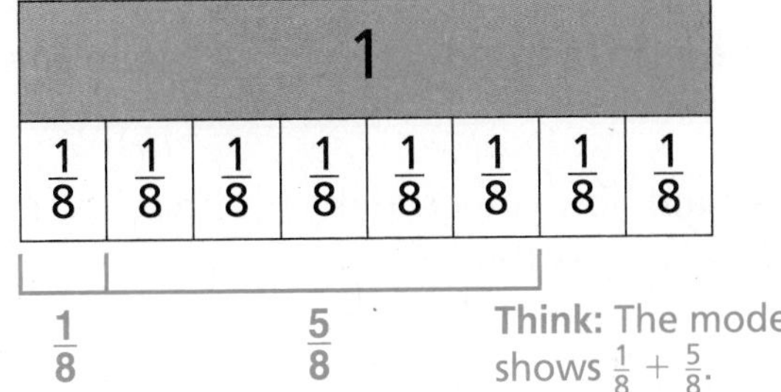

$\frac{1}{8}$ $\frac{5}{8}$

Think: The model shows $\frac{1}{8} + \frac{5}{8}$.

How many $\frac{1}{8}$-size parts are shaded? ______

Write the sum. $\frac{1}{8} + \frac{5}{8} = \frac{}{8}$

So, Ms. Clark used ______ of the bread.

1. Explain how the numerator of the sum is related to the fraction strip model.

____

____

Math Talk Mathematical Practices

Explain why $\frac{1}{8} + \frac{5}{8} \neq \frac{6}{16}$.

2. Explain how the denominator of the sum is related to the fraction strip model.

____

____

Example

Jacob needs two strips of wood to make masts for a miniature sailboat. One mast will be $\frac{3}{6}$ foot long. The other mast will be $\frac{2}{6}$ foot long. He has a strip of wood that is $\frac{4}{6}$ foot long. Is this strip of wood long enough to make both masts?

Shade the model to show $\frac{3}{6} + \frac{2}{6}$.

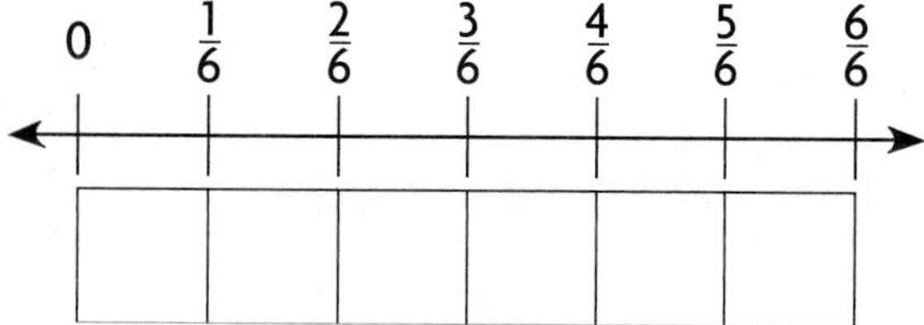

Write the sum. $\frac{3}{6} + \frac{2}{6} = \frac{\quad}{6}$

Is the sum less than or greater than $\frac{4}{6}$? __________

So, the strip of wood __________ long enough to make both masts.

3. Explain how you used the number line to determine if the sum was less than $\frac{4}{6}$.

____

____

4. What if each mast was $\frac{2}{6}$ foot long? Could Jacob use the strip of wood to make both masts? Explain.

____

Share and Show

1. Adrian's cat ate $\frac{3}{5}$ of a bag of cat treats in September and $\frac{1}{5}$ of the same bag of cat treats in October. What part of the bag of cat treats did Adrian's cat eat in both months?

Use the model to find the sum $\frac{3}{5} + \frac{1}{5}$.

How many fifth-size pieces are shown? ______

$\frac{3}{5} + \frac{1}{5} = \frac{\quad}{5}$ of a bag

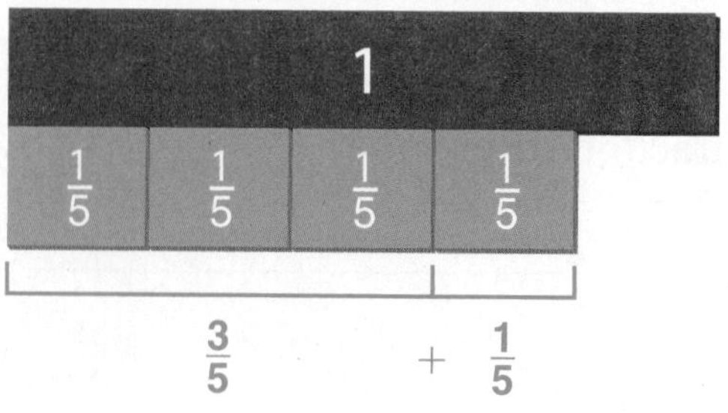

Name ____________________

Use the model to find the sum.

2.

1			
$\frac{1}{4}$	$\frac{1}{4}$	$\frac{1}{4}$	$\frac{1}{4}$

$\frac{1}{4}$ + $\frac{2}{4}$

$\frac{1}{4} + \frac{2}{4} =$ ______

3.

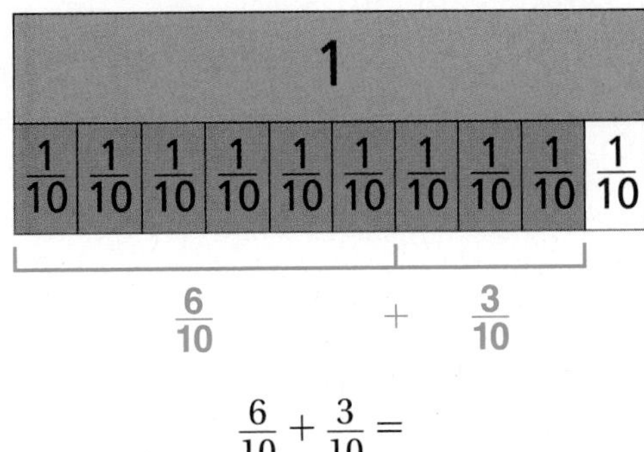

$\frac{6}{10} + \frac{3}{10} =$ ______

Find the sum. Use models to help.

4. $\frac{3}{6} + \frac{3}{6} =$ ______

5. $\frac{5}{8} + \frac{2}{8} =$ ______

6. $\frac{1}{3} + \frac{1}{3} =$ ______

Math Talk — **Mathematical Practices**

Explain how to add $\frac{2}{6} + \frac{3}{6}$.

On Your Own

Find the sum. Use models to help.

7. $\frac{5}{8} + \frac{2}{8} =$ ______

8. $\frac{2}{5} + \frac{2}{5} =$ ______

9. $\frac{4}{6} + \frac{1}{6} =$ ______

10. $\frac{1}{10} + \frac{4}{10} =$ ______

11. $\frac{1}{4} + \frac{1}{4} =$ ______

12. $\frac{5}{12} + \frac{5}{12} =$ ______

Problem Solving • Applications

13. THINK SMARTER A sum has five addends. Each addend is a unit fraction. The sum is 1. What are the addends?

____

14. THINK SMARTER In a survey, $\frac{4}{12}$ of the students chose Friday and $\frac{5}{12}$ chose Saturday as their favorite day of the week. What fraction shows the students who chose Friday or Saturday as their favorite day? Shade the model to show your answer.

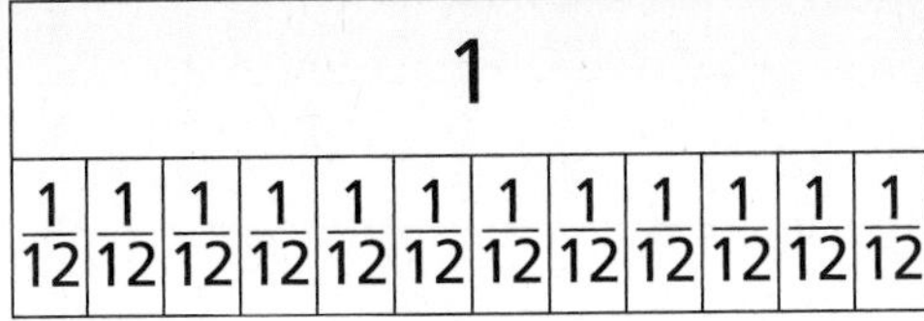

__________ of the students chose Friday or Saturday.

15. MATHEMATICAL PRACTICE 4 **Model Mathematics** Jin is putting colored sand in a jar. She filled $\frac{2}{10}$ of the jar with blue sand and $\frac{4}{10}$ of the jar with pink sand. Describe one way to model the part of the jar filled with sand.

____

____

Connect to Art

Stained Glass Windows

Have you ever seen a stained glass window in a building or home? Artists have been designing stained glass windows for hundreds of years.

Help design the stained glass sail on the boat below.

Materials ■ color pencils

Look at the eight triangles in the sail. Use the guide below to color the triangles:

- $\frac{2}{8}$ blue
- $\frac{3}{8}$ red
- $\frac{2}{8}$ orange
- $\frac{1}{8}$ yellow

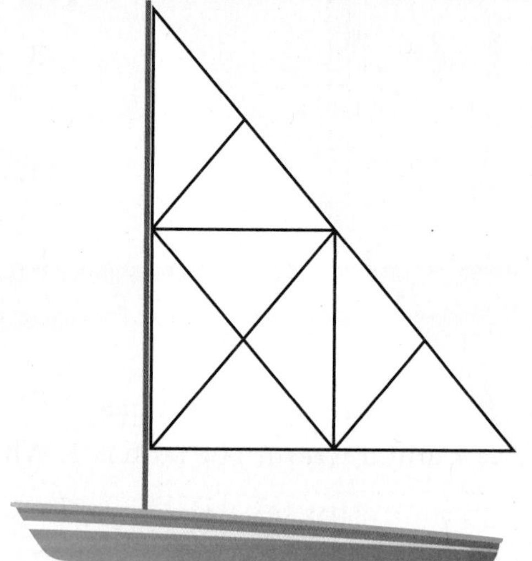

16. MATHEMATICAL PRACTICE 4 **Write an Equation** Write an equation that shows the fraction of triangles that are red or blue.

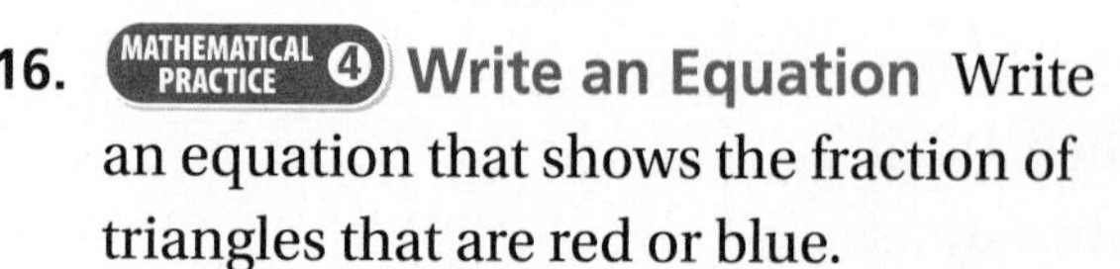

____

17. GO DEEPER What color is the greatest part of the sail? Write a fraction for that color. How do you know that fraction is greater than the other fractions? Explain.

____

____

____

FOR MORE PRACTICE:
Standards Practice Book

Name ______________________________

Subtract Fractions Using Models

Essential Question How can you subtract fractions with like denominators using models?

Numbers and Operations—Fractions—4.NF.3d *Also 4.MD.2*

MATHEMATICAL PRACTICES
MP.1, MP.2, MP.4, MP.5

Unlock the Problem

A rover needs to travel $\frac{5}{8}$ mile to reach its destination. It has already traveled $\frac{3}{8}$ mile. How much farther does the rover need to travel?

Compare fractions to find the difference.

STEP 1 Shade the model.

Shade the model to show the total distance.

Then shade the model to show how much distance the rover has already covered.

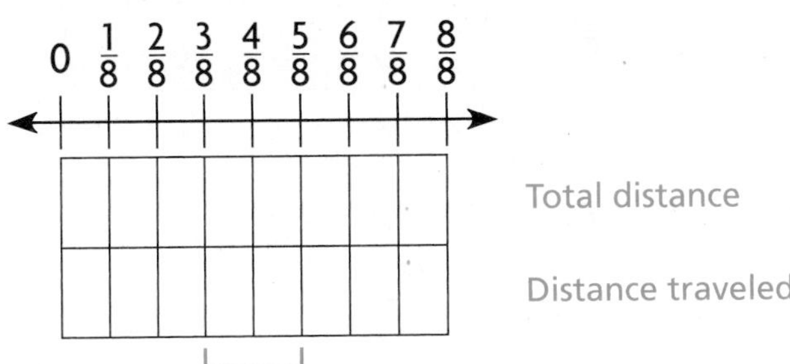

Think: The difference is ______.

STEP 2 Write the difference.

$$\frac{5}{8} - \frac{3}{8} = \frac{\square}{8}$$

So, the rover needs to travel ______ mile farther.

1. Explain how the model shows how much farther the rover needs to travel.

____

____

2. Explain how you can use the model to find $\frac{6}{8} - \frac{2}{8}$.

____

____

Example

Sam ordered a small pizza, which was cut into 6 equal slices. He ate $\frac{2}{6}$ of the pizza and put the rest away for later. How much of the pizza did he put away for later?

Find $1 - \frac{2}{6}$.

- How much pizza did Sam begin with? ______
- How many slices are in the whole? ______
- How many slices did Sam eat? ______

One Way Use a picture.

Shade 1 whole.

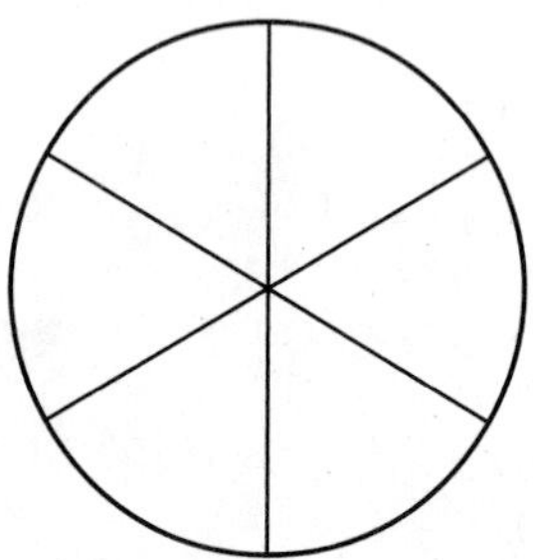

Cross out the parts Sam ate.

Think: He ate $\frac{2}{6}$ of the pizza, or 2 sixth-size parts.

How many sixth-size parts are left? ______

Another Way Use fraction strips.

Use six $\frac{1}{6}$-size parts to model the whole pizza.

1					
$\frac{1}{6}$	$\frac{1}{6}$	$\frac{1}{6}$	$\frac{1}{6}$	$\frac{1}{6}$	$\frac{1}{6}$

How many $\frac{1}{6}$-size parts should you cross out to model the slices Sam ate? ______

How many $\frac{1}{6}$-size parts are left? ______

Write the difference.

$1 - \frac{\quad}{\quad} = \frac{\quad}{\quad}$

So, Sam put ______ of the pizza away for later.

Math Talk **Mathematical Practices**

Explain why it makes sense to think of 1 whole as $\frac{6}{6}$ in this problem.

3. Explain how the equation $\frac{6}{6} - \frac{2}{6} = \frac{4}{6}$ is related to the problem situation.

______

______

4. Sam ate $\frac{2}{3}$ of the pizza and put the rest away for later. Explain how you can use the circle to find how much of the pizza Sam put away for later.

______

______

______

Name ______________________________

Share and Show

1. Lisa needs $\frac{4}{5}$ pound of shrimp to make shrimp salad. She has $\frac{1}{5}$ pound of shrimp. How much more shrimp does Lisa need to make the salad?

   0 $\frac{1}{5}$ $\frac{2}{5}$ $\frac{3}{5}$ $\frac{4}{5}$ $\frac{5}{5}$

   Subtract $\frac{4}{5} - \frac{1}{5}$. Use the model to help.

   Shade the model to show how much shrimp Lisa needs.

   Then shade the model to show how much shrimp Lisa has. Compare the difference between the two shaded rows.

   $\frac{4}{5} - \frac{1}{5} = \frac{\square}{5}$ pound

   Lisa needs ______ pound more shrimp.

Use the model to find the difference.

2. $\frac{3}{6} - \frac{2}{6} = \frac{\square}{6}$

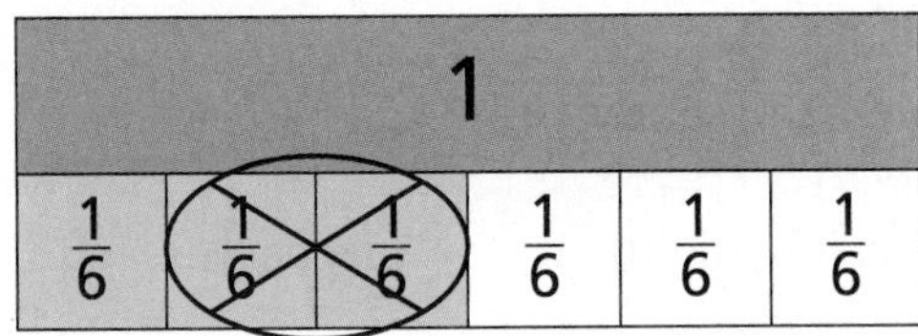

3. $\frac{8}{10} - \frac{3}{10} = \frac{\square}{10}$

   1

   1/10 1/10 1/10 1/10 1/10 1/10 1/10 1/10 1/10 1/10

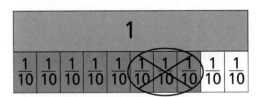

Subtract. Use models to help.

4. $\frac{5}{8} - \frac{2}{8} =$ ______

5. $\frac{7}{12} - \frac{2}{12} =$ ______

6. $\frac{3}{4} - \frac{2}{4} =$ ______

Mathematical Practices

Explain why the numerator changes when you subtract fractions with like denominators, but the denominator doesn't.

On Your Own

Subtract. Use models to help.

7. $\frac{2}{3} - \frac{1}{3} =$ ______

8. $\frac{7}{8} - \frac{5}{8} =$ ______

9. THINK SMARTER Explain how you could find the unknown addend in $\frac{2}{6} +$ ______ $= 1$ without using a model.

____

____

____

Unlock the Problem Real World

10. GO DEEPER Mrs. Ruiz served a pie for dessert two nights in a row. The drawings below show the pie after her family ate dessert on each night. What fraction of the pie did they eat on the second night?

First night **Second night**

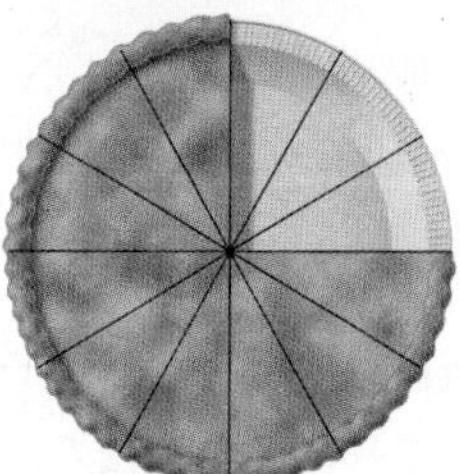

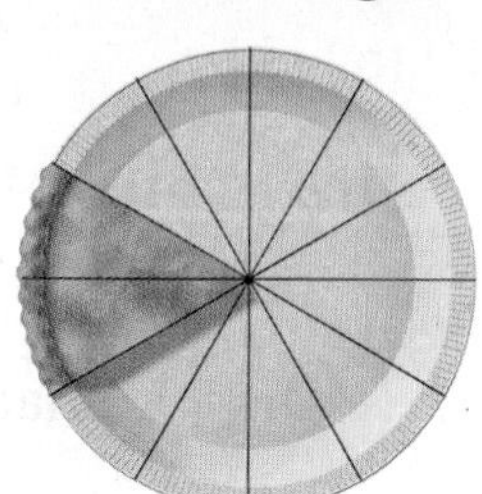

a. What do you need to know? ______________________

____

b. How can you find the number of pieces eaten on the second night? ______________________

____

c. Explain the steps you used to solve the problem.

____

____

____

d. Complete the sentences.

After the first night, _______ pieces were left.

After the second night, _______ pieces were left.

So, _______ of the pie was eaten on the second night.

11. MATHEMATICAL PRACTICE 6 **Make Connections Between Models** Judi ate $\frac{7}{8}$ of a small pizza and Jack ate $\frac{2}{8}$ of a second small pizza. How much more of a pizza did Judi eat?

____

12. THINK SMARTER Keiko sewed $\frac{3}{4}$ yard of lace on her backpack. Pam sewed $\frac{1}{4}$ yard of lace on her backpack. Shade the model to show how much more lace Keiko sewed on her backpack than Pam.

1			
$\frac{1}{4}$	$\frac{1}{4}$	$\frac{1}{4}$	$\frac{1}{4}$

Keiko sewed __________ yard more lace on her backpack than Pam.

FOR MORE PRACTICE: Standards Practice Book

Name ______

Add and Subtract Fractions

Essential Question How can you add and subtract fractions with like denominators?

Numbers and Operations—Fractions—4.NF.3d

MATHEMATICAL PRACTICES
MP.1, MP.2, MP.4

Unlock the Problem

Julie is making a poster for a book report. The directions say to use $\frac{1}{5}$ of the poster to describe the setting, $\frac{2}{5}$ of the poster to describe the characters, and the rest of the poster to describe the plot. What part of the poster will she use to describe the plot?

Example Use a model.

Shade ______ to represent the part for the setting.

Shade ______ to represent the part for the characters.

1				
$\frac{1}{5}$	$\frac{1}{5}$	$\frac{1}{5}$	$\frac{1}{5}$	$\frac{1}{5}$

- Write an equation for the part of the poster used for the setting and characters. ______
- What does the part of the model that is not shaded represent?

  ______
- Write an equation for the part of the poster she will use for the plot.

  ______

So, Julie will use ______ of the poster to describe the plot.

Mathematical Practices

Why should Julie divide her poster into 5 equal parts instead of 3 equal parts? **Explain.**

1. **What's the Error?** Luke says $\frac{1}{5} + \frac{2}{5} = \frac{3}{10}$. Describe his error.

______

______

______

Common Denominators Fractions with common denominators represent wholes divided into the same number of equal-size parts. To add or subtract fractions with the same denominator, you can add or subtract the number of parts given in the numerators.

Example Complete each equation.

Words	Fractions
1 fourth-size part + 2 fourth-size parts = ______ fourth-size parts	$\frac{1}{4} + \frac{2}{4} = \frac{\square}{4}$
3 sixth-size parts + 2 sixth-size parts = ______	$\frac{3}{6} + \frac{2}{6} = \frac{\square}{\square}$
7 tenth-size parts − 4 tenth-size parts = ______	$\frac{\square}{\square} - \frac{\square}{\square} = \frac{\square}{\square}$

Share and Show

Math Talk Mathematical Practices

Explain why $\frac{11}{12} - \frac{5}{6} \neq \frac{6}{6}$.

1. 9 twelfth-size parts − 5 twelfth-size parts = ______

$\frac{9}{12} - \frac{5}{12} =$ ______

Find the sum or difference.

2. $\frac{3}{12} + \frac{8}{12} =$ ______
3. $\frac{1}{3} + \frac{1}{3} =$ ______
4. $\frac{3}{4} - \frac{1}{4} =$ ______
5. $\frac{2}{6} + \frac{2}{6} =$ ______
6. $\frac{3}{8} + \frac{1}{8} =$ ______
7. $\frac{6}{10} - \frac{2}{10} =$ ______

On Your Own

Find the sum or difference.

8. $\frac{1}{2} + \frac{1}{2} =$ ______
9. $\frac{5}{6} - \frac{4}{6} =$ ______
10. $\frac{4}{5} - \frac{2}{5} =$ ______
11. $\frac{1}{10} + \frac{3}{10} =$ ______
12. $\frac{5}{12} - \frac{1}{12} =$ ______
13. $\frac{3}{8} + \frac{2}{8} =$ ______

Practice: Copy and Solve **Find the sum or difference.**

14. $\frac{1}{4} + \frac{1}{4} =$ ______
15. $\frac{9}{10} - \frac{5}{10} =$ ______
16. $\frac{1}{12} + \frac{7}{12} =$ ______

Name ______________________________

Problem Solving • Applications

17. MATHEMATICAL PRACTICE 6 A city worker is painting a stripe down the center of Main Street. Main Street is $\frac{8}{10}$ mile long. The worker painted $\frac{4}{10}$ mile of the street. **Explain** how to find what part of a mile is left to paint.

____

____

____

18. THINK SMARTER **Sense or Nonsense?** Brian says that when you add or subtract fractions with the same denominator, you can add or subtract the numerators and keep the same denominator. Is Brian correct? Explain.

____

____

____

____

____

19. GO DEEPER The length of a rope was $\frac{6}{8}$ yard. Jeff cut the rope into 3 pieces. Each piece is a different length measured in eighths of a yard. What is the length of each piece of rope?

____

20. THINK SMARTER For 20a–20d, choose Yes or No to show if the sum or difference is correct.

20a. $\frac{3}{5} + \frac{1}{5} = \frac{4}{5}$ ○ Yes ○ No

20b. $\frac{1}{4} + \frac{2}{4} = \frac{3}{8}$ ○ Yes ○ No

20c. $\frac{5}{8} - \frac{4}{8} = \frac{1}{8}$ ○ Yes ○ No

20d. $\frac{4}{9} - \frac{2}{9} = \frac{6}{9}$ ○ Yes ○ No

Sense or Nonsense?

21. Harry says that $\frac{1}{4} + \frac{1}{8} = \frac{2}{8}$. Jane says $\frac{1}{4} + \frac{1}{8} = \frac{3}{8}$. Whose answer makes sense? Whose answer is nonsense? Explain your reasoning. Draw a model to help.

Harry

$\frac{1}{4} + \frac{1}{8} = \frac{2}{8}$

Jane

$\frac{1}{4} + \frac{1}{8} = \frac{3}{8}$

Model

Harry

Jane

FOR MORE PRACTICE:
Standards Practice Book

Name ____________________

Vocabulary

Choose the best term from the box.

Vocabulary
fraction
simplest form
unit fraction

1. A ______________ always has a numerator of 1. (p. 283)

Concepts and Skills

Write the fraction as a sum of unit fractions. (4.NF.3b)

2. $\frac{3}{10} =$ ______________

3. $\frac{6}{6} =$ ______________

Use the model to write an equation. (4.NF.3a)

4. 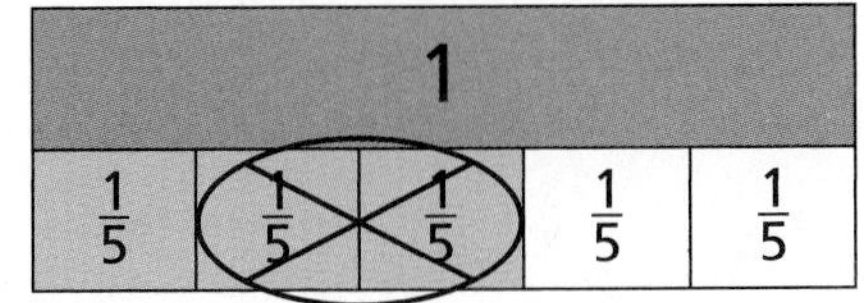

____

5. 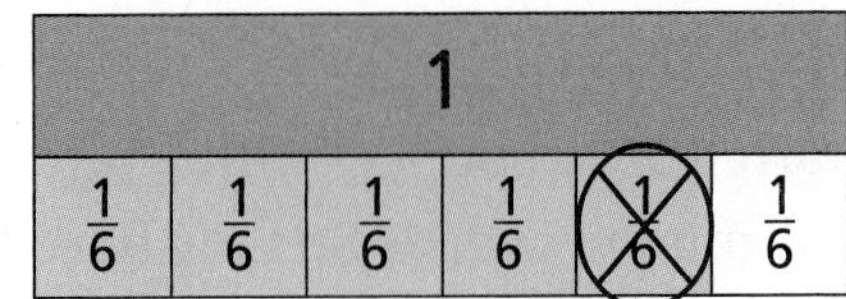

____

Use the model to solve the equation. (4.NF.3a)

6. $\frac{3}{8} + \frac{2}{8} =$ ______

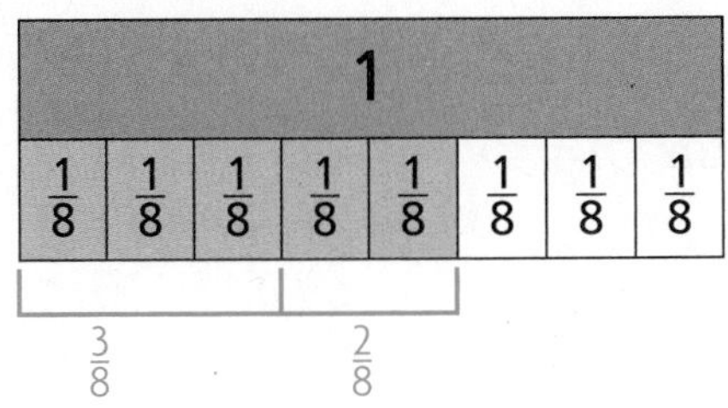

7. $\frac{4}{10} + \frac{5}{10} =$ ______

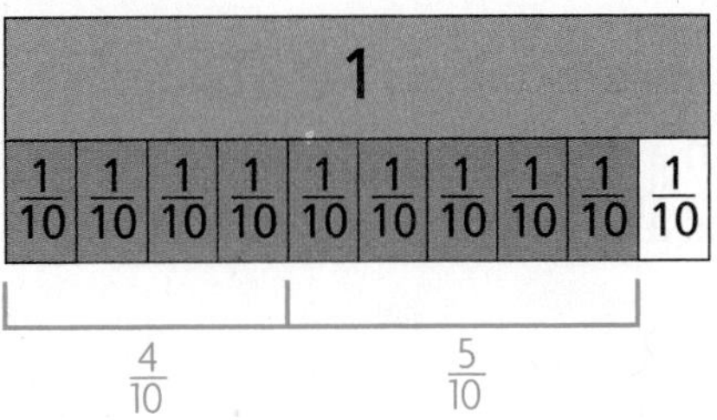

Find the sum or difference. (4.NF.3d)

8. $\frac{9}{12} - \frac{7}{12} =$ ______________

9. $\frac{2}{3} + \frac{1}{3} =$ ______________

10. $\frac{1}{5} + \frac{3}{5} =$ ______

11. $\frac{2}{6} + \frac{2}{6} =$ ______________

12. $\frac{4}{4} - \frac{2}{4} =$ ______________

13. $\frac{7}{8} - \frac{4}{8} =$ ______

14. Tyrone mixed $\frac{7}{12}$ quart of red paint with $\frac{1}{12}$ quart of yellow paint. How much paint does Tyrone have in the mixture? (4.NF.3d)

____

15. Jorge lives $\frac{6}{8}$ mile from school and $\frac{2}{8}$ mile from a ballpark. How much farther does Jorge live from school than from the ballpark? (4.NF.3d)

____

16. Su Ling started an art project with 1 yard of felt. She used $\frac{5}{6}$ yard. How much felt does Su Ling have left? (4.NF.3d)

____

17. Eloise hung artwork on $\frac{2}{5}$ of a bulletin board. She hung math papers on $\frac{1}{5}$ of the same bulletin board. What part of the bulletin board has artwork or math papers? (4.NF.3d)

____

Name ____________________

Rename Fractions and Mixed Numbers

Essential Question How can you rename mixed numbers as fractions greater than 1 and rename fractions greater than 1 as mixed numbers?

Numbers and Operations—Fractions—4.NF.3b *Also 4.MD.2*

MATHEMATICAL PRACTICES
MP.1, MP.4

Unlock the Problem

Mr. Fox has $2\frac{3}{6}$ loaves of corn bread. Each loaf was cut into $\frac{1}{6}$-size pieces. If he has 14 people over for dinner, is there enough bread for each person to have 1 piece?

- What is the size of 1 piece of bread relative to the whole?

____

- How much bread does Mr. Fox need for 14 people?

____

A **mixed number** is a number represented by a whole number and a fraction. You can write a mixed number as a fraction.

To find how many $\frac{1}{6}$-size pieces are in $2\frac{3}{6}$, write $2\frac{3}{6}$ as a fraction.

Example Write a mixed number as a fraction.

THINK	MODEL AND RECORD
STEP 1 Model $2\frac{3}{6}$.	1 | 1 | $\frac{1}{6}$ $\frac{1}{6}$ $\frac{1}{6}$ 1, 1, $\frac{3}{6}$ $2\frac{3}{6}$ = ____ + ____ + $\frac{\_\_}{\_\_}$
STEP 2 Find how many $\frac{1}{6}$-size pieces are in each whole. Model $2\frac{3}{6}$ using only $\frac{1}{6}$-size pieces.	1 | 1 | $\frac{1}{6}$ $\frac{1}{6}$ $\frac{1}{6}$ $\frac{1}{6}$ $\frac{1}{6}$ $\frac{1}{6}$ $\frac{1}{6}$ $\frac{1}{6}$ $\frac{1}{6}$ | $\frac{1}{6}$ $\frac{1}{6}$ $\frac{1}{6}$ $\frac{1}{6}$ $\frac{1}{6}$ $\frac{1}{6}$ | $\frac{1}{6}$ $\frac{1}{6}$ $\frac{1}{6}$ $\frac{6}{6}$, $\frac{6}{6}$, $\frac{3}{6}$ $2\frac{3}{6}$ = $\frac{\_\_}{\_\_}$ + $\frac{\_\_}{\_\_}$ + $\frac{\_\_}{\_\_}$
STEP 3 Find the total number of $\frac{1}{6}$-size pieces in $2\frac{3}{6}$.	Think: Find $\frac{6}{6} + \frac{6}{6} + \frac{3}{6}$. $2\frac{3}{6}$ = $\frac{\_\_}{\_\_}$

There are ______ sixth-size pieces in $2\frac{3}{6}$.

So, there is enough bread for 14 people to each have 1 piece.

Mathematical Practices

Explain how to write $1\frac{1}{4}$ as a fraction without using a model.

Example Write a fraction greater than 1 as a mixed number.

To weave a bracelet, Charlene needs 7 pieces of brown thread. Each piece of thread must be $\frac{1}{3}$ yard long. How much thread should she buy to weave the bracelet?

Write $\frac{7}{3}$ as a mixed number.

THINK	MODEL AND RECORD
STEP 1 Model $\frac{7}{3}$.	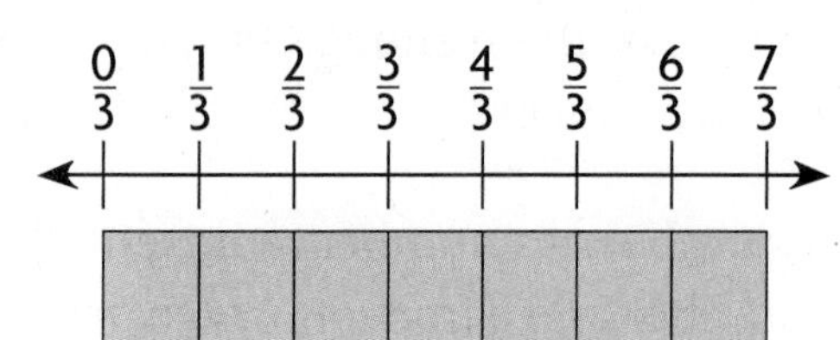 $\frac{7}{3} = \_\_ + \_\_ + \_\_ + \_\_ + \_\_ + \_\_ + \_\_$
STEP 2 Find how many wholes are in $\frac{7}{3}$, and how many thirds are left over.	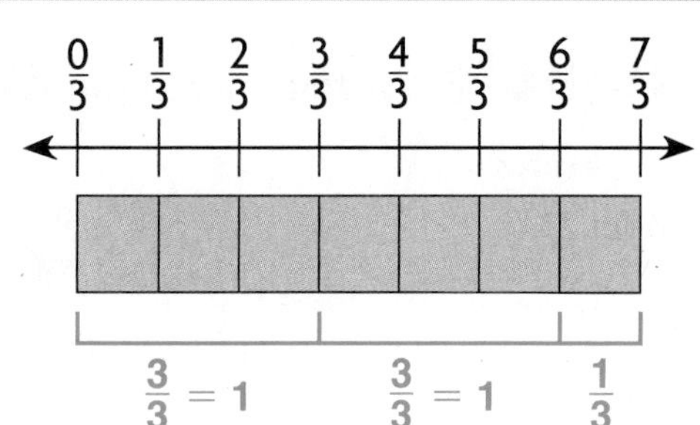 $\frac{7}{3} = \_\_\_\_ + \_\_\_\_ + \_\_$
STEP 3 Write $\frac{7}{3}$ as a mixed number.	$\frac{7}{3} = \_\_\frac{\_\_}{\_\_}$

So, Charlene should buy ______ yards of thread.

Share and Show

Write the unknown numbers. Write mixed numbers above the number line and fractions greater than one below the number line.

1.

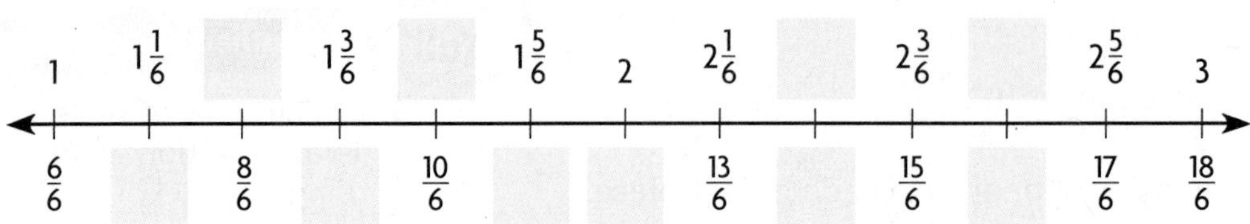

Name ________________________________

Write the mixed number as a fraction.

2. $1\frac{1}{8}$ ______

3. $1\frac{3}{5}$ ______

✓ 4. $1\frac{2}{3}$ ______

Write the fraction as a mixed number.

5. $\frac{11}{4}$ ______

6. $\frac{6}{5}$ ______

✓ 7. $\frac{13}{10}$ ______

Mathematical Practices

Describe how you can compare $1\frac{3}{5}$ and $\frac{7}{5}$.

On Your Own

Write the mixed number as a fraction.

8. $2\frac{7}{10}$ ______

9. $3\frac{2}{3}$ ______

10. $4\frac{2}{5}$ ______

Write the fraction as a mixed number.

11. $\frac{9}{5}$ ______

12. $\frac{11}{10}$ ______

13. $\frac{12}{2}$ ______

MATHEMATICAL PRACTICE 8 Use Repeated Reasoning **Algebra** **Find the unknown numbers.**

14. $\frac{13}{7} = 1\frac{\square}{7}$ ______

15. $\square\frac{5}{6} = \frac{23}{6}$ ______

16. $\frac{57}{11} = \square\frac{\square}{11}$ ______

Problem Solving • Applications Real World

Use the recipe to solve 17–19.

Energy Squares
$1\frac{1}{3}$ cups honey
$1\frac{1}{2}$ cups peanut butter
1 cup dry milk
$3\frac{1}{4}$ cups bran cereal

17. MATHEMATICAL PRACTICE 2 **Reason Quantitatively** Cal is making energy squares. How many $\frac{1}{2}$ cups of peanut butter are used in the recipe?

____

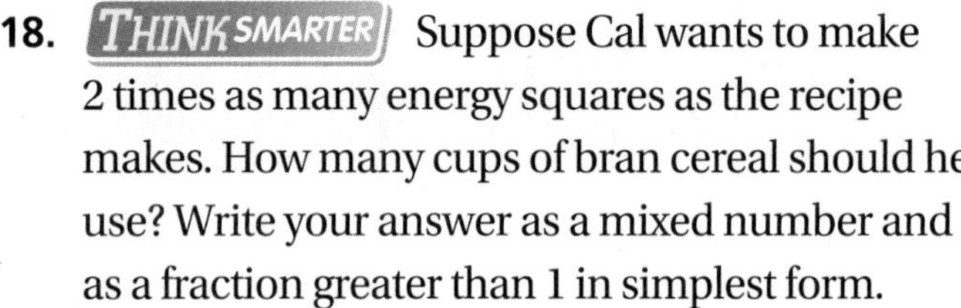

18. THINK SMARTER Suppose Cal wants to make 2 times as many energy squares as the recipe makes. How many cups of bran cereal should he use? Write your answer as a mixed number and as a fraction greater than 1 in simplest form.

____

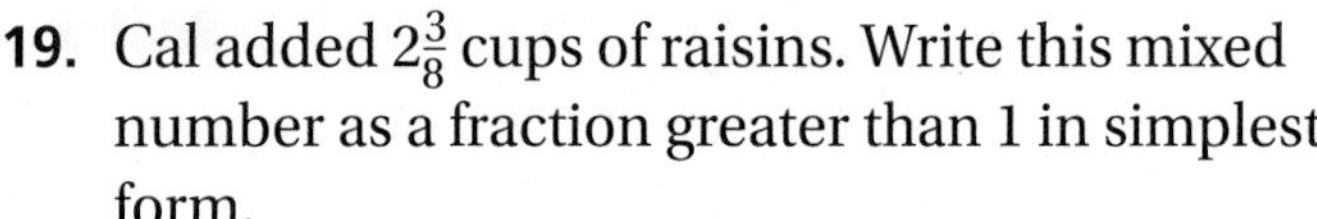

19. Cal added $2\frac{3}{8}$ cups of raisins. Write this mixed number as a fraction greater than 1 in simplest form.

____

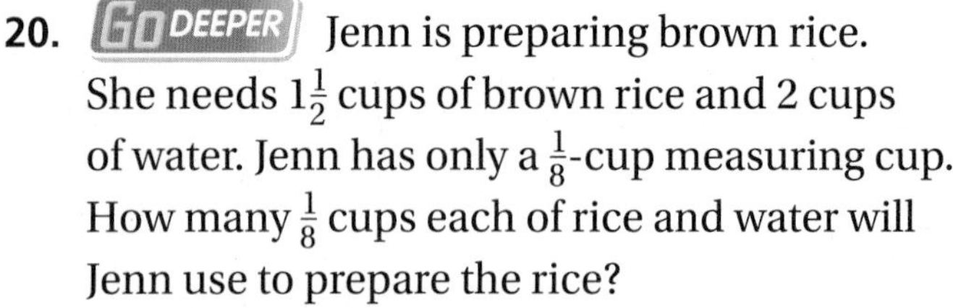

20. GO DEEPER Jenn is preparing brown rice. She needs $1\frac{1}{2}$ cups of brown rice and 2 cups of water. Jenn has only a $\frac{1}{8}$-cup measuring cup. How many $\frac{1}{8}$ cups each of rice and water will Jenn use to prepare the rice?

____

WRITE ▸ Math • Show Your Work

21. THINK SMARTER Draw a line to show the mixed number and fraction that have the same value.

$1\frac{2}{5}$	$2\frac{3}{8}$	$4\frac{1}{3}$	$1\frac{2}{3}$
•	•	•	•
•	•	•	•
$\frac{30}{3}$	$\frac{13}{3}$	$\frac{4}{3}$	$\frac{8}{5}$

FOR MORE PRACTICE: Standards Practice Book

Name ________________________________

Add and Subtract Mixed Numbers

Essential Question How can you add and subtract mixed numbers with like denominators?

Numbers and Operations—Fractions—4.NF.3c *Also 4.MD.2*

MATHEMATICAL PRACTICES
MP.2, MP.4, MP.8

Unlock the Problem (Real World)

After a party, there were $1\frac{4}{6}$ quesadillas left on one tray and $2\frac{3}{6}$ quesadillas left on another tray. How many quesadillas were left?

- What operation will you use?

____

- Is the sum of the fractional parts of the mixed numbers greater than 1?

____

Example Add mixed numbers.

THINK	MODEL	RECORD
STEP 1 Add the fractional parts of the mixed numbers.	Think: Shade to model $\frac{4}{6} + \frac{3}{6}$. 	$1\frac{4}{6}$ $+ 2\frac{3}{6}$ ——— $\frac{\square}{\square}$
STEP 2 Add the whole-number parts of the mixed numbers.	Think: Shade to model 1 + 2. 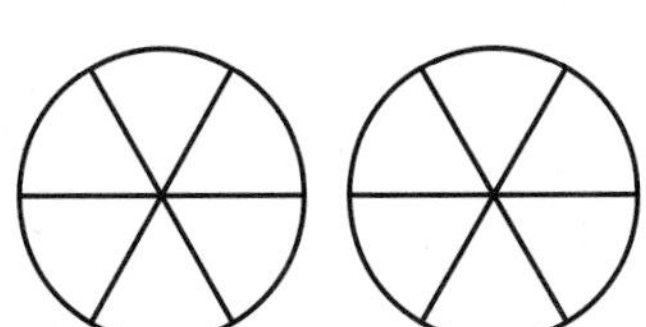	$1\frac{4}{6}$ $+ 2\frac{3}{6}$ ——— $\square\frac{7}{6}$
STEP 3 Rename the sum.	Think: $\frac{7}{6}$ is greater than 1. Group the wholes together to rename the sum. The model shows a total of ___ wholes and $\frac{\square}{\square}$ left over.	$3\frac{7}{6} = 3 + \frac{6}{6} + \frac{\square}{\square}$ $= 3 + 1 + \frac{\square}{\square} = \square\frac{\square}{\square}$

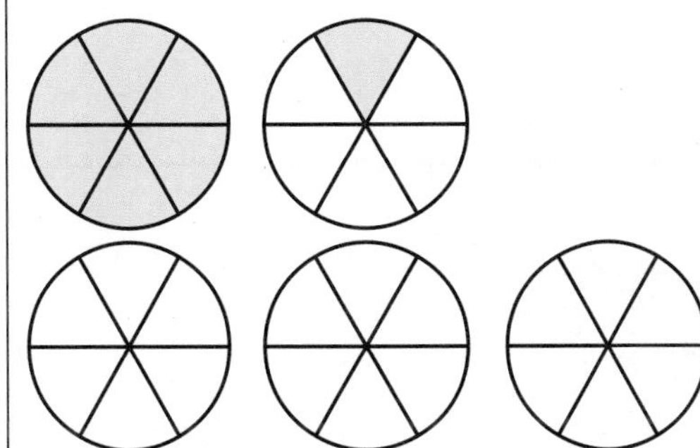

So, ______ quesadillas were left.

Math Talk — **Mathematical Practices**

When modeling sums such as $\frac{4}{6}$ and $\frac{3}{6}$, why is it helpful to combine parts into wholes when possible? **Explain.**

Example Subtract mixed numbers.

Alejandro had $3\frac{4}{6}$ quesadillas. His family ate $2\frac{3}{6}$ of the quesadillas. How many quesadillas are left?

Find $3\frac{4}{6} - 2\frac{3}{6}$.

Shade the model to show $3\frac{4}{6}$.

Then cross out $2\frac{3}{6}$ to model the subtraction.

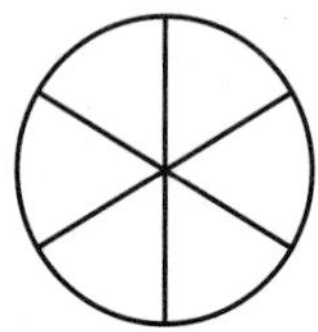
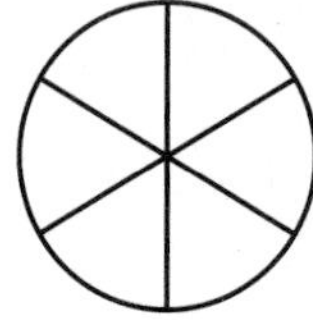
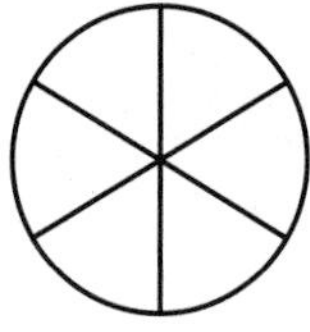
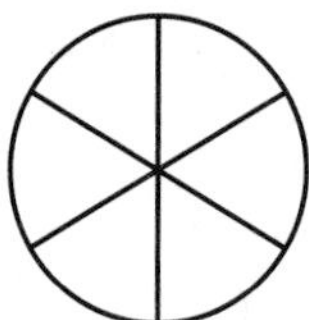

The difference is ______.

RECORD

Subtract the fractional parts of the mixed numbers.

Then subtract the whole-number parts of the mixed numbers.

$$\begin{array}{r} 3\frac{4}{6} \\ -\ 2\frac{3}{6} \\ \hline \square\frac{\square}{\square} \end{array}$$

So, there are ______ quesadillas left.

Share and Show

Write the sum as a mixed number with the fractional part less than 1.

1. $1\frac{1}{6}$ $+3\frac{3}{6}$ Add whole numbers. Add fractions.

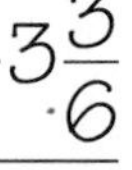

$\square + \square$ $\square + \square$

$\square + \square = $ ______

2. $1\frac{4}{5}$ $+7\frac{2}{5}$

3. $2\frac{1}{2}$ $+3\frac{1}{2}$

Name ______________________________

Find the difference.

4. $3\frac{7}{12}$ $-2\frac{5}{12}$

5. $4\frac{2}{3}$ $-3\frac{1}{3}$

6. $6\frac{9}{10}$ $-3\frac{7}{10}$

Math Talk **Mathematical Practices**

Explain how adding and subtracting mixed numbers is different from adding and subtracting fractions.

On Your Own

Write the sum as a mixed number with the fractional part less than 1.

7. $7\frac{4}{6}$ $+4\frac{3}{6}$

8. $8\frac{1}{3}$ $+3\frac{2}{3}$

9. $5\frac{4}{8}$ $+3\frac{5}{8}$

10. $3\frac{5}{12}$ $+4\frac{2}{12}$

Find the difference.

11. $5\frac{7}{8}$ $-2\frac{3}{8}$

12. $5\frac{7}{12}$ $-4\frac{1}{12}$

13. $3\frac{5}{10}$ $-1\frac{3}{10}$

14. $7\frac{3}{4}$ $-2\frac{2}{4}$

Practice: Copy and Solve **Find the sum or difference.**

15. $1\frac{3}{8} + 2\frac{7}{8}$

16. $6\frac{5}{8} - 4$

17. $9\frac{1}{2} + 8\frac{1}{2}$

18. $6\frac{3}{5} + 4\frac{3}{5}$

19. $8\frac{7}{10} - \frac{4}{10}$

20. $7\frac{3}{5} - 6\frac{3}{5}$

Problem Solving • Applications Real World

Solve. Write your answer as a mixed number.

WRITE ▸Math
Show Your Work

21. MATHEMATICAL PRACTICE 1 **Make Sense of Problems** The driving distance from Alex's house to the museum is $6\frac{7}{10}$ miles. What is the round-trip distance?

____

22. THINK SMARTER The driving distance from the sports arena to Kristina's house is $10\frac{9}{10}$ miles. The distance from the sports arena to Luke's house is $2\frac{7}{10}$ miles. How much greater is the driving distance between the sports arena and Kristina's house than between the sports arena and Luke's house?

____

23. Pedro biked from his house to the nature preserve, a distance of $23\frac{4}{5}$ miles. Sandra biked from her house to the lake, a distance of $12\frac{2}{5}$ miles. How many fewer miles did Sandra bike than Pedro?

____

24. GO DEEPER During the Martinez family trip, they drove from home to a ski lodge, a distance of $55\frac{4}{5}$ miles, and then drove an additional $12\frac{4}{5}$ miles to visit friends. If the family drove the same route back home, what was the distance traveled during their trip?

____

25. THINK SMARTER For 25a–25d, select True or False for each statement.

25a. $2\frac{3}{8} + 1\frac{6}{8}$ is equal to $4\frac{1}{8}$. ○ True ○ False

25b. $3\frac{6}{12} + 1\frac{4}{12}$ is equal to $2\frac{2}{12}$. ○ True ○ False

25c. $5\frac{5}{6} - 2\frac{4}{6}$ is equal to $1\frac{3}{6}$. ○ True ○ False

25d. $5\frac{5}{8} - 3\frac{2}{8}$ is equal to $2\frac{3}{8}$. ○ True ○ False

FOR MORE PRACTICE:
Standards Practice Book

Name ____________________

Subtraction with Renaming

Essential Question How can you rename a mixed number to help you subtract?

Numbers and Operations—Fractions—4.NF.3c *Also 4.MD.2*

MATHEMATICAL PRACTICES
MP.3, MP.4

Unlock the Problem (Real World)

Ramon, Chandler, and Chase go bike riding on weekends. On one weekend, Chase rode his bike for 3 hours, Chandler rode her bike for $2\frac{1}{4}$ hours, and Ramon rode his bike for $1\frac{3}{4}$ hours. How much longer did Chandler ride her bike than Ramon did?

- Which operation will you use?

____

- In the problem, circle the numbers that you need to use to find a solution.

Use a model. Find $2\frac{1}{4} - 1\frac{3}{4}$.

Shade the model to show how long Chandler rode her bike.
Then shade the model to show how long Ramon rode his bike.

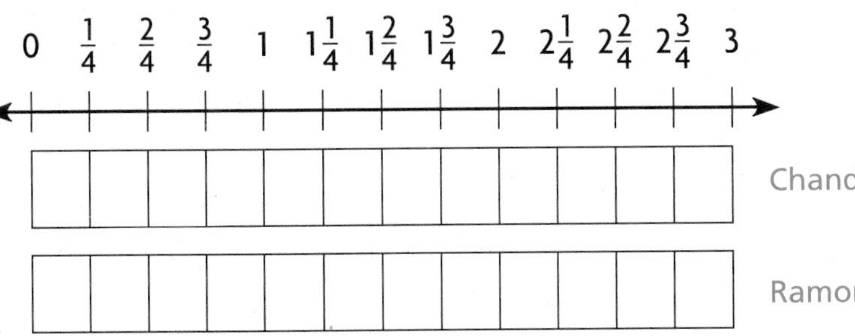

Think: The difference is _______.

So, Chandler rode her bike _______ hour longer than Ramon did.

1. If you have 1 fourth-size part, can you take away 3 fourth-size parts? Explain.

____

____

Math Talk — Mathematical Practices

Explain how you can find how much longer Chase rode his bike than Chandler did.

2. If you have 1 whole and 1 fourth-size part, can you take away 3 fourth-size parts? Explain.

____

____

One Way Rename the first mixed number.

Find the difference. $5\frac{1}{8} - 3\frac{3}{8}$

STEP 1

Rename $5\frac{1}{8}$ as a mixed number with a fraction greater than 1.

Think:

$5\frac{1}{8} = 4 + 1 + \frac{1}{8}$

$= 4 + \frac{\square}{8} + \frac{1}{8}$

$= \square$

STEP 2

Subtract the mixed numbers.

$5\frac{1}{8} = \square$

$-3\frac{3}{8} = -3\frac{3}{8}$

$\square$

Math Talk Mathematical Practices

Explain why you need to rename $5\frac{1}{8}$.

Another Way Rename both mixed numbers.

Find the difference. $3\frac{4}{12} - 1\frac{6}{12}$

STEP 1

Rename both mixed numbers as fractions greater than 1.

$3\frac{4}{12} = \frac{\square}{12}$ $\quad 1\frac{6}{12} = \frac{\square}{12}$

STEP 2

Subtract the fractions greater than 1.

$\frac{\square}{12}$

$-\frac{\square}{12}$

$\square$

- Explain how you could rename 5 to subtract $3\frac{1}{4}$.

Name ______________________________

Share and Show

1. Rename both mixed numbers as fractions. Find the difference.

$$3\frac{3}{6} = \frac{\square}{6}$$
$$-1\frac{4}{6} = -\frac{\square}{6}$$

Find the difference.

2. $1\frac{1}{3} - \frac{2}{3}$

3. $4\frac{7}{10} - 1\frac{9}{10}$

4. $3\frac{5}{12} - \frac{8}{12}$

Math Talk — Mathematical Practices

Describe how you would model $\frac{13}{6} - \frac{8}{6}$.

On Your Own

Find the difference.

5. $8\frac{1}{10} - 2\frac{9}{10}$

6. $2 - 1\frac{1}{4}$

7. $4\frac{1}{5} - 3\frac{2}{5}$

Practice: Copy and Solve Find the difference.

8. $4\frac{1}{6} - 2\frac{5}{6}$

9. $6\frac{9}{12} - 3\frac{10}{12}$

10. $3\frac{3}{10} - \frac{7}{10}$

11. $4 - 2\frac{3}{5}$

12. $5\frac{1}{4} - 2\frac{3}{4}$

13. $3\frac{9}{12} - 1\frac{11}{12}$

14. $7\frac{3}{10} - 4\frac{7}{10}$

15. $2\frac{3}{8} - 1\frac{5}{8}$

Problem Solving • Applications

Rename the fractions to solve.

Many instruments are coiled or curved so that they are easier for the musician to play, but they would be quite long if straightened out completely.

16. MATHEMATICAL PRACTICE 1 **Analyze Relationships** Trumpets and cornets are brass instruments. Fully stretched out, the length of a trumpet is $5\frac{1}{4}$ feet and the length of a cornet is $4\frac{2}{4}$ feet. The trumpet is how much longer than the cornet?

____

17. THINK SMARTER Tubas, trombones, and French horns are brass instruments. Fully stretched out, the length of a tuba is 18 feet, the length of a trombone is $9\frac{11}{12}$ feet, and the length of a French horn is $17\frac{1}{12}$ feet. The tuba is how much longer than the French horn? The French horn is how much longer than the trombone?

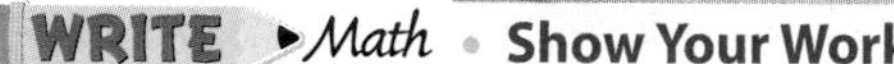

____

18. GO DEEPER The pitch of a musical instrument is related to its length. In general, the greater the length of a musical instrument, the lower its pitch. Order the brass instruments identified on this page from lowest pitch to the highest pitch.

____

Personal Math Trainer

19. THINK SMARTER + Alicia had $3\frac{1}{6}$ yards of fabric. After making a tablecloth, she had $1\frac{4}{6}$ yards of fabric. Alicia said she used $2\frac{3}{6}$ yards of fabric for the tablecloth. Do you agree? Explain.

____

____

____

FOR MORE PRACTICE: Standards Practice Book

Name ________________

Fractions and Properties of Addition

Essential Question How can you add fractions with like denominators using the properties of addition?

Numbers and Operations—Fractions—4.NF.3c

MATHEMATICAL PRACTICES
MP.2, MP.7

CONNECT The Associative and Commutative Properties of Addition can help you group and order addends to find sums mentally. You can use mental math to combine fractions that have a sum of 1.

- The Commutative Property of Addition states that when the order of two addends is changed, the sum is the same. For example, $4 + 5 = 5 + 4$.
- The Associative Property of Addition states that when the grouping of addends is changed, the sum is the same. For example, $(5 + 8) + 4 = 5 + (8 + 4)$.

The map shows four lighthouses in the Florida Keys and their distances apart in miles. The Dry Tortugas Lighthouse is the farthest west, and the Alligator Reef Lighthouse is the farthest east.

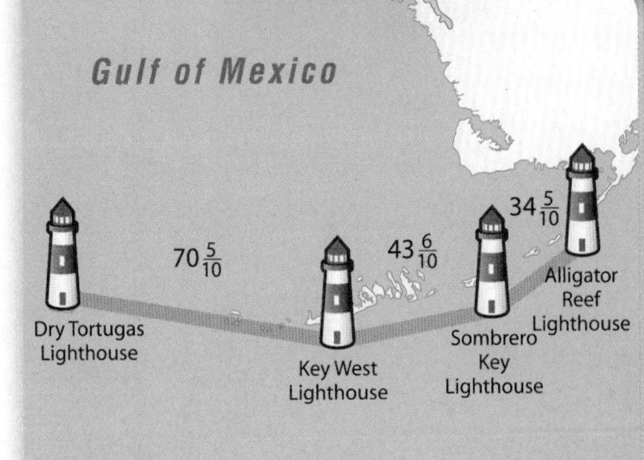

What is the distance from the Dry Tortugas Lighthouse to the Alligator Reef Lighthouse, traveling between the four lighthouses?

Use the properties to order and group.

Add. $70\frac{5}{10} + 43\frac{6}{10} + 34\frac{5}{10}$

$70\frac{5}{10} + 43\frac{6}{10} + 34\frac{5}{10} =$ ______ + ______ + ______

Use the Commutative Property to order the addends so that the fractions with a sum of 1 are together.

$=$ (______ + ______) + ______

Use the Associative Property to group the addends that you can add mentally.

$=$ (______) + ______

Add the grouped numbers, and then add the other mixed number.

$=$ ______

Write the sum.

So, the distance from the Dry Tortugas Lighthouse to the Alligator Reef Lighthouse, traveling between the four lighthouses, is ______ miles.

Try This! **Use the properties and mental math to solve. Show each step, and name the property used.**

$1\frac{1}{3} + (2 + 3\frac{2}{3})$

Share and Show

1. Complete. Name the property used.

$\left(3\frac{4}{10} + 5\frac{2}{10}\right) + \frac{6}{10} = \left(5\frac{2}{10} + 3\frac{4}{10}\right) + \_\_\_\_$ ____________

$= 5\frac{2}{10} + \left(3\frac{4}{10} + \_\_\_\_\right)$ ____________

$= 5\frac{2}{10} + \_\_\_\_$

$= \_\_\_\_$

Math Talk **Mathematical Practices**

Describe how you could use the properties to find the sum $1\frac{1}{3} + 2\frac{5}{8} + 1\frac{2}{3}$.

Use the properties and mental math to find the sum.

2. $\left(2\frac{7}{8} + 3\frac{2}{8}\right) + 1\frac{1}{8}$

3. $1\frac{2}{5} + \left(1 + \frac{3}{5}\right)$

4. $5\frac{3}{6} + (5\frac{5}{6} + 4\frac{3}{6})$

✓5. $(1\frac{1}{4} + 1\frac{1}{4}) + 2\frac{3}{4}$

6. $(12\frac{4}{9} + 1\frac{2}{9}) + 3\frac{5}{9}$

✓7. $\frac{3}{12} + (1\frac{8}{12} + \frac{9}{12})$

Name ______________________

On Your Own

Use the properties and mental math to find the sum.

8. $\left(45\frac{1}{3} + 6\frac{1}{3}\right) + 38\frac{2}{3}$

9. $\frac{1}{2} + \left(103\frac{1}{2} + 12\right)$

10. $\left(3\frac{5}{10} + 10\right) + 11\frac{5}{10}$

11. $1\frac{4}{10} + \left(37\frac{3}{10} + \frac{6}{10}\right)$

12. $\left(\frac{3}{12} + 10\frac{5}{12}\right) + \frac{9}{12}$

13. $5\frac{7}{8} + \left(6\frac{3}{8} + \frac{1}{8}\right)$

Problem Solving • Applications

Use the expressions in the box for 14–15.

14. Which property of addition would you use to regroup the addends in Expression A?

____

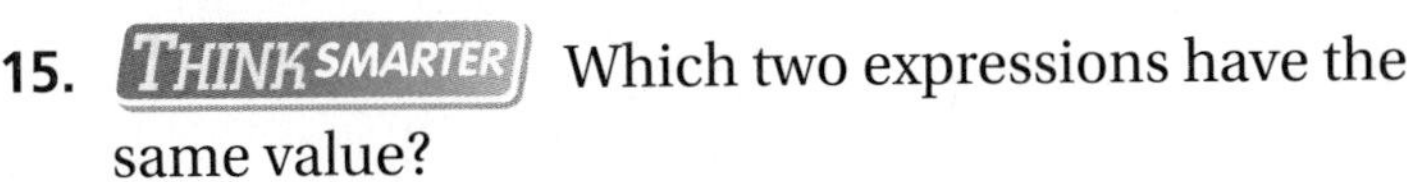

15. THINK SMARTER Which two expressions have the same value?

____

A	$\frac{1}{8} + \left(\frac{7}{8} + \frac{4}{8}\right)$
B	$\frac{1}{2} + 2$
C	$\frac{3}{7} + \left(\frac{1}{2} + \frac{4}{7}\right)$
D	$\frac{1}{3} + \frac{4}{3} + \frac{2}{3}$

16. THINK SMARTER Match the equation with the property used.

$\frac{6}{12} + (\frac{6}{12} + \frac{3}{12}) = (\frac{6}{12} + \frac{6}{12}) + \frac{3}{12}$ •

$3\frac{2}{5} + (5\frac{4}{5} + 2\frac{1}{5}) = 3\frac{2}{5} + (2\frac{1}{5} + 5\frac{4}{5})$ •   • Commutative Property

$(4\frac{1}{6} + 3\frac{5}{6}) + 2\frac{2}{6} = (3\frac{5}{6} + 4\frac{1}{6}) + 2\frac{2}{6}$ •   • Associative Property

$(1\frac{1}{8} + \frac{5}{8}) + 3\frac{3}{8} = 1\frac{1}{8} + (\frac{5}{8} + 3\frac{3}{8})$ •

Pose a Problem

17. GO DEEPER Costumes are being made for the high school musical. The table at the right shows the amount of fabric needed for the costumes of the male and female leads. Alice uses the expression $7\frac{3}{8} + 1\frac{5}{8} + 2\frac{4}{8}$ to find the total amount of fabric needed for the costume of the female lead.

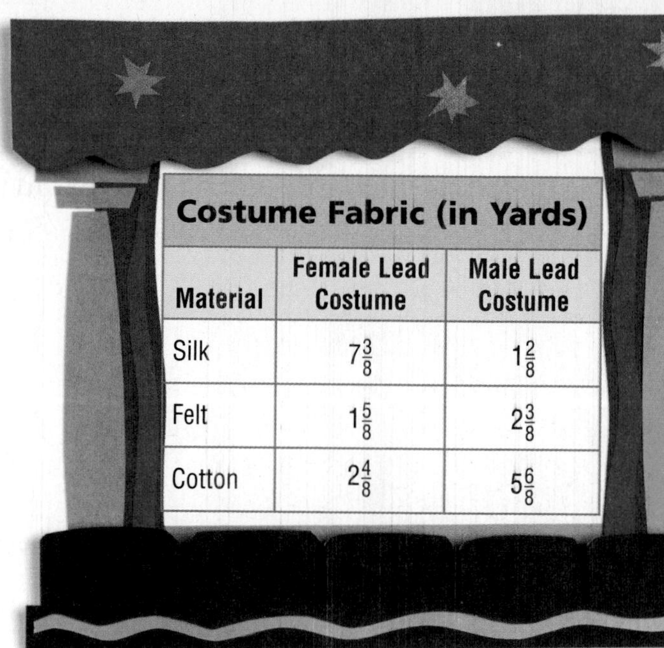

Costume Fabric (in Yards)		
Material	Female Lead Costume	Male Lead Costume
Silk	$7\frac{3}{8}$	$1\frac{2}{8}$
Felt	$1\frac{5}{8}$	$2\frac{3}{8}$
Cotton	$2\frac{4}{8}$	$5\frac{6}{8}$

To find the value of the expression using mental math, Alice used the properties of addition.

$$7\frac{3}{8} + 1\frac{5}{8} + 2\frac{4}{8} = \left(7\frac{3}{8} + 1\frac{5}{8}\right) + 2\frac{4}{8}$$

Alice added 7 + 1 and was able to quickly add $\frac{3}{8}$ and $\frac{5}{8}$ to the sum of 8 to get 9. She added $2\frac{4}{8}$ to 9, so her answer was $11\frac{4}{8}$.

So, the amount of fabric needed for the costume of the female lead actor is $11\frac{4}{8}$ yards.

Write a new problem using the information for the costume for the male lead actor.

Pose a Problem

Solve your problem. Check your solution.

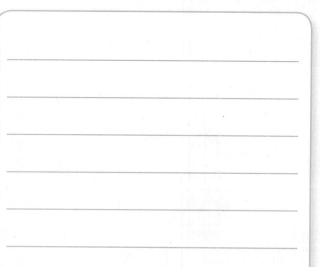

• MATHEMATICAL PRACTICE 7 **Identify Relationships** Explain how using the properties of addition makes both problems easier to solve.

FOR MORE PRACTICE: Standards Practice Book

Name ______________________

Problem Solving • Multistep Fraction Problems

Essential Question How can you use the strategy *act it out* to solve multistep problems with fractions?

Numbers and Operations—Fractions—4.NF.3d *Also 4.MD.2*

MATHEMATICAL PRACTICES
MP.1, MP.7

Unlock the Problem

A gift shop sells walnuts in $\frac{3}{4}$-pound bags. Ann will buy some bags of walnuts and repackage them into 1-pound bags. What is the least number of $\frac{3}{4}$-pound bags Ann could buy, if she wants to fill each 1-pound bag, without leftovers?

Read the Problem

What do I need to find?

I need to find how many __________ bags of walnuts Ann needs to make 1-pound bags of walnuts, without leftovers.

What information do I need to use?

The bags she will buy contain ______ pound of walnuts. She will repackage the walnuts into ______ -pound bags.

How will I use the information?

I can use fraction circles to __________ the problem.

Solve the Problem

Describe how to act it out. Use fraction circles.

One $\frac{3}{4}$-pound bag — Not enough for a 1-pound bag

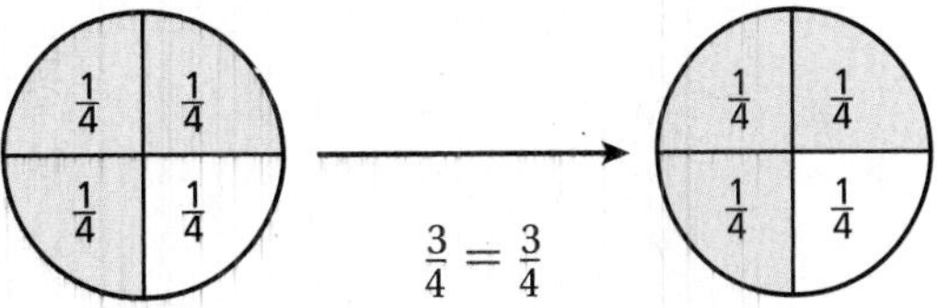

Two $\frac{3}{4}$-pound bags — One 1-pound bag with $\frac{2}{4}$ pound left over

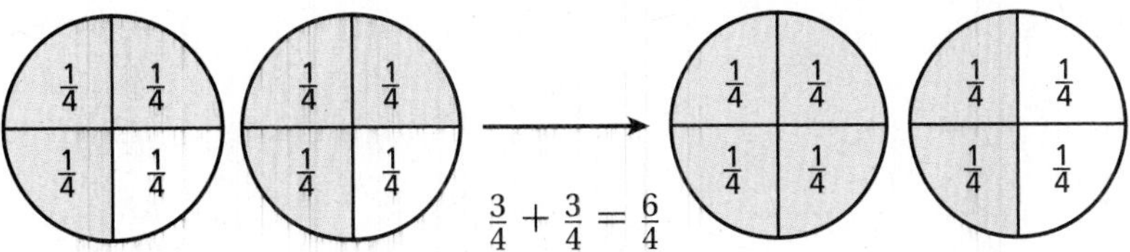

Three $\frac{3}{4}$-pound bags have $\frac{3}{4} + \frac{3}{4} + \frac{3}{4} = \frac{\square}{4}$ pounds of walnuts. This makes ______ 1-pound bags with ______ pound left over.

Four $\frac{3}{4}$-pound bags have $\frac{3}{4} + \frac{3}{4} + \frac{3}{4} + \frac{3}{4} = \frac{\square}{4}$-pounds of walnuts.

This makes ______ 1-pound bags with __________ left over.

So, Ann could buy ______ $\frac{3}{4}$-pound bags of walnuts.

Try Another Problem

At the end of dinner, a restaurant had several dishes of quiche, each with 2 sixth-size pieces of quiche. The chef was able to combine these pieces to make 2 whole quiches, with no leftovers. How many dishes did the chef combine?

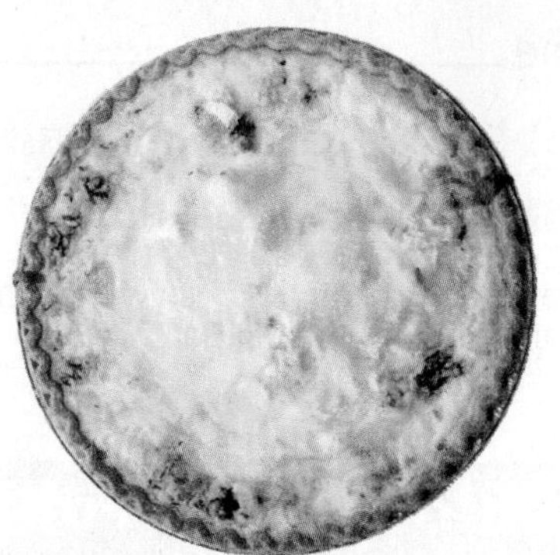

Read the Problem	Solve the Problem
What do I need to find?	**Describe how to act it out.**
What information do I need to use?	
How will I use the information?	

So, the chef combined ______ dishes each with $\frac{2}{6}$ quiche.

Name ______________________________

Share and Show

Unlock the Problem

- √ Underline the question.
- √ Circle the important facts.
- √ Cross out unneeded information.

1. Last week, Sia ran $1\frac{1}{4}$ miles each day for 5 days and then took 2 days off. Did she run at least 6 miles last week?

   First, model the problem. Describe your model.

   ____

   ____

   ____

   ____

   Then, regroup the parts in the model to find the number of whole miles Sia ran.

   Sia ran ______ whole miles and ______ mile.

   Finally, compare the total number of miles she ran to 6 miles.

   $6\frac{1}{4}$ miles ◯ 6 miles

   So, Sia ______ run at least 6 miles last week.

2. What if Sia ran only $\frac{3}{4}$ mile each day? Would she have run at least 6 miles last week? Explain.

   ____

   ____

3. A quarter is $\frac{1}{4}$ dollar. Noah has 20 quarters. How much money does he have? Explain.

   ____

   ____

   ____

4. THINK SMARTER How many $\frac{2}{5}$ parts are in 2 wholes?

   ____

WRITE ▸*Math* • **Show Your Work**

On Your Own

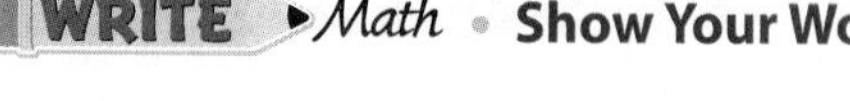

5. A company shipped 15,325 boxes of apples and 12,980 boxes of oranges. How many more boxes of apples than oranges did the company ship?

____

6. MATHEMATICAL PRACTICE 1 **Analyze** A fair sold a total of 3,300 tickets on Friday and Saturday. It sold 100 more on Friday than on Saturday. How many tickets did the fair sell on Friday?

____

7. THINK SMARTER Emma walked $\frac{1}{4}$ mile on Monday, $\frac{2}{4}$ mile on Tuesday, and $\frac{3}{4}$ mile on Wednesday. If the pattern continues, how many miles will she walk on Friday? Explain how you found the number of miles.

____

____

____

____

____

____

8. GO DEEPER Jared painted a mug $\frac{5}{12}$ red and $\frac{4}{12}$ blue. What part of the mug is **not** red or blue?

____

9. THINK SMARTER Choose the number that correctly completes the sentence.

Each day, Mrs. Hewes knits $\frac{1}{3}$ of a scarf in the morning and $\frac{1}{3}$ of a scarf in the afternoon.

It will take Mrs. Hewes [2 / 3 / 4] days to knit 2 scarves.

Name ______________________________

Chapter 7 Review/Test

1. A painter mixed $\frac{1}{4}$ quart of red paint with $\frac{3}{4}$ blue paint to make purple paint.

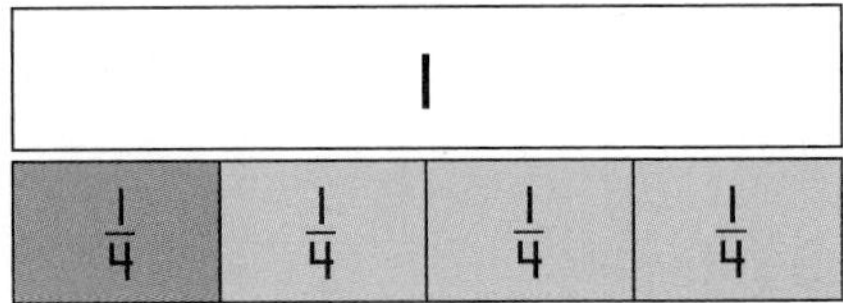

How much purple paint did the painter make?

☐ quart of purple paint

2. Ivan biked $1\frac{2}{3}$ hours on Monday, $2\frac{1}{3}$ hours on Tuesday, and $2\frac{2}{3}$ hours on Wednesday. What is the total number of hours Ivan spent biking?

Ivan spent ☐ hours biking.

3. Tricia had $4\frac{1}{8}$ yards of fabric to make curtains. When she finished she had $2\frac{3}{8}$ yards of fabric left. She said she used $2\frac{2}{8}$ yards of fabric for the curtains. Do you agree? Explain.

4. Miguel's class went to the state fair. The fairground is divided into sections. Rides are in $\frac{6}{10}$ of the fairground. Games are in $\frac{2}{10}$ of the fairground. Farm exhibits are in $\frac{1}{10}$ of the fairground.

Part A

Use the model. What fraction of the fairground is rides and games?

1									
$\frac{1}{10}$	$\frac{1}{10}$	$\frac{1}{10}$	$\frac{1}{10}$	$\frac{1}{10}$	$\frac{1}{10}$	$\frac{1}{10}$	$\frac{1}{10}$	$\frac{1}{10}$	$\frac{1}{10}$

The fraction of the fairground with games and rides is .

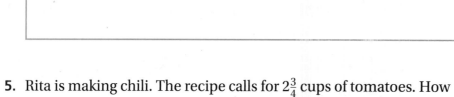

Part B

How much greater is the part of the fairground with rides than with farm exhibits? Explain how the model could be used to find the answer.

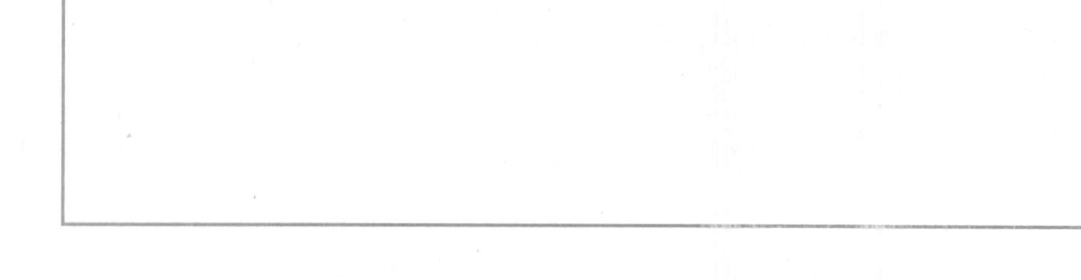

5. Rita is making chili. The recipe calls for $2\frac{3}{4}$ cups of tomatoes. How many cups of tomatoes, written as a fraction greater than one, are used in the recipe?

 cups

6. Lamar's mom sells sports equipment online. She sold $\frac{9}{10}$ of the sports equipment. Select a way $\frac{9}{10}$ can be written as a sum of fractions. Mark all that apply.

Ⓐ $\frac{1}{10} + \frac{1}{10} + \frac{1}{10} + \frac{1}{10} + \frac{2}{10}$

Ⓑ $\frac{3}{10} + \frac{2}{10} + \frac{3}{10} + \frac{1}{10}$

Ⓒ $\frac{2}{10} + \frac{2}{10} + \frac{2}{10} + \frac{2}{10}$

Ⓓ $\frac{4}{10} + \frac{1}{10} + \frac{1}{10} + \frac{3}{10}$

Ⓔ $\frac{4}{10} + \frac{3}{10} + \frac{1}{10} + \frac{1}{10} + \frac{1}{10}$

Ⓕ $\frac{2}{10} + \frac{2}{10} + \frac{2}{10} + \frac{3}{10}$

Name ____

7. Bella brought $\frac{8}{10}$ gallon of water on a hiking trip. She drank $\frac{6}{10}$ gallon of water. How much water is left?

☐ gallon

8. In a survey, $\frac{6}{10}$ of the students chose Saturday and $\frac{1}{10}$ chose Monday as their favorite day of the week. What fraction shows the students who chose Saturday or Monday as their favorite day?

Part A

Shade the model to show your answer.

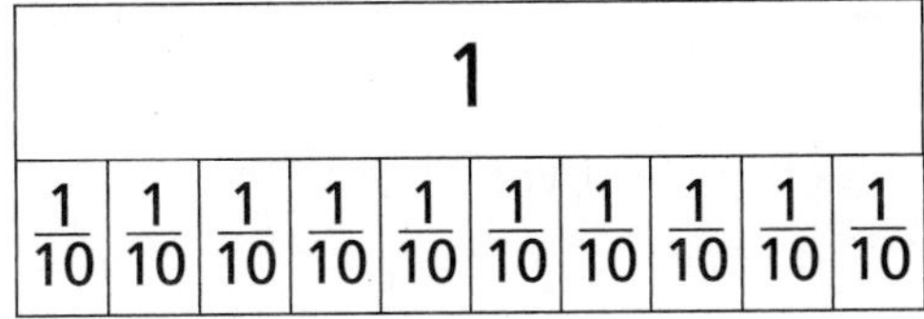

☐ of the students chose Monday or Saturday.

Part B

How are the numerator and denominator of your answer related to the model? Explain.

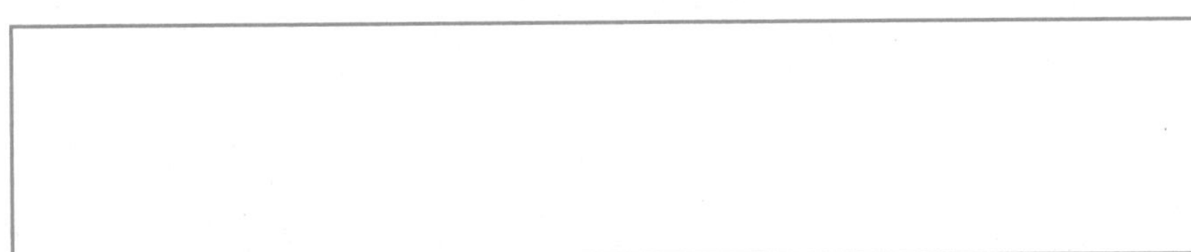

9. Match the equation with the property used.

$\frac{6}{10} + \left(\frac{4}{10} + \frac{3}{10}\right) = \left(\frac{6}{10} + \frac{4}{10}\right) + \frac{3}{10}$ •

$1\frac{1}{4} + \left(3 + 2\frac{1}{4}\right) = 1\frac{1}{4} + \left(2\frac{1}{4} + 3\right)$ •

$\left(2\frac{6}{10} + \frac{1}{10}\right) + 3\frac{9}{10} = 2\frac{6}{10} + \left(\frac{1}{10} + 3\frac{9}{10}\right)$ •

$\left(3\frac{4}{7} + 2\frac{1}{7}\right) + 6\frac{3}{7} = \left(2\frac{1}{7} + 3\frac{4}{7}\right) + 6\frac{3}{7}$ •

• Commutative Property

• Associative Property

10. For numbers 10a–10e, select Yes or No to show if the sum or difference is correct.

10a. $\frac{2}{8}+\frac{1}{8}=\frac{3}{8}$ ○ Yes ○ No

10b. $\frac{4}{5}+\frac{1}{5}=\frac{5}{5}$ ○ Yes ○ No

10c. $\frac{4}{6}+\frac{1}{6}=\frac{5}{12}$ ○ Yes ○ No

10d. $\frac{6}{12}-\frac{4}{12}=\frac{2}{12}$ ○ Yes ○ No

10e. $\frac{7}{9}-\frac{2}{9}=\frac{9}{9}$ ○ Yes ○ No

11. Gina has $5\frac{2}{6}$ feet of silver ribbon and $2\frac{4}{6}$ of gold ribbon. How much more silver ribbon does Gina have than gold ribbon?

 feet more silver ribbon

12. Jill is making a long cape. She needs $4\frac{1}{3}$ yards of blue fabric for the outside of the cape. She needs $3\frac{2}{3}$ yards of purple fabric for the lining of the cape.

Part A

Jill incorrectly subtracted the two mixed numbers to find how much more blue fabric than purple fabric she should buy. Her work is shown below.

$4\frac{1}{3}-3\frac{2}{3}=\frac{12}{3}-\frac{9}{3}=\frac{3}{3}$

Why is Jill's work incorrect?

Part B

How much more blue fabric than purple fabric should Jill buy? Show your work.

Name ______________________________

13. Russ has two jars of glue. One jar is $\frac{1}{5}$ full. The other jar is $\frac{2}{5}$ full.

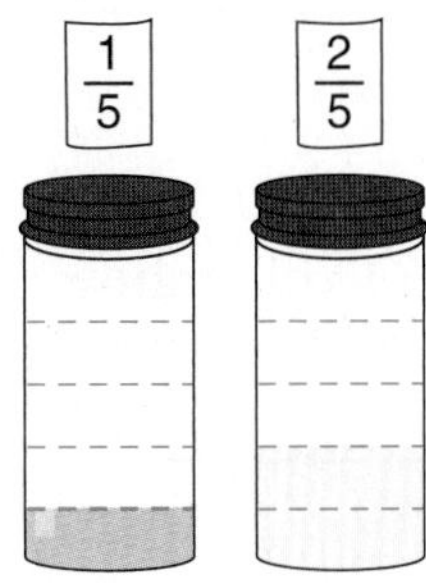

Use the fractions to write an equation to find the amount of glue Russ has.

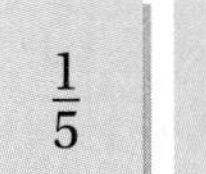
$\frac{1}{5}$ $\frac{2}{5}$ $\frac{3}{5}$ $\frac{4}{5}$

$\square + \square = \square$

14. Gertie ran $\frac{3}{4}$ mile during physical education class. Sarah ran $\frac{2}{4}$ mile during the same class. How much farther did Gertie run than Sarah? Shade the model to show your answer.

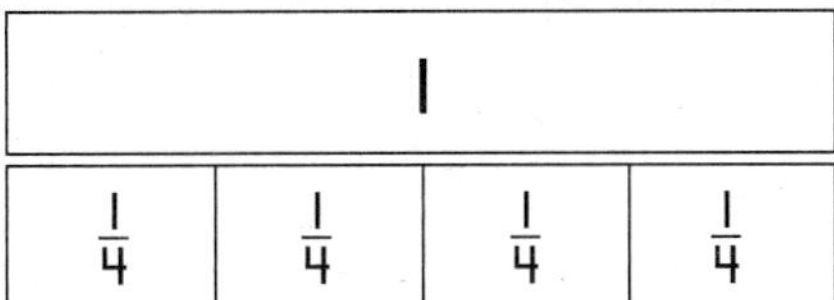

Gertie ran $\square$ mile farther than Sarah.

15. Teresa planted marigolds in $\frac{2}{8}$ of her garden and petunias in $\frac{3}{8}$ of her garden. What fraction of the garden has marigolds and petunias?

Teresa's garden has $\square$ marigolds and petunias.

16. Draw a line to show the mixed number and fraction that have the same value.

• $3\frac{2}{7}$ • $4\frac{5}{8}$ • $2\frac{3}{5}$ • $2\frac{3}{8}$

• $\frac{21}{8}$ • $\frac{37}{3}$ • $\frac{21}{7}$ • $\frac{37}{8}$

17. Each day, Tally's baby sister eats $\frac{1}{4}$ cup of rice cereal in the morning and $\frac{1}{4}$ cup of rice cereal in the afternoon.

It will take Tally's sister [2 / 3 / 4] days to eat 2 cups of rice cereal.

18. Three girls are selling cases of popcorn to earn money for a band trip. In week 1, Emily sold $2\frac{3}{4}$ cases, Brenda sold $4\frac{1}{4}$ cases, and Shannon sold $3\frac{1}{2}$ cases.

Part A

How many cases of popcorn have the girls sold in all? Explain how you found your answer.

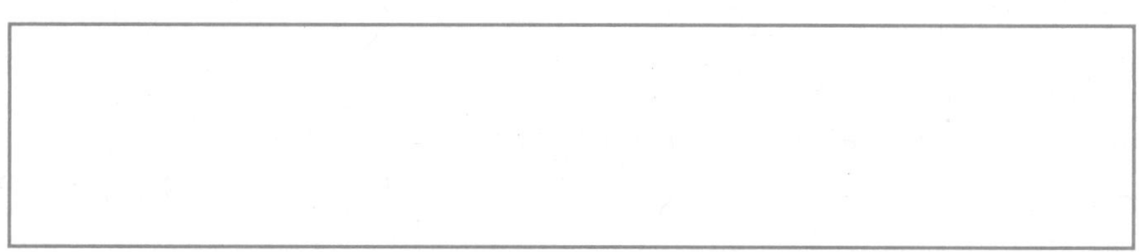

Part B

The girls must sell a total of 35 cases in order to have enough money for the trip. Suppose they sell the same amount in week 2 and week 3 of the sale as in week 1. Will the girls have sold enough cases of popcorn to go on the trip? Explain.

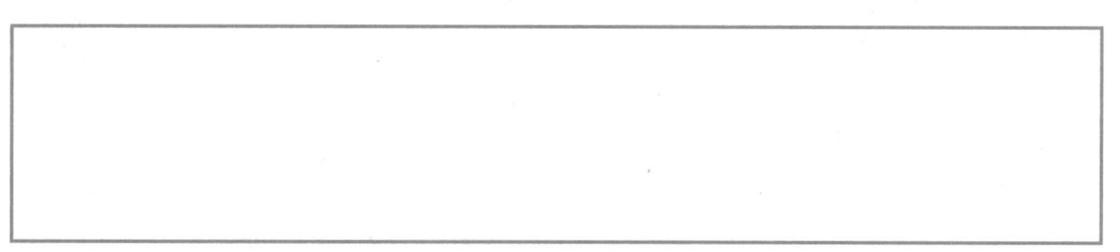

19. Henry ate $\frac{3}{8}$ of a sandwich. Keith ate $\frac{4}{8}$ of the same sandwich. How much more of the sandwich did Keith eat than Henry?

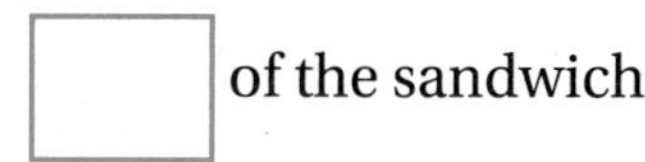

20. For numbers 20a–20d, choose True or False for each sentence.

20a.	$1\frac{4}{9} + 2\frac{6}{9}$ is equal to $4\frac{1}{9}$.	○ True	○ False
20b.	$3\frac{5}{6} + 2\frac{3}{6}$ is equal to $5\frac{2}{6}$.	○ True	○ False
20c.	$4\frac{5}{8} - 2\frac{4}{8}$ is equal to $2\frac{3}{8}$.	○ True	○ False
20d.	$5\frac{5}{8} - 3\frac{2}{8}$ is equal to $2\frac{3}{8}$.	○ True	○ False

21. Justin lives $4\frac{3}{5}$ miles from his grandfather's house. Write the mixed number as a fraction greater than one.

$4\frac{3}{5} =$ ☐

Chapter 8 Multiply Fractions by Whole Numbers

Show What You Know 

Check your understanding of important skills.

Name ______________________________

▶ Relate Addition to Multiplication **Complete.**

1. 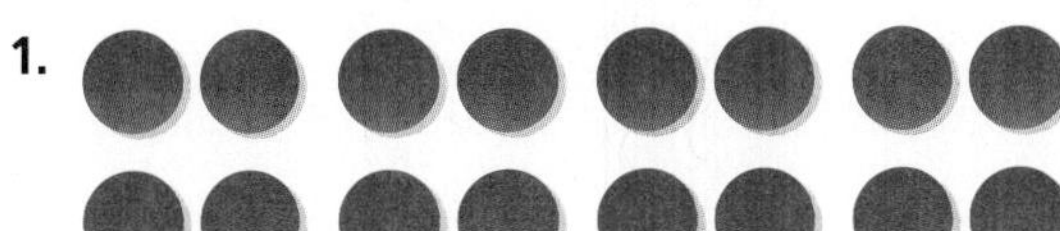

____ + ____ + ____ + ____ = ____

____ × ____ = ____

2. 

____ + ____ + ____ = ____

____ × ____ = ____

▶ Read and Write Mixed Numbers **Write a mixed number for the shaded part. Write a fraction for the unshaded part.**

3. Shaded: ______

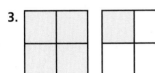

Unshaded: ______

4. 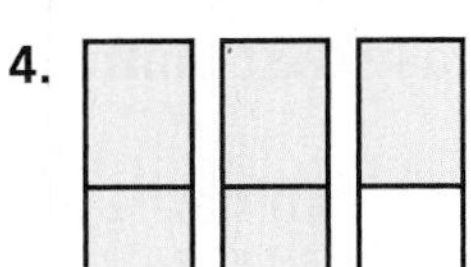

Shaded: ______

Unshaded: ______

▶ Model Fractions and Mixed Numbers **Write a fraction or mixed number for the model.**

5. 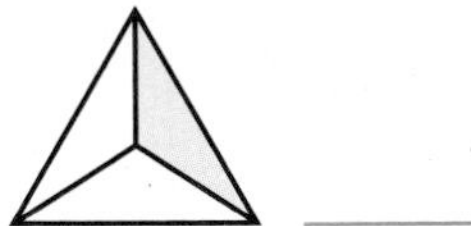 ______

6. 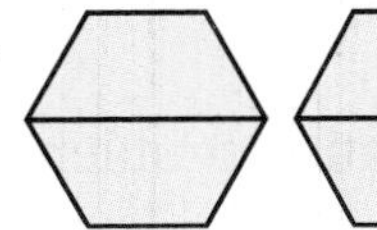 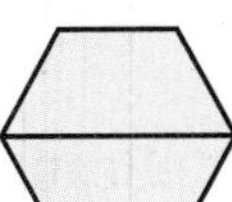 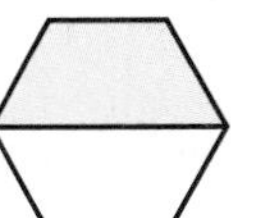 ______

Math Detective

The budget for Carter Museum's annual party is \$10,000. Food accounts for $\frac{1}{2}$ of the budget, beverages for $\frac{1}{4}$, and decorations for $\frac{1}{10}$ of the budget. The remainder is spent on staffing the party. Be a Math Detective. How much money is spent on staffing the party?

Personal Math Trainer
Online Assessment and Intervention

Vocabulary Builder

▶ Visualize It

Complete the bubble map using the review words.

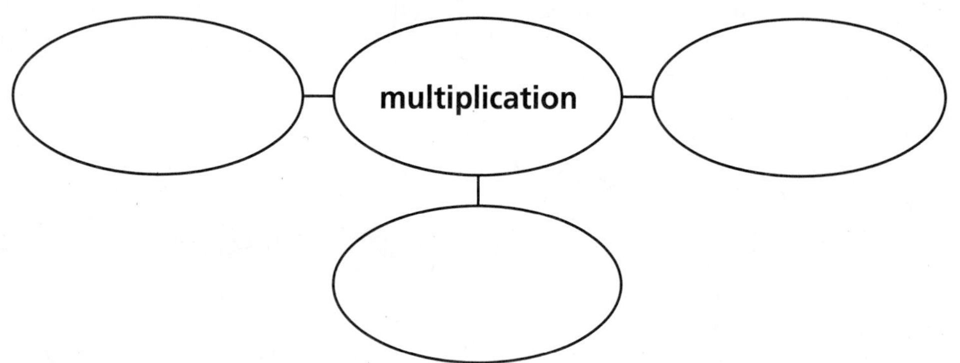

Review Words

fraction
Identity Property of Multiplication
multiple
product
unit fraction

▶ Understand Vocabulary

Write the word or phrase that matches the description.

1. A ________________ can name a part of a group or a whole.
2. You can write ________________ of 10 such as 10, 20, 30, and so on.
3. ________________ have one as the numerator.
4. The answer to a multiplication problem is called the ________________.
5. ________________________________ states that the product of any number and 1 is that number.

GO DIGITAL
• Interactive Student Edition
• Multimedia eGlossary

Name ____________________

Multiples of Unit Fractions

Essential Question How can you write a fraction as a product of a whole number and a unit fraction?

Numbers and Operations—Fractions—4.NF.4a

MATHEMATICAL PRACTICES
MP.2, MP.5

Unlock the Problem (Real World)

At a pizza party, each pizza was cut into 6 equal slices. At the end of the party, there was $\frac{5}{6}$ of a pizza left. Roberta put each of the leftover slices in its own freezer bag. How many bags did she use? What part of a pizza did she put in each bag?

- How many slices of pizza were eaten?

  ____

- What fraction of the pizza is 1 slice?

  ____

Example Write $\frac{5}{6}$ as the product of a whole number and a unit fraction.

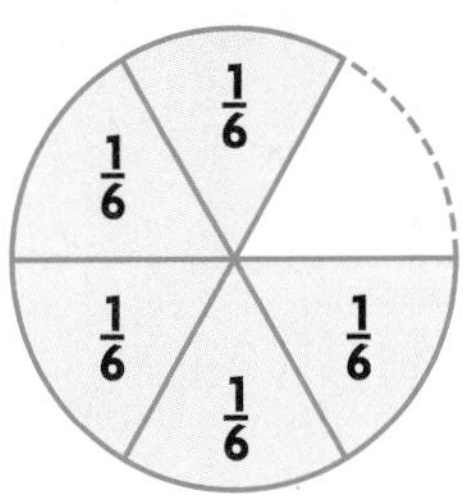

The picture shows $\frac{5}{6}$ or

______ sixth-size parts.

Each sixth-size part of the pizza can be shown by the

unit fraction ______.

You can use unit fractions to show $\frac{5}{6}$ in two ways.

$\frac{5}{6}$ = ______ + ______ + ______ + ______ + ______

$\frac{5}{6}$ = ______ $\times \frac{1}{6}$

The number of addends, or the multiplier, represents the number of bags used.

The unit fractions represent the part of a pizza in each bag.

So, Roberta used ______ bags. She put ______ of a pizza in each bag.

Remember

You can use multiplication to show repeated addition.

3×4 means $4 + 4 + 4$.

4×2 means $2 + 2 + 2 + 2$.

Math Talk — **Mathematical Practices**

Explain how you can write $\frac{3}{2}$ as a mixed number.

- Explain how you can write $\frac{3}{2}$ as the product of a whole number and a unit fraction.

____

____

____

Multiples The product of a number and a counting number is a multiple of the number. You have learned about multiples of whole numbers.

The products 1×4, 2×4, 3×4, and so on are multiples of 4. The numbers 4, 8, 12, and so on are multiples of 4.

You can also find multiples of unit fractions.

$1 \times \frac{1}{4}$ is $\frac{1}{4}$. Use models to write the next four multiples of $\frac{1}{4}$. Complete the last model.

$\frac{1}{4}$	$\frac{1}{4}$	$\frac{1}{4}$	$\frac{1}{4}$
$\frac{1}{4}$	$\frac{1}{4}$	$\frac{1}{4}$	$\frac{1}{4}$

$2 \times \frac{1}{4} = \frac{2}{4}$

$\frac{1}{4}$	$\frac{1}{4}$	$\frac{1}{4}$	$\frac{1}{4}$
$\frac{1}{4}$	$\frac{1}{4}$	$\frac{1}{4}$	$\frac{1}{4}$
$\frac{1}{4}$	$\frac{1}{4}$	$\frac{1}{4}$	$\frac{1}{4}$

$3 \times \frac{\square}{\square} = \frac{\square}{4}$

$\frac{1}{4}$	$\frac{1}{4}$	$\frac{1}{4}$	$\frac{1}{4}$
$\frac{1}{4}$	$\frac{1}{4}$	$\frac{1}{4}$	$\frac{1}{4}$
$\frac{1}{4}$	$\frac{1}{4}$	$\frac{1}{4}$	$\frac{1}{4}$
$\frac{1}{4}$	$\frac{1}{4}$	$\frac{1}{4}$	$\frac{1}{4}$

$4 \times \frac{\square}{\square} = \frac{\square}{4}$

$\frac{1}{4}$	$\frac{1}{4}$	$\frac{1}{4}$	$\frac{1}{4}$
$\frac{1}{4}$	$\frac{1}{4}$	$\frac{1}{4}$	$\frac{1}{4}$
$\frac{1}{4}$	$\frac{1}{4}$	$\frac{1}{4}$	$\frac{1}{4}$
$\frac{1}{4}$	$\frac{1}{4}$	$\frac{1}{4}$	$\frac{1}{4}$
$\frac{1}{4}$	$\frac{1}{4}$	$\frac{1}{4}$	$\frac{1}{4}$

$\square \times \frac{\square}{\square} = \frac{\square}{\square}$

Multiples of $\frac{1}{4}$ are $\frac{1}{4}$, ___, ___, ___, and ___.

Use a number line to write multiples of $\frac{1}{5}$.

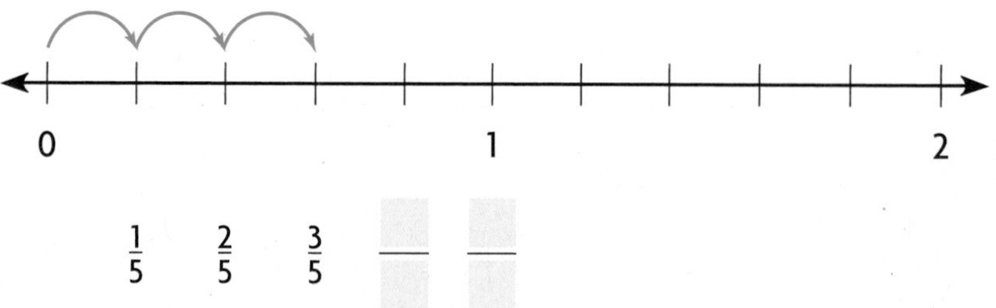

Multiples of $\frac{1}{5}$ are $\frac{1}{5}$, ___, ___, ___, and ___.

Name ______________________________

Share and Show

1. Use the picture to complete the equations.

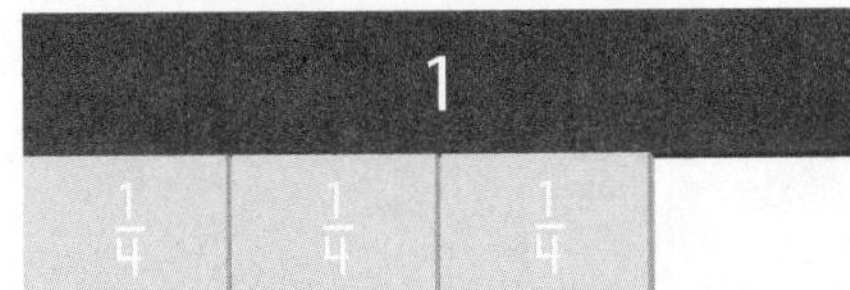

$\frac{3}{4} =$ ______ + ______ + ______

$\frac{3}{4} =$ ______ $\times \frac{1}{4}$

Write the fraction as a product of a whole number and a unit fraction.

2. $\frac{4}{5} =$ ______

3. $\frac{3}{10} =$ ______

4. $\frac{8}{3} =$ ______

List the next four multiples of the unit fraction.

5. $\frac{1}{6}$, ___, ___, ___, ___

6. $\frac{1}{3}$, ___, ___, ___, ___

Math Talk — **Mathematical Practices**

Explain why $\frac{8}{5}$ is a multiple of $\frac{1}{5}$.

On Your Own

Write the fraction as a product of a whole number and a unit fraction.

7. $\frac{5}{6} =$ ______

8. $\frac{9}{4} =$ ______

9. $\frac{3}{100} =$ ______

List the next four multiples of the unit fraction.

10. $\frac{1}{10}$, ___, ___, ___, ___

11. $\frac{1}{8}$, ___, ___, ___, ___

Problem Solving • Applications

12. MATHEMATICAL PRACTICE 6 Robyn uses $\frac{1}{2}$ cup of blueberries to make each loaf of blueberry bread. **Explain** how many loaves of blueberry bread she can make with $2\frac{1}{2}$ cups of blueberries.

____

13. GO DEEPER Nigel cut a loaf of bread into 12 equal slices. His family ate some of the bread and now $\frac{5}{12}$ of the loaf is left. Nigel wants to put each of the leftover slices in its own bag. How many bags does Nigel need?

____

14. THINK SMARTER Which fraction is a multiple of $\frac{1}{5}$? Mark all that apply.

○ $\frac{4}{5}$ ○ $\frac{5}{9}$

○ $\frac{5}{7}$ ○ $\frac{3}{5}$

Sense or Nonsense?

15. THINK SMARTER Whose statement makes sense? Whose statement is nonsense? Explain your reasoning.

There is no multiple of $\frac{1}{6}$ between $\frac{3}{6}$ and $\frac{4}{6}$.

$\frac{4}{5}$ is a multiple of $\frac{1}{4}$.

Gavin

Abigail

- For the statement that is nonsense, write a new statement that makes sense.

FOR MORE PRACTICE:
Standards Practice Book

Name ______________________________

Multiples of Fractions

Essential Question How can you write a product of a whole number and a fraction as a product of a whole number and a unit fraction?

Numbers and Operations—Fractions—4.NF.4b *Also 4.NF.4c*

MATHEMATICAL PRACTICES
MP.1, MP.2, MP.4

Unlock the Problem

Jen is making 4 pans of baked ziti. For each pan, she needs $\frac{2}{3}$ cup cheese. Her measuring cup can scoop $\frac{1}{3}$ cup of cheese. How many scoops of cheese does she need for the 4 pans?

Example 1 Use a model to write the product of $4 \times \frac{2}{3}$ as the product of a whole number and a unit fraction.

$\frac{1}{3}$	$\frac{1}{3}$	$\frac{1}{3}$

Think: $\frac{2}{3}$ is 2 third-size parts.

$\frac{2}{3}$ = ______ + ______ or 2 × ______.

There are 4 pans of baked ziti. Each pan needs $\frac{2}{3}$ cup cheese.

$\frac{1}{3}$	$\frac{1}{3}$	$\frac{1}{3}$	← 1 pan: $2 \times \frac{1}{3} = \frac{2}{3}$
$\frac{1}{3}$	$\frac{1}{3}$	$\frac{1}{3}$	← 2 pans: $2 \times 2 \times \frac{1}{3} = 4 \times \frac{1}{3} = \frac{4}{3}$
$\frac{1}{3}$	$\frac{1}{3}$	$\frac{1}{3}$	← 3 pans: $3 \times 2 \times \frac{1}{3} = 6 \times \frac{1}{3} = \frac{6}{3}$
$\frac{1}{3}$	$\frac{1}{3}$	$\frac{1}{3}$	← 4 pans: $4 \times 2 \times \frac{1}{3} = 8 \times \frac{1}{3} = \frac{8}{3}$

$4 \times \frac{2}{3} = 4 \times$ ______ $\times \frac{1}{3} =$ ______ $\times \frac{1}{3} = \frac{}{3}$

So, Jen needs ______ third-size scoops of cheese for 4 pans of ziti.

Math Talk — **Mathematical Practices**

Explain how this model of $4 \times \frac{2}{3}$ is related to a model of 4 × 2.

1. What if Jen decides to make 10 pans of ziti? Describe a pattern you could use to find the number of scoops of cheese she would need.

____

____

____

Multiples You have learned to write multiples of unit fractions. You can also write multiples of non-unit fractions.

Example 2 Use a number line to write multiples of $\frac{2}{5}$.

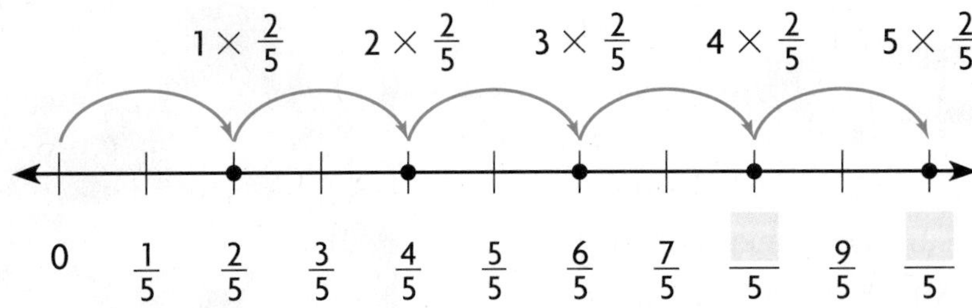

Think: Multiply $\frac{2}{5}$ by counting numbers.

Multiples of $\frac{2}{5}$ are $\frac{2}{5}$, ____, ____, ____, and ____.

$3 \times \frac{2}{5} = \frac{6}{5}$. Write $\frac{6}{5}$ as a product of a whole number and a unit fraction.

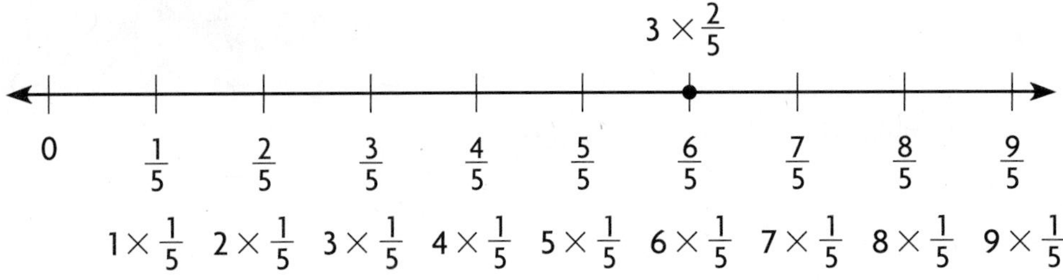

$3 \times \frac{2}{5} = \frac{6}{5} =$ _____ $\times$ _____

2. Explain how to use repeated addition to write the multiple of a fraction as the product of a whole number and a unit fraction.

____

____

Share and Show

1. Write three multiples of $\frac{3}{8}$.

$1 \times \frac{3}{8} =$ _____

$2 \times \frac{3}{8} =$ _____

$3 \times \frac{3}{8} =$ _____

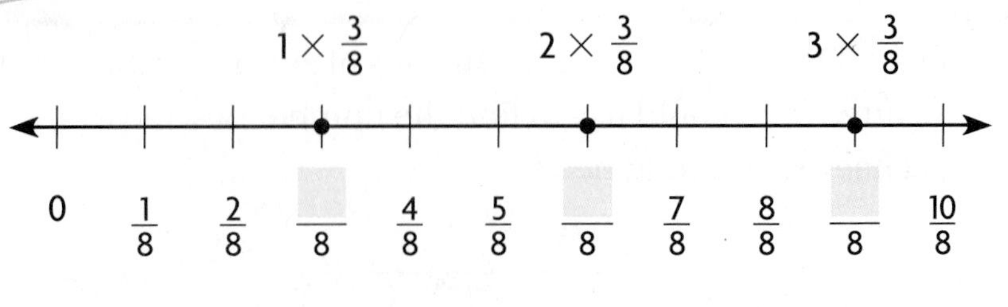

Multiples of $\frac{3}{8}$ are _____, _____, and _____.

Name ______________________

List the next four multiples of the fraction.

2. $\frac{3}{6}$, ___, ___, ___, ___

3. $\frac{2}{10}$, ___, ___, ___, ___

Write the product as the product of a whole number and a unit fraction.

4.

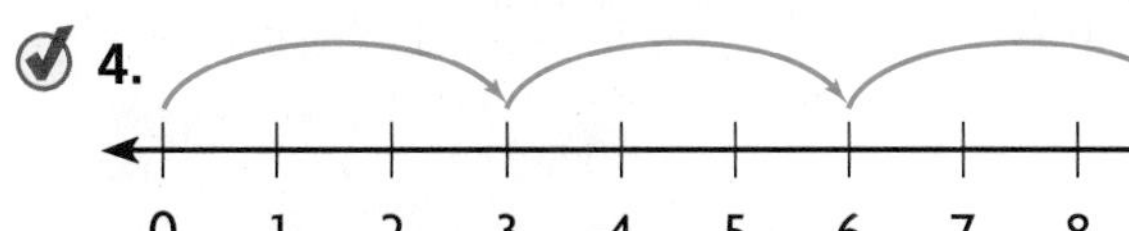

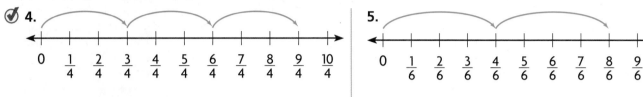

$3 \times \frac{3}{4} =$ ___________

5.

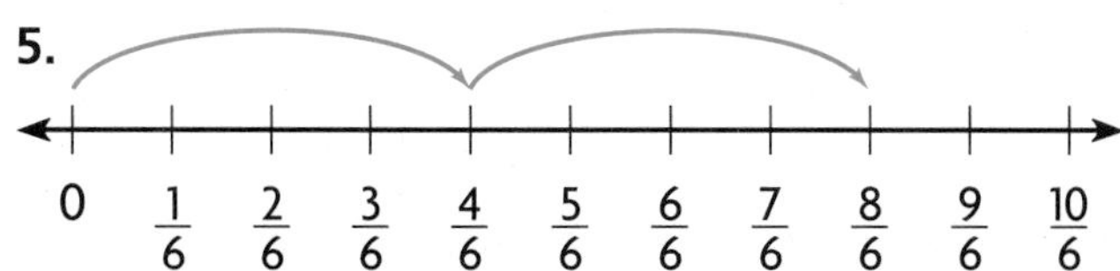

$2 \times \frac{4}{6} =$ ___________

Math Talk — **Mathematical Practices**

Explain how to write a product of a whole number and a fraction as a product of a whole number and a unit fraction.

On Your Own

List the next four multiples of the fraction.

6. $\frac{4}{5}$, ___, ___, ___, ___

7. $\frac{2}{4}$, ___, ___, ___, ___

Write the product as the product of a whole number and a unit fraction.

8.

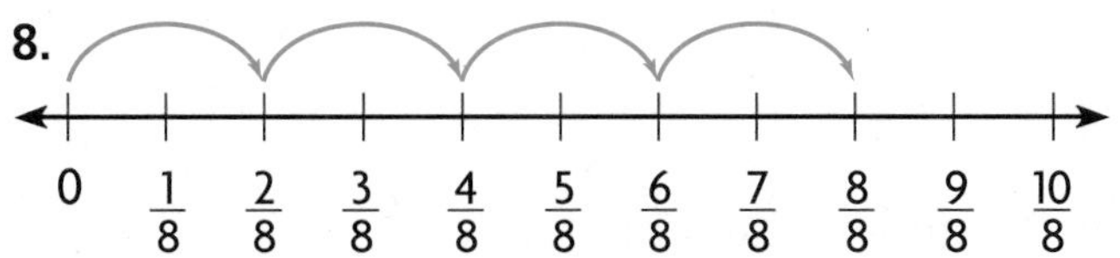

$4 \times \frac{2}{8} =$ ___________

9.

0 $\frac{1}{5}$ $\frac{2}{5}$ $\frac{3}{5}$ $\frac{4}{5}$ $\frac{5}{5}$ $\frac{6}{5}$ $\frac{7}{5}$ $\frac{8}{5}$ $\frac{9}{5}$ $\frac{10}{5}$

$3 \times \frac{3}{5} =$ ___________

10. MATHEMATICAL PRACTICE 8 **Use Repeated Reasoning** Are $\frac{6}{10}$ and $\frac{6}{30}$ multiples of $\frac{3}{10}$? Explain.

____

____

11. GO DEEPER Which is greater, $4 \times \frac{2}{7}$ or $3 \times \frac{3}{7}$? Explain.

____

Unlock the Problem 

12. THINKSMARTER Josh is watering his plants. He gives each of 2 plants $\frac{3}{5}$ pint of water. His watering can holds $\frac{1}{5}$ pint. How many times will he fill his watering can to water both plants?

a. What do you need to find?

____

b. What information do you need to use?

____

____

c. How can drawing a model help you solve the problem?

____

____

____

____

____

____

____

d. Show the steps you use to solve the problem.

e. Complete the sentence.

Josh will fill his watering can ______ times.

Personal Math Trainer

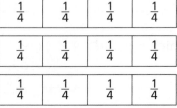

13. THINKSMARTER+ Alma is making 3 batches of tortillas. She adds $\frac{3}{4}$ cup of water to each batch. The measuring cup holds $\frac{1}{4}$ cup. How many times must Alma measure $\frac{1}{4}$ cup of water to have enough for the tortillas? Shade the model to show your answer.

$\frac{1}{4}$	$\frac{1}{4}$	$\frac{1}{4}$	$\frac{1}{4}$

$\frac{1}{4}$	$\frac{1}{4}$	$\frac{1}{4}$	$\frac{1}{4}$

$\frac{1}{4}$	$\frac{1}{4}$	$\frac{1}{4}$	$\frac{1}{4}$

Alma must measure $\frac{1}{4}$ cup ☐ times.

FOR MORE PRACTICE: Standards Practice Book

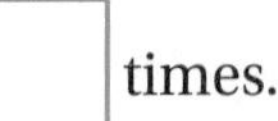

Name ___________________________

Mid-Chapter Checkpoint

Vocabulary

Vocabulary
multiple
product
unit fraction

Choose the best term from the box.

1. A ______________ of a number is the product of the number and a counting number. (p. 330)

2. A ______________ always has a numerator of 1. (p. 329)

Concepts and Skills

List the next four multiples of the unit fraction. (4.NF.4a)

3. $\frac{1}{2}$, ____, ____, ____, ____

4. $\frac{1}{5}$, ____, ____, ____, ____

Write the fraction as a product of a whole number and a unit fraction. (4.NF.4a)

5. $\frac{4}{10} =$ ____________

6. $\frac{8}{12} =$ ____________

7. $\frac{3}{4} =$ ____________

List the next four multiples of the fraction. (4.NF.4b)

8. $\frac{2}{5}$, ____, ____, ____, ____

9. $\frac{5}{6}$, ____, ____, ____, ____

Write the product as the product of a whole number and a unit fraction. (4.NF.4b)

10.

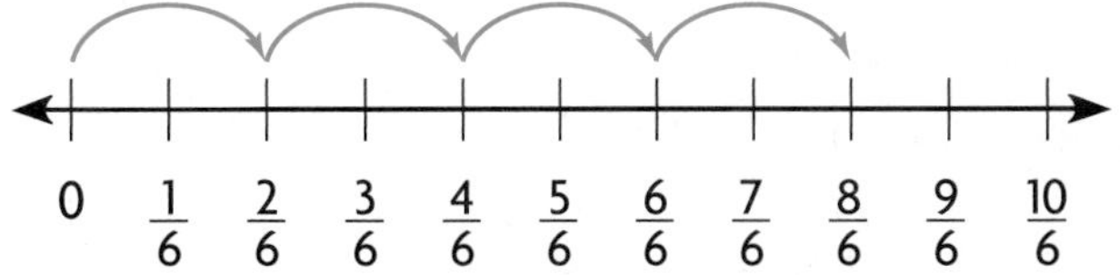

$4 \times \frac{2}{6} =$ ____________

11.

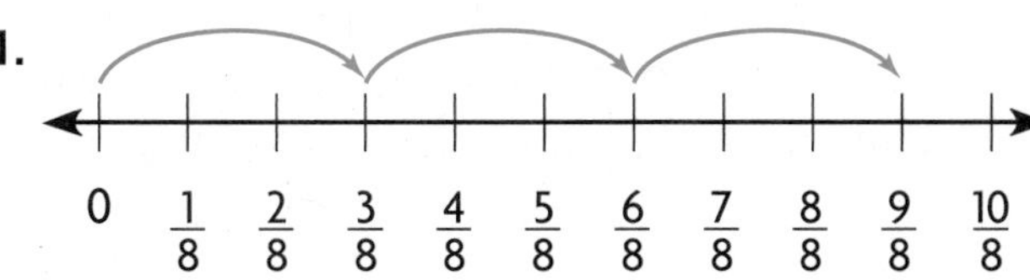

$3 \times \frac{3}{8} =$ ____________

12. Pedro cut a sheet of poster board into 10 equal parts. His brother used some of the poster board and now $\frac{8}{10}$ is left. Pedro wants to make a sign from each remaining part of the poster board. How many signs can he make? (4.NF.4a)

____

13. Ella is making 3 batches of banana milkshakes. She needs $\frac{3}{4}$ gallon of milk for each batch. Her measuring cup holds $\frac{1}{4}$ gallon. How many times will she need to fill the measuring cup to make all 3 batches of milkshakes? (4.NF.4b)

____

14. Darren cut a lemon pie into 8 equal slices. His friends ate some of the pie and now $\frac{5}{8}$ is left. Darren wants to put each slice of the leftover pie on its own plate. What part of the pie will he put on each plate? (4.NF.4a)

____

15. Beth is putting liquid fertilizer on the plants in 4 flowerpots. Her measuring spoon holds $\frac{1}{8}$ teaspoon. The directions say to put $\frac{5}{8}$ teaspoon of fertilizer in each pot. How many times will Beth need to fill the measuring spoon to fertilize the plants in the 4 pots? (4.NF.4b)

____

Name ______________________________

Lesson 8.3

Multiply a Fraction by a Whole Number Using Models

Essential Question How can you use a model to multiply a fraction by a whole number?

Numbers and Operations—Fractions—4.NF.4b *Also 4.NF.4c*

MATHEMATICAL PRACTICES
MP.1, MP.2, MP.4

Unlock the Problem

Rafael practices the violin for $\frac{3}{4}$ hour each day. He has a recital in 3 days. How much time will he practice in 3 days?

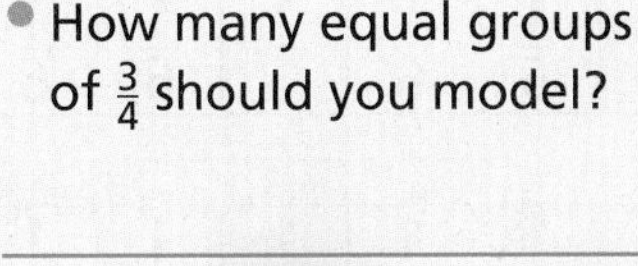

- How many equal groups of $\frac{3}{4}$ should you model?

____

Example 1 Use a model to multiply $3 \times \frac{3}{4}$.

Think: $3 \times \frac{3}{4}$ is 3 groups of $\frac{3}{4}$ of a whole. Shade the model to show 3 groups of $\frac{3}{4}$.

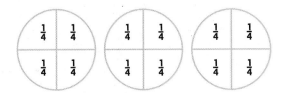

1 group of $\frac{3}{4}$ = ______

2 groups of $\frac{3}{4}$ = ______

3 groups of $\frac{3}{4}$ = ______

$3 \times \frac{3}{4}$ = ______

So, Rafael will practice for ______ hours in all.

Math Talk — Mathematical Practices

If you multiply $4 \times \frac{2}{6}$, is the product greater than or less than 4? **Explain.**

1. Explain how you can use repeated addition with the model to find the product $3 \times \frac{3}{4}$.

____

____

2. Rafael's daily practice of $\frac{3}{4}$ hour is in sessions that last for $\frac{1}{4}$ hour each. Describe how the model shows the number of practice sessions Rafael has in 3 days.

____

____

Example 2 Use a pattern to multiply.

You know how to use a model and repeated addition to multiply a fraction by a whole number. Look for a pattern in the table to discover another way to multiply a fraction by a whole number.

Multiplication Problem		Whole Number (Number of Groups)	Fraction (Size of Groups)	Product
$\frac{1}{6}$ $\frac{1}{6}$ $\frac{1}{6}$ $\frac{1}{6}$ $\frac{1}{6}$ $\frac{1}{6}$ $\frac{1}{6}$ $\frac{1}{6}$ $\frac{1}{6}$ $\frac{1}{6}$ $\frac{1}{6}$ $\frac{1}{6}$	$2 \times \frac{1}{6}$	2	$\frac{1}{6}$ of a whole	$\frac{2}{6}$
$\frac{1}{6}$ $\frac{1}{6}$ $\frac{1}{6}$ $\frac{1}{6}$ $\frac{1}{6}$ $\frac{1}{6}$ $\frac{1}{6}$ $\frac{1}{6}$ $\frac{1}{6}$ $\frac{1}{6}$ $\frac{1}{6}$ $\frac{1}{6}$	$2 \times \frac{2}{6}$	2	$\frac{2}{6}$ of a whole	$\frac{4}{6}$
$\frac{1}{6}$ $\frac{1}{6}$ $\frac{1}{6}$ $\frac{1}{6}$ $\frac{1}{6}$ $\frac{1}{6}$ $\frac{1}{6}$ $\frac{1}{6}$ $\frac{1}{6}$ $\frac{1}{6}$ $\frac{1}{6}$ $\frac{1}{6}$	$2 \times \frac{3}{6}$	2	$\frac{3}{6}$ of a whole	$\frac{6}{6}$

When you multiply a fraction by a whole number, the numerator in the product is the product of the ______________ and the ______________ of the fraction. The denominator in the product is the same as the ______________ of the fraction.

3. How do you multiply a fraction by a whole number without using a model or repeated addition?

____

____

4. Describe two different ways to find the product $4 \times \frac{2}{3}$.

____

____

____

Name ____________________

Share and Show

1. Find the product of $3 \times \frac{5}{8}$.

1 group of $\frac{5}{8} = \frac{\square}{8}$

2 groups of $\frac{5}{8} = \frac{\square}{8}$

3 groups of $\frac{5}{8} = \frac{\square}{8}$

$3 \times \frac{5}{8} =$ ______

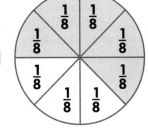

3 groups of $\frac{5}{8}$

Multiply.

2.

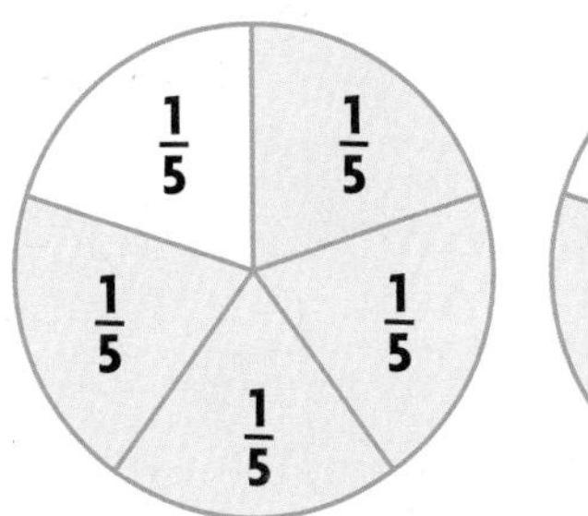

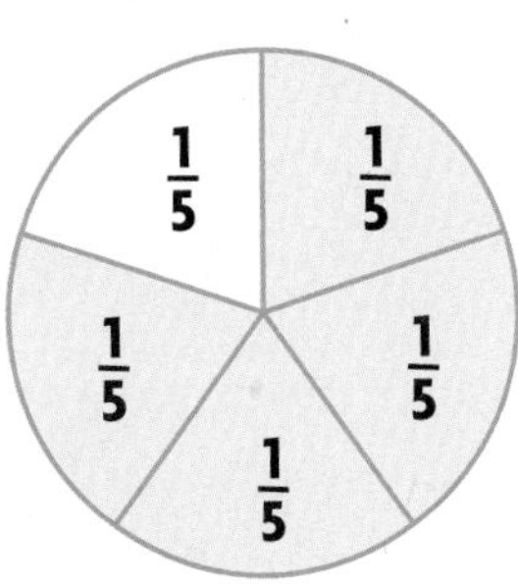

$2 \times \frac{4}{5} =$ ______

3.

$\frac{1}{3}$	$\frac{1}{3}$	$\frac{1}{3}$
$\frac{1}{3}$	$\frac{1}{3}$	$\frac{1}{3}$
$\frac{1}{3}$	$\frac{1}{3}$	$\frac{1}{3}$
$\frac{1}{3}$	$\frac{1}{3}$	$\frac{1}{3}$

$4 \times \frac{2}{3} =$ ______

4. $5 \times \frac{3}{10} =$ ______

5. $4 \times \frac{5}{6} =$ ______

Math Talk — Mathematical Practices

Describe how to model Exercise 5.

On Your Own

Multiply.

6. $2 \times \frac{7}{12} =$ ______

7. $6 \times \frac{3}{8} =$ ______

8. $5 \times \frac{2}{4} =$ ______

9. $3 \times \frac{4}{6} =$ ______

10. $2 \times \frac{5}{10} =$ ______

11. $4 \times \frac{2}{5} =$ ______

MATHEMATICAL PRACTICE 7 Look for a Pattern **Algebra** Write the unknown number.

12. $\square \times \frac{2}{3} = \frac{12}{3}$

13. $5 \times \frac{\square}{4} = \frac{10}{4}$

14. $2 \times \frac{7}{\square} = \frac{14}{8}$

Unlock the Problem

15. THINK SMARTER Lisa makes clothes for pets. She needs $\frac{5}{6}$ yard of fabric to make 1 dog coat. How much fabric does she need to make 3 dog coats?

a. What do you need to find?

____

b. What information do you need?

____

c. Show the steps you use to solve the problem.

d. Complete the sentence.

Lisa needs ______ yards of fabric to make 3 dog coats.

16. GO DEEPER Manuel's small dog eats $\frac{2}{4}$ bag of dog food in 1 month. His large dog eats $\frac{3}{4}$ bag of dog food in 1 month. How many bags do both dogs eat in 6 months?

____

17. THINK SMARTER Select the correct product for the equation.

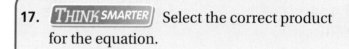

$\frac{24}{12}$ $\frac{18}{12}$ $\frac{24}{7}$ $\frac{18}{7}$

$9 \times \frac{2}{12} = $ ☐ $3 \times \frac{6}{7} = $ ☐

$6 \times \frac{4}{7} = $ ☐ $8 \times \frac{3}{12} = $ ☐

FOR MORE PRACTICE:
Standards Practice Book

Name ______________________________

Multiply a Fraction or Mixed Number by a Whole Number

Essential Question How can you multiply a fraction by a whole number to solve a problem?

Numbers and Operations—Fractions—4.NF.4c

MATHEMATICAL PRACTICES
MP.1, MP.4

Unlock the Problem

Christina is planning a dance routine. At the end of each measure of music, she will make a $1\frac{1}{4}$ turn. How many turns will she make after the first 3 measures of music?

- Will Christina make more or less than $1\frac{1}{4}$ turns in 3 measures of music?

____

- What operation will you use to solve the problem?

____

You can multiply a mixed number by a whole number.

Example

STEP 1 Write and solve an equation.

$3 \times 1\frac{1}{4} = 3 \times \frac{\square}{\square} = \frac{\square}{\square}$ Write $1\frac{1}{4}$ as a fraction. Multiply.

STEP 2 Write the product as a mixed number.

$\frac{15}{4} = \underbrace{\frac{1}{4} + \frac{1}{4} + \frac{1}{4} + \frac{1}{4}}_{1} + \underbrace{\_\_ + \_\_ + \_\_ + \_\_}_{1} + \underbrace{\_\_ + \_\_ + \_\_ + \_\_}_{1} + \frac{1}{4} + \frac{1}{4} + \frac{1}{4}$

$= \square + \frac{\square}{\square}$ Combine the wholes. Then combine the remaining parts.

$= \square\frac{\square}{\square}$ Write the mixed number.

So, Christina will make ______ turns.

Mathematical Practices

Explain how writing the mixed number as a fraction in Step 2 is related to division.

1. If you multiply $3 \times \frac{1}{4}$, is the product greater than or less than 3? Explain.

____

____

2. Explain how you can tell that $3 \times 1\frac{1}{4}$ is greater than 3 without finding the exact product.

____

Rename Mixed Numbers and Fractions You can use multiplication and division to rename fractions and mixed numbers.

Remember

The Identity Property of Multiplication states that the product of any number and 1 is that number.

Write $8\frac{1}{5}$ as a fraction.

$8\frac{1}{5} = 8 + \frac{1}{5}$

$= (8 \times \_\_\_\_) + \frac{1}{5}$ Use the Identity Property of Multiplication.

$= \left(8 \times \frac{\square}{\square}\right) + \frac{1}{5}$ Rename 1.

$= \frac{\square}{\square} + \frac{\square}{\square}$ Multiply.

$= \frac{\square}{\square}$ Add.

Write $\frac{32}{5}$ as a mixed number.

Find how many groups of $\frac{5}{5}$ are in $\frac{32}{5}$.

- Divide 32 by 5.
- The quotient is the number of wholes in $\frac{32}{5}$.
- The remainder is the number of fifths left over.

$5\overline{)32}$ = $\square$ r $\square$

$- \square$

$\square$

There are 6 groups of $\frac{5}{5}$, or 6 wholes.
There are 2 fifths, or $\frac{2}{5}$ left over.

$\frac{32}{5} = \square\frac{\square}{\square}$

Try This! **Find $5 \times 2\frac{2}{3}$. Write the product as a mixed number.**

$5 \times 2\frac{2}{3} = 5 \times \_\_\_\_$ Write $2\frac{2}{3}$ as a fraction.

$= \_\_\_\_$ Multiply.

$= \_\_\_\_$ Divide the numerator by 3.

3. Explain why your solution to $5 \times 2\frac{2}{3} = 13\frac{1}{3}$ is reasonable.

4. **Sense or Nonsense?** To find $5 \times 2\frac{2}{3}$, Dylan says he can find $(5 \times 2) + \left(5 \times \frac{2}{3}\right)$. Does this make sense? Explain.

Name ______________________________

Share and Show

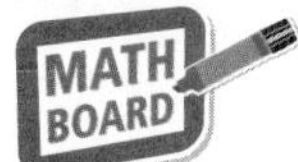

1. $2 \times 3\frac{2}{3} = 2 \times$ ______

   $=$ ______

   $=$ ______

Multiply. Write the product as a mixed number.

2. $6 \times \frac{2}{5} =$ ______
3. $3 \times 2\frac{3}{4} =$ ______
4. $2 \times 1\frac{5}{6} =$ ______

Math Talk — Mathematical Practices

Explain how you know your answer to Exercise 3 is reasonable.

On Your Own

Multiply. Write the product as a mixed number.

5. $4 \times \frac{5}{8} =$ ______
6. $6 \times \frac{5}{12} =$ ______
7. $3 \times 2\frac{1}{2} =$ ______
8. $2 \times 2\frac{2}{3} =$ ______
9. $5 \times 1\frac{2}{4} =$ ______
10. $4 \times 2\frac{2}{5} =$ ______

MATHEMATICAL PRACTICE 7 Look for a Pattern **Algebra** **Write the unknown number.**

11. $\square \times 2\frac{1}{3} = 9\frac{1}{3}$
12. $3 \times 2\frac{2}{\square} = 7\frac{2}{4}$
13. $3 \times \square\frac{3}{8} = 4\frac{1}{8}$

14. Describe two different ways to write $\frac{7}{3}$ as a mixed number.

____

____

____

____

____

Problem Solving • Applications

Use the recipe for 15–18.

15. Otis plans to make 3 batches of sidewalk chalk. How much plaster of Paris does he need?

16. **What's the Question?** The answer is $\frac{32}{3}$.

17. THINK SMARTER Patty has 2 cups of warm water. Is that enough water to make 4 batches of sidewalk chalk? Explain how you know without finding the exact product.

Sidewalk Chalk Recipe

$\frac{3}{4}$ cup warm water

$1\frac{1}{2}$ cups plaster of Paris

$2\frac{2}{3}$ tablespoons powdered paint

18. GO DEEPER Rita makes sidewalk chalk 2 days a week. Each of those days, she spends $1\frac{1}{4}$ hours making the chalk. How much time does Rita spend making sidewalk chalk in 3 weeks?

Personal Math Trainer

19. THINK SMARTER + Oliver has music lessons Monday, Wednesday, and Friday. Each lesson is $\frac{3}{4}$ of an hour. Oliver says he will have lessons for $3\frac{1}{2}$ hours this week. Without multiplying, explain how you know Oliver is incorrect.

FOR MORE PRACTICE: Standards Practice Book

Name ____________________

Problem Solving • Comparison Problems with Fractions

Essential Question How can you use the strategy *draw a diagram* to solve comparison problems with fractions?

Numbers and Operations—Fractions—4.NF.4c

MATHEMATICAL PRACTICES
MP.1, MP.2

Unlock the Problem

The deepest part of the Grand Canyon is about $1\frac{1}{6}$ miles deep. The deepest part of the ocean is located in the Mariana Trench, in the Pacific Ocean. The deepest part of the ocean is almost 6 times as deep as the deepest part of the Grand Canyon. About how deep is the deepest part of the ocean?

Read the Problem

What do I need to find?

I need to find ____________________

____

____

What information do I need to use?

The deepest part of the Grand Canyon is about ______ miles deep.

The deepest part of the ocean is about ______ times as deep.

How will I use the information?

I can ____________________ to compare the depths.

Solve the Problem

Draw a bar model. Compare the depth of the deepest part of the Grand Canyon and the deepest part of the ocean, in miles.

__________ $1\frac{1}{6}$

__________ | ___ | ___ | ___ | ___ | ___ | ___ |

m

Write an equation and solve.

m is the deepest part of __________, in miles.

$m =$ ______ ______ Write an equation.

$m =$ ______ ______ Write the mixed number as a fraction.

$m =$ ______ Multiply.

$m =$ ______ Write the fraction as a whole number.

So, the deepest part of the ocean is about ______ miles deep.

Try Another Problem

Mountains are often measured by the distance they rise above sea level. Mount Washington rises more than $1\frac{1}{10}$ miles above sea level. Mount Everest rises about 5 times as high. About how many miles above sea level does Mount Everest rise?

Read the Problem	Solve the Problem
What do I need to find?	
What information do I need to use?	
How will I use the information?	

So, Mount Everest rises about ______ miles above sea level.

- How did drawing a diagram help you solve the problem?

____

____

Math Talk **Mathematical Practices**

Explain how you could use the strategy *act it out* to find the height of Mount Everest.

Name ___________________________

Share and Show

Unlock the Problem

√ Use the Problem Solving MathBoard.
√ Underline important facts.

1. Komodo dragons are the heaviest lizards on earth. A baby Komodo dragon is $1\frac{1}{4}$ feet long when it hatches. Its mother is 6 times as long. How long is the mother?

   First, draw a bar model to show the problem.

   Then, write the equation you need to solve.

   ____

   Finally, find the length of the mother Komodo dragon.

   The mother Komodo dragon is ______ feet long.

2. THINK SMARTER What if a male Komodo dragon is 7 times as long as the baby Komodo dragon? How long is the male? How much longer is the male than the mother?

   ____

3. The smallest hummingbird is the Bee hummingbird. It has a mass of about $1\frac{1}{2}$ grams. A Rufous hummingbird's mass is 3 times the mass of the Bee hummingbird. What is the mass of a Rufous hummingbird?

   ____

4. Sloane needs $\frac{3}{4}$ hour to drive to her grandmother's house. It takes her 5 times as long to drive to her cousin's house. How long does it take to drive to her cousin's house?

   ____

WRITE ▸ Math
Show Your Work

On Your Own

Use the table for 5 and 6.

Payton has a variety of flowers in her garden. The table shows the average heights of the flowers.

Flower	Height
tulip	$1\frac{1}{4}$ feet
daisy	$2\frac{1}{2}$ feet
tiger lily	$3\frac{1}{3}$ feet
sunflower	$7\frac{3}{4}$ feet

5. MATHEMATICAL PRACTICE 1 **Make Sense of Problems** What is the difference between the height of the tallest flower and the height of the shortest flower in Payton's garden?

____

WRITE Math
Show Your Work

6. THINK SMARTER Payton says her average sunflower is 7 times the height of her average tulip. Do you agree or disagree with her statement? Explain your reasoning.

____

____

____

7. GO DEEPER Miguel ran $1\frac{3}{10}$ miles on Monday. On Friday, Miguel ran 3 times as far as he did on Monday. How much farther did Miguel run on Friday than he did on Monday?

____

Personal Math Trainer

8. THINK SMARTER + The table shows the lengths of different types of turtles at a zoo.

Turtle Name	Type of Turtle	Length
Tuck	Common Snapping Turtle	$1\frac{1}{6}$ feet
Lolly	Leatherback Sea Turtle	$5\frac{5}{6}$ feet
Daisy	Loggerhead Sea Turtle	$3\frac{1}{2}$ feet

For numbers 8a–8d, select True or False for each statement.

8a. Daisy is 4 times as long as Tuck. ○ True ○ False

8b. Lolly is 5 times as long as Tuck. ○ True ○ False

8c. Daisy is 3 times as long as Tuck. ○ True ○ False

8d. Lolly is 2 times as long as Daisy. ○ True ○ False

FOR MORE PRACTICE:
Standards Practice Book

Name ________________________________

Chapter 8 Review/Test

1. What are the next four multiples of $\frac{1}{8}$?

2. Marta is making 3 servings of fruit salad. She adds $\frac{3}{8}$ cup blueberries for each serving. Her measuring cup holds $\frac{1}{8}$ cup. How many times must Marta measure $\frac{1}{8}$ cup of blueberries to have enough for the fruit salad? Shade the models to show your answer.

$\frac{1}{8}$	$\frac{1}{8}$	$\frac{1}{8}$	$\frac{1}{8}$	$\frac{1}{8}$	$\frac{1}{8}$	$\frac{1}{8}$	$\frac{1}{8}$

$\frac{1}{8}$	$\frac{1}{8}$	$\frac{1}{8}$	$\frac{1}{8}$	$\frac{1}{8}$	$\frac{1}{8}$	$\frac{1}{8}$	$\frac{1}{8}$

$\frac{1}{8}$	$\frac{1}{8}$	$\frac{1}{8}$	$\frac{1}{8}$	$\frac{1}{8}$	$\frac{1}{8}$	$\frac{1}{8}$	$\frac{1}{8}$

Marta must measure $\frac{1}{8}$ cup __________ times.

3. Mickey exercises $\frac{3}{4}$ hour every day. How many hours does he exercise in 8 days?

__________ hours

GO DIGITAL Assessment Options Chapter Test

4. Molly is baking for the Moms and Muffins event at her school. She will bake 4 batches of banana muffins. She needs $1\frac{3}{4}$ cups of bananas for each batch of muffins.

Part A

Molly completed the multiplication below and said she needed 8 cups of bananas for 4 batches of muffins. What is Molly's error?

$$4 \times 1\frac{3}{4} = 4 \times \frac{8}{4} = \frac{32}{4} = 8$$

Part B

What is the correct number of cups Molly needs for 4 batches of muffins? Explain how you found your answer.

5. Which fraction is a multiple of $\frac{1}{9}$? Mark all that apply.

○ $\frac{3}{9}$ ○ $\frac{9}{12}$ ○ $\frac{2}{9}$

○ $\frac{4}{9}$ ○ $\frac{9}{10}$ ○ $\frac{9}{9}$

6. Mimi recorded a soccer game that lasted $1\frac{2}{3}$ hours. She watched it 3 times over the weekend to study the plays. How many hours did Mimi spend watching the soccer game? Show your work.

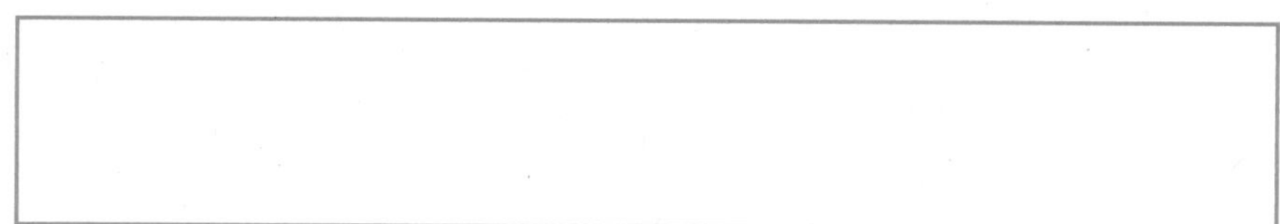

7. Theo is comparing shark lengths. He learned that a horn shark is $2\frac{3}{4}$ feet long. A blue shark is 4 times as long. Complete the model. Then find the length of a blue shark.

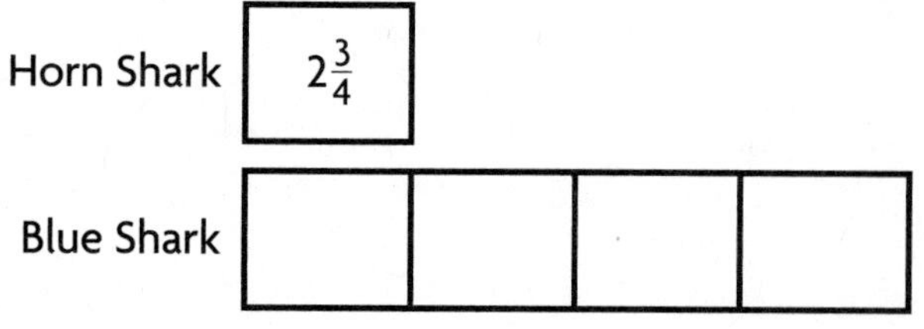

A blue shark is ☐ feet long.

Name ______________________________

8. Joel made a number line showing the multiples of $\frac{3}{5}$.

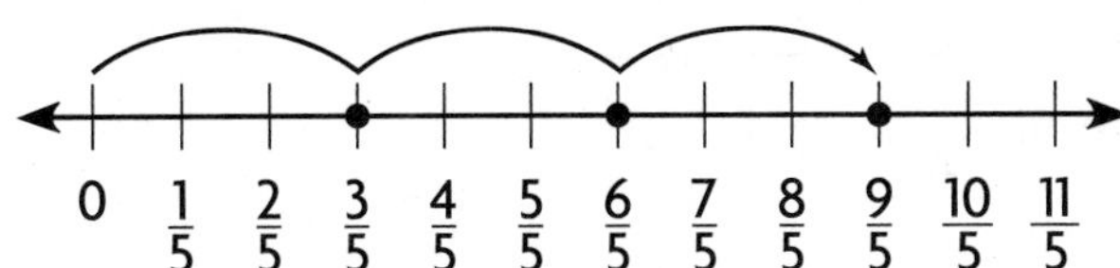

The product $2 \times \frac{3}{5}$ is shown by the fraction ☐ on the number line.

9. Bobby has baseball practice Monday, Wednesday, and Friday. Each practice is $2\frac{1}{2}$ hours. Bobby says he will have practice for 4 hours this week.

Part A

Without multiplying, explain how you know Bobby is incorrect.

Part B

How long will Bobby have baseball practice this week? Write your answer as a mixed number. Show your work.

10. Look at the number line. Write the missing fractions.

11. Ana's dachshund weighed $5\frac{5}{8}$ pounds when it was born. By age 4, the dog weighed 6 times as much. Fill each box with a number or symbol from the list to show how to find the weight of Ana's dog at age 4. Not all numbers and symbols may be used.

$5\frac{5}{8}$	4	5	6
$6\frac{5}{8}$	+	=	×

weight = ☐ ☐ ☐

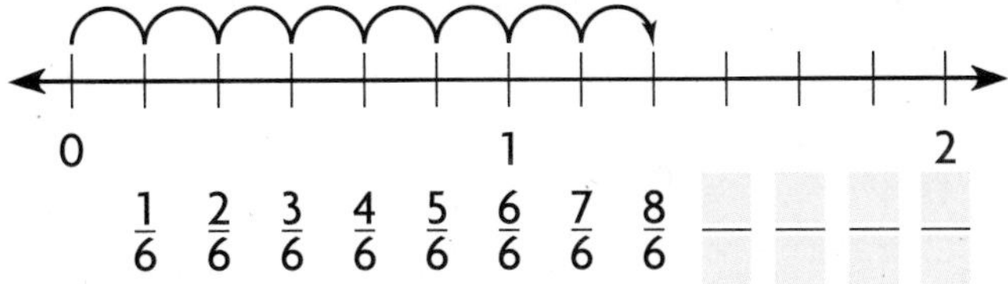

12. Asta made a fraction number line to help her find $3 \times \frac{4}{5}$.

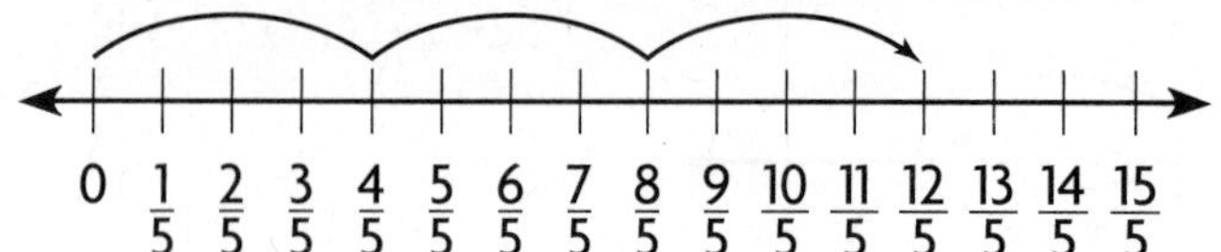

Select a way to write $3 \times \frac{4}{5}$ as the product of a whole number and a unit fraction.

$3 \times \frac{4}{5} =$ | $4 \times \frac{3}{5}$ / $12 \times \frac{1}{5}$ / $6 \times \frac{1}{5}$

13. Yusif wanted to give $\frac{1}{3}$ of his total toy car collection to 2 of his friends. How many of his toy cars will he give away?

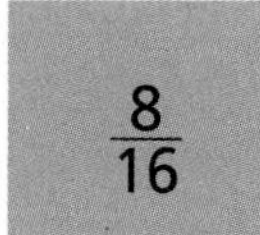

14. Select the correct product for the equation.

$\frac{8}{16}$ $\frac{32}{8}$ $\frac{16}{8}$ $\frac{20}{8}$

$4 \times \frac{5}{8} =$ ☐ $4 \times \frac{4}{8} =$ ☐

Name ______________________________

15. The lengths of different types of snakes at a zoo are shown in the table.

Snake's Name	Type of Snake	Length
Kenny	Kenyan Sand Boa	$1\frac{1}{2}$ feet
Bobby	Ball Python	$4\frac{1}{2}$ feet
Puck	Blood Python	$7\frac{1}{2}$ feet

For numbers 15a–15d, select True or False for the statement.

15a. Bobby is 4 times as long as Kenny. ○ True ○ False

15b. Bobby is 3 times as long as Kenny. ○ True ○ False

15c. Puck is 5 times as long as Kenny. ○ True ○ False

15d. Puck is 2 times as long as Bobby. ○ True ○ False

16. Hank used $3\frac{1}{2}$ bags of seed to plant grass in his front yard. He used 3 times as much seed to plant grass in his back yard. How much seed did Hank need for the backyard?

__________ bags

17. Jess made a big kettle of rice and beans. He used $1\frac{1}{2}$ cups of beans. He used 4 times as much rice.

Part A

Draw a model to show the problem.

Part B

Use your model to write an equation. Then solve the equation to find the amount of rice Jess needs.

18. Mrs. Burnham is making modeling clay for her class. She needs $\frac{2}{3}$ cup of warm water for each batch.

Part A

Mrs. Burnham has a 1-cup measure that has no other markings. Can she make 6 batches of modeling clay using only the 1-cup measure? Describe two ways you can find the answer.

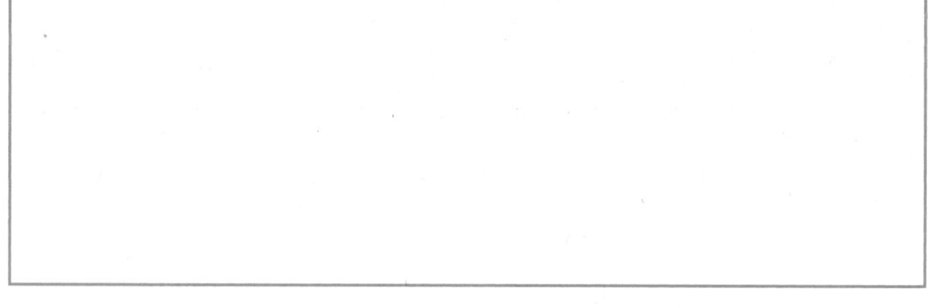

Part B

The modeling clay recipe also calls for $\frac{1}{2}$ cup of cornstarch. Nikki says Mrs. Burnham will also need 4 cups of cornstarch. Do you agree or disagree? Explain.

19. Donna buys some fabric to make place mats. She needs $\frac{1}{5}$ yard of each type of fabric. She has 9 different types of fabrics to make her design. Use the following equation. Write the number in the box to make the statement true.

$$\frac{9}{5} = \_\_\_\_\_\_ \times \frac{1}{5}$$

20. Mr. Tuyen uses $\frac{5}{8}$ of a tank of gas each week to drive to and from his job. How many tanks of gas does Mr. Tuyen use in 5 weeks? Write your answer two different ways.

Mr. Tuyen uses ________ or ________ tanks of gas.

21. Rico is making 4 batches of salsa. Each batch needs $\frac{2}{3}$ cup of corn. He only has a $\frac{1}{3}$-cup measure. How many times must Rico measure $\frac{1}{3}$ cup of corn to have enough for all of the salsa?

 times

Chapter 9

Relate Fractions and Decimals

Show What You Know

Check your understanding of important skills.

Name ______________________

▶ Count Coins **Find the total value.**

1. Total value: __________

2. Total value: __________

▶ Equivalent Fractions

Write two equivalent fractions for the picture.

3. __________

4. __________

▶ Fractions with Denominators of 10

Write a fraction for the words. You may draw a picture.

5. three tenths __________

6. six tenths __________

7. eight tenths __________

8. nine tenths __________

The Hudson River Science Barge, docked near New York City, provides a demonstration of how renewable energy can be used to produce food for large cities. Vegetables grown on the barge require ______ of the water needed by field crops. Be a Math Detective. Use these clues to find the fraction and decimal for the missing amount.

- The number is less than one and has two decimal places.
- The digit in the hundredths place has a value of $\frac{5}{100}$.
- The digit in the tenths place has a value of $\frac{2}{10}$.

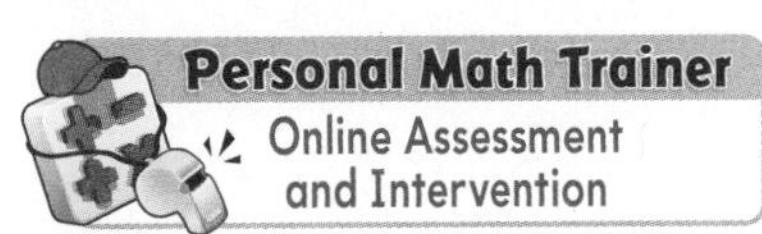

Vocabulary Builder

▶ Visualize It

Complete the Semantic Map by using words with a ✓.

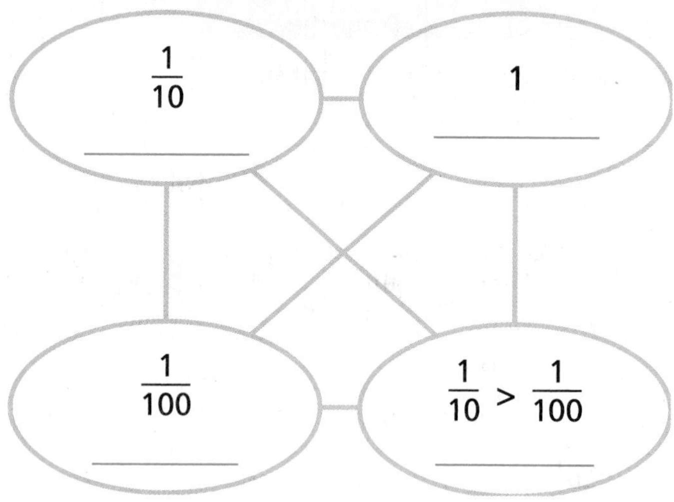

Review Words

✓ compare
equivalent fractions
fraction
place value
✓ whole

Preview Words

decimal
decimal point
equivalent decimals
✓ hundredth
✓ tenth

▶ Understand Vocabulary

Draw a line to match each word with its definition.

Word	Definition
1. decimal	• Two or more decimals that name the same amount
2. decimal point	• One part out of one hundred equal parts
3. tenth	• A number with one or more digits to the right of the decimal point
4. hundredth	• One part out of ten equal parts
5. equivalent decimals	• A symbol used to separate dollars from cents in money amounts and to separate the ones and the tenths places in decimals

GO DIGITAL
• Interactive Student Edition
• Multimedia eGlossary

Name ______________________________

Relate Tenths and Decimals

Essential Question How can you record tenths as fractions and decimals?

Number and Operations—Fractions—4.NF.6

MATHEMATICAL PRACTICES
MP.2, MP.3, MP.4

Unlock the Problem

Ty is reading a book about metamorphic rocks. He has read $\frac{7}{10}$ of the book. What decimal describes the part of the book Ty has read?

A **decimal** is a number with one or more digits to the right of the **decimal point**. You can write tenths and hundredths as fractions or decimals.

One Way Use a model and a place-value chart.

Fraction

Shade $\frac{7}{10}$ of the model.

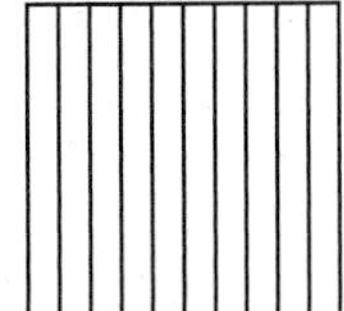

Think: The model is divided into 10 equal parts. Each part represents one **tenth**.

Write: ______________

Read: seven tenths

Decimal

$\frac{7}{10}$ is 7 tenths.

Ones	.	Tenths	Hundredths
	.		

decimal point

Write: ______________

Read: ______________

Another Way Use a number line.

Label the number line with decimals that are equivalent to the fractions. Locate the point $\frac{7}{10}$.

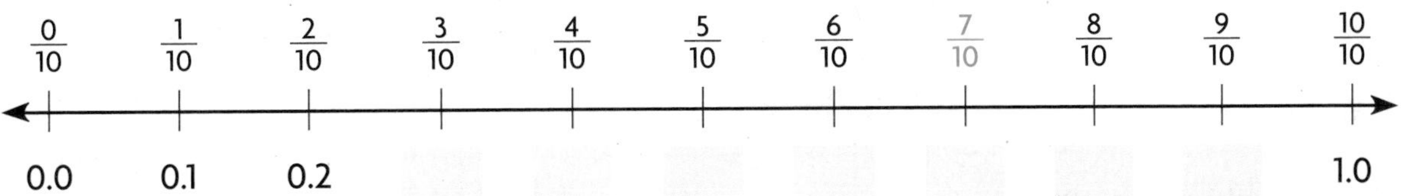

________ names the same amount as $\frac{7}{10}$.

So, Ty read 0.7 of the book.

Math Talk **Mathematical Practices**

Explain how the size of one whole is related to the size of one tenth.

- How can you write 0.1 as a fraction? Explain.

____

Tara rode her bicycle $1\frac{6}{10}$ miles. What decimal describes how far she rode her bicycle?

You have already written a fraction as a decimal. You can also write a mixed number as a decimal.

One Way Use a model and a place-value chart.

Fraction

Shade $1\frac{6}{10}$ of the model.

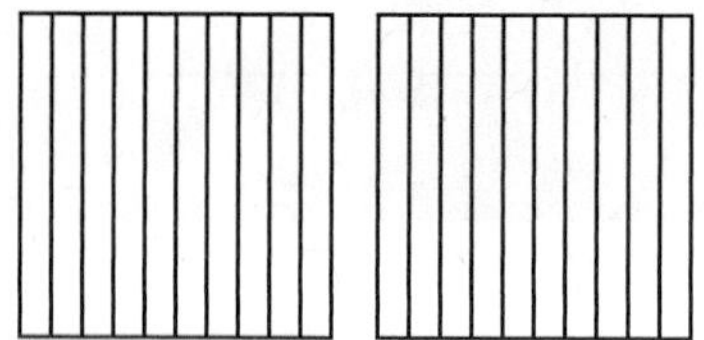

Write: ______________

Read: one and six tenths

Decimal

$1\frac{6}{10}$ is 1 whole and 6 tenths.

Think: Use the ones place to record wholes.

Ones	.	Tenths	Hundredths
	.		

Write: ______________

Read: ______________

Another Way Use a number line.

Label the number line with equivalent mixed numbers and decimals. Locate the point $1\frac{6}{10}$.

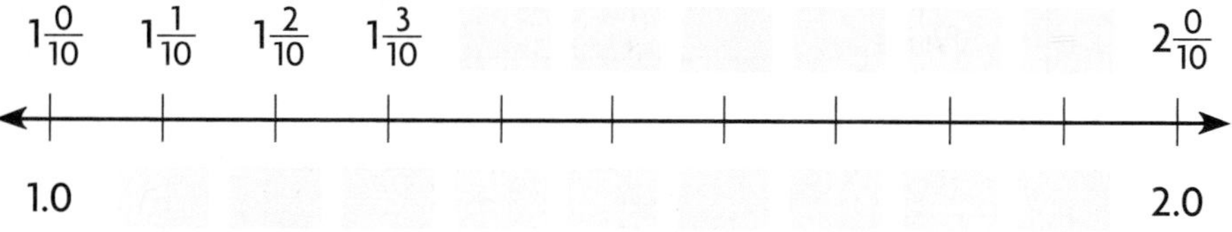

______ names the same amount as $1\frac{6}{10}$.

So, Tara rode her bicycle ______ miles.

Try This! Write 1 as a fraction and as a decimal.

Shade the model to show 1.

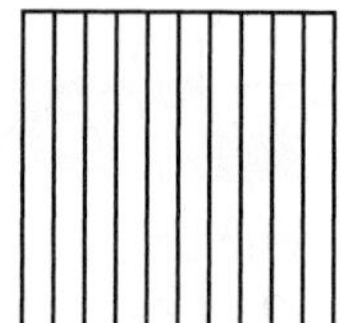

Fraction: ______________

Think: 1 is 1 whole and 0 tenths.

Ones	.	Tenths	Hundredths
	.		

Decimal: ______________

Name ______________________________

Share and Show

1. Write five tenths as a fraction and as a decimal.

   Fraction: ______ Decimal: ______

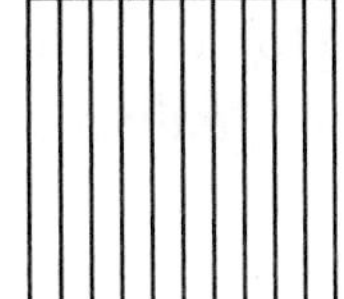

Ones	.	Tenths	Hundredths
	.		

Write the fraction or mixed number and the decimal shown by the model.

2. 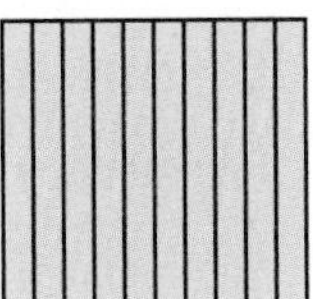 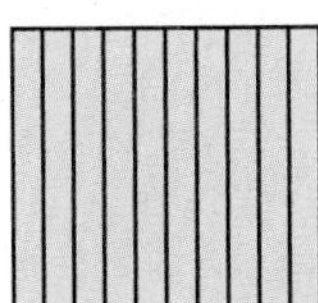 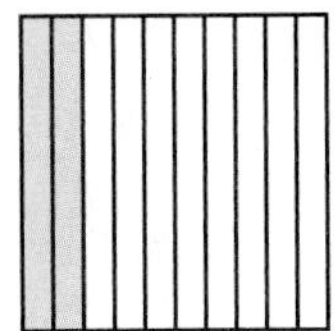

   ______ ______

3. 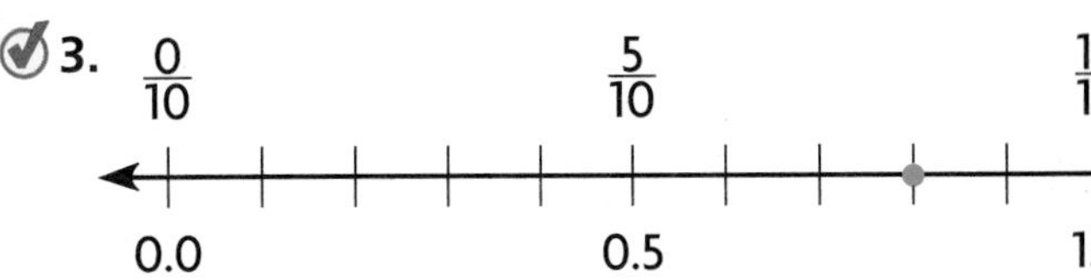

   ______ ______

Math Talk **Mathematical Practices**

How can you write $1\frac{3}{10}$ as a decimal? **Explain.**

On Your Own

Write the fraction or mixed number and the decimal shown by the model.

4. 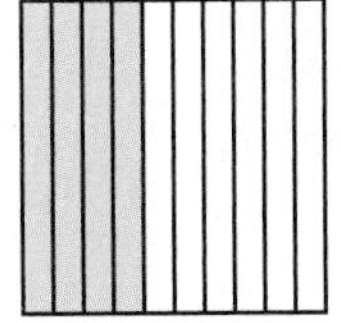

   ______ ______

5. 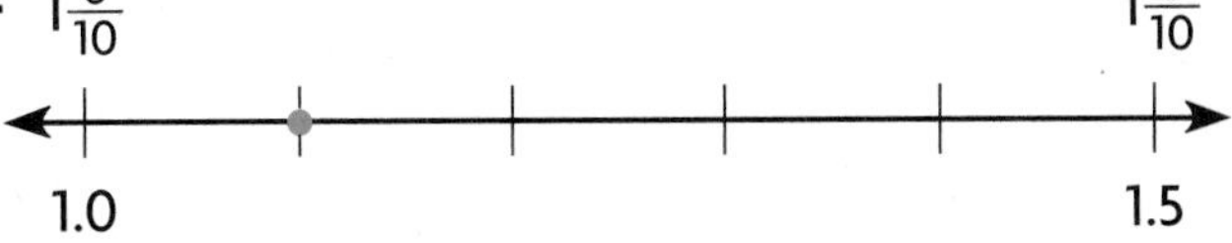

   ______ ______

6. 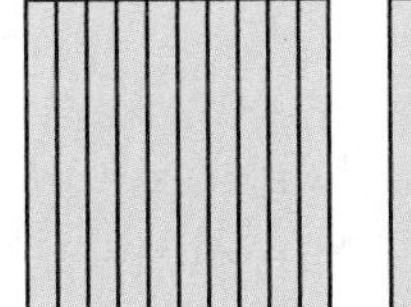 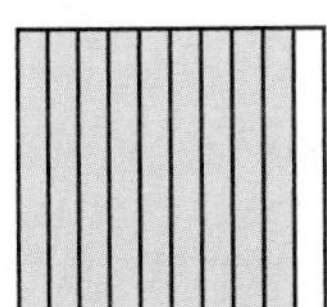

   ______ ______

7. 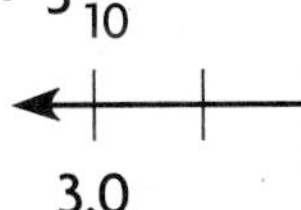 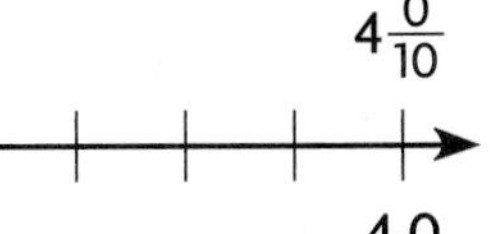

   ______ ______

Practice: Copy and Solve **Write the fraction or mixed number as a decimal.**

8. $5\frac{9}{10}$
9. $\frac{1}{10}$
10. $\frac{7}{10}$
11. $8\frac{9}{10}$
12. $\frac{6}{10}$
13. $6\frac{3}{10}$
14. $\frac{5}{10}$
15. $9\frac{7}{10}$

Problem Solving • Applications

Use the table for 16–19.

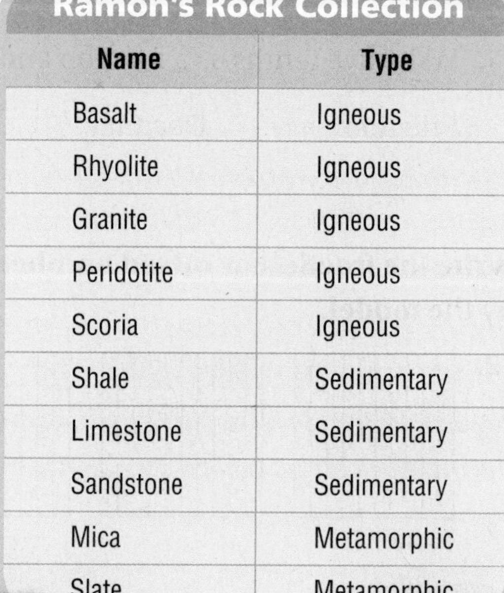

Name	Type
Basalt	Igneous
Rhyolite	Igneous
Granite	Igneous
Peridotite	Igneous
Scoria	Igneous
Shale	Sedimentary
Limestone	Sedimentary
Sandstone	Sedimentary
Mica	Metamorphic
Slate	Metamorphic

Ramon's Rock Collection

16. What part of the rocks listed in the table are igneous? Write your answer as a decimal.

17. Sedimentary rocks make up what part of Ramon's collection? Write your answer as a fraction and in word form.

18. THINK SMARTER What part of the rocks listed in the table are metamorphic? Write your answer as a fraction and as a decimal.

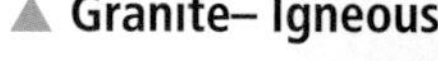
▲ Granite– Igneous

▲ Mica–Metamorphic

19. MATHEMATICAL PRACTICE 5 **Communicate** Niki wrote the following sentence in her report: "Metamorphic rocks make up 2.0 of Ramon's rock collection." Describe her error.

▲ Sandstone– Sedimentary

20. GO DEEPER Josh paid for three books with two $20 bills. He received $1 in change. Each book was the same price. How much did each book cost?

21. THINK SMARTER Select a number shown by the model. Mark all that apply.

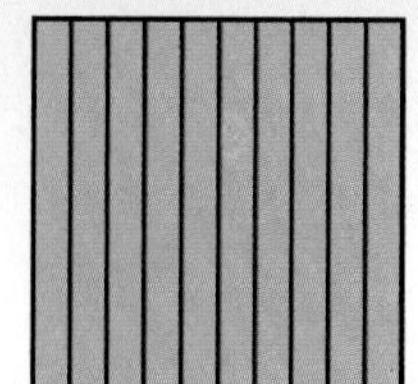 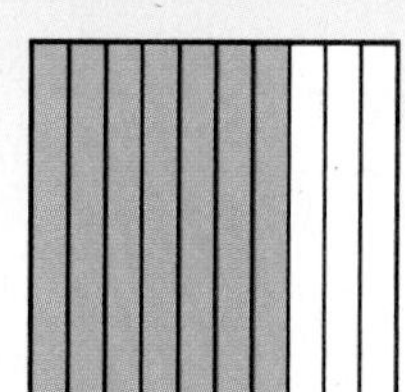

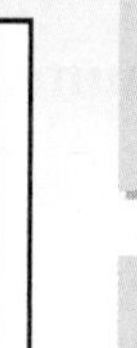

- $1\frac{7}{10}$
- $\frac{70}{10}$
- 1.7
- 7
- 0.7
- $\frac{17}{10}$

FOR MORE PRACTICE: Standards Practice Book

Name ____________________

Relate Hundredths and Decimals

Essential Question How can you record hundredths as fractions and decimals?

Number and Operations—Fractions—4.NF.6

MATHEMATICAL PRACTICES
MP.4, MP.6, MP.7

Unlock the Problem (Real World)

In the 2008 Summer Olympic Games, the winning time in the men's 100-meter butterfly race was only $\frac{1}{100}$ second faster than the second-place time. What decimal represents this fraction of a second?

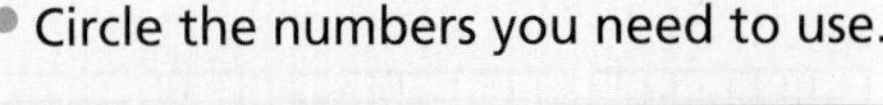

• Circle the numbers you need to use.

You can write hundredths as fractions or decimals.

One Way Use a model and a place-value chart.

Fraction

Shade $\frac{1}{100}$ of the model.

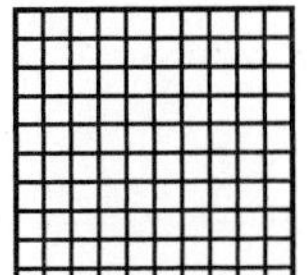

Think: The model is divided into 100 equal parts. Each part represents one **hundredth**.

Write: ____________

Read: one hundredth

Decimal

Complete the place-value chart. $\frac{1}{100}$ is 1 hundredth.

Ones	.	Tenths	Hundredths
0	.	0	1

Write: ____________

Read: one hundredth

Another Way Use a number line.

Label the number line with equivalent decimals. Locate the point $\frac{1}{100}$.

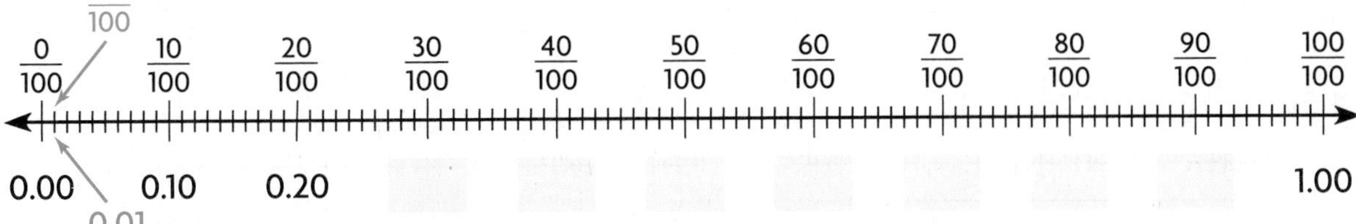

Math Talk **Mathematical Practices**

Explain how the size of one tenth is related to the size of one hundredth.

________ names the same amount as $\frac{1}{100}$.

So, the winning time was ________ second faster.

Alicia won her 400-meter freestyle race by $4\frac{25}{100}$ seconds. How can you write this mixed number as a decimal?

One Way Use a model and a place-value chart.

Mixed Number

Shade the model to show $4\frac{25}{100}$.

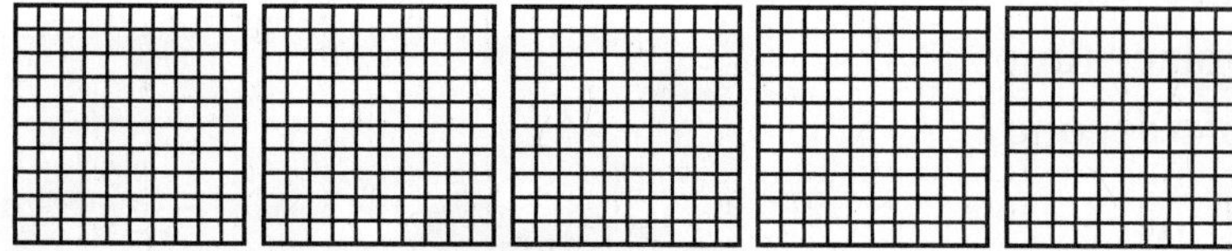

Write: ______________________

Read: four and twenty-five hundredths

Decimal

Complete the place-value chart.

Think: Look at the model above. $4\frac{25}{100}$ is 4 wholes and 2 tenths 5 hundredths.

Ones	.	Tenths	Hundredths
	.		

Write: ______________________

Read: ______________________

Another Way Use a number line.

Label the number line with equivalent mixed numbers and decimals. Locate the point $4\frac{25}{100}$.

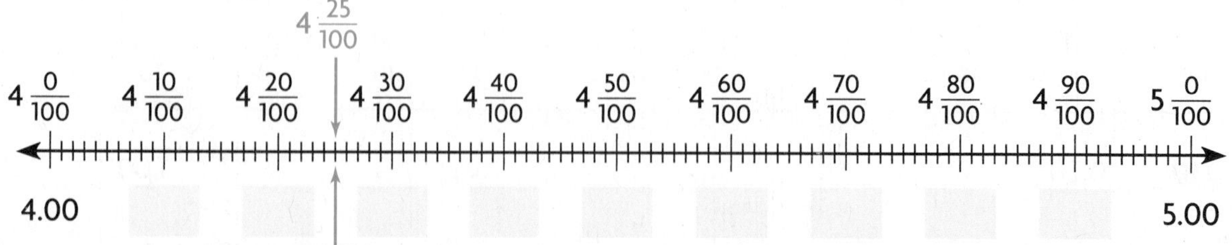

________ names the same amount as $4\frac{25}{100}$.

So, Alicia won her race by ________ seconds.

Name ______________________________

Share and Show

1. Shade the model to show $\frac{31}{100}$.

   Write the amount as a decimal. __________

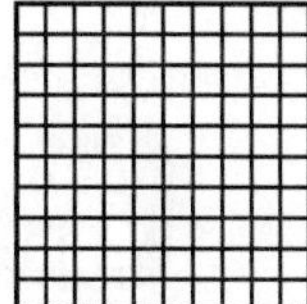

Ones	.	Tenths	Hundredths
	.		

Write the fraction or mixed number and the decimal shown by the model.

2. 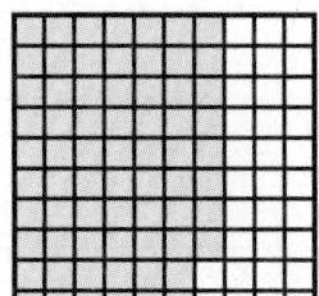 __________ __________

3. 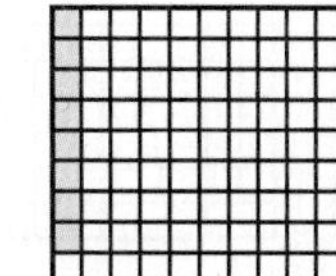 __________ __________

4. 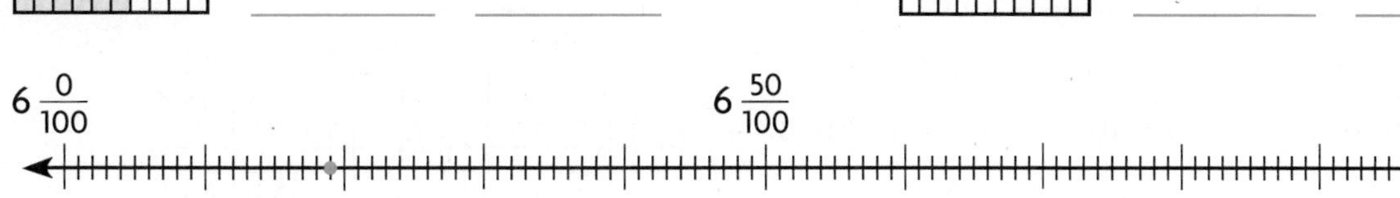

__________ __________

Math Talk — Mathematical Practices

Are 0.5 and 0.50 equivalent? **Explain.**

On Your Own

Write the fraction or mixed number and the decimal shown by the model.

5.  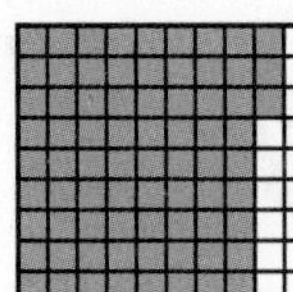 __________ __________

6. 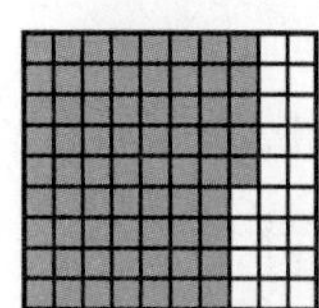 __________ __________

7. 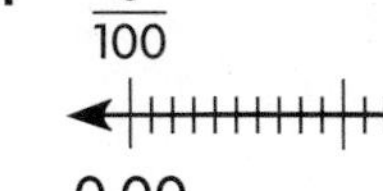  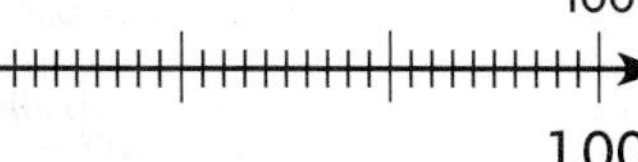

__________ __________

Practice: Copy and Solve **Write the fraction or mixed number as a decimal.**

8. $\frac{9}{100}$
9. $4\frac{55}{100}$
10. $\frac{10}{100}$
11. $9\frac{33}{100}$
12. $\frac{92}{100}$
13. $14\frac{16}{100}$

Problem Solving • Applications

14. THINK SMARTER Shade the grids to show three different ways to represent $\frac{16}{100}$ using models.

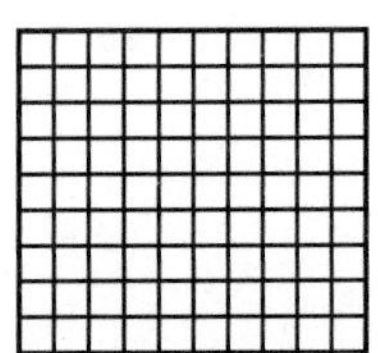 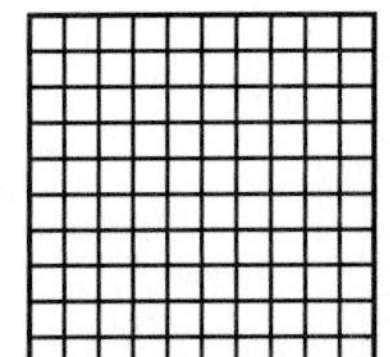 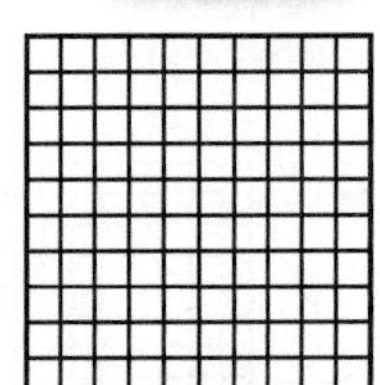

15. MATHEMATICAL PRACTICE 1 **Describe Relationships** Describe how one whole, one tenth, and one hundredth are related.

16. THINK SMARTER Shade the model to show $1\frac{24}{100}$. Then write the mixed number in decimal form.

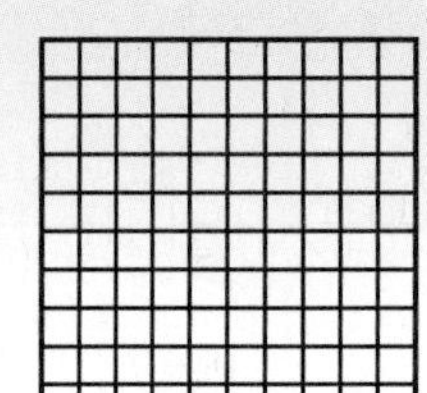 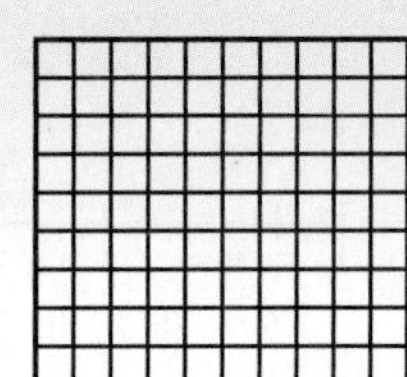 

Sense or Nonsense?

17. GO DEEPER The Memorial Library is 0.3 mile from school. Whose statement makes sense? Whose statement is nonsense? Explain your reasoning.

Gabe said he was going to walk 3 tenths mile to the Memorial Library after school.

Tara said she was going to walk 3 miles to the Memorial Library after school.

FOR MORE PRACTICE: Standards Practice Book

Name ______________________

Equivalent Fractions and Decimals

Essential Question How can you record tenths and hundredths as fractions and decimals?

Number and Operations—Fractions—4.NF.5 *Also 4.NF.6*

MATHEMATICAL PRACTICES
MP.2, MP.4, MP.6, MP.8

Unlock the Problem (Real World)

Daniel spent a day hiking through a wildlife preserve. During the first hour of the hike, he drank $\frac{6}{10}$ liter of water. How many hundredths of a liter did he drink?

- Underline what you need to find.
- How can you represent hundredths?

____

One Way Write $\frac{6}{10}$ as an equivalent fraction with a denominator of 100.

MODEL

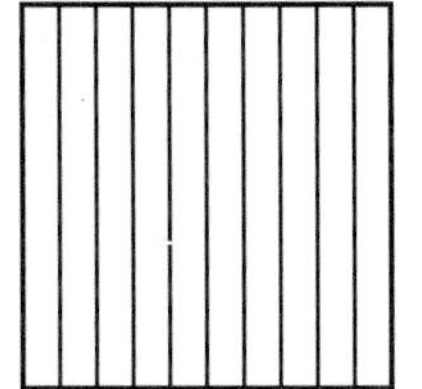

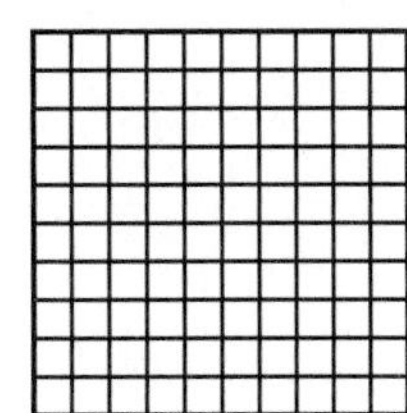

$$\frac{6}{10} = \frac{\square}{100}$$

RECORD

$$\frac{6}{10} = \frac{6 \times \square}{10 \times \square} = \frac{\square}{100}$$

Another Way Write $\frac{6}{10}$ as a decimal.

Think: 6 tenths is the same as 6 tenths 0 hundredths.

Ones	.	Tenths	Hundredths

So, Daniel drank ______, or ______ liter of water.

Math Talk **Mathematical Practices**

Explain how you can write 0.2 as hundredths.

- Explain why 6 tenths is equivalent to 60 hundredths.

____

____

Jasmine collected 0.30 liter of water in a jar during a rainstorm. How many tenths of a liter did she collect?

Equivalent decimals are decimals that name the same amount. You can write 0.30 as a decimal that names tenths.

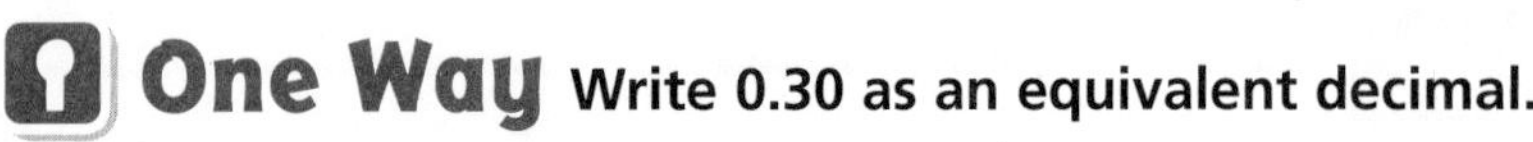

One Way **Write 0.30 as an equivalent decimal.**

Show 0.30 in the place-value chart.

Ones	.	Tenths	Hundredths

Think: There are no hundredths.

0.30 is equivalent to ______ tenths.

Write 0.30 as ______.

Another Way **Write 0.30 as a fraction with a denominator of 10.**

STEP 1 Write 0.30 as a fraction.

0.30 is ______ hundredths.

30 hundredths written as a fraction is ______.

STEP 2 Write $\frac{30}{100}$ as an equivalent fraction with a denominator of 10.

Think: 10 is a common factor of the numerator and the denominator.

$$\frac{30}{100} = \frac{30 \div \square}{100 \div \square} = \frac{\square}{10}$$

So, Jasmine collected ______, or ______ liter of water.

Share and Show

1. Write $\frac{4}{10}$ as hundredths.

Write $\frac{4}{10}$ as an equivalent fraction.

$$\frac{4}{10} = \frac{4 \times \square}{10 \times \square} = \frac{\square}{100}$$

Fraction: ____________

Write $\frac{4}{10}$ as a decimal.

Ones	.	Tenths	Hundredths
	.		

Decimal: ____________

Name ______________________________

Write the number as hundredths in fraction form and decimal form.

2. $\frac{7}{10}$ ______

3. 0.5 ______

4. $\frac{3}{10}$ ______

Write the number as tenths in fraction form and decimal form.

5. 0.40 ______

6. $\frac{80}{100}$ ______

7. $\frac{20}{100}$ ______

On Your Own

Math Talk — Mathematical Practices

Can you write 0.25 as tenths? Explain.

Practice: Copy and Solve Write the number as hundredths in fraction form and decimal form.

8. $\frac{8}{10}$

9. $\frac{2}{10}$

10. 0.1

Practice: Copy and Solve Write the number as tenths in fraction form and decimal form.

11. $\frac{60}{100}$

12. $\frac{90}{100}$

13. 0.70

THINK SMARTER Write the number as an equivalent mixed number with hundredths.

14. $1\frac{4}{10}$ ______

15. $3\frac{5}{10}$ ______

16. $2\frac{9}{10}$ ______

Problem Solving • Applications

17. THINK SMARTER Carter says that 0.08 is equivalent to $\frac{8}{10}$. Describe and correct Carter's error.

18. THINK SMARTER For numbers 18a–18e, choose True or False for the statement.

18a. 0.6 is equivalent to $\frac{6}{100}$. ○ True ○ False

18b. $\frac{3}{10}$ is equivalent to 0.30. ○ True ○ False

18c. $\frac{40}{100}$ is equivalent to $\frac{4}{10}$. ○ True ○ False

18d. 0.40 is equivalent to $\frac{4}{100}$. ○ True ○ False

18e. 0.5 is equivalent to 0.50. ○ True ○ False

Connect to Science

Inland Water

How many lakes and rivers does your state have? The U.S. Geological Survey defines inland water as water that is surrounded by land. The Atlantic Ocean, the Pacific Ocean, and the Great Lakes are not considered inland water.

19. WRITE ▸Math Just over $\frac{2}{100}$ of the entire United States is inland water. Write $\frac{2}{100}$ as a decimal.

20. MATHEMATICAL PRACTICE 6 Can you write 0.02 as tenths? **Explain.**

21. About 0.17 of the area of Rhode Island is inland water. Write 0.17 as a fraction.

22. GO DEEPER Louisiana's lakes and rivers cover about $\frac{1}{10}$ of the state. Write $\frac{1}{10}$ as hundredths in words, fraction form, and decimal form.

FOR MORE PRACTICE: Standards Practice Book

Name ______________________________

Relate Fractions, Decimals, and Money

Essential Question How can you relate fractions, decimals, and money?

Number and Operations—Fractions—4.NF.6

MATHEMATICAL PRACTICES
MP.2, MP.4, MP.6

Unlock the Problem

Together, Julie and Sarah have \$1.00 in quarters. They want to share the quarters equally. How many quarters should each girl get? How much money is this?

Remember

1 dollar = 100 cents
1 quarter = 25 cents
1 dime = 10 cents
1 penny = 1 cent

Use the model to relate money, fractions, and decimals.

4 quarters = 1 dollar = \$1.00

\$0.25 \$0.25 \$0.25 \$0.25

1 quarter is $\frac{25}{100}$, or $\frac{1}{4}$ of a dollar.

2 quarters are $\frac{50}{100}$, $\frac{2}{4}$, or $\frac{1}{2}$ of a dollar.

$\frac{1}{2}$ of a dollar = \$0.50, or 50 cents.

Circle the number of quarters each girl should get.

So, each girl should get 2 quarters, or \$ __________.

Examples Use money to model decimals.

1 dollar

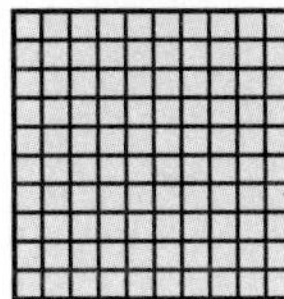

\$1.00, or

__________ cents

10 dimes = 1 dollar

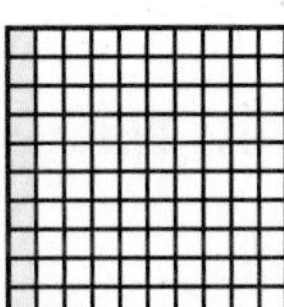

1 dime = $\frac{1}{10}$, or 0.10 of a dollar

\$ __________, or 10 cents

100 pennies = 1 dollar

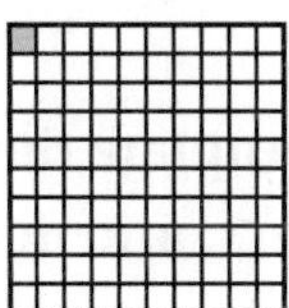

1 penny = $\frac{1}{100}$, or 0.01 of a dollar

\$ __________, or 1 cent

Math Talk **Mathematical Practices**

If you have 68 pennies, what part of a dollar do you have? **Explain.**

Relate Money and Decimals Think of dollars as ones, dimes as tenths, and pennies as hundredths.

$1.56

Dollars	.	Dimes	Pennies
1	.	5	6

Think: $1.56 = 1 dollar and 56 pennies

There are 100 pennies in 1 dollar.
So, $1.56 = 156 pennies.

1.56 dollars

Ones	.	Tenths	Hundredths
1	.	5	6

Think: 1.56 = 1 one and 56 hundredths

There are 100 hundredths in 1 one.
So, 1.56 = 156 hundredths.

More Examples

Shade the decimal model to show the money amount. Then write the money amount and a fraction in terms of dollars.

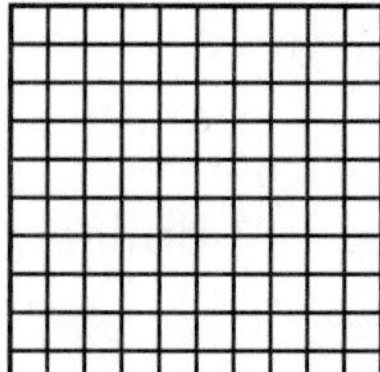

______, or $\frac{21}{100}$ of a dollar

B

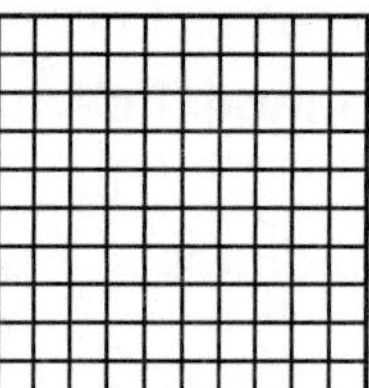

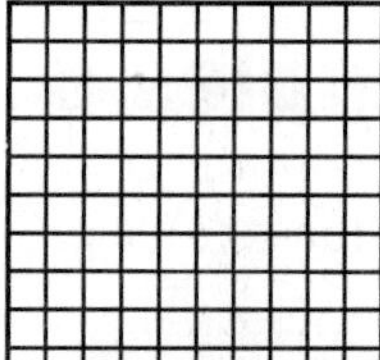

$1.46, or $1\frac{}{100}$ dollars

Try This! **Complete the table to show how money, fractions, mixed numbers, and decimals are related.**

$ Bills and Coins	Money Amount	Fraction or Mixed Number	Decimal
	$0.03		0.03
	$0.25	$\frac{25}{100}$, or $\frac{1}{4}$	
2 quarters 1 dime		$\frac{60}{100}$, or $\frac{6}{10}$	
2 $1 bills 5 nickels			

Mathematical Practices

Would you rather have $0.25 or $\frac{3}{10}$ of a dollar? **Explain.**

Name ______________________________

Share and Show

1. Write the amount of money as a decimal in terms of dollars.

5 pennies = $\frac{5}{100}$ of a dollar = __________ of a dollar.

Write the total money amount. Then write the amount as a fraction or a mixed number and as a decimal in terms of dollars.

2. 

_____ _____ _____

✓3. 

_____ _____ _____

Write as a money amount and as a decimal in terms of dollars.

4. $\frac{92}{100}$ _____ _____

5. $\frac{7}{100}$ _____ _____

6. $\frac{16}{100}$ _____ _____

✓7. $\frac{53}{100}$ _____ _____

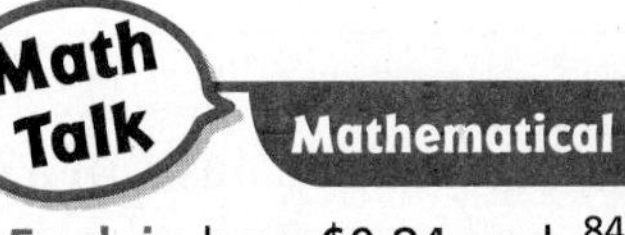

Explain how \$0.84 and $\frac{84}{100}$ of a dollar are related.

On Your Own

Write the total money amount. Then write the amount as a fraction or a mixed number and as a decimal in terms of dollars.

8.    

_____ _____ _____

9.   

_____ _____ _____

Write as a money amount and as a decimal in terms of dollars.

10. $\frac{27}{100}$ _____ _____

11. $\frac{4}{100}$ _____ _____

12. $\frac{75}{100}$ _____ _____

13. $\frac{100}{100}$ _____ _____

Write the total money amount. Then write the amount as a fraction and as a decimal in terms of dollars.

14. 1 quarter 6 dimes 8 pennies

_____ _____ _____

15. 3 dimes 5 nickels 20 pennies

_____ _____ _____

MATHEMATICAL PRACTICE 6 Make Connections **Algebra** **Complete to tell the value of each digit.**

16. \$1.05 = ______ dollar + ______ pennies, 1.05 = ______ one + ______ hundredths

17. \$5.18 = ______ dollars + ______ dime + ______ pennies

5.18 = ______ ones + ______ tenth + ______ hundredths

Problem Solving • Applications

Use the table for 18–19.

18. The table shows the coins three students have. Write Nick's total amount as a fraction in terms of dollars.

____

Pocket Change

Name	Quarters	Dimes	Nickels	Pennies
Kim	1	3	2	3
Tony	0	6	1	6
Nick	2	4	0	2

19. THINK SMARTER Kim spent $\frac{40}{100}$ of a dollar on a snack. Write as a money amount the amount she has left.

____

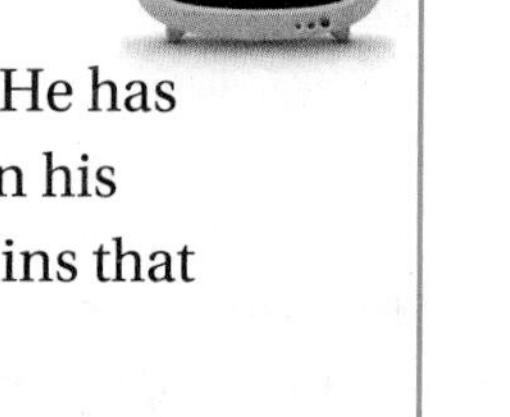

20. GO DEEPER Travis has $\frac{1}{2}$ of a dollar. He has at least two different types of coins in his pocket. Draw two possible sets of coins that Travis could have.

21. THINK SMARTER Complete the table.

\$ Bills and Coins	Money Amount	Fraction or Mixed Number	Decimal
6 pennies		$\frac{6}{100}$	0.06
	\$0.50		0.50
		$\frac{70}{100}$ or $\frac{7}{10}$	0.70
3 \$1 bills 9 pennies			3.09

Name ___________________________

Problem Solving • Money

Essential Question How can you use the strategy *act it out* to solve problems that use money?

Measurement and Data—4.MD.2

MATHEMATICAL PRACTICES
MP.1, MP.4, MP.5

Unlock the Problem

Together, Marnie and Serena have $1.20. They want to share the money equally. How much money will each girl get?

Use the graphic organizer to solve the problem.

Read the Problem

What do I need to find?

I need to find the ______________________

____

What information do I need to use?

I need to use the total amount, ______, and divide the amount into ______ equal parts.

How will I use the information?

I will use coins to model the __________ and act out the problem.

Solve the Problem

You can make $1.20 with 4 quarters and 2 ______.

Circle the coins to show two sets with equal value.

So, each girl gets ______ quarters and ______ dime. Each girl gets $______.

- Describe another way you could act out the problem with coins.

____

____

Try Another Problem

Josh, Tom, and Chuck each have $0.40. How much money do they have together?

Read the Problem	Solve the Problem
What do I need to find?	
What information do I need to use?	
How will I use the information?	

- How can you solve the problem using dimes and nickels?

____

____

Math Talk **Mathematical Practices**

What other strategy might you use to solve the problem? **Explain.**

Name ______________________________

Unlock the Problem

√ Circle the question.
√ Underline the important facts.
√ Cross out unneeded information.

Share and Show

1. Juan has $3.43. He is buying a paint brush that costs $1.21 to paint a model race car. How much will Juan have after he pays for the paint brush?

First, use bills and coins to model $3.43.

Next, you need to subtract. Remove bills and coins that have a value of $1.21. Mark Xs to show what you remove.

Last, count the value of the bills and coins that are left. How much will Juan have left?

____

WRITE ▸*Math*
Show Your Work

2. What if Juan has $3.43, and he wants to buy a paint brush that costs $2.28? How much money will Juan have left then? Explain.

____

____

____

____

____

3. Sophia has $2.25. She wants to give an equal amount to each of her 3 young cousins. How much will each cousin receive?

____

On Your Own

4. Marcus saves $13 each week. In how many weeks will he have saved at least $100?

5. MATHEMATICAL PRACTICE 1 **Analyze Relationships** Hoshi has $50. Emily has $23 more than Hoshi. Karl has $16 less than Emily. How much money do they have all together?

6. THINK SMARTER Four girls have $5.00 to share equally. How much money will each girl get? Explain.

WRITE ▸ Math
Show Your Work

7. GO DEEPER What if four girls want to share $5.52 equally? How much money will each girl get? Explain.

Personal Math Trainer

8. THINK SMARTER + Aimee and three of her friends find three quarters and one nickel on the ground. If Aimee and her friends share the money equally, how much will each person get? Explain how you found your answer.

Name ___________________________________

Mid-Chapter Checkpoint

Vocabulary

Choose the best term from the box to complete the sentence.

Vocabulary
decimal
decimal point
hundred
hundredth

1. A symbol used to separate the ones and the tenths place is called a _______________. (p. 359)

2. The number 0.4 is written as a _______________. (p. 359)

3. A _______________ is one of one hundred equal parts of a whole. (p. 363)

Concepts and Skills

Write the fraction or mixed number and the decimal shown by the model. (4.NF.6)

4. 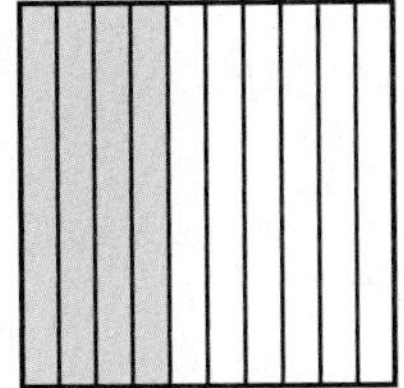

_______ _______

5. 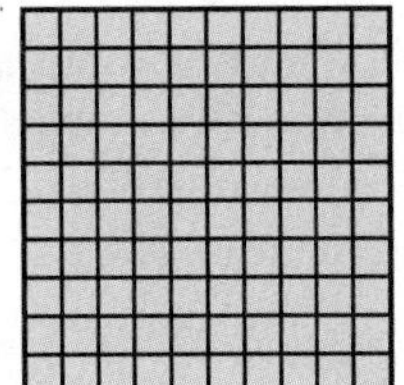 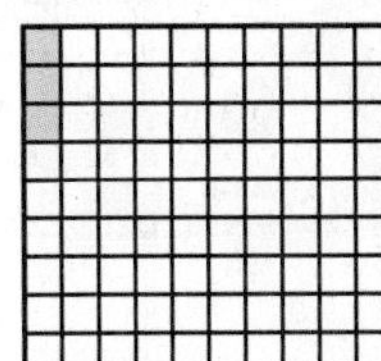

_______ _______

Write the number as hundredths in fraction form and decimal form. (4.NF.5)

6. $\frac{8}{10}$ _______________

7. 0.5 _______________

8. $\frac{6}{10}$ _______________

Write the fraction or mixed number as a money amount, and as a decimal in terms of dollars. (4.NF.6)

9. $\frac{65}{100}$ _______________

10. $1\frac{48}{100}$ _______________

11. $\frac{4}{100}$ _______________

12. Ken's turtle competed in a 0.50-meter race. His turtle had traveled $\frac{49}{100}$ meter when the winning turtle crossed the finish line. What is $\frac{49}{100}$ written as a decimal? (4.NF.6)

____

13. Alex lives eight tenths of a mile from Sarah. What is eight tenths written as a decimal? (4.NF.6)

____

14. What fraction, in hundredths, is equivalent to $\frac{1}{10}$? (4.NF.5)

____

15. Elaine found the following in her pocket. How much money was in her pocket? (4.NF.6)

____

16. Three girls share \$0.60. Each girl gets the same amount. How much money does each girl get? (4.MD.2)

____

17. The deli scale weighs meat and cheese in hundredths of a pound. Sam put $\frac{5}{10}$ pound of pepperoni on the deli scale. What weight does the deli scale show? (4.NF.5)

____

Name ____________________

Add Fractional Parts of 10 and 100

Essential Question How can you add fractions when the denominators are 10 or 100?

Number and Operations—Fractions—4.NF.5 *Also 4.MD.2*

MATHEMATICAL PRACTICES
MP.2, MP.6, MP.7, MP.8

Unlock the Problem

The fourth grade classes are painting designs on tile squares to make a mural. Mrs. Kirk's class painted $\frac{3}{10}$ of the mural. Mr. Becker's class painted $\frac{21}{100}$ of the mural. What part of the mural is painted?

You know how to add fractions with parts that are the same size. You can use equivalent fractions to add fractions with parts that are not the same size.

Example 1 Find $\frac{3}{10} + \frac{21}{100}$.

STEP 1 Write $\frac{3}{10}$ and $\frac{21}{100}$ as a pair of fractions with a common denominator.

Think: 100 is a multiple of 10. Use 100 as the common denominator.

$$\frac{3}{10} = \frac{3 \times \square}{10 \times \square} = \frac{\square}{100}$$

Think: $\frac{21}{100}$ already has 100 in the denominator.

STEP 2 Add.

Think: Write $\frac{3}{10} + \frac{21}{100}$ using fractions with a common denominator.

$$\frac{30}{100} + \frac{21}{100} = \frac{\square}{100}$$

So, $\frac{\square}{100}$ of the mural is painted.

Math Talk **Mathematical Practices**

When adding tenths and hundredths, can you always use 100 as a common denominator? **Explain.**

Try This! Find $\frac{4}{100} + \frac{1}{10}$.

A Write $\frac{1}{10}$ as $\frac{10}{100}$.

$$\frac{1}{10} = \frac{1 \times \square}{10 \times \square} = \frac{\square}{100}$$

B Add.

$$\frac{\square}{100} + \frac{10}{100} = \frac{\square}{100}$$

So, $\frac{4}{100} + \frac{10}{100} = \frac{14}{100}$

Example 2 Add decimals.

Sean lives 0.5 mile from the store. The store is 0.25 mile from his grandmother's house. Sean is going to walk to the store and then to his grandmother's house. How far will he walk?

Find 0.5 + 0.25.

STEP 1 Write 0.5 + 0.25 as a sum of fractions.

Think: 0.5 is 5 tenths. **Think:** 0.25 is 25 hundredths.

$0.5 = \frac{\square}{\square}$ $0.25 = \frac{\square}{\square}$

Write 0.5 + 0.25 as $\frac{\square}{\square} + \frac{\square}{\square}$

STEP 2 Write $\frac{5}{10} + \frac{25}{100}$ as a sum of fractions with a common denominator.

Think: Use 100 as a common denominator. Rename $\frac{5}{10}$.

$$\frac{5}{10} = \frac{5 \times \square}{10 \times \square} = \frac{\square}{100}$$

Write $\frac{5}{10} + \frac{25}{100}$ as $\frac{\square}{\square} + \frac{\square}{\square}$.

STEP 3 Add.

$$\frac{50}{100} + \frac{25}{100} = \frac{\square}{\square}$$

STEP 4 Write the sum as a decimal.

$$\frac{75}{100} = \underline{\quad}$$

So, Sean will walk ______ mile.

Math Talk **Mathematical Practices**

Explain why you can think of \$0.25 as either $\frac{1}{4}$ dollar or $\frac{25}{100}$ dollar.

Try This! **Find \$0.25 + \$0.40.**

\$0.25 + \$0.40 = ______

Remember

A money amount less than a dollar can be written as a fraction of a dollar.

Name ____________________

Share and Show

1. Find $\frac{7}{10} + \frac{5}{100}$.

Think: Write the addends as fractions with a common denominator.

$\frac{\square}{100} + \frac{\square}{100} = \frac{\square}{\square}$

Find the sum.

2. $\frac{1}{10} + \frac{11}{100} =$ ______

3. $\frac{36}{100} + \frac{5}{10} =$ ______

4. $0.16 + $0.45 = $______

5. $0.08 + $0.88 = $______

On Your Own

6. $\frac{6}{10} + \frac{25}{100} =$ ______

7. $\frac{7}{10} + \frac{7}{100} =$ ______

8. $\frac{19}{100} + \frac{4}{10} =$ ______

9. $\frac{3}{100} + \frac{9}{10} =$ ______

10. $0.55 + $0.23 = $______

11. $0.19 + $0.13 = $______

MATHEMATICAL PRACTICE 2 **Reason Quantitatively** **Algebra** Write the number that makes the equation true.

12. $\frac{20}{100} + \frac{\square}{10} = \frac{60}{100}$

13. $\frac{2}{10} + \frac{\square}{100} = \frac{90}{100}$

Problem Solving • Applications Real World

Use the table for 14–17.

14. THINK SMARTER Dean selects Teakwood stones and Buckskin stones to pave a path in front of his house. How many meters long will each set of one Teakwood stone and one Buckskin stone be?

Paving Stone Center	
Style	**Length (in meters)**
Rustic	$\frac{15}{100}$
Teakwood	$\frac{3}{10}$
Buckskin	$\frac{41}{100}$
Rainbow	$\frac{6}{10}$
Rose	$\frac{8}{100}$

15. The backyard patio at Nona's house is made from a repeating pattern of one Rose stone and one Rainbow stone. How many meters long is each pair of stones?

16. GO DEEPER For a stone path, Emily likes the look of a Rustic stone, then a Rainbow stone, and then another Rustic stone. How long will the three stones in a row be? Explain.

17. WRITE Math Which two stones can you place end-to-end to get a length of 0.38 meters? Explain how you found your answer.

18. THINK SMARTER Christelle is making a dollhouse. The dollhouse is $\frac{6}{10}$ meter high without the roof. The roof is $\frac{15}{100}$ meter high. What is the height of the dollhouse with the roof? Choose a number from each column to complete an equation to solve.

$\frac{6}{10} + \frac{15}{100} =$ [$\frac{6}{100}$ / $\frac{60}{100}$ / $\frac{61}{100}$] $+$ [$\frac{15}{10}$ / $\frac{5}{100}$ / $\frac{15}{100}$] $=$ [$\frac{65}{100}$ / $\frac{7}{10}$ / $\frac{75}{100}$] meter high.

FOR MORE PRACTICE: Standards Practice Book

Name ______________________________

Compare Decimals

Essential Question How can you compare decimals?

Number and Operations—Fractions—4.NF.7

MATHEMATICAL PRACTICES
MP.2, MP.4, MP.6

Unlock the Problem (Real World)

The city park covers 0.64 square mile. About 0.18 of the park is covered by water, and about 0.2 of the park is covered by paved walkways. Is more of the park covered by water or paved walkways?

- Cross out unnecessary information.
- Circle numbers you will use.
- What do you need to find?

____

____

One Way Use a model.

Shade 0.18. Shade 0.2.

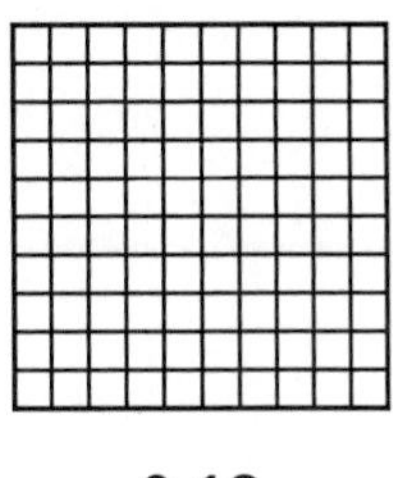

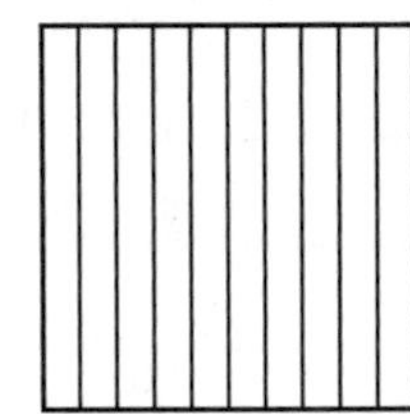

0.18 ◯ 0.2

Other Ways

A Use a number line.

Locate 0.18 and 0.2 on a number line.

Think: 2 tenths is equivalent to 20 hundredths.

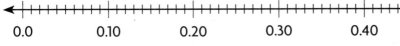

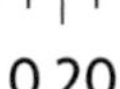

0.0 0.10 0.20 0.30 0.40 0.50

_____ is closer to 0, so 0.18 ◯ 0.2.

B Compare equal-size parts.

- 0.18 is _____ hundredths.
- 0.2 is 2 tenths, which is equivalent to _____ hundredths.

18 hundredths ◯ 20 hundredths, so 0.18 ◯ 0.2.

So, more of the park is covered by ______________.

Math Talk **Mathematical Practices**

How does the number of tenths in 0.18 compare to the number of tenths in 0.2? **Explain.**

Place Value You can compare numbers written as decimals by using place value. Comparing decimals is like comparing whole numbers. Always compare the digits in the greatest place-value position first.

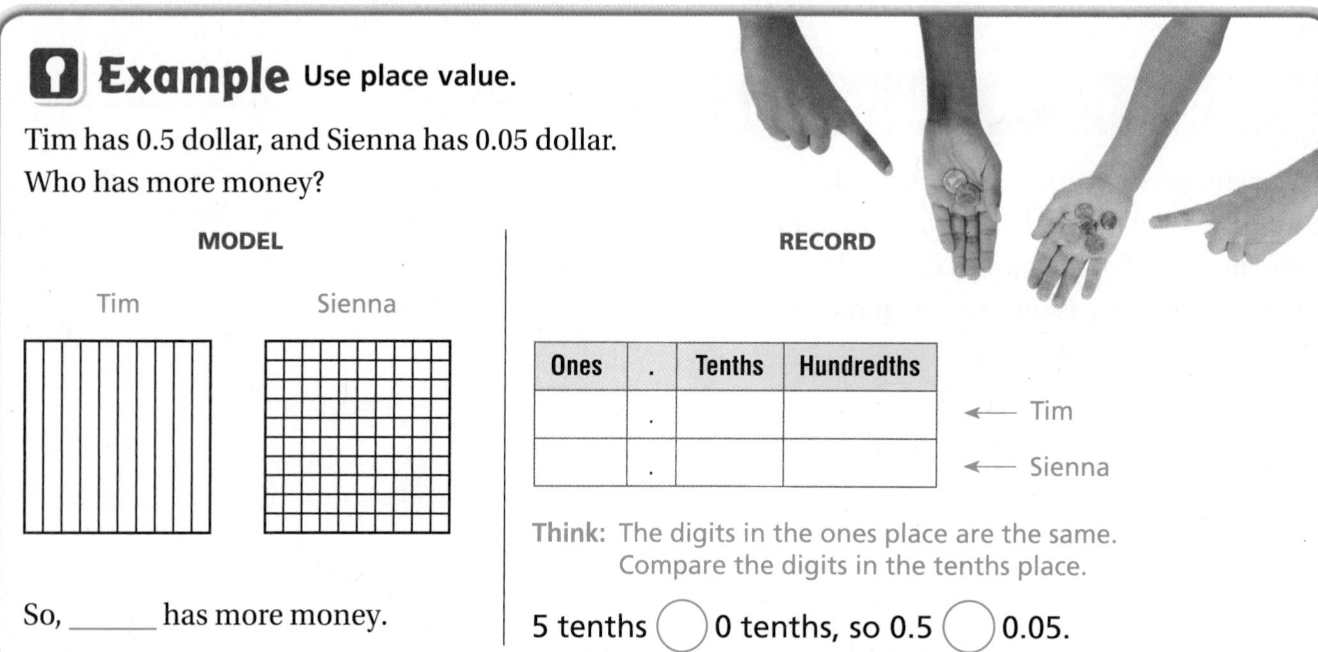

Example Use place value.
Tim has 0.5 dollar, and Sienna has 0.05 dollar. Who has more money?
MODEL
Tim
Sienna
So, ______ has more money.
RECORD
Ones
.
Tenths
Hundredths
Tim
Sienna
Think: The digits in the ones place are the same. Compare the digits in the tenths place.
5 tenths ◯ 0 tenths, so 0.5 ◯ 0.05.

- Compare the size of 1 tenth to the size of 1 hundredth. How could this help you compare 0.5 and 0.05? Explain.

____

____

____

Try This! **Compare 1.3 and 0.6. Write <, >, or =.**

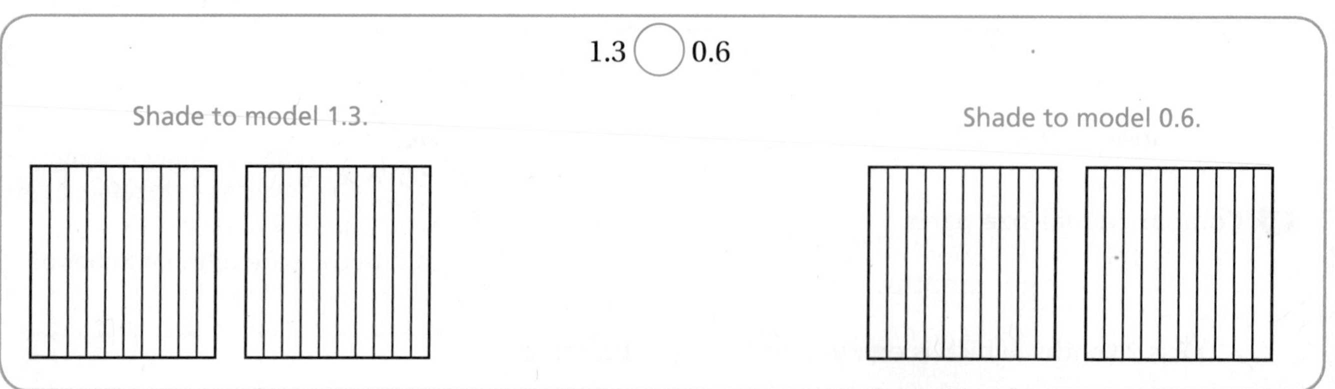

Shade to model 1.3.
Shade to model 0.6.

Math Talk **Mathematical Practices**

Explain how you could use place value to compare 1.3 and 0.6.

Name ______________________________

Share and Show

1. Compare 0.39 and 0.42. Write <, >, or =. Shade the model to help.

   0.39 ◯ 0.42

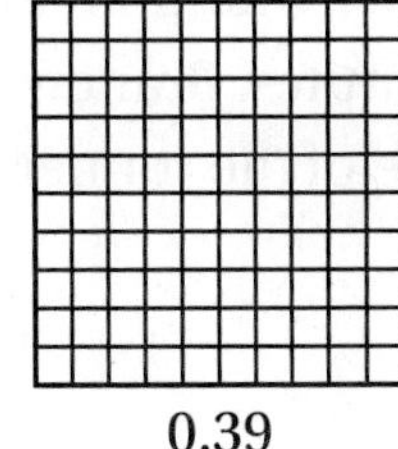
0.39

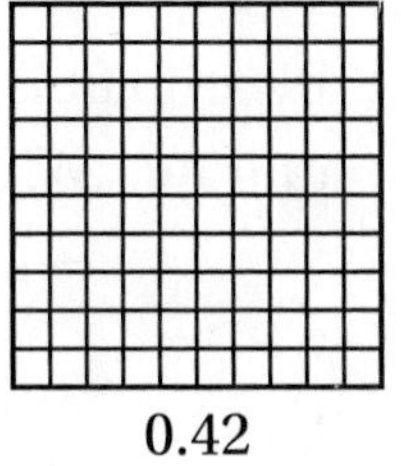
0.42

Compare. Write <, >, or =.

2. 0.26 ◯ 0.23

Ones	.	Tenths	Hundredths
	.		
	.		

✓ 3. 0.7 ◯ 0.54

Ones	.	Tenths	Hundredths
	.		
	.		

4. 1.15 ◯ 1.3

Ones	.	Tenths	Hundredths
	.		
	.		

✓ 5. 4.5 ◯ 2.89

Ones	.	Tenths	Hundredths
	.		
	.		

Math Talk — **Mathematical Practices**

Can you compare 0.39 and 0.42 by comparing only the tenths? **Explain.**

On Your Own

Compare. Write <, >, or =.

6. 0.9 ◯ 0.81
7. 1.06 ◯ 0.6
8. 0.25 ◯ 0.3
9. 2.61 ◯ 3.29
10. 0.38 ◯ 0.83
11. 1.9 ◯ 0.99
12. 1.11 ◯ 1.41
13. 0.8 ◯ 0.80

MATHEMATICAL PRACTICE 2 **Reason Quantitatively** **Compare. Write <, >, or =.**

14. 0.30 ◯ $\frac{3}{10}$
15. $\frac{4}{100}$ ◯ 0.2
16. 0.15 ◯ $\frac{1}{10}$
17. $\frac{1}{8}$ ◯ 0.8

Unlock the Problem

18. THINK SMARTER Ricardo and Brandon ran a 1500-meter race. Ricardo finished in 4.89 minutes. Brandon finished in 4.83 minutes. What was the time of the runner who finished first?

a. What are you asked to find? ____________________

b. What do you need to do to find the answer? ____________________

____

c. Solve the problem.

d. What was the time of the runner who finished first?

____

e. Look back. Does your answer make sense? Explain.

____

____

____

____

19. GO DEEPER The Venus flytrap closes in 0.3 second and the waterwheel plant closes in 0.2 second. What decimal is halfway between 0.2 and 0.3? Explain.

____

____

____

____

Personal Math Trainer

20. THINK SMARTER + For numbers 20a–20c, select True or False for the inequality.

20a. $0.5 > 0.53$ ○ True ○ False

20b. $0.35 < 0.37$ ○ True ○ False

20c. $\$1.35 > \$0.35$ ○ True ○ False

FOR MORE PRACTICE: Standards Practice Book

Name ________________________________

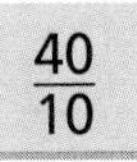

Chapter 9 Review/Test

1. Select a number shown by the model. Mark all that apply.

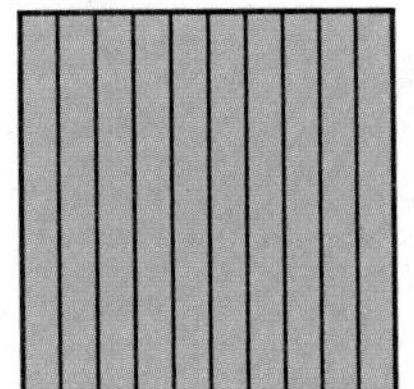 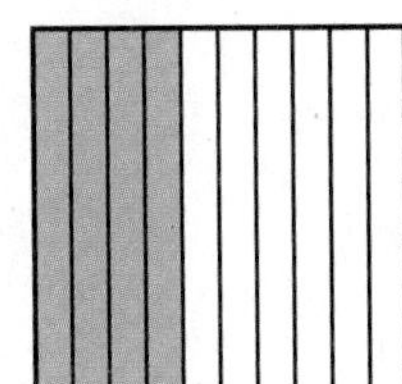

$\frac{14}{10}$	$\frac{40}{10}$	1.4
$1\frac{4}{10}$	14	4.1

2. Rick has one dollar and twenty-seven cents to buy a notebook. Which names this money amount in terms of dollars? Mark all that apply.

Ⓐ 12.7
Ⓑ 1.027
Ⓒ \$1.27
Ⓓ 1.27
Ⓔ $1\frac{27}{100}$
Ⓕ $\frac{127}{10}$

3. For numbers 3a–3e, select True or False for the statement.

3a.	0.9 is equivalent to 0.90.	○ True	○ False
3b.	0.20 is equivalent to $\frac{2}{100}$.	○ True	○ False
3c.	$\frac{80}{100}$ is equivalent to $\frac{8}{10}$.	○ True	○ False
3d.	$\frac{6}{10}$ is equivalent to 0.60.	○ True	○ False
3e.	0.3 is equivalent to $\frac{3}{100}$.	○ True	○ False

GO DIGITAL Assessment Options Chapter Test

4. After selling some old books and toys, Gwen and her brother Max had 5 one-dollar bills, 6 quarters, and 8 dimes. They agreed to divide the money equally.

Part A

What is the total amount of money that Gwen and Max earned? Explain.

Part B

Max said that he and Gwen cannot get equal amounts of money because 5 one-dollar bills cannot be divided evenly. Do you agree with Max? Explain.

5. Harrison rode his bike $\frac{6}{10}$ of a mile to the park. Shade the model. Then write the decimal to show how far Harrison rode his bike.

Harrison rode his bike ________ mile to the park.

6. Amaldo spent $\frac{88}{100}$ of a dollar on a souvenir pencil from Zion National Park in Utah. What is $\frac{88}{100}$ written as a decimal in terms of dollars?

7. Tran has $5.82. He is saving for a video game that costs $8.95.

Tran needs ________ more to have enough money for the game.

Name ______________________________

8. Cheyenne lives $\frac{7}{10}$ mile from school. A fraction in hundredths equal to $\frac{7}{10}$ is ________.

9. Write a decimal in tenths that is **less** than 2.42 but **greater** than 2.0.

____

10. Kylee and two of her friends are at a museum. They find two quarters and one dime on the ground.

Part A

If Kylee and her friends share the money equally, how much will each person get? Explain how you found your answer.

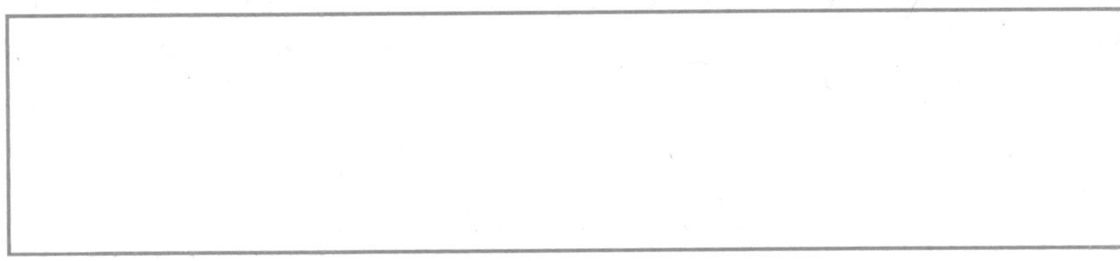

Part B

Kylee says that each person will receive $\frac{2}{10}$ of the money that was found. Do you agree? Explain.

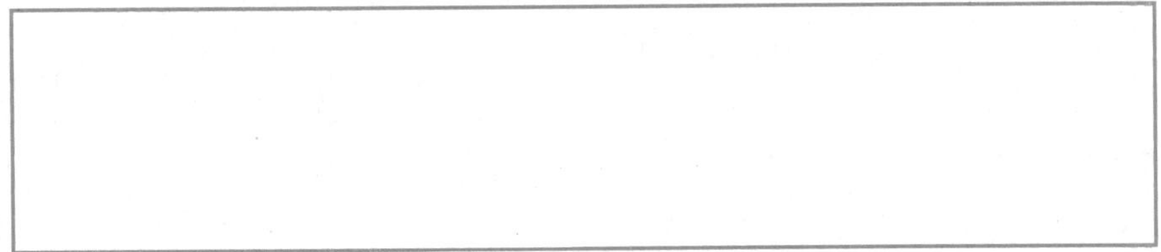

11. Shade the model to show $1\frac{52}{100}$. Then write the mixed number in decimal form.

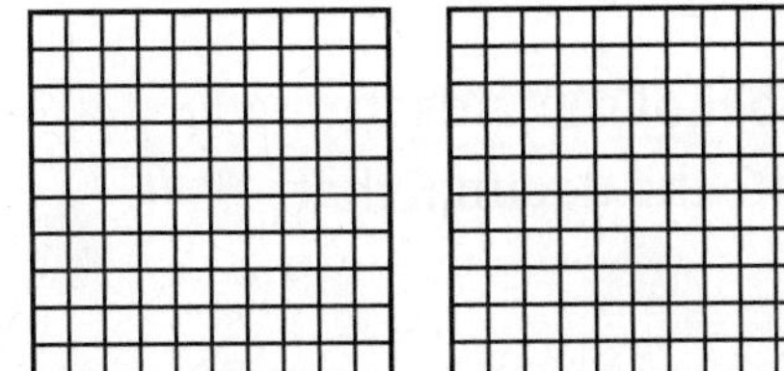

12. Henry is making a recipe for biscuits. A recipe calls for $\frac{5}{10}$ kilogram flour and $\frac{9}{100}$ kilogram sugar.

Part A

If Henry measures correctly and combines the two amounts, how much flour and sugar will he have? Show your work.

Part B

How can you write your answer as a decimal?

13. An orchestra has 100 musicians. $\frac{4}{10}$ of them play string instruments—violin, viola, cello, double bass, guitar, lute, and harp. What decimal is equivalent to $\frac{4}{10}$?

14. Complete the table.

$ Bills and Coins	Money Amount	Fraction or Mixed Number	Decimal
8 pennies		$\frac{8}{100}$	0.08
	$0.50		0.50
		$\frac{90}{100}$ or $\frac{9}{10}$	0.90
4 $1 bills 5 pennies			4.05

15. The point on the number line shows the number of seconds it took an athlete to run the forty-yard dash. Write the decimal that correctly names the point.

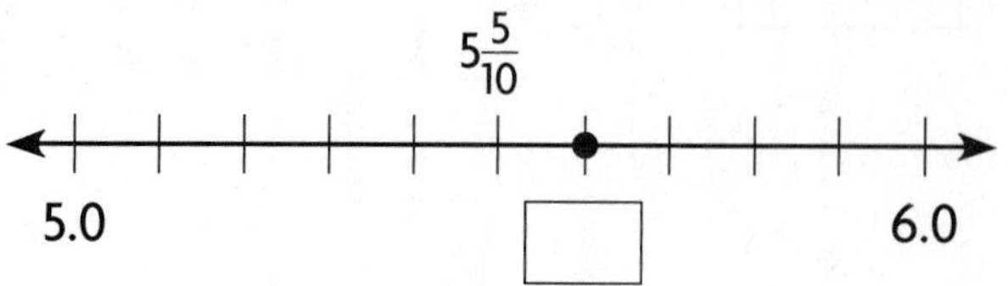

Name ____________________

16. Ingrid is making a toy car. The toy car is $\frac{5}{10}$ meter high without the roof. The roof is $\frac{18}{100}$ meter high. What is the height of the toy car with the roof? Choose a number from each column to complete an equation to solve.

$\frac{5}{10} + \frac{18}{100} =$ [$\frac{5}{100}$ / $\frac{15}{100}$ / $\frac{50}{100}$] $+$ [$\frac{18}{100}$ / $\frac{81}{100}$ / $\frac{18}{10}$] $=$ [$\frac{68}{10}$ / $\frac{32}{100}$ / $\frac{68}{100}$] meter high.

17. Callie shaded the model to represent the questions she answered correctly on a test. What decimal represents the part of the model that is shaded?

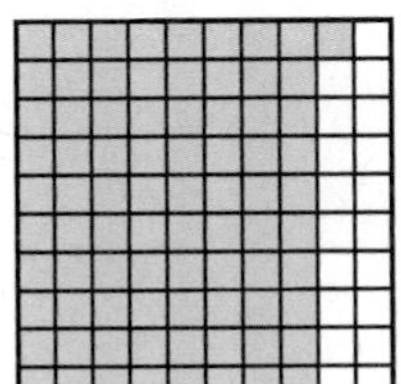

represents ☐

18. For numbers 18a–18f, select True or False for the inequality.

18a. $0.21 < 0.27$ ○ True ○ False

18b. $0.4 > 0.45$ ○ True ○ False

18c. $\$3.21 > \$0.2$ ○ True ○ False

18d. $1.9 < 1.90$ ○ True ○ False

18e. $0.41 = 0.14$ ○ True ○ False

18f. $6.2 > 6.02$ ○ True ○ False

19. Fill in the numbers to find the sum.

$\frac{4}{10} + \frac{\square}{100} = \frac{8}{\square}$

20. Steve is measuring the growth of a tree. He drew this model to show the tree's growth in meters. Which fraction, mixed number, or decimal does the model show? Mark all that apply.

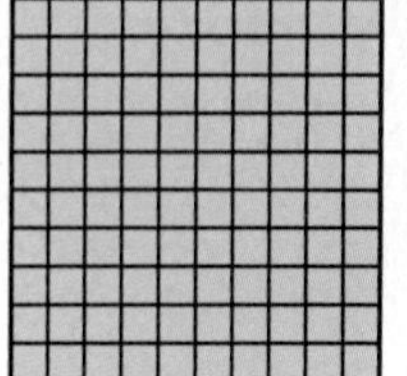
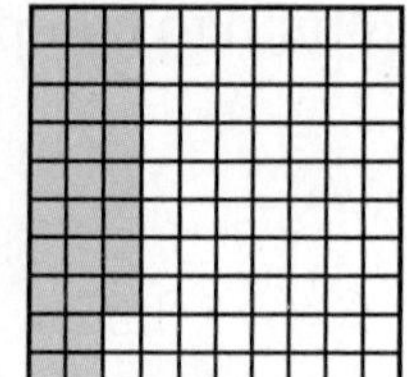

Ⓐ 1.28

Ⓑ 12.8

Ⓒ 0.28

Ⓓ $2\frac{8}{100}$

Ⓔ $1\frac{28}{100}$

Ⓕ $1\frac{28}{10}$

21. Luke lives 0.4 kilometer from a skating rink. Mark lives 0.25 kilometer from the skating rink.

Part A

Who lives closer to the skating rink? Explain.

Part B

How can you write each distance as a fraction? Explain.

Part C

Luke is walking to the skating rink to pick up a practice schedule. Then he is walking to Mark's house. Will he walk more than a kilometer or less than a kilometer? Explain.

Critical Area

Geometry, Measurement, and Data

CRITICAL AREA Understanding that geometric figures can be analyzed and classified based on their properties, such as having parallel sides, perpendicular sides, particular angle measures, and symmetry

Landscape architects can help design and plan outdoor spaces such as botanical gardens.

Project

Landscape Architects

When people who live and work in big cities take breaks, they leave their tall buildings to relax in patches of green. A city garden may be small, but it gives people a chance to enjoy the beauty of nature.

Get Started

Design a garden that covers a whole city block. Decide on features to have in your garden and where they will be located. Mark off parts of your garden for each feature. Then find the number of square units the feature covers and record it on the design. Use the Important Facts to help you.

Important Facts

Features of a City Garden

- Benches
- Flower garden
-  Paths
-  Shrub garden
- Snack bar
- Spring bulb garden
- Tree garden
-  Waterfall and fountain

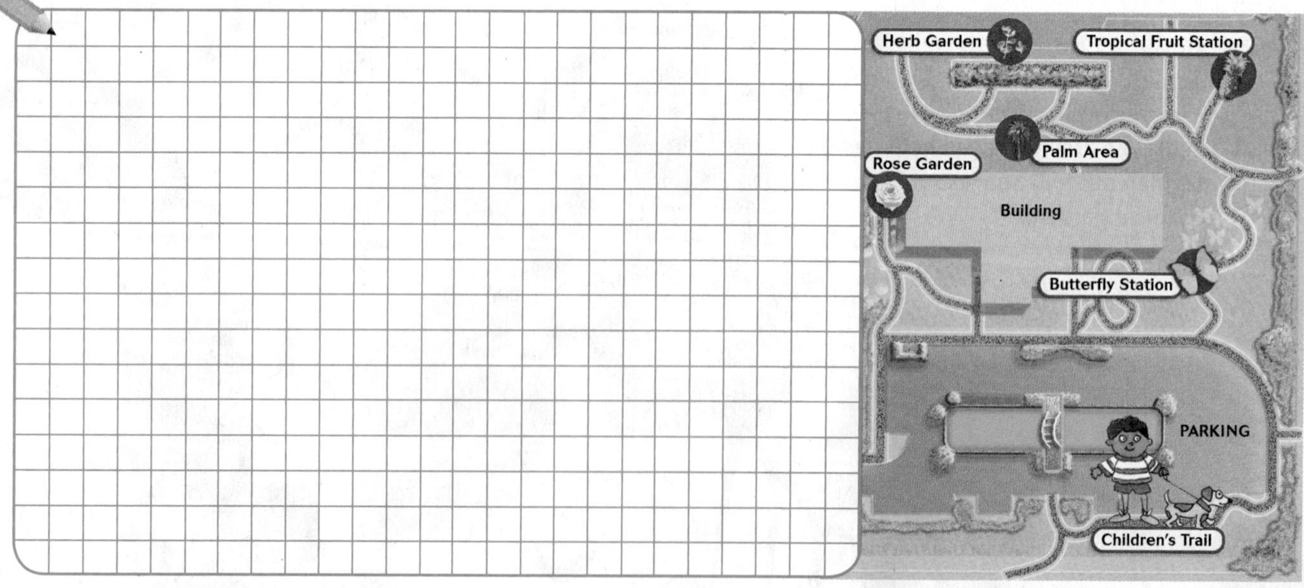

▲ This map is an example of how a city garden could be laid out.

Completed by ______________________________

Chapter 10

Two-Dimensional Figures

Show What You Know 

Check your understanding of important skills.

Name ______________________

▶ Sides and Vertices Write the number of vertices.

1. 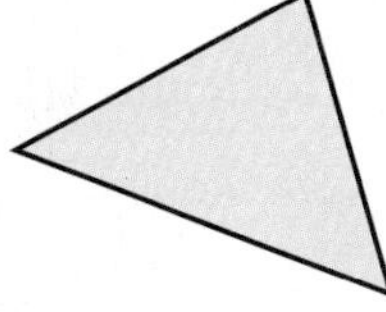

_____ vertices

2. 

_____ vertices

3. 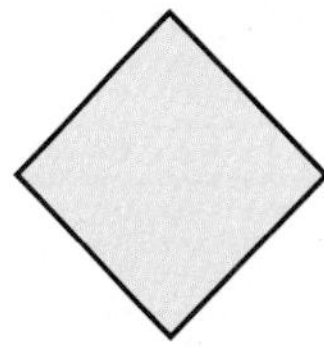

_____ vertices

▶ Number of Sides Write the number of sides.

4. 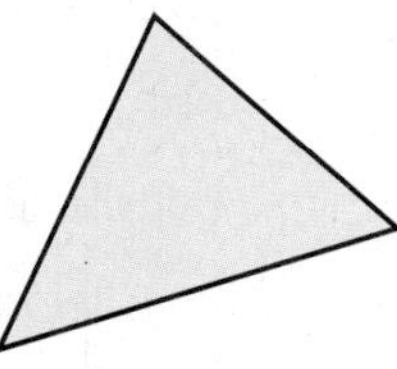

_____ sides

5. 

_____ sides

6. 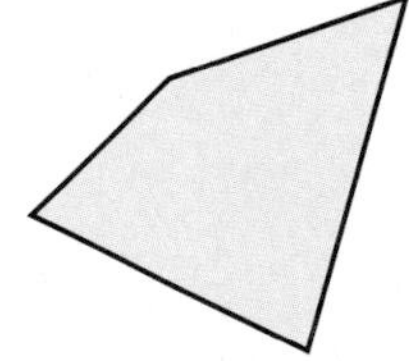

_____ sides

▶ Geometric Patterns Draw the next two shapes in the pattern.

7.  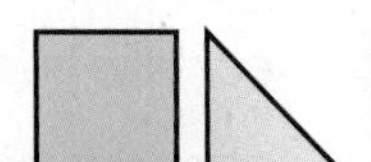  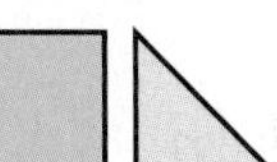    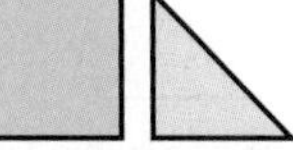

The Isle of Wight Natural History Centre, off the coast of England, has shells of every size, shape, and color. Many shells have symmetry. Be a Math Detective. Investigate this shell. Describe its shape in geometric terms. Then determine whether this shell has line symmetry.

Personal Math Trainer
Online Assessment and Intervention

Vocabulary Builder

▶ Visualize It

Complete the flow map by using the words with a ✓.

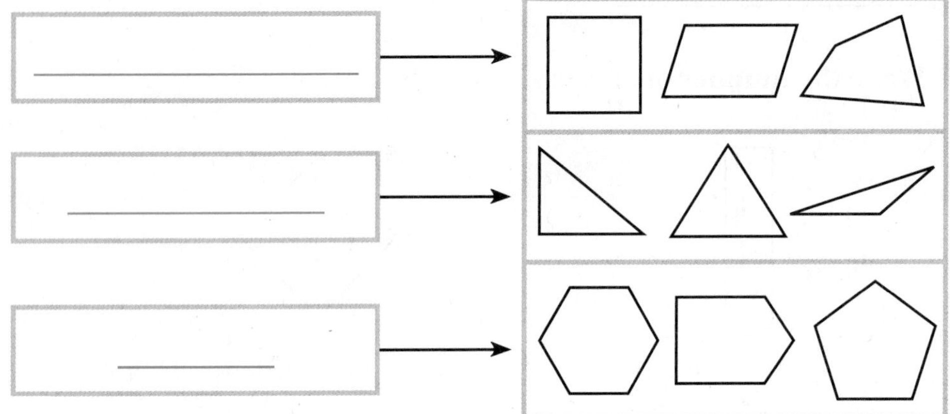

Review Words

✓ polygon
✓ triangle
✓ quadrilateral

Preview Words

acute angle
acute triangle
equilateral triangle
isosceles triangle
line
line segment
line symmetry
obtuse angle
obtuse triangle
parallel lines
parallelogram
perpendicular lines
ray
right angle
right triangle
scalene triangle
straight angle

▶ Understand Vocabulary

Complete the sentences by using preview words.

1. A shape has ____________________ if it can be folded about a line so that its two parts match exactly.

2. A figure that has no endpoints is called a ____________________.

3. A figure that has two endpoints is called a ____________________.

4. ____________________ are lines that never cross.

5. When two lines cross to form a square corner, the lines are ____________________.

• Interactive Student Edition
• Multimedia eGlossary

Name ______________________________

Lines, Rays, and Angles

Essential Question How can you identify and draw points, lines, line segments, rays, and angles?

Geometry—4.G.1

MATHEMATICAL PRACTICES
MP.4, MP.5, MP.6

Unlock the Problem

Everyday things can model geometric figures. For example, the period at the end of this sentence models a point. A solid painted stripe in the middle of a straight road models a line.

Term and Definition	Draw It	Read It	Write It	Example
A **point** is an exact location in space.	A •	point A	point A	
A **line** is a straight path of points that continues without end in both directions.	B, C	line BC line CB	$\overleftrightarrow{BC}$ $\overleftrightarrow{CB}$	
A **line segment** is part of a line between two endpoints.	D, E	line segment DE line segment ED	$\overline{DE}$ $\overline{ED}$	YIELD
A **ray** is a part of a line that has one endpoint and continues without end in one direction.	F, G	ray FG	$\overrightarrow{FG}$	ONE WAY

Activity 1 Draw and label $\overline{JK}$.

____

Mathematical Practices

Explain how lines, line segments, and rays are related.

- Is there another way to name $\overline{JK}$? Explain.

____

____

Angles

Term and Definition	Draw It	Read It	Write It	Example
An **angle** is formed by two rays or line segments that have the same endpoint. The shared endpoint is called the vertex.	P, Q, R	angle *PQR* angle *RQP* angle *Q*	$\angle PQR$ $\angle RQP$ $\angle Q$	

You can name an angle by the vertex. When you name an angle using 3 points, the vertex is always the point in the middle.

Angles are classified by the size of the opening between the rays.

A **right angle** forms a square corner.	A **straight angle** forms a line.	An **acute angle** is less than a right angle.	An **obtuse angle** is greater than a right angle and less than a straight angle.

Activity 2 Classify an angle.

Materials ■ paper

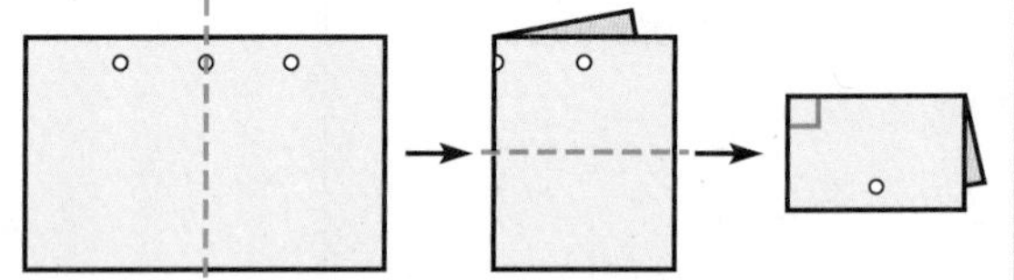

To classify an angle, you can compare it to a right angle.

Make a right angle by using a sheet of paper. Fold the paper twice evenly to model a right angle. Use the right angle to classify the angles below. Write *acute, obtuse, right,* or *straight.*

a. 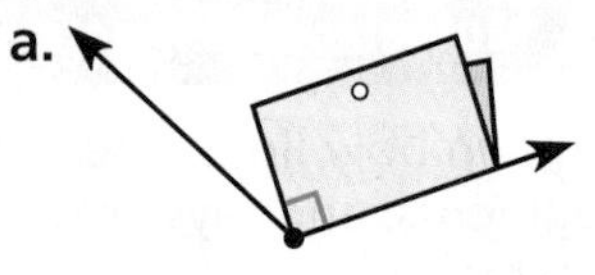
____

b. 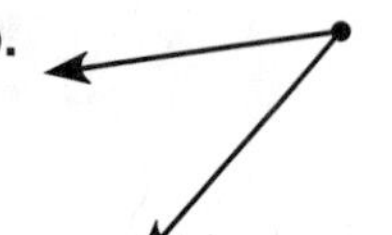
____

c. 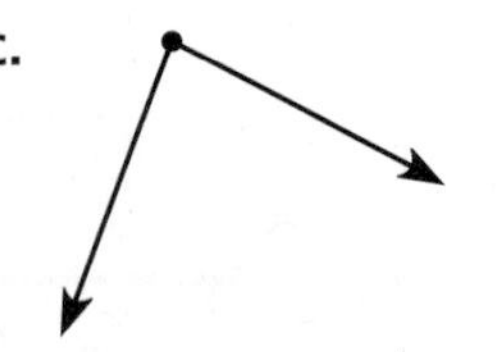
____

d. 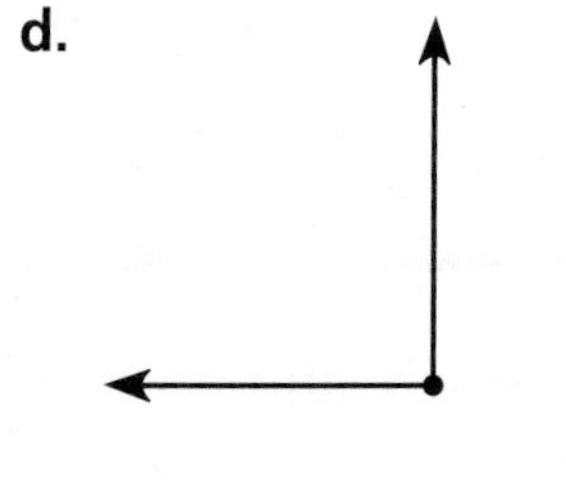
____

Name ______________________________

Share and Show

1. Draw and label $\overline{AB}$ in the space at the right.

   $\overline{AB}$ is a ______________________.

Draw and label an example of the figure.

2. $\overleftrightarrow{XY}$

3. obtuse $\angle K$

4. right $\angle CDE$

Use Figure *M* for 5 and 6.

5. Name a line segment.

   ____

6. Name a right angle.

   ____

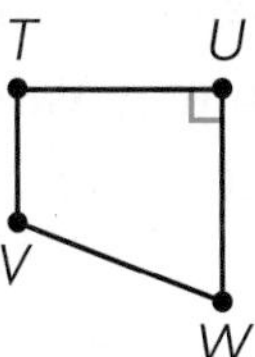

Figure *M*

On Your Own

Draw and label an example of the figure.

7. $\overrightarrow{PQ}$

8. acute $\angle RST$

9. straight $\angle WXZ$

Use Figure *F* for 10–15.

10. Name a ray.

    ____

11. Name an obtuse angle.

    ____

12. Name a line.

    ____

13. Name a line segment.

    ____

14. Name a right angle.

    ____

15. Name an acute angle.

    ____

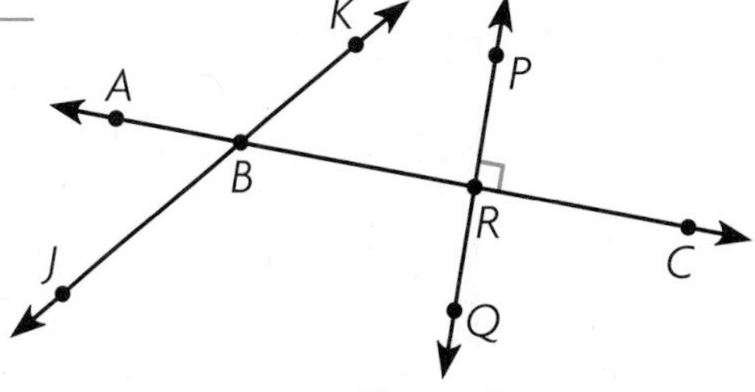

Figure *F*

Problem Solving • Applications

Use the picture of the bridge for 16 and 17.

16. Classify $\angle A$.

____

17. MATHEMATICAL PRACTICE 4 **Use Diagrams** Which angle appears to be obtuse? _______________

18. THINK SMARTER How many different angles are in Figure X? List them.

____

____

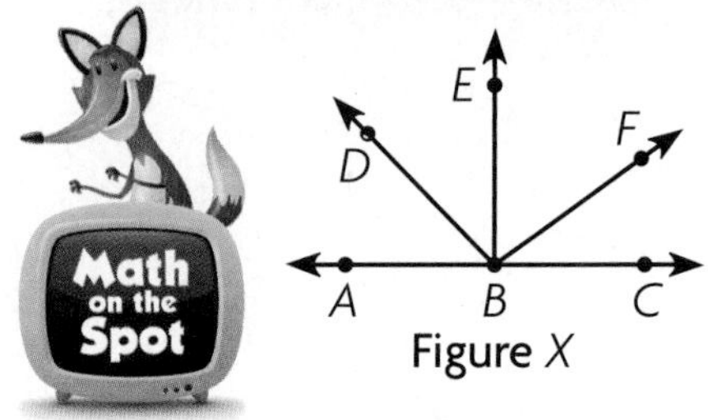

Figure X

19. GO DEEPER Vanessa drew the angle at the right and named it $\angle TRS$. Explain why Vanessa's name for the angle is incorrect. Write a correct name for the angle.

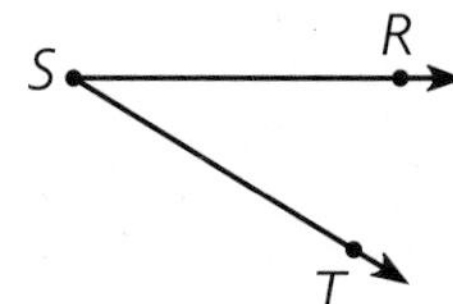

____

____

20. THINK SMARTER Write the word that describes the part of Figure A.

ray	line	line segment
acute angle	right angle	

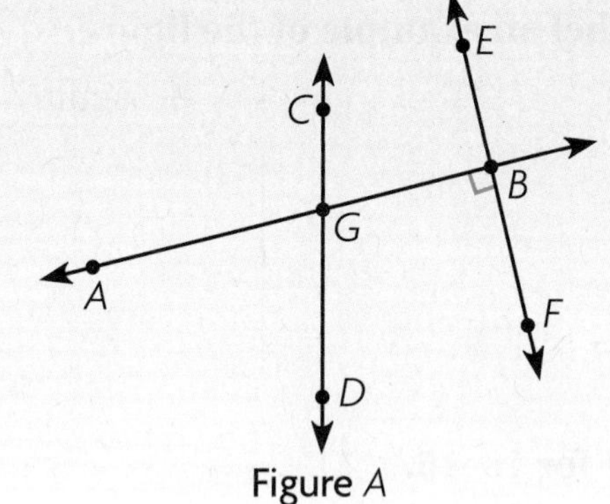

Figure A

$\overline{BG}$ [ ]

$\overleftrightarrow{CD}$ [ ]

$\angle FBG$ [ ]

$\overrightarrow{BE}$ [ ]

$\angle AGD$ [ ]

FOR MORE PRACTICE: Standards Practice Book

Name ______________________________

Classify Triangles by Angles

Essential Question How can you classify triangles by the size of their angles?

Geometry—4.G.2
Also 4.G.1

MATHEMATICAL PRACTICES
MP.3, MP.4, MP.6, MP.7

Unlock the Problem

A triangle is a polygon with three sides and three angles. You can name a triangle by the vertices of its angles.

Triangle	Possible Names	
(triangle with vertices A, B, C)	$\triangle ABC$	$\triangle ACB$
	$\triangle BCA$	$\triangle BAC$
	$\triangle CAB$	$\triangle CBA$

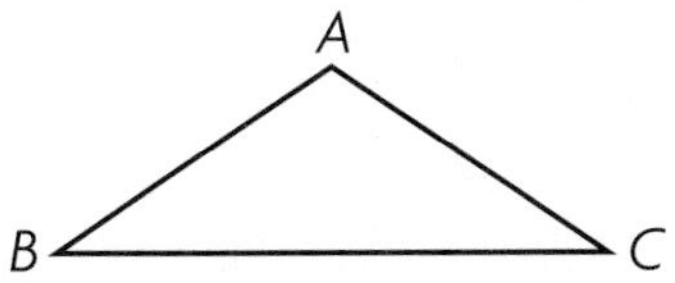

Read Math
When you see "$\triangle ABC$," say "triangle *ABC*."

An angle of a triangle can be right, acute, or obtuse.

Activity 1 Identify right, acute, and obtuse angles in triangles.

Materials ■ color pencils

Use the Triangle Color Guide to color the triangles below.

Triangle Color Guide	
RED	one right angle
BLUE	one obtuse angle
ORANGE	three acute angles

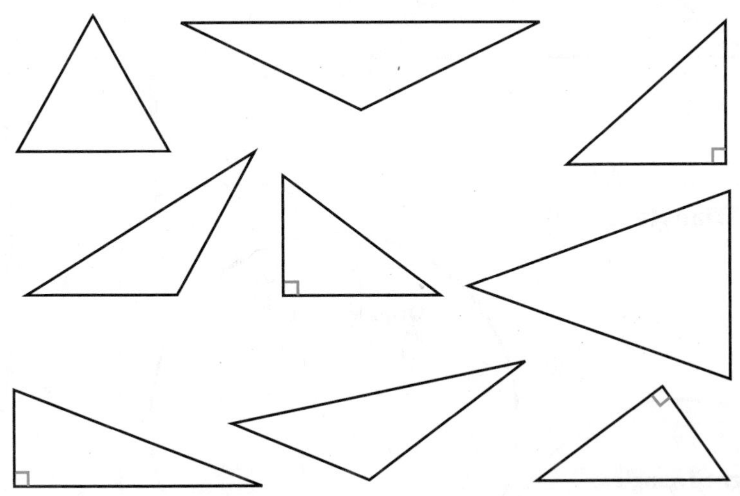

Math Talk **Mathematical Practices**
Can a triangle have more than one obtuse angle? Explain.

Try This!

a. Name the triangle with one right angle. ______

b. Name the triangle with one obtuse angle. ______

c. Name the triangle with three acute angles. ______

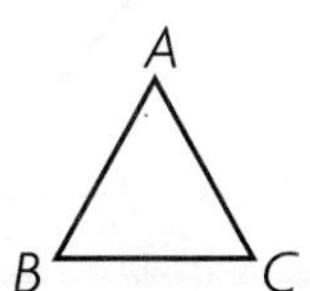

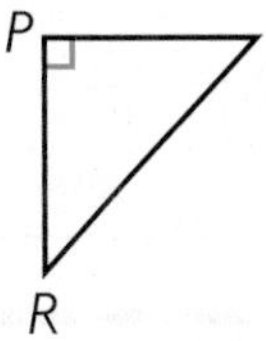

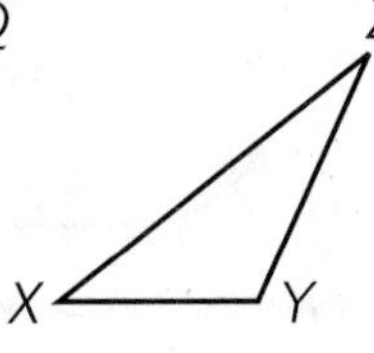

An **acute triangle** is a triangle with three acute angles.	An **obtuse triangle** is a triangle with one obtuse angle.	A **right triangle** is a triangle with one right angle.
Acute Triangle	**Obtuse Triangle**	**Right Triangle**

Activity 2 Use a Venn diagram to classify triangles.

Write the names of the triangles in the Venn diagram.

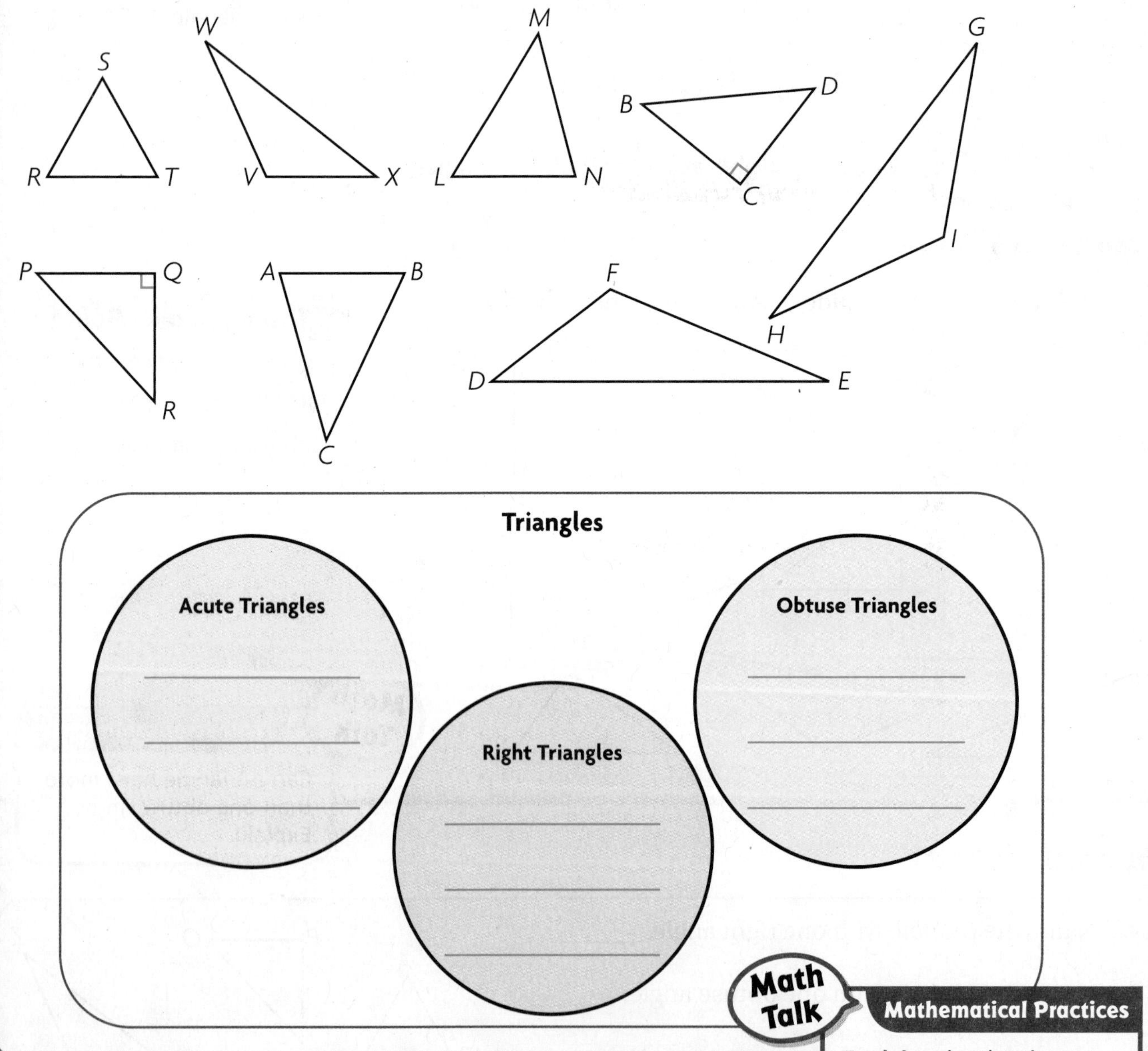

Math Talk **Mathematical Practices**

Explain why the three circles in this Venn diagram do not overlap.

Name ______________________________

Share and Show 

1. Name the triangle. Tell whether each angle is *acute*, *right*, or *obtuse*.

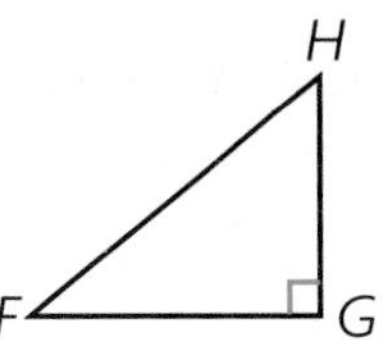

A name for the triangle is __________.

$\angle F$ is __________.

$\angle G$ is __________.

$\angle H$ is __________.

Classify each triangle. Write *acute, right,* or *obtuse*.

2.

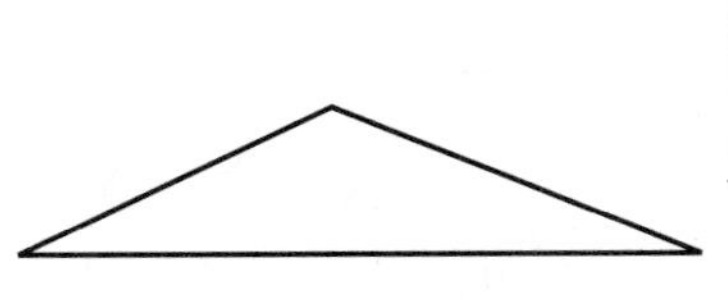

____

3.

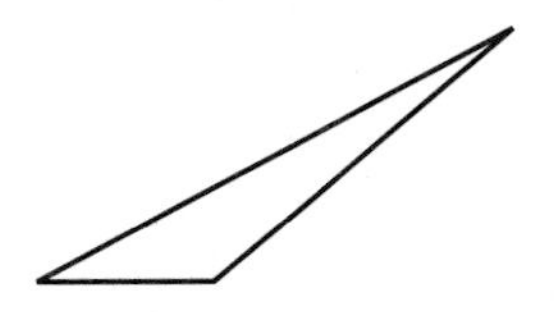

____

4.

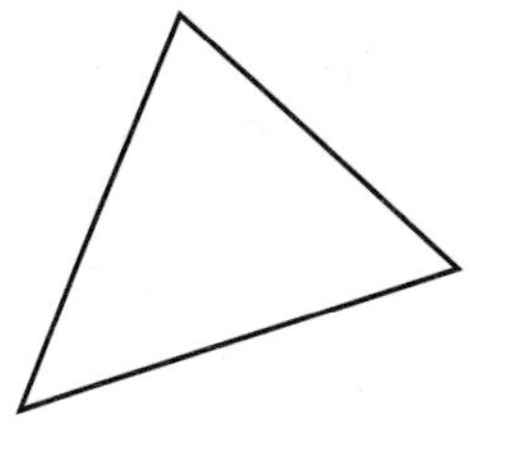

____

On Your Own

Classify each triangle. Write *acute, right,* or *obtuse*.

5.

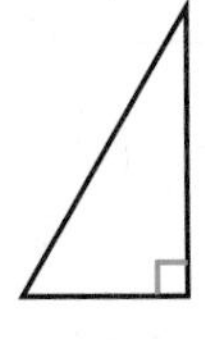

____

6.

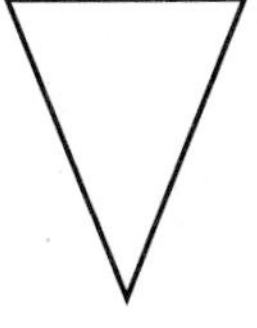

____

7.

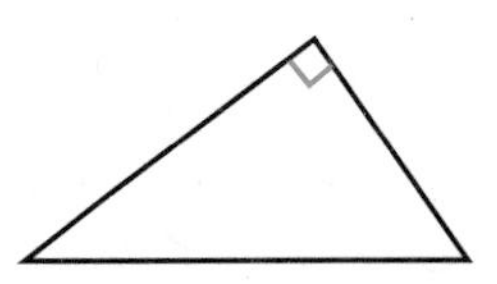

____

8. THINK SMARTER Cross out the figure that does not belong. Explain.

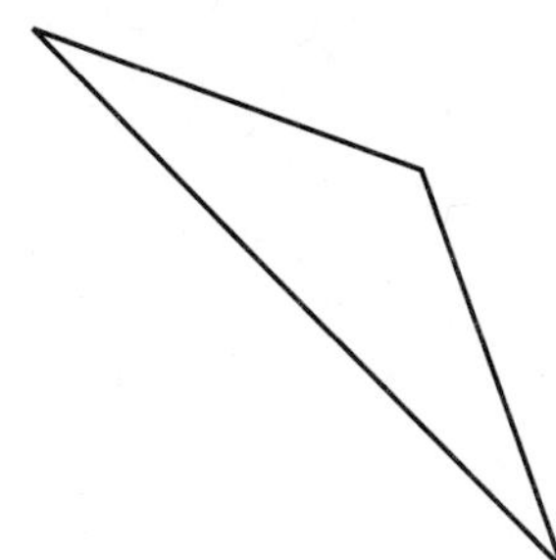

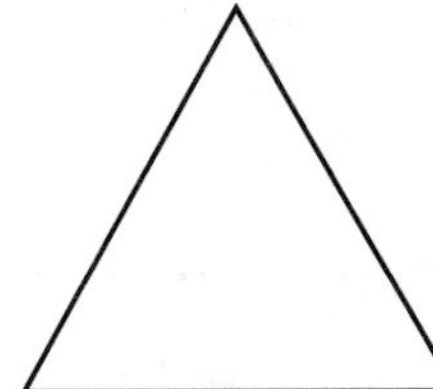

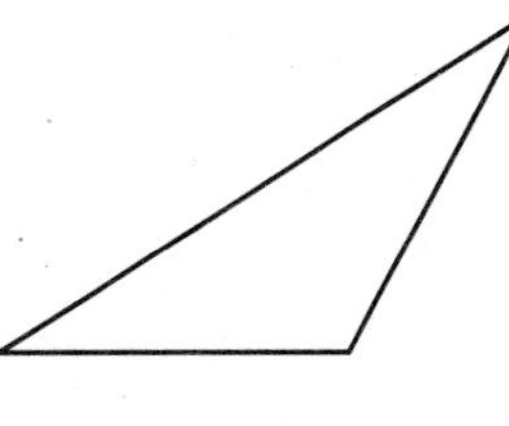

____

Problem Solving • Applications

Use the Venn diagram for 9–10.

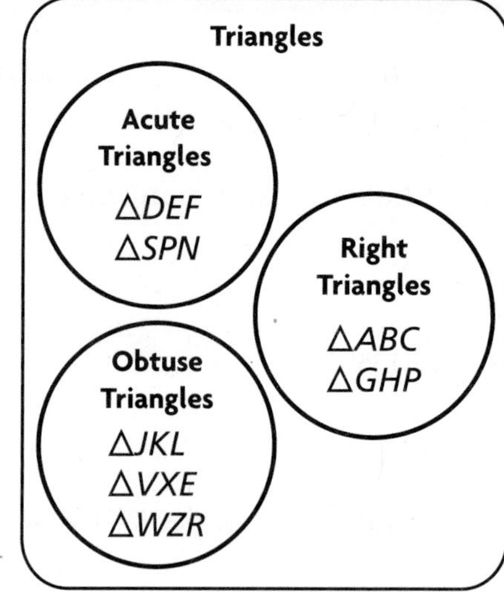

9. THINK SMARTER Which triangles do NOT have an obtuse angle? Explain.

10. MATHEMATICAL PRACTICE 6 How many triangles have *at least* two acute angles? **Explain.**

11. GO DEEPER Use the square shown at the right. Draw a line segment from point *M* to point *P*. Name and classify the triangles formed by the line segment.

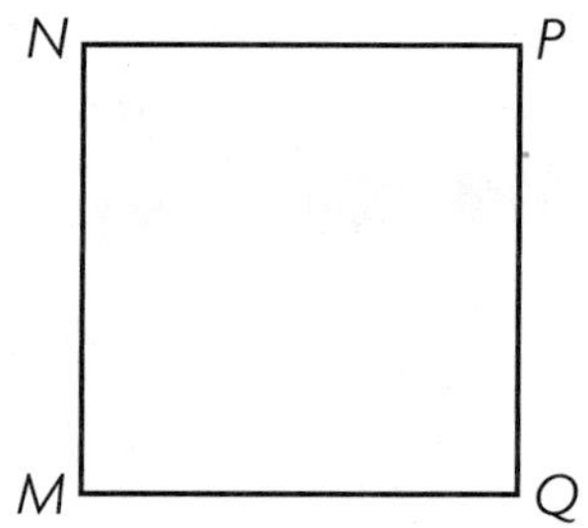

12. THINK SMARTER Write the letter of the triangle under its correct classification.

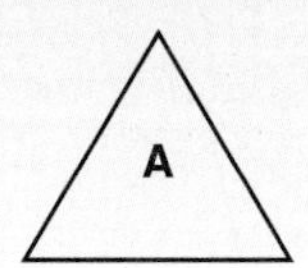

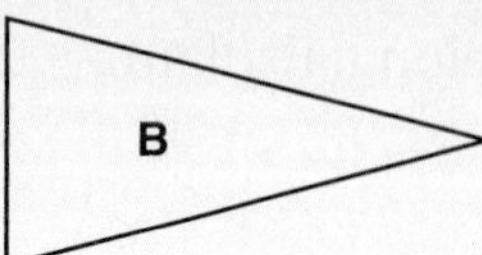

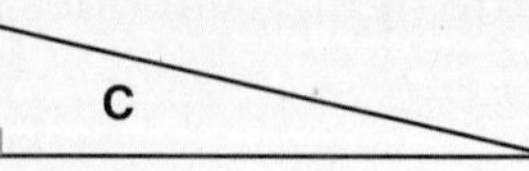

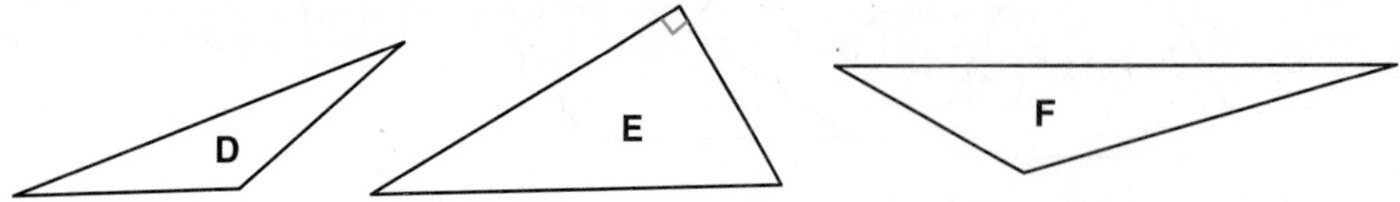

Acute Triangle	Obtuse Triangle	Right Triangle

FOR MORE PRACTICE:
Standards Practice Book

Name ______________________________

Classify Triangles by Sides

Essential Question How can you classify triangles by the length of their sides?

Geometry— 4.G.2

MATHEMATICAL PRACTICES
MP.3, MP.4, MP.6, MP.7

Unlock the Problem

A triangle can also be classified by the lengths of its sides.

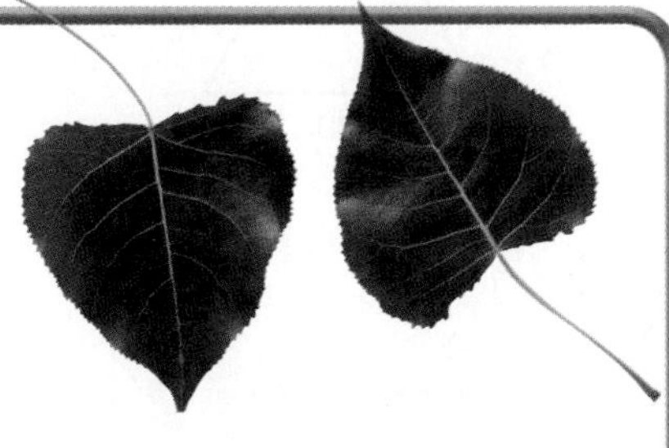

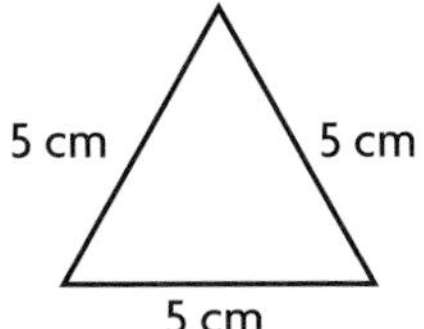

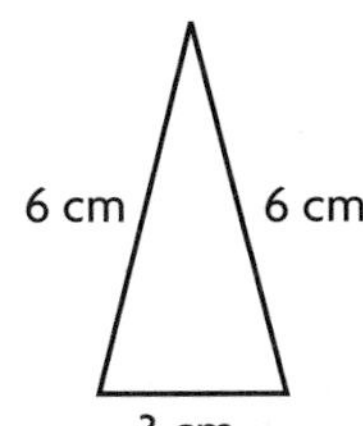

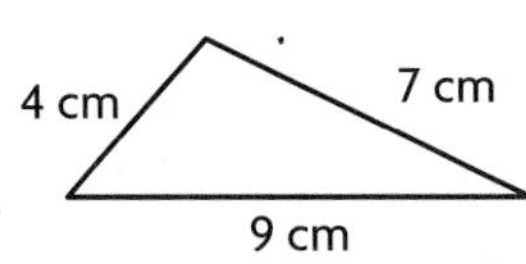

A triangle can have 3 sides that are the same length, 2 sides that are the same length, or no sides that are the same length.

Activity 1 Identify triangles that have 3 sides the same length, 2 sides the same length, or no sides the same length.

Materials ■ color pencils

Use the Triangle Color Guide to color the triangles below.

Triangle Color Guide	
Red	3 sides the same length
Blue	2 sides the same length
Orange	0 sides the same length

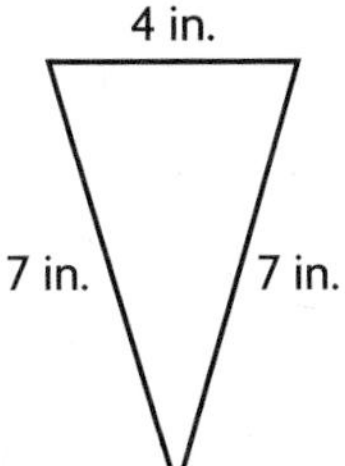

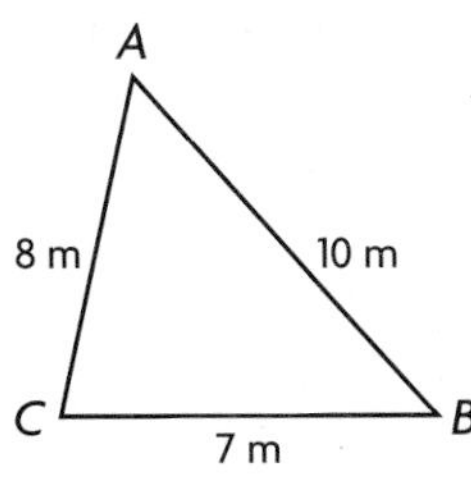

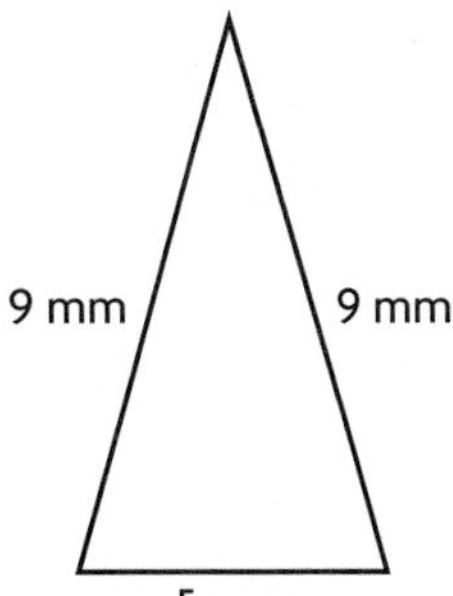

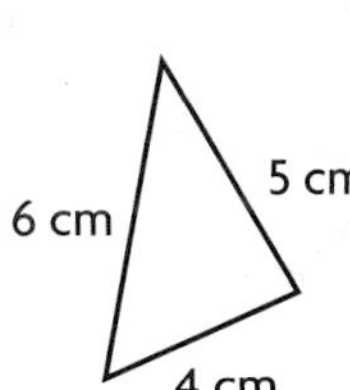

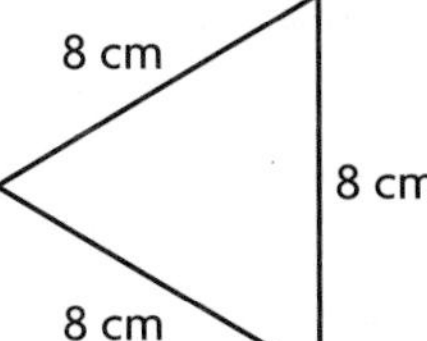

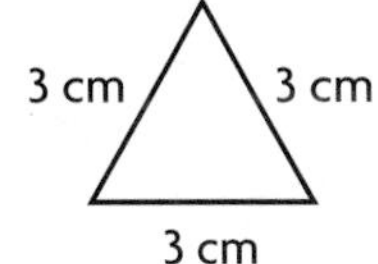

Try This!

a. Name the triangle that has no sides the same length. ______________

b. Name the triangle that has 3 sides the same length. ______________

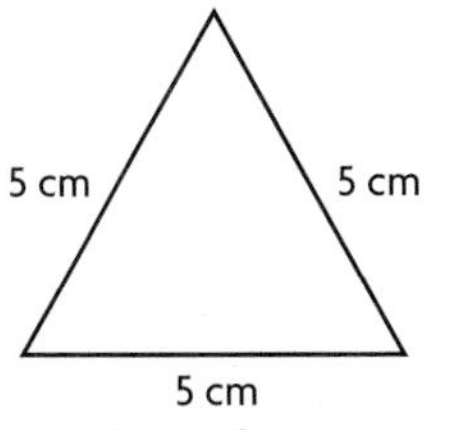

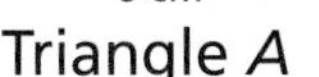

Triangle *A*

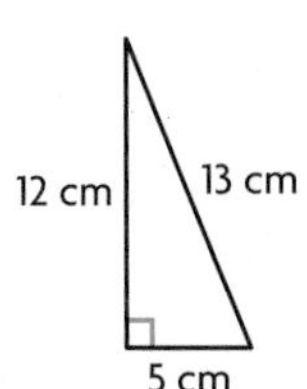

Triangle *B*

An **equilateral triangle** is a triangle that has 3 equal sides.

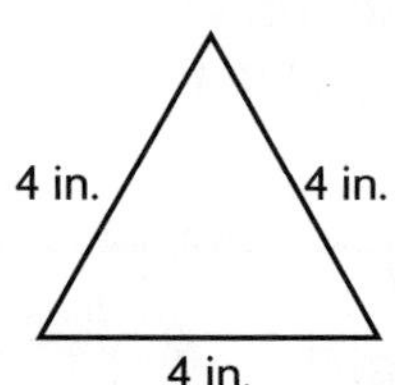

Equilateral Triangle

An **isosceles triangle** is a triangle that has 2 equal sides.

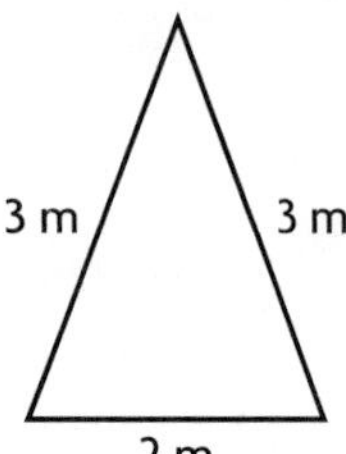

Isosceles Triangle

A **scalene triangle** is a triangle that has no equal sides.

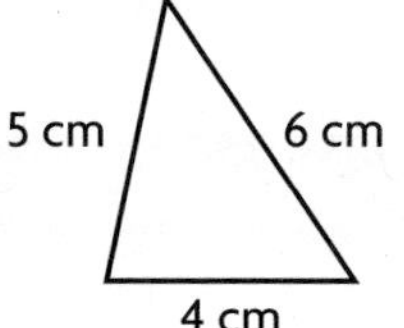

Scalene Triangle

Activity 2 Use a Venn diagram to classify triangles.

Write the names of the triangles in the Venn diagram

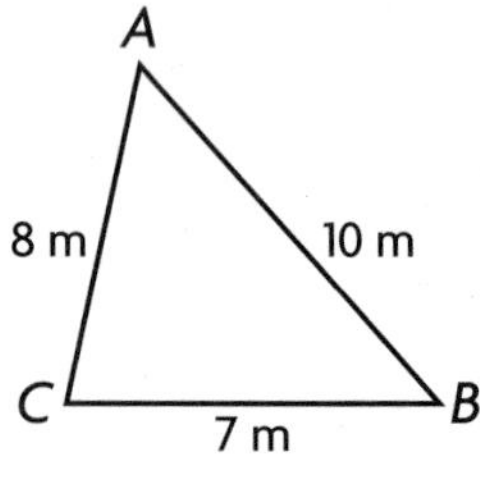

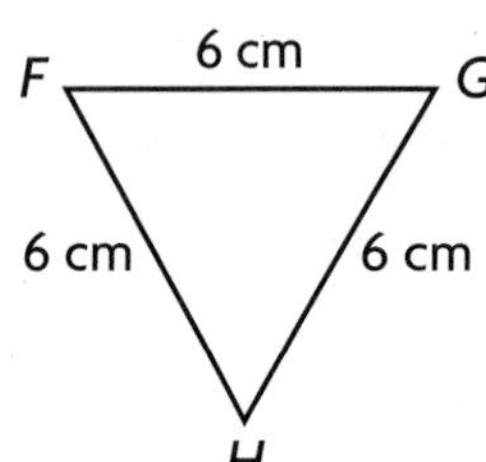

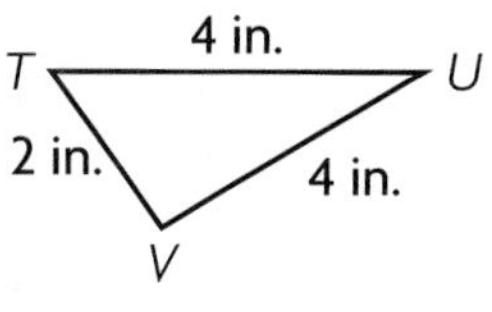

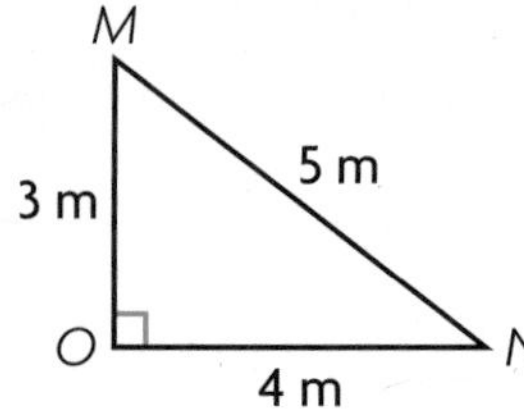

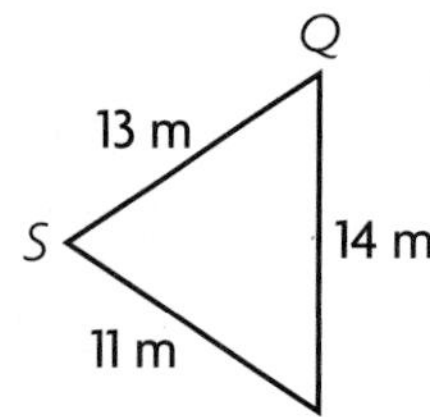

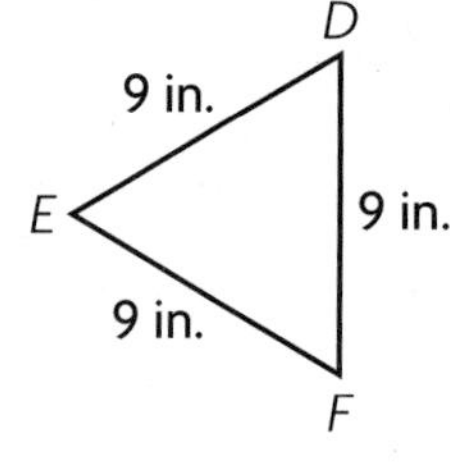

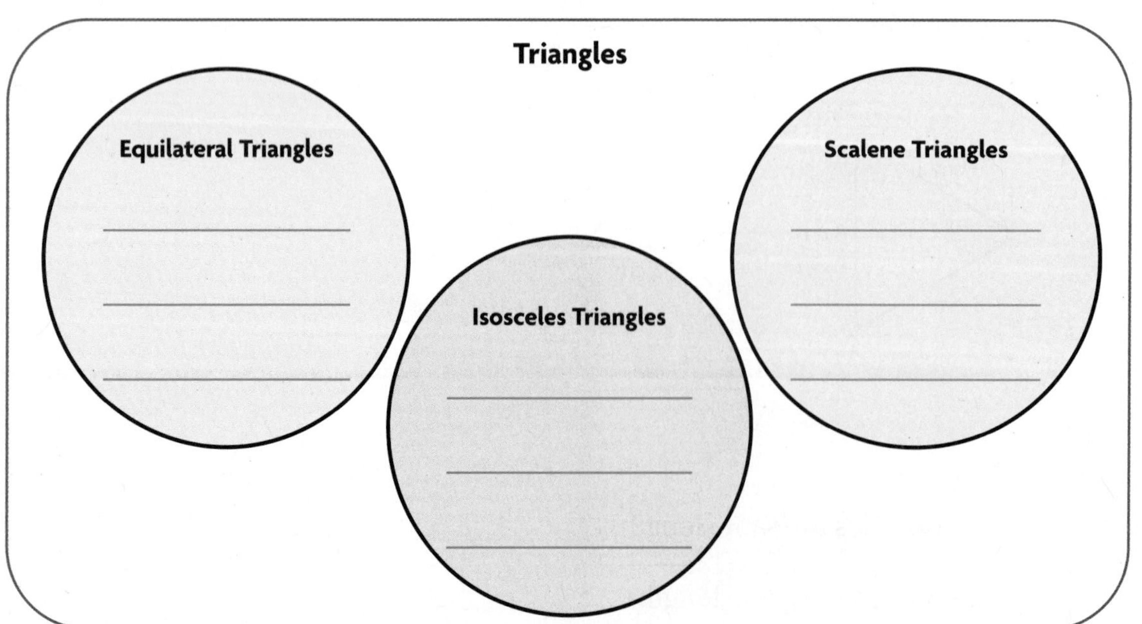

Name ______________________

Share and Show

1. Name the triangle at the right.
Write *equilateral, isosceles,* or *scalene.*

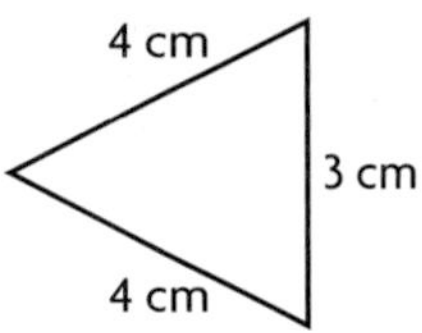

Think: How many equal sides does the triangle have?

____

Name the triangle. Write *equilateral, isosceles,* or *scalene.*

2. 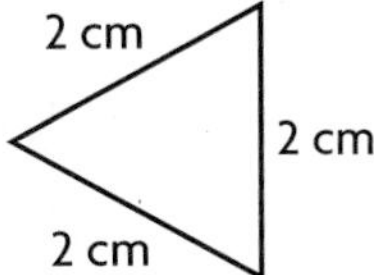

____

3. 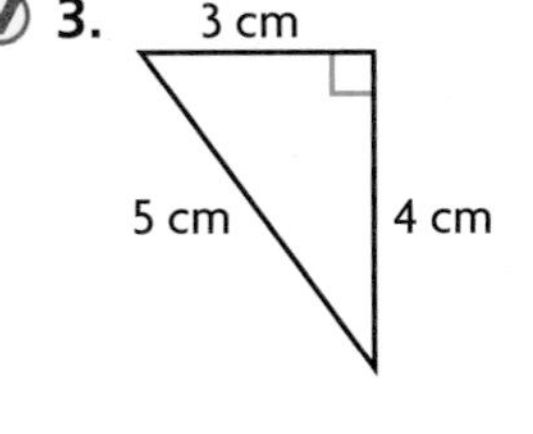

____

4. 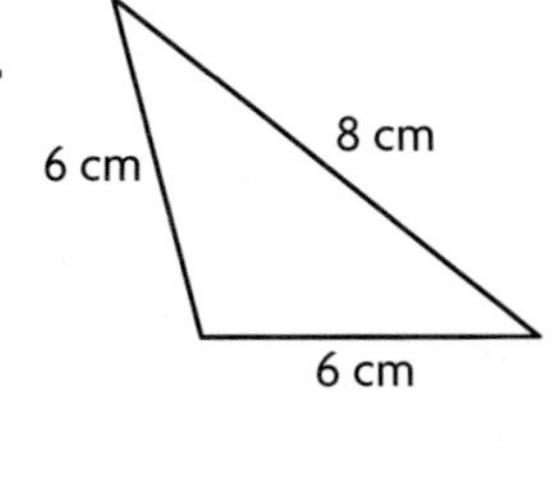

____

On Your Own

Name the triangle. Write *equilateral, isosceles,* or *scalene.*

5. 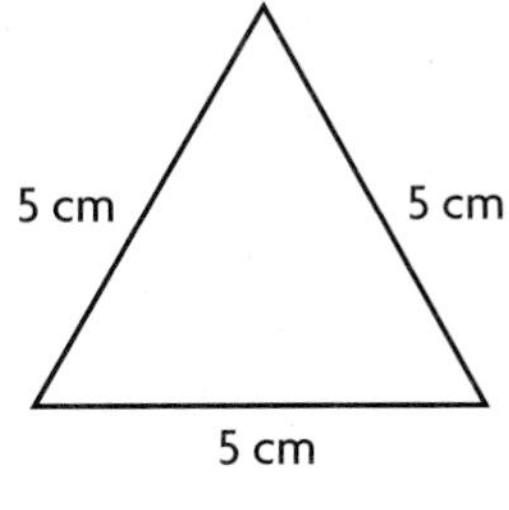

____

6. 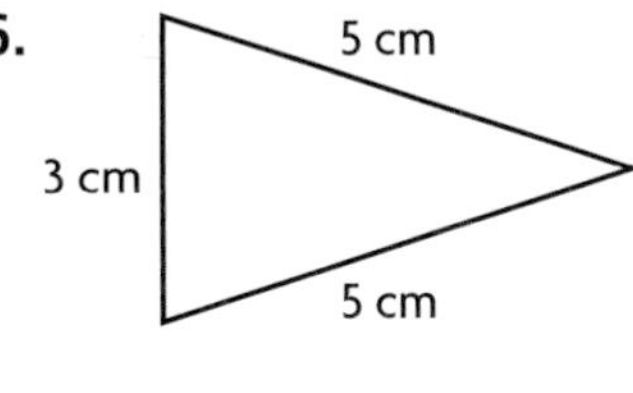

____

7. 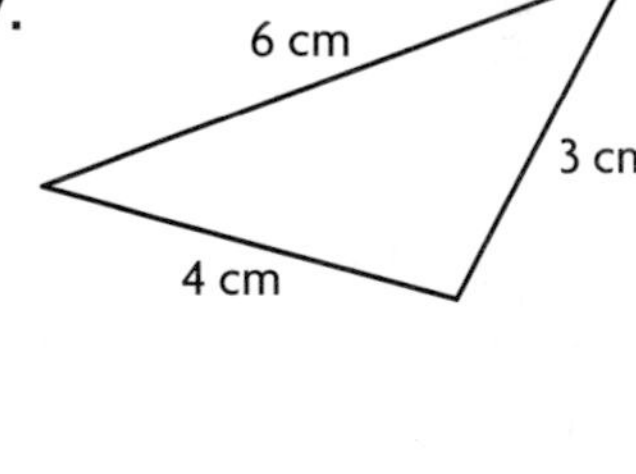

____

Name the triangle by the lengths of its sides. Write *equilateral, isosceles,* or *scalene.*

8. 12 inches, 12 inches, 12 inches

____

9. 4 inches, 6 inches, 6 inches

____

10. 9 inches, 5 inches, 7 inches

____

11. 14 inches, 7 inches, 14 inches

____

Problem Solving • Applications Real World

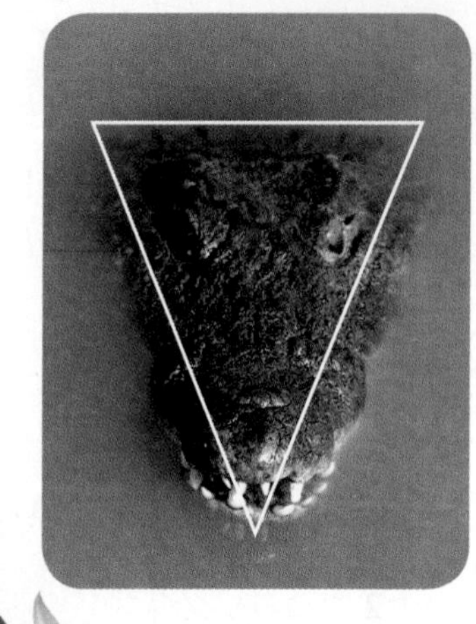

12. THINK SMARTER The American crocodile's head appears to be shaped like a triangle. Classify the shape of the head by the lengths of its sides. Write *isosceles, scalene,* or *equilateral.*

____

13. THINK SMARTER How are an equilateral triangle and a scalene triangle alike? How are they different? Explain your answer.

____

Math on the Spot

14. GO DEEPER I am a triangle. Two of my sides are 5 inches long. My third side is less than 5 inches. None of my angles are right angles. What two names do I have?

____

WRITE Math
Show Your Work

15. MATHEMATICAL PRACTICE 6 **Explain** how a triangle can be isosceles and obtuse.

____

16. THINK SMARTER Select the lengths that identify a scalene triangle. Mark all that apply.

Ⓐ 2 inches, 2 inches, 3 inches

Ⓑ 3 meters, 4 meters, 5 meters

Ⓒ 6 feet, 6 feet, 6 feet

Ⓓ 10 meters, 7 meters, 5 meters

Ⓔ 8 feet, 3 feet, 8 feet

FOR MORE PRACTICE:
Standards Practice Book

Name ______________________________

Parallel Lines and Perpendicular Lines

Essential Question How can you identify and draw parallel lines and perpendicular lines?

Geometry—
4.G.1

MATHEMATICAL PRACTICES
MP.4, MP.5, MP.6

Unlock the Problem

You can find models of lines in the world around you. For example, two streets that cross each other model intersecting lines. Metal rails on a train track that never cross model parallel lines.

▲ Maglev trains use magnets to lift them above the tracks while moving.

Term and Definition	Draw It	Read It	Write It
Intersecting lines are lines in a plane that cross at exactly one point. Intersecting lines form four angles.		Line *HI* intersects line *JK* at point *X*.	$\overleftrightarrow{HI}$ and $\overleftrightarrow{JK}$ intersect at point *X*
Parallel lines are lines in a plane that are always the same distance apart. Parallel lines never intersect.		Line *DE* is parallel to line *FG*.	$\overleftrightarrow{DE} \parallel \overleftrightarrow{FG}$ The symbol $\parallel$ means "is parallel to."
Perpendicular lines are lines in a plane that intersect to form four right angles.		Line *LM* is perpendicular to line *NO*.	$\overleftrightarrow{LM} \perp \overleftrightarrow{NO}$ The symbol $\perp$ means "is perpendicular to."

Try This! **Tell how the streets appear to be related. Write *perpendicular, parallel,* or *intersecting.***

- W 36th St and Broadway ______________________
- W 35th St and 7th Ave ______________________
- W 37th St and W 36th St ______________________

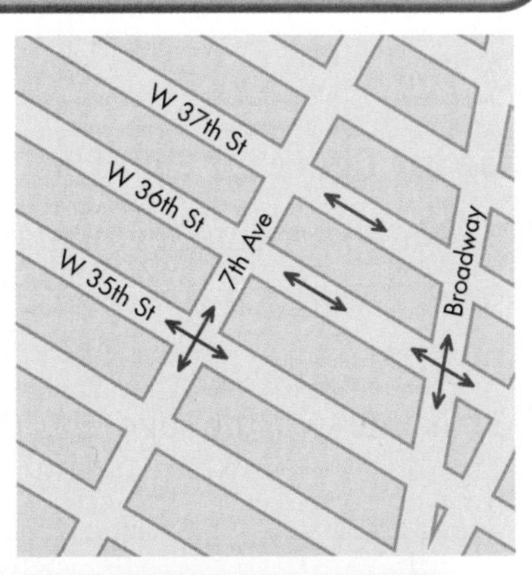

Math Talk **Mathematical Practices**

Can two rays be parallel? Explain.

Activity Draw and label $\overrightarrow{YX} \perp \overrightarrow{YZ}$ intersecting at point Y.

Materials ■ straightedge

STEP 1: Draw and label $\overrightarrow{YX}$.

STEP 2: Then draw and label $\overrightarrow{YZ}$.

STEP 3: Make sure $\overrightarrow{YX}$ and $\overrightarrow{YZ}$ intersect at point Y.

STEP 4: Make sure the rays are perpendicular.

- How can you check if two rays are perpendicular?

1. Name the figure you drew.

2. Can you classify the figure? Explain.

Share and Show

MATH BOARD

1. Draw and label $\overline{QR} \parallel \overline{ST}$.

   Think: Parallel lines never intersect. Parallel line segments are parts of parallel lines.

Use the figure for 2 and 3.

2. Name two line segments that appear to be parallel.

3. Name two line segments that appear to be perpendicular.

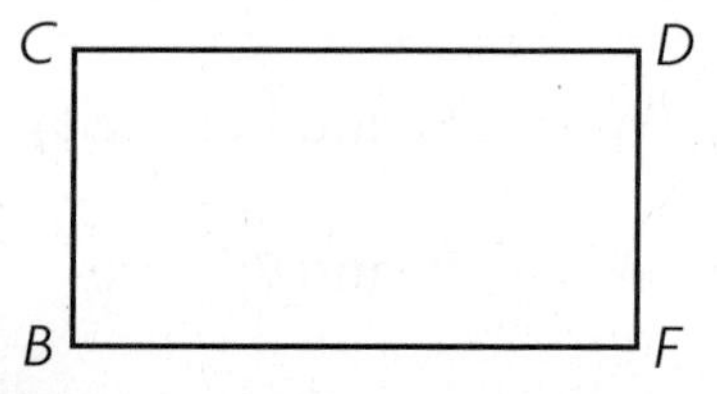

Math Talk **Mathematical Practices**

Explain how the symbols ⊥ and ∥ help you remember which relationships they describe.

Name ______________________

On Your Own

Use the figure for 4–5.

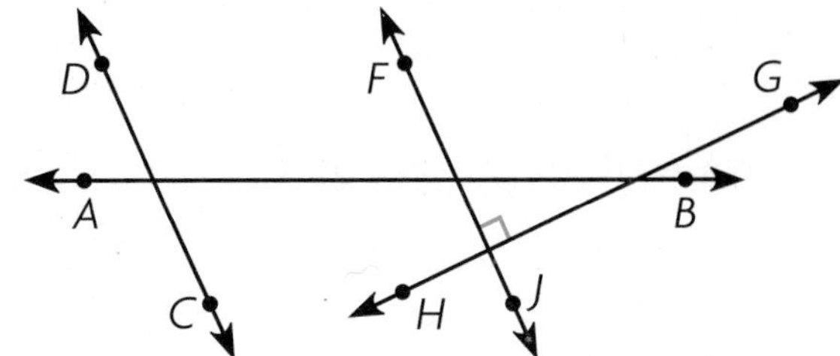

4. Name a pair of lines that are perpendicular. ______________

5. Name a pair of lines that appear to be parallel.

____

Draw and label the figure described.

6. $\overline{RS} \parallel \overline{TU}$

7. $\overrightarrow{KL}$ and $\overrightarrow{KM}$

8. $\overline{CD} \perp \overline{DE}$

9. $\overleftrightarrow{JK} \perp \overleftrightarrow{LM}$

10. $\overleftrightarrow{ST}$ intersecting $\overleftrightarrow{UV}$ at point X

11. $\overleftrightarrow{AB} \parallel \overleftrightarrow{FG}$

Problem Solving • Applications 

Use the figure for 12–13.

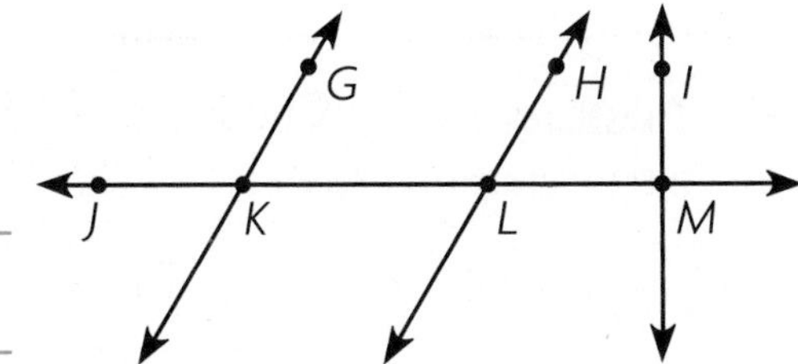

12. THINK SMARTER Dan says that $\overleftrightarrow{HL}$ is parallel to $\overleftrightarrow{IM}$. Is Dan correct? Explain.

____

____

13. GO DEEPER Name two intersecting line segments that are not perpendicular.

____

Use the house plan at the right for 14–16.

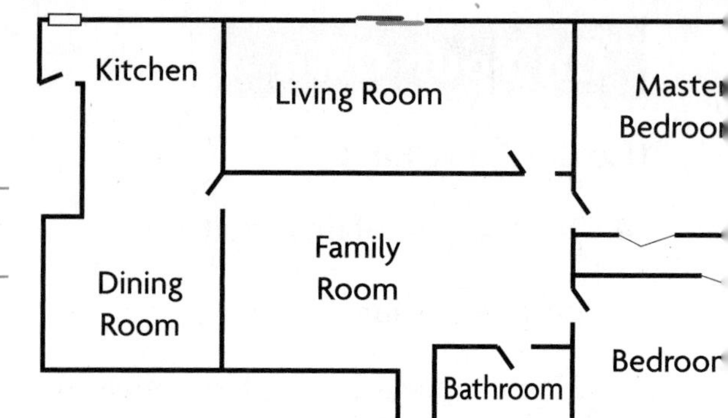

14. What geometric term describes a corner of the living room?

15. Name three parts of the plan that show line segments.

16. THINK SMARTER Name a pair of line segments that appear to be parallel.

Use the map at the right for 17–19.

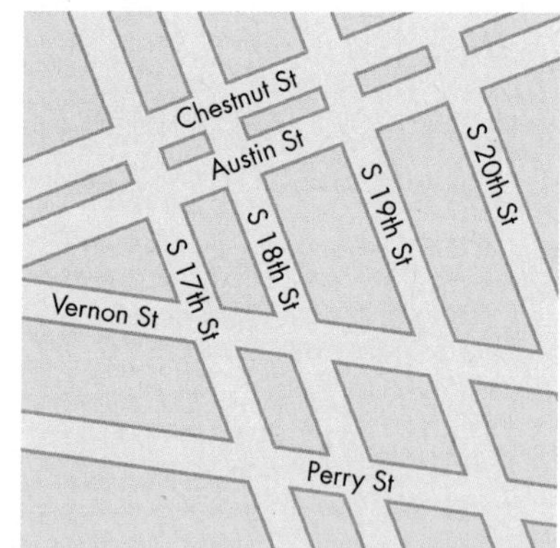

17. Name a street that appears to be parallel to S 17th Street.

18. MATHEMATICAL PRACTICE 4 **Use Diagrams** Name a street that appears to be parallel to Vernon Street.

19. Name a street that appears to be perpendicular to S 19th Street.

20. THINK SMARTER Choose the labels to make a true statement.

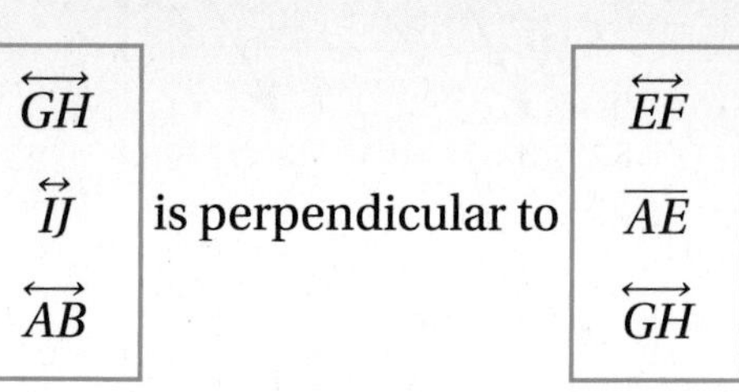

$\overleftrightarrow{GH}$ $\overleftrightarrow{IJ}$ $\overleftrightarrow{AB}$	is perpendicular to	$\overleftrightarrow{EF}$ $\overline{AE}$ $\overleftrightarrow{GH}$

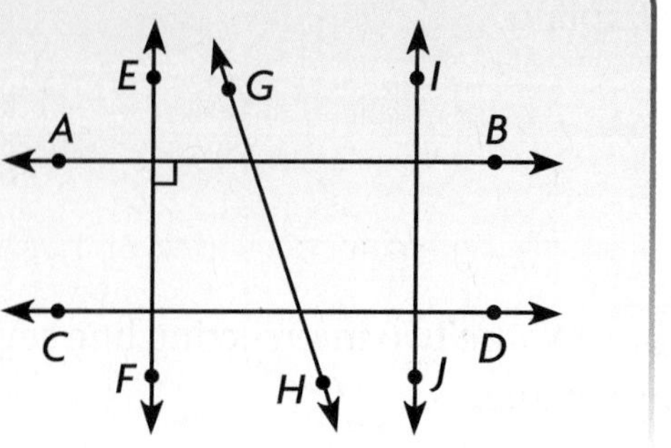

FOR MORE PRACTICE: Standards Practice Book

Name ______________________________

Classify Quadrilaterals

Essential Question How can you sort and classify quadrilaterals?

Geometry—4.G.2

MATHEMATICAL PRACTICES
MP.2, MP.4, MP.6

Unlock the Problem

A quadrilateral is a polygon with four sides and four angles. You can name a quadrilateral by the vertices of its angles.

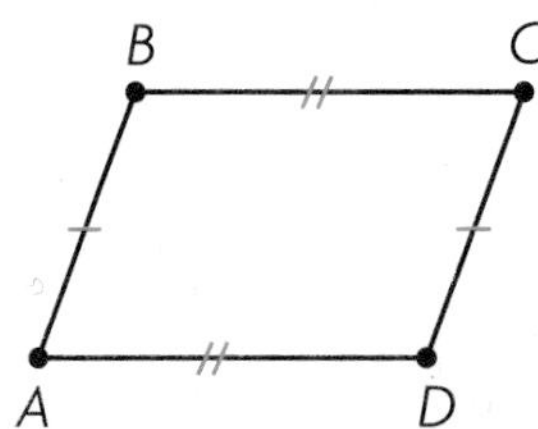

The tick marks on the line segments show that they have the same length. Sides *AD* and *BC* have the same length. Sides *AB* and *CD* have the same length.

Quadrilateral *ABCD* is a possible name for the figure shown at the right. Quadrilateral *ACBD* is not a possible name, since points *A* and *C* are not endpoints of the same side.

Assume that line segments that appear to be parallel are parallel.

Common Quadrilaterals

Trapezoid
- 1 pair of parallel sides

Parallelogram
- 2 pairs of parallel sides
- 2 pairs of sides of equal length

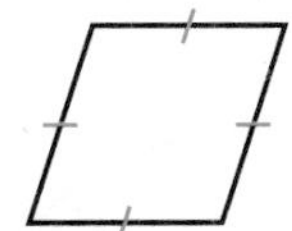

Rhombus
- 2 pairs of parallel sides
- 4 sides of equal length

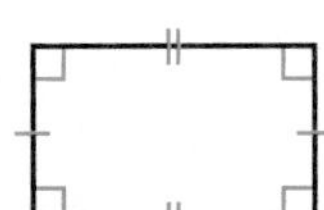

Rectangle
- 2 pairs of parallel sides
- 2 pairs of sides of equal length
- 4 right angles

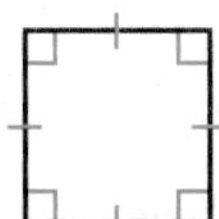

Square
- 2 pairs of parallel sides
- 4 sides of equal length
- 4 right angles

Materials ■ color pencils

Use the Quadrilateral Color Guide to color the quadrilaterals.

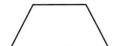

Quadrilateral Color Guide	
RED:	exactly 4 right angles
BLUE:	exactly 2 right angles
ORANGE:	exactly 1 right angle

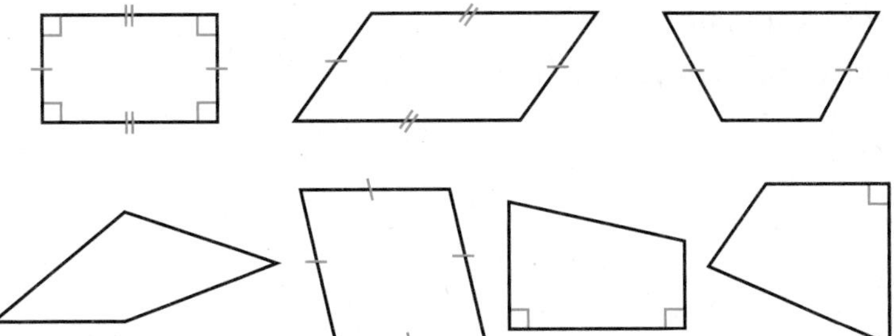

Math Talk **Mathematical Practices**

Can a quadrilateral have exactly 3 right angles? **Explain.**

Activity 2 Use a Venn diagram to sort quadrilaterals.

Write the names of the quadrilaterals in the Venn diagram.

Try This! **Classify each figure as many ways as possible. Write** ***quadrilateral, trapezoid, parallelogram, rhombus, rectangle,*** **or** ***square.***

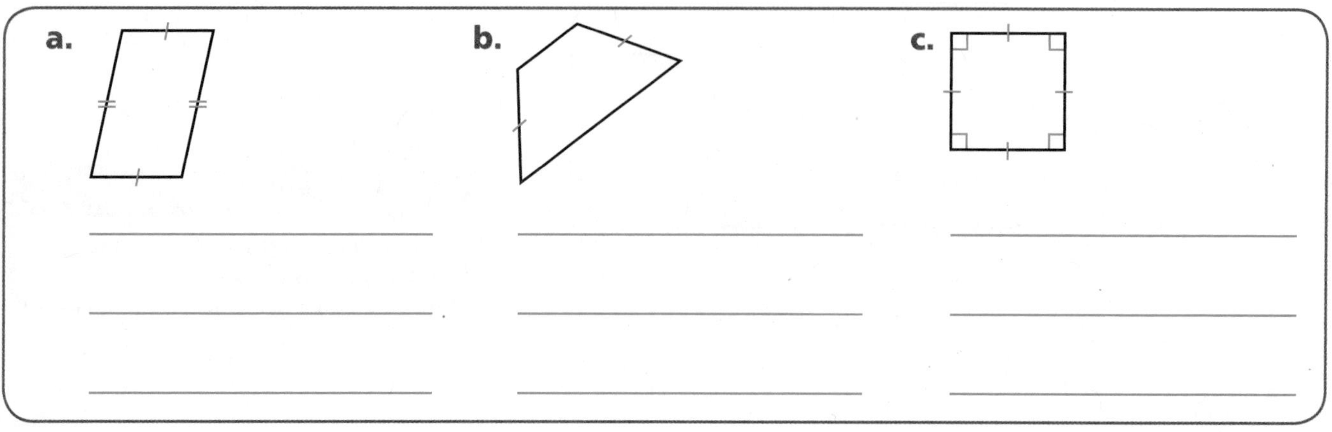

Name ________________________________

Share and Show

1. Tell whether the quadrilateral is also a trapezoid, parallelogram, rhombus, rectangle, or square.

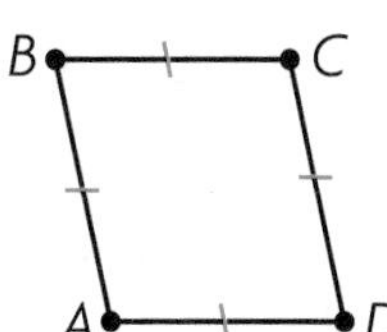

Think: ______ pairs of parallel sides

______ sides of equal length

______ right angles

Quadrilateral *ABCD* is also a ____________________.

Classify each figure as many ways as possible. Write *quadrilateral, trapezoid, parallelogram, rhombus, rectangle,* or *square.*

2. 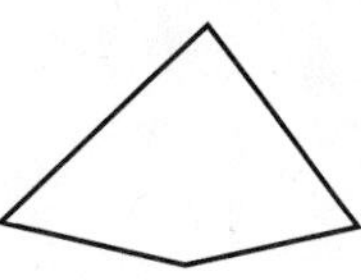

____

____

____

3. 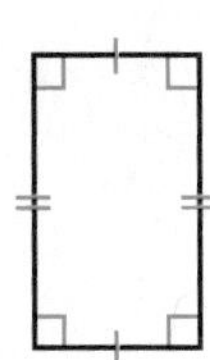

____

____

____

4. 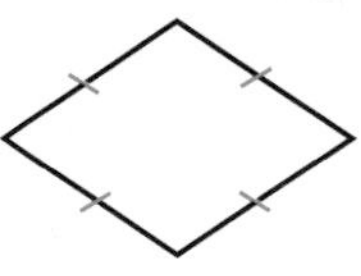

____

____

____

Math Talk **Mathematical Practices**

How would you classify a figure with 4 sides, none of which are parallel? **Explain.**

On Your Own

Classify each figure as many ways as possible.
Write *quadrilateral, trapezoid, parallelogram, rhombus, rectangle,* or *square.*

5. 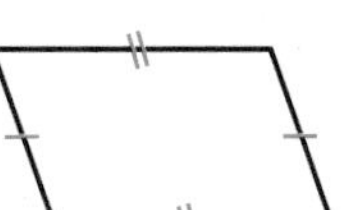

____

____

____

6. 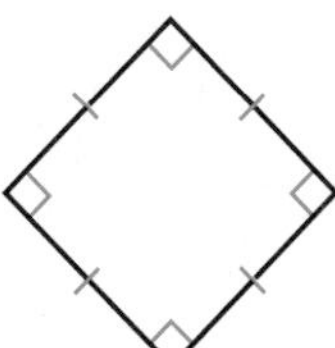

____

____

____

7. 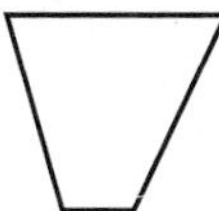

____

____

____

Problem Solving • Applications Real World

8. THINK SMARTER Explain how a rhombus and square are alike, and how they are different.

____

____

____

____

____

9. THINK SMARTER Classify the figure. Select all that apply.

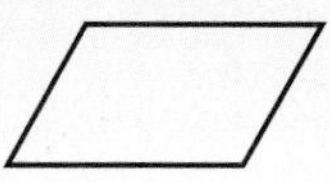

○ quadrilateral ○ rectangle
○ trapezoid ○ rhombus
○ parallelogram ○ square

Connect to Art

The Louvre Museum is located in Paris, France. Architect I.M. Pei designed the glass and metal structure at the main entrance of the museum. This structure is called the Louvre Pyramid.

Below is a diagram of part of the entrance to the Louvre Pyramid.

10. MATHEMATICAL PRACTICE 1 **Describe** the quadrilaterals you see in the diagram.

____

____

____

____

____

11. GO DEEPER How many triangles do you see in the diagram? Explain.

____

____

____

____

____

FOR MORE PRACTICE: Standards Practice Book

Name ____________________

Vocabulary

Choose the best term from the box to complete the sentence.

Vocabulary
acute angle
line segment
obtuse angle
ray
right angle
straight angle

1. A ________ is part of a line between two endpoints. (p.399)

2. A ________ forms a square corner. (p. 400)

3. An ________ is greater than a right angle and less than a straight angle. (p. 400)

4. The two-dimensional figure that has one endpoint is a ________. (p. 399)

5. An angle that forms a line is called a ________. (p. 400)

Concepts and Skills

6. On the grid to the right, draw a polygon that has 2 pairs of parallel sides, 2 pairs of sides equal in length, and 2 acute and 2 obtuse angles. Tell all the possible names for the figure. (4.G.2)

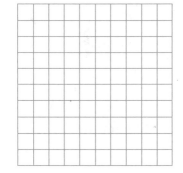

____

Draw the figure. (4.G.1)

7. parallel lines	8. obtuse $\angle ABC$	9. intersecting lines that are not perpendicular	10. acute $\angle RST$

11. Which triangle has no sides lengths of equal length? (4.G.2)

____

12. Which figure has 2 pairs of parallel sides, 2 pairs of sides of equal length, and 4 right angles? (4.G.2)

____

13. Which quadrilateral can have 2 pairs of parallel sides, all sides with equal length, and no right angles? (4.G.2)

____

14. What is the correct name of the figure shown? (4.G.1)

F *E*

____

15. Describe the angles of an obtuse triangle. (4.G.2)

____

____

____

____

Name ___________________________________

Line Symmetry

Essential Question How can you check if a shape has line symmetry?

Geometry—4.G.3

MATHEMATICAL PRACTICES
MP.2, MP.3, MP.5

Unlock the Problem

One type of symmetry found in geometric shapes is line symmetry. This sign is in the hills above Hollywood, California. Do any of the letters in the Hollywood sign show line symmetry?

A shape has **line symmetry** if it can be folded about a line so that its two parts match exactly.
A fold line, or a **line of symmetry**, divides a shape into two parts that are the same size and shape.

Activity Explore line symmetry.

Materials ■ pattern blocks ■ scissors

A **Does the letter W have line symmetry?**

STEP 1 Use pattern blocks to make the letter W.

STEP 2 Trace the letter.

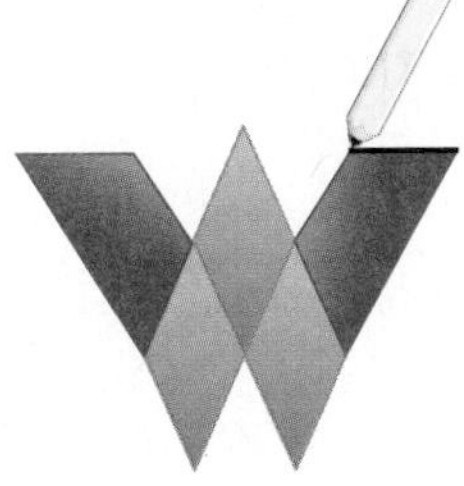

Math Idea

A vertical line goes up and down. ↕

A horizontal line goes left and right. ↔

A diagonal line goes through vertices of a polygon that are not next to each other. It can go up and down and left and right.

STEP 3 Cut out the tracing.

STEP 4 Fold the tracing over a vertical line.

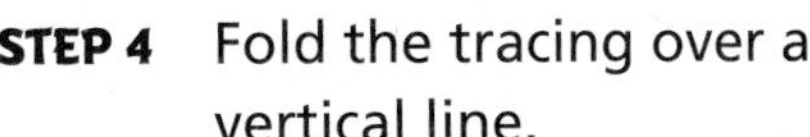

Think: The two parts of the folded W match exactly. The fold line is a line of symmetry.

So, the letter W ____________ line symmetry.

Math Talk **Mathematical Practices**

Why is it important to use a fold line to check if a shape has line symmetry?

B Does the letter L have line symmetry?

STEP 1

Use pattern blocks or grid paper to make the letter L.

STEP 2

Trace the letter.

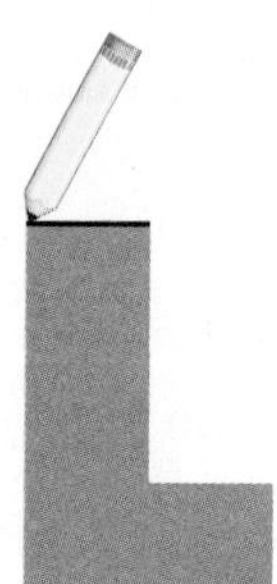

STEP 3

Cut out the tracing.

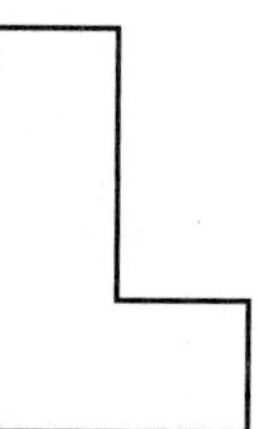

STEP 4

Fold the tracing over a vertical line.

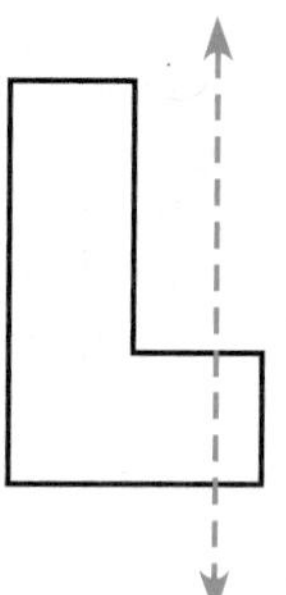

Do the two parts match exactly?

____

STEP 5

Then open it and fold it horizontally.

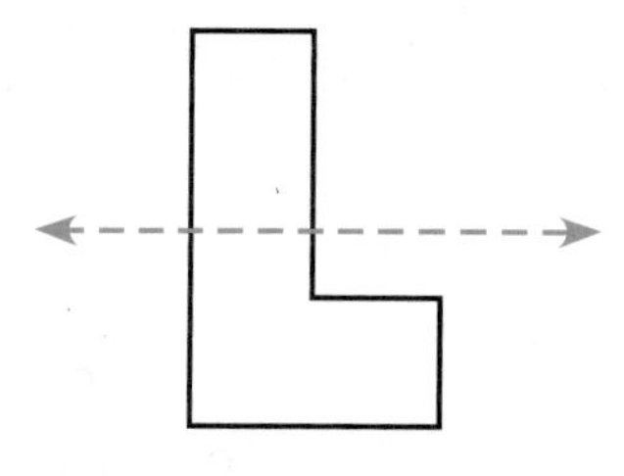

Do the two parts match exactly?

____

STEP 6

Then open it and fold it diagonally.

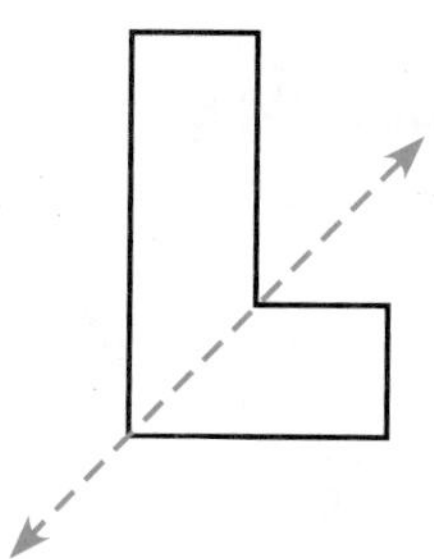

Do the two parts match exactly?

____

So, the letter L ______________ line symmetry.

1. Repeat Steps 1–6 for the remaining letters in HOLLYWOOD. Which letters have line symmetry?

____

2. Do any of the letters have more than one line of symmetry? Explain.

____

____

Remember

You can fold horizontally, vertically, or diagonally to determine if the parts match exactly.

Name ____________________

Share and Show

Tell whether the parts on each side of the line match. Is the line a line of symmetry? Write *yes* or *no*.

1. 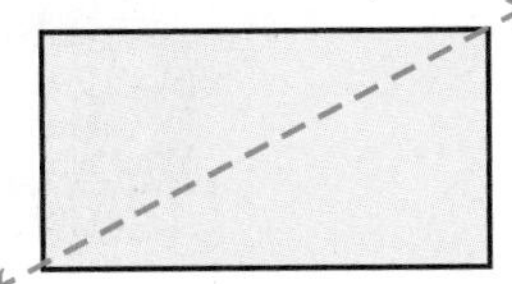
____

2. 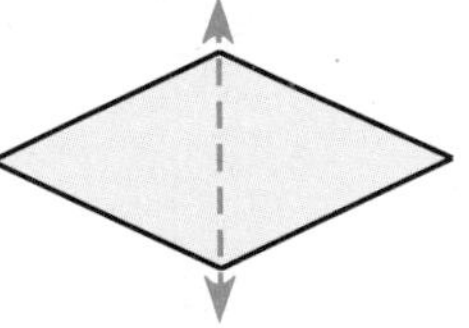
____

3. 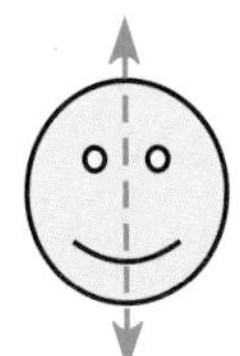
____

4. 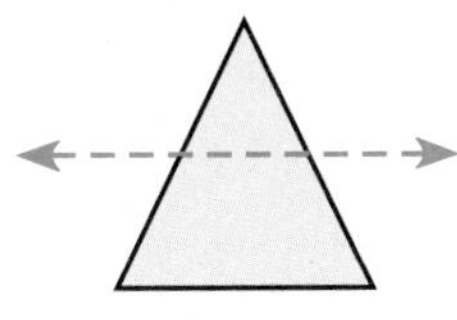
____

Tell if the blue line appears to be a line of symmetry. Write *yes* or *no*.

5. 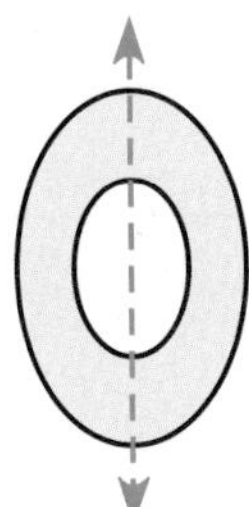
____

6. 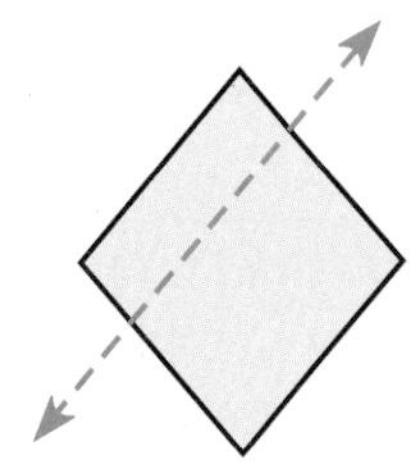
____

7. 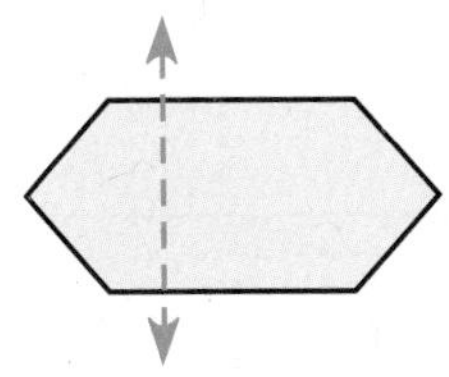
____

8. 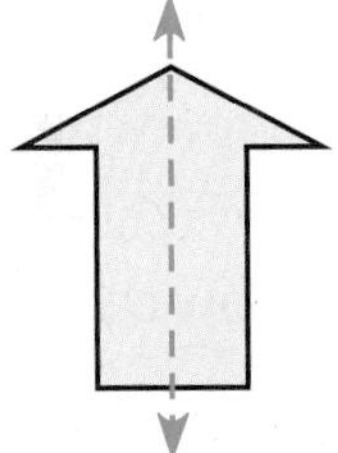
____

Math Talk — **Mathematical Practices**

Explain how you can use paper folding to check if a shape has line symmetry.

On Your Own

Tell if the blue line appears to be a line of symmetry. Write *yes* or *no*.

9. 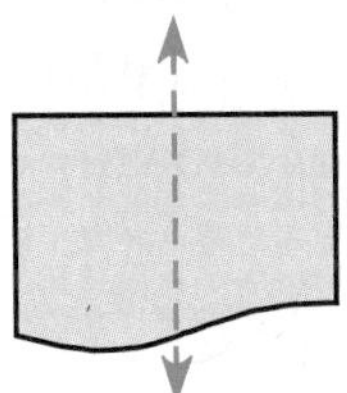
____

10. 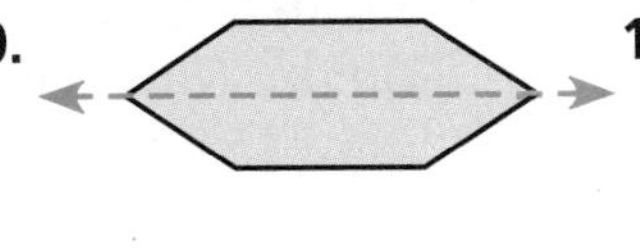
____

11. 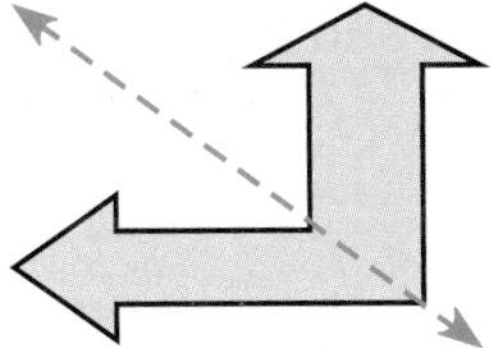
____

12. 
____

13. GO DEEPER Which best describes the symmetry in the letter I?

I

____

Unlock the Problem

14. Which shape has a correctly drawn line of symmetry?

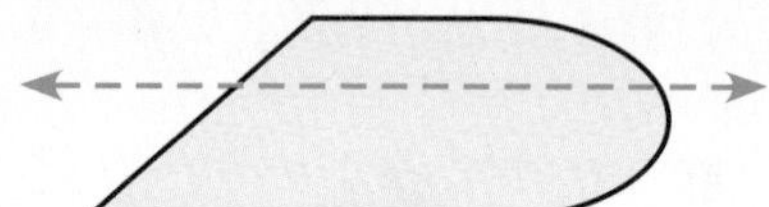

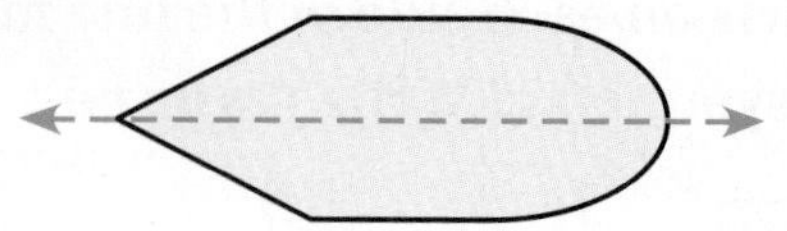

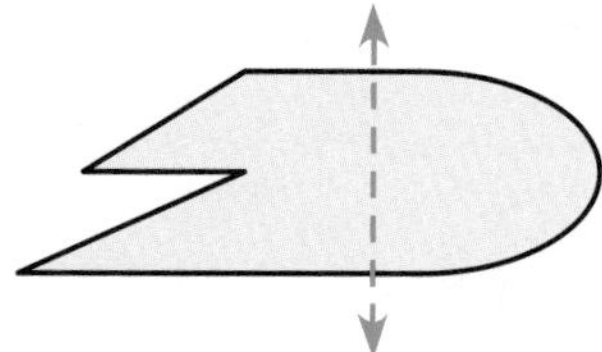

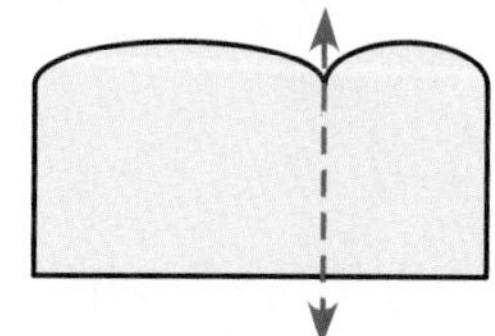

a. What do you need to find? ____________________

____

b. How can you tell if the line of symmetry is correct?

____

c. Tell how you solved the problem.

____

____

d. Circle the correct shape above.

15. MATHEMATICAL PRACTICE 2 **Reason Abstractly** Draw a line of symmetry in the figure shown.

Personal Math Trainer

16. THINK SMARTER + Evie's birthday is on the 18th of May. Since May is the 5th month, Evie wrote the date as shown.

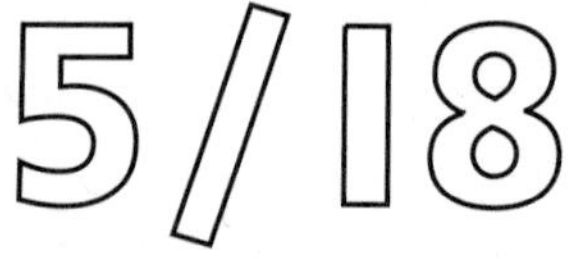

Evie says all the numbers she wrote have line symmetry. Is she correct? Explain.

____

____

____

FOR MORE PRACTICE:
Standards Practice Book

Name ____________________

Find and Draw Lines of Symmetry

Essential Question How do you find lines of symmetry?

Geometry—4.G.3

MATHEMATICAL PRACTICES
MP.1, MP.7, MP.8

Unlock the Problem

How many lines of symmetry does each polygon have?

Activity 1 Find lines of symmetry.

Materials ■ isometric and square dot paper ■ straightedge

STEP 1

Draw a triangle like the one shown, so all sides have equal length.

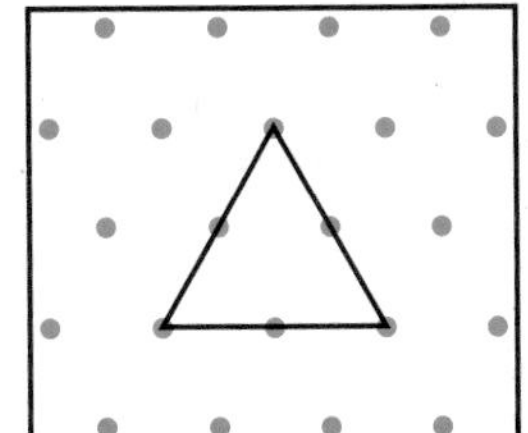

STEP 2

Fold the triangle in different ways to test for line symmetry. Draw along the fold lines that are lines of symmetry.

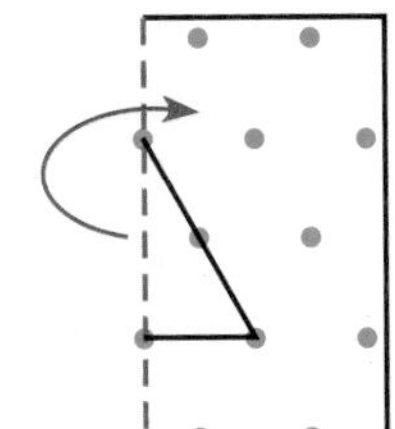

- Is there a line of symmetry if you fold the paper horizontally?

____

STEP 3

Repeat the steps for each polygon shown. Complete the table.

Polygon	Triangle	Square	Parallelogram	Rhombus	Trapezoid	Hexagon
Number of Sides	3					
Number of Lines of Symmetry	3					

- In a regular polygon, all sides are of equal length and all angles are equal. What do you notice about the number of lines of symmetry in regular polygons?

____

____

Math Talk **Mathematical Practices**

How many lines of symmetry does a circle have? **Explain.**

Activity 2 Make designs that have line symmetry.

Materials ■ pattern blocks

Make a design by using more than one pattern block.
Record your design. Draw the line or lines of symmetry.

ERROR Alert

To avoid errors, you may use a mirror to check for line symmetry.

Make a design with 2 lines of symmetry.

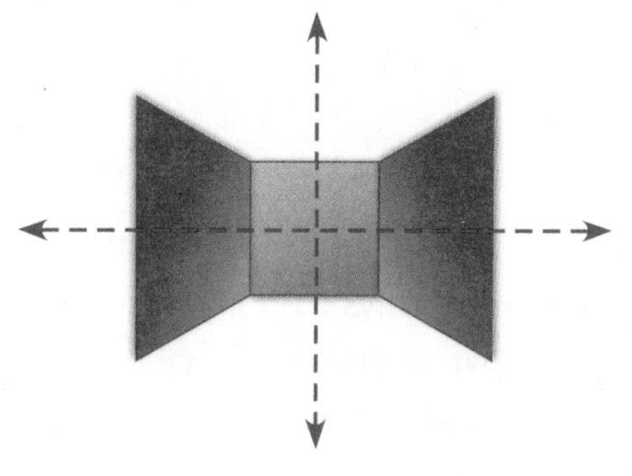

Make a design with 1 line of symmetry.

Make a design with more than 2 lines of symmetry.

Make a design with zero lines of symmetry.

Share and Show

1. The shape at the right has line symmetry. Draw the 2 lines of symmetry.

Name ___________________________

Tell whether the shape appears to have zero lines, 1 line, or more than 1 line of symmetry. Write *zero, 1,* or *more than 1.*

2.

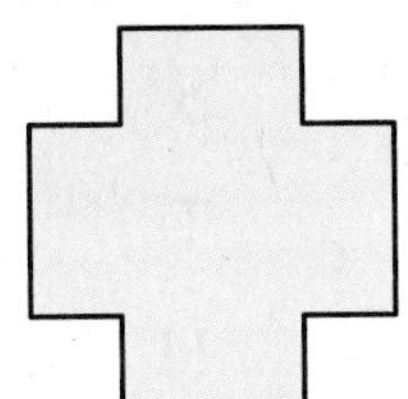

____

3.

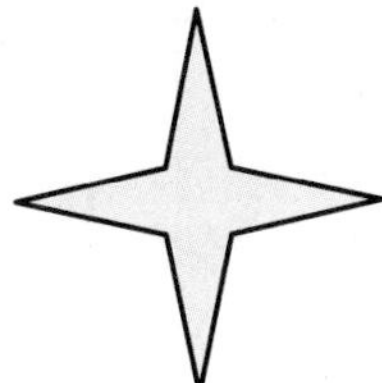

____

4.

____

5.

____

Math Talk **Mathematical Practices**

Explain how you can find lines of symmetry for a shape.

On Your Own

Tell whether the shape appears to have zero lines, 1 line, or more than 1 line of symmetry. Write *zero, 1,* or *more than 1.*

6.

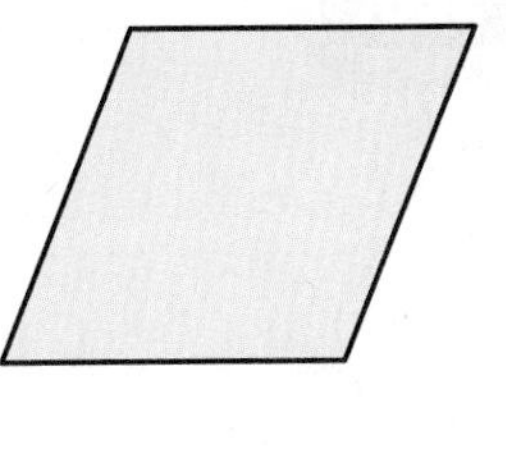

____

7.

____

8.

____

9.

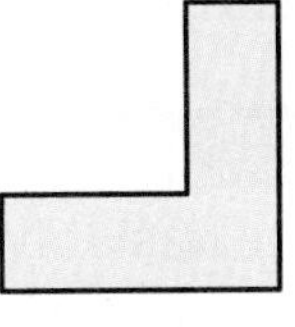

____

Practice: Copy and Solve **Does the design have line symmetry? Write *yes* or *no*. If your answer is *yes*, draw all lines of symmetry.**

10.

11.

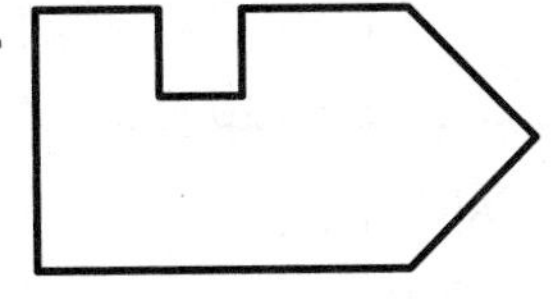

12.

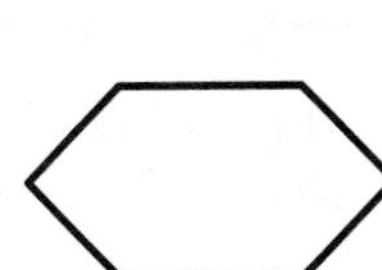

13.

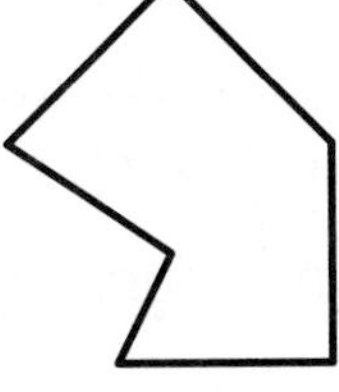

14. GO DEEPER Draw a figure that has 5 sides and exactly 1 line of symmetry.

Problem Solving • Applications

Use the chart for 15–17.

A	H	S
B	I	T
C	J	U
D	L	V
E	N	W

15. Which letters appear to have only 1 line of symmetry?

____

16. Which letters appear to have zero lines of symmetry?

____

17. THINK SMARTER The letter C has horizontal symmetry. The letter A has vertical symmetry. Which letters appear to have both horizontal and vertical symmetry?

____

18. MATHEMATICAL PRACTICE 3 **Verify the Reasoning of Others** Jeff says that the shape has only 2 lines of symmetry.

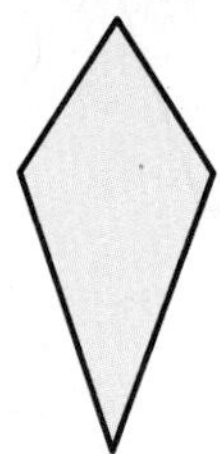

Does his statement make sense? Explain.

____

____

____

Personal Math Trainer

19. THINK SMARTER + Match each figure with the correct number of lines of symmetry it has.

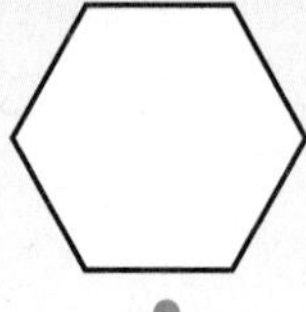

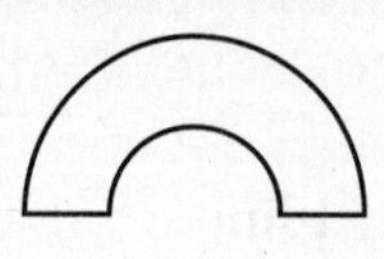

G

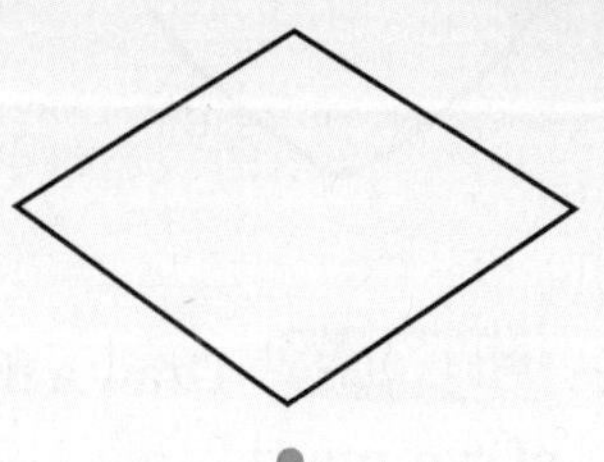

0 lines of symmetry	1 line of symmetry	2 lines of symmetry	More than 2 lines of symmetry

FOR MORE PRACTICE: Standards Practice Book

Name ______________________________

Problem Solving • Shape Patterns

Essential Question How can you use the strategy *act it out* to solve pattern problems?

Operations and Algebraic Thinking—4.OA.5

MATHEMATICAL PRACTICES
MP.4, MP.7, MP.8

Unlock the Problem

You can find patterns in fabric, pottery, rugs, and wall coverings. You can see patterns in shape, size, position, color, or number of figures.

Sofia will use the pattern below to make a wallpaper border. What might be the next three figures in the pattern?

Use the graphic organizer below to solve the problem.

Read the Problem

What do I need to find?	What information do I need to use?	How will I use the information?
I need to find the next three ____________ in the pattern.	I need to use the ____________ of each figure in Sofia's pattern.	I will use pattern blocks to model the ____________ and act out the problem.

Solve the Problem

Describe how you acted out the problem to solve it.

I used a trapezoid and triangle to model the first figure in the pattern. I used a ________________ and ________________ to model the second figure in the pattern. I continued to model the pattern by repeating the models of the first two figures.

These are the next three figures in the pattern.

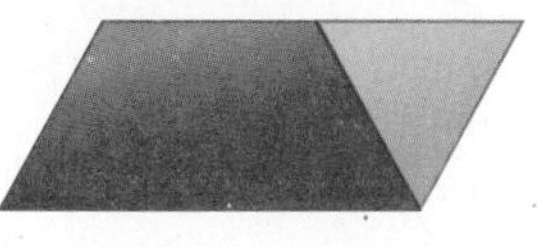 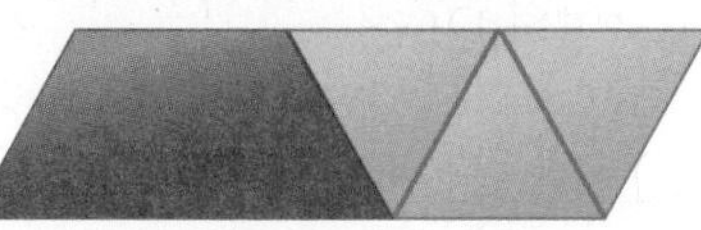 

Math Talk **Mathematical Practices**

Explain how you can describe the shape pattern using numbers.

Try Another Problem

Draw what might be the next figure in the pattern.

Figure: 1 2 3 4 ______ 5

How can you describe the pattern?

Read the Problem

What do I need to find?	What information do I need to use?	How will I use the information?

Solve the Problem

1. Use the figures to write a number pattern. Then describe the pattern in the numbers.

______

______

______

Math Talk **Mathematical Practices**

What other strategy could you use to solve the problem?

2. What might the tenth number in your pattern be? Explain.

______

______

Name ___________________________

Share and Show

Unlock the Problem

√ Use the Problem Solving MathBoard.
√ Underline the important facts.
√ Choose a strategy you know.

1. Marisol is making a pattern with blocks. What might the missing shape be?

First, look at the blocks.

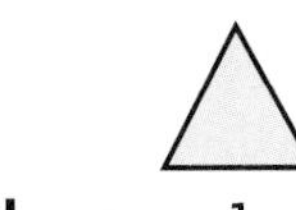
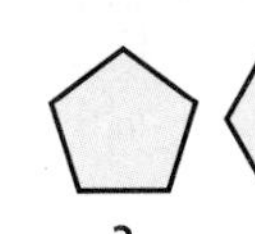
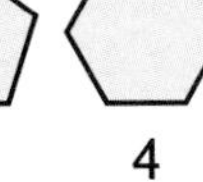
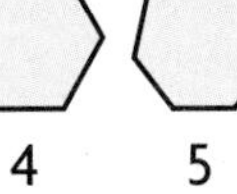

?

Shape: 1 2 3 4 5

Next, describe the pattern.

____

____

Finally, draw the missing shape.

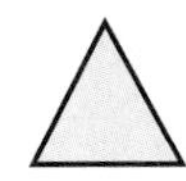

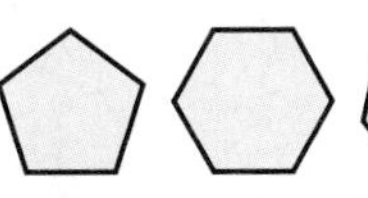

Shape: 1 2 3 4 5

2. Use the shapes to write a number pattern. Then describe the pattern in the numbers.

____

3. THINK SMARTER What if the pattern continued? Write an expression to describe the number of sides the sixth shape has in Marisol's pattern.

____

4. Sahil made a pattern using circles. The first nine circles are shown. Describe the pattern. If Sahil continues the pattern, what might the next three circles be?

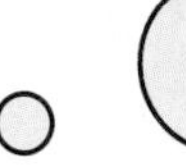
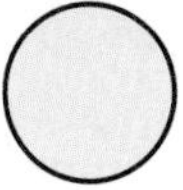

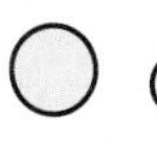

____

On Your Own

Use the toy quilt designs for 5–6.

5. THINK SMARTER Lu is making a quilt that is 20 squares wide and has 24 rows. The border of the quilt is made by using each toy design equally as often. Each square can hold one design. How many of each design does she use for the border?

____

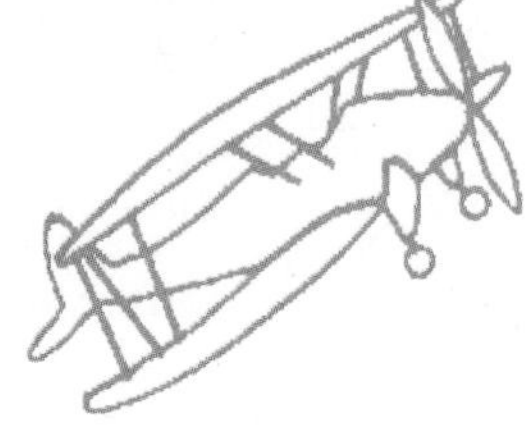
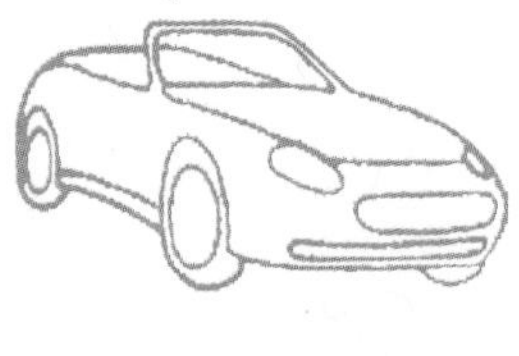

6. MATHEMATICAL PRACTICE 5 **Communicate** Starting in the first square of her quilt, Lu lined up her toy designs in this order: plane, car, fire truck, helicopter, crane, and wagon. Using this pattern unit, which design will Lu place in the fifteenth square? Explain how you found your answer.

____

____

____

____

7. GO DEEPER Missy uses 1 hexagonal, 2 rectangular, and 4 triangular pieces of fabric to make 1 bug design for a quilt. If she uses 70 pieces in all to make bug designs, how many of each shape does she use?

____

8. THINK SMARTER Norris drew the pattern shown.

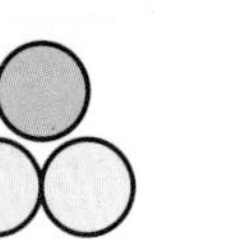
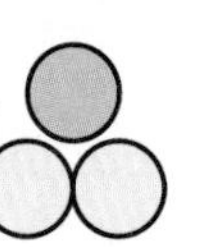
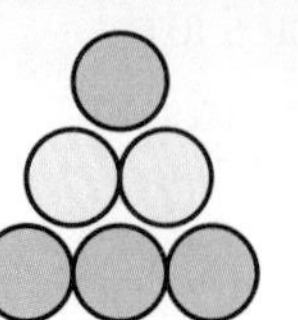
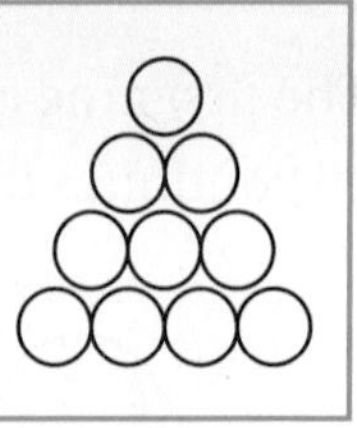
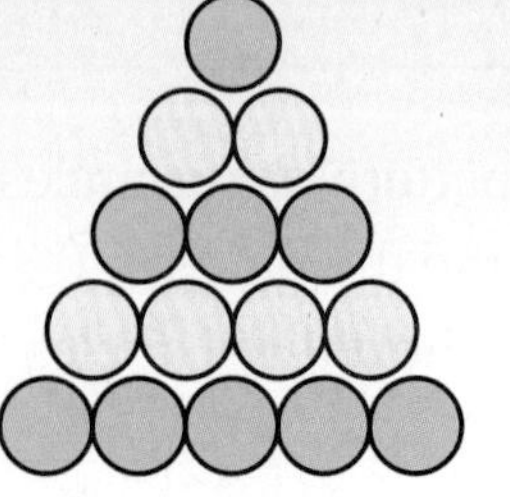

Label the circles to show the colors in the fourth figure of the pattern.

FOR MORE PRACTICE:
Standards Practice Book

Name ___________________________________

Chapter 10 Review/Test

1. Gavin is designing a kite. He sketched a picture of the kite. How many right angles does the kite appear to have?

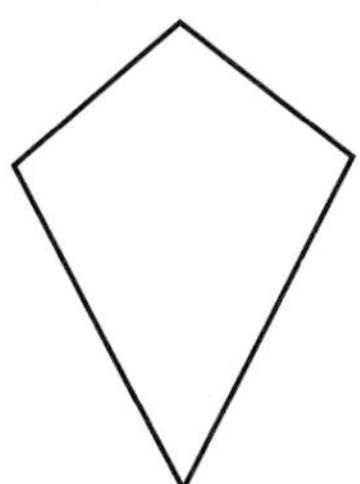

_____ right angles

2. Write the letter of the triangle under its correct classification.

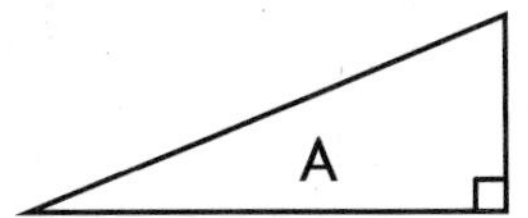

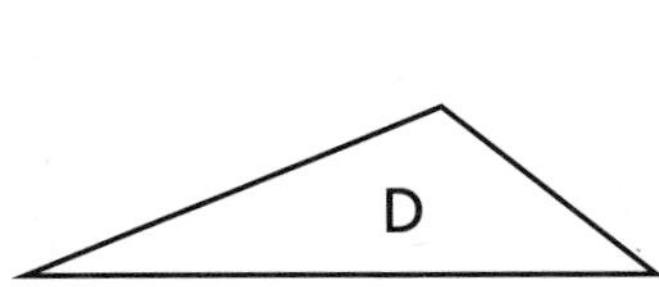

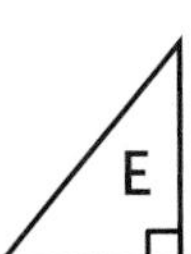

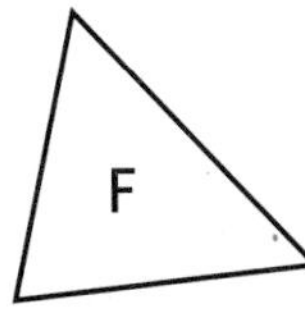

Acute Triangle	Obtuse Triangle	Right Triangle

3. Select the lengths that identify a scalene triangle. Mark all that apply.

Ⓐ 5 inches, 5 inches, 6 inches

Ⓑ 2 meters, 3 meters, 4 meters

Ⓒ 9 feet, 9 feet, 9 feet

Ⓓ 11 meters, 6 meters, 15 meters

Ⓔ 6 feet, 3 feet, 6 feet

GO DIGITAL Assessment Options Chapter Test

4. Write the word that describes the part of Figure A written below.

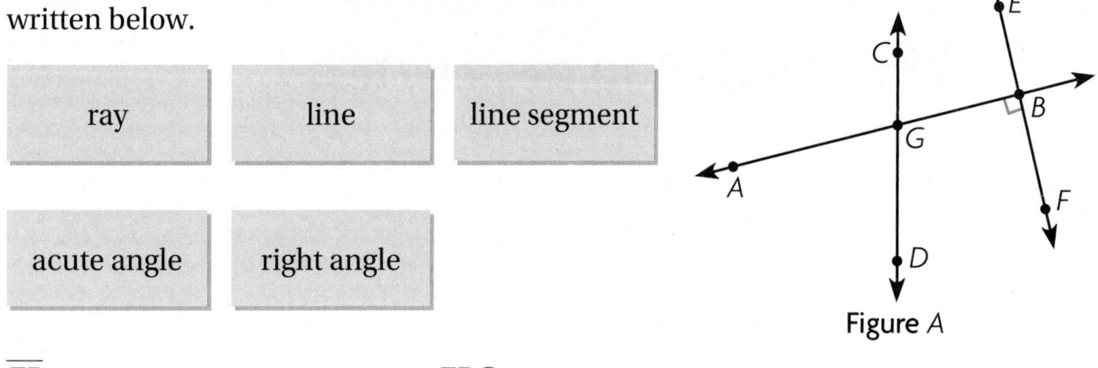

$\overline{EB}$ ______________ $\angle EBG$ ______________

$\overleftrightarrow{AB}$ ______________ $\angle CGB$ ______________

$\overrightarrow{GA}$ ______________

5. What term best describes the figure shown below?

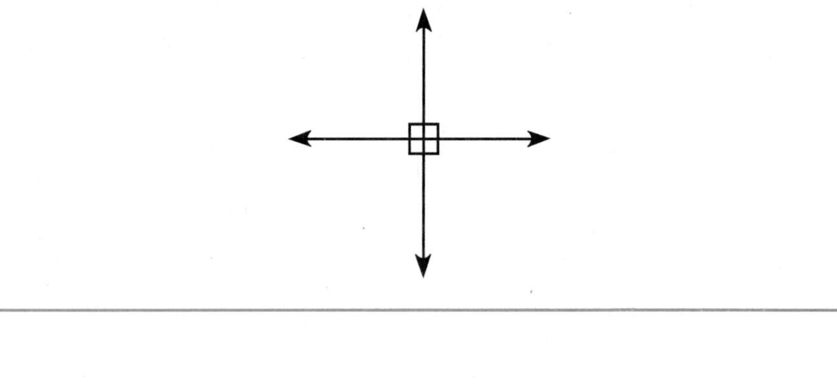

6. Naomi leaves for her trip to Los Angeles on the 12th day of August. Since August is the 8th month, Naomi wrote the date as shown.

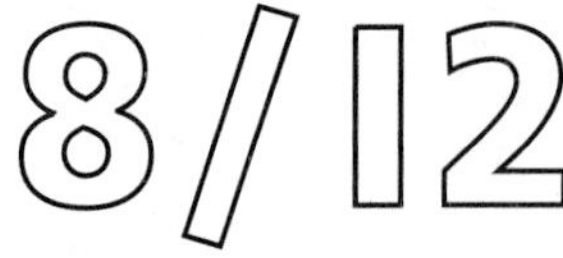

Naomi says all the numbers she wrote have line symmetry. Is she correct? Explain your thinking.

Name ________________________________

7. Max made a pennant that looks like a triangle. How can you classify the triangle based upon its angles?

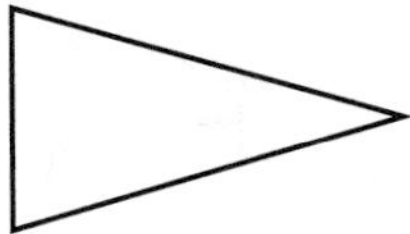

The triangle is a(n) ____________ triangle.

8. Choose the labels to make a true statement.

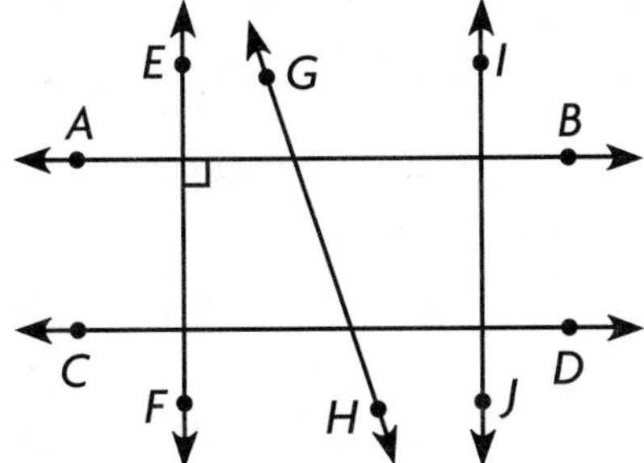

$\overleftrightarrow{GH}$ $\overleftrightarrow{CD}$ $\overleftrightarrow{AB}$	is parallel to	$\overleftrightarrow{EF}$ $\overleftrightarrow{CD}$ $\overleftrightarrow{GH}$	.

9. Classify the figure. Select all that apply.

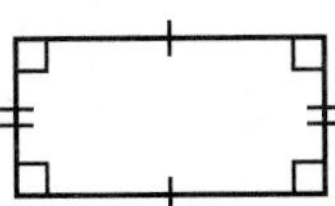

○ quadrilateral ○ rectangle

○ trapezoid ○ rhombus

○ parallelogram ○ square

10. Lily designed a deck in her backyard that looks like a quadrilateral that has only 1 pair of parallel sides. How can you classify the figure?

The quadrilateral is a ______________.

11. Match each figure with the correct number of lines of symmetry it has.

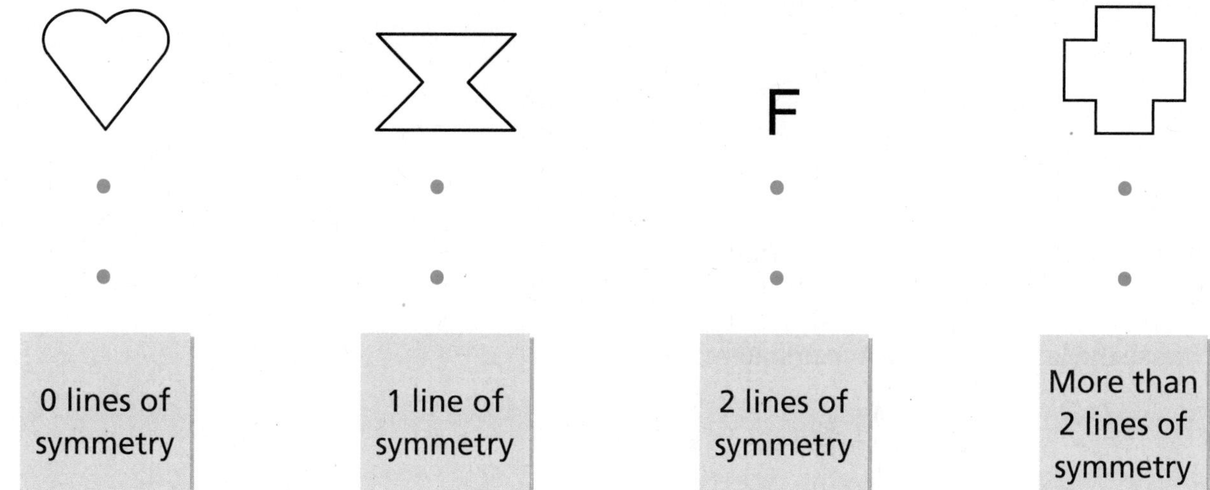

12. Barb drew the pattern shown.

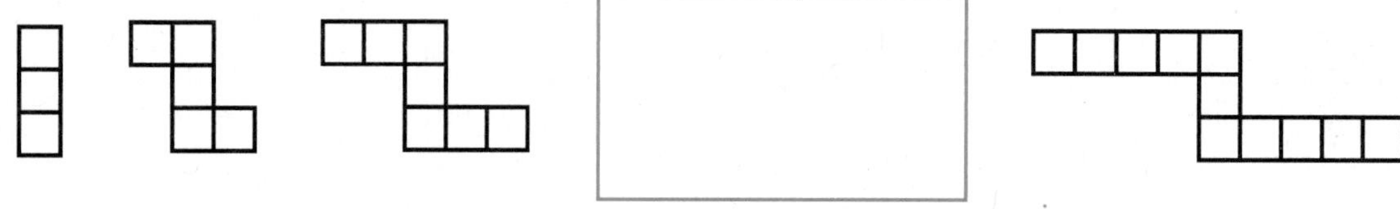

Use the square shown to draw the missing pattern. □

13. Claudia drew the figure below. Draw a line of symmetry on Claudia's figure.

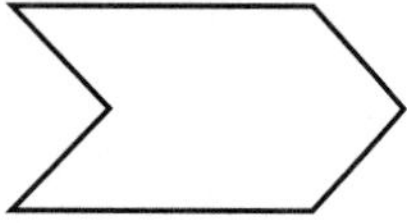

14. Write the word or words that best describe this figure.

15. How many acute angles does a right triangle have?

A right triangle has ______ acute angles.

Name ___________________________

16. Mike drew a figure with opposite sides parallel. Write the pairs of parallel sides. What figure is it?

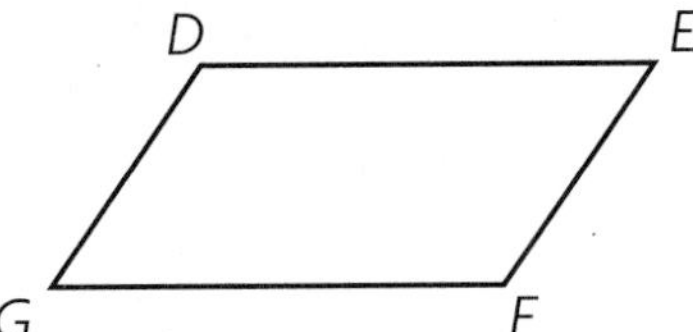

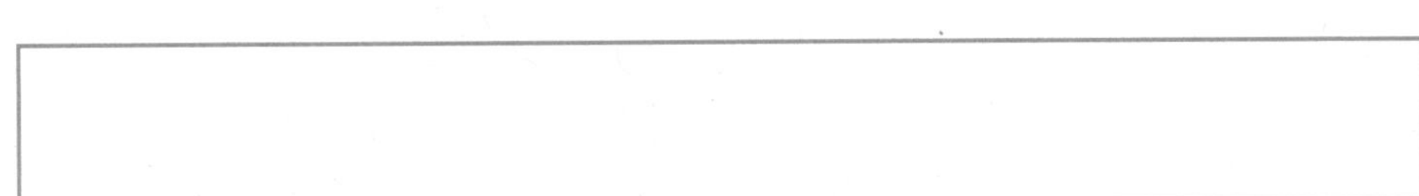

17. Circle the letter that does not have line symmetry.

DOTS

18. Joseph made a pattern using ovals and rectangles. The first four figures of his pattern are shown. Draw the next figure in the pattern.

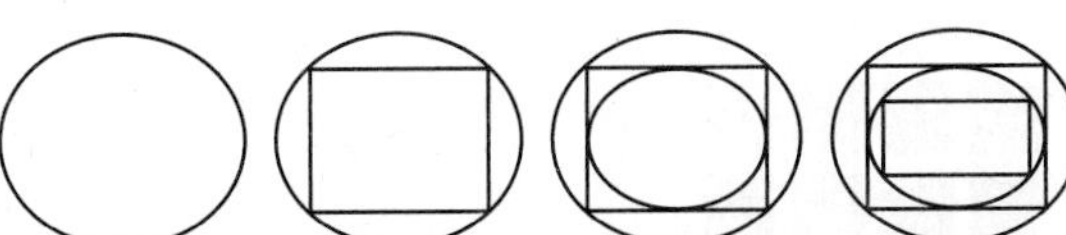

Figure 1 **Figure 2** **Figure 3** **Figure 4** **Figure 5**

19. Jeremy drew Figure 1 and Louisa drew Figure 2.

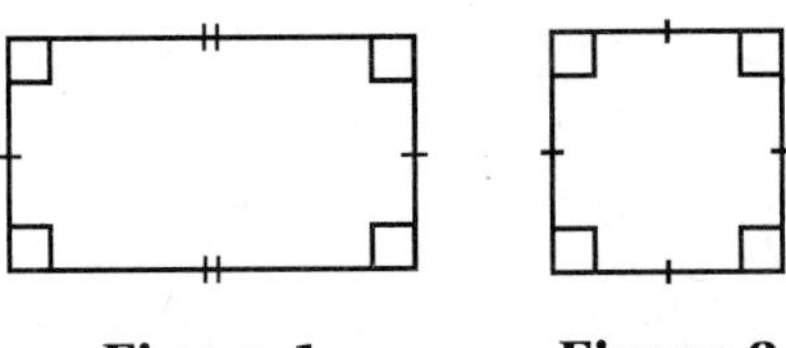

Figure 1 **Figure 2**

Part A

Jeremy says both figures are rectangles. Do you agree with Jeremy? Support your answer.

Part B

Louisa says both figures are rhombuses. Do you agree with Louisa? Support your answer.

20. Veronica found the number of lines of symmetry for the figure below. How many lines of symmetry does it have?

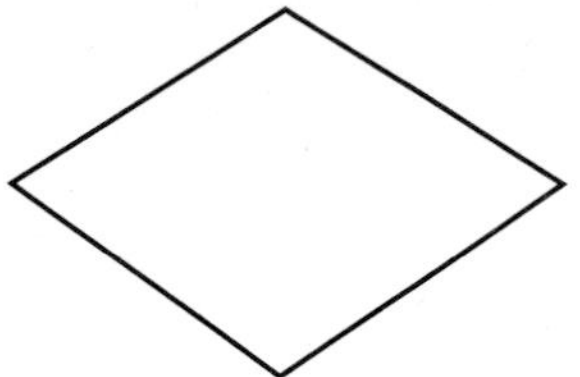

_____ lines of symmetry

21. Judy drew an isosceles triangle. One side of the triangle was 5 inches long. The other side of the triangle was 8 inches long. What could be the length of the third side of the triangle Judy drew? Explain your reasoning.

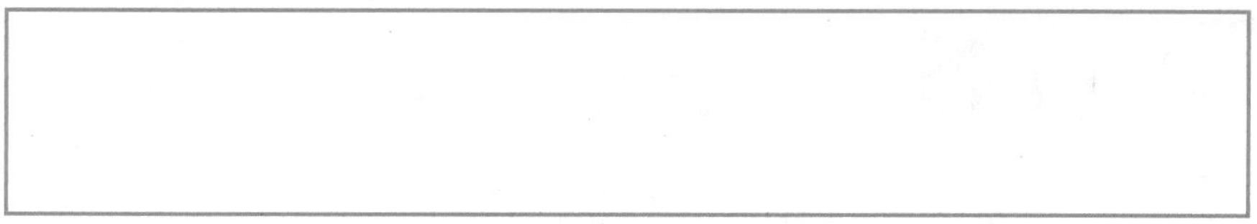

22. Jordan drew the pattern below.

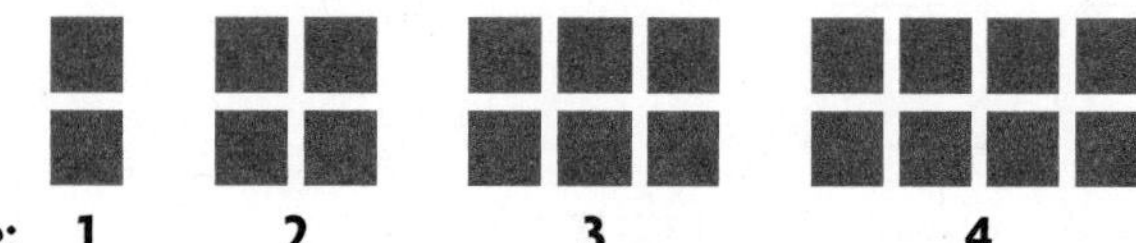

Part A

Describe the pattern.

Part B

Write a rule using numbers to find the number of squares in any figure in the pattern.

Part C

Draw Figure 5.

Chapter 11

Angles

Show What You Know 

Check your understanding of important skills.

Name ______________________

▶ Use a Metric Ruler Use a centimeter ruler to measure. Find the length in centimeters.

1. 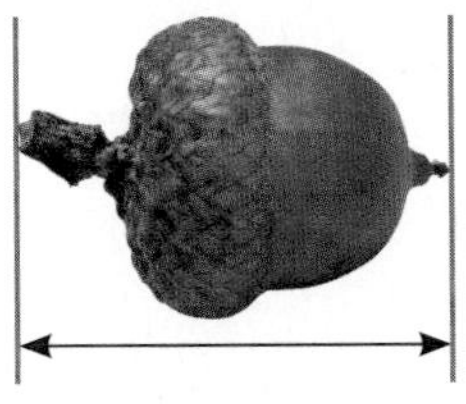

_____ centimeters

2. 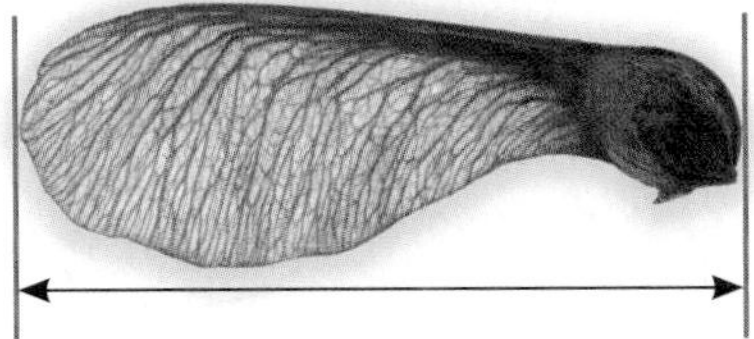

_____ centimeters

▶ Classify Angles Classify the angle. Write *acute, right,* or *obtuse*.

3. 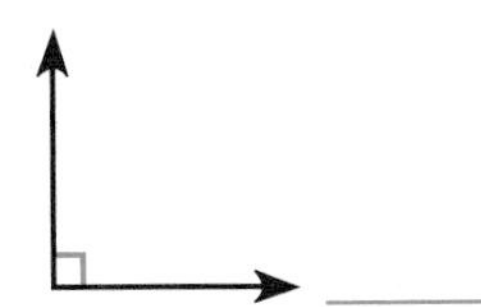 _______

4.  _______

5. 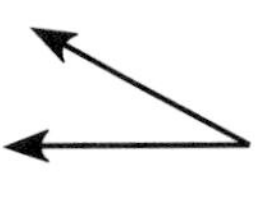 _______

▶ Parts of a Whole Write a fraction for each shaded part.

6. 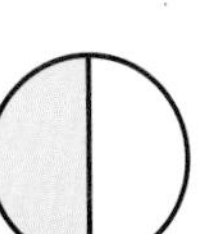 _______

7.  _______

8.  _______

9. 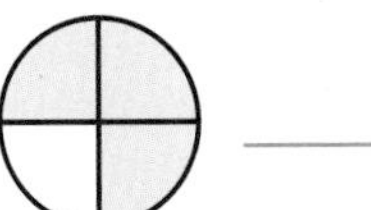 _______

The Sunshine Skyway Bridge crosses over Tampa Bay, Florida. Bridges and other building structures can model geometric figures. Be a Math Detective and investigate the bridge. Describe the geometric figures you see. Then classify the labeled angles and triangle.

Personal Math Trainer
Online Assessment and Intervention

Vocabulary Builder

▶ Visualize It

Complete the Bubble Map using review words.

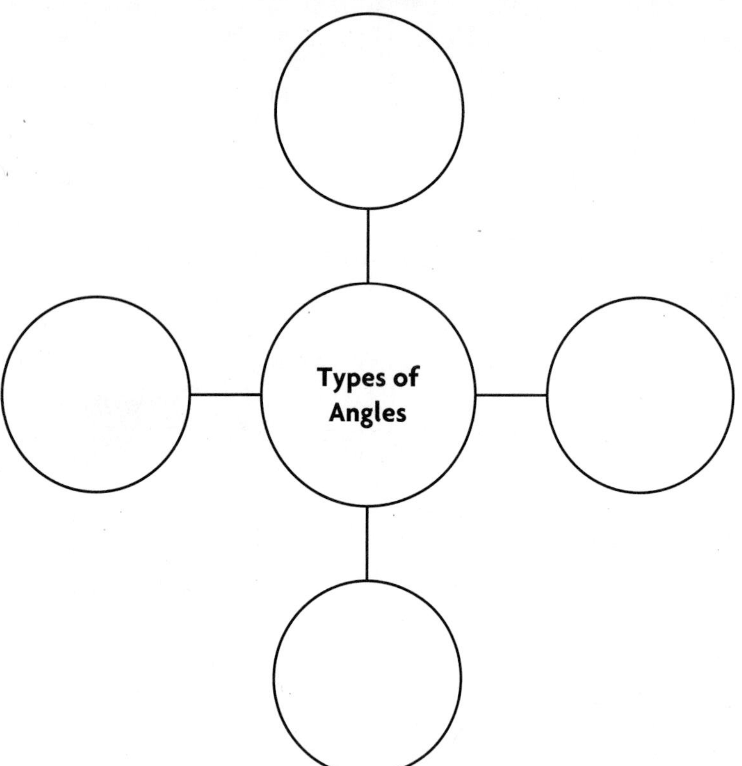

Review Words
acute
circle
obtuse
ray
right
straight
vertex

Preview Words
clockwise
counterclockwise
degree (°)
protractor

▶ Understand Vocabulary

Draw a line to match each word with its definition.

1. protractor
2. degree(°)
3. clockwise
4. counterclockwise

- In the same direction in which the hands of a clock move
- In the opposite direction in which the hands of a clock move
- A tool for measuring the size of an angle
- The unit used for measuring angles

GO DIGITAL
- Interactive Student Edition
- Multimedia eGlossary

Name ______________________

Angles and Fractional Parts of a Circle

Essential Question How can you relate angles and fractional parts of a circle?

Measurement and Data—4.MD.5a

MATHEMATICAL PRACTICES
MP.2, MP.3, MP.5

Hands On

Investigate

Materials ■ fraction circles

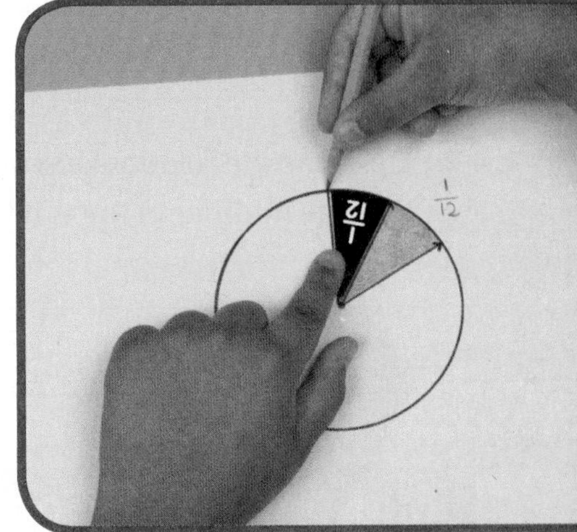

A. Place a $\frac{1}{12}$ piece on the circle. Place the tip of the fraction piece on the center of the circle. Trace the fraction piece to create an angle.

What parts of the fraction piece represent the rays of the angle? ______________

Where is the vertex of the angle?

____

B. Shade the angle formed by the $\frac{1}{12}$ piece. Label it $\frac{1}{12}$.

C. Place the $\frac{1}{12}$ piece back on the shaded angle. Turn it counterclockwise. **Counterclockwise** is the direction opposite from the way the hands move on a clock.

Trace the fraction piece in its new position. How many twelfths have you traced in all? ______ Label $\frac{2}{12}$.

D. Turn the fraction piece counterclockwise again and trace it. Label the total number of twelfths.

Continue until you reach the shaded angle.

How many times did you need to turn the $\frac{1}{12}$ piece to make a circle? __________

How many angles come together in the center of the circle? __________

Draw Conclusions

1. Compare the size of the angle formed by a $\frac{1}{4}$ piece and the size of the angle formed by a $\frac{1}{12}$ piece. Use a $\frac{1}{4}$ piece and your model on page 441 to help.

____

____

____

2. Describe the relationship between the size of the fraction piece and the number of turns it takes to make a circle.

____

____

Make Connections

You can relate fractions and angles to the hands of a clock.

Let the hands of the clock represent the rays of an angle. Each 5-minute mark represents a $\frac{1}{12}$ turn **clockwise**.

15 minutes elapse.

The minute hand makes a

__________ turn clockwise.

30 minutes elapse.

The minute hand makes a

__________ turn clockwise.

45 minutes elapse.

The minute hand makes a

__________ turn clockwise.

60 minutes elapse.

The minute hand makes a

__________ turn clockwise.

Math Talk **Mathematical Practices**

Explain how an angle formed in a circle using a $\frac{1}{4}$ fraction piece is like a $\frac{1}{4}$ turn and 15 minutes elapsing on a clock.

Name ____________________

Share and Show 

Tell what fraction of the circle the shaded angle represents.

1. 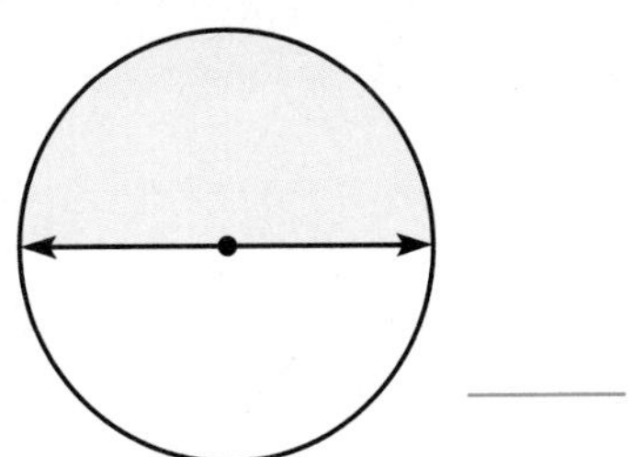

2. 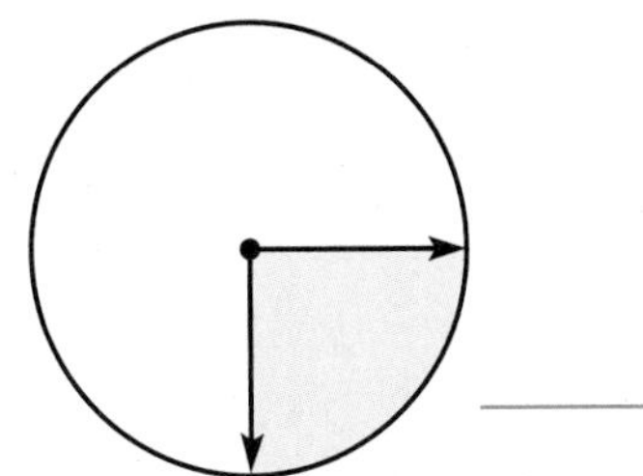

3. 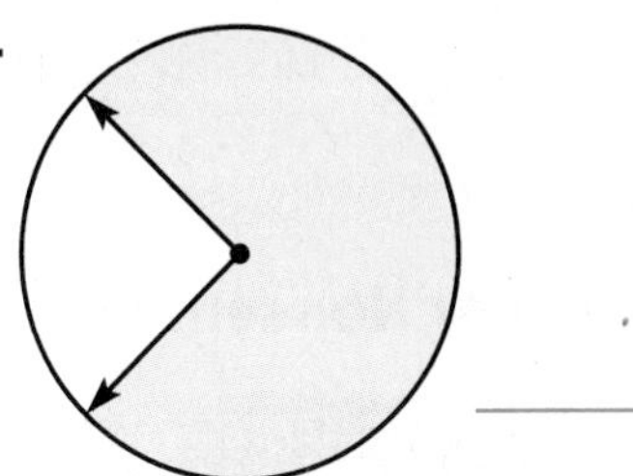

4. 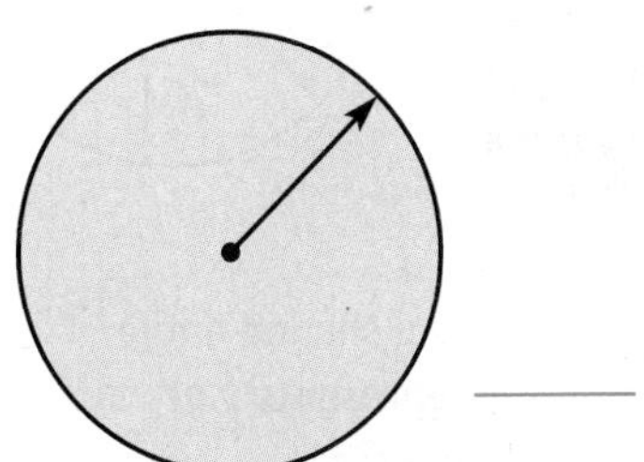

5. 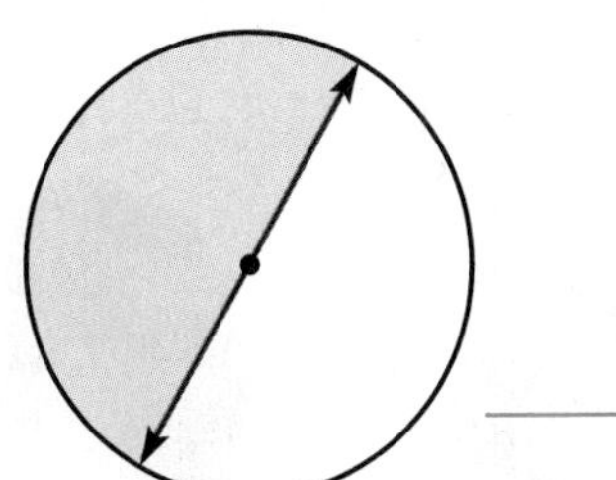

6. 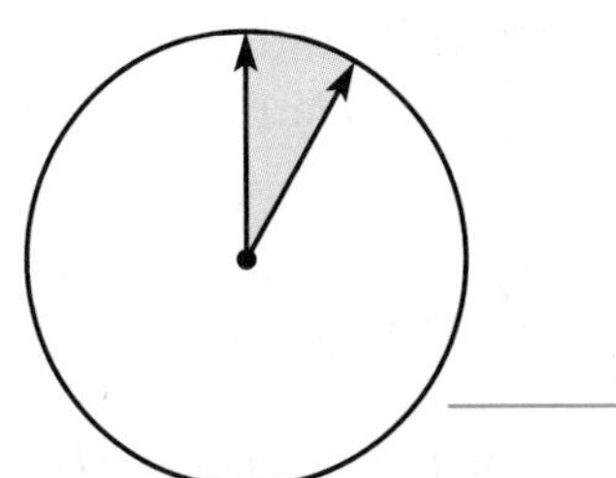

Tell whether the angle on the circle shows a $\frac{1}{4}$, $\frac{1}{2}$, $\frac{3}{4}$, or 1 full turn clockwise or counterclockwise.

7. 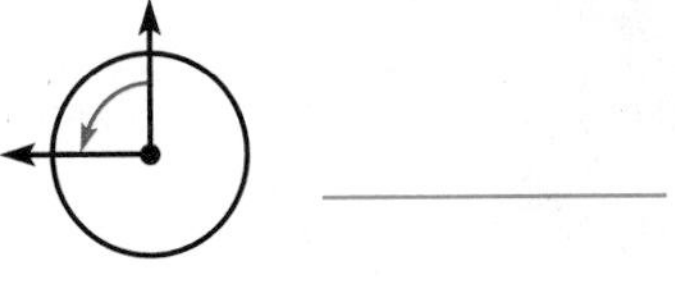

8. 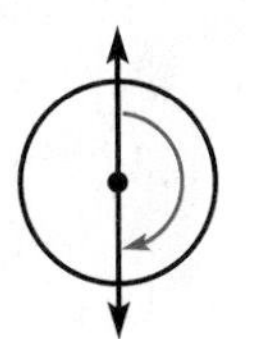

9. 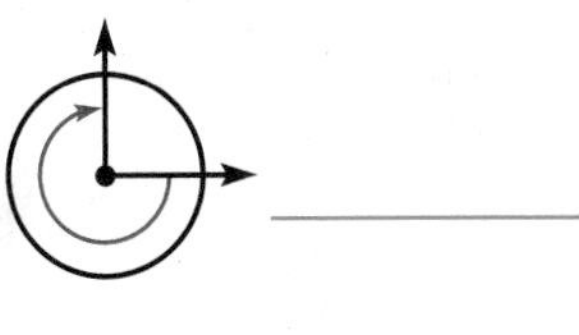

Problem Solving • Applications 

10. MATHEMATICAL PRACTICE 1 Susan watched the game from 1 P.M. to 1:30 P.M. **Describe** the turn the minute hand made.

11. GO DEEPER Compare the angles in Exercises 1 and 5. Does the position of the angle affect the size of the angle? Explain.

Personal Math Trainer

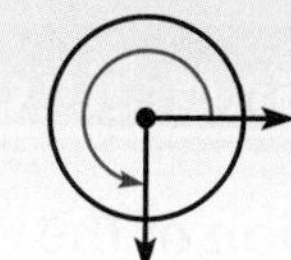

12. THINK SMARTER + Malcolm drew this angle on the circle. Which of the following describes the angle? Mark all that apply.

○ $\frac{3}{4}$ turn ○ clockwise

○ $\frac{1}{4}$ turn ○ counterclockwise

Sense or Nonsense?

13. THINK SMARTER Whose statement makes sense? Whose statement is nonsense? Explain your reasoning.

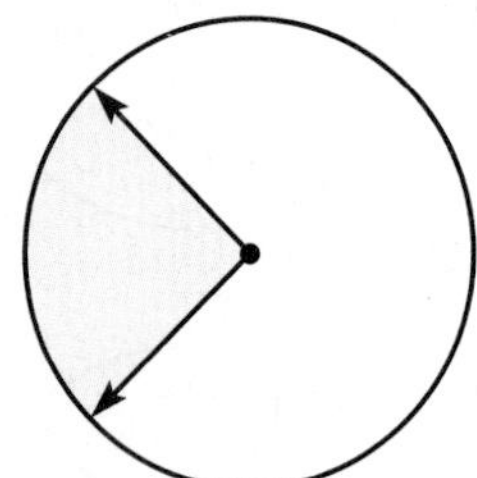

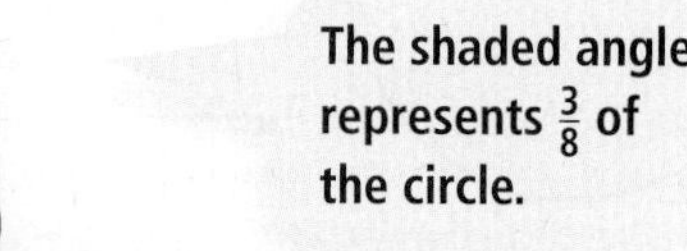

The shaded angle represents $\frac{3}{8}$ of the circle.

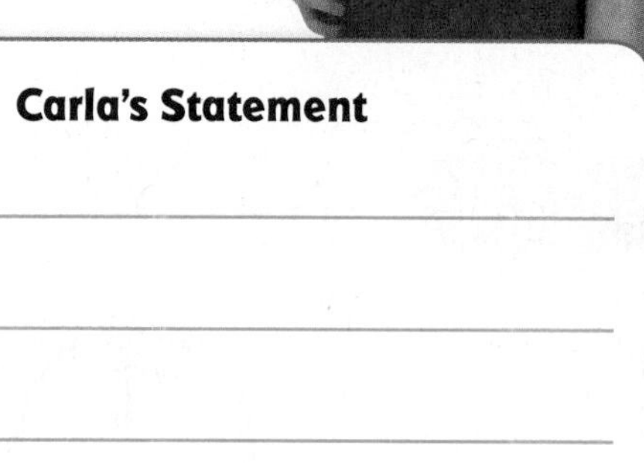

The shaded angle represents $\frac{1}{4}$ of the circle.

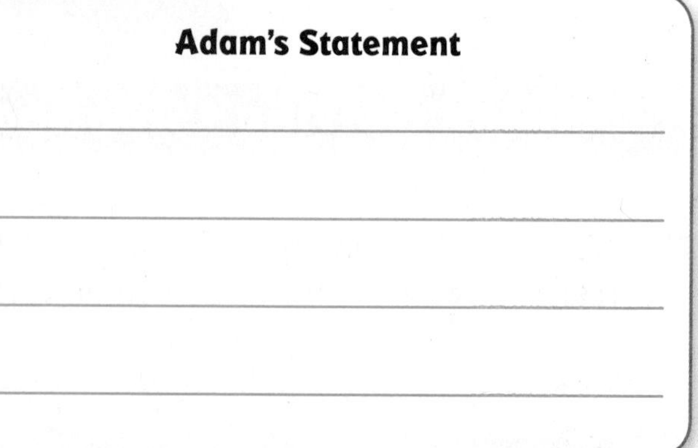

Carla's Statement

Adam's Statement

- For the statement that is nonsense, write a statement that makes sense.

- What is another way to describe the size of the angle? Explain.

FOR MORE PRACTICE: Standards Practice Book

Name ______________________________

Degrees

Essential Question How are degrees related to fractional parts of a circle?

Measurement and Data—4.MD.5a, 4.MD.5b

MATHEMATICAL PRACTICES
MP.1, MP.2, MP.5

CONNECT You can use what you know about angles and fractional parts of a circle to understand angle measurement. Angles are measured in units called **degrees**. Think of a circle divided into 360 equal parts. An angle that turns through $\frac{1}{360}$ of the circle measures 1 degree.

Math Idea
The symbol for degrees is °.

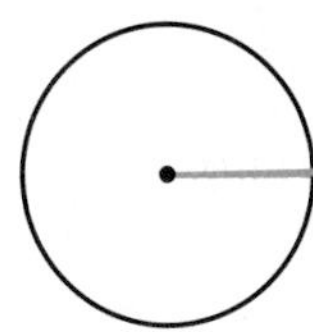

Unlock the Problem

The angle between two spokes on the bicycle wheel turns through $\frac{10}{360}$ of a circle. What is the measure of the angle formed between the spokes?

- What part of an angle does a spoke represent?

____

____

Example 1 Use fractional parts to find the angle measure.

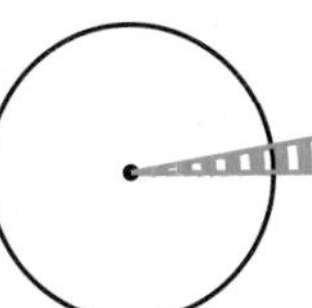

Each $\frac{1}{360}$ turn measures ______ degree.

Ten $\frac{1}{360}$ turns measure ______ degrees.

So, the measure of the angle between the spokes is ______.

Math Talk Mathematical Practices

How many degrees is the measure of an angle that turns through 1 whole circle? **Explain.**

▲ The Penny Farthing bicycle was built in the 1800s.

Example 2 Find the measure of a right angle.

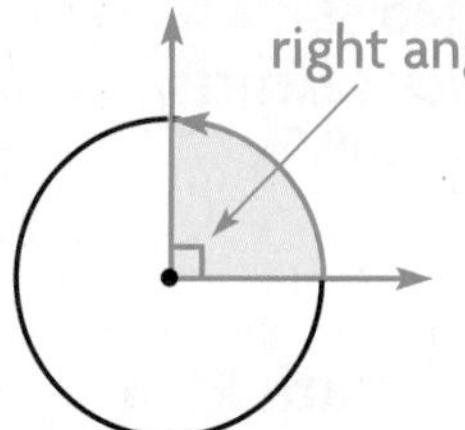

Think: Through what fraction of a circle

does a right angle turn? ______

STEP 1 Write $\frac{1}{4}$ as an equivalent fraction with 360 in the denominator.

$\frac{1}{4} = \frac{\square}{360}$ **Think:** 4 × 9 = 36, so 4 × ______ = 360.

STEP 2 Write $\frac{90}{360}$ in degrees.

An angle that turns through $\frac{1}{360}$ of a circle measures ______.

An angle that turns through $\frac{90}{360}$ of a circle measures ______.

So, a right angle measures ______.

Remember

To write an equivalent fraction, multiply the numerator and denominator by the same factor.

Try This! Find the measure of a straight angle.

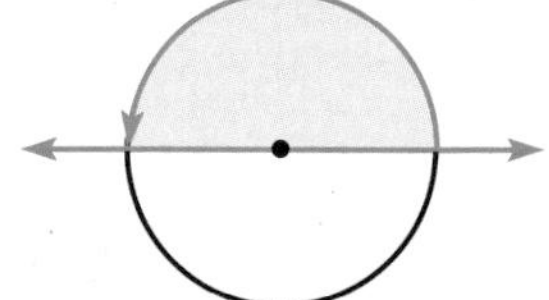

Through what fraction of a circle does a straight angle turn? ______

Write $\frac{1}{2}$ as an equivalent fraction with 360 in the denominator.

$\frac{1}{2} = \frac{\square}{360}$ **Think:** 2 × 18 = 36, so 2 × ______ = 360.

So, a straight angle measures ______.

1. How can you describe the measure of an acute angle in degrees?

2. How can you describe the measure of an obtuse angle in degrees?

Name ______________________________

Share and Show

1. Find the measure of the angle.

Through what fraction of a circle does the angle turn? ______

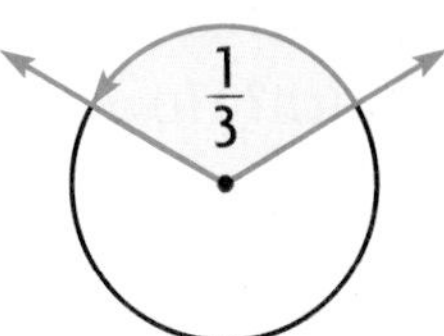

$\frac{1}{3} = \frac{\square}{360}$ Think: 3 × 12 = 36, so 3 × ______ = 360.

So, the measure of the angle is ______.

Tell the measure of the angle in degrees.

2.

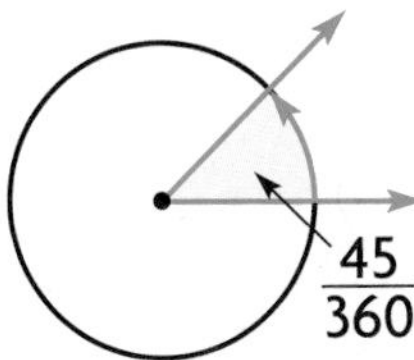

______

3.

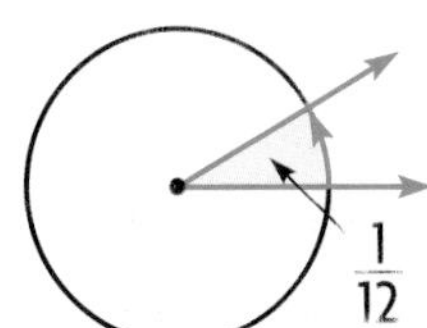

______

Math Talk **Mathematical Practices**

If an angle measures 60°, through what fraction of a circle does it turn? **Explain.**

On Your Own

Tell the measure of the angle in degrees.

4.

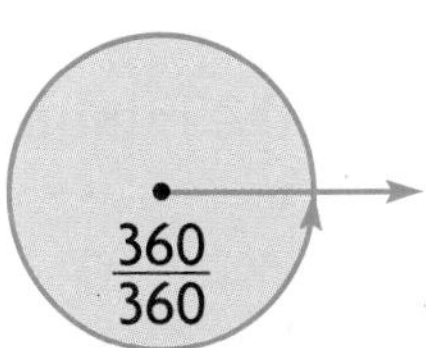

______

5.

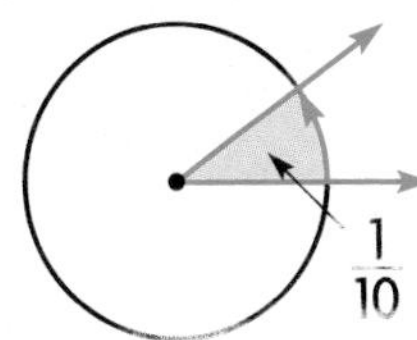

______

Classify the angle. Write *acute, obtuse, right,* or *straight.*

6.

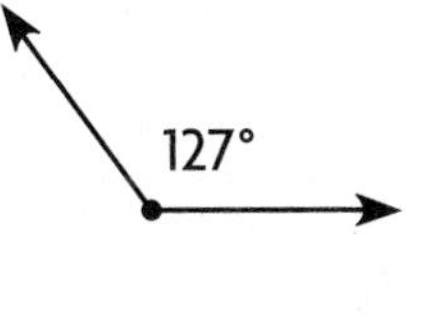

______

7.

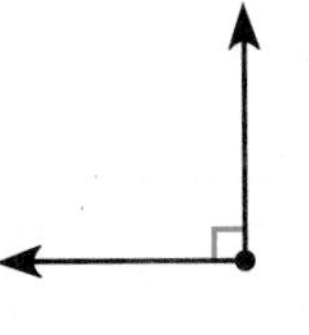

______

8.

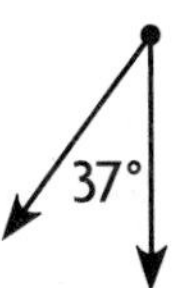

______

9.

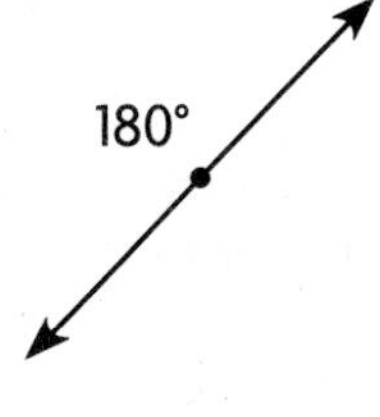

______

10. MATHEMATICAL PRACTICE 6 Is this an obtuse angle? **Explain.**

____

____

____

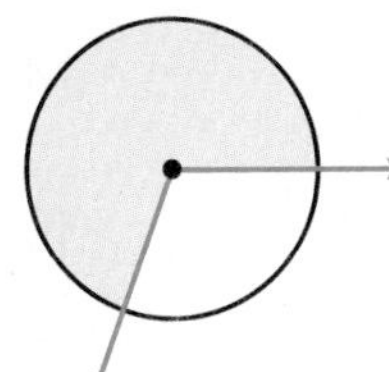

11. GO DEEPER Alex cut a circular pizza into 8 equal slices. He removed 2 of the slices of pizza. What is the measure of the angle made by the missing slices of pizza?

____

Unlock the Problem — Real World

12. THINK SMARTER Ava started reading at 3:30 P.M. She stopped for a snack at 4:15 P.M. During this time, through what fraction of a circle did the minute hand turn? How many degrees did the minute hand turn?

a. What are you asked to find? ____________________

____

b. What information can you use to find the fraction of a circle through which the minute hand turned?

____

____

c. How can you use the fraction of a circle through which the minute hand turned to find how many degrees it turned?

____

____

d. Show the steps to solve the problem.

STEP 1 $\frac{3 \times \square}{4 \times \square} = \frac{?}{360}$

STEP 2 $\frac{3 \times 90}{4 \times 90} = \frac{\square}{360}$

e. Complete the sentences.

From 3:30 P.M. to 4:15 P.M., the minute hand made a ______ turn clockwise.

The minute hand turned ______ degrees.

13. THINK SMARTER An angle represents $\frac{1}{15}$ of a circle. Select the number to show how to find the measure of the angle in degrees.

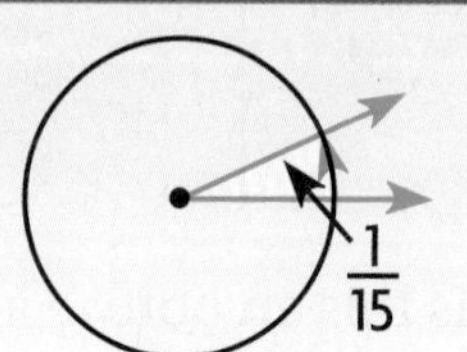

$\frac{1}{15} = \frac{1 \times \square}{15 \times \square} = \frac{\square}{360}$

20

24

30

The angle measures ____________.

FOR MORE PRACTICE: Standards Practice Book

Lesson 11.3

Name ______________________________

Measure and Draw Angles

Essential Question How can you use a protractor to measure and draw angles?

Measurement and Data—4.MD.6
MATHEMATICAL PRACTICES
MP.4, MP.5, MP.6,

Unlock the Problem Real World

Emma wants to make a clay sculpture of her daughter as she appears in the photo from her dance recital. How can she measure $\angle DCE$, or the angle formed by her daughter's arms?

A **protractor** is a tool for measuring the size of an angle.

Activity Measure $\angle DCE$ using a protractor.

Materials ■ protractor

STEP 1 Place the center point of the protractor on vertex *C* of the angle.

Align center point and vertex.

STEP 2 Align the 0° mark on the scale of the protractor with ray *CE*.

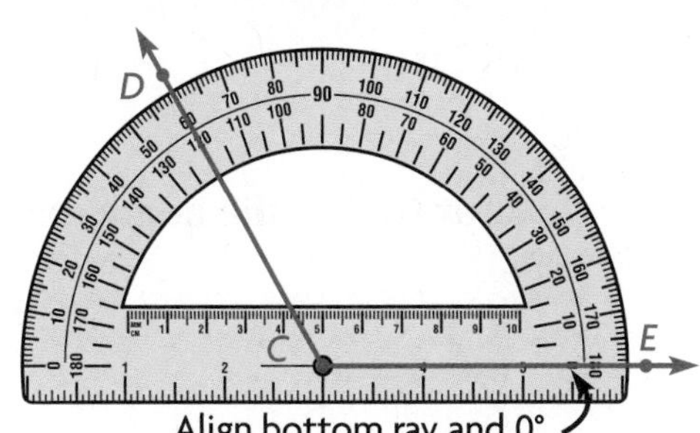

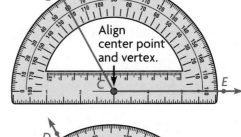

Align bottom ray and 0°.

STEP 3 Find where ray *CD* intersects the same scale. Read the angle measure on that scale. Extend the ray if you need to.

m$\angle DCE$ = ______

Read m$\angle DCE$ as "the measure of angle *DCE*".

Read the scale.

So, the angle formed by Emma's daughter's arms is ______.

Math Talk Mathematical Practices

Can you line up either ray of the angle with the protractor when measuring? **Explain.**

Draw Angles You can also use a protractor to draw an angle of a given measure.

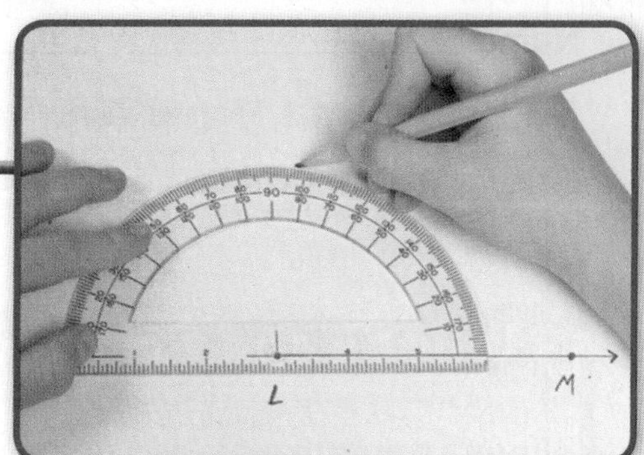

Activity Draw ∠*KLM* with a measure of 82°.

Materials ■ protractor

STEP 1 Use the straight edge of the protractor to draw and label ray *LM*.

STEP 2 Place the center point of the protractor on point *L*. Align ray *LM* with the 0° mark on the protractor.

STEP 3 Using the same scale, mark a point at 82°. Label the point *K*.

STEP 4 Use the straight edge of the protractor to draw ray *LK*.

Share and Show

1. Measure ∠*ABC*.

   Place the center of the protractor on point ______.

   Align ray *BC* with ______.

   Read where ____________ intersects the same scale.

   So, m∠*ABC* is ______.

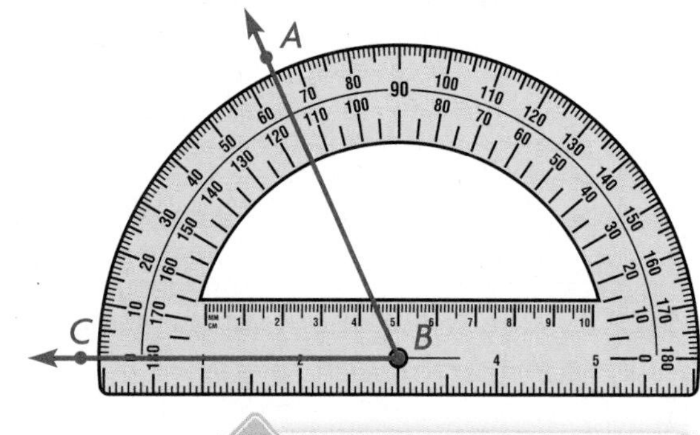

ERROR Alert

Be sure to use the correct scale on the protractor. Ask yourself: Is the measure reasonable?

Use a protractor to find the angle measure.

2. 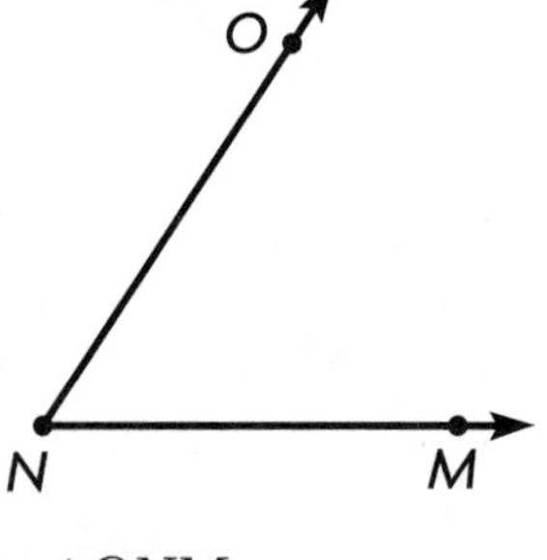

   m∠*ONM* = ______

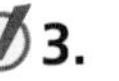3. 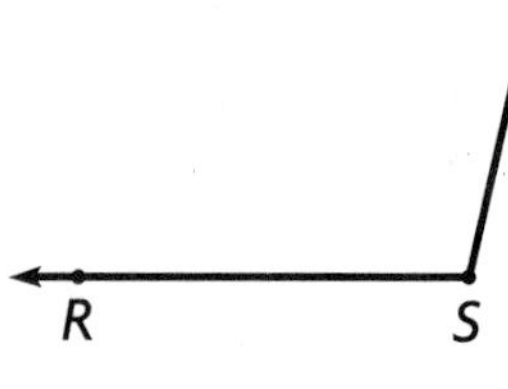

   m∠*TSR* = ______

Use a protractor to draw the angle.

4. 170°

5. 78°

Math Talk **Mathematical Practices**

Describe how drawing and measuring angles are similar.

Name ___________________________________

On Your Own

Use a protractor to find the angle measure.

6.

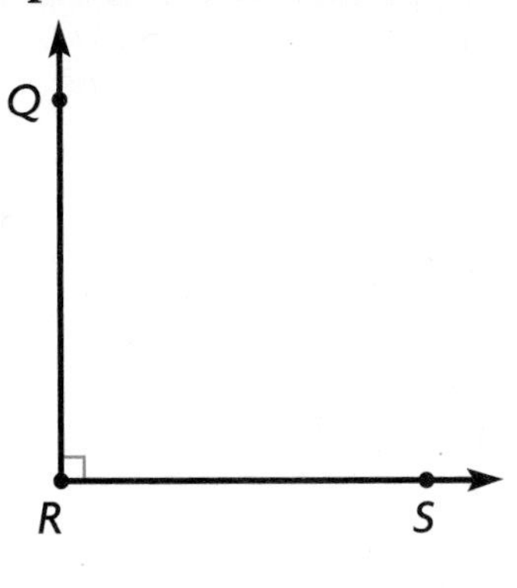

m∠QRS = ______

7.

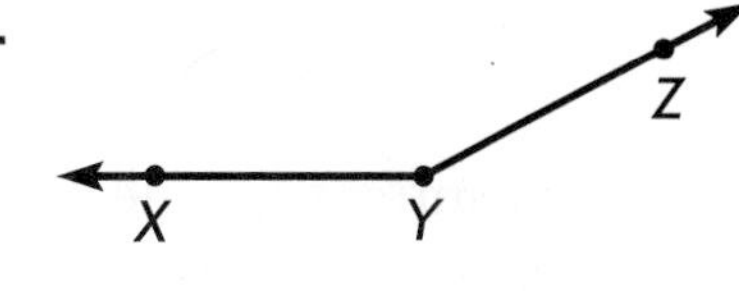

m∠XYZ = ______

Use a protractor to draw the angle.

8. 115°

9. 67°

Draw an example of each. Label the angle with its measure.

10. an acute angle

11. an obtuse angle

12. a straight angle

13. a right angle

14. THINK SMARTER Draw an angle with a measure of 0°. Describe your drawing.

____

____

Math on the Spot

Problem Solving • Applications Real World

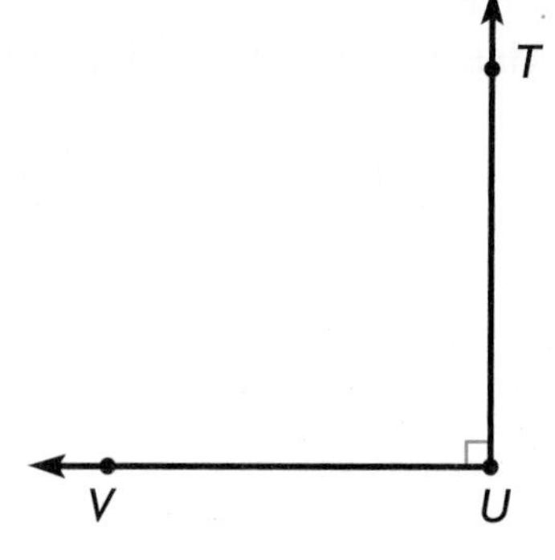

15. GO DEEPER Hadley wants to divide this angle into three angles with equal measure. What will the measure of each angle be?

______

16. MATHEMATICAL PRACTICE 6 Tracy measured an angle as 50° that was actually 130°. **Explain** her error.

______

______

17. THINK SMARTER Choose the word or number to complete a true statement about $\angle QRS$.

$\angle QRS$ is a(n) [acute / obtuse / right] angle that has a measure of [45°. / 115°. / 135°.]

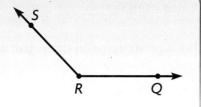

Connect to Science

Earth's Axis

Earth revolves around the sun yearly. The Northern Hemisphere is the half of Earth that is north of the equator. The seasons of the year are due to the tilt of Earth's axis.

Use the diagrams and a protractor for 18–20.

Northern Hemisphere

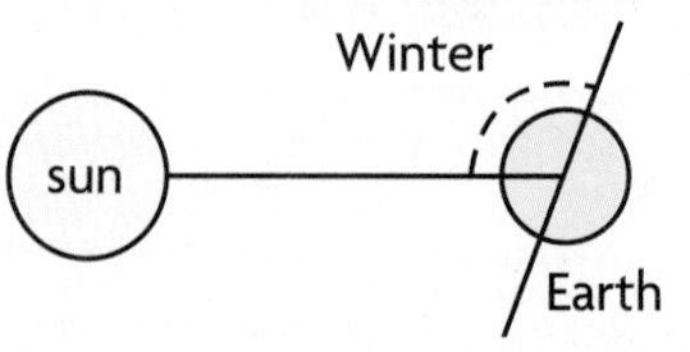

18. In the Northern Hemisphere, Earth's axis is tilted away from the sun on the first day of winter, which is often on December 21. What is the measure of the marked angle on the first day of winter, the shortest day of the year?

______

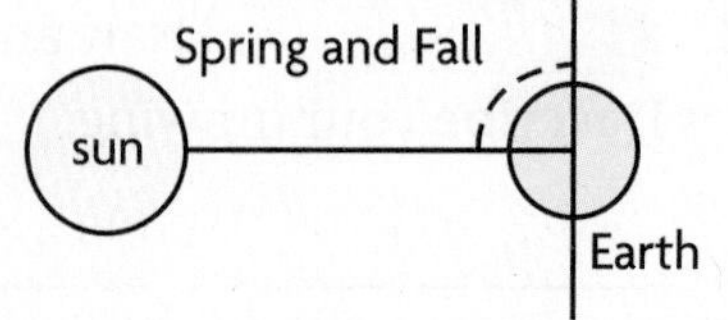

19. Earth's axis is not tilted away from or toward the sun on the first days of spring and fall, which are often on March 20 and September 22. What is the measure of the marked angle on the first day of spring or fall?

______

FOR MORE PRACTICE: Standards Practice Book

Name ________________________________

Mid-Chapter Checkpoint

Vocabulary

Choose the best term from the box.

Vocabulary
clockwise
counterclockwise
degree (°)
protractor

1. The unit used to measure an angle is called a ______________. (p. 445)

2. ______________________ is the opposite of the direction in which the hands of a clock move. (p. 441)

3. A ____________________ is a tool for measuring the size of an angle. (p. 449)

Concepts and Skills

Tell whether the angle on the circle shows a $\frac{1}{4}$, $\frac{1}{2}$, $\frac{3}{4}$, or 1 full turn clockwise or counterclockwise. (4.MD.5a)

4. 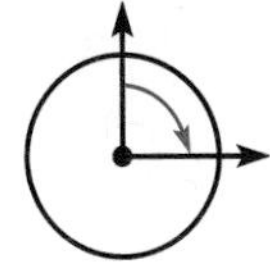

____

____

5. 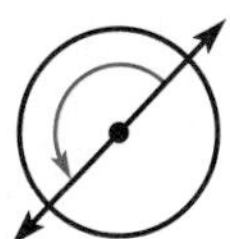

____

____

6. 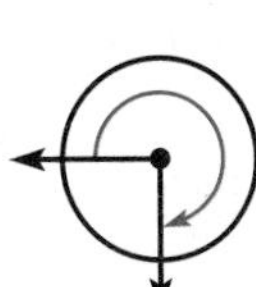

____

____

7. 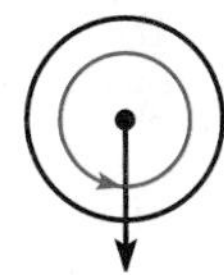

____

____

Tell the measure of the angle in degrees. (4.MD.5a, 4.MD.5b)

8. 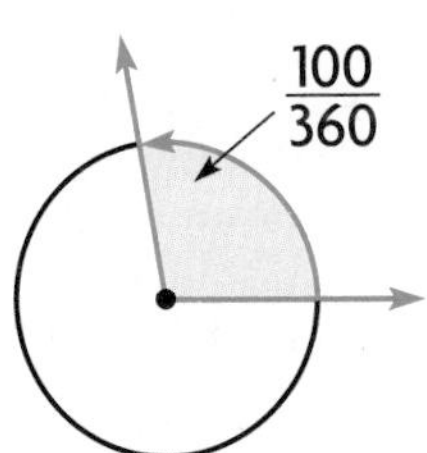

____

9. 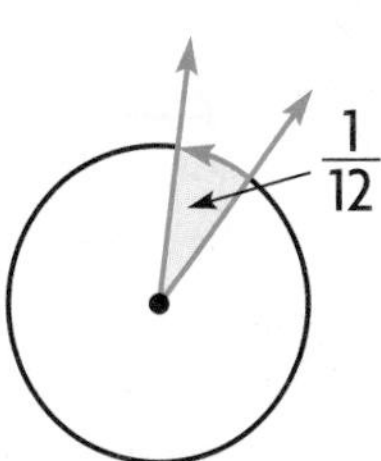

____

Use a protractor to draw the angle. (4.MD.6)

10. 75°

11. 127°

12. Phillip watched a beach volleyball game from 1:45 P.M. to 2:00 P.M. How many degrees did the minute hand turn?
(4.MD.5a, 4.MD.5b)

13. What angle does this piece of pie form? (4.MD.5a, 4.MD.5b)

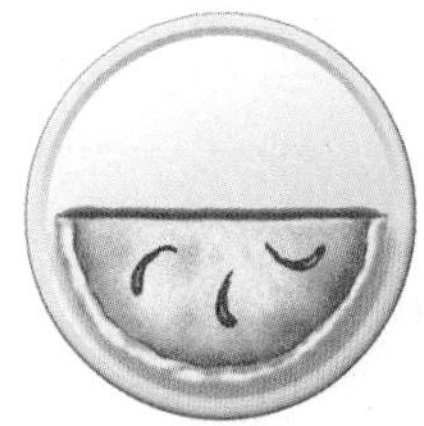

14. What is m$\angle CBT$? Use a protractor to help you. (4.MD.6)

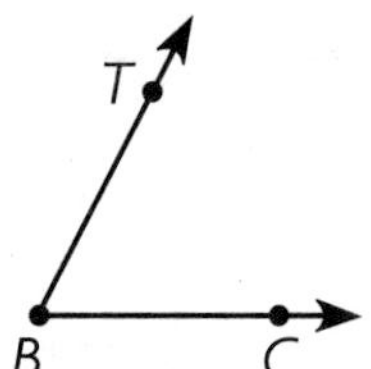

Name ____________________

Join and Separate Angles

Essential Question How can you determine the measure of an angle separated into parts?

Measurement and Data—4.MD.7

MATHEMATICAL PRACTICES
MP.2, MP.4, MP.5

Investigate

Hands On

Materials ■ construction paper ■ scissors ■ protractor

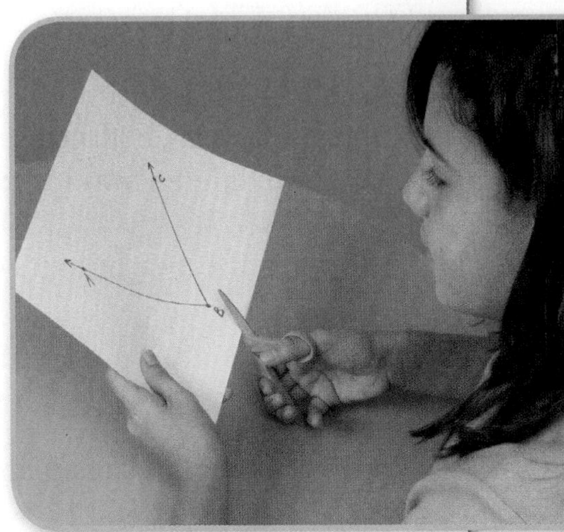

A. Use construction paper. Draw an angle that measures exactly 70°. Label it $\angle ABC$.

B. Cut out $\angle ABC$.

C. Separate $\angle ABC$ by cutting it into two parts. Begin cutting at the vertex and cut between the rays.

What figures did you form? ____________

D. Use a protractor to measure the two angles you formed.

Record the measures. ____________

E. Find the sum of the angles you formed.

____ + ____ = ____

part + part = whole

Math Idea

You can think of $\angle ABC$ as the whole and the two angles you formed as the parts of the whole.

F. Join the two angles. Compare m$\angle ABC$ to the sum of the measures of its parts. Explain how they compare.

____

____

____

____

Draw Conclusions

1. What if you cut $\angle ABC$ into two different angles? What can you conclude about the sum of the measures of these two angles? Explain.

___

___

___

2. THINK SMARTER Seth cut $\angle ABC$ into 3 parts. Draw a model that shows two different ways he could have separated his angle.

3. Write a sentence that compares the measure of an angle to the sum of its parts.

___

___

Make Connections

Materials ■ protractor

You can write the measure of the angles shown in a circle as a sum.

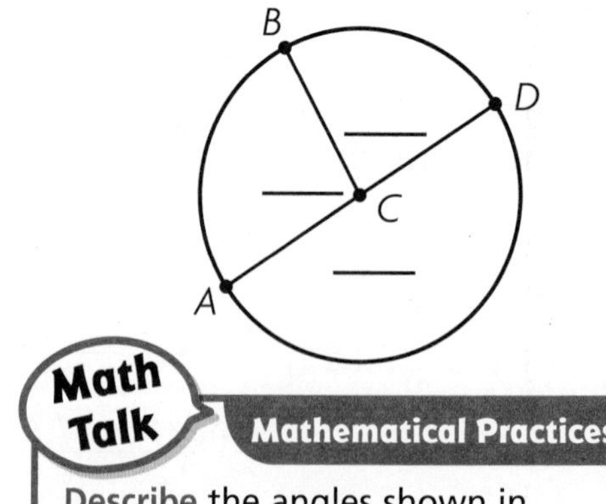

STEP 1 Use a protractor to find the measure of each angle.

STEP 2 Label each angle with its measure.

STEP 3 Write the sum of the angle measures as an equation.

_____ + _____ + _____ = _____

part + part + part = whole

Math Talk | **Mathematical Practices**

Describe the angles shown in the circle above using the words *whole* and *part*.

Name

Share and Show

Add to find the measure of the angle. Write an equation to record your work.

1.

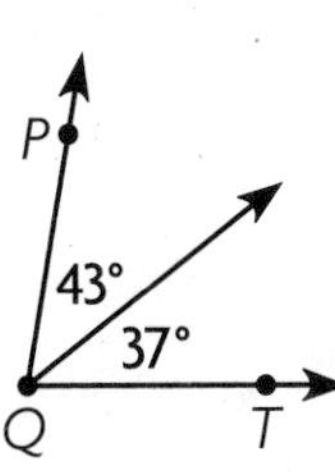

m∠*PQT* = ______

2.

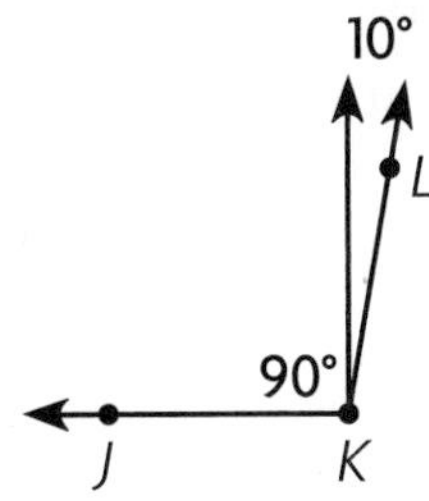

m∠*JKL* = ______

3.

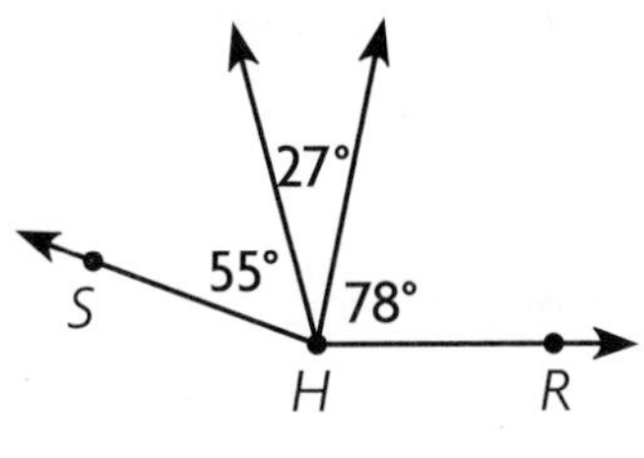

m∠*RHS* = ______

Use a protractor to find the measure of each angle. Label each angle with its measure. Write the sum of the angle measures as an equation.

4.

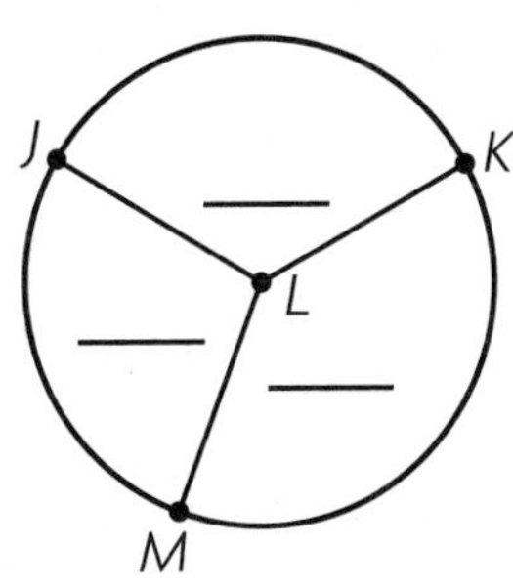

5.

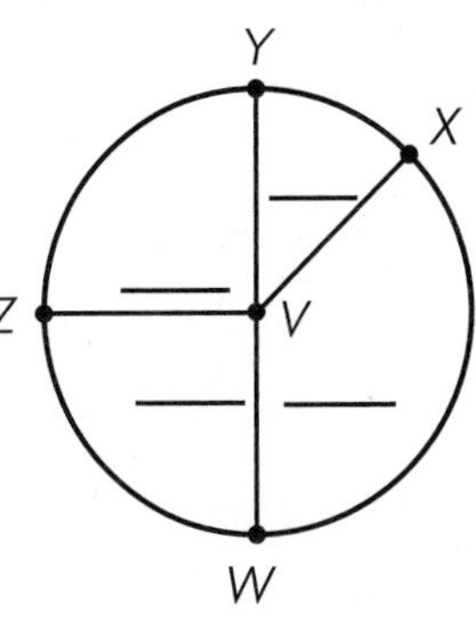

Problem Solving • Applications

6. MATHEMATICAL PRACTICE 4 **Use Diagrams** What is m∠*QRT*?

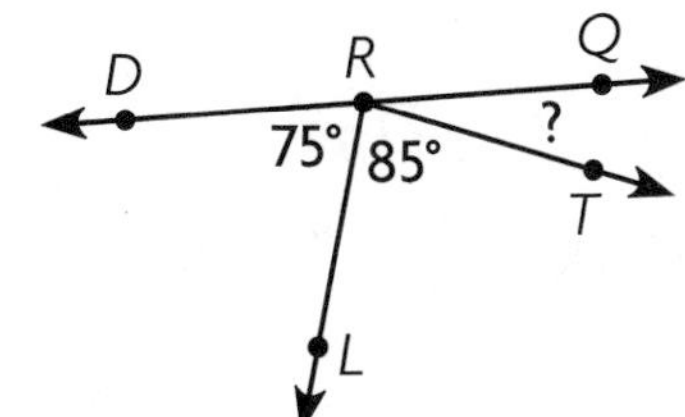

7. GO DEEPER Look back at Exercise 1. Suppose you joined an angle measuring 10° to ∠*PQT*. Draw the new angle, showing all three parts. What type of angle is formed?

Unlock the Problem

8. THINK SMARTER Stephanie, Kay, and Shane each ate an equal-sized piece of a pizza. The measure of the angle of each piece was 45°. When the pieces were together, what is the measure of the angle they formed?

a. What are you asked to find? ____________________

____

b. What information do you need to use? ____________________

____

____

c. Tell how you can use addition to solve the problem. ____________________

____

____

____

d. Complete the sentence. The three pieces of pizza formed a __________ angle.

9. What is the measure of $\angle XZW$? Write an equation to record your work.

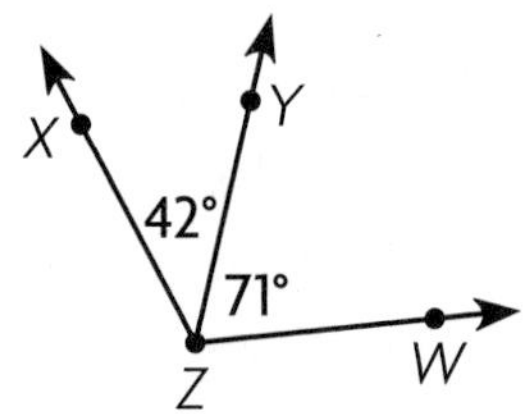

____

Personal Math Trainer

10. THINK SMARTER + What is $m\angle PRS$? Use equations to explain and check your answer.

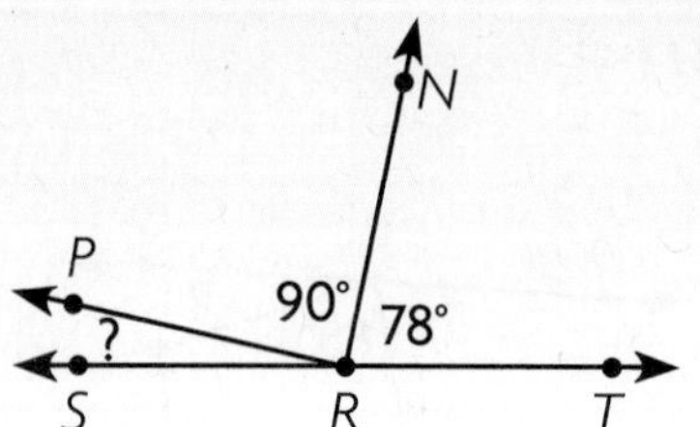

FOR MORE PRACTICE: Standards Practice Book

Name ________________________________

Problem Solving • Unknown Angle Measures

Essential Question How can you use the strategy *draw a diagram* to solve angle measurement problems?

Measurement and Data—4.MD.7

MATHEMATICAL PRACTICES
MP.1, MP.4

Unlock the Problem

Mr. Tran is cutting a piece of kitchen tile as shown at the right. He needs tiles with 45° angles to make a design. After the cut, what is the angle measure of the part left over? Can Mr. Tran use both pieces in the design?

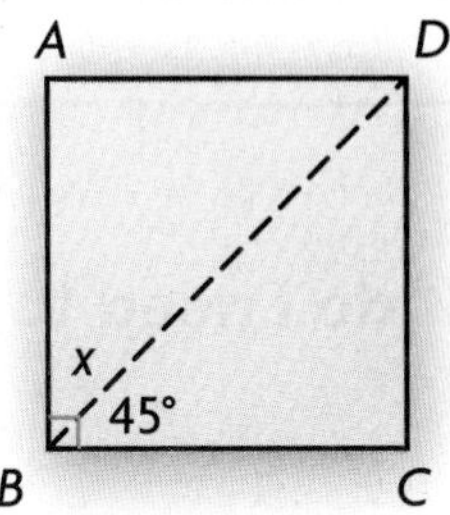

Use the graphic organizer below to solve the problem.

Read the Problem

What do I need to find?	What information do I need to use?	How will I use the information?
I need to find ______ ______	I can use the measures of the angles I know. ______ ______	I can draw a bar model and use the information to ______ ______

Solve the Problem

I can draw a bar model to represent the problem.
Then I can write an equation to solve the problem.

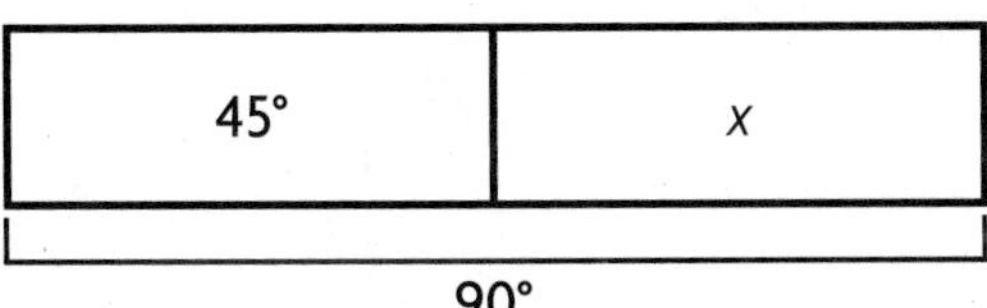

$m\angle ABD + m\angle CBD = m\angle ABC$

$x +$ ______ $=$ ______

$x =$ ______

The $m\angle ABD =$ ______.

Since both tiles measure ______, Mr. Tran can use both pieces in the design.

Mathematical Practices

What other equation can you write to solve the problem? **Explain.**

Try Another Problem

Marisol is building a frame for a sandbox, but the boards she has are too short. She must join two boards together to build a side as shown. At what angle did she cut the first board?

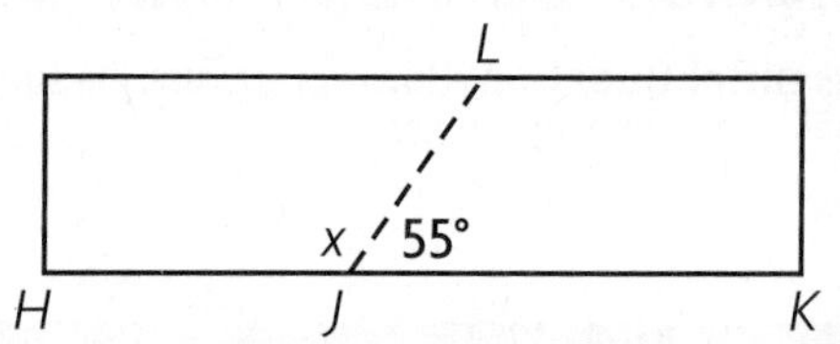

Read the Problem		
What do I need to find?	**What information do I need to use?**	**How will I use the information?**

Solve the Problem

- Explain how you can check the answer to the problem.

Name ___________________________

Share and Show

1. Laura cuts a square out of scrap paper as shown. What is the angle measure of the piece left over?

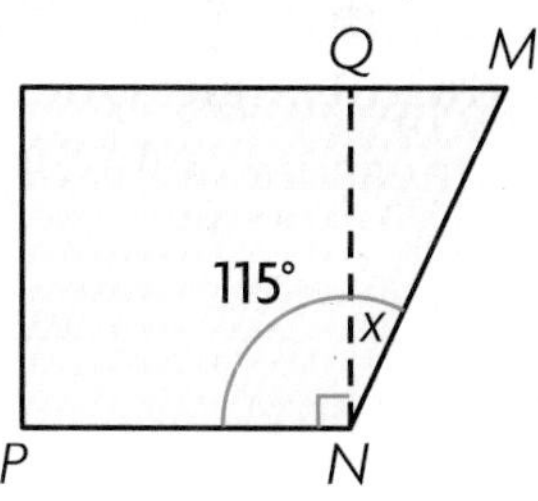

First, draw a bar model to represent the problem.

Next, write the equation you need to solve.

____

____

Last, find the angle measure of the piece left over.

$m\angle MNQ =$ ______

So, the angle measure of the piece left over is ______.

2. Jackie trimmed a piece of scrap metal to make a straight edge as shown. What is the measure of the piece she trimmed off?

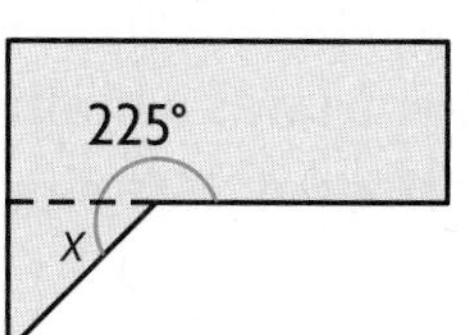

____

On Your Own

3. THINK SMARTER What if Laura cut a smaller square as shown? Would $m\angle MNQ$ be different? Explain.

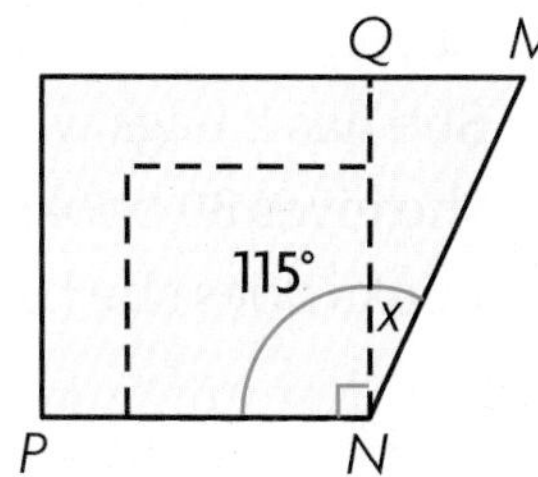

____

____

____

4. GO DEEPER The map shows Marco's paper route. When Marco turns right onto Center Street from Main Street, what degree turn does he make? **Hint:** Draw a dashed line to extend Oak Street to form a 180° angle.

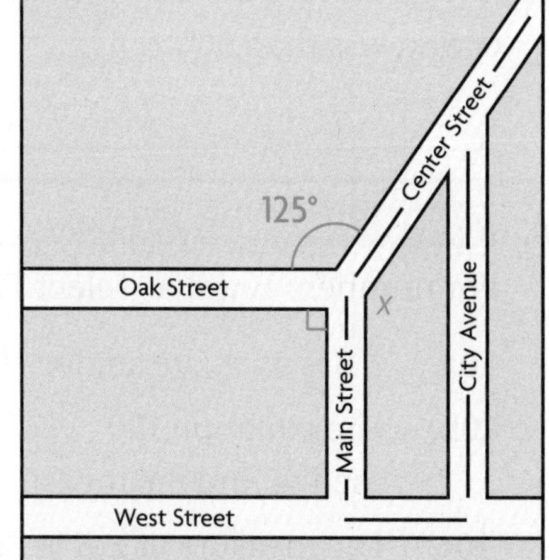

____

Problem Solving • Applications

5. MATHEMATICAL PRACTICE 4 **Write an Equation** Two angles form a straight angle. One angle measures 89°. What is the measure of the other angle? Explain.

6. **Pose a Problem** Look back at Problem 5. Write a similar problem about two angles that form a right angle.

WRITE ▸Math • Show Your Work

7. Sam paid $20 for two t-shirts. The price of each t-shirt was a multiple of 5. What are the possible prices of the t-shirts?

8. Zayna has 3 boxes with 15 art books in each box. She has 2 bags with 11 math books in each bag. If she gives 30 books away, how many art and math books does she have left?

9. **What's the Question?** It measures greater than 0° and less than 90°.

10. THINK SMARTER Two angles, $\angle A$ and $\angle B$, form a straight angle. $\angle A$ measures 65°. For numbers 10a–10c, select True or False for the statement.

10a.	$\angle B$ is an acute angle.	○ True	○ False
10b.	The equation $180° - 65° = x°$ can be used to find the measure of $\angle B$.	○ True	○ False
10c.	The measure of $\angle B$ is 125°.	○ True	○ False

FOR MORE PRACTICE: Standards Practice Book

Name ______________________________

Chapter 11 Review/Test

1. An angle represents $\frac{1}{12}$ of a circle. Use the numbers to show how to find the measure of the angle in degrees.

$$\frac{1}{12} = \frac{1 \times \square}{12 \times \square} = \frac{\square}{360}$$

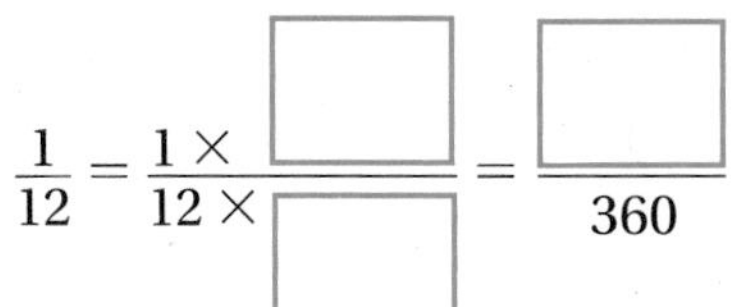

24

30

36

The angle measure is ______.

2. Match the measure of each $\angle C$ with the measure of $\angle D$ that forms a straight angle.

$\angle C$	$\angle D$
	145°
122°	75°
35°	148°
62°	58°
105°	55°
	118°

3. Katie drew an obtuse angle. Which could be the measure of the angle she drew? Mark all that apply.

Ⓐ 35°

Ⓑ 157°

Ⓒ 180°

Ⓓ 92°

4. Draw an angle that represents a $\frac{1}{4}$ turn counterclockwise on the circle.

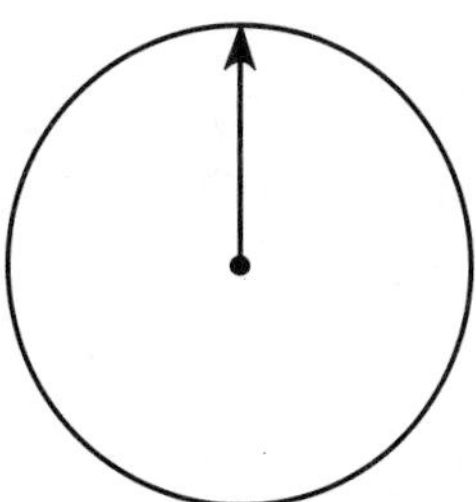

GO DIGITAL Assessment Options Chapter Test

5. Renee drew the figure shown. For 5a–5c, select Yes or No to tell whether the statement is true.

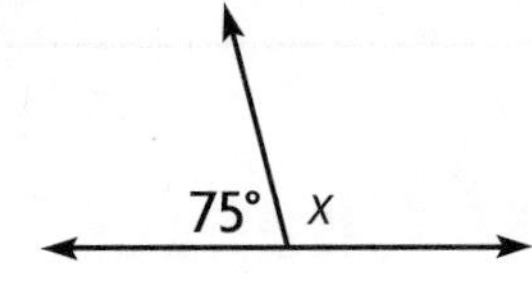

5a. The measure of a straight angle is 180°. ○ Yes ○ No

5b. To find the measure of x, Renee can subtract 75° from 180°. ○ Yes ○ No

5c. The measure of x is 115°. ○ Yes ○ No

6. Trey drew this figure with a protractor.

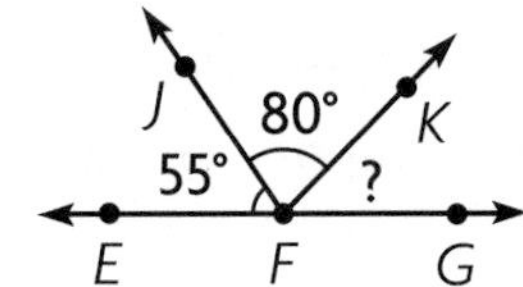

Part A

Write an equation that can be used to find m$\angle KFG$.

Part B

What is the measure of $\angle KFG$? Describe how you solved the equation and how you can check your answer.

7. Use a protractor to find the measure of the angle.

The angle measures ______.

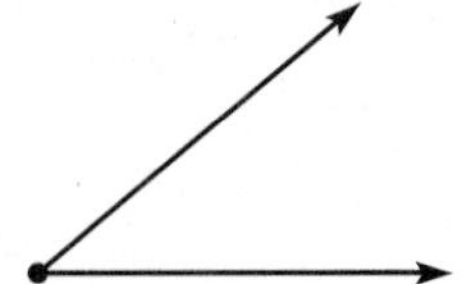

Name ____________________

8. Alex drew this angle on the circle. Which describes the angle? Mark all that apply.

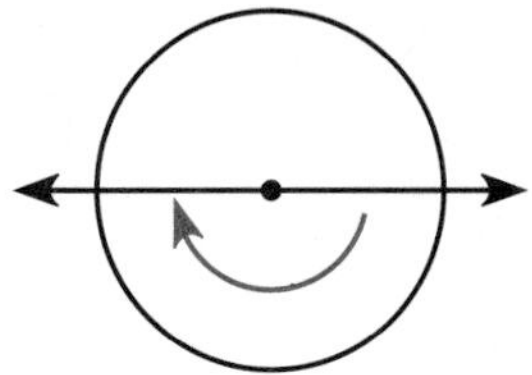

(A) $\frac{1}{4}$ turn

(B) $\frac{1}{2}$ turn

(C) clockwise

(D) counterclockwise

9. Miles has a piece of paper that is $\frac{1}{4}$ of a large circle. He cuts the paper into three equal parts from the center point of the circle. What is the angle measure of each part?

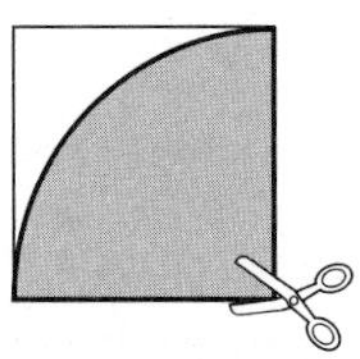

The angle measures ______.

10. Use a protractor to find the measure of each angle. Write each angle and its measure in a box ordered by the measure of the angles from least to greatest.

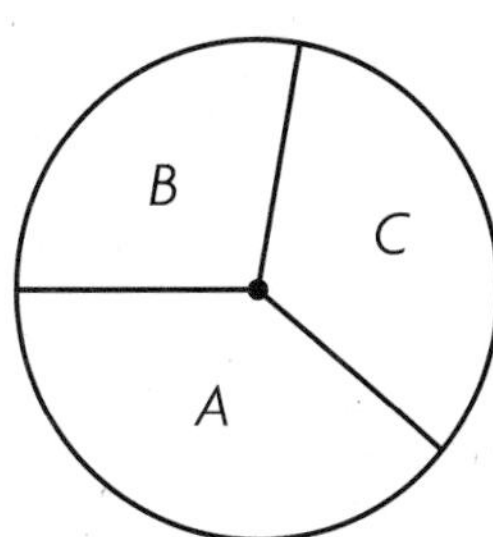

Angle: Measure:	Angle: Measure:	Angle: Measure:

11. Use the numbers and symbols to write an equation that can be used to find the measure of the unknown angle.

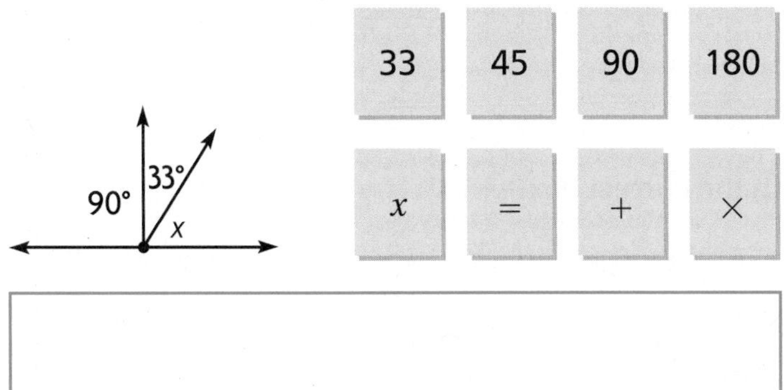

What is the measure of the unknown angle? ______

12. Choose the word or number to complete a true statement about $\angle JKL$.

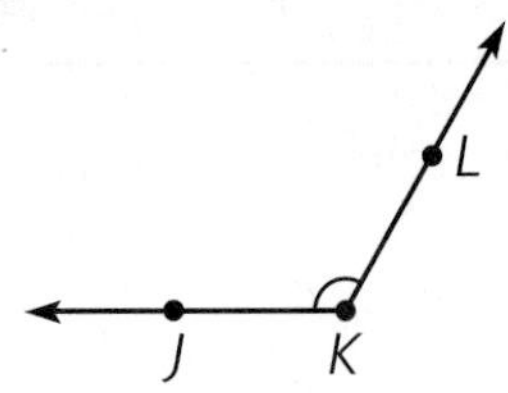

	acute		60°.
$\angle JKL$ is a(n)	obtuse	angle that has a measure of	120°.
	right		135°.

13. Vince began practicing piano at 5:15 P.M. He stopped at 5:35 P.M. How many degrees did the minute hand turn during Vince's practice time? Explain how you found your answer.

Start

Stop

14. An angle measures 125°. Through what fraction of a circle does the angle turn?

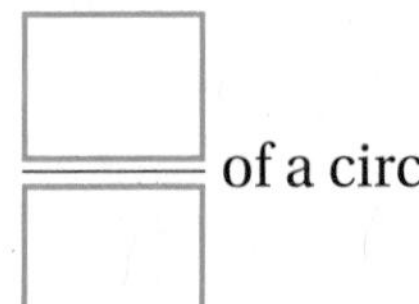
of a circle

15. Write the letter for each angle measure in the correct box.

Ⓐ 125° Ⓑ 90° Ⓒ 180° Ⓓ 30° Ⓔ 45° Ⓕ 95°

acute	obtuse	right	straight

Name ____________________

16. For numbers 16a–16b, select the fraction that makes a true statement about the figure.

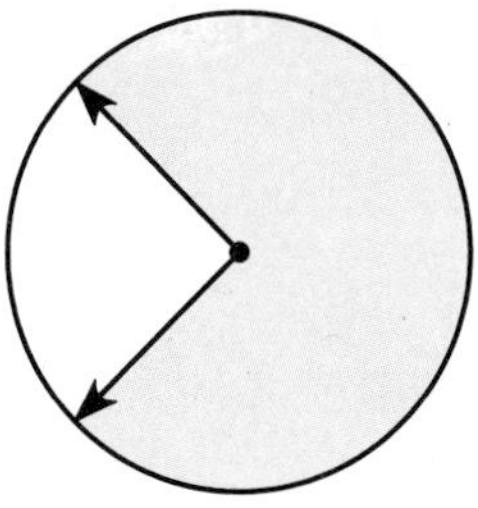

Figure 1 Figure 2

16a. The angle in Figure 1 represents a [$\frac{1}{4}$ / $\frac{1}{2}$ / $\frac{3}{4}$] turn.

16b. The angle in Figure 2 represents a [$\frac{1}{4}$ / $\frac{1}{2}$ / $\frac{3}{4}$] turn.

17. Melanie cuts a rectangle out of a piece of scrap paper as shown. She wants to calculate the angle measure of the piece that is left over.

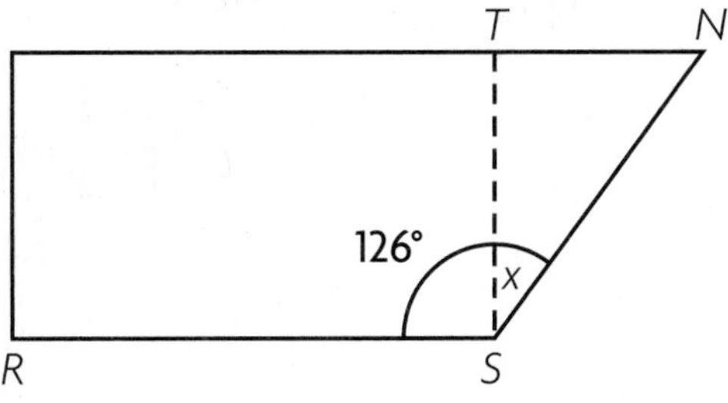

Part A

Draw a bar model to represent the problem.

Part B

Write and solve an equation to find *x*.

The angle measures ______.

18. Two angles, $\angle A$ and $\angle B$, form a right angle. $\angle A$ measures 32°. For numbers 18a–18c, select True or False for the statement.

18a.	$\angle B$ is an acute angle.	○ True	○ False
18b.	The equation $180° - 32° = x°$ can be used to find the measure of $\angle B$.	○ True	○ False
18c.	The measure of $\angle B$ is 58°.	○ True	○ False

19. A circle is divided into parts. Which sum could represent the angle measures that make up the circle? Mark all that apply.

Ⓐ $120° + 120° + 120° + 120°$

Ⓑ $25° + 40° + 80° + 105° + 110°$

Ⓒ $33° + 82° + 111° + 50° + 84°$

Ⓓ $40° + 53° + 72° + 81° + 90° + 34°$

20. Use a protractor to find the unknown angle measures.

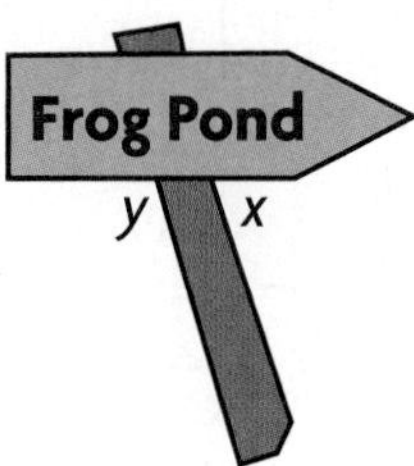

$x =$ ______ $y =$ ______

What do you notice about the measures of the unknown angles? Is this what you would have expected? Explain your reasoning.

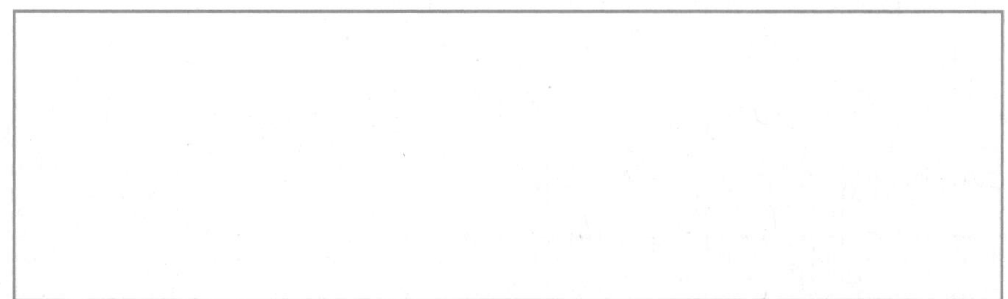

Chapter 12

Relative Sizes of Measurement Units

Show What You Know

Check your understanding of important skills.

Name ______________________

▶ Time to the Half Hour Read the clock. Write the time.

1. 
____

2. 
____

3. 
____

▶ Multiply by 1-Digit Numbers Find the product.

4. $\begin{array}{r} 84 \\ \times\ 7 \\ \hline \end{array}$

5. $\begin{array}{r} 536 \\ \times\ \ 8 \\ \hline \end{array}$

6. $\begin{array}{r} 748 \\ \times\ \ 5 \\ \hline \end{array}$

7. $\begin{array}{r} 2{,}524 \\ \times\ \ \ 2 \\ \hline \end{array}$

8. $\begin{array}{r} 360 \\ \times\ \ 9 \\ \hline \end{array}$

9. $\begin{array}{r} 296 \\ \times\ 3 \\ \hline \end{array}$

10. $\begin{array}{r} \$1{,}428 \\ \times\ \ \ 4 \\ \hline \end{array}$

11. $\begin{array}{r} 64 \\ \times\ 5 \\ \hline \end{array}$

Math Detective

A team was given a bucket of water and a sponge. The team had 1 minute to fill an empty half-gallon bucket with water using only the sponge. The line plot shows the amount of water squeezed into the bucket. Be a Math Detective. Did the team squeeze enough water to fill the half-gallon bucket?

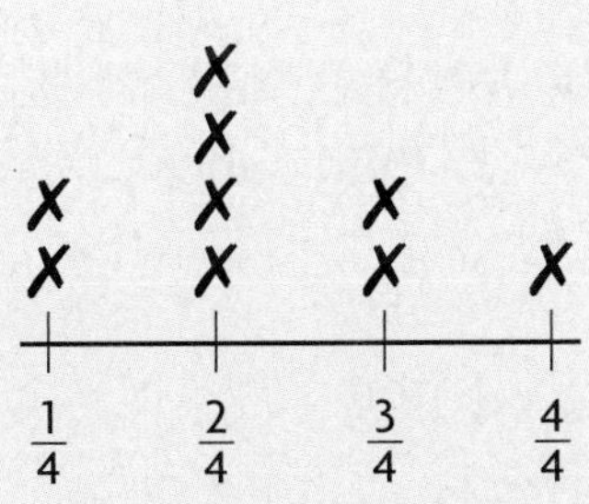

Amount of Water Squeezed into the Bucket (in cups)

Personal Math Trainer
Online Assessment and Intervention

Vocabulary Builder

▶ Visualize It

Complete the Brain Storming diagram by using words with a ✓.

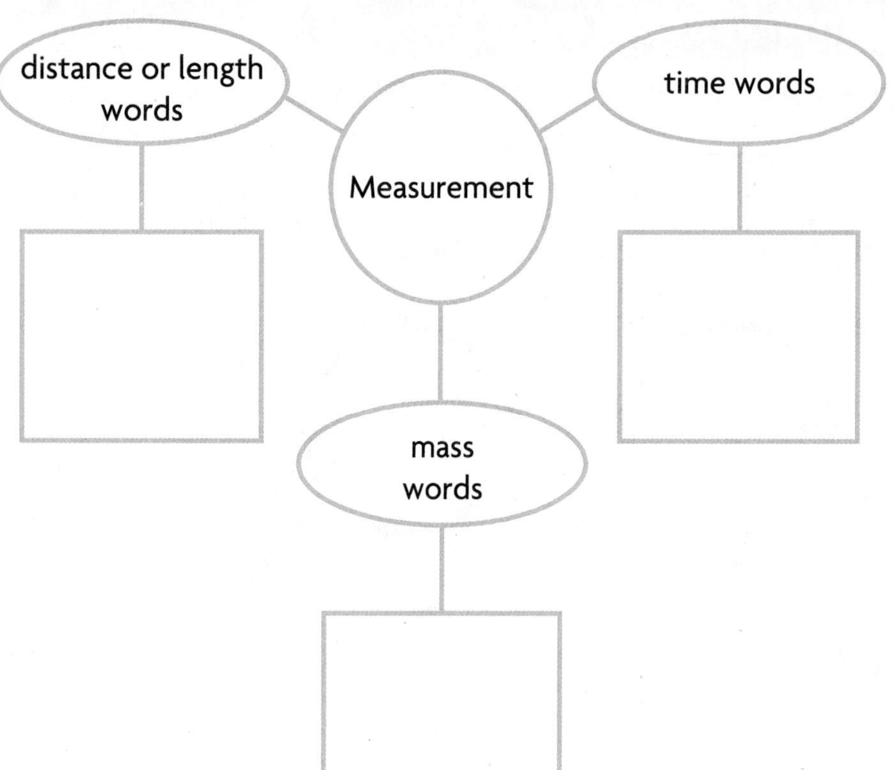

Review Words

- ✓ A.M.
- ✓ centimeter
- ✓ elapsed time
- ✓ foot
- ✓ gram
- ✓ hour
- ✓ inch
- ✓ kilogram
- ✓ meter
- ✓ minute
- ✓ P.M.
- ✓ yard

Preview Words

- cup
- decimeter
- fluid ounce
- gallon
- half gallon
- line plot
- milliliter
- millimeter
- ounce
- pint
- pound
- quart
- second
- ton

▶ Understand Vocabulary

Draw a line to match each word with its definition.

1. decimeter
2. second
3. fluid ounce
4. ton
5. line plot

- A customary unit for measuring liquid volume
- A graph that shows the frequency of data along a number line
- A customary unit used to measure weight
- A small unit of time
- A metric unit for measuring length or distance

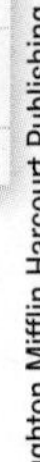

GO DIGITAL
- Interactive Student Edition
- Multimedia eGlossary

Lesson 12.1

Name ______________________________

Measurement Benchmarks

Essential Question How can you use benchmarks to understand the relative sizes of measurement units?

Measurement and Data—4.MD.1

MATHEMATICAL PRACTICES
MP.1, MP.5

Unlock the Problem (Real World)

Jake says the length of his bike is about four yards. Use the benchmark units below to determine if Jake's statement is reasonable.

Customary Units of Length			
1 in. about 1 inch	 1 ft about 1 foot	1 yd about 1 yard	1 mile in about 20 minutes

A **mile** is a customary unit for measuring length or distance. The benchmark shows the distance you can walk in about 20 minutes.

A baseball bat is about one yard long. Since Jake's bike is shorter than four times the length of a baseball bat, his bike is shorter than four yards long.

So, Jake's statement ______ reasonable.

Jake's bike is about ______ baseball bats long.

Example 1 Use the benchmark customary units.

Customary Units of Liquid Volume				
1 cup = 8 fluid ounces	1 pint	1 quart	1 half gallon	1 gallon

• About how much liquid is in a mug of hot chocolate? ______________

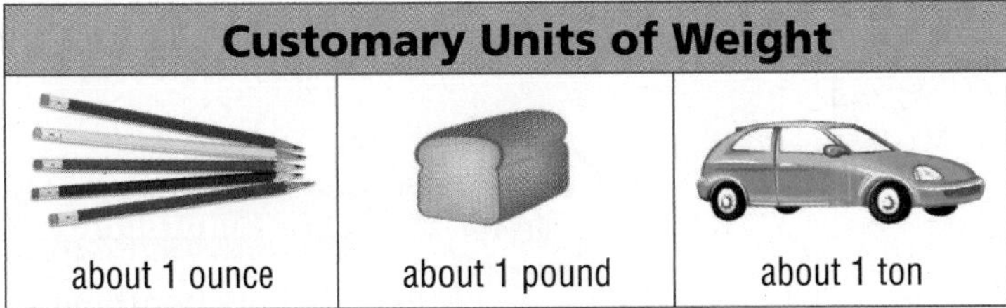

Customary Units of Weight		
about 1 ounce	about 1 pound	about 1 ton

• About how much does a grapefruit weigh? ______________

Math Talk **Mathematical Practices**

Order the units of weight from heaviest to lightest. Use benchmarks to **explain** your answer.

Benchmarks for Metric Units Like place value, the metric system is based on multiples of ten. Each unit is 10 times as large as the next smaller unit. Below are some common metric benchmarks.

Example 2 Use the benchmark metric units.

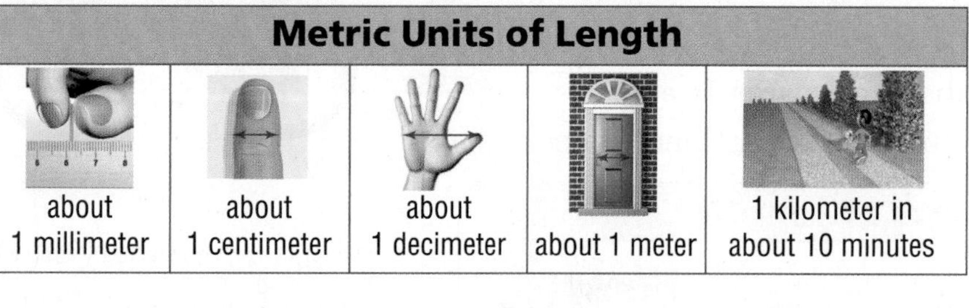

Metric Units of Length				
about 1 millimeter	about 1 centimeter	about 1 decimeter	about 1 meter	1 kilometer in about 10 minutes

A **kilometer** is a metric unit for measuring length or distance. The benchmark shows the distance you can walk in about 10 minutes.

- Is the length of your classroom greater than or less than one kilometer?

____

Metric Units of Liquid Volume	
1 milliliter	1 liter

- About how much medicine is usually in a medicine bottle?

about 120 _______________

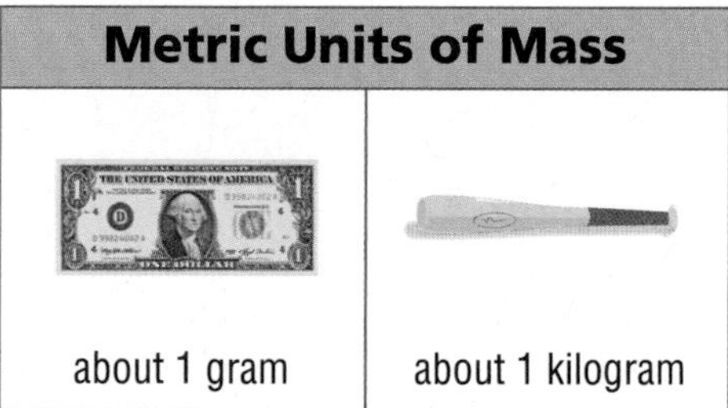

Metric Units of Mass	
about 1 gram	about 1 kilogram

- About how much is the mass of a paper clip?

____

Math Talk **Mathematical Practices**

Explain how benchmark measurements can help you decide which unit to use when measuring.

Name ___________________________

Share and Show

Use benchmarks to choose the metric unit you would use to measure each.

Metric Units
centimeter
meter
kilometer
gram
kilogram
milliliter
liter

1. mass of a strawberry

____

✓ 2. length of a cell phone

____

Circle the better estimate.

3. width of a teacher's desk

10 meters or 1 meter

4. the amount of liquid a punch bowl holds

2 liters or 20 liters

✓ 5. distance between Seattle and San Francisco

6 miles or 680 miles

Mathematical Practices

Explain why you would use kilometers instead of meters to measure the distance across the United States.

On Your Own

Use benchmarks to choose the customary unit you would use to measure each.

Customary Units
inch
foot
yard
ounce
pound
cup
gallon

6. length of a football field

____

7. weight of a pumpkin

____

Circle the better estimate.

8. weight of a watermelon

4 pounds or 4 ounces

9. the amount of liquid a fish tank holds

10 cups or 10 gallons

Complete the sentence. Write *more* or *less*.

10. Matthew's large dog weighs _____________ than one ton.

11. The amount of liquid a sink can hold is _____________ than one cup of water.

12. A paper clip has a mass of _____________ than one kilogram.

Problem Solving • Applications

For 13–15, use benchmarks to explain your answer.

13. THINK SMARTER Cristina is making macaroni and cheese for her family. Would Cristina use 1 pound of macaroni or 1 ounce of macaroni?

____

____

14. Which is the better estimate for the length of a kitchen table, 200 centimeters or 200 meters?

____

____

15. GO DEEPER Jodi wants to weigh her dog and measure its height. Which two units should she use?

____

16. MATHEMATICAL PRACTICE 1 **Evaluate Reasonableness** Dalton used benchmarks to estimate that there are more cups than quarts in one gallon. Is Dalton's estimate reasonable? Explain.

____

____

17. THINK SMARTER Select the correct word to complete the sentence.

Justine is thirsty after running two miles.

She should drink [1 liter / 1 meter / 100 milliliters] of water.

FOR MORE PRACTICE:
Standards Practice Book

Name ____________________________

Customary Units of Length

Essential Question How can you use models to compare customary units of length?

Measurement and Data—4.MD.1
Also 4.MD.2

MATHEMATICAL PRACTICES
MP.1, MP.2, MP.5

Unlock the Problem

You can use a ruler to measure length. A ruler that is 1 foot long shows 12 inches in 1 foot. A ruler that is 3 feet long is called a yardstick. There are 3 feet in 1 yard.

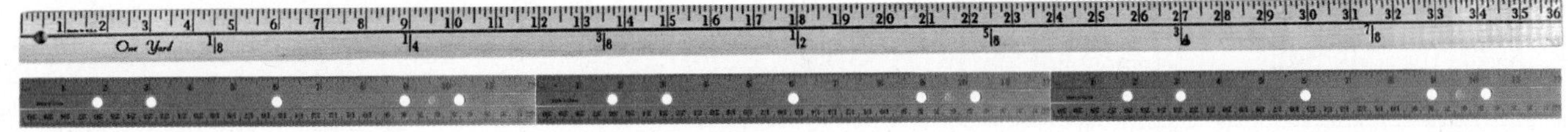

How does the size of a foot compare to the size of an inch?

Activity

Materials ■ 1-inch grid paper ■ scissors ■ tape

STEP 1 Cut out the paper inch tiles. Label each tile 1 inch.

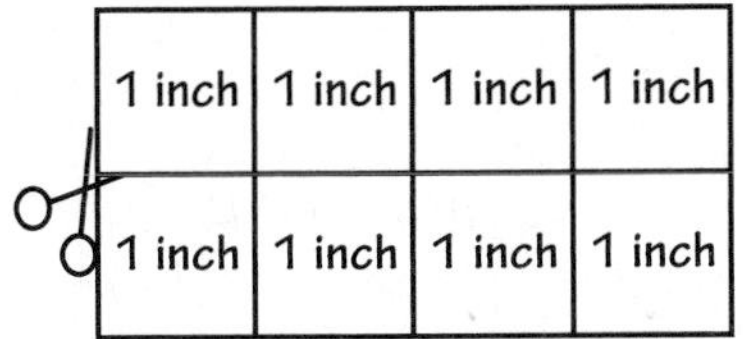

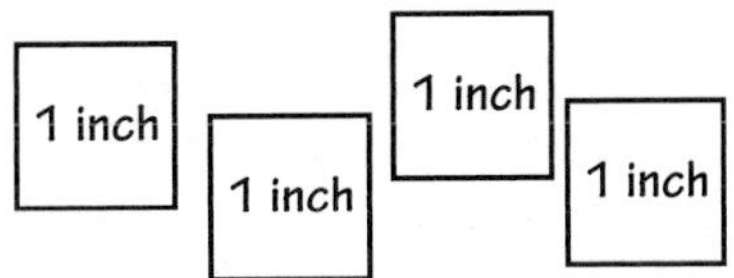

STEP 2 Place 12 tiles end-to-end to build 1 foot. Tape the tiles together.

1 foot

1 inch	1 inch	1 inch	1 inch	1 inch	1 inch	1 inch	1 inch	1 inch	1 inch	1 inch	1 inch

STEP 3 Compare the size of 1 foot to the size of 1 inch.

1 foot

1 inch	1 inch	1 inch	1 inch	1 inch	1 inch	1 inch	1 inch	1 inch	1 inch	1 inch	1 inch

1 inch

1 inch

Think: You need 12 inches to make 1 foot.

So, 1 foot is ______ times as long as 1 inch.

Math Talk **Mathematical Practices**

How many inches would you need to make a yard? **Explain.**

Example Compare measures.

Emma has 4 feet of thread. She needs 50 inches of thread to make some bracelets. How can she determine if she has enough thread to make the bracelets?

Since 1 foot is 12 times as long as 1 inch, you can write feet as inches by multiplying the number of feet by 12.

STEP 1 Make a table that relates feet and inches.

Feet	Inches
1	12
2	
3	
4	
5	

Think:

1 foot × 12 = 12 inches

2 feet × 12 = ______

3 feet × ______ = ______

4 feet × ______ = ______

5 feet × ______ = ______

STEP 2 Compare 4 feet and 50 inches.

4 feet

50 inches

Think: Write each measure in inches and compare using <, >, or =.

______  ______

Emma has 4 feet of thread. She needs 50 inches of thread.

4 feet is ______ than 50 inches.

So, Emma ______ enough thread to make the bracelets.

Mathematical Practices

Explain how making a table helped you solve the problem.

- What if Emma had 5 feet of thread? Would she have enough thread to make the bracelets? Explain.

______

______

______

Name ______________________________

Share and Show

1. Compare the size of a yard to the size of a foot. Use a model to help.

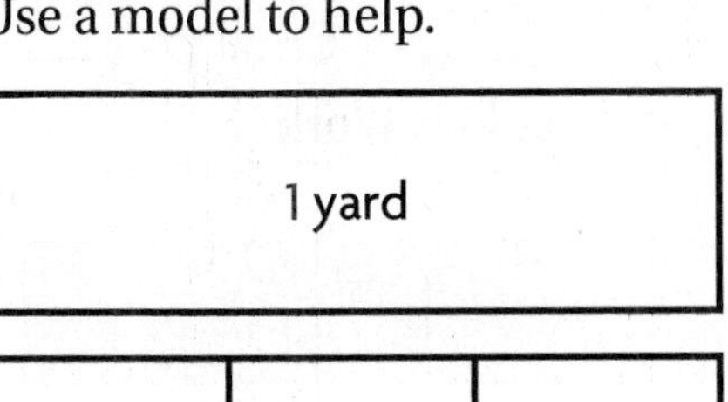

Customary Units of Length
1 foot (ft) = 12 inches (in.) 1 yard (yd) = 3 feet 1 yard (yd) = 36 inches

1 yard is _____ times as long as _____ foot.

Complete.

2. 2 feet = _____ inches
3. 3 yards = _____ feet
4. 7 yards = _____ feet

Mathematical Practices

If you measured the length of your classroom in yards and then in feet, which unit would have a greater number of units? **Explain.**

On Your Own

Complete.

5. 4 yards = _____ feet
6. 10 yards = _____ feet
7. 7 feet = _____ inches

MATHEMATICAL PRACTICE 4 **Use Symbols Algebra** **Compare using <, >, or =.**

8. 1 foot ◯ 13 inches
9. 2 yards ◯ 6 feet
10. 6 feet ◯ 60 inches

Problem Solving • Applications

11. THINK SMARTER Joanna has 3 yards of fabric. She needs 100 inches of fabric to make curtains. Does she have enough fabric to make curtains? Explain. Make a table to help.

____

____

____

Yards	Inches
1	
2	
3	

12. THINK SMARTER Select the measures that are equal. Mark all that apply.

Ⓐ 4 feet
Ⓑ 12 yards
Ⓒ 36 feet
Ⓓ 480 inches
Ⓔ 15 feet
Ⓕ 432 inches

13. **GO DEEPER** Jasmine and Luke used fraction strips to compare the size of a foot to the size of an inch using fractions. They drew models to show their answers. Whose answer makes sense? Whose answer is nonsense? Explain your reasoning.

Jasmine's Work

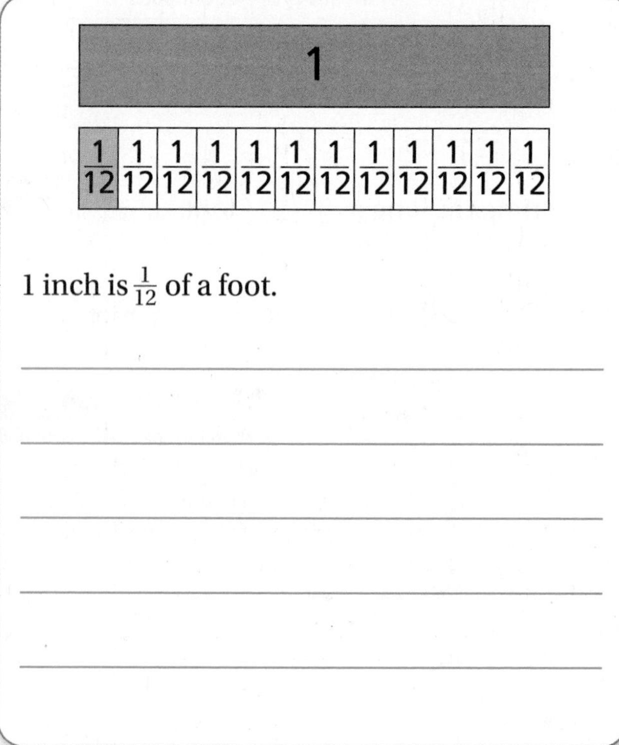

1 inch is $\frac{1}{12}$ of a foot.

Luke's Work

1

$\frac{1}{3}$ | $\frac{1}{3}$ | $\frac{1}{3}$

1 inch is $\frac{1}{3}$ of a foot.

a. **MATHEMATICAL PRACTICE 3 Apply** For the answer that is nonsense, write an answer that makes sense.

b. Look back at Luke's model. Which two units could you compare using his model? Explain.

FOR MORE PRACTICE: Standards Practice Book

Name ______________________________

Customary Units of Weight

Essential Question How can you use models to compare customary units of weight?

Measurement and Data—4.MD.1
Also 4.MD.2

MATHEMATICAL PRACTICES
MP.1, MP.6, MP.7

Unlock the Problem

Ounces and **pounds** are customary units of weight. How does the size of a pound compare to the size of an ounce?

▲ You can use a spring scale to measure weight.

Activity

Materials ■ color pencils

The number line below shows the relationship between pounds and ounces.

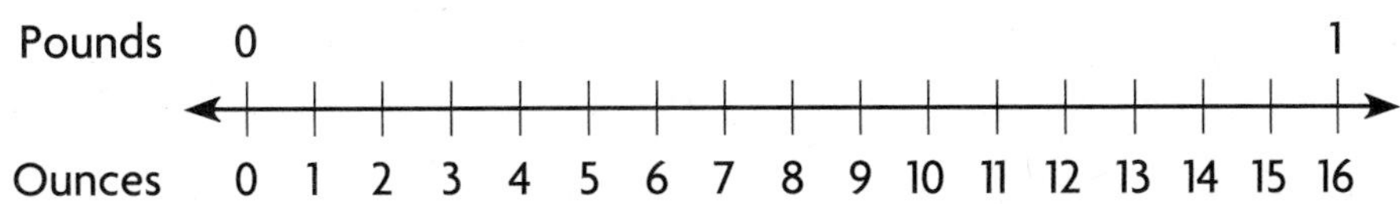

STEP 1 Use a color pencil to shade 1 pound on the number line.

STEP 2 Use a different color pencil to shade 1 ounce on the number line.

STEP 3 Compare the size of 1 pound to the size of 1 ounce.

You need ______ ounces to make ______ pound.

So, 1 pound is ______ times as heavy as 1 ounce.

Math Talk **Mathematical Practices**

Which is greater, 9 pounds or 9 ounces? **Explain.**

- MATHEMATICAL PRACTICE 6 **Explain** how the number line helped you to compare the sizes of the units.

____

____

____

____

Example Compare measures.

Nancy needs 5 pounds of flour to bake pies for a festival. She has 90 ounces of flour. How can she determine if she has enough flour to bake the pies?

STEP 1 Make a table that relates pounds and ounces.

Pounds	Ounces
1	16
2	
3	
4	
5	

Think:

1 pound × 16 = 16 ounces

2 pounds × 16 = ______

3 pounds × ______ = ______

4 pounds × ______ = ______

5 pounds × ______ = ______

STEP 2 Compare 90 ounces and 5 pounds.

90 ounces → ______ ◯ ______ ← 5 pounds

Think: Write each measure in ounces and compare using <, >, or =.

Nancy has 90 ounces of flour. She needs 5 pounds of flour.

90 ounces is ______ than 5 pounds.

So, Nancy ______ enough flour to make the pies.

Try This! There are 2,000 pounds in 1 **ton**.
Make a table that relates tons and pounds.

Tons	Pounds
1	2,000
2	
3	

1 ton is ______ times as heavy as 1 pound.

Name ________________________________

Share and Show

Customary Units of Weight
1 pound (lb) = 16 ounces (oz)
1 ton (T) = 2,000 pounds

1. 4 tons = __________ pounds

   Think: 4 tons × __________ = __________

Complete.

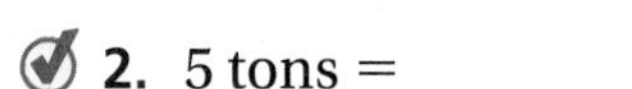

2. 5 tons = __________ pounds

3. 6 pounds = __________ ounces

Math Talk — **Mathematical Practices**

What equation can you use to solve Exercise 4? **Explain.**

On Your Own

Complete.

4. 7 pounds = __________ ounces

5. 6 tons = __________ pounds

Use Symbols **Algebra** **Compare using >, <, or =.**

6. 1 pound ◯ 15 ounces

7. 2 tons ◯ 2 pounds

Problem Solving • Applications

8. A landscaping company ordered 8 tons of gravel. They sell the gravel in 50-pound bags. How many pounds of gravel did the company order?

   ____

9. THINK SMARTER If you could draw a number line that shows the relationship between tons and pounds, what would it look like? Explain.

   ____

   ____

   ____

10. THINK SMARTER Write the symbol that compares the weights correctly.

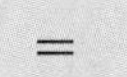

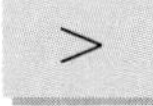

160 ounces ______ 10 pounds

600 pounds ______ 3 tons

11. GO DEEPER Alexis bought $\frac{1}{2}$ pound of grapes. How many ounces of grapes did she buy?

Dan drew the number line below to solve the problem. He says his model shows that there are 5 ounces in $\frac{1}{2}$ pound. What is his error?

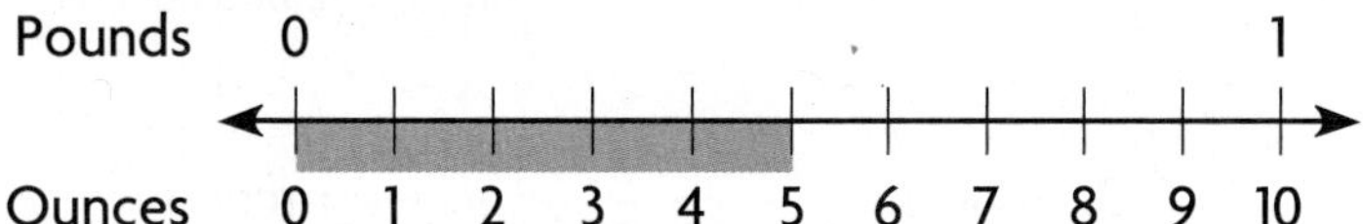

Look at the way Dan solved the problem. Find and describe his error.

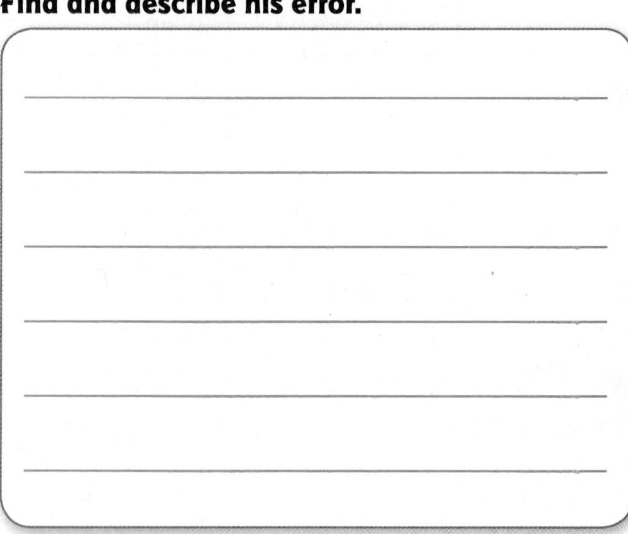

Draw a correct number line and solve the problem.

So, Alexis bought ______ ounces of grapes.

- MATHEMATICAL PRACTICE 6 Look back at the number line you drew. How many ounces are in $\frac{1}{4}$ pound? **Explain.**

FOR MORE PRACTICE: Standards Practice Book

Name ____________________________________

Customary Units of Liquid Volume

Essential Question How can you use models to compare customary units of liquid volume?

Measurement and Data—4.MD.1
Also 4.MD.2

MATHEMATICAL PRACTICES
MP.3, MP.7, MP.8

Unlock the Problem

Liquid volume is the measure of the space a liquid occupies. Some basic units for measuring liquid volume are **gallons**, **half gallons**, **quarts**, **pints**, and **cups**.

1 cup = 8 fluid ounces
1 pint = 2 cups
1 quart = 4 cups

The bars below model the relationships among some units of liquid volume. The largest units are gallons. The smallest units are **fluid ounces**.

1 gallon

1 gallon															
1 half gallon								1 half gallon							
1 quart				1 quart				1 quart				1 quart			
1 pint		1 pint		1 pint		1 pint		1 pint		1 pint		1 pint		1 pint	
1 cup	1 cup	1 cup	1 cup	1 cup	1 cup	1 cup	1 cup	1 cup	1 cup	1 cup	1 cup	1 cup	1 cup	1 cup	1 cup
8 fluid ounces	8 fluid ounces	8 fluid ounces	8 fluid ounces	8 fluid ounces	8 fluid ounces	8 fluid ounces	8 fluid ounces	8 fluid ounces	8 fluid ounces	8 fluid ounces	8 fluid ounces	8 fluid ounces	8 fluid ounces	8 fluid ounces	8 fluid ounces

Example How does the size of a gallon compare to the size of a quart?

STEP 1 Draw two bars that represent this relationship. One bar should show gallons and the other bar should show quarts.

STEP 2 Shade 1 gallon on one bar and shade 1 quart on the other bar.

STEP 3 Compare the size of 1 gallon to the size of 1 quart.

So, 1 gallon is ______ times as much as 1 quart.

Math Talk — **Mathematical Practices**

Describe the pattern in the units of liquid volume.

Example Compare measures.

Serena needs to make 3 gallons of lemonade for the lemonade sale. She has a powder mix that makes 350 fluid ounces of lemonade. How can she decide if she has enough powder mix?

STEP 1 Use the model on page 483. Find the relationship between gallons and fluid ounces.

1 gallon = ______ cups

1 cup = ______ fluid ounces

1 gallon = ______ cups × ______ fluid ounces

1 gallon = ______ fluid ounces

STEP 2 Make a table that relates gallons and fluid ounces.

Gallons	Fluid Ounces
1	128
2	
3	

Think:

1 gallon = 128 fluid ounces

2 gallons × 128 = ______ fluid ounces

3 gallons × 128 = ______ fluid ounces

STEP 3 Compare 350 fluid ounces and 3 gallons.

350 fluid ounces   3 gallons

Think: Write each measure in fluid ounces and compare using <, >, or =.

______________ ◯ ______________

Serena has enough mix to make 350 fluid ounces. She needs to make 3 gallons of lemonade.

350 fluid ounces is ______ than 3 gallons.

So, Serena ______________ enough mix to make 3 gallons of lemonade.

Name ______________________

Share and Show

1. Compare the size of a quart to the size of a pint. Use a model to help.

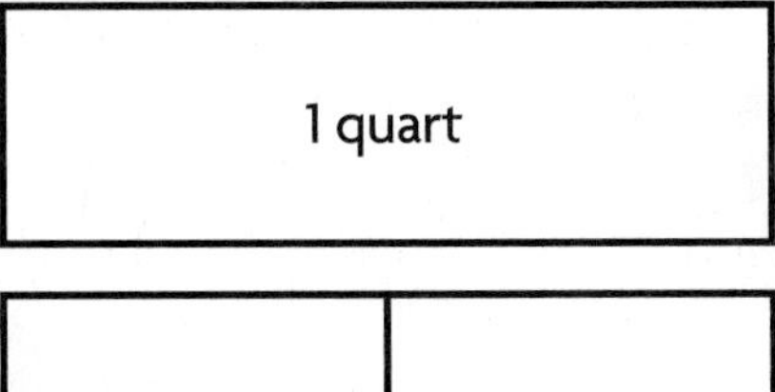

Customary Units of Liquid Volume
1 cup (c) = 8 fluid ounces (fl oz)
1 pint (pt) = 2 cups
1 quart (qt) = 2 pints
1 quart (qt) = 4 cups
1 gallon (gal) = 4 quarts
1 gallon (gal) = 8 pints
1 gallon (gal) = 16 cups

1 quart is ______ times as much as ______ pint.

Complete.

2. 2 pints = ______ cups
3. 3 gallons = ______ quarts
4. 6 quarts = ______ cups

Mathematical Practices

Explain how the conversion chart above relates to the bar model in Exercise 1.

On Your Own

Complete.

5. 4 gallons = ______ pints
6. 5 cups = ______ fluid ounces

Use Symbols **Algebra** **Compare using >, <, or =.**

7. 2 gallons ◯ 32 cups
8. 4 pints ◯ 6 cups
9. 5 quarts ◯ 11 pints

Problem Solving • Applications

10. THINK SMARTER A soccer team has 25 players. The team's thermos holds 4 gallons of water. If the thermos is full, is there enough water for each player to have 2 cups? Explain. Make a table to help.

____

____

____

Gallons	Cups
1	
2	
3	
4	

11. MATHEMATICAL PRACTICE 3 **Verify the Reasoning of Others** Whose statement makes sense? Whose statement is nonsense? Explain your reasoning.

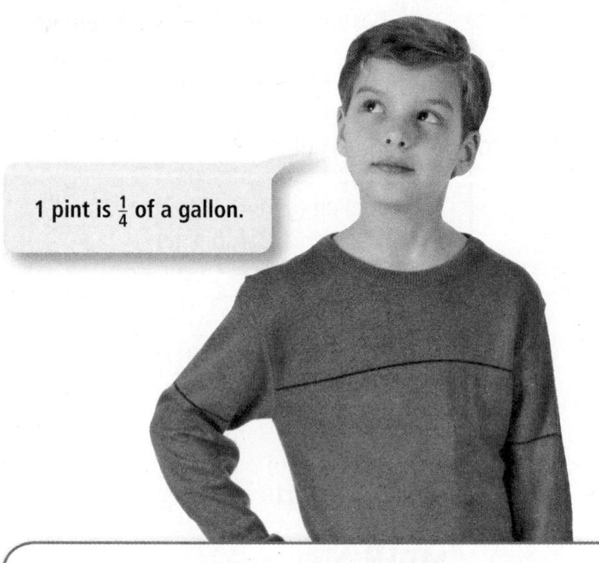
1 pint is $\frac{1}{4}$ of a gallon.

1 pint is $\frac{1}{8}$ of a gallon.

Zach's Statement	Angela's Statement

12. GO DEEPER Peter's glasses each hold 8 fluid ounces. How many glasses of juice can Peter pour from a bottle that holds 2 quarts?

13. THINK SMARTER + A pitcher contains 5 quarts of water. Josy says the pitcher contains 10 cups of water. Explain Josy's error. Then find the correct number of cups the pitcher contains.

FOR MORE PRACTICE:
Standards Practice Book

Name ______

Line Plots

Essential Question How can you make and interpret line plots with fractional data?

Measurement and Data—4.MD.4
Also 4.MD.2

MATHEMATICAL PRACTICES
MP.4, MP.5, MP.7

Unlock the Problem (Real World)

The data show the lengths of the buttons in Jen's collection. For an art project, she wants to know how many buttons are longer than $\frac{1}{4}$ inch.

You can use a line plot to solve the problem. A **line plot** is a graph that shows the frequency of data along a number line.

Length of Buttons in Jen's Collection (in inches)
$\frac{1}{4}, \frac{3}{4}, \frac{1}{4}, \frac{4}{4}, \frac{1}{4}, \frac{4}{4}$

Make a line plot to show the data.

Example 1

STEP 1 Order the data from least to greatest length and complete the tally table.

______

Buttons in Jen's Collection	
Length (in inches)	Tally
$\frac{1}{4}$	
$\frac{3}{4}$	
$\frac{4}{4}$	

STEP 2 Label the fraction lengths on the number line below from the least value of the data to the greatest.

STEP 3 Plot an *X* above the number line for each data point. Write a title for the line plot.

___ ___ ___ ___

______

So, ______ buttons are longer than $\frac{1}{4}$ inch.

Math Talk Mathematical Practices

Explain how you labeled the numbers on the number line in Step 2.

1. How many buttons are in Jen's collection? ______

2. What is the difference in length between the longest button and the shortest button in Jen's collection? ______

Think: To find the difference, subtract the numerators. The denominators stay the same.

Example 2

Some of the students in Ms. Lee's class walk to school. The data show the distances these students walk. What distance do most students walk?

Distance Students Walk to School (in miles)
$\frac{1}{2}$, $\frac{1}{2}$, $\frac{1}{4}$, $\frac{3}{4}$, $\frac{1}{4}$, $\frac{1}{2}$, $\frac{1}{2}$

Make a line plot to show the data.

STEP 1 Order the data from least to greatest distance and complete the tally table.

____

Distance Students Walk to School	
Distance (in miles)	Tally

STEP 2 Label the fraction lengths on the number line below from the least value of the data to the greatest.

STEP 3 Plot an *X* above the number line for each data point. Write a title for the line plot.

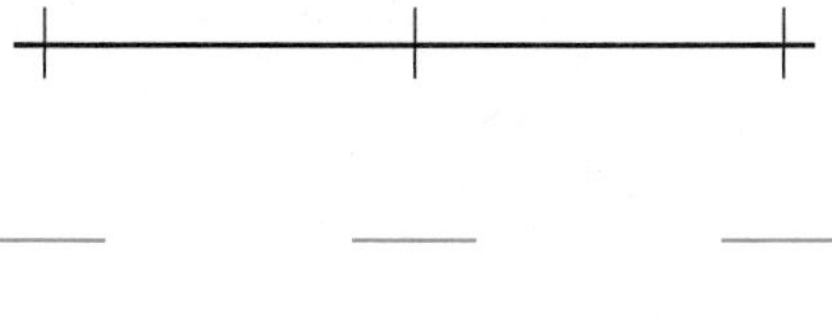

So, most students walk ____________.

3. How many more students walk $\frac{1}{2}$ mile than $\frac{1}{4}$ mile to school?

____

4. What is the difference between the longest distance and the shortest distance that students walk?

____

5. What if a new student joins Ms. Lee's class who walks $\frac{3}{4}$ mile to school? How would the line plot change? Explain.

____

Name ______________________________

Share and Show

1. A food critic collected data on the lengths of time customers waited for their food. Order the data from least to greatest time. Make a tally table and a line plot to show the data.

Time Customers Waited for Food (in hours)
$\frac{1}{2}, \frac{1}{4}, \frac{3}{4}, \frac{1}{4}, \frac{1}{4}, \frac{1}{2}, 1$

Time Customers Waited for Food	
Time (in hours)	Tally

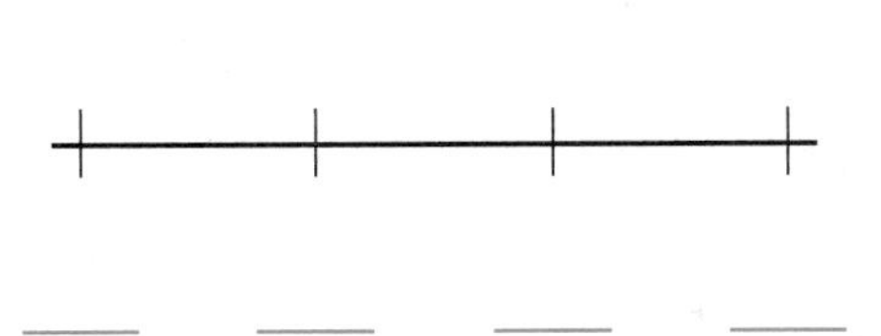

Math Talk — Mathematical Practices

Explain how the line plot helped you answer the question for Exercise 2.

Use your line plot for 2 and 3.

2. On how many customers did the food critic collect data? ____________

3. What is the difference between the longest time and the shortest time that customers waited? ____________

On Your Own

4. MATHEMATICAL PRACTICE 4 **Use Models** The data show the lengths of the ribbons Mia used to wrap packages. Make a tally table and a line plot to show the data.

Ribbon Length Used to Wrap Packages (in yards)
$\frac{1}{6}, \frac{2}{6}, \frac{5}{6}, \frac{3}{6}, \frac{2}{6}, \frac{6}{6}, \frac{3}{6}, \frac{2}{6}$

Ribbon Used to Wrap Packages	
Length (in yards)	Tally

5. What is the difference in length between the longest ribbon and the shortest ribbon Mia used? ____________

Unlock the Problem — Real World

6. GO DEEPER The line plot shows the distances the students in Mr. Boren's class ran at the track in miles. Altogether, did the students run more or less than 5 miles?

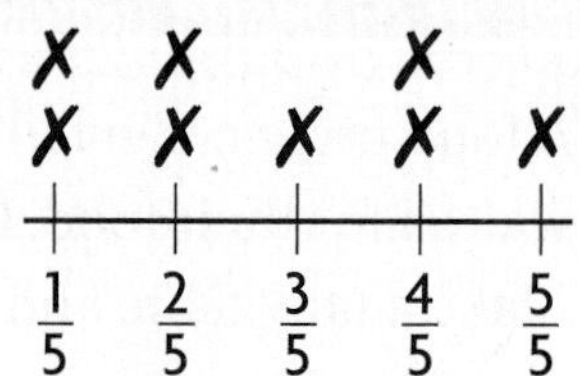

Distance Students Ran at the Track (in miles)

a. What are you asked to find? ______________________

____

b. What information do you need to use? ______________________

____

c. How will the line plot help you solve the problem? ______________________

____

d. What operation will you use to solve the problem? ______________________

e. Show the steps to solve the problem.

____

____

f. Complete the sentences.

The students ran a total of ______ miles.

______ miles ______ 5 miles; so, altogether the students ran ______ than 5 miles.

7. THINK SMARTER Lena collects antique spoons. The line plot shows the lengths of the spoons in her collection. If she lines up all of her spoons in order of size, what is the size of the middle spoon? Explain.

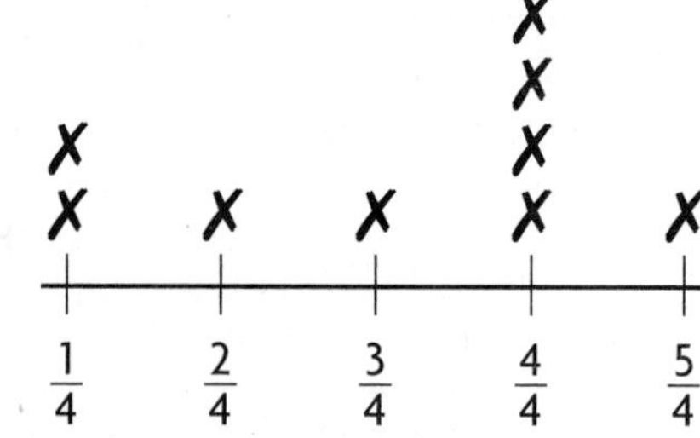

Length of Spoons (in feet)

____

____

Personal Math Trainer

8. THINK SMARTER + The table shows the distances some students hiked. Complete the line plot to show the data.

Distance Students Hiked (in miles)
$\frac{4}{8}$, $\frac{5}{8}$, $\frac{7}{8}$, $\frac{7}{8}$, $\frac{5}{8}$, $\frac{6}{8}$, $\frac{7}{8}$, $\frac{7}{8}$, $\frac{6}{8}$

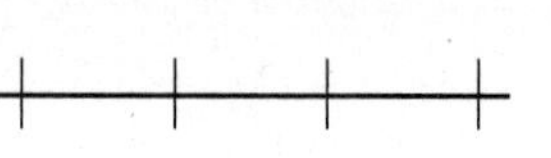

Distance Students Hiked

FOR MORE PRACTICE: Standards Practice Book

Name ______________________

Mid-Chapter Checkpoint

Vocabulary

Choose the best term from the box to complete the sentence.

Vocabulary
pint
pound
yard

1. A __________ is a customary unit used to measure weight. (p. 479)

2. The cup and the __________ are both customary units for measuring liquid volume. (p. 483)

Concepts and Skills

Complete the sentence. Write *more* or *less*. (4.MD.1)

3. A cat weighs __________ than one ounce.

4. Serena's shoe is __________ than one yard long.

Complete. (4.MD.1)

5. 5 feet = ______ inches

6. 4 tons = ______ pounds

7. 4 cups = ______ pints

8. Mrs. Byrne's class went raspberry picking. The data show the weights of the cartons of raspberries the students picked. Make a tally table and a line plot to show the data. (4.MD.4)

Weight of Cartons of Raspberries Picked (in pounds)
$\frac{3}{4}, \frac{1}{4}, \frac{2}{4}, \frac{4}{4}, \frac{1}{4}, \frac{1}{4}, \frac{2}{4}, \frac{3}{4}, \frac{3}{4}$

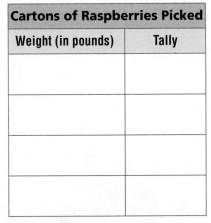

Cartons of Raspberries Picked

Weight (in pounds)	Tally

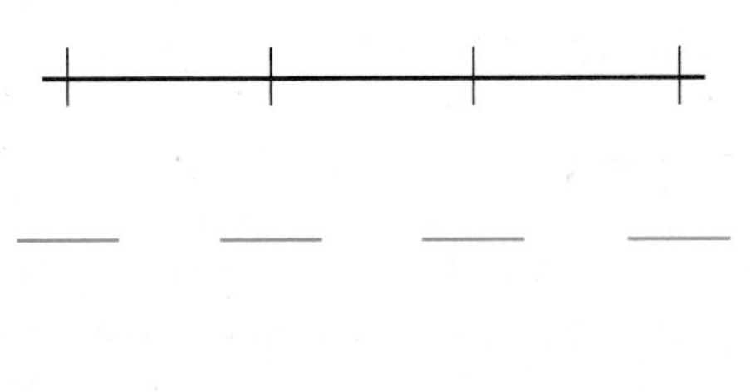

Use your line plot for 9 and 10. (4.MD.4)

9. What is the difference in weight between the heaviest carton and lightest carton of raspberries? __________

10. How many pounds of raspberries did Mrs. Byrne's class pick in all? __________

11. A jug contains 2 gallons of water. How many quarts of water does the jug contain? (4.MD.1)

____

12. Serena bought 4 pounds of dough to make pizzas. The recipe gives the amount of dough needed for a pizza in ounces. How many ounces of dough did she buy? (4.MD.1)

____

13. Vaughn threw the shot put 9 yards at a track meet. The official used a tape measure to measure the distance in feet. How many feet did he throw the shot put? (4.MD.1)

____

14. The watering can that Carlos uses in his vegetable garden holds 5 of a certain unit of liquid volume. When full, how much water is in the watering can? (4.MD.1)

____

Name ____________________

Metric Units of Length

Essential Question How can you use models to compare metric units of length?

Measurement and Data—4.MD.1
Also 4.MD.2

MATHEMATICAL PRACTICES
MP.1, MP.7, MP.8

Investigate

Materials ■ ruler (meter) ■ scissors ■ tape

Meters (m), **decimeters** (dm), centimeters (cm), and **millimeters** (mm) are all metric units of length.

Build a meterstick to show how these units are related.

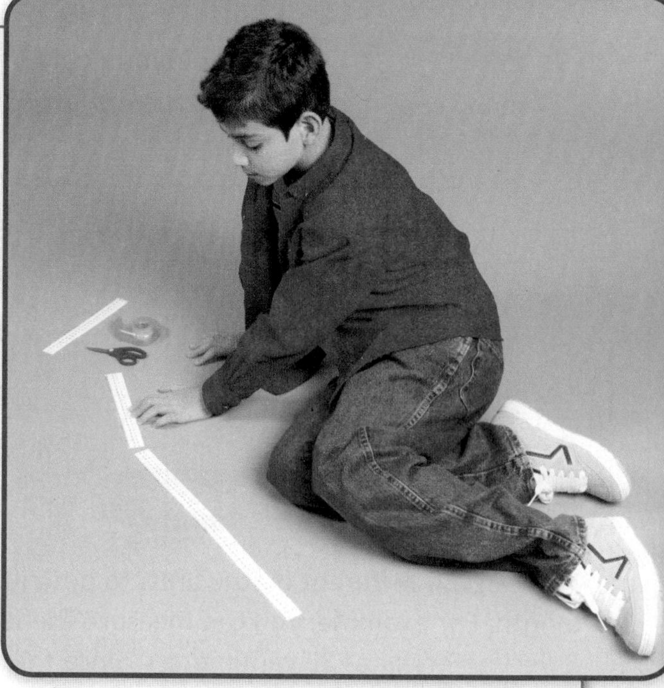

A. Cut out the meterstick strips.

B. Place the strips end-to-end to build 1 meter. Tape the strips together.

C. Look at your meter strip. What patterns do you notice about the sizes of the units?

1 meter is ______ times as long as 1 decimeter.

1 decimeter is ______ times as long as 1 centimeter.

1 centimeter is ______ times as long as 1 millimeter.

Describe the pattern you see.

____

____

Math Idea
If you lined up 1,000 metersticks end-to-end, the length of the metersticks would be 1 kilometer.

Draw Conclusions

1. Compare the size of 1 meter to the size of 1 centimeter. Use your meterstick to help.

____

2. Compare the size of 1 meter to the size of 1 millimeter. Use your meterstick to help.

____

____

3. THINK SMARTER What operation could you use to find how many centimeters are in 3 meters? Explain.

____

____

____

____

Make Connections

You can use different metric units to describe the same length. For example, you can measure the length of a book as 3 decimeters or as 30 centimeters. Since the metric system is based on the number 10, decimals or fractions can be used to describe metric lengths as equivalent units.

Think of 1 meter as one whole. Use your meter strip to write equivalent units as fractions and decimals.

1 meter = 10 decimeters

Each decimeter is

______ or ______ of a meter.

1 meter = 100 centimeters

Each centimeter is

______ or ______ of a meter.

Complete the sentence.

- A length of 51 centimeters is ______ or ______ of a meter.
- A length of 8 decimeters is ______ or ______ of a meter.
- A length of 82 centimeters is ______ or ______ of a meter.

Math Talk — Mathematical Practices

Explain how you are able to locate and write decimeters and centimeters as parts of a meter on the meterstick.

Name ______________________

Share and Show

Metric Units of Length
1 centimeter (cm) = 10 millimeters (mm)
1 decimeter (dm) = 10 centimeters
1 meter (m) = 10 decimeters
1 meter (m) = 100 centimeters
1 meter (m) = 1,000 millimeters

Complete.

1. 2 meters = ______ centimeters

2. 3 centimeters = ______ millimeters

3. 5 decimeters = ______ centimeters

MATHEMATICAL PRACTICE 4 Use Symbols **Algebra** **Compare using $<$, $>$, or $=$.**

4. 4 meters ◯ 40 decimeters

5. 5 centimeters ◯ 5 millimeters

6. 6 decimeters ◯ 65 centimeters

7. 7 meters ◯ 700 millimeters

Describe the length in meters. Write your answer as a fraction and as a decimal.

8. 65 centimeters = ______ or ______ meter

9. 47 centimeters = ______ or ______ meter

10. 9 decimeters = ______ or ______ meter

11. 2 decimeters = ______ or ______ meter

Problem Solving • Applications

12. Lucille runs the 50-meter dash in her track meet. How many decimeters long is the race?

____

13. GO DEEPER Alexis is knitting a blanket 2 meters long. Every 2 decimeters, she changes the color of the yarn to make stripes. How many stripes will the blanket have? Explain.

____

____

____

14. THINK SMARTER Julianne's desk is 75 centimeters long. She says her desk is 7.5 meters long. Describe her error.

15. THINK SMARTER Write the equivalent measurements in each column.

5,000 millimeters | 500 centimeters | 50 centimeters
$\frac{55}{100}$ meter | 0.500 meter | 0.55 meter
$\frac{500}{1,000}$ meter | 550 millimeters | 50 decimeters

5 meters	55 centimeters	500 millimeters

16. THINK SMARTER Aruna was writing a report on pecan trees. She made the table of information to the right.

Write a problem that can be solved by using the data.

Pecan Tree	
Average Measurements	
Length of nuts	3 cm to 5 cm
Height	21 m to 30 m
Width of trunk	18 dm
Width of leaf	10 cm to 20 cm

Pose a problem.

Solve your problem.

- MATHEMATICAL PRACTICE 1 **Describe** how you could change the problem by changing a unit in the problem. Then solve the problem.

FOR MORE PRACTICE:
Standards Practice Book

Name ______________________

Metric Units of Mass and Liquid Volume

Essential Question How can you compare metric units of mass and liquid volume?

Measurement and Data—4.MD.1
Also 4.MD.2

MATHEMATICAL PRACTICES
MP.2, MP.7

Unlock the Problem

Mass is the amount of matter in an object. Metric units of mass include kilograms (kg) and grams (g). Liters (L) and **milliliters** (mL) are metric units of liquid volume.

The charts show the relationship between these units.

Metric Units of Mass
1 kilogram (kg) = 1,000 grams (g)

Metric Units of Liquid Volume
1 liter (L) = 1,000 milliliters (mL)

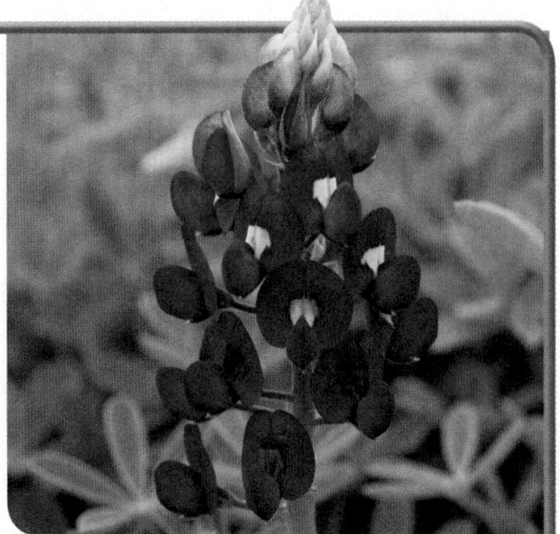

Example 1 Compare kilograms and grams.

Becky planted a flower garden full of bluebonnets. She used 9 kilograms of soil. How many grams of soil is that?

number of kilograms		grams in 1 kilogram		total grams
9	×	1,000	=	______

So, Becky used ______ grams of soil to plant her bluebonnets.

- Are kilograms heavier or lighter than grams?

______

- Will the number of grams be greater than or less than the number of kilograms?

______

- What operation will you use to solve the problem?

______

Example 2 Compare liters and milliliters.

Becky used 5 liters of water to water her bluebonnet garden. How many milliliters of water is that?

number of liters		milliliters in 1 liter		total milliliters
5	×	1,000	=	______

So, Becky used ______ milliliters of water.

Math Talk **Mathematical Practices**

Compare the size of a kilogram to the size of a gram. Then compare the size of a liter to the size of a milliliter.

Share and Show

1. There are 3 liters of water in a pitcher. How many milliliters of water are in the pitcher?

   There are ______ milliliters in 1 liter. Since I am changing

   from a larger unit to a smaller unit, I can __________ 3 by 1,000 to find the number of milliliters in 3 liters.

   So, there are ______ milliliters of water in the pitcher.

Complete.

2. 4 liters = ______ milliliters

3. 6 kilograms = ______ grams

Math Talk — **Mathematical Practices**

Explain how you found the number of grams in 6 kilograms in Exercise 3.

On Your Own

Complete.

4. 8 kilograms = ______ grams

5. 7 liters = ______ milliliters

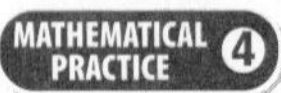

Use Symbols Algebra Compare using <, >, or =.

6. 1 kilogram ◯ 900 grams

7. 2 liters ◯ 2,000 milliliters

Look for a Pattern Algebra Complete.

8.

Liters	Milliliters
1	1,000
2	
3	
	4,000
5	
6	
	7,000
8	
9	
10	

9.

Kilograms	Grams
1	1,000
2	
	3,000
4	
5	
6	
7	
	8,000
9	
10	

Name ________________________________

Problem Solving • Applications

10. Frank wants to fill a fish tank with 8 liters of water. How many milliliters is that?

____

11. Kim has 3 water bottles. She fills each bottle with 1 liter of water. How many milliliters of water does she have?

____

12. Jared's empty backpack has a mass of 3 kilograms. He doesn't want to carry more than 7 kilograms on a trip. How many grams of equipment can Jared pack?

____

WRITE ▸ Math
Show Your Work

13. GO DEEPER A large cooler contains 20 liters of iced tea and a small cooler contains 5 liters of iced tea. How many more milliliters of iced tea does the large cooler contain than the small cooler?

____

14. THINK SMARTER A 500-gram bag of granola costs $4, and a 2-kilogram bag of granola costs $15. What is the least expensive way to buy 2,000 grams of granola? Explain.

____

____

____

____

15. MATHEMATICAL PRACTICE 3 **Verify the Reasoning of Others** The world's largest apple had a mass of 1,849 grams. Sue said the mass was greater than 2 kilograms. Does Sue's statement make sense? Explain.

____

____

____

____

Unlock the Problem

16. THINK SMARTER Lori bought 600 grams of cayenne pepper and 2 kilograms of black pepper. How many grams of pepper did she buy in all?

black pepper   cayenne pepper

a. What are you asked to find?

____

b. What information will you use?

____

c. Tell how you might solve the problem.

____

____

____

d. Show how you solved the problem.

____

____

____

____

e. Complete the sentences.

Lori bought ______ grams of cayenne pepper.

She bought ______ grams of black pepper.

______ + ______ = ______ grams

So, Lori bought ______ grams of pepper in all.

17. WRITE ▸Math Jill has two rocks. One has a mass of 20 grams and the other has a mass of 20 kilograms. Which rock has the greater mass? Explain.

____

____

____

18. THINK SMARTER For numbers 18a–18c, choose Yes or No to tell whether the measurements are equivalent.

18a. 5,000 grams and 5 kilograms ○ Yes ○ No

18b. 300 milliliters and 3 liters ○ Yes ○ No

18c. 8 grams and 8,000 kilograms ○ Yes ○ No

Name ______________________________

Units of Time

Essential Question How can you use models to compare units of time?

Measurement and Data—4.MD.1
Also 4.MD.2
MATHEMATICAL PRACTICES
MP.1, MP.5, MP.7

Unlock the Problem

The analog clock below has an hour hand, a minute hand, and a **second** hand to measure time. The time is 4:30:12.

- Are there more minutes or seconds in one hour?

____

Read Math

Read 4:30:12 as 4:30 and 12 seconds, or 30 minutes and 12 seconds after 4.

There are 60 seconds in a minute and 60 minutes in an hour. The clocks show how far the hands move for each length of time.

Start Time: 3:00:00

1 second elapses.

The time is now 3:00:01.

1 minute, or 60 seconds, elapses. The second hand has made a full turn clockwise.

The time is now 3:01:00.

1 hour, or 60 minutes, elapses. The minute hand has made a full turn clockwise.

The time is now 4:00:00.

Example 1 How does the size of an hour compare to the size of a second?

There are ______ minutes in an hour.

There are ______ seconds in a minute.

60 minutes × ______ = ______ seconds

Think: Multiply the number of minutes in an hour by the number of seconds in a minute.

There are ______ seconds in a hour.

So, 1 hour is ______ times as long as 1 second.

Mathematical Practices

How many full turns clockwise does a minute hand make in 3 hours? **Explain.**

Example 2 Compare measures.

Larissa spent 2 hours on her science project.
Cliff spent 200 minutes on his science project.
Who spent more time?

STEP 1 Make a table that relates hours and minutes.

Hours	Minutes
1	60
2	
3	

STEP 2 Compare 2 hours and 200 minutes.

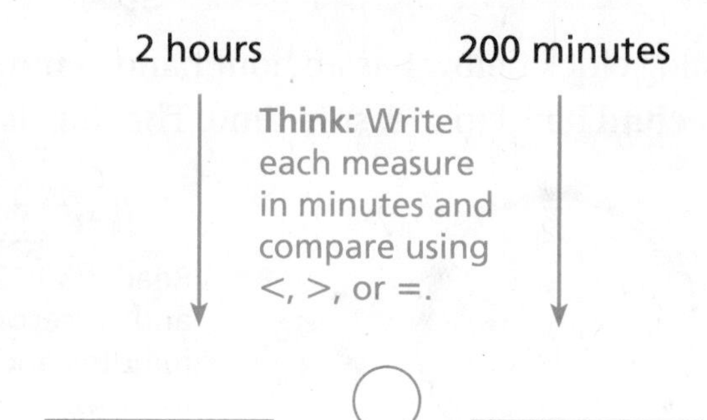

2 hours is ______ than 200 minutes.

So, ______ spent more time than ___________ on the science project.

Activity Compare the length of a week to the length of a day.

Materials ■ color pencils

The number line below shows the relationship between days and weeks.

STEP 1 Use a color pencil to shade 1 week on the number line.

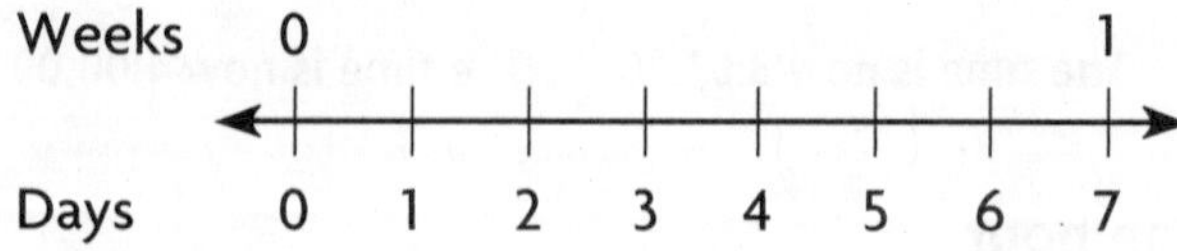

____

STEP 2 Use a different color pencil to shade 1 day on the number line.

____

STEP 3 Compare the size of 1 week to the size of 1 day.

There are ______ days in ______ week.

So, 1 week is ______ times as long as 1 day.

Name ____________________

Share and Show 

Units of Time
1 minute (min) = 60 seconds (s) 1 hour (hr) = 60 minutes 1 day (d) = 24 hours 1 week (wk) = 7 days 1 year (yr) = 12 months (mo) 1 year (yr) = 52 weeks

1. Compare the length of a year to the length of a month. Use a model to help.

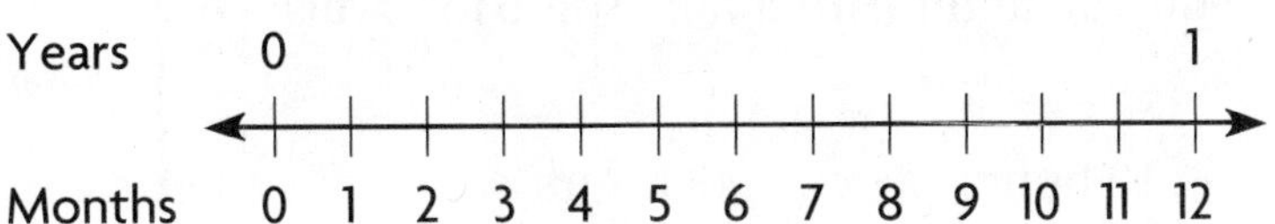

1 year is ______ times as long as ______ month.

Math Talk **Mathematical Practices**

Explain how the number line helped you compare the length of a year and the length of a month.

Complete.

2. 2 minutes = ______ seconds

3. 4 years = ______ months

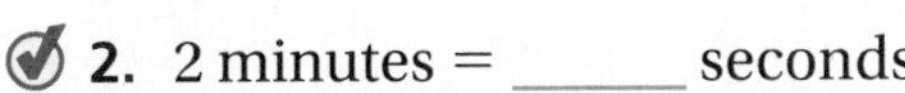

On Your Own

Complete.

4. 3 minutes = ______ seconds

5. 4 hours = ______ minutes

 **Use Symbols** **Algebra** **Compare using >, <, or =.**

6. 3 years ◯ 35 months

7. 2 days ◯ 40 hours

Problem Solving • Applications 

8. GO DEEPER Damien has lived in the apartment building for 5 years. Ken has lived there for 250 weeks. Who has lived in the building longer? Explain. Make a table to help.

____

____

Years	Weeks
1	
2	
3	
4	
5	

9.  How many hours are in a week? Explain.

____

____

10. MATHEMATICAL PRACTICE 5 **Communicate** Explain how you know that 9 minutes is less than 600 seconds.

---

11. THINK SMARTER Draw lines to match equivalent time intervals. Some intervals might not have a match.

1 hour • 2 hours • 5 hours • 12 hours • 48 hours •

• 2 days • 120 minutes • 4 days • 3,600 seconds • 300 minutes

Connect to Science

One day is the length of time it takes Earth to make one complete rotation. One year is the time it takes Earth to revolve around the sun. To make the calendar match Earth's orbit time, there are leap years. Leap years add one extra day to the year. A leap day, February 29, is added to the calendar every four years.

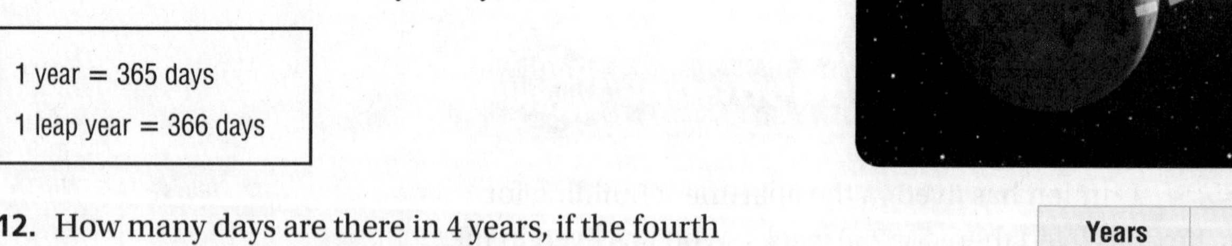

1 year = 365 days
1 leap year = 366 days

12. How many days are there in 4 years, if the fourth year is a leap year? Explain. Make a table to help.

Years	Days
1	
2	
3	
4	

---

13. Parker was born on February 29, 2008. The second time he is able to celebrate on his actual birthday is in 2016. How many days old will Parker be on February 29, 2016?

FOR MORE PRACTICE: Standards Practice Book

Name ______________________________

Problem Solving • Elapsed Time

Essential Question How can you use the strategy *draw a diagram* to solve elapsed time problems?

Measurement and Data—4.MD.2
Also 4.MD.1

MATHEMATICAL PRACTICES
MP.3, MP.5, MP.8

Unlock the Problem

Dora and her brother Kyle spent 1 hour and 35 minutes doing yard work. Then they stopped for lunch at 1:20 P.M. At what time did they start doing yard work?

Use the graphic organizer to help you solve the problem.

Read the Problem

What do I need to find?	What information do I need to use?	How will I use the information?
I need to find the time that Dora and Kyle ______________.	I need to use the ______________ and the time that they ______________.	I can draw a time line to help me count backward and find the ______________.

Solve the Problem

I draw a time line that shows the end time 1:20 P.M. Next, I count backward 1 hour and then 5 minutes at a time until I have 35 minutes.

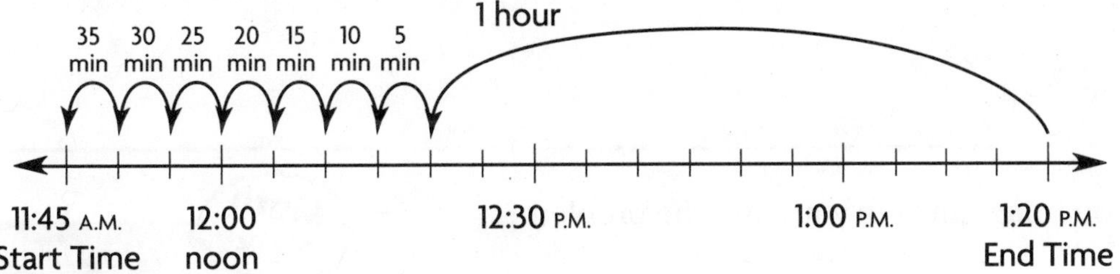

So, Dora and her brother Kyle started doing yard work at ______________.

1. What if Dora and Kyle spent 50 minutes doing yard work and they stopped for lunch at 12:30 P.M.? What time would they have started doing yard work?

____

Try Another Problem

Ben started riding his bike at 10:05 A.M. He stopped 23 minutes later when his friend Robbie asked him to play kickball. At what time did Ben stop riding his bike?

Read the Problem

What do I need to find?	What information do I need to use?	How will I use the information?

Solve the Problem

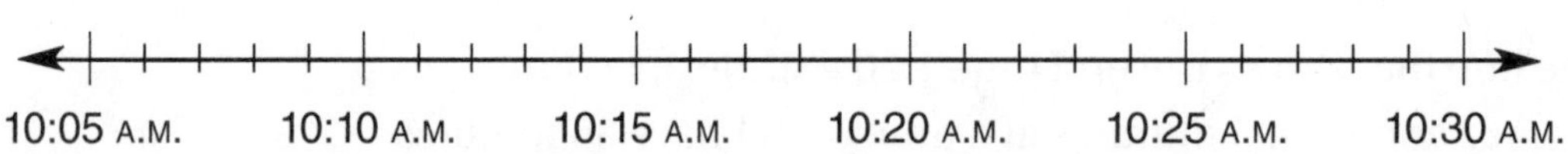

2. How did your diagram help you solve the problem?

____

____

____

Math Talk **Mathematical Practices**

Describe another way you could find the time an activity started or ended given the elapsed time and either the start or end time.

Name ______________________________

Share and Show

Unlock the Problem

- ✓ Use the Problem Solving MathBoard.
- ✓ Choose a strategy you know.
- ✓ Underline important facts.

1. Evelyn has dance class every Saturday. It lasts 1 hour and 15 minutes and is over at 12:45 P.M. At what time does Evelyn's dance class begin?

First, write the problem you need to solve.

____

Next, draw a time line to show the end time and the elapsed time.

Finally, find the start time.

Evelyn's dance class begins at ____________ .

2. THINK SMARTER What if Evelyn's dance class started at 11:00 A.M. and lasted 1 hour and 25 minutes? At what time would her class end? Describe how this problem is different from Problem 1.

____

____

3. Beth got on the bus at 8:06 A.M. Thirty-five minutes later, she arrived at school. At what time did Beth arrive at school?

____

____

4. Lyle went fishing for 1 hour and 30 minutes until he ran out of bait at 6:40 P.M. At what time did Lyle start fishing?

____

____

On Your Own

5. Mike and Jed went skiing at 10:30 A.M. They skied for 1 hour and 55 minutes before stopping for lunch. At what time did Mike and Jed stop for lunch?

____

6. GO DEEPER Mike can run a mile in 12 minutes. He starts his run at 11:30 AM. and runs 4 miles. What time does Mike finish his run?

____

7. MATHEMATICAL PRACTICE 5 **Communicate** Explain how you can use a diagram to determine the start time when the end time is 9:00 A.M. and the elapsed time is 26 minutes. What is the start time?

____

____

____

____

WRITE Math
Show Your Work

8. THINK SMARTER Bethany finished her math homework at 4:20 P.M. She did 25 multiplication problems in all. If each problem took her 3 minutes to do, at what time did Bethany start her math homework?

____

9. THINK SMARTER Vincent began his weekly chores on Saturday morning at 11:20 A.M. He finished 1 hour and 10 minutes later. Draw a time line to show the end time.

Vincent finished his chores at ___________ P.M.

Name ______________________

Mixed Measures

Essential Question How can you solve problems involving mixed measures?

Measurement and Data—4.MD.2
Also 4.MD.1
MATHEMATICAL PRACTICES
MP.1, MP.2, MP.8

Unlock the Problem

Herman is building a picnic table for a new campground. The picnic table is 5 feet 10 inches long. How long is the picnic table in inches?

- Is the mixed measure greater than or less than 6 feet?

____

- How many inches are in 1 foot?

____

Change a mixed measure.

Think of 5 feet 10 inches as 5 feet + 10 inches.

Write feet as inches.

5 feet
+ 10 inches

Think: 5 feet × 12 = 60 inches →

____ inches
+ ____ inches
____ inches

So, the picnic table is ______ inches long.

Example 1 Add mixed measures.

Herman built the picnic table in 2 days. The first day he worked for 3 hours 45 minutes. The second day he worked for 2 hours 10 minutes. How long did it take him to build the table?

STEP 1 Add the minutes.

3 hr 45 min
+ 2 hr 10 min
____ min

STEP 2 Add the hours.

3 hr 45 min
+ 2 hr 10 min
____ hr 55 min

So, it took Herman ______________________ to build the table.

Math Talk **Mathematical Practices**

How is adding mixed measures similar to adding tens and ones? How is it different? **Explain.**

- What if Herman worked an extra 5 minutes on the picnic table? How long would he have worked on the table then? Explain.

____

____

Example 2 Subtract mixed measures.

Alicia is building a fence around the picnic area. She has a pole that is 6 feet 6 inches long. She cuts off 1 foot 7 inches from one end. How long is the pole now?

STEP 1 Subtract the inches.

Think: 7 inches is greater than 6 inches. You need to regroup to subtract.

6 ft 6 in. = 5 ft 6 in. + 12 in.

= 5 ft _____ in.

```
   5  18
   6 ft 6 in.
 − 1 ft 7 in.
 ------------
          in.
```

STEP 2 Subtract the feet.

```
   5  18
   6 ft 6 in.
 − 1 ft 7 in.
 ------------
     ft 11 in.
```

So, the pole is now _____________________ long.

ERROR Alert

Be sure to check that you are regrouping correctly. There are 12 inches in 1 foot.

Try This! Subtract.

3 pounds 5 ounces − 1 pound 2 ounces

Share and Show

1. A truck is carrying 2 tons 500 pounds of steel. How many pounds of steel is the truck carrying?

Think of 2 tons 500 pounds as 2 tons + 500 pounds.
Write tons as pounds.

```
  2 tons        Think: 2 tons × 2,000 =  →          pounds
+ 500 pounds    _________ pounds                 +  pounds
                                                 ----------
                                                    pounds
```

So, the truck is carrying __________ pounds of steel.

Name ______________________

Rewrite each measure in the given unit.

2. 1 yard 2 feet

   ______ feet

3. 3 pints 1 cup

   ______ cups

4. 3 weeks 1 day

   ______ days

Add or subtract.

5. 2 lb 4 oz
   + 1 lb 6 oz

6. 3 gal 2 qt
   − 1 gal 3 qt

7. 5 hr 20 min
   − 3 hr 15 min

Math Talk — Mathematical Practices

How do you know when you need to regroup to subtract? Explain.

On Your Own

Rewrite each measure in the given unit.

8. 1 hour 15 minutes

   ______ minutes

9. 4 quarts 2 pints

   ______ pints

10. 10 feet 10 inches

    ______ inches

Add or subtract.

11. 2 tons 300 lb
    − 1 ton 300 lb

12. 10 gal 8 c
    + 8 gal 9 c

13. 7 lb 6 oz
    − 2 lb 12 oz

Problem Solving • Applications

14. MATHEMATICAL PRACTICE 3 Apply Ahmed fills 6 pitchers with juice. Each pitcher contains 2 quarts 1 pint. How many pints of juice does he have in all?

    ____

15. **Sense or Nonsense?** Sam and Dave each solve the problem at the right. Sam says the sum is 4 feet 18 inches. Dave says the sum is 5 feet 6 inches. Whose answer makes sense? Whose answer is nonsense? Explain.

    2 ft 10 in.
    + 2 ft 8 in.

    ____

    ____

16. THINK SMARTER Jackson has a rope 1 foot 8 inches long. He cuts it into 4 equal pieces. How many inches long is each piece?

    ____

Unlock the Problem Real World

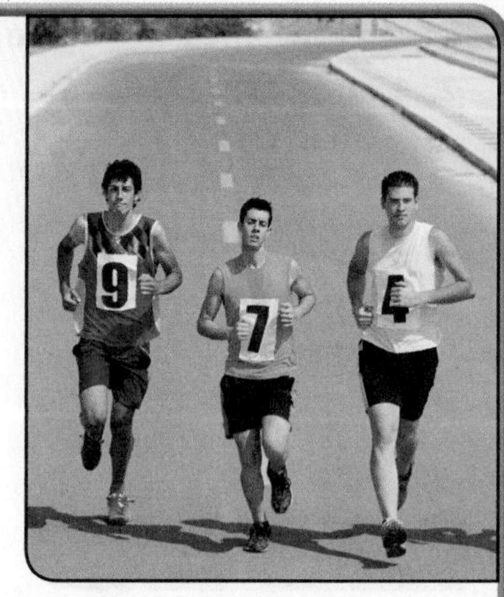

17. Theo is practicing for a 5-kilometer race. He runs 5 kilometers every day and records his time. His normal time is 25 minutes 15 seconds. Yesterday it took him only 23 minutes 49 seconds. How much faster was his time yesterday than his normal time?

a. What are you asked to find?

____

____

b. What information do you know?

____

____

c. How will you solve the problem?

____

d. Solve the problement.

____

e. Fill in the sentence.

Yesterday, Theo ran 5 kilometers in a time that was ___________ faster than his normal time.

18. GO DEEPER Don has 5 pieces of pipe. Each piece is 3 feet 6 inches long. If Don joins the pieces end to end to make one long pipe, how long will the new pipe be?

____

Personal Math Trainer

19. THINK SMARTER + Ana mixes 2 quarts 1 pint of apple juice and 1 quart 3 cups of cranberry juice. Will her mixture be able to fit in a 1 gallon pitcher? Explain.

____

____

____

____

____

FOR MORE PRACTICE: Standards Practice Book

ALGEBRA
Lesson 12.11

Name ______________________

Patterns in Measurement Units

Essential Question How can you use patterns to write number pairs for measurement units?

Measurement and Data—4.MD.1

MATHEMATICAL PRACTICES
MP.4, MP.5, MP.7

CONNECT The table at the right relates yards and feet. You can think of the numbers in the table as number pairs. 1 and 3, 2 and 6, 3 and 9, 4 and 12, and 5 and 15 are number pairs.

Yards	Feet
1	3
2	6
3	9
4	12
5	15

The number pairs show the relationship between yards and feet. 1 yard is equal to 3 feet, 2 yards is equal to 6 feet, 3 yards is equal to 9 feet, and so on.

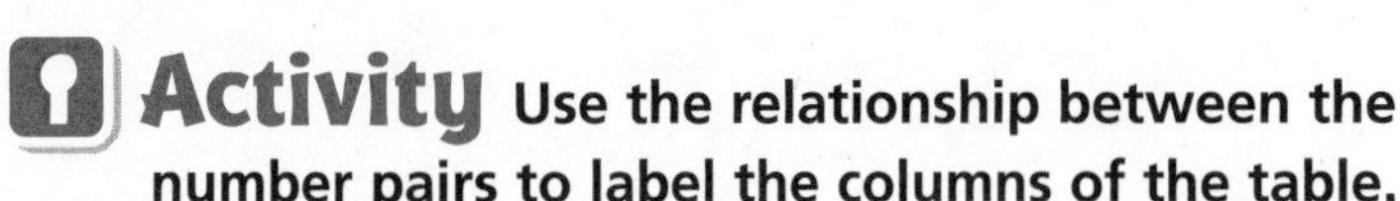

Unlock the Problem (Real World)

Lillian made the table below to relate two units of time. What units of time does the pattern in the table show?

Activity Use the relationship between the number pairs to label the columns of the table.

______	______
1	7
2	14
3	21
4	28
5	35

- List the number pairs.

  ____

- Describe the relationship between the numbers in each pair.

  ____

  ____

- Label the columns of the table.

Think: What unit of time is 7 times as great as another unit?

Math Talk — Mathematical Practices

Look at each number pair in the table. Could you change the order of the numbers in the number pairs? **Explain** why or why not.

Try This! Jasper made the table below to relate two customary units of liquid volume. What customary units of liquid volume does the pattern in the table show?

- List the number pairs.

____

- Describe the relationship between the numbers in each pair.

____

____

____

- Label the columns of the table.

____	____
1	4
2	8
3	12
4	16
5	20

Think: What customary unit of liquid volume is 4 times as great as another unit?

- What other units could you have used to label the columns of the table above? Explain.

____

____

____

Share and Show

1. The table shows a pattern for two units of time. Label the columns of the table with the units of time.

Think: What unit of time is 24 times as great as another unit?

____	____
1	24
2	48
3	72
4	96
5	120

Math Talk **Mathematical Practices**

Explain how you labeled the columns of the table.

Name ______________________________

Each table shows a pattern for two customary units. Label the columns of the table.

2.

______	______
1	2
2	4
3	6
4	8
5	10

3.

______	______
1	16
2	32
3	48
4	64
5	80

On Your Own

Each table shows a pattern for two units of time. Label the columns of the table.

4.

______	______
1	60
2	120
3	180
4	240
5	300

5.

______	______
1	12
2	24
3	36
4	48
5	60

Each table shows a pattern for two metric units of length. Label the columns of the table.

6.

______	______
1	10
2	20
3	30
4	40
5	50

7.

______	______
1	100
2	200
3	300
4	400
5	500

8. GO DEEPER List the number pairs for the table in Exercise 6. Describe the relationship between the numbers in each pair.

____

____

____

9. What's the Error? Maria wrote *Weeks* as the label for the first column of the table and *Years* as the label for the second column. Describe her error.

?	?
1	52
2	104
3	156
4	208
5	260

10. MATHEMATICAL PRACTICE 3 **Verify the Reasoning of Others** The table shows a pattern for two metric units. Lou labels the columns *Meters* and *Millimeters*. Zayna labels them *Liters* and *Milliliters*. Whose answer makes sense? Whose answer is nonsense? Explain.

?	?
1	1,000
2	2,000
3	3,000
4	4,000
5	5,000

11. THINK SMARTER Look at the following number pairs: 1 and 365, 2 and 730, 3 and 1,095. The number pairs describe the relationship between which two units of time? Explain.

12. THINK SMARTER The tables show patterns for some units of measurement. Write the correct labels in each table.

Ounces | Days | Feet | Gallons | Hours | Inches | Pounds | Quarts

____	____
1	12
2	24
3	36
4	48

____	____
1	24
2	48
3	72
4	96

____	____
1	4
2	8
3	12
4	16

Name ________________________________

Chapter 12 Review/Test

1. Mrs. Miller wants to estimate the width of the steps in front of her house. Select the best benchmark for her to use.

   (A) her fingertip

   (B) the thickness of a dime

   (C) the width of a license plate

   (D) how far she can walk in 20 minutes

2. Franco played computer chess for 3 hours. Lian played computer chess for 150 minutes. Compare the times spent playing computer chess. Complete the sentence.

   ____________ played for ______________ longer than ____________.

3. Select the measures that are equal. Mark all that apply.

   (A) 6 feet

   (B) 15 yards

   (C) 45 feet

   (D) 600 inches

   (E) 12 feet

   (F) 540 inches

4. Jackie made 6 quarts of lemonade. Jackie says she made 3 pints of lemonade. Explain Jackie's error. Then find the correct number of pints of lemonade.

GO DIGITAL Assessment Options Chapter Test

5. Josh practices gymnastics each day after school. The data shows the lengths of time Josh practiced gymnastics for 2 weeks.

Time Practicing Gymnastics (in hours)
$\frac{1}{4}$, $\frac{1}{4}$, $\frac{3}{4}$, $\frac{3}{4}$, $\frac{1}{2}$, 1, 1, 1, $\frac{3}{4}$, 1

Part A

Make a tally table and line plot to show the data.

Time Practicing Gymnastics	
Time (in hours)	Tally

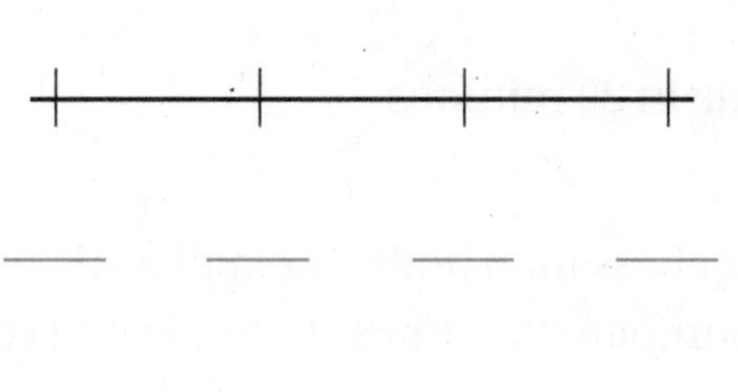

Part B

Explain how you used the tally table to label the numbers and plot the *X*s.

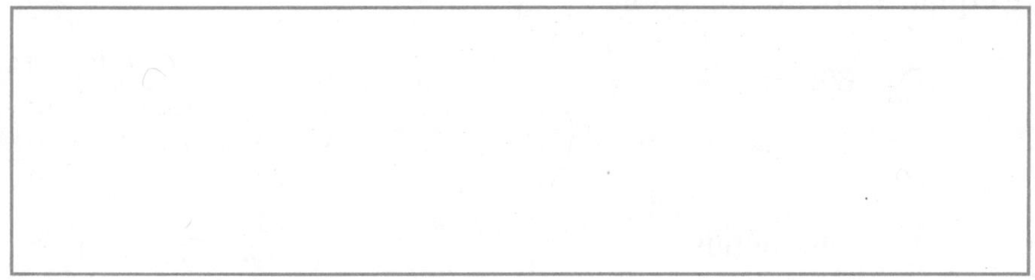

Part C

What is the difference between the longest time and shortest time Josh spent practicing gymnastics?

______ hour

6. Select the correct word to complete the sentence.

Juan brings a water bottle with him to soccer practice.

A full water bottle holds [1 liter / 10 milliliters / 1 meter] of water.

Name ________________________________

7. Write the symbol that compares the weights correctly.

<	=	>

128 ounces ______ 8 pounds

8,000 pounds ______ 3 tons

8. Dwayne bought 5 yards of wrapping paper. How many inches of wrapping paper did he buy?

______ inches

9. A sack of potatoes weighs 14 pounds 9 ounces. After Wendy makes potato salad for a picnic, the sack weighs 9 pounds 14 ounces. What is the weight of the potatoes Wendy used for the potato salad? Write the numbers to show the correct subtraction.

4	5	11	13	19	25	39

☐	☐
14 pounds	9 ounces
− 9 pounds	14 ounces
☐ pounds	☐ ounces

10. Sabita made this table to relate two customary units of liquid volume.

______	______
1	2
2	4
3	6
4	8
5	10

Part A

List the number pairs for the table. Then describe the relationship between the numbers in each pair.

Part B

Label the columns of the table. Explain your answer.

11. The table shows the distances some students swam in miles. Complete the line plot to show the data.

Distance Students Swam(in miles)
$\frac{1}{8}$, $\frac{2}{8}$, $\frac{3}{8}$, $\frac{3}{8}$, $\frac{5}{8}$, $\frac{3}{8}$, $\frac{2}{8}$, $\frac{4}{8}$, $\frac{3}{8}$, $\frac{1}{8}$, $\frac{4}{8}$, $\frac{4}{8}$

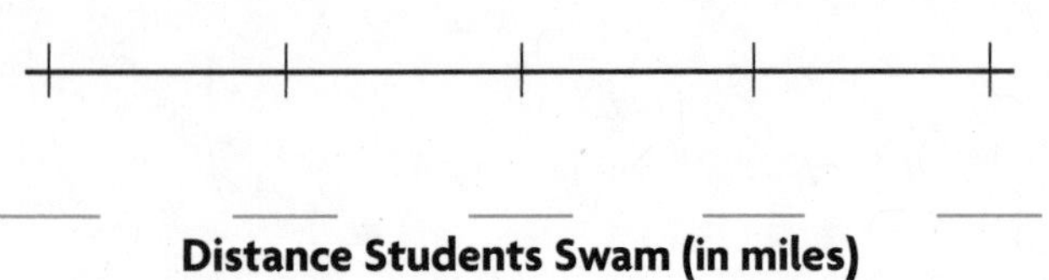

____ ____ ____ ____ ____

Distance Students Swam (in miles)

What is the difference between the longest distance and the shortest distance the students swam?

☐ mile

12. An elephant living in a wildlife park weighs 4 tons. How many pounds does the elephant weigh?

_____ pounds

13. Katia bought two melons. She says the difference in mass between the melons is 5,000 grams. Which two melons did Katia buy?

Ⓐ watermelon: 8 kilograms

Ⓑ cantaloupe: 5 kilograms

Ⓒ honeydew: 3 kilograms

Ⓓ casaba melon: 2 kilograms

Ⓔ crenshaw melon: 1 kilogram

14. Write the equivalent measurements in each column.

3,000 millimeters	300 centimeters	30 centimeters
$\frac{35}{100}$ meter	0.300 meter	0.35 meter
$\frac{300}{1,000}$ meter	350 millimeters	30 decimeters

3 meters	35 centimeters	300 millimeters

Name ____________________

15. Cheryl is making a mixed fruit drink for a party. She mixes 7 pints each of apple juice and cranberry juice. How many fluid ounces of mixed fruit drink does Cheryl make?

______ fluid ounces

16. Hamid's soccer game will start at 11:00 A.M., but the players must arrive at the field three-quarters of an hour early to warm up. The game must end by 1:15 P.M.

Part A

Hamid says he has to be at the field at 9:45 A.M. is Hamid correct? Explain your answer.

Part B

The park closes at 6:30 P.M. There is a 15-minute break between each game played at the park, and each game takes the same amount of time as Hamid's soccer game. How many more games can be played before the park closes? Explain your answer.

17. For numbers 17a–17e, select Yes or No to tell whether the measurements are equivalent.

17a.	7,000 grams and 7 kilograms	○ Yes	○ No
17b.	200 milliliters and 2 liters	○ Yes	○ No
17c.	6 grams and 6,000 kilograms	○ Yes	○ No
17d.	5 liters and 5,000 milliliters	○ Yes	○ No
17e.	2 milliliters and 2,000 liters	○ Yes	○ No

18. Draw lines to match equivalent time intervals.

$\frac{1}{2}$ hour	2 hours	3 hours	8 hours	72 hours
3 days	180 minutes	1,800 seconds	480 minutes	7,200 seconds

19. Anya arrived at the library on Saturday morning at 11:10 A.M. She left the library 1 hour 20 minutes later. Draw a time line to show the end time.

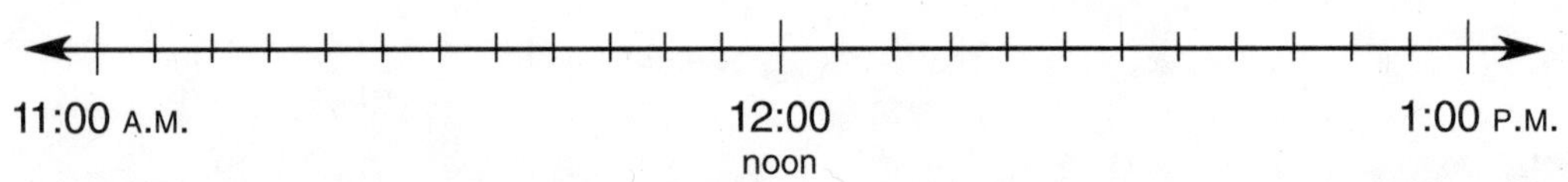

Anya left the library at ______ P.M.

20. The tables show patterns for some units of measurement. Write the correct labels in each table.

Pints | Days | Feet | Cups | Week | Yards | Inches | Quarts

1	3
2	6
3	9
4	12

1	7
2	14
3	21
4	28

1	4
2	8
3	12
4	16

21. An Olympic swimming pool is 25 meters wide. How many decimeters wide is an Olympic swimming pool?

______ decimeters wide

22. Frankie is practicing for a 5-kilometer race. His normal time is 31 minutes 21 seconds. Yesterday it took him only 29 minutes 38 seconds.

How much faster was Frankie yesterday than his normal time?

____

Chapter 13

Algebra: Perimeter and Area

Show What You Know 

Check your understanding of important skills.

Name ______________________

▶ Missing Factors Find the missing factor.

1.  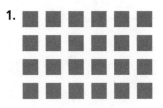

_____ $\times 6 = 24$

2. 

$3 \times$ _____ $= 27$

▶ Add Whole Numbers Find the sum.

3. $17 + 153 + 67 =$ ________

4. $8 + 78 + 455 =$ ________

5. $211 + 52 + 129 + 48 =$ ________

6. $42 + 9 + 336 + 782 =$ ________

▶ Multiply Whole Numbers Find the product.

7. 78×6

8. 29×7

9. 42×5

10. 57×9

Math Detective

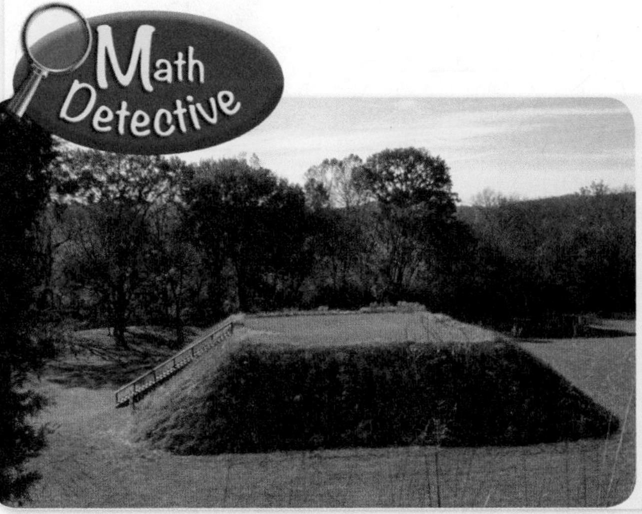

Native Americans once lived near Cartersville, Georgia, in an area that is now a state park. They constructed burial mounds that often contained artifacts, such as beads, feathers, and copper ear ornaments. One of the park's mounds is 63 feet in height. Be a Math Detective. If the top of the mound is rectangular in shape with a perimeter of 322 yards, what could be the side lengths of the rectangle?

Personal Math Trainer
Online Assessment and Intervention

Vocabulary Builder

▶ Visualize It

Sort words with a ✓ using the Venn diagram.

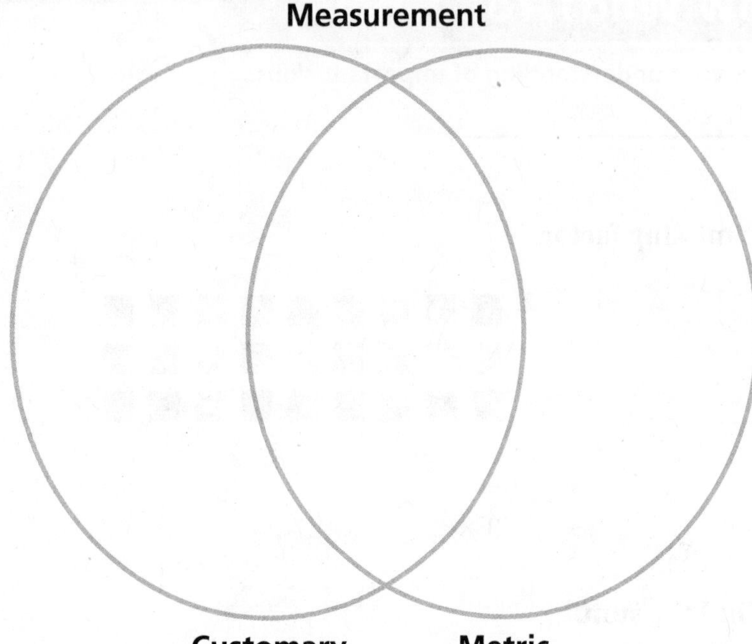

Review Words

✓ centimeter
✓ foot
✓ inch
✓ kilometer
✓ meter
✓ mile
✓ yard

Preview Words

✓ area
base
✓ formula
✓ height
✓ perimeter
square unit

▶ Understand Vocabulary

Write the word or term that answers the riddle.

1. I am the number of square units needed to cover a surface.

____

2. I am the distance around a shape.

____

3. I am a unit of area that measures 1 unit by 1 unit.

____

4. I am a set of symbols that expresses a mathematical rule.

____

GO DIGITAL • Interactive Student Edition • Multimedia eGlossary

Name ______________________

Perimeter

Essential Question How can you use a formula to find the perimeter of a rectangle?

Measurement and Data—4.MD.3

MATHEMATICAL PRACTICES
MP.1, MP.7, MP.8

Unlock the Problem

Julio is putting a stone border around his rectangular garden. The length of the garden is 7 feet. The width of the garden is 5 feet. How many feet of stone border does Julio need?

- Circle the numbers you will use.
- What are you asked to find?

____

____

Perimeter is the distance around a shape.

To find how many feet of stone border Julio needs, find the perimeter of the garden.

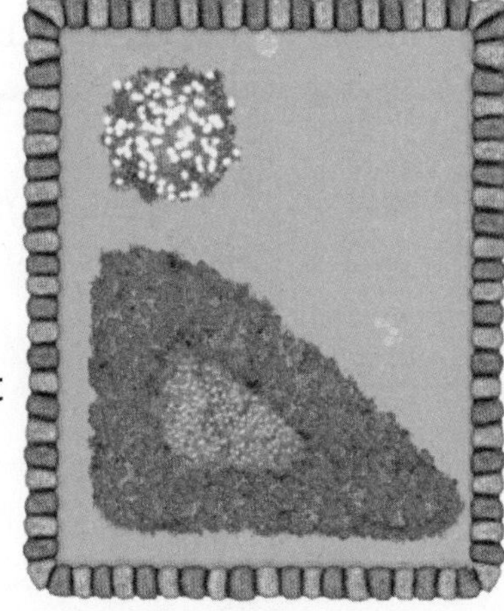

Use addition.

Perimeter of a Rectangle = length + width + length + width

$7 + 5 + 7 + 5 =$ ______

The perimeter is ______ feet.

So, Julio needs ______ feet of stone border.

Use multiplication.

A Find Perimeter of a Rectangle

Perimeter = (2 × length) + (2 × width)

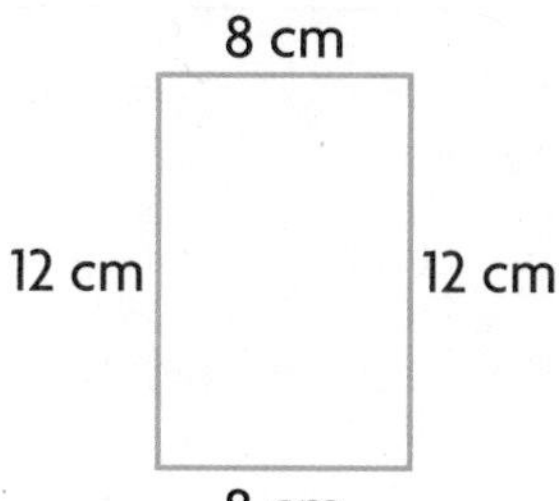

Perimeter $= (2 \times 12) + (2 \times 8)$

$= 24 + 16$

$=$ ______

So, the perimeter is ______ centimeters.

B Find Perimeter of a Square

Perimeter = 4 × one side

16 in.

16 in. 16 in.

16 in.

Perimeter $= 4 \times 16$

$=$ ______

So, the perimeter is ______ inches.

Mathematical Practices

Explain how using addition and using multiplication to find the perimeter of a rectangle are related.

Use a Formula A **formula** is a mathematical rule. You can use a formula to find perimeter.

$P = (2 \times l) + (2 \times w)$

↑ perimeter ↑ length ↑ width

width

length

Example Find the perimeter of the rectangle.

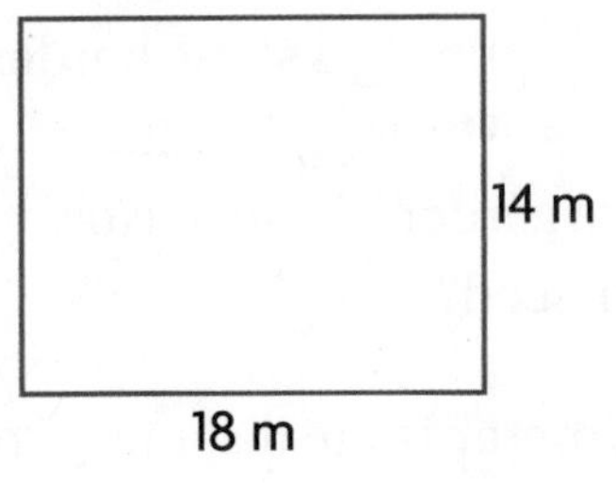

$P = (2 \times l) + (2 \times w)$

$= (2 \times$ ______ $) + (2 \times$ ______ $)$ Think: Write the measures you know.

$=$ ______ $+$ ______ Think: Do what is in parentheses first.

$=$ ______

The perimeter of the rectangle is __________.

1. Can you use the Distributive Property to write the formula $P = (2 \times l) + (2 \times w)$ another way? Explain.

____

____

____

____

Try This! **Write a formula for the perimeter of a square.**

Use the letter ______ for perimeter.

Use the letter ______ for the length of a side.

Formula: ____________________

2. Justify the formula you wrote for the perimeter of a square.

____

____

____

____

Name ________________________________

Share and Show

Formulas for Perimeter

Rectangle:
$P = (2 \times l) + (2 \times w)$ or
$P = 2 \times (l + w)$

Square:
$P = 4 \times s$

1. Find the perimeter of the rectangle.

$P = (\_\_\_ \times \_\_\_) + (\_\_\_ \times \_\_\_)$

$= (\_\_\_ \times \_\_\_) + (\_\_\_ \times \_\_\_)$

$= \_\_\_ + \_\_\_$

$= \_\_\_$

8 ft

4 ft

The perimeter is ______ feet.

Find the perimeter of the rectangle or square.

2. 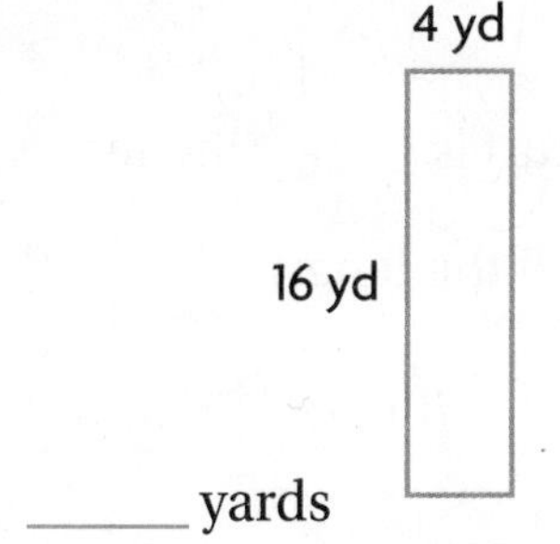

______ yards

3. 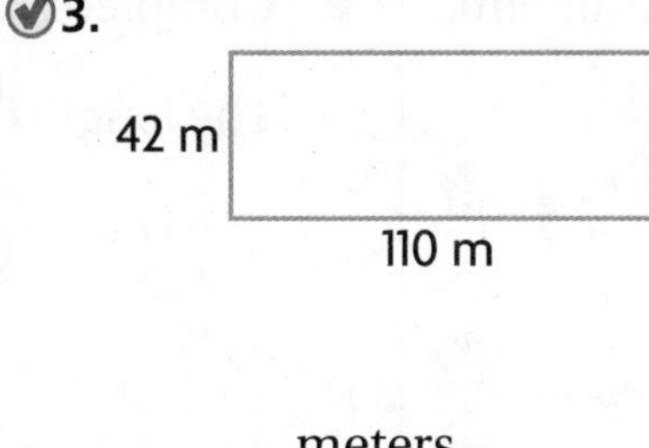

______ meters

4. 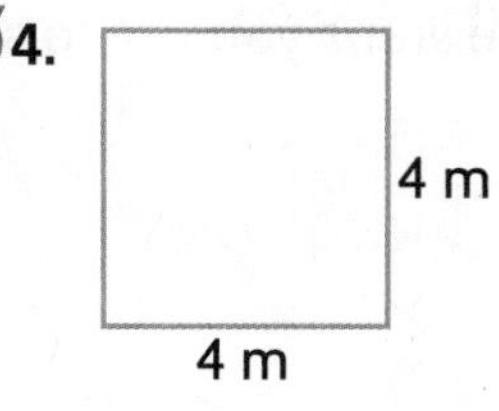

______ meters

Math Talk Mathematical Practices

Can you use the formula $P = (2 \times l) + (2 \times w)$ to find the perimeter of a square? **Explain.**

On Your Own

Find the perimeter of the rectangle or square.

5. 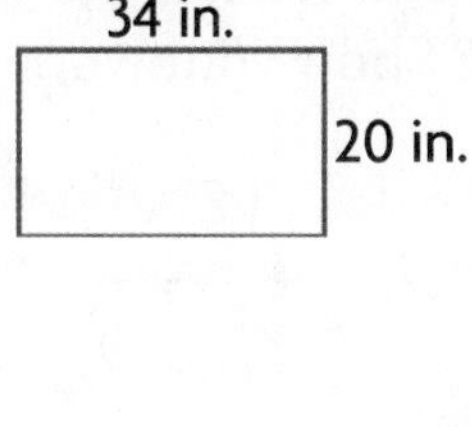

______ inches

6. 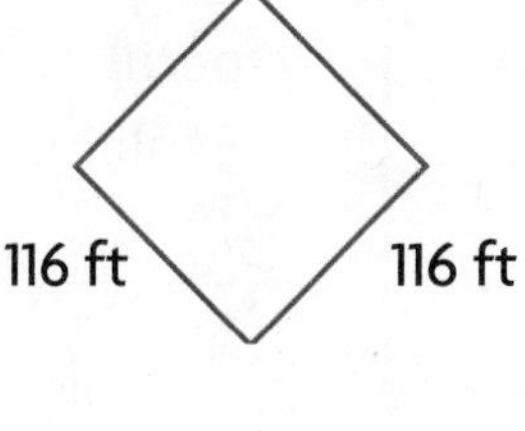

______ feet

7. 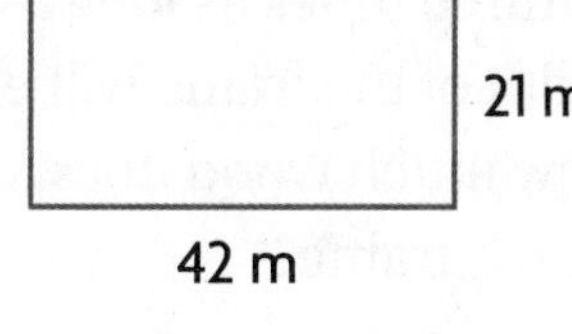

______ meters

8. Robert wants to put lights around the edge of his yard. The yard is 40 feet long and 25 feet wide. How many feet of lights does he need?

____

9. MATHEMATICAL PRACTICE 1 **Analyze** What is the side length of a square with a perimeter of 60 meters?

____

Unlock the Problem Real World

10. THINK SMARTER Alejandra plans to sew fringe on a scarf. The scarf is shaped like a rectangle. The length of the scarf is 48 inches.The width is one half the length. How much fringe does Alejandra need?

a. Draw a picture of the scarf, and label the given measurements on your drawing.

b. What do you need to find?

____

c. What formula will you use?

____

d. Show the steps you use to solve the problem.

e. Complete.

The length of the scarf is _____ inches.

The width is one half the length,

or _____ ÷ 2 = _____ inches.

So, the perimeter is (_____ × _____) +

(_____ × _____) = _____ inches.

f. Alejandra needs __________ of fringe.

11. GO DEEPER Marcia will make a frame for her picture. The picture frame will be three times as long as it is wide. The width of the frame will be 5 inches. How much wood does Marcia need for the frame?

____

12. THINK SMARTER Maya is building a sandbox that is 36 inches wide. The length is four times the width. What is the perimeter of the sandbox? Show your work. Explain.

FOR MORE PRACTICE:
Standards Practice Book

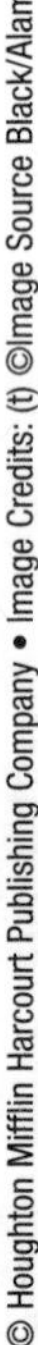

Name ______________________________

Area

Essential Question How can you use a formula to find the area of a rectangle?

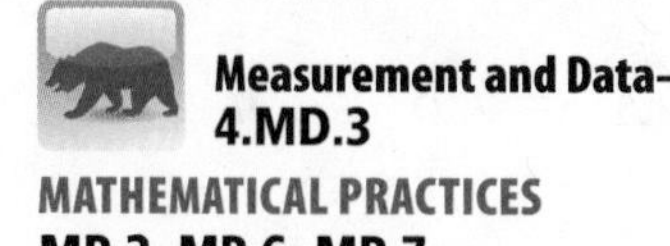

MATHEMATICAL PRACTICES
MP.3, MP.6, MP.7

Unlock the Problem

The **base, *b*,** of a two-dimensional figure can be any side. The **height, *h*,** is the measure of a perpendicular line segment from the base to the top of the figure.

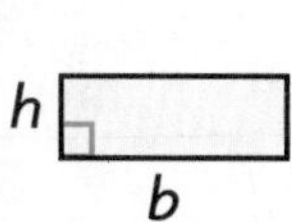

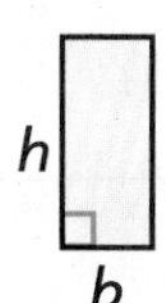

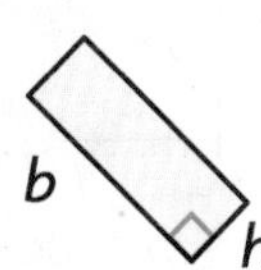

Remember

Perpendicular lines and perpendicular line segments form right angles.

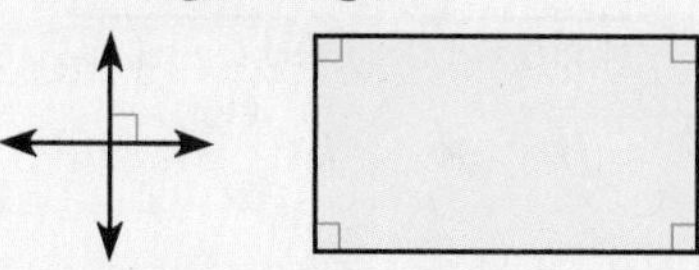

Area is the number of **square units** needed to cover a flat surface without gaps or overlaps. A square unit is a square that is 1 unit long and 1 unit wide. To find the area of a figure, count the number of square units inside the figure.

1 unit
1 unit 1 unit
1 unit

How are the base, height, and area of a rectangle related?

Complete the table to find the area.

Figure	Base	Height	Area
	5 units		

1. What relationship do you see among the base, height, and area?

____

____

Math Talk **Mathematical Practices**

How do you decide which side of a rectangle to use as the base?

2. Write a formula for the area of a rectangle. Use the letter *A* for area. Use the letter *b* for base. Use the letter *h* for height.

Formula: ______________________________

Use a Formula You can use a formula to find the area.

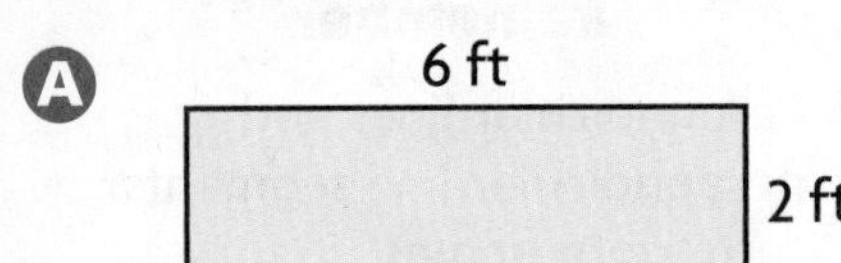

height

base

Math Idea

You can think of the base and height of a rectangle as length (l) and width (w), since the length and width are perpendicular. You can write the formula for the area (A) of a rectangle as $A = l \times w$.

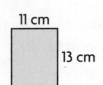

Examples Use a formula to find the area of a rectangle and a square.

A

6 ft

2 ft

$A = b \times h$

$= \_\_\_\_ \times \_\_\_\_$

$= \_\_\_\_$

The area is ________.

B

2 m

2 m

$A = b \times h$

$= \_\_\_\_ \times \_\_\_\_$

$= \_\_\_\_$

The area is ________.

Try This! Write a formula for the area of a square.

Use the letter ____ for area.

Use the letter ____ for the length of a side.

Formula: ________________

Share and Show

1. Find the area of the rectangle.

$A = b \times \_\_\_\_$

$= \_\_\_\_ \times \_\_\_\_$

$= \_\_\_\_$

11 cm

13 cm

Name ______________________________

Formulas for Area

Rectangle: $A = b \times h$ | Square: $A = s \times s$

Find the area of the rectangle or square.

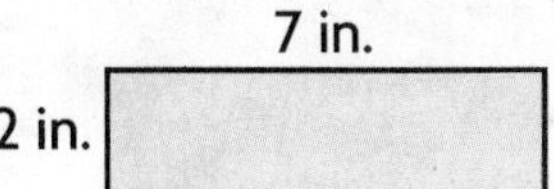

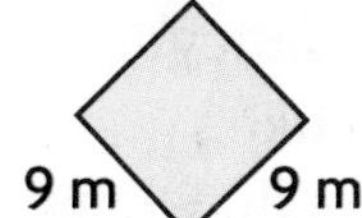

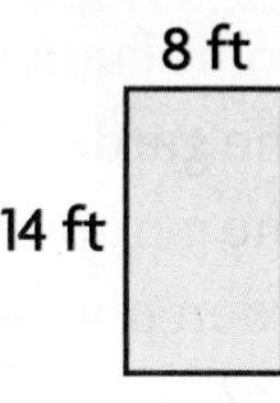

Math Talk — **Mathematical Practices**

Explain how to find the area of a square if you only know the length of one side is 23 feet.

On Your Own

Find the area of the rectangle or square.

5.

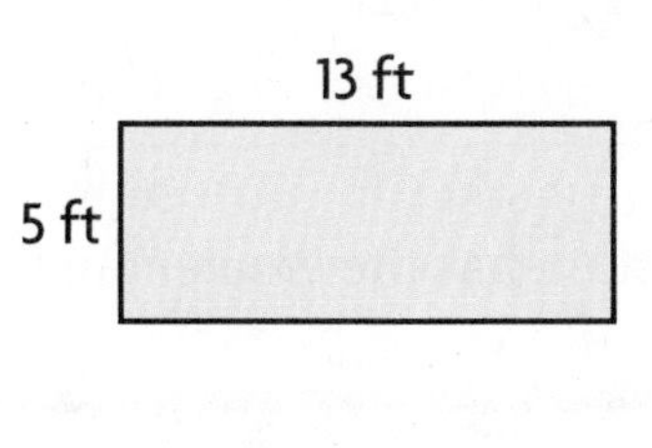

6.

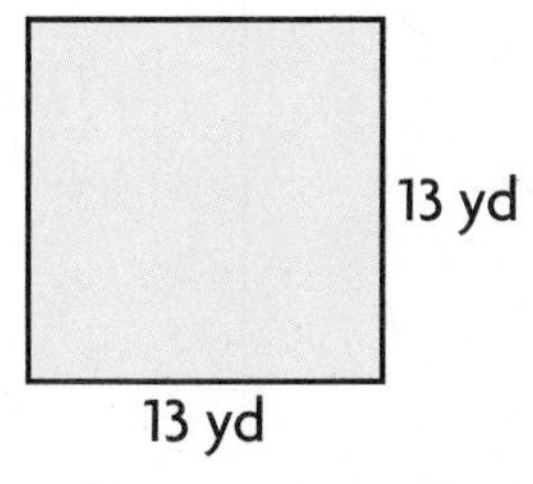

7.

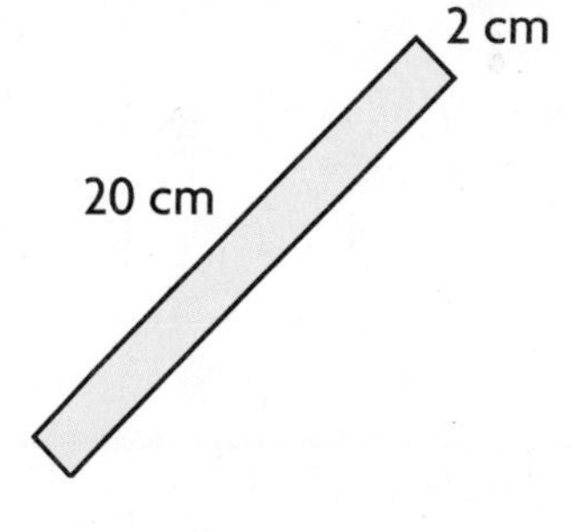

Practice: Copy and Solve **Find the area of the rectangle.**

8. base: 16 feet

height: 6 feet

9. base: 9 yards

height: 17 yards

10. base: 14 centimeters

height: 11 centimeters

11. Frank will paint a wall that measures 10 feet by 14 feet. What is the area of the wall that Frank will paint?

12. MATHEMATICAL PRACTICE 2 **Reason Quantitatively** Carmen sewed a square baby quilt that measures 36 inches on each side. What is the area of the quilt?

Unlock the Problem Real World

13. THINK SMARTER Nancy and Luke are drawing plans for rectangular flower gardens. In Nancy's plan, the garden is 18 feet by 12 feet. In Luke's plan, the garden is 15 feet by 15 feet. Who drew the garden plan with the greater area? What is the area?

a. What do you need to find? ______________________

____

b. What formula will you use? ______________________

c. What units will you use to write the answer? ______________________

d. Show the steps to solve the problem.

e. Complete the sentences.

The area of Nancy's garden is

______________________.

The area of Luke's garden is

______________________.

__________ garden has the greater area.

14. GO DEEPER Victor wants to buy fertilizer for his yard. The yard is 35 feet by 55 feet. The directions on the bag of fertilizer say that one bag will cover 1,250 square feet. How many bags of fertilizer should Victor buy to be sure that he covers the entire yard?

____

15. THINK SMARTER Tuan is an artist. He is painting on a large canvas which is 45 inches wide. The height of the canvas is 9 inches less than the width. What is the area of Tuan's canvas?

__________ square inches

FOR MORE PRACTICE: Standards Practice Book

Name ______________________________

Area of Combined Rectangles

Essential Question How can you find the area of combined rectangles?

Measurement and Data—4.MD.3

MATHEMATICAL PRACTICES
MP.1, MP.4, MP.5

Unlock the Problem Real World

Jan is visiting a botanical garden with her family. The diagram shows two rectangular sections of the garden. What is the total area of the two sections?

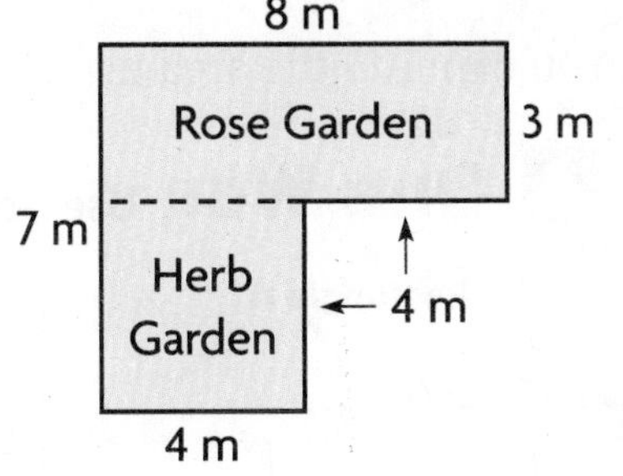

There are different ways to find the area of combined rectangles.

One Way Count square units.

Materials ■ grid paper

- Draw the garden on grid paper. Then find the area of each section by counting squares inside the shape.

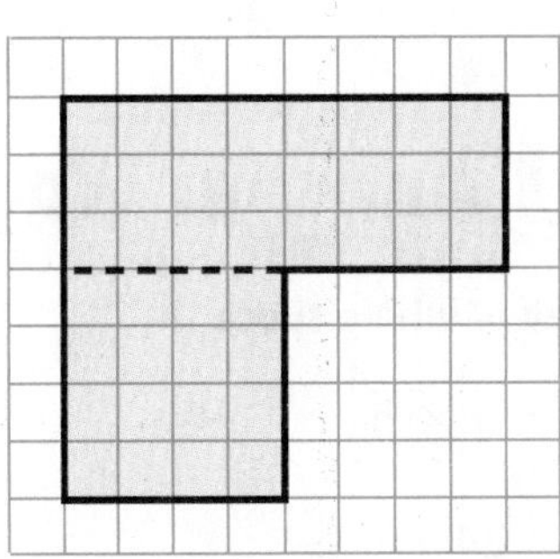
1 square = 1 square meter

Rose Garden

Area = ______ square meters

Herb Garden

Area = ______ square meters

- Add the areas.

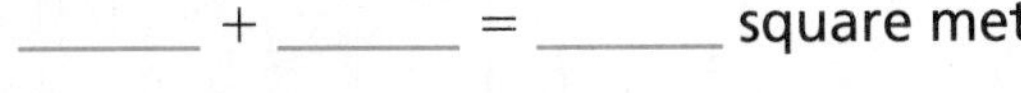

______ + ______ = ______ square meters

Another Way Use the area formula for a rectangle.

A **Rose Garden**

$A = b \times h$

$= \_\_\_\_ \times \_\_\_\_$

$=$ ______ square meters

B **Herb Garden**

$A = b \times h$

$= \_\_\_\_ \times \_\_\_\_$

$=$ ______ square meters

- Add the areas.

______ + ______ = ______ square meters

So, the total area is ______ square meters.

Math Talk **Mathematical Practices**

Is there another way you could divide the figure to find the total area? **Explain.**

Example

Greg is laying carpet in the space outside his laundry room. The diagram shows where the carpet will be installed. The space is made of combined rectangles. What is the area of the carpeted space?

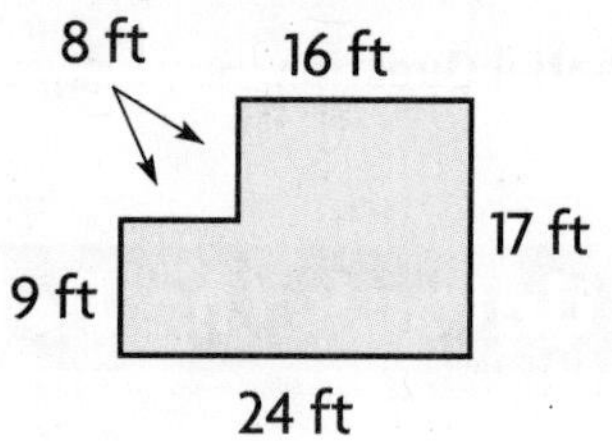

You can find the area using addition or subtraction.

One Way Use addition.

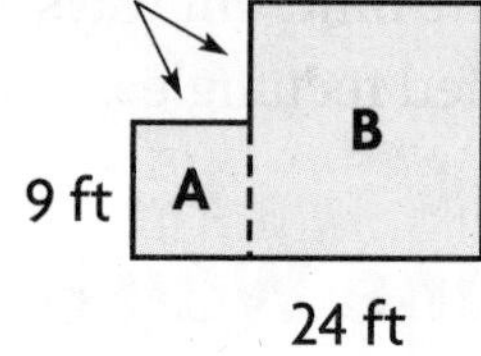

Rectangle A	**Rectangle B**
$A = b \times h$	$A = b \times h$
$= 8 \times$ ______	$=$ ______ $\times 17$
$=$ ______	$=$ ______

Sum of the areas:

______ + ______ = ______ square feet

Another Way Use subtraction.

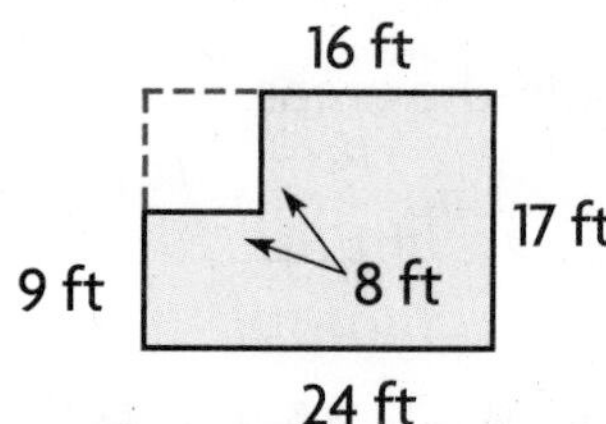

Area of whole space	**Area of missing section**
$A = b \times h$	$A = b \times h$
$= 24 \times$ ______	$=$ ______ $\times$ ______
$=$ ______	$=$ ______

Difference between the areas:

______ − ______ = ______ square feet

So, the area of the carpeted space is ______ square feet.

- Is there another way you could divide the figure to find the total area? Explain.

______

______

______

______

Name ____________________

Share and Show

1. Explain how to find the total area of the figure.

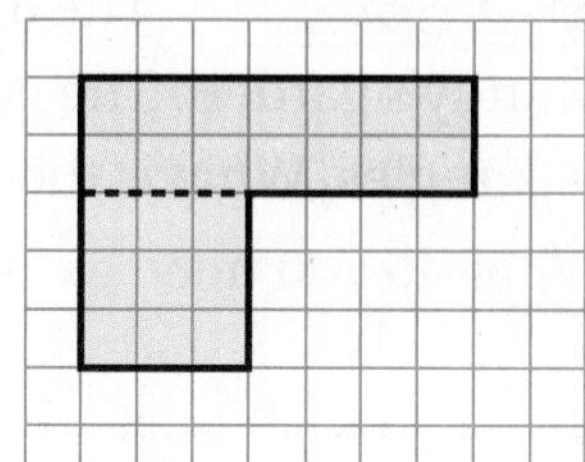

Find the area of the combined rectangles.

2.

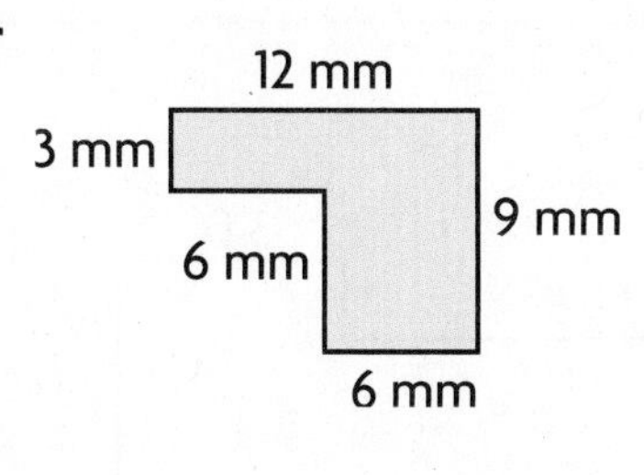

3.

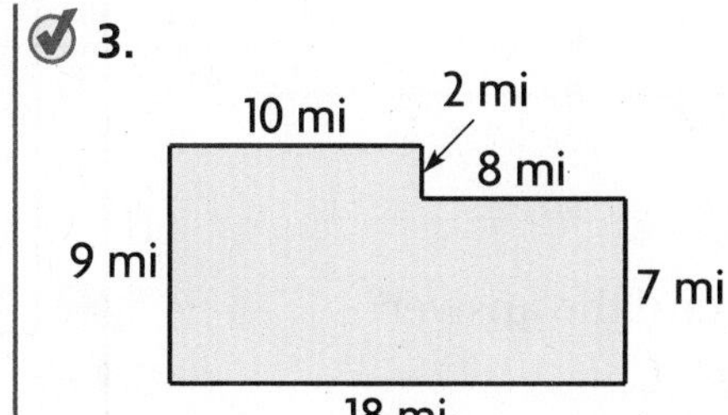

4.

4 ft 4 ft 4 ft

8 ft 8 ft 8 ft

16 ft

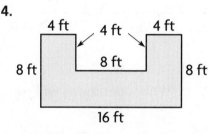

Math Talk Mathematical Practices

Describe the characteristics of combined rectangles.

On Your Own

Find the area of the combined rectangles.

5. MATHEMATICAL PRACTICE 6 **Attend to Precision** Jamie's mom wants to enlarge her rectangular garden by adding a new rectangular section. The garden is now 96 square yards. What will the total area of the garden be after she adds the new section?

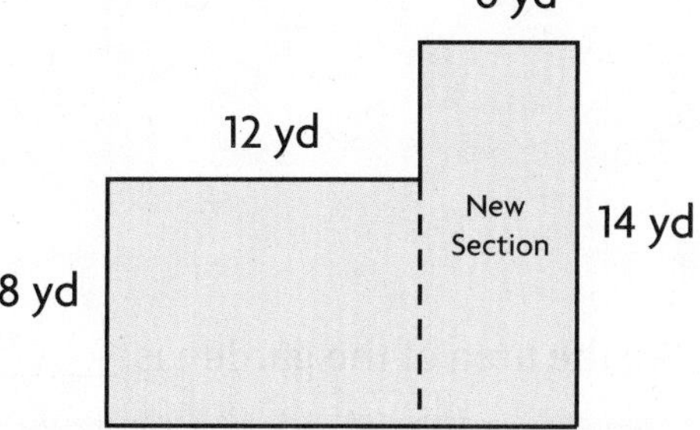

6. GO DEEPER Explain how to find the perimeter and area of the combined rectangles at the right.

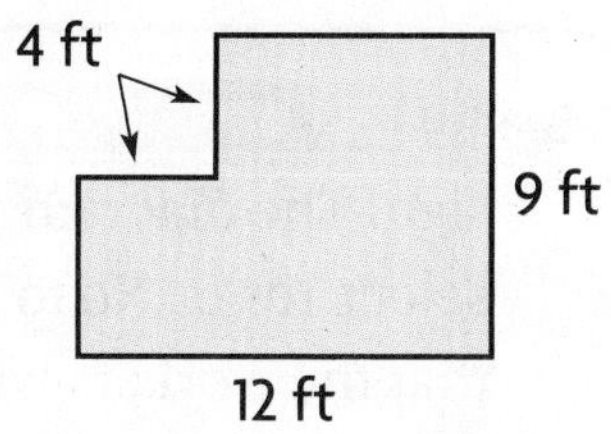

Unlock the Problem 

7. THINK SMARTER The diagram shows the layout of Mandy's garden. The garden is the shape of combined rectangles. What is the area of the garden?

a. What do you need to find?

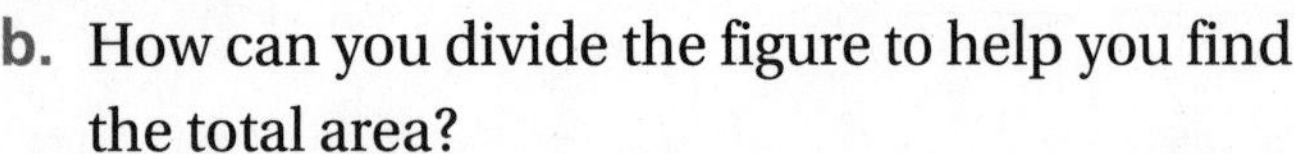

b. How can you divide the figure to help you find the total area?

____

____

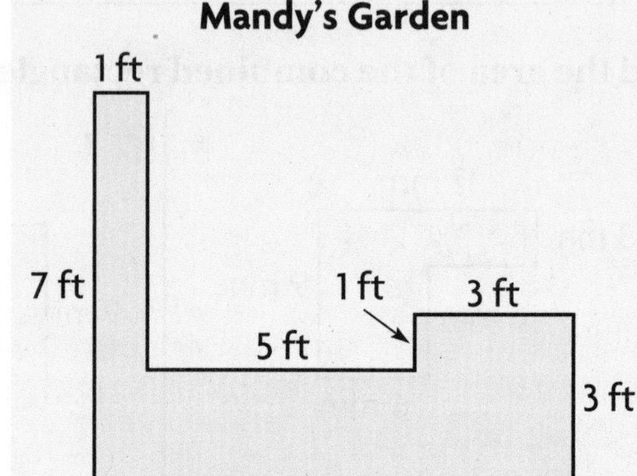

c. What operations will you use to find the answer?

____

d. Draw a diagram to show how you divided the figure. Then show the steps to solve the problem.

So, the area of the garden is ______________.

Personal Math Trainer

8. THINK SMARTER + Workers are painting a large letter L for an outdoor sign. The diagram shows the dimensions of the L. For numbers 8a–8c, select Yes or No to tell whether you can add the products to find the area that the workers will paint.

8a. 2×8 and 2×4 ○ Yes ○ No

8b. 2×6 and 2×8 ○ Yes ○ No

8c. 2×6 and 6×2 ○ Yes ○ No

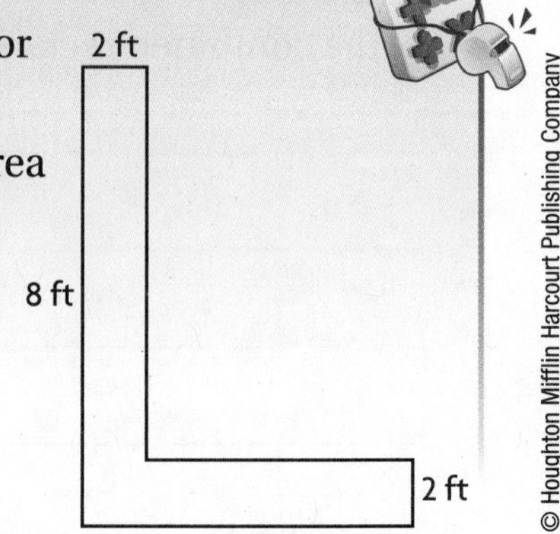

FOR MORE PRACTICE: Standards Practice Book

Name ______________________________

Mid-Chapter Checkpoint

Vocabulary

Choose the best term from the box.

Vocabulary
area
base
formula
perimeter
square unit (sq un)

1. A square that is 1 unit wide and 1 unit long is a

   ______________. (p. 529)

2. The ______________ of a two-dimensional figure can be any side. (p. 529)

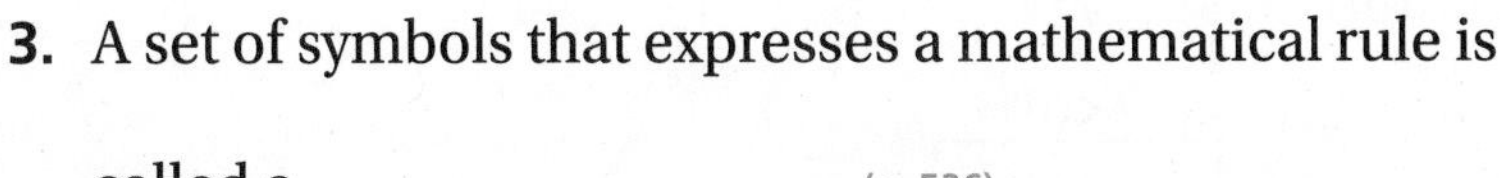

3. A set of symbols that expresses a mathematical rule is

   called a ______________. (p. 526)

4. The ______________ is the distance around a shape. (p. 525)

Concepts and Skills

Find the perimeter and area of the rectangle or square. (4.MD.3)

5.

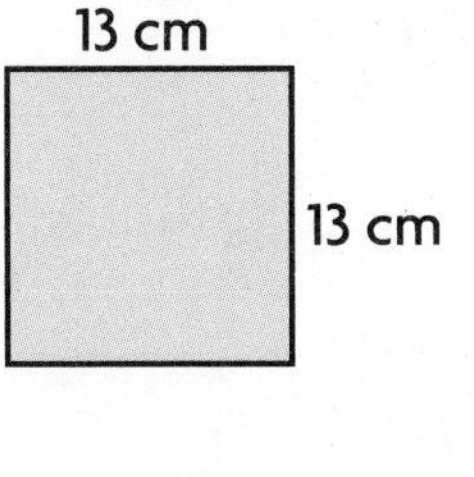

____

6.

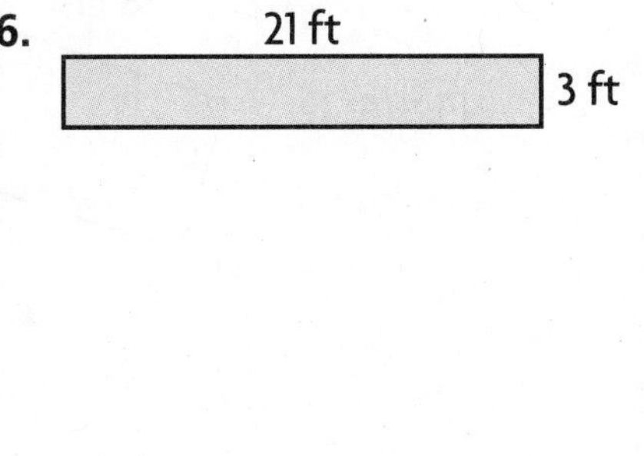

____

7.

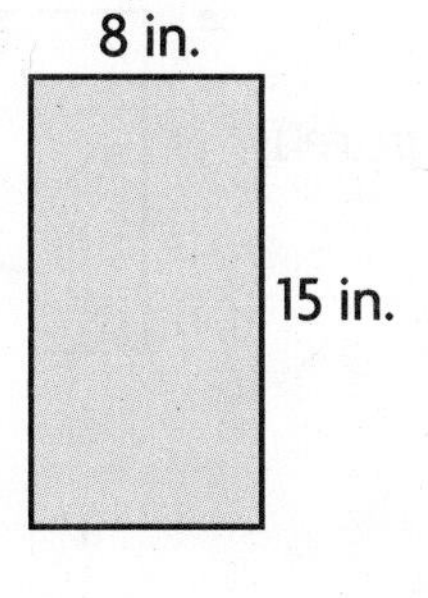

____

Find the area of the combined rectangles. (4.MD.3)

8.

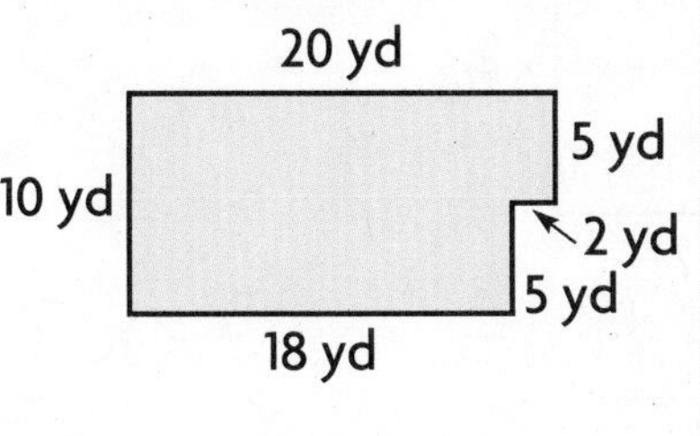

____

9.

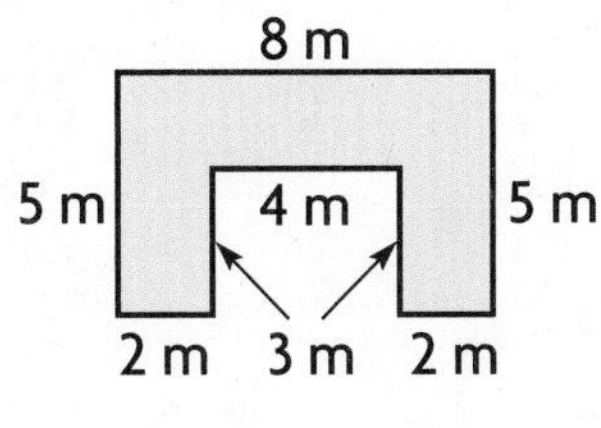

____

10.

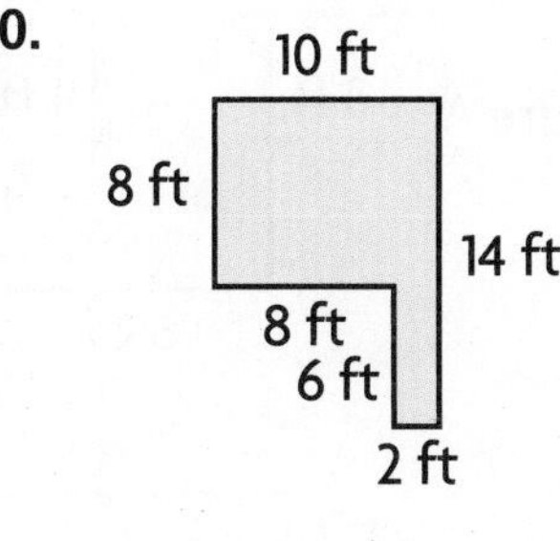

____

11. Which figure has the greatest perimeter? (4.MD.3)

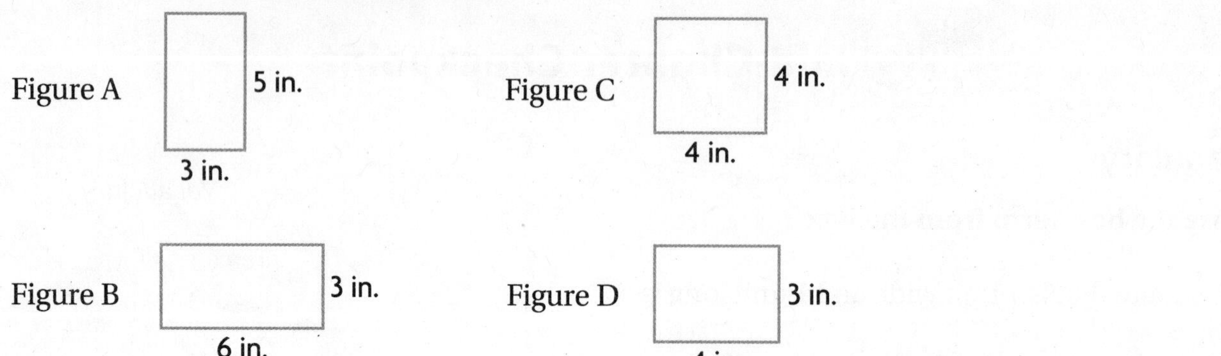

____

12. Which figure has an area of 108 square centimeters? (4.MD.3)

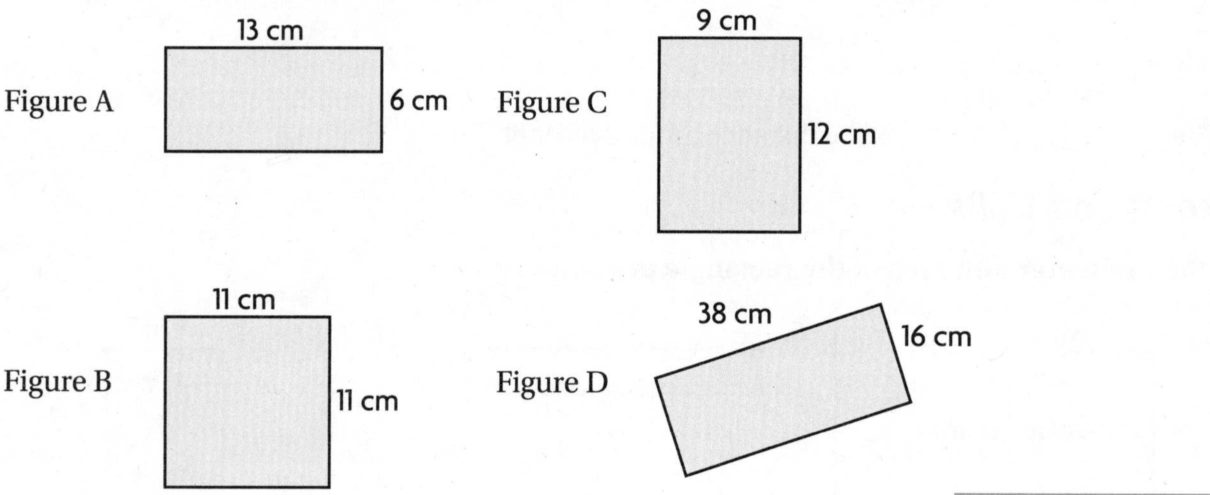

____

13. Which of the combined rectangles has an area of 40 square feet? (4.MD.3)

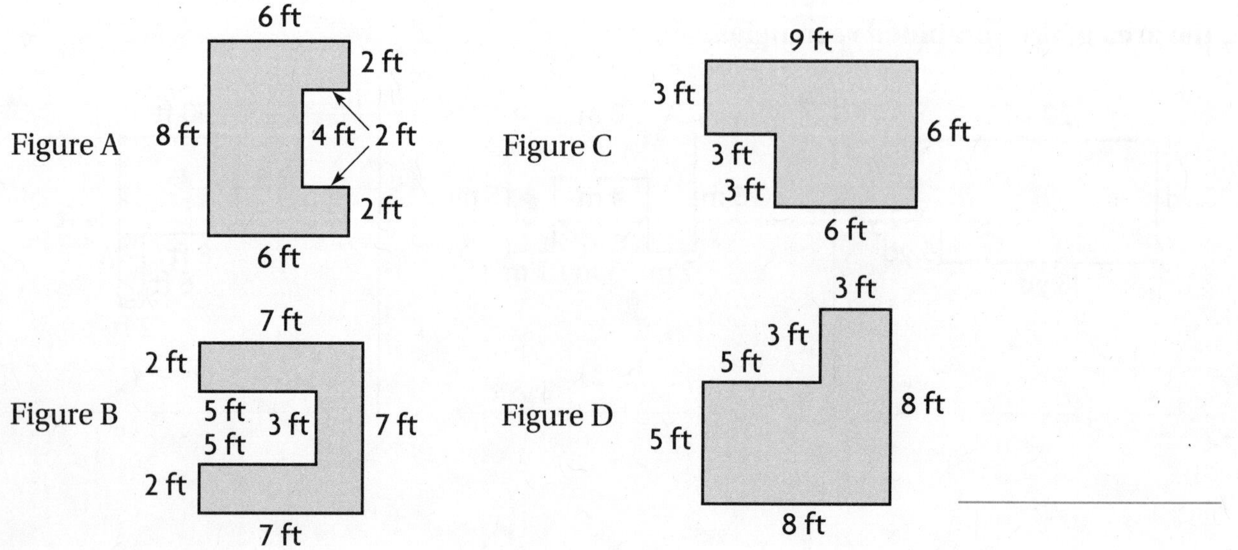

____

Name ___________________________

Find Unknown Measures

Essential Question How can you find an unknown measure of a rectangle given its area or perimeter?

Measurement and Data—4.MD.3

MATHEMATICAL PRACTICES
MP.2, MP.4, MP.7

Unlock the Problem — Real World

Tanisha is painting a mural that is in the shape of a rectangle. The mural covers an area of 54 square feet. The base of the mural measures 9 feet. What is its height?

Use a formula for area.

- What do you need to find?

  ____

- What information do you know?

  ____

Example 1 Find an unknown measure given the area.

MODEL

Think: Label the measures you know. Use n for the unknown.

$A =$ ______ $h =$ ______

9

$b =$ ______

RECORD

Use the model to write an equation and solve.

______ = ______ ______ Write the formula for area.

______ = ______ ______ Use the model to write an equation.

54 = 9 × ______ What times 9 equals 54?

The value of n is ______.

Think: n is the height of the mural.

So, the height of the mural is ______ feet.

Math Talk — Mathematical Practices

Explain how you can use division to find an unknown factor.

1. What if the mural were in the shape of a square with an area of 81 square feet? What would the height of the mural be? Explain.

____

____

2. Explain how you can find an unknown side length of any square, when given only the area of the square.

____

____

____

Example 2 Find an unknown measure given the perimeter.

Gary is building an outdoor pen in the shape of a rectangle for his dog. He will use 24 meters of fencing. The pen will be 3 meters wide. How long will the pen be?

Use a formula for perimeter.

MODEL

Think: Label the measures you know. Use n for the unknown.

$w =$ ______

$l =$ ______

$P =$ ______

RECORD

Use the model to write an equation and solve.

$P = (2 \times l) + (2 \times w)$

______ = (______ ______) + (______ ______)

______ = (______ ______) + ______

Think: $(2 \times n)$ is an unknown addend.

$24 =$ ______ $+ 6$ Think: What is $24 - 6$?

The value of $(2 \times n)$ is 18.

To find the value of n, find the unknown factor.

$2 \times$ ______ $= 18$

The value of n is ______.

Think: n is the length of the pen.

So, the pen will be ______ long.

ERROR Alert

Check that you are using the correct formula. Are you given the area or the perimeter?

Try This! The perimeter of a square is 24 feet. Find the side length.

Draw a model.	Write an equation.
	$P = 4 \times s$

Name ______________________________

Share and Show

1. Find the unknown measure. The area of the rectangle is 36 square feet.

   $A = b \times h$

   _____ $= b \times$ _____

   The base of the rectangle is __________.

   3 ft

   ?

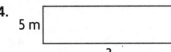

Find the unknown measure of the rectangle.

2. 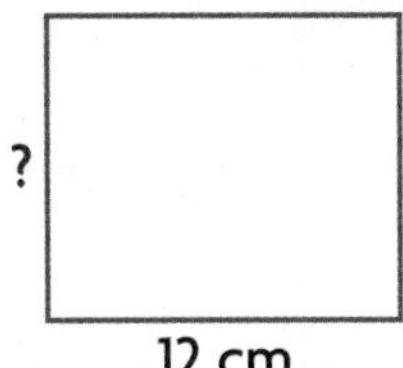

   ?

   12 cm

   Perimeter = 44 centimeters

   width = ______________

3. 9 in.

   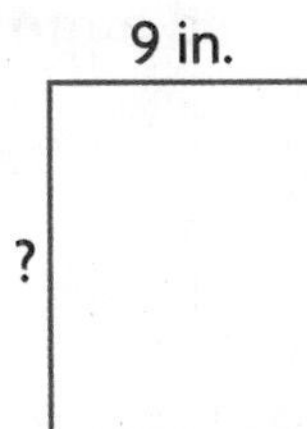

   ?

   Area = 108 square inches

   height = ______________

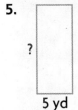

4. 5 m

   ?

   Area = 90 square meters

   base = ______________

Math Talk **Mathematical Practices**

Explain how using the area formula helps you find the base of a rectangle when you know its area and height.

On Your Own

5. ?

   5 yd

   Perimeter = 34 yards

   length = ______________

6. 

   8 ft

   ?

   Area = 96 square feet

   base = ______________

7. 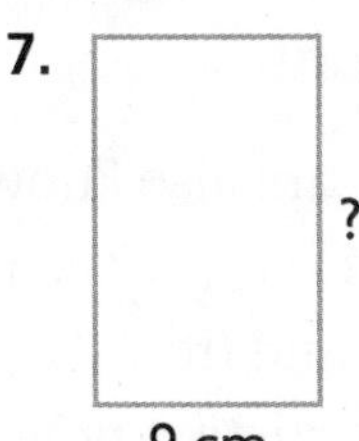

   ?

   9 cm

   Area = 126 square centimeters

   height = ______________

8. **GO DEEPER** A square has an area of 49 square inches. Explain how to find the perimeter of the square.

____

____

____

____

Problem Solving • Applications

9. MATHEMATICAL PRACTICE 7 **Identify Relationships** The area of a swimming pool is 120 square meters. The width of the pool is 8 meters. What is the length of the pool in centimeters?

____

Personal Math Trainer

10. THINK SMARTER + An outdoor deck is 7 feet wide. The perimeter of the deck is 64 feet. What is the length of the deck? Use the numbers to write an equation and solve. A number may be used more than once.

7	9	5	14	25	50	64

$P = (2 \times l) + (2 \times w)$

$\square = (2 \times l) + (2 \times \square)$

$\square = 2 \times l + \square$

$\square = 2 \times l$

$\square = l$

So, the length of the deck is ________ feet.

Connect to Science

Mountain Lions

Mountain lions are also known as cougars, panthers, or pumas. Their range once was from coast to coast in North America and from Argentina to Alaska. Hunting and habitat destruction now restricts their range to mostly mountainous, unpopulated areas.

Mountain lions are solitary animals. A male's territory often overlaps two females' territories but never overlaps another male's. The average size of a male's territory is 108 square miles, but it may be smaller or larger depending on how plentiful food is.

11. THINK SMARTER A male mountain lion has a rectangular territory with an area of 96 square miles. If his territory is 8 miles wide, what is the length of his territory? ________

FOR MORE PRACTICE: Standards Practice Book

Name ______________________

PROBLEM SOLVING
Lesson 13.5

Problem Solving • Find the Area

Essential Question How can you use the strategy *solve a simpler problem* to solve area problems?

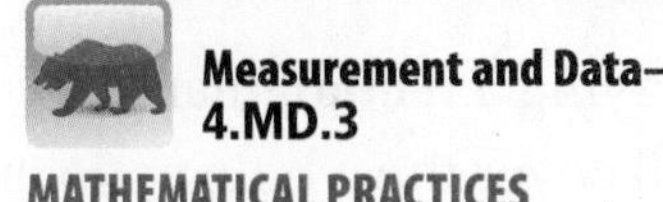

Measurement and Data—4.MD.3

MATHEMATICAL PRACTICES
MP.1, MP.4, MP.6

Unlock the Problem

A landscaper is laying grass for a rectangular playground. The grass will cover the whole playground except for a square sandbox. The diagram shows the playground and sandbox. How many square yards of grass will the landscaper use?

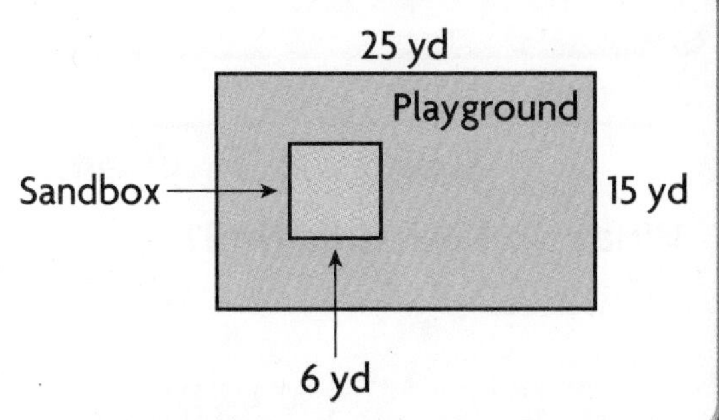

Use the graphic organizer below to solve the problem.

Read the Problem

What do I need to find?

I need to find how many __________ the landscaper will use.

What information do I need to use?

The grass will cover the __________.

The grass will not cover the __________.

The length and width of the playground are __________ and __________.

The side length of the square sandbox is __________.

How will I use the information?

I can solve simpler problems.

Find the area of the __________.

Find the area of the __________.

Then __________ the area of the __________ from the area of the __________.

Solve the Problem

First, find the area of the playground.

$A = b \times h$

$=$ ______ $\times$ ______

$=$ ______ square yards

Next, find the area of the sandbox.

$A = s \times s$

$=$ ______ $\times$ ______

$=$ ______ square yards

Last, subtract the area of the sandbox from the area of the playground.

$$\begin{array}{r} 375 \\ -\ 36 \\ \hline \end{array}$$

______ square yards

So, the landscaper will use __________ __________ of grass to cover the playground.

Mathematical Practices

Explain how the strategy helped you to solve the problem.

Try Another Problem

Zach is laying a rectangular brick patio for a new museum. Brick will cover the whole patio except for a rectangular fountain, as shown in the diagram. How many square meters of brick does Zach need?

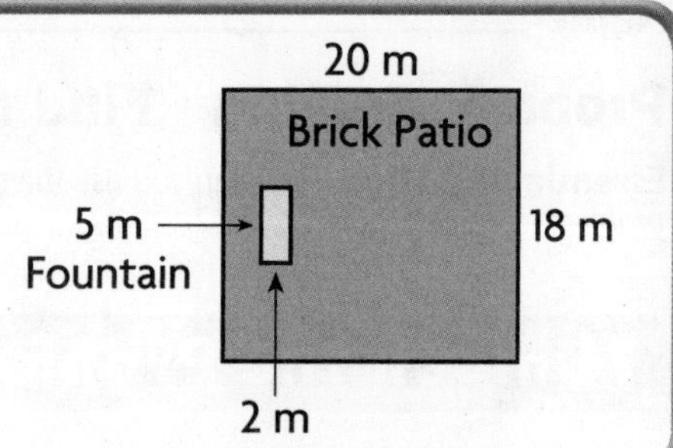

Read the Problem	Solve the Problem
What do I need to find?	
What information do I need to use?	
How will I use this information?	

- How many square meters of brick does Zach need? Explain.

Name ________________________________

Share and Show

Unlock the Problem

- √ Use the Problem Solving MathBoard
- √ Underline important facts.
- √ Choose a strategy you know.

1. Lila is wallpapering one wall of her bedroom, as shown in the diagram. She will cover the whole wall except for the doorway. How many square feet of wallpaper does Lila need?

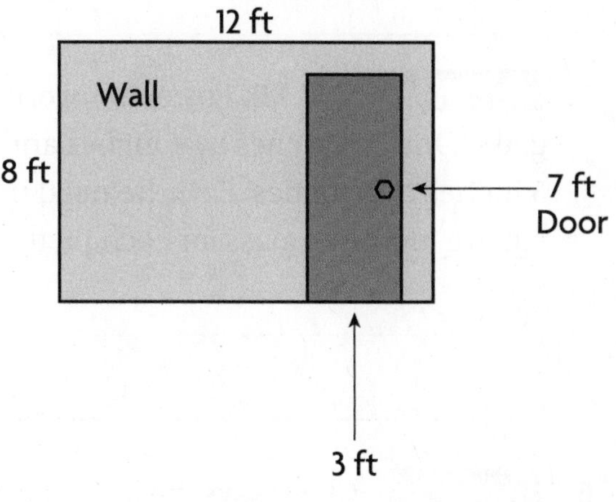

First, find the area of the wall.

$A = b \times h$

$=$ ______ $\times$ ______

$=$ ______ square feet

Next, find the area of the door.

$A = b \times h$

$=$ ______ $\times$ ______

$=$ ______ square feet

Last, subtract the area of the door from the area of the wall.

______ $-$ ______ $=$ ______ square feet

So, Lila needs ________________ of wallpaper.

2. What if there was a square window on the wall with a side length of 2 feet? How much wallpaper would Lila need then? Explain.

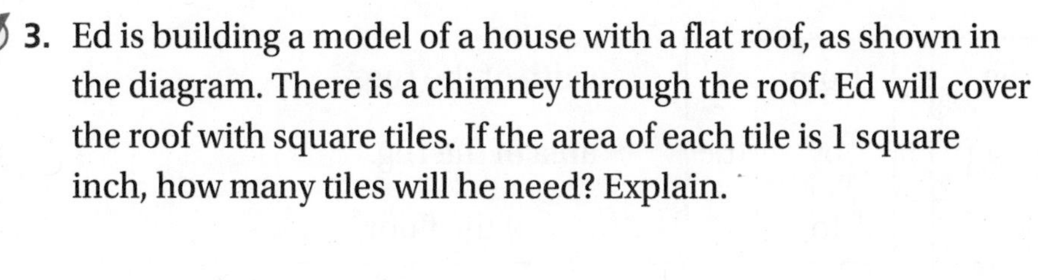

3. Ed is building a model of a house with a flat roof, as shown in the diagram. There is a chimney through the roof. Ed will cover the roof with square tiles. If the area of each tile is 1 square inch, how many tiles will he need? Explain.

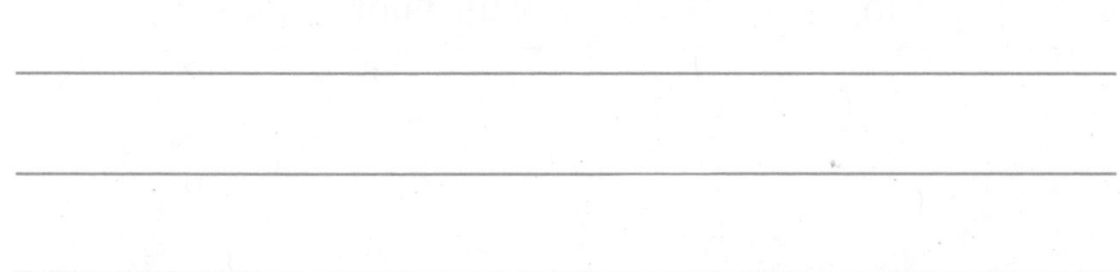

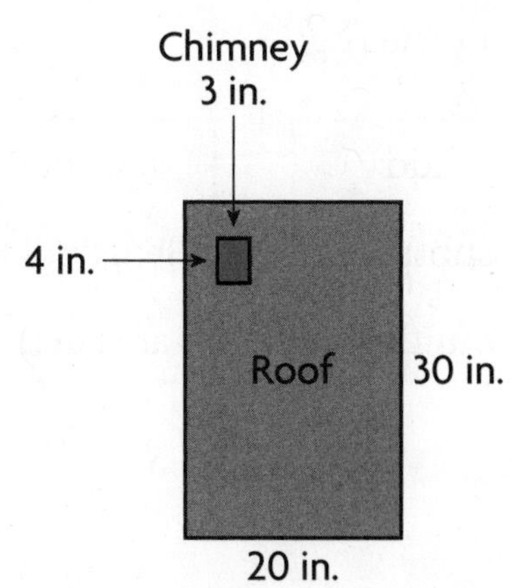

On Your Own

4. MATHEMATICAL PRACTICE 1 **Make Sense of Problems** Lia has a dog and a cat. Together, the pets weigh 28 pounds. The dog weighs 3 times as much as the cat. How much does each pet weigh?

____

5. THINK SMARTER Mr. Foster is covering two pictures with glass. One is 6 inches by 4 inches and the other one is 5 inches by 5 inches. Does he need the same number of square inches of glass for each picture? Explain.

____

____

WRITE Math
Show Your Work

6. GO DEEPER Claire says the area of a square with a side length of 100 centimeters is greater than the area of a square with a side length of 1 meter. Is she correct? Explain.

____

____

____

7. THINK SMARTER A rectangular floor is 12 feet long and 11 feet wide. Janine places a rug that is 9 feet long and 7 feet wide and covers part of the floor in the room. Select the word(s) to complete the sentence.

To find the number of square feet of the floor that is NOT covered by the rug,

add / subtract / multiply	the	area of the rug / length of the rug / area of the floor	from / by / to	the	width of the rug. / area of the rug. / area of the floor.

Name ________________________________

Chapter 13 Review/Test

1. For numbers 1a–1e, select Yes or No to indicate if a rectangle with the given dimensions would have a perimeter of 50 inches.

1a.	length: 25 inches	width: 2 inches	○ Yes	○ No
1b.	length: 20 inches	width: 5 inches	○ Yes	○ No
1c.	length: 17 inches	width: 8 inches	○ Yes	○ No
1d.	length: 15 inches	width: 5 inches	○ Yes	○ No
1e.	length: 15 inches	width: 10 inches	○ Yes	○ No

2. The swimming club's indoor pool is in a rectangular building. Marco is laying tile around the rectangular pool.

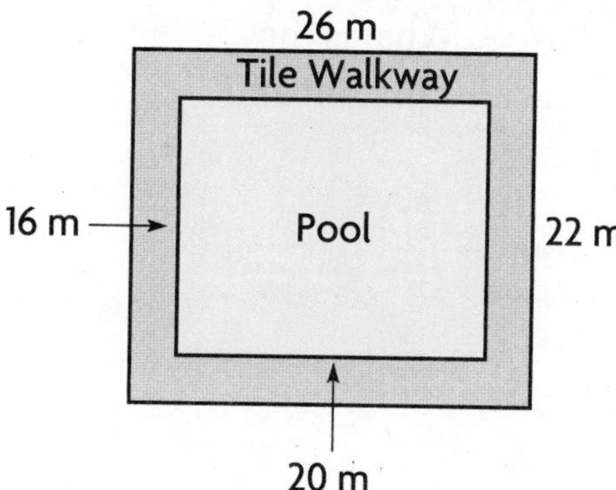

Part A

What is the area of the pool and the area of the pool and the walkway? Show your work.

Part B

How many square meters of tile will Marco need for the walkway? Explain how you found your answer.

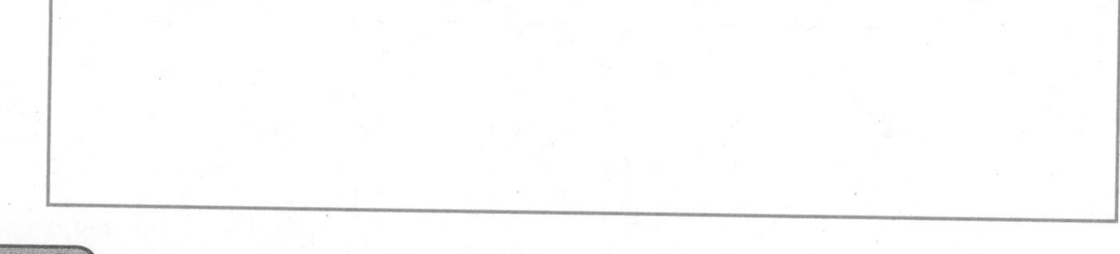

3. Match the dimensions of the rectangles in the top row with the correct area or perimeter in the bottom row.

length: 5 cm width: 9 cm	length: 6 cm width: 6 cm	length: 6 cm width: 5 cm	length: 9 cm width: 6 cm
area = 36 sq cm	perimeter = 22 cm	perimeter = 30 cm	area = 45 sq cm

4. Kyleigh put a large rectangular sticker on her notebook. The height of the sticker measures 18 centimeters. The base is half as long as the height. What area of the notebook does the sticker cover?

______ square centimeters

5. A rectangular flower garden in Samantha's backyard has 100 feet around its edge. The width of the garden is 20 feet. What is the length of the garden? Use the numbers to write an equation and solve. A number may be used more than once.

10 | 20 | 50 | 30 | 40 | 60 | 100

$P = (2 \times l) + (2 \times w)$

$\square = (2 \times l) + (2 \times \square)$

$\square = 2 \times l + \square$

$\square = 2 \times l$

$\square = l$

So, the length of the garden $\square$ feet.

6. Gary drew a rectangle with a perimeter of 20 inches. Then he tried to draw a square with a perimeter of 20 inches.

Draw 3 different rectangles that Gary could have drawn. Then draw the square, if possible.

Name ______________________________

7. Ami and Bert are drawing plans for rectangular vegetable gardens. In Ami's plan, the garden is 13 feet by 10 feet. In Bert's plan the garden is 12 feet by 12 feet. For numbers 7a–7d, select True or False for each statement.

7a.	The area of Ami's garden is 130 square feet.	○ True	○ False
7b.	The area of Bert's garden is 48 square feet.	○ True	○ False
7c.	Ami's garden has a greater area than Bert's garden.	○ True	○ False
7d.	The area of Bert's garden is 14 square feet greater than Ami's.	○ True	○ False

8. A farmer planted corn in a square field. One side of the field measures 32 yards. What is the area of the cornfield? Show your work.

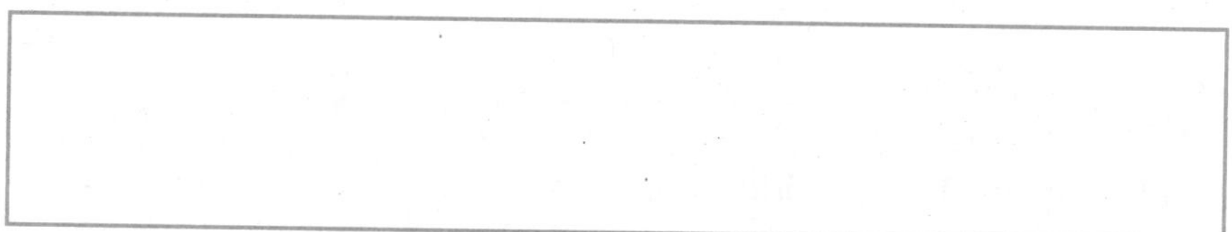

9. Harvey bought a frame in which he put his family's picture.

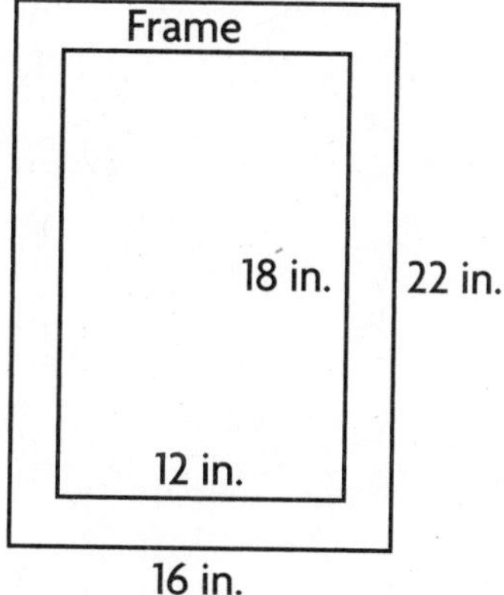

What is the area of the frame not covered by the picture?

______ square inches

10. Kelly has 236 feet of fence to use to enclose a rectangular space for her dog. She wants the width to be 23 feet. Draw a rectangle that could be the space for Kelly's dog. Label the length and the width.

11. The diagram shows the dimensions of a new parking lot at Helen's Health Food store.

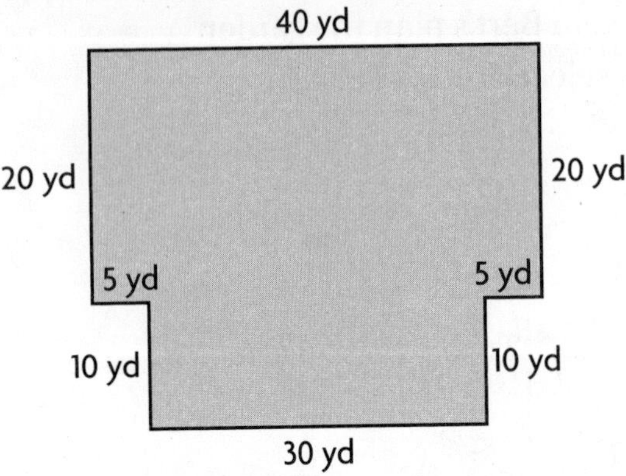

Use either addition or subtraction to find the area of the parking lot. Show your work.

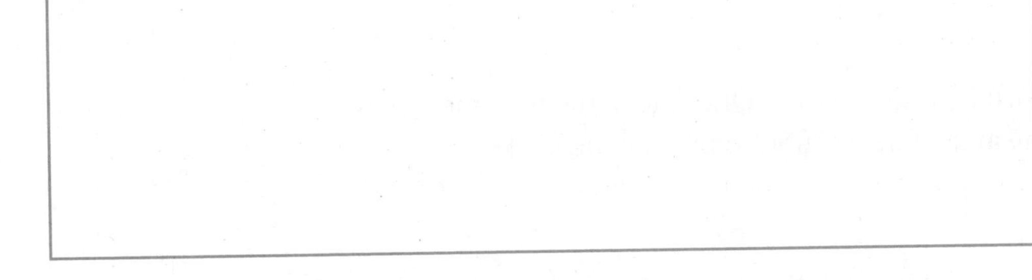

12. Chad's bedroom floor is 12 feet long and 10 feet wide. He has an area rug on his floor that is 7 feet long and 5 feet wide. Which statement tells how to find the amount of the floor that is not covered by the rug? Mark all that apply.

Ⓐ Add 12×10 and 7×5.

Ⓑ Subtract 35 from 12×10

Ⓒ Subtract 10×5 from 12×7.

Ⓓ Add $12 + 10 + 7 + 5$.

Ⓔ Subtract 7×5 from 12×10.

Ⓕ Subtract 12×10 from 7×5.

13. A row of plaques covers 120 square feet of space along a wall. If the plaques are 3 feet tall, what length of the wall do they cover?

______ feet

Name ________________________________

14. Ms. Bennett wants to buy carpeting for her living room and dining room.

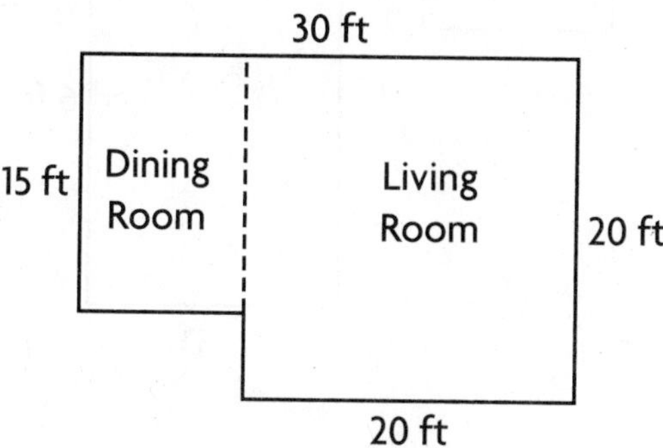

Explain how she can find the amount of carpet she needs to cover the floor in both rooms. Then find the amount of carpet she will need.

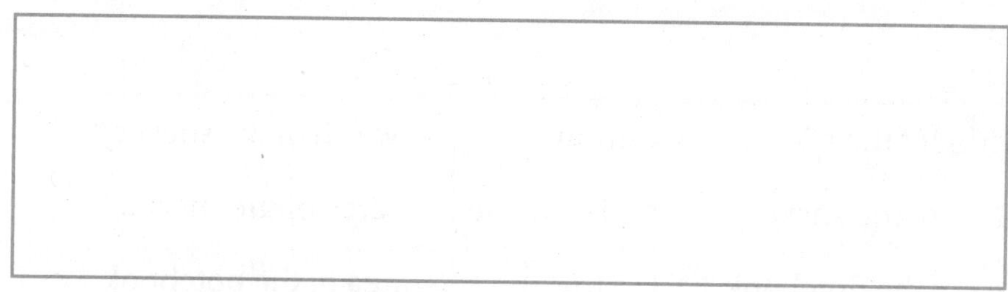

15. Lorenzo built a rectangular brick patio. He is putting a stone border around the edge of the patio. The width of the patio is 12 feet. The length of the patio is two feet longer than the width.

How many feet of stone will Lorenzo need? Explain how you found your answer.

16. Which rectangle has a perimeter of 10 feet? Mark all that apply.

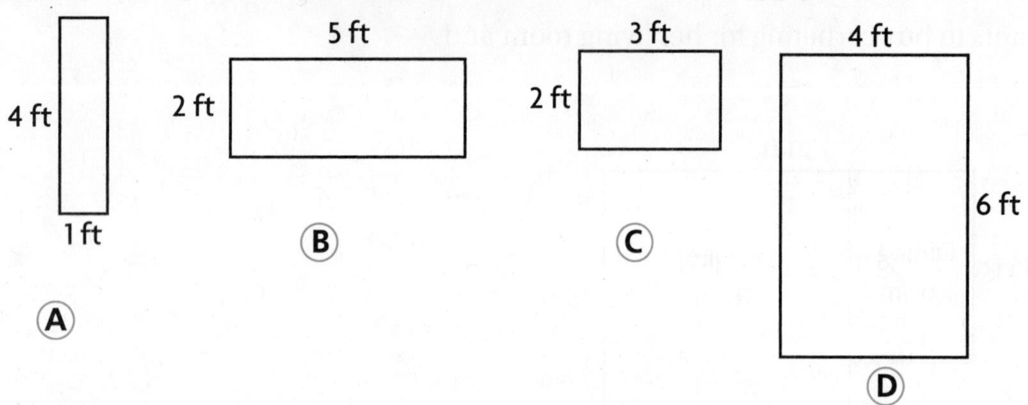

17. A folder is 11 inches long and 8 inches wide. Alyssa places a sticker that is 2 inches long and 1 inch wide on the notebook. Choose the words that correctly complete the sentence.

To find the number of square inches of the folder that is NOT covered by the sticker,

add subtract multiply	the	width of the sticker area of the sticker area of the notebook	from by to	the	width of the sticker. area of the sticker. area of the notebook.

18. Tricia is cutting her initial from a piece of felt.

8 cm
1 cm 1 cm
3 cm 3 cm
5 cm

For numbers 18a–18c, select Yes or No to tell whether you can add the products to find the number of square centimeters Tricia needs.

18a. 1×8 and 5×2 ○ Yes ○ No

18b. 3×5 and 1×8 ○ Yes ○ No

18c. 2×5 and 1×3 and 1×3 ○ Yes ○ No

19. Mr. Butler posts his students' artwork on a bulletin board.

The width and length of the bulletin board are whole numbers. What could be the dimensions of the bulletin board Mr. Butler uses?

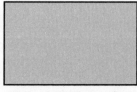

Area = 15 square feet

Glossary

Pronunciation Key

a	add, map	ē	equal, tree	m	move, seem	o͞o	pool, food	ů	pull, book
ā	ace, rate	f	fit, half	n	nice, tin	p	pit, stop	û(r)	burn, term
â(r)	care, air	g	go, log	ng	ring, song	r	run, poor	yo͞o	fuse, few
ä	palm, father	h	hope, hate	o	odd, hot	s	see, pass	v	vain, eve
b	bat, rub	i	it, give	ō	open, so	sh	sure, rush	w	win, away
ch	check, catch	ī	ice, write	ô	order, jaw	t	talk, sit	y	yet, yearn
d	dog, rod	j	joy, ledge	oi	oil, boy	th	thin, both	z	zest, muse
e	end, pet	k	cool, take	ou	pout, now	th	this, bathe	zh	vision, pleasure
		l	look, rule	o͝o	took, full	u	up, done		

ə the schwa, an unstressed vowel representing the sound spelled *a* in *above*, *e* in *sicken*, *i* in *possible*, *o* in *melon*, *u* in *circus*

Other symbols:
- • separates words into syllables
- ′ indicates stress on a syllable

acute angle [ə•kyo͞ot′ ang′gəl] **ángulo agudo** An angle that measures greater than 0° and less than 90°
Example:

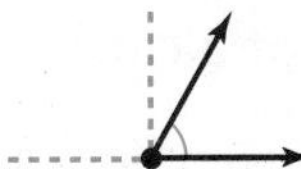

acute triangle [ə•kyo͞ot′ trī′ang•gəl] **triángulo acutángulo** A triangle with three acute angles
Example:

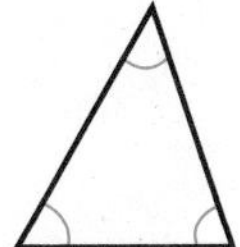

addend [a′dend] **sumando** A number that is added to another in an addition problem
Example: 2 + 4 = 6;
2 and 4 are addends.

addition [ə•di′shən] **suma** The process of finding the total number of items when two or more groups of items are joined; the opposite operation of subtraction

A.M. [ā•em′] **a.m.** The times after midnight and before noon

analog clock [anəl• ôg kläk] **reloj analógico** A tool for measuring time, in which hands move around a circle to show hours, minutes, and sometimes seconds
Example:

angle [ang′gəl] **ángulo** A shape formed by two line segments or rays that share the same endpoint
Example:

area [âr′ē•ə] **área** The number of square units needed to cover a flat surface
Example:

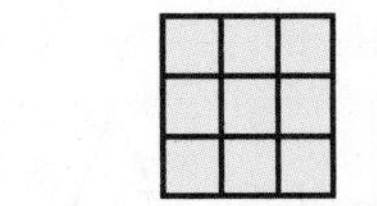

area = 9 square units

array [ə•rā′] **matriz** An arrangement of objects in rows and columns
Example:

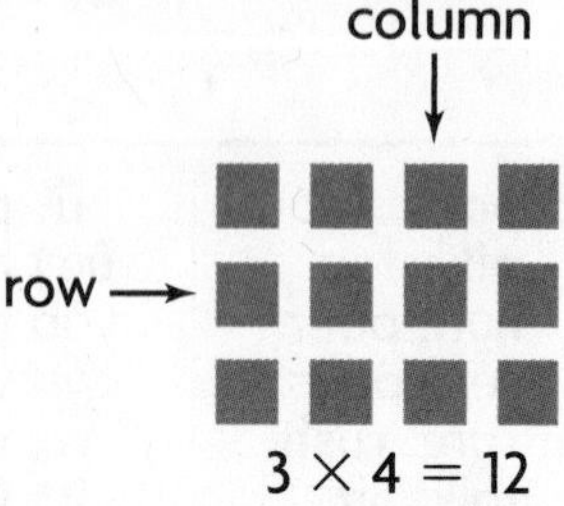

Associative Property of Addition [ə•sō′shē•āt•iv präp′ər•tē əv ə•dish′ən] **propiedad asociativa de la suma** The property that states that you can group addends in different ways and still get the same sum
Example: 3 + (8 + 5) = (3 + 8) + 5

Associative Property of Multiplication [ə•sō′shē•ə•tiv präp′ər•tē əv mul•tə•pli•kā′shən] **propiedad asociativa de la multiplicación** The property that states that you can group factors in different ways and still get the same product
Example: 3 × (4 × 2) = (3 × 4) × 2

B

bar graph [bär graf] **gráfica de barras** A graph that uses bars to show data
Example:

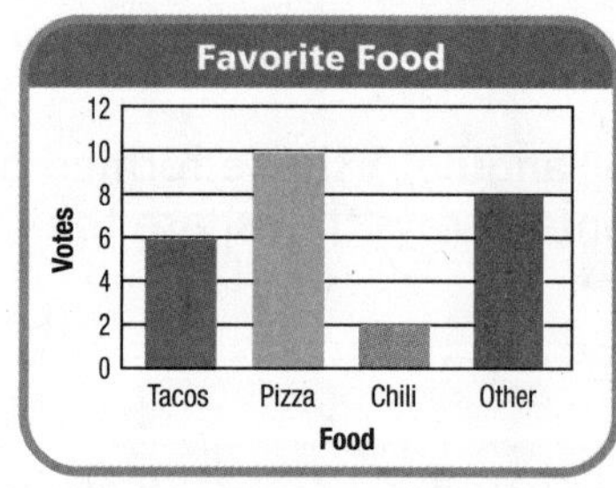

base [bās] **base** A polygon's side or a two-dimensional shape, usually a polygon or circle, by which a three-dimensional shape is measured or named
Examples:

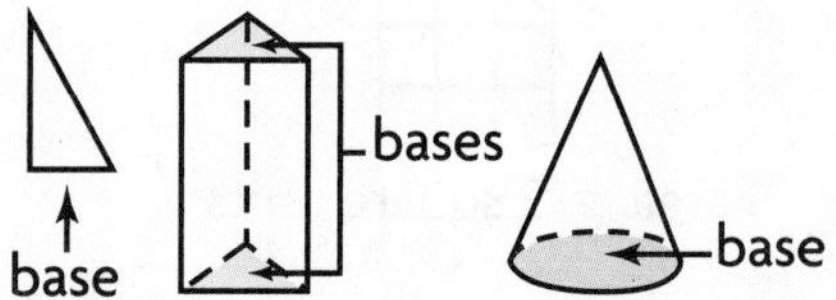

benchmark [bench′märk] **punto de referencia** A known size or amount that helps you understand a different size or amount

C

calendar [kal′ən•dər] **calendario** A table that shows the days, weeks, and months of a year

capacity [kə•pas′i•tē] **capacidad** The amount a container can hold when filled

Celsius (°C) [sel′sē•əs] **Celsius** A metric scale for measuring temperature

centimeter (cm) [sen′tə•mēt•ər] **centímetro (cm)** A metric unit for measuring length or distance
1 meter = 100 centimeters
Example:

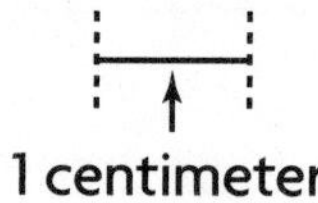

cent sign (¢) [sent sīn] **símbolo de centavo** A symbol that stands for *cent* or *cents*
Example: 53¢

clockwise [kläk′wīz] **en el sentido de las manecillas del reloj** In the same direction in which the hands of a clock move

closed shape [klōzd shāp] **figura cerrada** A two-dimensional shape that begins and ends at the same point
Examples:

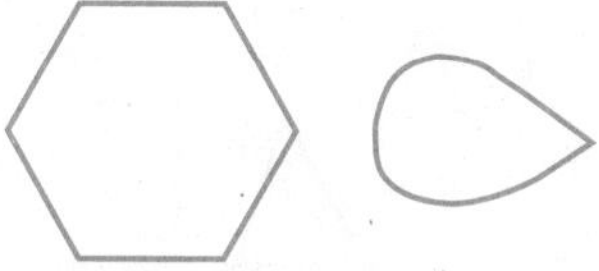

common denominator [käm′ən dē•näm′ə•nāt•ər] **denominador común** A common multiple of two or more denominators
Example: Some common denominators for $\frac{1}{4}$ and $\frac{5}{6}$ are 12, 24, and 36.

common factor [käm′ən fak′tər] **factor común** A number that is a factor of two or more numbers

common multiple [käm′ən mul′tə•pəl] **múltiplo común** A number that is a multiple of two or more numbers

Commutative Property of Addition [kə•myōōt′ə•tiv präp′ər•tē əv ə•dish′ən] **propiedad conmutativa de la suma** The property that states that when the order of two addends is changed, the sum is the same
Example: $4 + 5 = 5 + 4$

Commutative Property of Multiplication [kə•myōōt′ə•tiv präp′ər•tē əv mul•tə•pli•kā′shən] **propiedad conmutativa de la multiplicación** The property that states that when the order of two factors is changed, the product is the same
Example: $4 \times 5 = 5 \times 4$

compare [kəm•pâr′] **comparar** To describe whether numbers are equal to, less than, or greater than each other

compatible numbers [kəm•pat′ə•bəl num′bərz] **números compatibles** Numbers that are easy to compute mentally

composite number [kəm•päz′it num′bər] **número compuesto** A number having more than two factors
Example: 6 is a composite number, since its factors are 1, 2, 3, and 6.

corner [kôr′nər] **esquina** See *vertex*.

counterclockwise [kount•er•kläk′wīz] **en sentido contrario a las manecillas del reloj** In the opposite direction in which the hands of a clock move

counting number [kount′ing num′bər] **número natural** A whole number that can be used to count a set of objects (1, 2, 3, 4, . . .)

cube [kyōōb] **cubo** A three-dimensional shape with six square faces of the same size
Example:

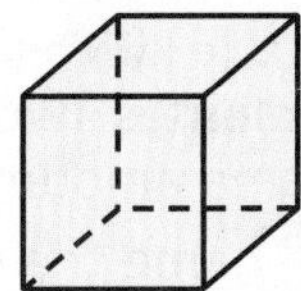

cup (c) [kup] **taza (tz)** A customary unit used to measure capacity and liquid volume
1 cup = 8 ounces

data [dāt′ə] **datos** Information collected about people or things

decagon [dek′ə•gän] **decágono** A polygon with ten sides and ten angles

decimal [des′ə•məl] **decimal** A number with one or more digits to the right of the decimal point

decimal point [des′ə•məl point] **punto decimal** A symbol used to separate dollars from cents in money amounts, and to separate the ones and the tenths places in a decimal
Example: 6.4
↑ decimal point

decimeter (dm) [des′i•mēt•ər] **decímetro (dm)** A metric unit for measuring length or distance
1 meter = 10 decimeters

degree (°) [di•grē′] **grado (°)** The unit used for measuring angles and temperatures

denominator [dē•näm′ə•nāt•ər] **denominador** The number below the bar in a fraction that tells how many equal parts are in the whole or in the group
Example: $\frac{3}{4}$ ← denominator

diagonal [dī•ag′ə•nəl] **diagonal** A line segment that connects two vertices of a polygon that are not next to each other
Example:

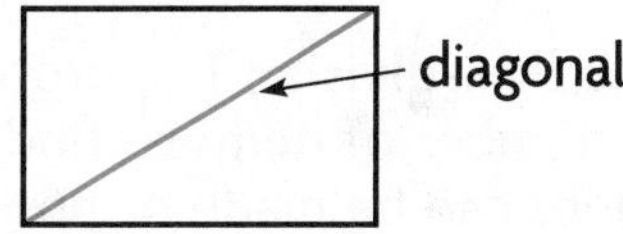

difference [dif′ər•əns] **diferencia** The answer to a subtraction problem

digit [dij′it] **dígito** Any one of the ten symbols 0, 1, 2, 3, 4, 5, 6, 7, 8, or 9 used to write numbers

digital clock [dij′i•təl kläk] **reloj digital** A clock that shows time to the minute, using digits
Example:

dime [dīm] **moneda de 10¢** A coin worth 10 cents and with a value equal to that of 10 pennies; 10¢
Example:

dimension [də•men′shən] **dimensión** A measure in one direction

Distributive Property [di•strib′yōō•tiv präp′ər•tē] **propiedad distributiva** The property that states that multiplying a sum by a number is the same as multiplying each addend by the number and then adding the products
Example: $5 \times (10 + 6) = (5 \times 10) + (5 \times 6)$

divide [də•vīd′] **dividir** To separate into equal groups; the opposite operation of multiplication

dividend [dəv′ə•dend] **dividendo** The number that is to be divided in a division problem
Example: $36 \div 6$; $6\overline{)36}$; the dividend is 36.

divisible [də•viz′ə•bəl] **divisible** A number is divisible by another number if the quotient is a counting number and the remainder is zero
Example: 18 is divisible by 3.

division [də•vi′zhən] **división** The process of sharing a number of items to find how many equal groups can be made or how many items will be in each equal group; the opposite operation of multiplication

divisor [də•vī′zər] **divisor** The number that divides the dividend
Example: $15 \div 3$; $3\overline{)15}$; the divisor is 3.

dollar [däl′ər] **dólar** Paper money worth 100 cents and equal to 100 pennies; $1.00
Example:

elapsed time [ē•lapst′ tīm] **tiempo transcurrido** The time that passes from the start of an activity to the end of that activity

endpoint [end′point] **extremo** The point at either end of a line segment or the starting point of a ray

equal groups [ē′kwəl grōōpz] **grupos iguales** Groups that have the same number of objects

equal parts [ē′kwəl pärts] **partes iguales** Parts that are exactly the same size

equal sign (=) [ē′kwəl sīn] **signo de igualdad** A symbol used to show that two numbers have the same value
Example: 384 = 384

equal to [ē′kwəl tōō] **igual a** Having the same value
Example: 4 + 4 is equal to 3 + 5.

equation [ē•kwā′zhən] **ecuación** A number sentence which shows that two quantities are equal
Example: 4 + 5 = 9

equilateral triangle [ē•kwə•la′tə•rəl trī′ang•gəl] **triángulo equilátero** A triangle with 3 equal sides
Example:

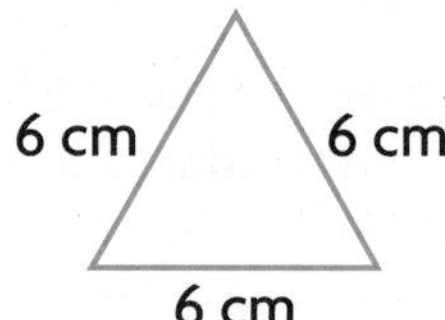

equivalent [ē•kwiv′ə•lənt] **equivalente** Having the same value or naming the same amount

equivalent decimals [ē•kwiv′ə•lənt des′ə•məlz] **decimales equivalentes** Two or more decimals that name the same amount

equivalent fractions [ē•kwiv′ə•lənt frak′shənz] **fracciones equivalentes** Two or more fractions that name the same amount
Example: $\frac{3}{4}$ and $\frac{6}{8}$ name the same amount.

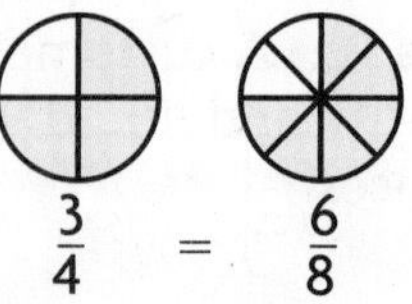

$\frac{3}{4} = \frac{6}{8}$

estimate [es′tə•māt] *verb* **estimar** To find an answer that is close to the exact amount

estimate [es′tə•mit] *noun* **estimación** A number that is close to the exact amount

even [ē′vən] **par** A whole number that has a 0, 2, 4, 6, or 8 in the ones place

expanded form [ek•span′did fôrm] **forma desarrollada** A way to write numbers by showing the value of each digit
Example: 253 = 200 + 50 + 3

expression [ek•spresh′ən] **expresión** A part of a number sentence that has numbers and operation signs but does not have an equal sign

fact family [fakt fam′ə•lē] **familia de operaciones** A set of related multiplication and division equations, or addition and subtraction equations
Example: $7 \times 8 = 56$ $8 \times 7 = 56$
$56 \div 7 = 8$ $56 \div 8 = 7$

factor [fak′tər] **factor** A number that is multiplied by another number to find a product

Fahrenheit (°F) [fâr′ən•hīt] **Fahrenheit** A customary scale for measuring temperature

fluid ounce (fl oz) [flo͞o′id ouns] **onza fluida (fl oz)** A customary unit used to measure liquid capacity and liquid volume
1 cup = 8 fluid ounces

foot (ft) [fo͝ot] **pie (ft)** A customary unit used for measuring length or distance
1 foot = 12 inches

formula [fôr′myo͞o•lə] **fórmula** A set of symbols that expresses a mathematical rule
Example: Area = base × height, or $A = b \times h$

fraction [frak′shən] **fracción** A number that names a part of a whole or part of a group
Example:

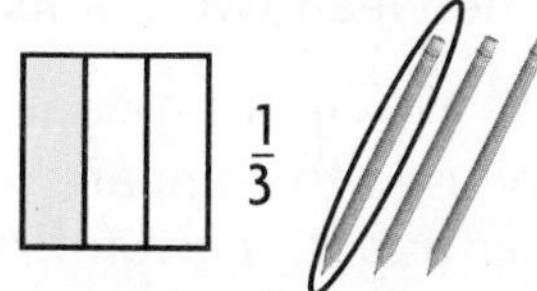

fraction greater than 1 [frak′shən grāt′ər than wun] **fracción mayor que 1** A number which has a numerator that is greater than its denominator

frequency table [frē′kwən•sē tā′bəl] **tabla de frecuencia** A table that uses numbers to record data about how often something happens
Example:

Favorite Color	
Color	**Frequency**
Blue	10
Red	7
Green	5
Other	3

gallon (gal) [gal′ən] **galón (gal)** A customary unit for measuring capacity and liquid volume
1 gallon = 4 quarts

gram (g) [gram] **gramo (g)** A metric unit for measuring mass
1 kilogram = 1,000 grams

greater than sign (>) [grāt′ər than sīn] **signo de mayor que** A symbol used to compare two quantities, with the greater quantity given first
Example: $6 > 4$

grid [grid] **cuadrícula** Evenly divided and equally spaced squares on a shape or flat surface

H

half gallon [haf gal′ən] **medio galón** A customary unit for measuring capacity and liquid volume
1 half gallon = 2 quarts

half hour [haf our] **media hora** 30 minutes
Example: 4:00 to 4:30 is one half hour.

half-square unit [haf skwâr yo͞o′nit] **media unidad cuadrada** Half of a unit of area with dimensions of 1 unit × 1 unit

height [hīt] **altura** The measure of a perpendicular from the base to the top of a two-dimensional shape

hexagon [hek′sə•gän] **hexágono** A polygon with six sides and six angles
Examples:

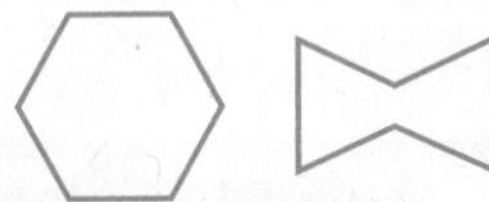

horizontal [hôr•i•zänt′l] **horizontal** In the direction from left to right

hour (hr) [our] **hora (hr)** A unit used to measure time
1 hour = 60 minutes

hundredth [hun′drədth] **centésimo** One of one hundred equal parts
Example:

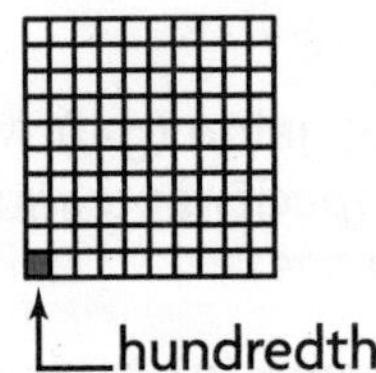

Identity Property of Addition [ī•den′tə•tē präp′ər•tē əv ə•dish′ən] **propiedad de identidad de la suma** The property that states that when you add zero to any number, the sum is that number
Example: 16 + 0 = 16

Identity Property of Multiplication [ī•den′tə•tē präp′ər•tē əv mul•tə•pli•kā′shən] **propiedad de identidad de la multiplicación** The property that states that the product of any number and 1 is that number
Example: 9 × 1 = 9

inch (in.) [inch] **pulgada (pulg)** A customary unit used for measuring length or distance
Example:

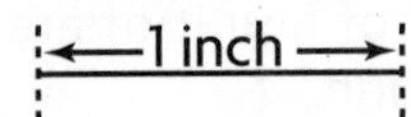

intersecting lines [in•tər•sekt′ing līnz] **líneas secantes** Lines that cross each other at exactly one point
Example:

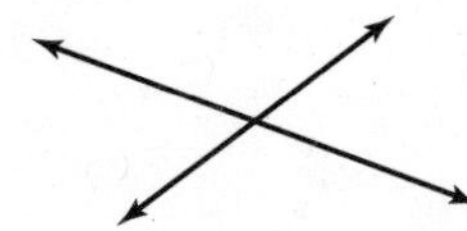

inverse operations [in′vûrs äp•ə•rā′shənz] **operaciones inversas** Operations that undo each other, such as addition and subtraction or multiplication and division
Example: 6 × 8 = 48 and 48 ÷ 6 = 8

isosceles triangle [ī•sä′sə•lēz trī′ang•gəl] **triángulo isósceles** A triangle with two equal sides
Example:

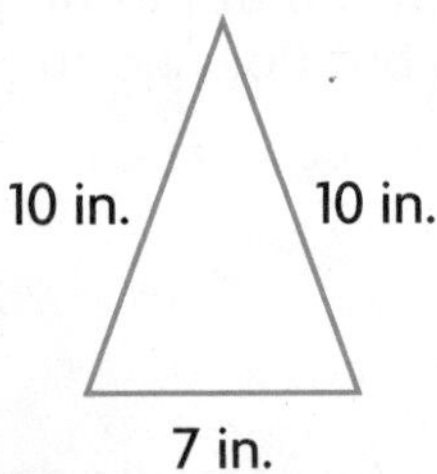

Word History

When you look at the sides of an ***isosceles*** triangle, you see that two sides are equal in length. The Greek root ***iso-*** means "same or equal," and ***skelos*** means "leg."

key [kē] **clave** The part of a map or graph that explains the symbols

kilogram (kg) [kil′ō•gram] **kilogramo (kg)** A metric unit for measuring mass
1 kilogram = 1,000 grams

kilometer (km) [kə•läm′ət•ər] **kilómetro (km)** A metric unit for measuring length or distance
1 kilometer = 1,000 meters

length [lengkth] **longitud** The measurement of the distance between two points

less than sign (<) [les than sīn] **signo de menor que** A symbol used to compare two quantities, with the lesser quantity given first
Example: 3 < 7

line [līn] **línea** A straight path of points in a plane that continues without end in both directions with no endpoints
Example:

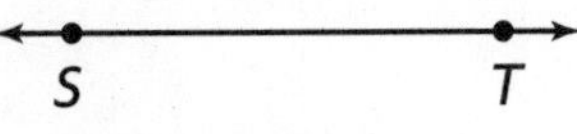

line graph [līn graf] **gráfica lineal** A graph that uses line segments to show how data change over time

line of symmetry [līn əv sim′ə•trē] **eje de simetría** An imaginary line on a shape about which the shape can be folded so that its two parts match exactly
Example:

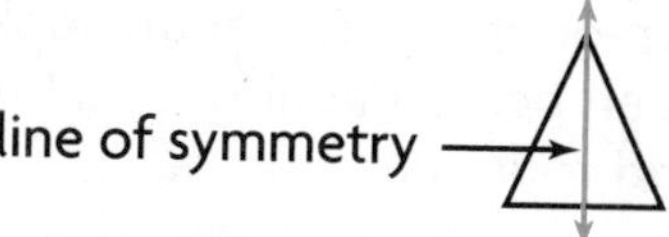

line plot [līn plöt] **diagrama de puntos** A graph that records each piece of data on a number line
Example:

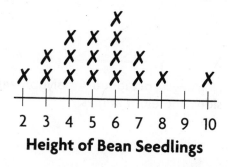

2 3 4 5 6 7 8 9 10
Height of Bean Seedlings

line segment [līn seg′mənt] **segmento** A part of a line that includes two points called endpoints and all the points between them
Example:

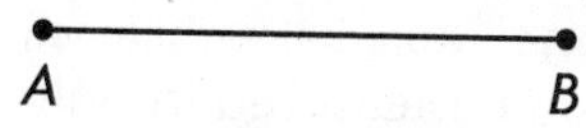

line symmetry [līn sim′ə•trē] **simetría axial** What a shape has if it can be folded about a line so that its two parts match exactly

linear units [lin′ē•ər yo͞o′nits] **unidades lineales** Units that measure length, width, height, or distance

liquid volume [lik′wid väl′yo͞om] **volumen de un líquido** The measure of the space a liquid occupies

liter (L) [lēt′ər] **litro (L)** A metric unit for measuring capacity and liquid volume
1 liter = 1,000 milliliters

mass [mas] **masa** The amount of matter in an object

meter (m) [mēt′ər] **metro (m)** A metric unit for measuring length or distance
1 meter = 100 centimeters

midnight [mid′nīt] **medianoche** 12:00 at night

mile (mi) [mīl] **milla (mi)** A customary unit for measuring length or distance
1 mile = 5,280 feet

milliliter (mL) [mil′i•lēt•ər] **mililitro (mL)** A metric unit for measuring capacity and liquid volume
1 liter = 1,000 milliliters

millimeter (mm) [mil′i•mēt•ər] **milímetro (mm)** A metric unit for measuring length or distance
1 centimeter = 10 millimeters

million [mil′yən] **millón** The counting number after 999,999; 1,000 thousands; written as 1,000,000

millions [mil′yənz] **millones** The period after thousands

minute (min) [min′it] **minuto (min)** A unit used to measure short amounts of time
1 minute = 60 seconds

mixed number [mikst num′bər] **número mixto** An amount given as a whole number and a fraction

multiple [mul′tə•pəl] **múltiplo** The product of a number and a counting number is called a multiple of the number
Example:

$\begin{array}{r}3\\ \times\ 1\\ \hline 3\end{array}\quad \begin{array}{r}3\\ \times\ 2\\ \hline 6\end{array}\quad \begin{array}{r}3\\ \times\ 3\\ \hline 9\end{array}\quad \begin{array}{r}3\\ \times\ 4\\ \hline 12\end{array}$ ← counting numbers / ← multiples of 3

multiplication [mul•tə•pli•kā′shən] **multiplicación** A process to find the total number of items in equal-sized groups, or to find the total number of items in a given number of groups when each group contains the same number of items; multiplication is the inverse of division

multiply [mul′tə•plī] **multiplicar** To combine equal groups to find how many in all; the opposite operation of division

N

nickel [nik′əl] **moneda de 5¢** A coin worth 5 cents and with a value equal to that of 5 pennies; 5¢
Example:

noon [no͞on] **mediodía** 12:00 in the day

not equal to sign (≠) [not ē′kwəl to͞o sīn] **signo de no igual a** A symbol that indicates one quantity is not equal to another
Example: $12 \times 3 \neq 38$

number line [num′bər līn] **recta numérica** A line on which numbers can be located
Example:

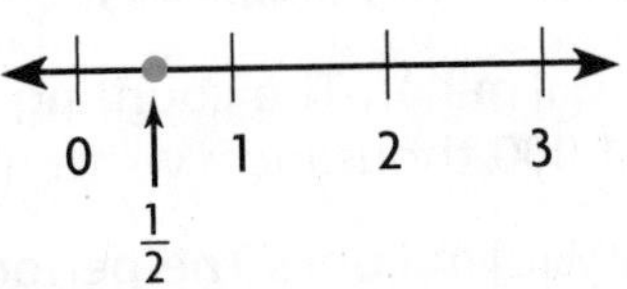

number sentence [num′bər sent′ns] **enunciado numérico** A sentence that includes numbers, operation symbols, and a greater than or less than symbol or an equal sign
Example: $5 + 3 = 8$

numerator [no͞o′mər•āt•ər] **numerador** The number above the bar in a fraction that tells how many parts of the whole or group are being considered

Example: $\frac{2}{3}$ ← numerator

O

obtuse angle [äb•to͞os′ ang′gəl] **ángulo obtuso** An angle that measures greater than 90° and less than 180°
Example:

Word History

The Latin prefix ***ob-*** means "against." When combined with ***-tusus***, meaning "beaten," the Latin word ***obtusus***, from which we get ***obtuse***, means "beaten against." This makes sense when you look at an obtuse angle, because the angle is not sharp or acute. The angle looks as if it has been beaten against and become blunt and rounded.

obtuse triangle [äb•to͞os′ trī′ang•gəl] **triángulo obtusángulo** A triangle with one obtuse angle

Example:

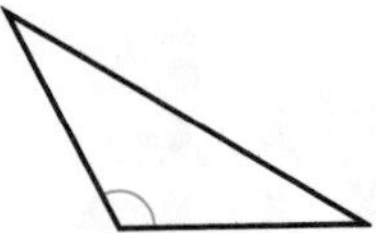

octagon [äk′tə•gän] **octágono** A polygon with eight sides and eight angles
Examples:

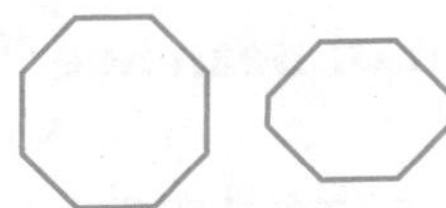

odd [od] **impar** A whole number that has a 1, 3, 5, 7, or 9 in the ones place

one-dimensional [wun də•men′shə•nəl] **unidimensional** Measured in only one direction, such as length
Examples:

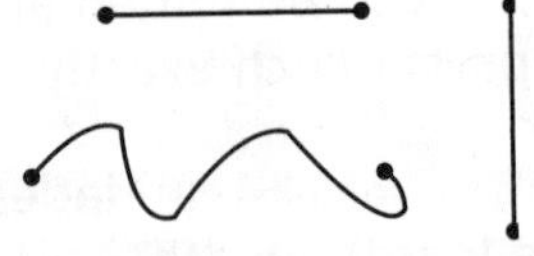

open shape [ō′pən shāp] **figura abierta** A shape that does not begin and end at the same point
Examples:

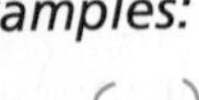 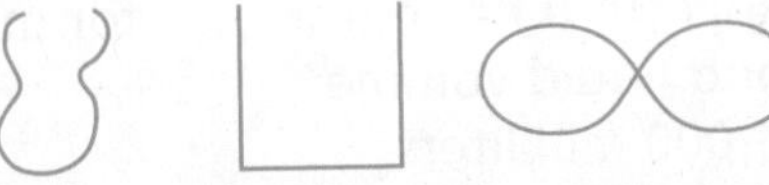

order [ôr′dər] **orden** A particular arrangement or placement of things one after the other

order of operations [ôr′dər əv äp•ə•rā′shənz] **orden de las operaciones** A special set of rules which gives the order in which calculations are done

ounce (oz) [ouns] **onza (oz)** A customary unit for measuring weight
1 pound = 16 ounces

parallel lines [pâr′ə•lel līnz] **líneas paralelas** Lines in the same plane that never intersect and are always the same distance apart
Example:

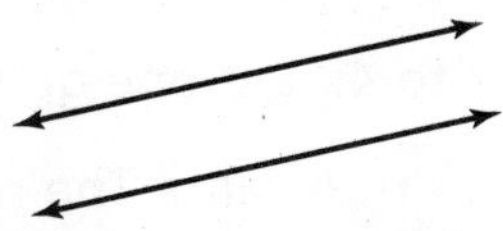

Word History

Euclid, an early Greek mathematician, was one of the first to explore the idea of parallel lines. The prefix ***para-*** means "beside or alongside." This prefix helps you understand the meaning of the word ***parallel***.

parallelogram [pâr•ə•lel′ə•gram] **paralelogramo** A quadrilateral whose opposite sides are parallel and of equal length
Example:

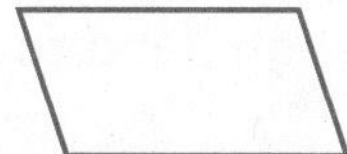

parentheses [pə•ren′thə•sēz] **paréntesis** The symbols used to show which operation or operations in an expression should be done first

partial product [pär′shəl präd′əkt] **producto parcial** A method of multiplying in which the ones, tens, hundreds, and so on are multiplied separately and then the products are added together

partial quotient [pär′shəl kwō′shənt] **cociente parcial** A method of dividing in which multiples of the divisor are subtracted from the dividend and then the quotients are added together

pattern [pat′ərn] **patrón** An ordered set of numbers or objects; the order helps you predict what will come next
Examples: 2, 4, 6, 8, 10

pattern unit [pat′ərn yo͞o′nit] **unidad de patrón** The part of a pattern that repeats
Example:

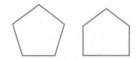

pentagon [pen′tə•gän] **pentágono** A polygon with five sides and five angles
Examples:

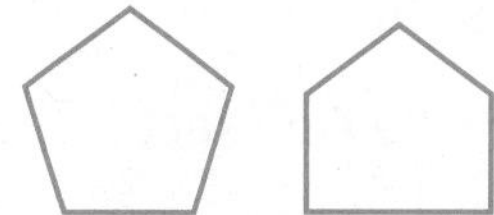

perimeter [pə•rim′ə•tər] **perímetro** The distance around a shape

period [pir′ē•əd] **período** Each group of three digits in a multi-digit number; periods are usually separated by commas or spaces.
Example: 85,643,900 has three periods.

perpendicular lines [pər•pən•dik′yo͞o•lər līnz] **líneas perpendiculares** Two lines that intersect to form four right angles
Example:

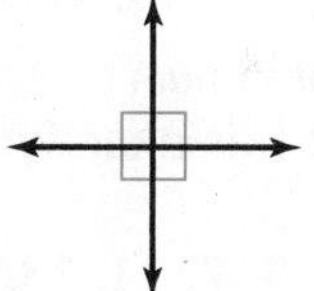

picture graph [pik′chər graf] **gráfica con dibujos** A graph that uses symbols to show and compare information
Example:

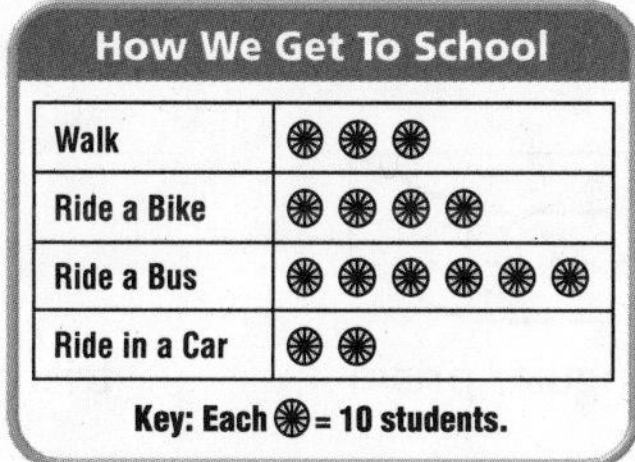

pint (pt) [pīnt] **pinta (pt)** A customary unit for measuring capacity and liquid volume
1 pint = 2 cups

place value [plās val′yo͞o] **valor posicional** The value of a digit in a number, based on the location of the digit

plane [plān] **plano** A flat surface that extends without end in all directions
Example:

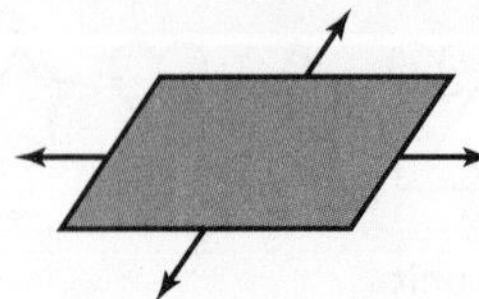

plane shape [plān shāp] **figura plana** See *two-dimensional figure.*

P.M. [pē•em] **p.m.** The times after noon and before midnight

point [point] **punto** An exact location in space

polygon [päl′i•gän] **polígono** A closed two-dimensional shape formed by three or more straight sides that are line segments
Examples:

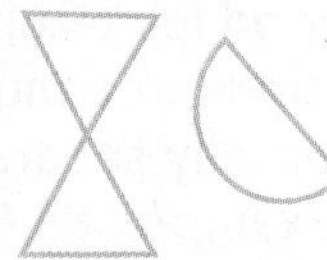

Polygons Not Polygons

pound (lb) [pound] **libra (lb)** A customary unit for measuring weight
1 pound = 16 ounces

prime number [prīm num′bər] **número primo** A number that has exactly two factors: 1 and itself
Examples: 2, 3, 5, 7, 11, 13, 17, and 19 are prime numbers. 1 is not a prime number.

prism [priz′əm] **prisma** A solid figure that has two same size, same polygon-shaped bases, and other faces that are all rectangles
Examples:

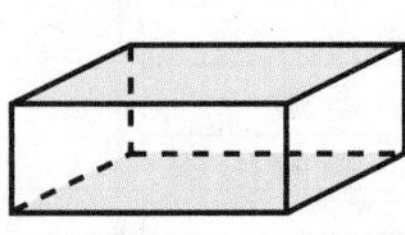

rectangular prism

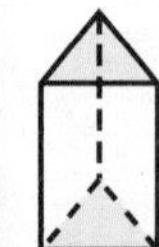

triangular prism

product [präd′əkt] **producto** The answer to a multiplication problem

protractor [prō′trak•tər] **transportador** A tool for measuring the size of an angle

quadrilateral [kwä•dri•lat′ər•əl] **cuadrilátero** A polygon with four sides and four angles

quart (qt) [kwôrt] **cuarto (ct)** A customary unit for measuring capacity and liquid volume
1 quart = 2 pints

quarter hour [kwôrt′ər our] **cuarto de hora** 15 minutes
Example: 4:00 to 4:15 is one quarter hour

quotient [kwō′shənt] **cociente** The number, not including the remainder, that results from dividing
Example: 8 ÷ 4 = 2; 2 is the quotient.

ray [rā] **semirrecta** A part of a line; it has one endpoint and continues without end in one direction
Example:

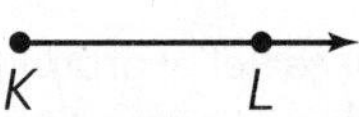

rectangle [rek′tang•gəl] **rectángulo** A quadrilateral with two pairs of parallel sides, two pairs of sides of equal length, and four right angles
Example:

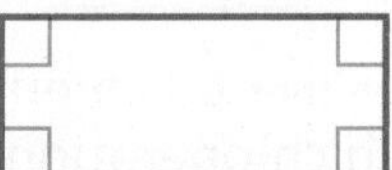

rectangular prism [rek•tang′gyə•lər priz′əm] **prisma rectangular** A three-dimensional shape in which all six faces are rectangles
Example:

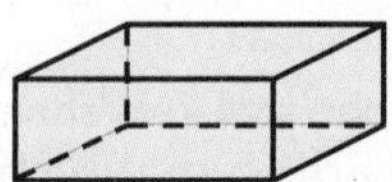

regroup [rē•grōōp′] **reagrupar** To exchange amounts of equal value to rename a number
Example: 5 + 8 = 13 ones or 1 ten 3 ones

regular polygon [reg′yə•lər päl′i•gän] **polígono regular** A polygon that has all sides that are equal in length and all angles equal in measure
Examples:

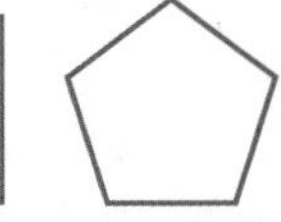

related facts [ri•lāt′id fakts] **operaciones relacionadas** A set of related addition and subtraction, or multiplication and division, number sentences
Examples: 4 × 7 = 28 28 ÷ 4 = 7
7 × 4 = 28 28 ÷ 7 = 4

remainder [ri•mān′dər] **residuo** The amount left over when a number cannot be divided equally

rhombus [räm′bəs] **rombo** A quadrilateral with two pairs of parallel sides and four sides of equal length
Example:

right angle [rīt ang′gəl] **ángulo recto** An angle that forms a square corner
Example:

right triangle [rīt trī′ang•gəl] **triángulo rectángulo** A triangle with one right angle
Example:

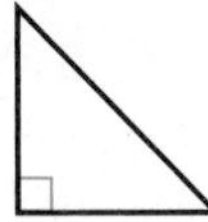

round [round] **redondear** To replace a number with another number that tells about how many or how much

rule [ro͞ol] **regla** A procedure (usually involving arithmetic operations) to determine an output value from an input value

scale [skāl] **escala** A series of numbers placed at fixed distances on a graph to help label the graph

scalene triangle [skā′lēn trī′ang•gəl] **triángulo escaleno** A triangle with no equal sides
Example:

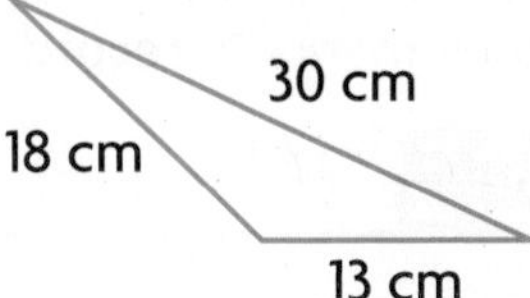

second (sec) [sek′ənd] **segundo (seg)** A small unit of time
1 minute = 60 seconds

simplest form [sim′pləst fôrm] **mínima expresión** A fraction is in simplest form when the numerator and denominator have only 1 as a common factor

solid shape [sä′lid shāp] **cuerpo geométrico** See *three-dimensional figure.*

square [skwâr] **cuadrado** A quadrilateral with two pairs of parallel sides, four sides of equal length, and four right angles
Example:

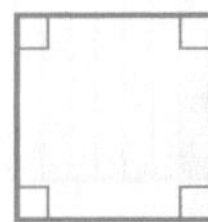

square unit [skwâr yo͞o′nit] **unidad cuadrada** A unit of area with dimensions of 1 unit × 1 unit

standard form [stan′dərd fôrm] **forma normal** A way to write numbers by using the digits 0–9, with each digit having a place value *Example:* 3,540 ← standard form

straight angle [strāt ang′gəl] **ángulo llano** An angle whose measure is 180°
Example:

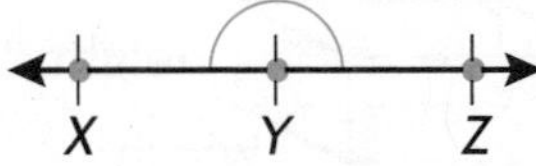

subtraction [səb•trak′shən] **resta** The process of finding how many are left when a number of items are taken away from a group of items; the process of finding the difference when two groups are compared; the opposite operation of addition

sum [sum] **suma o total** The answer to an addition problem

survey [sûr′vā] **encuesta** A method of gathering information

tally table [tal′ē tā′bəl] **tabla de conteo** A table that uses tally marks to record data

Word History

Some people keep score in card games by making marks on paper (IIII). These marks are known as tally marks. The word ***tally*** is related to ***tailor***, from the Latin ***talea***, meaning "twig." In early times, a method of keeping count was by cutting marks into a piece of wood or bone.

temperature [tem′pər•ə•chər] **temperatura** The degree of hotness or coldness usually measured in degrees Fahrenheit or degrees Celsius

tenth [tenth] **décimo** One of ten equal parts
Example:

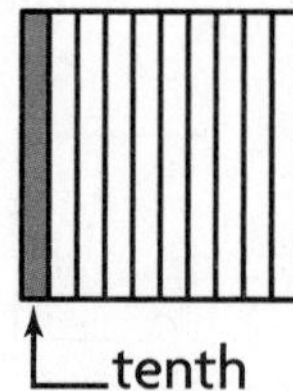

term [tûrm] **término** A number or object in a pattern

thousands [thou′zəndz] **miles** The period after the ones period in the base-ten number system

three-dimensional [thrē də•men′shə•nəl] **tridimensional** Measured in three directions, such as length, width, and height
Example:

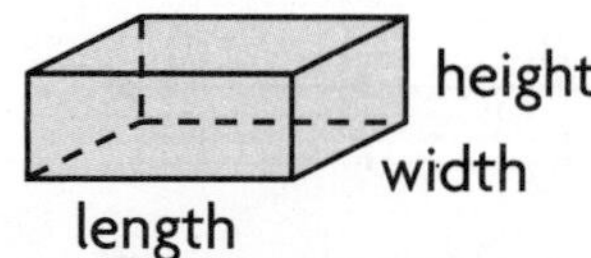

three-dimensional figure [thrē də•men′shə•nəl fig′yər] **figura tridimensional** A figure having length, width, and height

ton (T) [tun] **tonelada (t)** A customary unit used to measure weight
1 ton = 2,000 pounds

trapezoid [trap′i•zoid] **trapecio** A quadrilateral with exactly one pair of parallel sides
Examples:

triangle [trī′ang•gəl] **triángulo** A polygon with three sides and three angles
Examples:

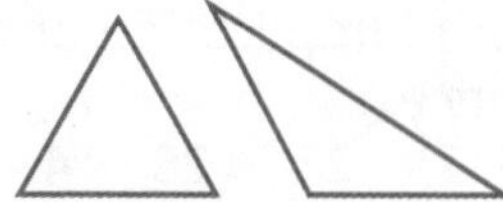

two-dimensional [to͞o də•men′shə•nəl] **bidimensional** Measured in two directions, such as length and width
Example:

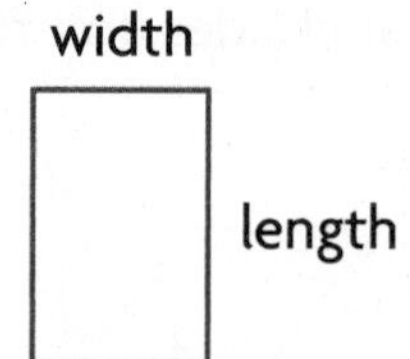

two-dimensional figure [to͞o də•men′shə•nəl fig′yər] **figura bidimensional** A figure that lies in a plane; a shape having length and width

unit fraction [yo͞o′nit frak′shən] **fracción unitaria** A fraction that has a numerator of one

variable [vâr′ē•ə•bəl] **variable** A letter or symbol that stands for a number or numbers

Venn diagram [ven dī′ə•gram] **diagrama de Venn** A diagram that shows relationships among sets of things
Example:

2-Digit Numbers **Even Numbers**

35 17 29 | 12 10 | 8 6 4

vertex [vûr′teks] **vértice** The point at which two rays of an angle meet or two (or more) line segments meet in a two-dimensional shape
Examples:

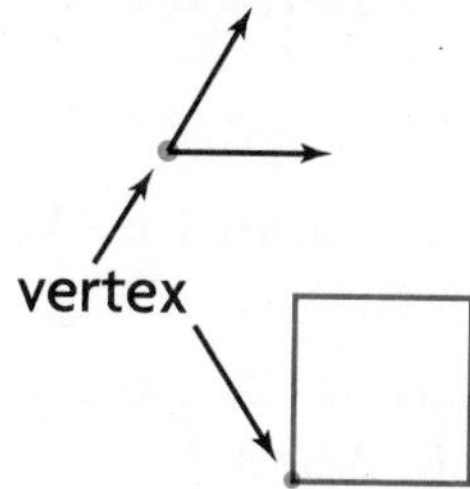

vertical [vûr′ti•kəl] **vertical** In the direction from top to bottom

weight [wāt] **peso** How heavy an object is

whole [hōl] **entero** All of the parts of a shape or group

word form [wûrd fôrm] **en palabras** A way to write numbers by using words
Example: Four hundred fifty-three thousand, two hundred twelve

yard (yd) [yärd] **yarda (yd)** A customary unit for measuring length or distance
1 yard = 3 feet

Zero Property of Multiplication [zē′rō präp′ər•tē əv mul•tə•pli•kā′shən] **propiedad del cero de la multiplicación** The property that states that the product of 0 and any number is 0
Example: $0 \times 8 = 0$

Correlations

CALIFORNIA COMMON CORE STATE STANDARDS

Standards You Will Learn

Mathematical Practices		Student Edition Lessons
MP.1	Make sense of problems and persevere in solving them.	Lessons 1.6, 2.5, 3.7, 5.6, 7.6, 8.3, 9.5, 11.2, 12.8
MP.2	Reason abstractly and quantitatively.	Lessons 1.4, 2.12, 3.5, 4.1, 4.8, 6.1, 7.9, 10.5, 11.4, 12.10
MP.3	Construct viable arguments and critique the reasoning of others.	Lessons 1.8, 3.6, 4.7, 6.6, 7.8, 10.3, 11.1, 12.4, 12.9
MP.4	Model with mathematics.	Lessons 1.5, 1.8, 2.3, 4.12, 6.4, 7.4, 8.2, 9.7, 10.8, 12.5
MP.5	Use appropriate tools strategically.	Lessons 1.4, 2.3, 3.2, 5.6, 7.3, 7.4, 9.5, 10.6, 11.4, 12.9
MP.6	Attend to precision.	Lessons 2.4, 4.7, 5.2, 5.4, 6.3, 9.2, 10.3, 10.5, 13.2
MP.7	Look for and make use of structure.	Lessons 1.1, 2.5, 2.7, 4.1, 4.10, 5.5, 6.1, 7.10, 9.2, 12.5, 13.1
MP.8	Look for and express regularity in repeated reasoning.	Lessons 1.6, 1.8, 2.3, 3.3, 4.7, 6.2, 7.7, 10.8, 12.4, 13.1

Standards You Will Learn

Student Edition Lessons

Domain: Operations and Algebraic Thinking		
Use the four operations with whole numbers to solve problems		
4.OA.1	Interpret a multiplication equation as a comparison, e.g., interpret $35 = 5 \times 7$ as a statement that 35 is 5 times as many as 7 and 7 times as many as 5. Represent verbal statements of multiplicative comparisons as multiplication equations.	Lesson 2.1
4.OA.2	Multiply or divide to solve word problems involving multiplicative comparison, e.g., by using drawings and equations with a symbol for the unknown number to represent the problem, distinguishing multiplicative comparison from additive comparison.	Lessons 2.2, 4.12
4.OA.3	Solve multistep word problems posed with whole numbers and having whole-number answers using the four operations, including problems in which remainders must be interpreted. Represent these problems using equations with a letter standing for the unknown quantity. Assess the reasonableness of answers using mental computation and estimation strategies including rounding.	Lessons 2.9, 2.12, 3.7, 4.3
Gain familiarity with factors and multiples.		
4.OA.4	Find all factor pairs for a whole number in the range 1–100. Recognize that a whole number is a multiple of each of its factors. Determine whether a given whole number in the range 1–100 is a multiple of a given one-digit number. Determine whether a given whole number in the range 1–100 is prime or composite.	Lessons 5.1, 5.2, 5.3, 5.4, 5.5
Generate and analyze patterns.		
4.OA.5	Generate a number or shape pattern that follows a given rule. Identify apparent features of the pattern that were not explicit in the rule itself.	Lessons 5.6, 10.8

Standards You Will Learn

Student Edition Lessons

Domain: Number and Operations in Base Ten		
Generalize place value understanding for multi-digit whole numbers.		
4.NBT.1	Recognize that in a multi-digit whole number, a digit in one place represents ten times what it represents in the place to its right.	Lessons 1.1, 1.5
4.NBT.2	Read and write multi-digit whole numbers using base-ten numerals, number names, and expanded form. Compare two multi-digit numbers based on meanings of the digits in each place, using >, =, and < symbols to record the results of comparisons.	Lessons 1.2, 1.3
4.NBT.3	Use place value understanding to round multi-digit whole numbers to any place.	Lesson 1.4
Use place value understanding and properties of operations to perform multi-digit arithmetic.		
4.NBT.4	Fluently add and subtract multi-digit whole numbers using the standard algorithm.	Lessons 1.6, 1.7, 1.8
4.NBT.5	Multiply a whole number of up to four digits by a one-digit whole number, and multiply two two-digit numbers, using strategies based on place value and the properties of operations. Illustrate and explain the calculation by using equations, rectangular arrays, and/or area models.	Lessons 2.3, 2.4, 2.5, 2.6, 2.7, 2.8, 2.10, 2.11, 3.1, 3.2, 3.3, 3.4, 3.5, 3.6
4.NBT.6	Find whole-number quotients and remainders with up to four-digit dividends and one-digit divisors, using strategies based on place value, the properties of operations, and/or the relationship between multiplication and division. Illustrate and explain the calculation by using equations, rectangular arrays, and/or area models.	Lessons 4.1, 4.2, 4.4, 4.5, 4.6, 4.7, 4.8, 4.9, 4.10, 4.11

Standards You Will Learn

Student Edition Lessons

Number and Operations—Fractions		
Extend understanding of fraction equivalence and ordering.		
4.NF.1	Explain why a fraction *a*/*b* is equivalent to a fraction $(n \times a)/(n \times b)$ by using visual fraction models, with attention to how the number and size of the parts differ even though the two fractions themselves are the same size. Use this principle to recognize and generate equivalent fractions.	Lessons 6.1, 6.2, 6.3, 6.4, 6.5
4.NF.2	Compare two fractions with different numerators and different denominators, e.g., by creating common denominators or numerators, or by comparing to a benchmark fraction such as 1/2. Recognize that comparisons are valid only when the two fractions refer to the same whole. Record the results of comparisons with symbols $>$, $=$, or $<$, and justify the conclusions, e.g., by using a visual fraction model.	Lessons 6.6, 6.7, 6.8

Standards You Will Learn

Student Edition Lessons

Domain: Number and Operations–Fractions

Build fractions from unit fractions by applying and extending previous understandings of operations on whole numbers.

Standard	Description	Student Edition Lessons
4.NF.3	Understand a fraction *a/b* with $a > 1$ as a sum of fractions 1/*b*.	
	a. Understand addition and subtraction of fractions as joining and separating parts referring to the same whole.	Lesson 7.1
	b. Decompose a fraction into a sum of fractions with the same denominator in more than one way, recording each decomposition by an equation. Justify decompositions, e.g., by using a visual fraction model. *Examples: 3/8 = 1/8 + 1/8 + 1/8; 3/8 = 1/8 + 2/8; 2 1/8 = 1 + 1 + 1/8 = 8/8 + 8/8 + 1/8.*	Lessons 7.2, 7.6
	c. Add and subtract mixed numbers with like denominators, e.g., by replacing each mixed number with an equivalent fraction, and/or by using properties of operations and the relationship between addition and subtraction.	Lessons 7.7, 7.8, 7.9
	d. Solve word problems involving addition and subtraction of fractions referring to the same whole and having like denominators, e.g., by using visual fraction models and equations to represent the problem.	Lessons 7.3, 7.4, 7.5, 7.10
4.NF.4	Apply and extend previous understandings of multiplication to multiply a fraction by a whole number.	
	a. Understand a fraction *a/b* as a multiple of 1/*b*.	Lesson 8.1
	b. Understand a multiple of *a/b* as a multiple of 1/*b*, and use this understanding to multiply a fraction by a whole number.	Lessons 8.2, 8.3
	c. Solve word problems involving multiplication of a fraction by a whole number, e.g., by using visual fraction models and equations to represent the problem.	Lessons 8.4, 8.5

Standards You Will Learn		Student Edition Lessons
Domain: Number and Operations—Fractions		
Understand decimal notation for fractions, and compare decimal fractions.		
4.NF.5	Express a fraction with denominator 10 as an equivalent fraction with denominator 100, and use this technique to add two fractions with respective denominators 10 and 100.	Lessons 9.3, 9.6
4.NF.6	Use decimal notation for fractions with denominators 10 or 100.	Lessons 9.1, 9.2, 9.4
4.NF.7	Compare two decimals to hundredths by reasoning about their size. Recognize that comparisons are valid only when two decimals refer to the same whole. Record the results of comparisons with the symbols $>$, $=$, or $<$, and justify the conclusions, e.g., by using the number line or another visual model.	Lesson 9.7
Domain: Measurement and Data		
Solve problems involving measurement and conversion of measurements from a larger unit to a smaller unit.		
4.MD.1	Know relative sizes of measurement units within one system of units including km, m, cm; kg, g; lb, oz.; l, ml; hr, min, sec. Within a single system of measurement, express measurements in a larger unit in terms of a smaller unit. Record measurement equivalents in a two-column table.	Lessons 12.1, 12.2, 12.3, 12.4, 12.6, 12.7, 12.8, 12.11
4.MD.2	Use the four operations to solve word problems involving distances, intervals of time, liquid volumes, masses of objects, and money, including problems involving simple fractions or decimals, and problems that require expressing measurements given in a larger unit in terms of a smaller unit. Represent measurement quantities using diagrams such as number line diagrams that feature a measurement scale.	Lessons 9.5, 12.9, 12.10
4.MD.3	Apply the area and perimeter formulas for rectangles in real world and mathematical problems.	Lessons 13.1, 13.2, 13.3, 13.4, 13.5

Standards You Will Learn

Standards You Will Learn		Student Edition Lessons
Domain: Measurement and Data		
Represent and interpret data.		
4.MD.4	Make a line plot to display a data set of measurements in fractions of a unit (1/2, 1/4, 1/8). Solve problems involving addition and subtraction of fractions by using information presented in line plots.	Lesson 12.5
Geometric measurement: understand concepts of angle and measure angles.		
4.MD.5	Recognize angles as geometric shapes that are formed wherever two rays share a common endpoint, and understand concepts of angle measurement:	
	a. An angle is measured with reference to a circle with its center at the common endpoint of the rays, by considering the fraction of the circular arc between the points where the two rays intersect the circle. An angle that turns through 1/360 of a circle is called a "one-degree angle," and can be used to measure angles.	Lessons 11.1, 11.2
	b. An angle that turns through *n* one-degree angles is said to have an angle measure of *n* degrees.	Lesson 11.2
4.MD.6	Measure angles in whole-number degrees using a protractor. Sketch angles of specified measure.	Lesson 11.3
4.MD.7	Recognize angle measure as additive. When an angle is decomposed into non-overlapping parts, the angle measure of the whole is the sum of the angle measures of the parts. Solve addition and subtraction problems to find unknown angles on a diagram in real world and mathematical problems, e.g., by using an equation with a symbol for the unknown angle measure.	Lessons 11.4, 11.5

Standards You Will Learn

Student Edition Lessons

Domain: Geometry		
Draw and identify lines and angles, and classify shapes by properties of their lines and angles.		
4.G.1	Draw points, lines, line segments, rays, angles (right, acute, obtuse), and perpendicular and parallel lines. Identify these in two-dimensional figures.	Lessons 10.1, 10.4
4.G.2	Classify two-dimensional figures based on the presence or absence of parallel or perpendicular lines, or the presence or absence of angles of a specified size. Recognize right triangles as a category, and identify right triangles. (Two-dimensional shapes should include special triangles, e.g., equilateral, isosceles, scalene, and special quadrilaterals, e.g., rhombus, square, rectangle, parallelogram, trapezoid.)	Lessons 10.2, 10.3, 10.5
4.G.3	Recognize a line of symmetry for a two-dimensional figure as a line across the figure such that the figure can be folded along the line into matching parts. Identify line-symmetric figures and draw lines of symmetry.	Lessons 10.6, 10.7

Index

A

B

D

E

F

O

P

V

Table of Measures

METRIC	CUSTOMARY
Length	
1 centimeter (cm) = 10 millimeters (mm)	1 foot (ft) = 12 inches (in.)
1 meter (m) = 1,000 millimeters	1 yard (yd) = 3 feet, or 36 inches
1 meter = 100 centimeters	1 mile (mi) = 1,760 yards, or 5,280 feet
1 meter = 10 decimeters (dm)	
1 kilometer (km) = 1,000 meters	
Capacity and Liquid Volume	
1 liter (L) = 1,000 milliliters (mL)	1 cup (c) = 8 fluid ounces (fl oz)
	1 pint (pt) = 2 cups
	1 quart (qt) = 2 pints, or 4 cups
	1 half gallon = 2 quarts
	1 gallon (gal) = 2 half gallons, or 4 quarts
Mass/Weight	
1 kilogram (kg) = 1,000 grams (g)	1 pound (lb) = 16 ounces (oz)
	1 ton (T) = 2,000 pounds

TIME

1 minute (min) = 60 seconds (sec)
1 half hour = 30 minutes
1 hour (hr) = 60 minutes
1 day (d) = 24 hours
1 week (wk) = 7 days
1 year (yr) = 12 months (mo), or about 52 weeks
1 year = 365 days
1 leap year = 366 days
1 decade = 10 years
1 century = 100 years

MONEY

1 penny = 1¢, or $0.01
1 nickel = 5¢, or $0.05
1 dime = 10¢, or $0.10
1 quarter = 25¢, or $0.25
1 half dollar = 50¢, or $0.50
1 dollar = 100¢, or $1.00

SYMBOLS

$<$	is less than	$\perp$	is perpendicular to
$>$	is greater than	$\parallel$	is parallel to
$=$	is equal to	$\overleftrightarrow{AB}$	line *AB*
$\neq$	is not equal to	$\overrightarrow{AB}$	ray *AB*
¢	cent or cents	$\overline{AB}$	line segment *AB*
$	dollar or dollars	$\angle ABC$	angle *ABC* or angle *B*
°	degree or degrees	$\triangle ABC$	triangle *ABC*

FORMULAS

Perimeter		Area	
Polygon	$P =$ sum of the lengths of sides	Rectangle	$A = b \times h$
Rectangle	$P = (2 \times l) + (2 \times w)$ or $P = 2 \times (l + w)$		
Square	$P = 4 \times s$